THE SABR BOOK OF
UMPIRES
AND
UMPIRING

Edited by Larry R. Gerlach and Bill Nowlin

Associate editors: Dennis Bingham and Len Levin

Society for American Baseball Research, Inc.
Phoenix, AZ

The SABR Book on Umpires and Umpiring
Edited by Larry R. Gerlach and Bill Nowlin
Associate editors: Dennis Bingham and Len Levin

ISBN 978-1-943816-45-3
(Ebook ISBN 978-1-943816-44-6)

Cover and book design: Gilly Rosenthol

Photo credits:
Front cover: Brad Adams from Sonoma, California. High School Championship Game (De La Salle vs. California) at O.Co. Coliseum, Oakland, June 2, 2012. Photograhy by Dennis Lee.

Back cover: National Baseball Hall of Fame (Nestor Chylak making the call)

Courtesy of Andy Andres - 336
Courtesy of Perry Barber – 222, 228, 229
John Behrend – 211, 212
Courtesy of Boston Red Sox – 386
Noel Cilker - 186
Reynaldo Cruz – 208, 233
Matt Dirksen, Colorado Rockies – 428
Courtesy of Rob Edelman – 433, 436
Courtesy of Lorenz Evans – 181
Amy Guccione – 139
Chris Guccione – 365, 366
Michael Jacobs – 289
Courtesy of Stephen Johnson III - 80
Courtesy of Hank Levy – 189
Bain Collection, Library of Congress – 26, 166, 410, 412
Courtesy of Major League Baseball – 198, 199, 316, 317, 321, 324, 325
Courtesy of Shaun McCready – 247, 254
Courtesy of Byron Motley – 174
National Baseball Hall of Fame – 5, 13, 15, 23, 25, 31, 36, 48, 55, 63, 74, 83, 88, 97, 109, 120, 214,217, 222, 238, 377, 390.
Noir-Tech Research - 171
Bill Nowlin – 2, 131, 133, 136, 148, 151, 203, 237, 239, 240, 241, 255, 256, 257, 264, 275, 276, 282, 283, 299, 301, 304, 305, 338, 339, 340, 399, 442, 453, 454, 457, 464, 467, 468, 469.
Collection of Bill Nowlin - 102
Courtesy of Ben Phillips - 178
Society for American Baseball Research - 404
Spalding Collection, New York Public Library - 381
The Topps Company, Inc. – 440
Spencer Research Library, University of Kansas – 115
Courtesy of Bart Wilhelm - 279
YouTube - 426

Society for American Baseball Research
Cronkite School at ASU
555 N. Central Ave. #416
Phoenix, AZ 85004
Phone: (602) 496-1460
Web: www.sabr.org
Facebook: Society for American Baseball Research
Twitter: @SABR

DEDICATION

For my sons, T. J. and Jonathan, fellow baseball fans.
—LG

To Emmet, who is more engaged with esports (video game sorts),
but who is co-editing SABR's book on 20 Game Losers.
—BN

Thanks to the following

Dan Brooks
Abby DeCiccio
Chris Gilligan
Matt Levin
Justin Long
Randy Marsh
Dan Rea
Brent Rice
Steve Rippley
Cathie Ross
Terry Samway
Tim Samway
Jim Sandoval
Dr. Charles Steinberg
Mike Teevan

and to the following current umpires, who were interviewed
during the course of the preparation of this book:

Lance Barksdale, Lance Barrett, Ted Barrett, Cory Blaser,
C. B. Bucknor, Vic Carapazza, Mark Carlson,
Gary Cederstrom, Chris Conroy, Fieldin Culbreth,
Bob Davidson, Kerwin Danley, Dana DeMuth, Laz Diaz,
Paul Emmel, Mike Estabrook, Chad Fairchild, Andy Fletcher,
Marty Foster, Greg Gibson, Brian Gorman, Chris Guccione,
Angel Hernandez, Ed Hickox, John Hirschbeck, James Hoye,
Marvin Hudson, Dan Iassonga, Jim Joyce, Jeff Kellogg,
Brian Knight, Ron Kulpa, Will Little, Alfonso Marquez,
Jerry Meals, Bill Miller, Mike Muchlinski, Brian O'Nora,
David Rackley, Tony Randazzo, Mark Ripperger, D. J. Reyburn,
Jim Reynolds, Paul Schreiber, Dale Scott, Todd Tichenor,
John Tumpane, Larry Vanover, Mark Wegner, Bill Welke,
Tim Welke, Hunter Wendelstedt, Joe West, Mike Winters,
Quinn Wolcott, Jim Wolf, and fill-in umpires Sean Barber,
Toby Basner, Clint Fagan, Pat Hoberg, and Carlos Torres.

Contents

UMPIRES AND FAMILIES, AND UMPIRE HEALTH

HISTORICAL ITEMS

SOME CULTURAL PERSPECTIVES

CONVERSATIONS WITH UMPIRE CREWS

Introduction

By Larry R. Gerlach

5.01 Starting the Game ("Play Ball!")

At the time set for beginning the game the players of the home team shall take their defensive positions, the first batter of the visiting team shall take his position in the batter's box, the umpire-in-chief shall call "Play," and the game shall start.

Official Baseball Rules, 2016 Edition

"Play!" With that simple directive, umpires not only start a baseball game, but also ensure that it is played according to the rules. Although umpires are an essential component of the national pastime—no umpires, no organized game—they are little appreciated or understood, even by many ardent fans. Indeed "Blue," the traditional spectator's designation for an umpire, has historically been ridiculed for presumed incompetence or demonized for unpopular decisions. If organists no longer play "Three Blind Mice" à la Ebbets Field's Gladys Gooding, and the homicidal refrain "Kill the Umpire" is rarely heard, umpires still receive little respect for their game-time functions.

Even less appreciated is the umpiring profession—requiring initial attendance at a training school, lengthy apprenticeship in the minor leagues, arduous travel and familial stress of a career spent largely away from home, administrative procedures before and during games, and the systematic human and technological evaluations of performance.

While biographies and autobiographies of players and managers abound, with few exceptions anonymity characterizes the guardians of the game. Umpires are people, too, their personalities and private lives not add only a human dimension to the game but also insight into the character of those who have served since the 1840s.

In short, the umpire remains a conspicuously missing chapter in the otherwise extensively documented history of baseball. Astonishingly, James Kahn's *The Umpire Story* (1953) remains the lone general history. Over the course of more than 150 years, the history of baseball is reflected in the extraordinary development of the profession of umpiring from the initial presence of a gentleman arbiter charged with maintaining decorum to the emergence of the tough-minded lone rules enforcer of the formative professional era; from the creation of multi-member crews and the dominance of individual personalities and styles prior to World War II; and from the postwar emergence of the training schools, unionization, and the appearance of African American and Latino umpires to the current financial security and technological enhancements of a modern profession.

And at each stage umpires and umpiring mirrored the transformation of the game itself within the larger American society. For all the changes, and there were many, there remained one constant: the integrity and dedication—indeed love of the game—of those who by enforcing the rules made it possible to play the game in an orderly fashion. To Jacques Barzun's famous dictum—"whoever wants to know the heart and mind of America had better learn baseball"—one might add: "whoever wants to know baseball had better learn about umpires."

This volume is something of a companion to *Can He Play? A Look at Baseball Scouts and Their Profession*, a previous SABR publication that called attention to another group of important if neglected contributors to the national pastime. Intended partially to fill the void, herein are biographies of prominent umpires including the 10 members of the National Baseball Hall of Fame; accounts of major historical events and lists of performance records; cultural and literary representations; interviews with contemporary individual umpires and crews as well as ballpark support personnel; and the descriptions of current administrative and technological supervisory systems. While the material predominantly deals with major-league baseball, there are also accounts of other professional, amateur, and international umpiring.

Although the book provides an expansive view of umpires and their profession past and present, selectivity governed inclusions. The contents reflect the editors' inclinations as well the research contributions of SABR members. Undoubtedly some readers will regret that this umpire or that topic has been omitted, but hopefully all will appreciate and benefit from what has been included. And hopefully, in keeping with SABR's core mission, the book will inspire additional biographical and historical research into an essential, if neglected, component of the national pastime.

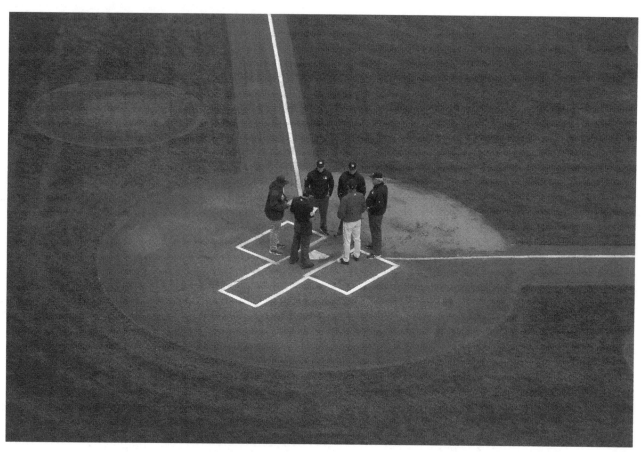

Plate conference, TOR at BOS, October 2, 2016 – the last game of the regular season. Umpires: HP – Chris Guccione, 1B – Brian Gorman, 2B – Mark Carlson, 3B – Quinn Wolcott.

Al Barlick

By David Vincent

Al Barlick rose from a Midwestern coal-mining family to a long career as a major-league umpire and eventual election to baseball's Hall of Fame, the sixth umpire to be so honored. He gave his adult life to baseball and umpiring, working 57 years (1936-1993) in the game.

Albert Joseph Barlick was born on April 2, 1915, in Springfield, Illinois, the fifth and youngest son of John Barlick (c. 1879-1953) and Louise Gorence (1883-1966). John Barlick, an Austrian immigrant, worked for 50 years at the Peabody No. 59 bituminous mine.

Young Al dropped out of high school after two years to help support his family. He joined the Civilian Conservation Corps, a Depression-era federal work program, spending six months in Washington State and six more in Wisconsin. When an older brother died, Al returned home and went to work in the coal mine as his father's helper.

Growing up in Springfield, Barlick and a friend, Pat Ciotti, had devised a backyard game in which they used a flat board for a bat and pitched kernels of corn from about 35 feet away. The pitcher also called balls and strikes. In 1935 Jack Rossiter, who ran the Springfield Municipal Baseball League, needed umpires. Ciotti recommended the 20-year-old Barlick, who was given a tryout and, eventually, a job.

In August 1936 the Class D Northeast Arkansas League needed a replacement umpire after one of the league's arbiters fell ill. Barlick was recommended to the league's president, Joe Bertig, and was hired for the last four weeks of the season. He hitchhiked from Springfield to the league office in Paragould, Arkansas. In 1937 Barlick jumped to the Class B Piedmont League, where he spent two seasons, then to the International League after the 1938 season. That league farmed him out to the Eastern League for the start of the 1939 campaign, but recalled him by June.

In September 1940 National League chief umpire Bill Klem was unable to work, so the league needed a fill-in. Barlick made his debut in a doubleheader at Shibe Park in Philadelphia on September 8. His debut game was the first major-league contest he had ever seen. (The complete list of games he umpired can be viewed on the Retrosheet.org website.)

In February 1941 Barlick married Jennie Marie Leffell. They had two daughters, Marlene (born c. 1943) and Kathleen (born c. 1945). At the time of Barlick's Hall of Fame induction in 1989, two of his grandsons were serving in the US Marine Corps.

The National League offered Barlick a contract for the 1941 season. At 26, he became one of the youngest umpires in major league history.

Barlick was behind the plate for the first game of a doubleheader in Pittsburgh on July 27, 1941. In the first inning, Brooklyn catcher Herman Franks objected to Barlick's strike zone and Barlick ejected him, the first time he had ejected someone from a major-league game. Bill Klem joined Barlick and his partners for three games in St. Louis starting on September 11, the last three games of Klem's career.

In just his second season, on July 6, 1942, Barlick was in the umpire crew for the All-Star Game, at the Polo Grounds in New York. It was the first of seven All-Star Games he umpired, and the only one for which he was not the home-plate umpire and crew chief. He worked at second base for the first half of the game and third base for the second half.

Barlick joined the US Coast Guard on November 5, 1943. He spent most of the next two years assigned to an 83-foot cutter based at the training station at the Coast Guard Academy in New London, Connecticut. When he was discharged in 1945, he had attained the rank of seaman 1st class. He returned to umpiring in 1946, and worked in his first World Series that season. At the time a four-man umpire crew worked in the Series. Barlick umpired at second base in the first game and worked behind the plate twice, including the Series-deciding seventh game, in which Enos Slaughter made his mad dash around the bases. Barlick ruled Slaughter safe at the plate.

Barlick worked at first base on April 15, 1947, Opening Day, as the Brooklyn Dodgers beat the Boston Braves, 5-3, in Brooklyn. The historic game marked the big-league debut of the Dodgers first baseman, Jackie Robinson. Thus, Barlick was the closest man on the field to Robinson as he became the first African-American to play in the majors in the 20th century.

Barlick umpired six no-hit games, the first of them as the home-plate umpire on June 18, 1947, as Ewell Blackwell of the Cincinnati Reds shut down the Boston Braves. In the other five no-nos, he umpired on the bases.

Barlick worked at first base in Pittsburgh on June 10, 1948, and, in the second inning, called a balk on Dodgers hurler Harry Taylor with the bases loaded, allowing a run to score. Dodgers manager Leo Durocher ran out on the field to argue the call with Barlick and was ejected. Before the game the next afternoon, Durocher started yelling at Barlick, renewing the argument from the previous evening. According to news reports on the game, Barlick was overheard saying something along the lines of "this thing is starting all over again" before tossing Durocher.

This was a continuation of a long-standing battle between the young umpire and the fiery Durocher. The arbiter ejected Durocher ten times during Durocher's career as a manager; in all, Barlick had 81 ejections.

In 1948 Barlick umpired 161 National League contests in a 154-game season. He worked 22 doubleheaders, including a four-day span starting September 19 in which he umpired four consecutive twin bills. He led all National League arbiters in games worked that summer.

On April 30, 1949, Rocky Nelson of the St. Louis Cardinals hit a sinking line drive to left-center in the top of the ninth at Wrigley Field, Chicago. Andy Pafko made a diving attempt at the ball, somersaulted, and came up running into the infield, thinking his

catch was the third out. However, Barlick ruled that he had not caught the ball. Pafko argued with the arbiter while holding onto the ball and Nelson ran the circuit for a two-run inside-the-park homer that provided the Redbirds with a 4-3 victory.

Barlick made his second All-Star Game appearance on July 12, 1949, at Ebbets Field in Brooklyn. This was the first time six umpires worked the midsummer classic, and Barlick was the home-plate umpire. This game was played in an intermittent drizzle and was sloppily played because of the conditions. The tradition at the time was that the umpires rotated positions after 4½ innings. Instead of taking another position, Barlick left the contest and the right-field line was left uncovered, which was not unusual at the time. No reason was disclosed for his departure.

At the end of the 1950 season, Barlick made his second appearance in the World Series as the New York Yankees swept the Philadelphia Phillies in four games. He worked only in the outfield, two games along the left-field line and two along the right-field line. When the World Series umpire crew expanded from four to six arbiters in 1947, it was the practice that two of the umpires, deemed as "alternates," worked only in the outfield. This practice was changed for the 1964 fall classic, when the current system of rotating all six umpires around the field was instituted.

On May 6, 1951, Barlick and his partners were at the Polo Grounds in New York for a doubleheader between the Giants and the visiting Cincinnati Reds. The first contest lasted ten innings, with the Reds scoring in the top of the tenth on a solo homer by Virgil Stallcup. In the bottom of the frame, Whitey Lockman singled to lead off the inning and advanced to second on Alvin Dark's sacrifice. However, Reds second baseman Connie Ryan, who had made the putout at first on Dark, walked down to second with the ball hidden in his glove. He asked Lockman to step off the bag so he could straighten it, and the unsuspecting Lockman did so. Ryan tagged Lockman on the hidden-ball trick to complete a double play and negate the sacrifice. When Barlick called Lockman out, the enraged Giants stormed the umpire, led by their manager, Leo Durocher. Eventually, Barlick ejected his old nemesis and the game ended on the next play. Two days later Durocher and Lockman were fined by the league for their actions. The Durocher ejection was the first of 12 by Barlick during the 1951 season. He led all NL umpires in ejections that year, the only time he ejected more than eight people in one campaign.

Barlick was chosen for the World Series in 1951 for the second consecutive year. This year, he was part of the four-man rotating crew in the infield in the six-game, all-New York series. He worked behind the plate in Game Four, which was played at the Polo Grounds.

Barlick was behind the plate at Shibe Park, Philadelphia, for the 1952 All-Star Game. This was his third appearance at an All-Star Game and his second time starting a game behind the plate. In the middle of the fifth inning, the umpires changed positions and he moved to second base. The start of the game had been delayed 20 minutes by rain and, at the end of the fifth inning, there was a 56-minute rain delay before the game was called off, with the National League ahead, 3-2.

Barlick umpired the 1954 World Series, a four-game sweep by the New York Giants over the Cleveland Indians. He was behind the plate for Game One, a ten-inning affair at the Polo Grounds.

On July 12, 1955, Barlick was once again behind the plate to start the All-Star Game. After 4½ innings, he swapped places with third-base umpire Bill Summers of the American League. The game, played at County Stadium in Milwaukee, was won by the NL, 6-5, in 12 innings on a game-ending homer by Stan Musial.

On September 25, 1955, Barlick and Lee Ballanfant worked their last game together. They umpired 1,633 games together in the major leagues, starting with Barlick's debut in 1940. At the time, only Beans Reardon and Larry Goetz had worked more games as partners (1,913) and, at the end of the 2013 season, Barlick and Ballanfant are third on the list of partners. Joe Brinkman and Derryl Cousins top the list with 2,123 games together.

Al Barlick.

Barlick missed the 1956 and 1957 seasons because of a heart problem, described in various news accounts as either an enlarged heart or a mild heart attack. He spent the time operating a gas station called Barlick & Petrone in Springfield, Illinois. He returned to the National League in 1958 as a crew chief. At the end of the season, Barlick umpired the 1958 World Series, a seven-game set won by the New York Yankees over the Milwaukee Braves.

In 1959 the major leagues held two All-Star Games and Barlick was the plate umpire to start the first game, played on July 7 at Forbes Field in Pittsburgh. (He swapped with third-base umpire Joe Paparella in the middle of the fifth inning.)

On September 20, 1959, Barlick was in San Francisco with Jocko Conlan's crew for the last game played at Seals Stadium. It was an important game in the standings because the hometown Giants, the visiting Los Angeles Dodgers, and the Milwaukee Braves (who were in Philadelphia that day) were all fighting for the National League pennant. At the start of the day, the Giants and Dodgers were tied for first place and the Braves were a half-game behind. The Dodgers never trailed in the contest and took a one-game lead over the Giants. At the end of the season, the Dodgers and Braves played a best-of-three series to determine the league champion. The two senior umpires in the league, Barlick and Conlan, were chosen to work the series, along with a veteran group of four other umpires.

On August 15, 1960, Barlick's crew was in Cincinnati for a doubleheader between the Braves and the Reds. In the first game, Barlick was umpiring at third base when Frank Robinson of the Reds slid hard into third attempting to stretch a double into a triple. Eddie Mathews tagged Robinson out and decided that the latter had come in too hard to the bag, so Mathews started punching the runner. Barlick ejected Mathews for fighting in one of the most memorable brawls in major-league history.

The National League umpire staff expanded in 1961 in anticipation of the addition of two teams in 1962. The league decided to season some arbiters before the league expansion. Barlick's crew worked with various other umpires for many games as a five-man crew, with the extra umpire stationed down the left-field line. On July 4 the crew was at Wrigley Field in Chicago for a doubleheader between the San Francisco Giants and the Cubs. For those games, the fifth man on the crew was stationed in center field. Barlick's reasoning, according to *The Sporting News*, was to give the outfield umpire a better angle to view balls hit near the wall. Many fans would reach over the wall and touch balls in flight, so this angle gave the arbiter a better chance to rule on those situations. This was before netting was installed near the top of the wall.

On July 26, 1961, *The Sporting News* published the results of a poll to determine the best umpires. In the opinion of the managers and coaches, Al Barlick was rated as the most respected in the National League and won the top rating in five other categories in the poll: best caller of balls and strikes, best on the bases, best knowledge of rules, best at being in the right position, and most serious-minded. He was tied for the best with Shag Crawford in the category of

making the most deliberate decisions. In the opinion of the writers polled, Barlick was at the top of four lists: most respected, best on bases, best knowledge of the rules, and making deliberate decisions.

When asked about the poll, Barlick, the senior National League umpire at the time, called it a disgrace. He criticized what he called the ill-informed opinions of the writers and some of the categories in the poll, including the most sarcastic, the hardest to talk to, the biggest grandstander, and the worst pop-off. His comments drew a lot of negative responses from writers, as might be expected.

Barlick was quoted by Ray Kelly in the *Philadelphia Evening Bulletin* as saying: "The very idea of the ratings is unfair in that they place labels on hard-working officials who always try to do a good job. What, for instance, has neatness of appearance to do with sound officiating on the field? What constitutes respect? Does refusal to take abuse from a manager or player signify respect and is that respect forfeited when the player or manager is thrown out of the game?"

At the start of the 1962 season, Barlick's crew umpired the first game at Dodger Stadium in Los Angeles. At the end of the season, the San Francisco Giants and Dodgers were tied and played a best-of-three series to determine the winner of the NL pennant. Barlick was chosen to work the playoff series, and for the third time in nine years, he was the crew chief for the World Series. This seven-game series started at San Francisco's Candlestick Park; it was the first time that the Series had been played in the Bay Area and Barlick umpired behind the plate for that initial contest.

In 1963 the National League mandated that the umpires crack down on balks by pitchers. This created a lot of arguments on the field. On May 4 Barlick was behind the plate for a game in Milwaukee between the Chicago Cubs and the Braves. Milwaukee starting pitcher Bob Shaw was called for a balk in the top of the first inning, three times in the third, and again in the fifth. In the third, the Cubs' Billy Williams had walked and the three balks sent him around to score. In the fifth inning, after setting a record with his fifth balk of the game, Shaw walked Andre Rodgers to load the bases and then Nelson Mathews to force in the go-ahead run for the Braves. Shaw objected to Barlick's strike zone and was ejected by the arbiter.

A week later Barlick was quoted by Les Biederman in *The Sporting News*: "We umps have to shoulder too much blame, yet all we do is enforce the rules. We don't write the rules, just make certain none is violated. Now everybody is on us about the balks. Our instructions are to call balks when the pitcher fails to pause in his delivery with men on base, and we're following orders. What would you do if your boss told you to do something and you didn't follow through? What happens to a player who fails to follow instructions from a manager? It's just as simple as that."

On June 15, 1963, his crew worked a game in Cincinnati between the Reds and the New York Mets. At 3 o'clock the next morning, Barlick called Fred Fleig, the secretary of the National League, and, according to various news accounts, told him: "I am fed up with things and I am going to quit and go home." League President Warren Giles told reporters later that day that he had tried to contact Barlick without success but hoped that he would change his mind because "he is an excellent umpire and a fine person." At the time, there was no supervisor of umpires in the league, unlike the American League, which had a supervisor. The NL umpires were dissatisfied with Giles' administration and felt that he failed to back them up when there was a controversy.

The balk situation was one of those controversial issues. Giles had ordered the arbiters to call the rule the way it was written, and so well over 100 were called in the first few weeks of the season. Commissioner Ford Frick convened an emergency meeting of the rules committee to reword the balk rule and bring it into conformity with standard practice. The umpires felt that Giles caused the problem and then failed to defend them once the trouble started. On June 17 Giles announced that he had spoken with Barlick, who was at his home in Springfield. Giles released a statement saying: "A misunderstanding has been cleared up. I asked Barlick to spend two or three days with his family. He will rejoin his crew in Chicago on June 21." Giles refused to elaborate on the misunderstanding.

The time at home for the umpire was a rarity. Most years, Barlick would leave for spring training in February or March and not return home until the beginning of October or later. On the last day of the 1963 season, he said he was not sure if he would return the following year. He had umpired 20 seasons in the National League and, at 48 years old, was the senior arbiter in the league in terms of service. When he returned home to Springfield, he took a job at the city's Water, Light and Power Department as a public-relations representative. By mid-January, however, Barlick had told the league that he would be back for the 1964 season.

In October 1963 the first umpires union was formed. The Association of National Baseball League Umpires included only National League umpires and was no doubt a reflection of the umpires' opinion of the state of relations between them and Warren Giles. The union's board of directors comprised Barlick, Jocko Conlan, Henry "Shag" Crawford, Augie Donatelli, and Tom Gorman. Conlan and Barlick were the two most senior umpires in the league at the time, since both joined the staff in 1941.

The purpose of the union as stated in its Illinois incorporation papers was "(t)o improve the general conditions pertaining to the relationship of the National Baseball League Umpires with the National League of Professional Baseball Clubs and to further aid in the constructive improvement of the game of National League Baseball."

This union was replaced with the Major League Umpires Association, which was recognized by both leagues in 1970 and represented all umpires. This organization was disbanded and replaced with the World Umpires Association in 2000.

In 1965 Barlick and his crew opened the season in Houston, as the Astros hosted the Philadelphia Phillies at their new ballpark, the Astrodome. This was the first indoor stadium in the major leagues and the senior member of the league umpiring staff, Al Barlick, worked behind the plate for the initial contest.

On May 28, 1966, Barlick's mother, Louise, died at her home in Springfield. Barlick went home after the game of May 25 to be with his ailing mother and returned to work on June 3, missing nine games. On July 12 Barlick was behind the plate for the All-Star Game, played at the newly opened Busch Stadium in St. Louis. As was the practice, the umpires changed positions in the middle of the fifth inning, with Barlick moving to third base.

Six days later, he was behind the plate for a game at Connie Mack Stadium in Philadelphia between the Los Angeles Dodgers and the Phillies. In the bottom of the seventh inning, Dick Allen was on second base when a pitch got by Dodgers catcher John Roseboro for a passed ball. Barlick called the pitch a foul ball, so Roseboro did not run after the ball immediately. By the time he retrieved the ball, Allen had scored from second base. However, Barlick called time and placed Allen at third, explaining to the Phillies what he had done and that Allen would only have reached third without the umpire's gaffe. Allen scored minutes later on a sacrifice fly.

Barlick missed the last two weeks of the 1966 season due to high blood pressure. He worked his last game on September 15 in Chicago and traveled to Houston for the next series. However, on September 17, he went home and was admitted to the hospital for a series of tests, which showed no damage to his heart. Barlick rested during the fall and later decided he was fit enough to go back to work in 1967. The 135 games Barlick umpired in 1966 represented the lowest total of his career for one season, excluding his partial season in 1940 before he joined the National League staff in 1941.

Barlick was chosen to umpire the 1967 World Series, his seventh and final time in the fall classic. In the second inning of the first game, played at Boston's Fenway Park, Barlick stopped the contest briefly because a teenager was watching the game from atop the left-field wall just to the fair side of the foul pole. This was before the addition of the Monster Seats above the wall, when there was only a net.

On September 13, 1968, a fifth umpire was added to Barlick's crew. Just as in 1961, the league decided to give some umpires big-league experience before they were needed on the field the following season. Each member of the crew was to take a day off in rotation and they worked that way until September 24, when all five umpires were on the field. The crew worked together for the last five games of the season.

After the season, Barlick accompanied the St. Louis Cardinals on a five-week tour of Japan. In one game, Lou Brock protested a strike call by the arbiter, so Barlick took Brock's hat and bat, gave Brock his umpire cap, and stepped into the batter's box. The crowd loved this prearranged set piece.

During the 1969 season, Barlick umpired 166 games, including 20 doubleheaders. The 166 games were the most in any season of Barlick's career. With the expansion in 1969, each league was split into two divisions and the division winners played a round of playoff games to determine the World Series participants. The NL version of the League Championship Series started on October 4 with Al Barlick as the crew chief.

After the 1969 season, Barlick announced that he would retire if the pension plan for umpires was set up sufficiently. If not, he told reporters, "I'll hang around. They're not going to leave me in the middle of the street." However, he returned to work in 1970 and, on June 28, he was in Pittsburgh for the final game played at Forbes Field. The Chicago Cubs and the Pirates played a doubleheader that day, with Barlick behind the plate for the first game. Two days later, the crew was in Cincinnati as the Reds opened their new home, Riverfront Stadium.

The 1970 All-Star Game was played at Riverfront Stadium on July 14, and Barlick was the crew chief and home-plate umpire. This was his seventh All-Star Game appearance, which is the most by any umpire, tied with longtime American League arbiter Bill Summers. Summers worked behind the plate for all of his games, while Barlick was the plate umpire six times. The 1970 game ended with the famous play in which Pete Rose crashed into catcher Ray Fosse, scoring the winning run when Fosse dropped the ball.

In February 1971 Barlick accepted the Umpire of the Year Award at the Al Somers Umpire School.

The selection was based on a poll of the major-league umpires. As he accepted the award, Barlick said: "I've never accepted an award before. This is a true, honorable, sincere award because it is given to an umpire by umpires. That's why it is very special." He continued: "Bill Klem told me I'd meet some people in baseball I'd like. I'd meet some I didn't like. But to help them all, because in doing that you'll be helping all baseball."

Barlick returned to the field in 1971 for his 28th and final year, even though he was a year past the retirement age. On May 31 the crew worked a game in Cincinnati between the Houston Astros and the hometown Reds. Barlick, who had been the plate umpire on the previous afternoon, worked at third base this day. During the game, Reds coach Alex Grammas was sarcastically praising Barlick's strike zone of the previous day, so Barlick ejected Grammas.

The crew was at Wrigley Field for a Sunday afternoon game between the Philadelphia Phillies and the Chicago Cubs on September 26. Barlick worked behind the plate that day in the final game of his career, as the Phillies won, 5-1. The rest of the crew went to New York for three days, but Barlick did not work that series, having taken the advice of his teammates to go home early.

Al Barlick worked 4,227 games in the major leagues, which at the time was the fourth most of all time. He worked with 49 different umpires, including more than 1,000 games with four different umpires: Lee Ballanfant (1,633), Stan Landes (1,229), Augie Donatelli (1,104), and Ed Vargo (1,009).

On December 9, 1971, National League President Chub Feeney announced that Barlick was retiring from active duty as an umpire. The league hired him to supervise and scout umpires, a job he held for 22 years. During his time as supervisor, he hired many umpires who had long major-league careers. According to Bruce Froemming, who worked on Barlick's crew in 1971, Barlick was "very proud of the staff he built."

Froemming also talked about how easy Barlick made the transition from the minors to the majors. He "was a good teacher for the young guys" and "down to earth" with them, helping them get acclimated to life in the big leagues.

During spring training in 1988, Barlick was eating dinner with some umpires. He asked Mike Winters, a minor-league umpire working major-league spring games, to bring the bottom of his strike zone up a quarter-inch the next day. Winters looked at Barlick for a bit and then realized he had been had. Barlick was only joking with him because "no one is that good with their strike zone."

In 1989 Al Barlick was elected to the Hall of Fame by the Veterans Committee. He was the sixth umpire to be so honored, after Bill Klem, Tommy Connolly, Billy Evans, Jocko Conlan, and Cal Hubbard. In 1991 Barlick was made a charter member of the Springfield (Illinois) Sports Hall of Fame.

On September 10, 1995, a ceremony was held at Wrigley Field, Chicago, to retire numbers for three Hall of Fame umpires who worked in the National League: Bill Klem (No. 1), Jocko Conlan (2) and Al Barlick (3). Note that these were not numbers actually worn by those arbiters but done to honor them.

At the end of that month, the Babe Ruth Museum in Baltimore held a weekend card show as part of its celebration of the centennial of Ruth's birth. The museum gathered many Hall of Famers for autograph sessions during the three-day event and Barlick was one of them. The Hall of Famers waited in a backstage room before doing their session with the public. Many players who came into the room, upon seeing Barlick sitting quietly at the side of the room, made a detour and stopped to say hello. Most addressed him as "Mr. Barlick" and asked how he was doing. Barlick once said: "I think I earned the players' respect and that's the ultimate in life, isn't it? I didn't care if they liked me or disliked me, as long as I had their respect." The reaction of those Hall of Fame players that day in Baltimore certainly proved that respect.

Weeks later, Al Barlick died in Springfield on December 27, 1995, at the age of 80. He had collapsed at home and was pronounced dead at a hospital. Cardiac arrest had stilled his growling, booming voice, one of the loudest in the big leagues. His body was cremated and his ashes scattered by the family.

Barlick was fond of saying: "There are umpires and there are those who hold the title." No one doubts that Barlick was an umpire. In fact, Bruce Froemming described Barlick as "an umpire's umpire."

In addition to the 49 umpires with whom he shared the field, Barlick mentored many umpires who were still working in the major leagues as of 2014. His legacy in the game lives on in those people.

SOURCES

Biederman, Les, "Umps Shoulder Too Much Blame," *The Sporting News,* May 11, 1963.

Dolson, Frank, "Barlick a Loveable Tough Guy," *Philadelphia Inquirer,* July 27, 1989.

Froemming, Bruce N., phone interview with the author, January 27, 2011.

Holtzman, Jerome, "How Al Barlick Entered the 'Hall,'" *Chicago Tribune,* March 12, 1989.

"Japan Land of Fun for Gift-Laden Cards," *The Sporting News,* December 14, 1968.

Kelly, Ray, "Rating of Umpires Called Disgrace by Barlick," *Philadelphia Evening Bulletin,* July 24, 1961.

Koppett, Leonard, "Al Barlick: An Ump Calls Himself Out," *New York Times,* June 17, 1963.

Miller, Tony, "An Interview with HOF Umpire Al Barlick," *Sports Collectors Digest,* December 25, 1992.

Retrosheet website retrosheet.org (umpire data and game schedules).

Vincent, David, Lyle Spatz, and David Smith,. *The Midsummer Classic: The Complete History of Baseball's All-Star Game* (Lincoln, Nebraska: Bison Books, 2001).

Wind, Herbert Warren, "How an Umpire Gets That Way," *Saturday Evening Post,* August 8, 1953.

Winters, Michael J., phone interview with the author, January 25, 2011.

Nestor Chylak

by Herb Wilson

"Considered by many to be the nonpareil umpire of the Post-War Era. A model of consistency with invariable accuracy both behind the plate and on the bases." Those words on Nestor Chylak's Baseball Hall of Fame plaque describe him well. An American League umpire from 1954 through 1978, Chylak was highly respected by managers, players, and league officials for his skills at keeping the game moving and avoiding being the center of attention.[1] His posthumous election to the Hall, the eighth umpire so honored, was a testament to his umpiring accomplishments.[2]

Chylak was born on May 11, 1922, in Olyphant, Pennsylvania, near Scranton in the northeastern part of the state. His parents, of Ukrainian descent, were Nestor George Chylak Sr. and Nellie (Shipskie) Chylak, both first-generation Americans.[3] His father operated a bar.[4]

Nestor was the oldest of five children. He had two sisters, Mae and Julie, and two brothers, Gene and Joseph, who died at the age of 2.[5]

Chylak attended Rutgers University briefly in 1939-1940, but his studies were interrupted by military service in World War II.[6] A sergeant in an Army Ranger battalion, Chylak served in the Army in the European theater and was wounded on January 3, 1945, during the Battle of the Bulge, when fragments of a tree hit by shrapnel smashed into his face.[7] For 10 days, he could not see, but eventually recovered his eyesight. Chylak was awarded a Purple Heart for his wound and a Silver Star for gallantry in action.[8]

Chylak almost never talked about the horrors of the battlefield. His son Bill thought Nestor's generosity and kindness to people grew out of his loneliness on the road, but another son, Bob, said the friends their father lost in battle had something to do with it.[9]

Returning to the United States after the war, Chylak briefly resumed his college studies at the University of Scranton, but did not finish his degree.[10] He wanted to play baseball, but a shoulder injury prevented him from doing so. He decided to try umpiring.[11] In 1946 Chylak began umpiring amateur baseball games in the Northeastern Pennsylvania League. He decided to pursue umpiring as a career, beginning in the minor leagues in 1947. He began in the Pony League (1947-1948), moved to the Canadian-American League (early 1949), the New England League (1949), and then the Triple-A International League in 1952-53. On April 13, 1954, at Griffith Stadium in Washington, Chylak made his debut in the American League. He worked third base in the 10-inning game, the Senators prevailing over the Yankees, 5-3.[12]

Thus began a major-league career that spanned 25 years and 3,857 regular-season games. Chylak was a home-plate umpire for 974 games.[13] He was a crew chief for 14 years, mentoring rookie and younger umpires.[14]

Chylak's son Bob cited his father's on-field demeanor as a key to his success. He was decisive, consistent, authoritative, and unflappable. He let players have their say and then moved on. Once a manager or player stopped arguing, he let the dispute drop.[15]

Chylak had the baseball rulebook memorized by paragraph and by section, ensuring that he knew the rules cold. His preparation meant he never lost an argument, even to well-informed managers like Earl Weaver.[16] Chylak was proud of the fact that he never threw Weaver out of a game.[17] In his 25 years as a major-league umpire, Chylak ejected only 24 players, managers, and coaches, and ejection rate among the lowest in major-league history.[18]

Chylak's sense of humor served him well as an umpire. He had a ready wit. He once said, "The way I see it, an umpire must be perfect on the first day of the season and then get better every day."[19] At the Umpire Exhibit at the Hall of Fame, a plaque gives this Chylak quip: "This must be the only job in

Nestor Chylak.

America that everybody knows how to do better than the guy who's doing it."[20]

When Chylak died in 1982, Commissioner Bowie Kuhn said, "Few have ever been more respected in his field. Everyone looked up to him, and I developed more respect every time I saw him in a World Series or All-Star Game."[21] When Chylak was inducted into the Hall of Fame, Harmon Killebrew called him "one of the best umpires in the American League for years and years," and added, "I think he had a great rapport with the players."[22] Jim Palmer said, "I think anybody who ever played while Nestor umpired understood how much he loved the game and how much he loved people."[23] Brooks Robinson called him "my favorite umpire."[24]

Yogi Berra called Chylak "an umpire's umpire," saying, "He kept the game under control, but he would also listen to you when you had a beef."[25] But fellow umpire Don Denkinger said he was "a pitcher's umpire." Chylak's philosophy was to never call a strike a ball. Former player and coach Dick Tracewski opined that Chylak thought it was acceptable to call a ball a strike once in a while, but never the opposite because it slowed the game down.

In a time when selection for postseason and All-Star Games was based on merit, Chylak was chosen to umpire in five World Series, three League Championship Series, and six All-Star Games. His first World Series was in 1957, when he worked the left- and right-field lines for all seven games of the Yankees-Braves Series. Chylak also umpired in the 1960, 1966, 1971, and 1977 World Series, serving as crew chief in 1971 and 1977.[26]

Chylak umpired in the American League for his whole major-league career; he retired long before the umpiring staffs were consolidated. He was behind the plate for the first major-league game in Toronto, in Exhibition Stadium in 1977, a contest made memorable by a snowstorm during the game. He called balls and strikes in Sandy Koufax's last major-league contest, Gamne Two of the 1966 World Series.[27] Chylak was the plate umpire when Bert Campaneris threw his bat at pitcher Lerrin LaGrow during a 1972 playoff game. Nestor ejected both players.

He was the third-base umpire for the 1974 "Ten Cent Beer Night" game between Cleveland and the Texas Rangers on June 4, 1974.[28] The players were doused by beer by midgame. Hundreds of inebriated fans stormed the field in the ninth inning. Both teams fled the field for their own safety. The fans stole the bases and threw objects including bottles, rocks, cups, radio batteries and folding chairs. Chylak was struck in the head and cut by part of a stadium chair and also hit in the hand by a rock. The crew chief, he realized that order could not be restored and forfeited the game (tied at the time) to Texas.[29]

Chylak's career ended in Toronto in July 1978 when he became ill working a night game after a spell of difficult travel. His umpire colleagues asserted that he suffered a mild stroke, but family members said he was suffering from exhaustion.[30]

After retiring from the field, Chylak became an assistant supervisor of umpires for the American League. He was present in Chicago on Disco Demolition night, July 12, 1979. Between games disco records were blown up on the field. Then thousands of spectators stormed the field and a riot was on. Chylak informed Bill Veeck, the owner of the White Sox, that the second game could not be played. Despite Veeck's protest, the American League president Lee MacPhail upheld Chylak's decision. The next day MacPhail ordered the second game forfeited to Detroit rather than rescheduled.

In retirement, Chylak became a member of the Sports Illustrated Speakers' Bureau,[31] speaking about the intangible lessons he had learned from his years umpiring baseball. His son Bill said that his father was the biggest politician on behalf of baseball there ever was.

Chylak gave baseballs, bats, and other memorabilia to friends, family, and sometimes even total strangers. Chylak visited patients in the Veterans Hospital in Plains, Pennsylvania, each week. During the offseason he spoke to Little Leaguers, Boy Scouts, and others without charge.[32] As evidenced by baseballs and cards signed by Chylak on auction on eBay, Chylak signed his autograph with the words "Play Hard and Fair."

Chylak died at home in Dunmore, Pennsylvania, of an apparent heart attack on February 17, 1982, three months before his 60th birthday. He is buried in SS. Cyril and Methodius Catholic Cemetery in Peckville, Pennsylvania. Chylak was survived by his wife, the former Sophie Shemet, and his two sons.[33]

Chylak was inducted into the National Baseball Hall of Fame in July 1999 after election by the Veterans Committee. (A committee in his home area had begun lobbying the Veterans Committee on behalf of Chylak, collecting signatures and letters of endorsement.)[34] Chylak's son Bob spoke at the induction ceremony.[35]

NOTES

1   William C. Kashatus, *Diamonds in the Coalfields: 21 Remarkable Baseball Players, Managers, and Umpires From Northeast Pennsylvania* (Jefferson, North Carolina: McFarland Publishers, 2001), 88.

2   "A Tribute to Nestor Chylak," chylak.maslar-online.com. Accessed October 3, 2014.

3   Borys Krawczeniuk, "The Right Call," *Scranton Sunday Times,* July 25, 1999.

4   "A Tribute to Nestor Chylak."

5   Ibid.

6   Gary Bedingfield, "Nestor Chylak," http://www.baseballinwartime.com/player_biographies/chylak_nestor.htm. Accessed October 5, 2016

7   "A Tribute to Nestor Chylak."

8   Kashatus, 64.

9   "The Right Call."

10 Kashatus, 40.

11 "A Tribute to Nestor Chylak."

12 Kashatus, 56-57. See Retrosheet.org for details on each game of Chylak's major-league career.

13 Sean Lahman, The Baseball Archive, seanlahman.com/baseball-archive/statistics/. Accessed October 4, 2014. Chylak's first assignment working the plate was in the first game of a doubleheader at Fenway Park on April 18, 1954.

14 "A Tribute to Nestor Chylak."

15 Kashatus, 88.

16 Krawczeniuk, "Brooks Says Nestor Was the Best," *Scranton Sunday Times,* July 25, 1999.

17 Bob Chylak, text of Hall of Fame induction speech, July 25, 1999, chylak.maslar-online.com/.

18 retrosheet.org/boxesetc/index.html#Umpires.

19 Chylak obituary, *Ellensburg* (Washington) *Daily Record,* February 18, 1982.

20 "A Tribute to Nestor Chylak."

21 Ibid.

22 Mike Crist, "Nestor Was the Ump the Players Wanted," *Scranton Sunday Times,* July 26, 1999.

23 Ibid.

24 Krawczeniuk, "Brooks Says Nestor Was the Best."

25 "A Tribute to Nestor Chylak."

26 Ibid.

27 Ibid.

28 Kashatus, *Diamonds in the Coalfields,* 89.

29 Randy Galloway, "Unruly Fans Cause Forfeit," *Dallas Morning News,* June 5, 1974: B1.

30 Ibid.

31 Kashatus, *Diamonds in the Coalfields,* 126.

32 "The Right Call."

33 "A Tribute to Nestor Chylak."

34 Mike Crist, "A Day in the Sun," *Scranton Tribune,* July 26, 1999.

35 Bob Chylak, Hall of Fame induction speech, *Scranton Sunday Times,* July 26, 1999.

Jocko Conlan

By Rodney Johnson

ocko Conlan always wanted to be a ballplayer. He never dreamed about becoming an umpire until the opportunity presented itself by accident. He parlayed that chance into a Hall of Fame career that spanned 25 big-league seasons. A *Sporting News* book once wrote of Conlan, "He was a master psychologist in the charged-up world of the baseball diamond, knowing when to cajole, when to rebuff, and when to ignore. He knew the rules as well as any umpire but he also used the feel of the rules as they applied to plays and players."[1]

Born on December 6, 1899, John Bertrand Conlan was the son of a Chicago policeman. The youngest of nine children, he was named after his uncle John. Sister Mary Bertrand, a nun who was a good friend of his mother, inspired his middle name. When John was 3 his father died at 49, leaving his mother to raise nine children. "My mother was a wonderful woman," recalled Conlan. "My mother did all our washing and sewing and baking and she kept us all together."[2] The family matriarch lived to be 88 years old.

Conlan grew up playing ball with All Saints Parochial School. He pitched and played first base. Fred Lindstrom, who later played with the Giants, was the team's third baseman. When he was 13, Johnny spent his summer at White Sox Park picking up bats and shagging balls at morning practices. His lucky day came when coach Kid Gleason forgot a glove on the ground. "Oh[,] it was nice and shiny and oily," remembered Conlan. "I had never had a big-league glove on my hand or even seen one up close. … I shoved the glove under my overalls and walked out of the park."[3]

The glove was right-handed so Conlan traded it for $2 and a lefty glove. Fifteen years later, when he was playing for Newark and Gleason was coaching for the Athletics, the two crossed paths at an exhibition game in Miami. After confessing the theft, Conlan received absolution of sorts. "That was the greatest glove I ever had," lamented Gleason. "Let me tell you something, kid. If that glove helped make a ballplayer out of you, I'm glad you swiped it."[4]

Johnny went on to play outfield at De La Salle High School and for semipro teams around Chicago. Johnny's brother Joe was a good amateur pitcher and played in the semipro Midwest League with Jocko. In 1920 Joe had a tryout with the Brooklyn Dodgers and pitched in a spring-training game in Florida against the New York Yankees. Joe claimed that the longest home run Babe Ruth ever hit came against him in that game. But Joe had just got married and soon moved back to Chicago, where he, like his father, became a policeman. Johnny also tried his hand in the ring as an amateur boxer.

Matty Fitzpatrick, an umpire in the Midwest League, recommended Johnny to Tulsa of the Class-A Western League, where he was signed to play in 1920 but never did. Conlan was actually traded at a train station. Both Tulsa and Wichita were passing through Union Station in Kansas City when it was discovered that the Wichita Jobbers' roster was a man short and Tulsa's was a man over, so Conlan just switched teams. Johnny spent most of the season with the Jobbers and hit .247 in 117 games. The naïve 20-year-old made a big mistake late in the season. His brother was on his way back to Chicago to get married and stopped by to pick up Johnny. The youngster jumped the team and went home with Joe. The team suspended him, which meant that he had to sit out a year. Johnny couldn't afford not to play so he went back to the semipro Midwest League in 1921. This was a mistake by the still naïve youngster. After returning to Wichita for the 1922 season, he was once again suspended for violating his original suspension. He played in just 10 games. His case was heard at the minor-league winter meetings in December and he was reinstated for the 1923 season. Johnny rapped out 204 hits and batted .311, the first of seven minor-league seasons in which he hit over .300.

In 1924 Conlan's contract was sold to Rochester of the International League, where he played for George Stallings, whom he called "the smartest, the most intelligent, greatest baseball man I ever met in my life."[5]

Conlan played three seasons for Stallings. The first year, 1924, he led the IL in hits, runs, and stolen bases. For his efforts he was paid $2,500. After holding out, he got a raise to $5,200 for the next season. By all accounts, Conlan was a speedy, strong-armed center fielder. At 5-feet-7 and 165 pounds, his diminutive stature seemed to be all that kept him out of the big leagues for 14 seasons. In 1925 it looked as though Conlan would get his chance with Cincinnati. A deal was set to send him to the Reds but when he was injured on a play at the plate, the Reds canceled the deal. Conlan's Rochester years also yielded a nickname that would become iconic: Jocko. "There was a sportswriter on the *Democrat and Chronicle* named Corri," explained Conlan. "He was the fellow who hung the name 'Jocko' on me." Another Jocko, Arthur Joseph "Jocko" Conlon, went to Harvard and played second base for the Boston Braves in 1923. Like Johnny, he was small in stature at 5-feet-7 and 145 pounds. The sportswriter Corri, who was from Maine, likely picked up on the similarities of size and name. The "original" Jocko spelled his name slightly differently, with o-n rather than a-n. "It seemed to fit. I wouldn't know what to do now if I didn't have Jocko as part of my name," wrote Conlan in his autobiography.[6]

On January 12, 1926, Jocko wed Ruth Anderson. The couple would have two children, John Jr. and Nona. John Bertrand Conlan Jr. went on to graduate from Harvard Law School and become a US congressman from Arizona. Jocko and Ruth's children gave them seven grandchildren.

After Rochester, Jocko spent three years playing for Newark. He hit over .300 all three seasons, reaching a career high .321 in 1927. In 1930 Conlan was traded to Toledo of the American Association, where he played for one season under manager Casey Stengel. His season was cut short by an injury he suffered while sliding into third on a triple. Conlan stayed in the game and scored on a sacrifice fly. It was

Jocko Conlan.

only then that it was discovered that he had a broken ankle. Jocko finished his minor-league playing career in 1931 and '32 with Montreal of the IL.

In 1934 Jocko finally got his chance in the big leagues. He sat out the 1933 season (he worked as a Chicago playground instructor), but got back in the game when the injury-depleted White Sox signed him as a reserve outfielder in midseason. While growing up just blocks from what became Comiskey Park, it was always his dream to play for the Sox. On July 6, 1934, the 34-year-old rookie made his major-league debut, against the Cleveland Indians at League Park. The last-place White Sox (25-49) toppled the Indians (37-35), 7-5. Jocko led off and played right field, going 1-for-5 with an RBI against Ralph Winegarner. In all, Conlan played in 63 games, 53 of them as a starter. Although his first start was as a right fielder, he worked only three games in right and started 49 games in center. Among his teammates were Luke Appling, Al Simmons, and Jimmy Dykes, who was also the manager. On September 16 in the second game of a doubleheader, Jocko had four hits in a 12-10 win against the Red Sox at Comiskey Park.

Lefty Grove pitched the final 3⅔ innings in relief and took the loss. He also had three other games in which he stroked three hits. For the season, Jocko batted .249 in 225 at-bats.

Conlan was back for the 1935 season and although he played in more games, he came to the plate nearly 100 times fewer. He was deployed as a pinch-hitter 28 times and twice as a pinch-runner. He started 30 games in the outfield and batted .286 in 140 at-bats. His greatest day as a player came on August 20, 1935, at Comiskey Park against the Philadelphia Athletics. In the first game of a doubleheader, Conlan played right field and batted seventh. He went 4-for-4 with a double and two stolen bases (including a steal of home) in a 13-4 White Sox win. For an encore he went 3-for-4 with three RBIs and a double in the nightcap to lead the White Sox to a sweep. He had one more shining moment near the end of the season. On August 26 he had three hits off Lefty Gomez of the Yankees in the first game of a doubleheader. Jocko threw and batted left-handed and was very much a platoon player. In his 82 career starts, only five came against left-handed starting pitchers.

Perhaps Conlan's most significant on-field performance came when he wasn't in the lineup. On July 28 in St. Louis, the White Sox were playing a doubleheader against the Browns. The heat was stifling—114 degrees by some accounts. Jocko was on the bench nursing a thumb injury he had suffered while wrestling with his best friend on the team, Ted Lyons. Of course, manager Jimmy Dykes thought that Jocko hurt his thumb diving for a ball in practice. The sore thumb may have been the start to a Hall of Fame career.

Red Ormsby was the home-plate umpire and Harry Geisel was on the bases in a two-man crew. Ormsby was overcome by the heat and had to be carried from the field. He was unable to answer the bell for the second game, and Conlan volunteered to take Ormsby's place on the bases. "I'll umpire," said Conlan. "I can't play anyway."[7] By custom and rule, players could be enlisted to umpire when one of the crew had to leave the game. Both Dykes and Browns skipper Rogers Hornsby agreed to let Conlan take a

spot on the bases. Geisel went behind the plate, Ollie Bejma, a reserve infielder for the Browns, was at first base and Jocko was stationed at third. (It might be added that Jocko umpired in his White Sox uniform that game.) While the Browns were hopelessly mired in last place, the Chisox were in third place just 5½ games out of the lead, so it was an important game. The Browns beat the White Sox, 4-3. The next day, while Ormsby recovered, Jocko once again umpired at third base with Harry Geisel behind the plate and Grover Hartley, a Browns coach, at first. The White Sox won 7-2 in spite of a triple play pulled off by the Browns. The league paid Conlan $50 for his first foray into the umpiring profession.

As a player, Jocko earned $3,000 in 1934 and $3,600 in 1935. In November he drew his release from the White Sox but along with it came a surprise offer. Perhaps inspired by Conlan's two-day umpiring stint, White Sox general manager Harry Grabiner suggested to him that since his career was winding down, maybe he should think about becoming an umpire. Jocko had never really considered being an umpire. He thought he would always be a player and then a manager. Grabiner explained that umpires, unlike players at the time, could earn a pension if they stuck with the job for a number of years. Major-league umpires at the time earned a pension of $100 a year for each year of service. "That means if you stay 18 seasons, you'd retire on $1,800 a year," explained Grabiner.[8] That meant an income of $150 a month. That sounded good to Jocko and he decided to give it a try.

Grabiner helped set up a meeting with American League President Will Harridge to talk about the job. Conlan thought he was going to get an umpiring job in the American League so he was surprised when Harridge explained that he would have to get some experience in the minors first. Taking on former big-league pitcher Firpo Marberry, who had no umpiring experience, had burned the league before. "[H]e looked great—on the bases. But when he went behind the plate he was nothing," said Conlan.[9] "We won't take an umpire on again unless he has experience," Harridge told Conlan. "You'll have to go to the minor leagues for that, Jocko."[10]

After a couple of days Conlan accepted the offer and in 1936 he started the season as an umpire in the New York-Penn League at a salary of $300 per month—$225 paid by the minor league and $75 paid by the American League. Jocko was married with two children and making $1,500 a season.

Conlan's minor-league journey lasted five years. He umpired in the New York-Pennsylvania League in 1936-37 and the American Association in 1938 through '40. Along the journey he thought that he would become an American League umpire, but it didn't work out that way.

After just one year as an umpire, Jocko got an offer from the Chicago Cubs to manage in the minor leagues. Clarence "Pants" Rowland, then a Cubs scout, encouraged him to give up umpiring and take a job with the Cubs managing their Southern Association team in Birmingham. Jocko turned down the offer to continue umpiring.

Tommy Connolly, the supervisor of umpires for the American League, came to Columbus, Ohio, to watch Jocko and his partner, Ernie Stewart, work. As Conlan and his supervisor walked to the train station after the game, Connolly told Jocko that he was a "finished performer."[11] It wasn't long after that Conlan found out what Connolly had meant by "finished." That winter Stewart and Texas League umpire Art Passarella received American League assignments for the 1941 season. Jocko was disappointed that he had been passed over.

On December 5, 1940, the day before his birthday, Jocko's fortunes changed. At about midnight a phone call from an old connection changed everything. Pants Rowland was on the phone with an unexpected invitation. "Ford Frick (National League president) wants to see you in the Palmer House at one o'clock tomorrow," Rowland told him.[12] At their meeting, Frick offered Conlan a job as a National League umpire. The next day at the hotel where the winter meetings were going on, Conlan ran into Connolly. Without breathing a word of his job offer from the National League, Jocko asked why he didn't get pro-

moted to the American League. "I'm sorry, Jocko," Connolly said. "The American League thinks you're just a bit too short for an umpire."[13] Of course this seemed hypocritical to Conlan, who at 5-feet-7½-inches was a half-inch taller than Connolly. Jocko never forgave Connolly. Conlan considered Klem, the National League umpire supervisor, to be his mentor.

So it was that Jocko became a National League umpire in 1941. It was the beginning of a 25-year big-league umpiring career. During this time he umpired in five World Series: 1945, 1950, 1954, 1957, and 1961; six All-Star Games: 1943 1947, 1950, 1953, 1958, and 1962 (second game); and four National League playoffs: 1946, 1951, 1959, and 1962.

Unlike Klem, who claimed to never have made a wrong decision, Conlan said that he just never "admitted" making one. "If you know in your heart that you called one wrong, you just try to call the next one right. Never 'even up.' That just makes two wrong decisions," said Conlan.[14]

Conlan soon became one of the most recognizable figures on the diamond. In addition to the diminutive figure he cut on the diamond, his polka-dot bow tie was instantly recognizable. Later in his career you could always tell when Jocko was behind the plate because he was the last National League umpire who was permitted to use the big balloon chest protector after all others had switched to the smaller, under-the-shirt model. This was more due to need rather than style. He twice suffered from broken collarbones and was granted permission to continue using the larger chest protector.

In addition to his appearance, Conlan's mechanics set him apart from other umpires. Wrote Oscar Ruhl in *The Sporting News*: "Jocko Conlan has what is perhaps the most picturesque and distinctive gesture in calling a strike, clenching his fist and throwing it up and back like an engineer pulling the throttle."[15] Southpaw Conlan was also noted for making his strike calls with his left hand.

Many fans may remember Conlan for his career-long feud with Dodgers and Giants manager Leo Durocher. The conflict reached a boiling point in April of 1961 when Durocher, by this time a Dodgers coach, got into a shin-kicking match with Conlan. Durocher had been out of baseball for five years and claimed that he had been blackballed. When Leo returned, he and Conlan picked up right where they had left off. The Pittsburgh Pirates were visiting Los Angeles. In the fourth inning, Norm Larker hit a popup and Pirates catcher Hal Smith couldn't quite get to the ball as it dropped in fair territory about three yards down the first base line. The ball then bounced foul without being touched. Larker ran all the way to second base and Conlan correctly called a foul ball. The Dodgers argued that Smith had touched the ball before it went foul. The field was cleared, order restored and Dodgers manager Walter Alston returned to the dugout. Conlan then walked over and threw Durocher out of the game, claiming he had thrown a towel onto the field, which Leo denied. Leo came out onto the field and a kicking match ensued. Conlan described the incident by saying, "I got kicked twice, and so did he."[16] Jocko was wearing shin guards, so Leo took the worst of the exchange.

In a 1954 interview, Conlan said, "You've got to have a thick skin and a strong heart. You've got to have and command respect. Without them, you're nothing."[17]

Their well-known dislike for each other went back many years. Durocher was fond of bringing celebrities to games and allowing them in the dugouts during pregame activates. Jocko was a by-the-book umpire and would not allow these celebs to stay once the game was to begin. One day in Brooklyn, Durocher had invited entertainer Danny Kaye to the game and asked Jocko if he could stay there for the game. Conlan, of course told him no. In 1962, with his tongue firmly in his cheek, Kaye recorded the song "D-O-D-G-E-R-S (Oh Really? No, O'Malley)." The song described a fictional game between the Giants and Dodgers. Jocko and Leo were both prominently featured. Of course the Dodgers won the game but not without some controversy involving Jocko and Leo.[18]

Conlan called Durocher "king of the complainers, troublemakers, arguers, and moaners."[19] In spite of their personal dislike for one another, there was respect. "As little as I think of Durocher, there is no question in my mind but that he always was a first-class manager," said Conlan. "If only he had behaved better, he would have gone down in baseball history as one of the great managers of all time."[20]

After Conlan's death, Durocher was generous in his remarks: "We had our battles on the field but we were good friends off the field. That's where it counts. He was a fine umpire and a fine man."[21]

Conlan traveled the world giving umpiring clinics in Europe and working exhibition games in Japan. Perhaps the trip he enjoyed the most was the one he took with the Dodgers in 1956. Games were played on Wake Island and in Hawaii and Tokyo. He enjoyed many of his relationships with the Dodgers including Pee Wee Reese, Gil Hodges, Don Drysdale, Sandy Koufax, and Duke Snider. One Dodger whom he never got along with well was Jackie Robinson. "I had a couple of run-ins with Jackie Robinson on that Japan trip, which is nothing new for Robinson and me," explained Conlan. "He was the most difficult ballplayer I ever had to deal with as an umpire. … Jackie was one of those players who could never accept a decision."[22]

By 1963 Jocko had developed a painful bone spur on his heel. He announced that 1964 would be his last season. After the season, Conlan began a restless retirement at his Scottsdale, Arizona, home. "You think you've been an important figure in the game over the years, and all of a sudden you're out of it. You're not important. You're not even a part of it any more," lamented Conlan.[23] So it came as a welcome call when National League President Bill Giles reached out to offer Jocko an encore of sorts in 1965. Giles let Jocko know that umpire Tom Gorman was sick and would be out for a couple of weeks. He asked if Jocko would be interested in filling in. Conlan jumped at the chance and those extra two weeks let Jocko leave on his own terms.

In retirement Conlan enjoyed playing golf, attending Cactus League spring training and observing umpires in the Arizona Instructional League. In 1974 he became the fourth umpire elected to the Baseball

Hall of Fame. One of the hallmarks of Conlan's career was to show respect and never curse. He described his philosophy to sportswriter Ed Prell. "I never cursed a ballplayer," said Conlan. "If a player cursed me, he was out. I never retaliated with profanity because that would make me equally guilty. When an umpire walks onto the field, he must have respect and it must be continued throughout the game."[24]

Just three months after his induction into the Hall of Fame, Conlan was in Los Angeles for the World Series. During the first game, he suffered a coronary occlusion and was taken to the hospital. As soon as he was well enough to travel, he was transferred to a hospital in Scottsdale, where he underwent open-heart surgery. Although he made a near full recovery, his activity slowed over the rest of his life. Jocko died on April 16, 1989, and is interred not far from Scottsdale Stadium at Green Acres Cemetery. Conlan served briefly in the US Navy during World War I. Though he doesn't even mention his service in his autobiography, it was deemed important enough that it was engraved on his gravestone. It reads "John Jocko Conlan," provides his birth and death dates, has a cross, and the inscription, "US Navy World War I." He is the only baseball Hall of Famer buried in Arizona. His wife, Ruth, died five years later.

NOTES

1   Paul MacFarlane, *Daguerrotypes of Great Stars of Baseball* (St. Louis: The Sporting News, 1971.)

2   Jocko Conlan and Robert W. Creamer, *Jocko* (Lincoln: University of Nebraska Press, 1967, 1997), 26.

3   *Jocko*, 25.

4   *Jocko*, 27.

5   *Jocko*, 32.

6   *Jocko*, 45.

7   *Jocko*, 17.

8   *Jocko*, 19.

9   *Jocko*, 20.

10 Ibid.

11 *Jocko*, 98.

12 *Jocko*, 100.

13 *Jocko*, 101.

14 Robert Cromie, "The Umpire Is Not Always Right," *Chicago Tribune*, February 27, 1955: 23.

15 Oscar Ruhl, "Scoreboard Magician Beats Umps to Punch," *The Sporting News*, March 3, 1948: 8.

16 Charles Maher, Associated Press, "Leo and Umpire Get Kick Out of Baseball," *Washington Evening Star*, April 17, 1961: A17.

17 Saul Pett, Associated Press, "Tale of Man Behind Mask—an Umpire," *Boston American*, September 19, 1954: 43.

18 baseball-almanac.com/poetry/dodgers.shtml.

19 *The Sporting News Baseball Guide 1990*, 300.

20 *Jocko*, 234.

21 Associated Press, "Famed Umpire Conlan Is Dead," *Mobile Register*, April 17, 1989: 3D.

22 *Jocko*, 151.

23 *Jocko*, 232.

24 Ed Prell, "Jocko, in Finest Hours, Lauds Giles and Klem," *The Sporting News*, February 16, 1974: 46.

Thomas Henry "Tommy" Connolly

By David W. Anderson

One of the important currents in the history of early 20th-century baseball is how many immigrants not only embraced their new home but also its national game. Hall of Fame umpire Tommy Connolly stands as a prime example of this fact.

Born in Manchester, England, on December 31, 1870, Thomas Henry Connolly immigrated to the United States in 1885. His father was a stonemason and the entire family, except one son who preceded them, came to the US aboard the Cunard Liner *Servia*.[1] They settled in Natick, Massachusetts, where his father became a salesman for Catholic church supplies and provided the family with a comfortable living.

Like most young Englishmen, including the famous sportswriter Henry Chadwick, Connolly played cricket while in Great Britain, but had never seen a baseball game before coming to America. In Natick he became batboy for a local team and developed an interest in studying the rules of baseball, reportedly from reading editions of *Sporting Life*. Unlike many early umpires who took up the profession once their playing days were over, Connolly never played any organized baseball. He turned his interest in baseball and fascination with the rules into a career. His interest in the rules and the knowledge he developed naturally, leading him to a successful umpiring career, both on and off the field. During the early 1890s Connolly umpired for the YMCA Club of Natick. His professional career began in 1894 in the New England League. Umpiring ability aside, ethnic solidarity was a crucial consideration and it was National League umpire Tim Hurst, also of Irish Catholic heritage, who recommended Connolly for his first professional assignment.

Connolly remained in the New England League until 1898, when he joined Hurst in the National League. Umpiring in the major leagues as much an ordeal as it was a job, because of player behavior and the lack of authority. Connolly resigned midway through the 1900 season after multiple disagreements with National League President Nicholas Young, who failed to support some of his on-field rulings. By the end of the year Connolly was officiating in the New York State League.

Fortunately for Connolly's umpiring career and for Organized Baseball itself, the new American League claimed major-league status. League President Ban Johnson promised umpires he hired that they would receive full support from the league office, and he opposed "rowdyism," a policy that suited Connolly. Though he had never seen Connolly umpire, Connie Mack, manager of the Philadelphia Athletics and himself an Irish Catholic, recommended that Johnson hire Connolly for the inaugural 1901 season. That began a half-century-plus of service with the junior circuit. Simply put, Tommy Connolly was one of the greatest umpires to ever take the field.

His hiring by Harridge came at a time when nearly every team in the league was unhappy with the quality of umpiring. To address the issue, Connolly instituted many reforms, including scouting the minor leagues for umpiring talent. When a prospect was identified, Connolly would often do the evaluation personally. His career was intertwined with Bill Klem's; the two men deserve credit for much of the changed status of umpires and umpiring in the major leagues. Most importantly, Connolly created an American League style of umpiring, which resulted in a heated rivalry with his National League counterpart Klem. Most notably, Connolly favored persuasive diplomacy in dealing with controversies and used the outside, "balloon" chest protector, while Klem was an authoritarian presence who insisted on the inside protector.

Because he worked in the league's first season, it is easy to note Connolly's career as one of firsts. It is an impressive list, especially when it is understood that his on-field performance justified many of the firsts. Connolly umpired the first American League game when Chicago hosted Cleveland. He later umpired inaugural games at Shibe Park in Philadelphia, Fenway Park in Boston, and Yankee Stadium in the Bronx. He and Hank O'Day were selected to officiate in the first modern World Series, in 1903. Connolly subsequently umpired in seven other fall classics. He umpired in the American League until June 1931, when he retired as a field umpire and was named American League umpire in chief by league President Will Harridge. He served in that post until he retired in January 1954.

He was behind the plate for four no-hitters, including the perfect game pitched by Cleveland's Addie Joss on October 2, 1908, in which Joss outpitched the Chicago White Sox' Big Ed Walsh in a 1-0 victory.

Connolly's baseball career spanned the time from when umpires worked games alone all the way to the modern four-man crews. It also spanned the time from when the profession was not highly regarded to the one that requires formal training and years of on-the-job experience.

Connolly described working alone as not being fun. He was mobbed many times. "Some umpires in those days didn't dare put the home boys out and I noticed they weren't around very long," he said. "They were what we called 'homers' and they had short careers."[2]

A smallish, slim man (he is reported as 5-feet-7, 170 pounds), Connolly always dressed formally with stiff collars with a tie split by a jeweled stickpin. When asked about his preference for formal dress, Connolly said he dressed carefully because he was representing an important phase of American life. Though not physically imposing, Connolly was able to garner the respect of players by his knowledge of the rules, fairness, and a firm manner. Devoutly religious, he attended Catholic Mass every morning, even during the baseball season.

During the Deadball Era, many umpires made their mark by ejecting players, coaches, managers, and sometimes fans. The primary reason for this was that they were working alone and had to do anything to keep control. In his first year, Connolly tossed 10 players but as he gained experience and respect he seldom had to resort to the thumb. Many accounts of his career note that he umpired 10 years without resorting to an ejection. Ty Cobb respected Connolly and once said, "You can go just so far with Tommy. Once you see his neck get red it's time to lay off."[3]

From 1901 to 1907, Connolly primarily worked games alone and preferred to do so until the time came when the league hired enough umpires to allow for two-man, and later three-man crews. As an umpire supervisor, Connolly was skeptical over the need for a fourth ump, saying three were enough; "…[J]ust perfect…" is how he put it. But the league office won that one.

Despite his preference, Connolly admitted later in his life that solo umpires had their hands full and often could not be in position to make a call. In describing play during the early Deadball days, Connolly said players took advantage of the single-umpire system by leaving base early on fly balls, cutting the second- or third-base corner to gain an edge, tripping base runners, and doing whatever else was required to gain an advantage.

Connolly noted that these tactics almost always caused altercations. He summed up: "An umpire just couldn't cover every base and everything that happened no matter how alert he was or how hard he tried. But we did the best we could. I have no regrets."[4]

Another view of Connolly came from the authors of *Baseball: The Biographical Encyclopedia*: "[H]e … believed in the quiet, dignified approach to umpiring, consciously forgoing grandstanding and controversy."[5] Another way of putting it was in Connolly's off-putting way of describing the umpire. "It may surprise you, but no one ever paid in to a ball park just to watch an umpire."[6]

Connolly always stood against rowdyism, and received strong backing from Ban Johnson. In

Tommy Connolly.

Baltimore in 1901, Joe McGinnity spat tobacco juice in Connolly's face. Johnson, coming to the umpire's defense, suspended McGinnity for 12 games.[7] Baltimore manager John McGraw, who had long been unhappy with Johnson's unwavering support of his umpires, eventually left the American League and became manager of the New York Giants the next season.

When he worked alone, Connolly would stay behind the plate when first base was open. With a runner on first, he would move to the back of the pitcher's mound. But unlike other Deadball Era umpires, Connolly would move back to the plate with a runner on second. Connolly reasoned he would be in better position to see a play at third and of course would then have the plate covered.

On the field Connolly was methodical and far from colorful. He would tell anyone who listened that no one ever bought a ticket to see an umpire. He once tossed Babe Ruth during the Bambino's early days with Boston. During those days Ruth would often visit with Connolly during the offseason. Anyone

familiar with Ruth knows he could not or would not remember a person's name and almost always referred to people as 'Kid.' But that did not apply to Connolly. The Babe would often greet him with "Hi yah, Tommy, you old son of a gun. Remember that day you tossed me?"[8]

While having a reputation as an excellent mentor for younger umpires, Connolly would also attempt to nurture young players as well. During the debut of a promising rookie who went on to a Hall of Fame career, Tommy called time to talk to the young hurler, who was catching grief from the opposing dugout for the crime of not toeing the mound properly. Going out to the mound, Connolly told the pitcher, "Son, there are right ways and wrong ways to pitch in this league. Let me show you the right way. I'll take care of that wrecking crew in the dugout and from what you've shown me today you'll be up here a long time." The rookie pitcher was Gettysburg Eddie Plank, who won over 300 big-league games.[9]

Another player Connolly encountered was Tris Speaker. In a close play, Speaker blew his top, accusing Connolly of being prejudiced against him and the Indians. Connolly, never raising his voice said, "Tris, you're out of the game, of course. And if you don't change your thinking, you'll be out of baseball."[10]

Connolly and the great center fielder did not speak for months, even though Speaker tried to apologize. Later in the season, Speaker wanted Connolly to umpire behind the plate. Connolly agreed. Tris knew that Connolly was the best.[11]

As an umpire supervisor, Connolly often had to judge talent. Though he was a small man, he preferred umps to have some size. He said a large umpire often makes a good impression on the field and that shorter umpires often have trouble working behind large catchers. He was a stickler on the rules but when asked to list what made a good umpire, he said, "If they're otherwise all right, what you have to teach them is poise. And another thing I tell 'em is not to have rabbit ears. Never mind that wrecking crew in the dugout. Just go about your job of calling 'em on the field."[12]

Former National League President and Commissioner Ford Frick described Connolly this way: "Tommy was a slight quiet little man in an era when most umpires were big, brawny, and boisterous. … He was a religious man too, in an age of violent argument and colorful profanity. … But he had a ready wit and a quiet sense of humor that usually quelled the most serious distractions."[13]

Connolly also was a fair judge of playing talent as well. Until his dying day, he would mention two players on his list of all-time greats. He called Walter Johnson the greatest pitcher he had ever seen, and Ty Cobb the best position player because Cobb could "beat you in so many ways."[14]

In 1953 Connolly and Klem, the most influential umpires in baseball history, the fathers of their respective league's umpiring traditions, both of whom were the only ones to have worked in five decades, were elected to the Baseball Hall of Fame, the first arbiters enshrined among the game's immortals. He was unable to attend the induction due to illness.

Connolly married Margaret Gavin in 1902 and they had seven children, four daughters and three sons. After Margaret died in 1943, he lived with two of his daughters. Upon his retirement in 1953, Connolly was awarded a gold pass to major-league games and when his schedule and health permitted was often seen at Fenway Park. He died at the age of 90 on April 28, 1961, in Natick of natural causes.

NOTES

1   Baseball Hall of Fame, umpires file Thomas Connolly biography file. Unless otherwise stated, most of the content is from the Baseball Hall of Fame.

2   Ibid.

3   David L. Porter, "Thomas Henry Connolly, Sr." in Porter, *Biographical Dictionary of American Sports* (Westport, Connecticut: Greenwood Press, 2000), 109-111.

4   Baseball Hall of Fame, umpires file Thomas Connolly biography file.

5   David Pietrusza, Matthew Silverman, and Michael Gershman, *Baseball: The Biographical Encyclopedia* (Kingston, New York: Total Baseball, 2000), 232.

6   Baseball Hall of Fame, umpires file Thomas Connolly biography file.

7   Donald Dewey and Nicholas Acocella, *The Biographical History of Baseball* (New York: Carroll and Graf Publishers, Inc., 1995), 93.

8   Ibid.

9   Ibid.

10 Arthur Daley, "Sports of the Times," *New York Times*, February 11, 1954.

11 Ibid.

12 Baseball Hall of Fame, umpires file Thomas Connolly biography file.

13 Ford C. Frick, *Games, Asterisks, and People: Memoirs of a Lucky Fan* (New York: Crown, 1973), 137.

14 Baseball Hall of Fame, umpires file Thomas Connolly biography file.

Billy Evans

By David W. Anderson

Billy Evans had one of the most varied nonplaying careers in baseball history. The third umpire to be inducted into the Hall of Fame, Evans umpired from 1906 to 1927 during most of the Deadball Era in the American League, and augmented his umpire's salary by writing a nationally syndicated sports column, "Billy Evans Says," as the sports editor of the Newspaper Enterprise Association. Prior to that, he had written columns that appeared in more than 100 newspapers across the country covering varied topics as player personalities, umpiring techniques, and the World Series. In doing this, he promoted and understanding of the game and its stars in the early 20th century. A popular offering was a frequent column on strategy and rules, with the pointed question, "What Would You Do?"[1]

Born in Chicago on February 10, 1884, William George Evans grew up in Youngstown, Ohio, where his father, a Welsh immigrant, worked as a superintendent in a Carnegie Steel mill. As a youngster he participated in YMCA sports programs and a local baseball team, the Youngstown Spiders, named after the Cleveland Spiders. Billy enrolled at Cornell University in 1901. Having excelled in baseball, football, and track in high school, Evans played freshman football and baseball at Cornell University. His baseball coach, former Baltimore Orioles player and future Detroit Tigers manager Hughie Jennings, called Evans a fine outfielder, but Billy's playing days ended with a football-related knee injury.

Evans spent 2½ years at Cornell studying law before his father's death forced him to leave school in 1902 to help support his family. He became a newspaper reporter, securing a job with the *Youngstown Vindicator* for $15 a week, and soon became the newspaper's sports editor.[2] Also in 1902, Evans began umpiring local baseball games. When the scheduled umpire failed to appear due to illness for an Ohio Protective Association game be-

tween the Youngstown Works club and a team from Homestead, Pennsylvania, Evans was persuaded to umpire the contest. He wound up working in the league as a substitute for a few more days, and was then hired as a regular umpire for $150 a month, a substantial increase from his newspaper salary.

In 1904 Evans joined the Class-C Ohio-Pennsylvania League. In 1905 he visited a clothing store in Youngstown owned by former Cleveland outfielder Jimmy McAleer, now manager of the St. Louis Browns, who told Evans he had seen him umpire and liked what he saw. McAleer recommended Evans to American League President Ban Johnson. McAleer had witnessed a game between Youngstown and Niles in which a Niles batter fell down after being hit by the pitcher. But Evans called the pitch a strike, ending the game. Evans had to be escorted from the field by police and Niles manager Charley Crowe.[3]

Acting on McAleer's advice, Johnson offered Evans $2,400 per year plus a $600 bonus to umpire in the American League in 1906. Evans said that looked like all the money in the world and claimed to break all speed records in getting his acceptance back to Johnson in a tersely-worded telegram reply saying, "Yes and thanks!"[4] Known as Big Boy Blue or the Boy Umpire, Evans was the youngest umpire to be hired by the majors when he joined the American League in 1906 at the age of 22. (*The Sporting News* obituary said that Evans rose from a Class-D minor league to the major leagues, but the *Encyclopedia of Minor League Baseball*[5] reports that the Ohio-Pennsylvania League was Class C.) Evans subsequently became, at 25, the youngest World Series umpire.

Being an umpire during the Deadball Era was not a comfortable position to be in as then a single umpire worked most games. Through his actions and on-field judgment, Evans built a reputation as one of the fairest arbiters in the game.[6]

Unique among his profession, Evans openly admitted that he was fallible and could make mis-

Billy Evans, 1914.

takes. The man behind the plate for Walter Johnson's first major-league game, Evans later confessed that Johnson's fastball sometimes came to the plate so quickly that he would close his eyes before making a call. "Why, do you know, Johnson was the only pitcher I ever closed my eyes on, in automatic self-defense, in spite of wearing a mask and having a catcher standing in front of me as extra protection," he once said.[7]

"The public wouldn't like the perfect umpire in every game," Evans contended. "It would kill off baseball's greatest alibi — 'We wuz robbed.'"

After Evans became a major-league umpire he had a confrontation with Hughie Jennings on May 22, 1907. "In the tenth Detroit's coaches sent [Boss] Schmidt in from second on [Charley] O'Leary's double but Umpire Evans, on [Monte] Cross' appeal, declared Schmidt out for not touching third base. The spectators swarmed the field and Evans had to call for police protection; at the same time he sent Manager [Hughie] Jennings to the club house."[8] Detroit won the game in the 11th and Jennings was suspended.

Evans quickly built a reputation as a "fair and square umpire" capable of handling any situation that arose on the diamond. He often said the trick of um-

piring relied upon three talents: the ability to study human nature and apply the findings, the ability to be at the right angle to make a call and the ability to bear no malice. Billy demonstrated this third skill in St. Louis in September 1907, when his skull was fractured by a bottle thrown by a 17-year-old fan after a controversial call. Ban Johnson came to St. Louis to announce he had hired an attorney and would prosecute the young offender. To his dismay, however, Evans refused to press charges, saying the youth's parents were nice people and the kid had apologized for throwing the bottle.[9]

But Evans was not a saint. If pushed he would not back down, and in September 1921 was involved in a fistfight with Ty Cobb under the stands after a game. Cobb was irate over a strike call in the late innings. During the argument Cobb reportedly told Evans that he would whip him right at home plate, but would not do so because he knew he would be suspended. Evans invited Cobb to the umpires' dressing room for the postgame festivities. The brawl itself took place under the stands, with players from both teams forming a ring for the combatants. According to some accounts of the incident, the fight ended in a draw, and was the bloodiest they had ever seen.

Cobb was suspended for the next game, which Evans umpired wearing bandages.[10]

Among his colleagues, Evans was well known as a mentor for young umpires, generous with his time and advice. Evans also became a strong advocate for the establishment of formal school training for umpires to meet the growing demand for officials. He was highly critical of Organized Baseball for doing little about the situation. Ironically, if the present-day umpire-school system existed during the Deadball Era, Evans would probably have never gotten a chance to umpire in the major leagues. Hall of Fame umpire Bill McGowan was quoted in the 2005 book, *Dean of Umpires: Bill McGowan*, as saying that being teamed with Evans early in his career was "the greatest break of my life" and "whatever I've accomplished in my life, I owe to Billy Evans … and Tommy Connolly."[11]

Yet Evans's umpiring philosophy sounds like something straight out of a handbook: "Good eyes, plenty of courage—mental and physical—a thorough knowledge of the playing rules, more than average portions of fair play, common sense and diplomacy, an entire lack of vindictiveness, plenty of confidence in your ability." Nonetheless, he was not afraid to admit his mistakes. He once called a ball foul before it stopped rolling. When the ball struck a pebble and bounced back into fair territory, the manager of the team at bat rushed onto the field, cursing Evans and demanding that he reverse his ruling. Billy responded, "Well, it would have been a fair ball yesterday and it will be fair tomorrow and for all years to come. But right now, unfortunately, it's foul because that's the way I called it."[12]

During his 22-year umpiring career, Evans umpired 3,319 games and umpired six World Series. He umpired four no-hitters as well as Walter Johnson's three consecutive shutouts of the New York Highlanders in 1908. A final point to Evans' umpiring career came from Fielder Jones, who often had arguments with him: "We always liked to meet up with Evans on the road and knew he was to umpire."[13]

Throughout his umpiring career, Evans continued to write about the game and the umpiring profession. He wrote frequent articles for the popular magazine *Collier's*, as well as for *The Sporting News*. He authored two books, *Knotty Problems of Baseball* (1950) and in 1947 *Umpiring From the Inside*, a superb umpire's manual that has withstood the test of time for its sound advice on the mechanics of umpiring and handling game situations. Among his tips for calling games were: You can't be too thorough a student of the playing rules. Never take your eye off the ball. Never flaunt your authority. Always work on the theory that the fans came out to see the players perform. Never look for trouble. Treat players with the same consideration that you expect from them. Hustle every minute you are on the ballfield.[14]

Evans retired as an umpire in 1927 to become general manager of the Cleveland Indians. It was the first time the term "general manager" was used; before that almost every club had a business manager.[15] During his nine years with Cleveland, the team showed steady improvement on the field and Evans was credited with signing Bob Feller, Tommy Henrich, Wes Ferrell, and Hal Trosky, among others. While attending Cleveland's Amateur All-Star Game in 1929 with his wife, Hazel, he asked her if any young players impressed her, and she said, "That good looking Viking over there."[16] The player was Joe Vosmik, who spent a 13-year career with the Indians, St. Louis Browns, Boston Red Sox, Brooklyn, and Washington.

Evans left the Indians in 1935 because of a salary dispute and accepted a job as farm director for the Boston Red Sox. His tenure was marked by conflicts with owner Tom Yawkey and manager Joe Cronin. His association with Boston ended in October 1940 when he was fired by Yawkey. His trouble with Cronin came after Evans had persuaded Boston to purchase the Louisville Triple-A franchise. The player wanted by Evans was Pee Wee Reese. In July 1939 Cronin traded Reese to Brooklyn, thus beginning a major feud with Evans.[17]

In 1941 Evans became the general manager of the Cleveland Rams of the NFL, but left the next year and became president of the Southern Association. From 1942 until 1946, while many other minor leagues went bankrupt because of the manpower shortage during World War II, the Southern Association increased attendance from 700,000 to over 2 million. Evans also rewrote *The Southern League Record Book* which he said, "is what I consider my No. 1 achievement while president, but my biggest thrill came in getting the League thru 1943. All but ten leagues had folded, and when we finished in the black, I was really happy."[18]

Evans got back to the major leagues in 1946 when he became executive vice president and general manager of the Detroit Tigers, a post he held until he retired in 1951. He sold slugger Hank Greenberg after the 1946 season for cash to the Pittsburgh Pirates, which was an unpopular move. Detroit never won a pennant during Evans's tenure, and after the team collapsed in 1951 he left baseball forever.

Always a dapper dresser, Evans, a devout Presbyterian, was known as a good family man, though his baseball activities often kept him away from his Cleveland home. He married Hazel Baldwin in 1908 and the couple had one child, Robert, who enjoyed a successful career as a radio executive. Evans died at 71 in Miami, Florida, on January 23, 1956, after suffering a massive stroke while visiting his son. He was buried in Knollwood Cemetery in Mayfield Heights, Ohio. His greatest honor came posthumously in 1973 with election as the third umpire enshrined in the National Baseball Hall of Fame (after Bill Klem and Tommy Connolly).

NOTES

1   Sources include Martin Appel and Burt Goldblatt, *Baseball's Best: The Hall of Fame Gallery* (New York: McGraw-Hill, 1977); Rich Marazzi's entry on Evans in Mike Shatzkin, ed., *The Ballplayers* (New York: Arbor House, 1990); Jonathan Fraser Light, *The Cultural Encyclopedia of Baseball* (Jefferson, North Carolina: McFarland Publishers, 2005); James M. Kahn, *The Umpire Story* (New York: Putnam, 1953); and Dan E. Krueckeberg, "William George 'Billy' Evans," in David L. Porter, ed., *Biographical Dictionary of American Sports: Baseball* (Westport, Connecticut: Greenwood Press, 1987), 169.

2   "Billy Evans, Renowned Baseball Figure, Dies," *Youngstown Vindicator*, January 24, 1956.

3   "Billy Evans, Scribe, Umpire and Executive, Dies at 71," *The Sporting News*, February 1, 1956.

4   Billy Evans file at the National Baseball Hall of Fame Library.

5   Lloyd Johnson and Miles Wolff, eds., *Encyclopedia of Minor League Baseball, Third Edition* (Durham, North Carolina: Baseball America, 2007).

6   "Here He Is—the Perfect Umpire—Billy Evans," *Chicago Sunday Record-Herald*, March 2, 1913; Grantland Rice, "About Umpires." This is undated but refers to Evans and others; Billy Evans file at the National Baseball Hall of Fame Library.

7   The Old Scout, "Evans Umpired With Eyes Shut," Billy Evans file at the National Baseball Hall of Fame Library.

8   "American League," *Sporting Life*, June 1, 1907.

9   Ed Bang, "Courage as Young Strike-Caller Brought Evans Big Time Chance," *The Sporting News*, February 1, 1956.

10 Billy Evans file at the National Baseball Hall of Fame Library.

11 Bob Luke, *Dean of Umpires: Bill McGowan* (Jefferson, North Carolina: McFarland Publishers, 2005).

12 Billy Evans file at the National Baseball Hall of Fame Library.

13 Billy Evans file at the National Baseball Hall of Fame Library.

14 Dave Anderson, "Seven timeless tips from a Hall of Famer," *Referee*, August 1999.

15 Lee Allen, "Cooperstown Corner," *The Sporting News*, November 4, 1967.

16 Jeff Carroll, *Sam Rice: A Biography of the Washington Senators Hall of Famer* (Jefferson, North Carolina: McFarland Publishers, 2007).

17 Glenn Stout and Richard A. Johnson, *Red Sox Century: The Definitive History of Baseball's Most Storied Franchise* (Boston and New York: Houghton-Mifflin Company, 2000), 214, 216, 221, and 225.

18 Jack Fleischer, "Evans Provided Southern With Major League Class," *Memphis Press Scimitar*, publication date not noted; in Billy Evans file at the National Baseball Hall of Fame Library.

Doug Harvey

By Alan Cohen

"The integrity of the game is the umpires. Nobody else. The entire integrity of the game is the umpires."

— Doug Harvey[1]

It was the late 1980s. The Cincinnati Reds had replaced the Big Red Machine with the Nasty Boys, and the Nastiest of the Nasty Boys was Rob Dibble. In the beginning of his career, Dibble had a habit of tapping his glove against his leg as he stood on the rubber. One day, the umpire was Doug Harvey. Harvey stepped out from behind home plate and strode to the mound. "Young man," he said, "the next time you do that, I will call a balk." Twenty-five years later, Dibble recalled his first meeting with God, and remembered Harvey as the pre-eminent umpire of his day, with an abundance of talent and patience.[2]

Harvey himself wrote. "I knew I wanted to be an umpire when I was six years old. My dad was an umpire—and a damn fine one—and I wanted to be just like him. I wanted nothing more than to be out on that field, and I umpired in the major leagues for thirty-one wonderful years, and for that I'm very grateful."[3]

Harold Douglas Harvey was the third of four sons, and he was born in South Gate, a suburb of Los Angeles, on March 13, 1930. His father, Harold W. Harvey, who had migrated from the Midwest to California at a young age, worked in trucking for the Union Ice Company, and the family lived in South Gate. Doug's mother, born Margaret Teters in Oklahoma, was from mixed Cherokee and Choctaw heritage. She worked as a waitress and then took a position a cashier at the local Safeway Supermarket. At an early age, the future umpire was called Doug, so as not to be confused with his father. At the age of 4, Doug was afflicted with nephritis, a kidney infection, and it took him almost two years to get well and

regain his strength. When Doug was 10, his father took another trucking job, and the family moved to El Centro, 170 miles away on the border with Mexico. During World War II, Harold Harvey was the civilian personnel director of the Camp Lockett Army Base.

In El Centro Harold umpired industrial league and high-school games when he wasn't working at Camp Lockett. After the war, he got a job selling tickets for the El Centro Imperials of the Class-C Sunset League, on occasion working as a stand-in umpire, getting a good reputation that didn't hurt Doug when he, still in high school, began umpiring semipro and Industrial League baseball games. In school Doug played all sports, was on the California state championship basketball team, as a junior and went on to attend El Centro Junior College. While in college he married Joan Manning, and shortly thereafter left school. He worked at several low-paying jobs and his marriage, which produced a son, Douglas Lee Harvey, ended in divorce within two years. Harvey was able to get a partial scholarship to San Diego State. He hit well enough in college (.378) to receive offers to play professional baseball, but he refused, wanting to stay close to home to attend to his sick mother and see his infant son as much as possible. A broken leg playing football ended his collegiate athletic career and, short of funds, he dropped out of college.

By 1956 Harvey's life was going nowhere. He was working odd jobs and umpiring amateur and semipro baseball whenever the opportunity presented itself. He decided to try to get a job as a professional umpire. He wrote letters but was getting no place when he got his first break. He umpired a game for the Southern California Baseball Championship. A Milwaukee Braves scout at the game, Johnny Moore, liked what he saw and put in a good word for Harvey. Not long after, he had a job in the Class-C California League for $250 a month.

Alimony and child support were such that Harvey had little in the way of funds and could not afford to go to umpiring school. Nevertheless, he set out to make himself the best umpire he could be. He committed himself not only to being authoritative and fair on the field but also to learning the rule book cover to cover. He was a no-nonsense fellow for whom name-calling was totally out of bounds and the cause for a quick ejection.

During his second year in the California League, Harvey met Joy Ann Glascock, a college student who was working at the ballpark in Bakersfield. It wasn't long before the two became engaged. On September 24, 1960, a year after Joy graduated from college, they were married.[4] They were still married more than half a century later.

In early 1961 Harvey got a job umpiring in the Arizona Instructional League. Once again, as was the case five years earlier, his style and acumen caught the eye of someone in a position to push him forward. This time it was 82-year-old Clarence Henry "Pants" Rowland, a former major-league manager, scout, American League umpire, and former president of the Pacific Coast League. On Rowland's recommendation, PCL President Dewey Soriano hired Harvey to work in the Pacific Coast League, a jump from Class C to Triple A.[5]

After the season, National League President Warren Giles secured a job for him as an umpire in the Puerto Rico Winter League. Harvey was highly regarded by league President Pedro Vasquez, and was hired to work in the National League, starting in 1962. He was assigned to Al Barlick's crew, joining Shag Crawford and Ed Vargo. Barlick and Harvey did not initially get along. Harvey discovered that Barlick was unhappy when Harvey was chosen over umpire Billy Williams, a Barlick favorite, to be promoted. Over the years, Barlick grew to appreciate Harvey's skills as an umpire.

His first game was on April 10, 1962, and it was the first time his father got to see him umpire professionally. Harvey, who was umpiring at third base that day, said, "It was as big a thrill for him as it was for me."[6]

Harvey set his own standards for positioning himself, calling a game, and talking with managers and players. He saw arguments as part of the game, and when there was a close call he fully expected to have a "discussion" with a complaining manager. As long as the discussion was civil and there was no name-calling, he would let the player or manager have his say.

It wasn't long before the 32-year-old arbiter ejected his first player. On May 9 the temperature was 38 degrees and the Pirates were playing the Braves at County Stadium in Milwaukee. Harvey was stationed at second base. With the game tied 1-1 in the third, the Braves took the lead on singles by Joe Torre, Frank Bolling, and Roy McMillan. Torre, trying to advance from first to third on McMillan's hit, was not far past second base when catcher Smoky Burgess grabbed left fielder Bob Skinner's throw and gunned down Torre as he tried to get back to second base. Torre disputed the call and his choice of words was deemed inappropriate by the rookie umpire.[7]

Thirty years later, in 1992, Torre was managing St. Louis. Harvey was in his final season and thought it would be appropriate for Torre, who had been his first ejection, to be his last. And on September 16, the time was right. (Both teams had been virtually eliminated from playoff contention.) Torre came out of the Cardinal dugout to "contest" a call, as pre-arranged (the cover story was that Torre questioned whether pinch-hitter Craig Wilson had been properly announced into the game), and Harvey gave him the heave-ho in the top of the ninth inning.[8]

One of Harvey's earliest memories as a major-league umpire came from a game he was umpiring between St. Louis and the Dodgers on May 11, 1962. In the second inning, Dodgers pitcher Stan Williams, had two strikes on the Cardinals batter, and the count was 1-and-2. The next pitch was coming straight for the plate, and Harvey prematurely called "strike three." At the last instant the pitch broke out of the strike zone. The batter quietly walked away and over his shoulder calmly said, "Young fella, I don't know what league you came from, but home plate is 17 inches wide, same as it is here. If you want to stay up here, wait until the ball crosses the plate before you call it."[9] The batter was Stan Musial, and the lesson was learned by the rookie umpire.

Toward the end of the 1962 season, the Harveys became parents for the first time when their son Scott was born. Harvey was umpiring in Pittsburgh and did not see his son until the baby was two weeks old. They later had another son, Todd.

What was Doug Harvey's worst day behind the plate? In 1988, 25 years after the fact, he told writer Jerome Holtzman about a game in Houston. In those days, the Colt .45's, as they were then called, were playing in a ballpark notorious for its heat and mosquitoes. Most games were played at night, and "the lights were like flashlights." He was tired that evening, having been on the road for 10 weeks, and had a child at home who was terribly ill. He "couldn't tell if it was a ball or strike." He "vowed that I would never let it happen again, and I haven't."[10]

In 1964 Harvey was transferred to Jocko Conlan's crew, and was teamed with Conlan, Tony Venzon, and Lee Weyer. When Conlan retired at the end of the season, he joined Shag Crawford's crew. He was on Crawford's crew for 12 seasons. During that first season, he was teamed with Crawford, Venzon, and Al Forman. Years later, Harvey said that Crawford was the best umpire he had worked with.[11]

Money wasn't good for umpires in the 1960s when Harvey was promoted to the National League. His salary during those first two years was $8,000 per year. To supplement his income, he became a basketball referee. He was a referee during the inaugural season of the American Basketball Association in 1967.

Harvey also was a strong force in the umpires union, which was formed in 1963, his second year in the league, and over the years fought hard to improve benefits for umpires. Umpires struck during the first games of the 1970 playoffs, and in 1979 they stayed on the sidelines during spring training, looking for better pay. Asked to comment about the replacement umpires, Harvey said, "It's like not having a police force in our society. The amateurs can't cope because they don't have our training."[12] In 1984 the umpires stayed out for the first games of the playoffs before

Doug Harvey.

Commissioner Peter Ueberroth agree to arbitrate the matter. Harvey was part of a four-man crew that, as part of the agreement, umpired the final game of the playoff between the Cubs and the Padres and agreed to be available for the World Series.[13]

In his time in the National League, Harvey called many historic games and interacted with the greats of the game. On August 22, 1965, with the Dodgers playing the Giants in San Francisco, Harvey was at third base. Juan Marichal led off for the Giants in the third inning. There had been unusually bad feelings between the two teams and Marichal had been pitching the Dodgers batters a bit close. On each of the first two pitches to Marichal, Dodgers catcher John Roseboro stepped behind Marichal when firing the ball back to the pitcher, blazing the ball past Marichal's ear. Marichal, enraged, hit Roseboro over the head with his bat. A brawl ensued with Harvey's crew chief, Crawford, the home-plate umpire, at the bottom of the pile. Harvey tried to play peacemaker, and locate his comrade. Crawford ejected Marichal.

Harvey's first of five World Series was in 1968, when the Tigers defeated the Cardinals. He also worked six All-Star games and nine League Championship Series.

As much a fan as an arbiter, Harvey was very much in the right place at the right time on September 30, 1972. He was umpiring at second base when the batter rifled a shot to left-center field for a double. The center fielder returned the ball to the infield. Harvey asked the shortstop for the ball, which he handed to the batter as he congratulated Roberto Clemente on his 3,000th hit.

In 1974 Harvey was named a crew chief. His first crew comprised Harry Wendelstedt, Nick Colosi, and Art Williams. Over time, he worked with two umpires, Paul Pryor and John McSherry, who had more seniority, but he was able to maintain camaraderie with them and with all the other umpires he worked with.

On July 14, 1978, Harvey ejected Dodgers pitcher Don Sutton after the umpires crew found three balls that were scuffed.. Sutton was often accused of doctoring the ball.

On September 20, 1979, Harvey's crew was umpiring a game in Philadelphia between the Pirates and Phillies. The teams had split two games and the Pirates needed a win to maintain their slim lead over Montreal in the NL Eastern Division. The game was tied going into the bottom of the sixth inning. With two runners on base, the Phillies' Keith Moreland, in a play "that defines what it's like to be an umpire,"[14] lined a ball toward the left-field corner. Home-plate umpire Harvey's view of the ball was blocked as the batter crossed in front of him. Third-base umpire Eric Gregg ruled the line drive had gone over the fence in fair territory, putting the Phillies up 4-1.

Bedlam erupted and Harvey was besieged by the angry Pirates. Gregg "looked like he was being attacked by wasps or yellow jackets, because back in those days the Pirates had those awful yellow-and-black uniforms," Harvey later wrote. The umpiring crew of Harvey, Gregg, Andy Olsen, and Frank Pulli

got together and reversed the call. None of them had gotten a good look. It was the Phillies' turn to erupt, charging the field, led by manager Dallas Green and one of Harvey's favorite players, Mike Schmidt. Harvey ejected Green, the Phillies protested the game, and Moreland struck out. In the next inning, the Phillies scored a run and won the game, 2-1, dropping the Pirates to second place. In retrospect, Harvey said that the play was "the closest I've ever come to being stumped."[15]

Harvey was never one to put up with nonsense. Philadelphia was playing the Cubs at Wrigley field in 1982 and Phillies reliever Ed Farmer was wild. Farmer had already walked two batters in the seventh and the count was 2-and-0 on a potential third baserunner when manager Pat Corrales removed him from the game. The departing Farmer hurled some expletives in Harvey's direction and was ejected, causing Corrales to exclaim, "How do you throw a guy out of the ballgame when he is already out?"[16]

Occasionally an umpire's call can change the outcome of a game, and on June 6, 1984, Harvey was umpiring at third base in a game between the Mets and the Pirates. With the score tied 1-1 in the bottom of the ninth inning and Pirates center fielder Lee Mazzilli on third base, Jason Thompson launched a fly ball to center fielder Mookie Wilson. Mazzilli tagged up and scored what appeared to be the winning run. The Mets appealed the play, saying that Mazzilli left too early. Harvey, sure that it was the right call, ruled in favor of the Mets, and New York went on to win the game 2-1in 13 innings. Harvey said, "That's a call that if there's any doubt in the umpire's mind, he won't make it. A call like that comes from the heart and guts."[17]

How did Harvey get to be known as "God"? One story has it that San Diego catcher Terry Kennedy had seen Harvey checking out a rain-soaked field during a rain delay and made a comment about "God's" walking on water. Another story has Whitey Herzog exclaiming, during an argument, "Who do you think you are—God?"[18]

Kennedy remembered well the game in question. It was May 28, 1984, and the Padres were in New

York for a series against the Mets. Before the first game, Mets GM Frank Cashen asked Harvey to do everything within his power to get in the first game of the series as even worse weather was forecast for the next two days.

Kennedy recalled, "Doug was behind the plate, and I asked him how long we were going to play in such bad conditions. He said we had to make this game official or we would be playing back-to-back doubleheaders. (When the Padres next visited New York, the teams played two doubleheaders in a row. Had the May 28 game been rained out, there would have been three doubleheaders.) After the game, I was asked about playing in those conditions (the teams completed nine innings with the Padres winning, 5-4) and I made a comment about how the Son of God knew more bad weather was coming and we should play through this. (There was one 63-minute delay in the fourth inning.)[19] It all started from that. Doug got wind of my comment and, instead of being insulted, he was actually pleased by it." Kennedy went on to say, "Doug was a good umpire and kept his skills even as he got older, which was rare. He too enjoyed being in the rarefied air of major-league baseball."[20]

By the time Harvey worked the National League Championship Series in 1986, use of the term was very widespread and even more respectful. As Jerome Holtzman noted in an article in 1985, "Many players and managers refer to Harvey as 'God,' because in 22 years in the National League he has yet to make a wrong call."[21]

In the NLCS that year, the New York Mets were facing the Houston Astros and having all sorts of trouble with the offerings of Mike Scott. As had been the case with Don Sutton, Scott was accused of doing a little slicing and dicing of the ball. Umpire Harvey was the crew chief and drew the Game One assignment behind home plate. Scott, the National League's most dominant pitcher that year, was so strongly believed by the Mets to be putting something extra and quite illegal on the ball that backup catcher Ed Hearn's sole task was to track down balls and look for evidence of scuffing. In the first inning

Gary Carter swung at strike two and asked Harvey to check the ball. Harvey examined the ball, and tossed it back to Scott. Carter struck out on the next pitch. Harvey elaborated: "Carter said, 'Harvey, Harvey, no way. Look at that ball.' So I looked at it. I purposely turned toward Carter. I turned it over one way, then the other. That ball was clean. The man just exploded two extraordinary pitches."[22]

Carter, in his book *A Dream Season*, said of Harvey: "He's tall with thick white hair and a face as stern as rock. He's one of the premier umpires, and he is never wrong. I mean he knows everything. A pitch will come in, a ball, and Harvey will say, 'That one missed by half an inch.' Half an inch? What eyes! He tries to be helpful. He'll study your stance, your swing, and say, 'You know, son, you're not holding your hands back enough.' He calls every ballplayer son."[23]

Mets catcher Ed Hearn said he was behind the plate one time when a pitch came in relatively low. Hearn thought it to be in the strike zone. Harvey called, "Ball!" Hearn questioned the call. Hearn had turned his glove fingers down to make the catch. Harvey said, "Look, son, you turn your hand down and it's never a strike."[24]

Harvey's last season was 1992 and he retired as the most respected umpire in the game. He had stated that his goal was to work 5,000 games and retire at age 65. However, his knees were giving him problems and, at 62, he informed National League President Bill White that he was unable to continue. After the All-Star Game, it was announced that he would retire at the end of the season. When he umpired his last game, in October 1962, it brought his count to 4,673 regular-season games, which at the time was the third most for a major-league umpire.

In all of his years of umpiring, Harvey never was involved in a no-hitter. The closest he ever came was in 1969.

In his retirement, Harvey encountered medical issues. After chewing tobacco much of his life, he was diagnosed with throat cancer in August 1997. Radiation therapy proved successful and at the end of his treatment, he committed himself toward educating young people on the dangers of chewing tobacco.

In 2010, Harvey became the ninth umpire inducted into the Baseball Hall of Fame. By then, his mobility was limited as he had suffered a couple of strokes. It was thought for a time that he would not be able to attend the induction ceremony, but he was able to go to Cooperstown to accept induction, along with Andre Dawson and longtime nemesis Whitey Herzog. In his biography, published in 2014, he said he had regained his mobility, survived a bout with pneumonia and "is hanging in there pretty good for an old guy who started out with twenty-two months in the hospital when I was four years old. I had to fight it then, and I've had to fight it all the way."[25]

Reflecting on his time in the game, Harvey observed in 2015 that umpires were considered "necessary evils" when he broke in. Now they get a month off, and are allowed time off for things such as the birth of a child. With the use of replays, most confrontations are avoided.[26]

In 1986 manager Whitey Herzog of the Cardinals presented Harvey with a cap inscribed, "We'll get along just fine as soon as you realize I'm God"[27]—That's basically it.

SOURCES

In addition to the sources cited in the Notes, the author consulted Ancestry.com, Baseball-Reference.com, and the following:

Books:

Hearn, Ed, with Gene Frenette. *Conquering Life's Curves: Baseball, Battles, and Beyond* (Indianapolis: Masters Press, 1996).

Kaiser, Ken, with David Fisher. *Planet of the Umps: A Baseball Life From Behind the Mask* (New York: St. Martin's Press, 2003).

Skipper, John C. *Umpires: Classic Baseball Stories from the Men Who Made the Calls* (Jefferson, North Carolina: McFarland Publishers, 1997).

Articles:

"Pittsburgh Second by a Half-Game: Phils Beat Pirates 2-1," *New York Times*, September 21, 1979: A21.

Blair, Sam. "Seeking Solace Amid the Storm," *Dallas Morning News*, July 25, 1978.

Coffey, Wayne. "Longtime Ump Harvey Says He Made the Right Call—Retirement," *New York Daily News*, October 18, 1992.

Walfoort, Cleon. "Strikeouts and Men Left on Base are Making Braves' Progress Slow," *Milwaukee Journal*, May 10, 1962: 16-17.

NOTES

1   Bruce Weber, *As They See 'Em: A Fan's Travels in the Land of Umpires* (New York: Scribner, 2009), 15.

2   Author interview with Rob Dibble, June 20, 2014.

3   Doug Harvey with Peter Golenbock, *They Called Me God: The Best Umpire Who Ever Lived* (New York: Gallery Books, 2014), 9.

4   Harvey, 67.

5   Harvey, 75.

6   Phil Collier, "Climb to Major Leagues Swift for Harvey, San Diego Umpire," *San Diego Union*, May 27, 1962: B-11.

7   Harvey, 188; *Racine* (Wisconsin) *Journal Times*, May 10, 1962: 1D

8   John Harper, "Cards Officially Eliminate the Mets," *New York Post*, September 17, 1992: 67.

9   Harvey, 124.

10 Jerome Holtzman, "A Chat With God Offers Salvation," *Chicago Tribune*, December 28, 1988: C1.

11 Author interview with Doug Harvey, March 15, 2015.

12 Jack Murphy, "Umpires See Anarchy Unless Pros Return," *San Diego Union*, April 13, 1979: C-1.

13 Jerome Holtzman, "Umps End Strike, Go to Arbitration," *Chicago Tribune*, October 8, 1984: C7.

14 Harvey, 229-233.

15 Ibid.

16 Jayson Stark, *Philadelphia Inquirer*, June 17, 1982.

17 Ken Rappoport (Associated Press), *The Index-Journal* (Greenwood, South, Carolina), June 7, 1984: 12.

18 Author interview with Bill Haller, June 18, 2015.

19 Murray Chass, *New York Times*, May 29, 1984: D15.

20 Letter to author from Terry Kennedy, June 2015.

21 Jerome Holtzman, *Chicago Tribune*, June 27, 1985: C3.

22 Bus Saidt, "Great Scott! Debate Over Scuffed Baseballs a Challenge to Game's Integrity," *Trenton* (New Jersey) *Evening Times*, October 14, 1986: B-1.

23 Gary Carter with John Hough Jr. *A Dream Season* (Orlando: Harcourt, Brace, Jovanovich, 1987), 14.

24 Author interview with Ed Hearn, April 24, 2015.

25 Harvey, 268.

26 Author interview with Doug Harvey, March 15, 2015.

27 "A Chat With God."

Cal Hubbard: Two Sport Immortal

By Dennis Bingham

"Who is the only person enshrined in both the Pro Football Hall of Fame *and* the National Baseball Hall of Fame?"

Cal Hubbard first earned acclaim as a bone-crushing tackle, then as a formidable umpire, and finally as an exceptional baseball executive. For nearly half a century his name was known by every self-respecting football or baseball fan. Alas, fame can be fleeting. Today, if sports fans are familiar with him at all it is probably as the answer to the above trivia question, but Hubbard deserves to be remembered more as just a means to win a barroom bet. To be bestowed the highest honor of a sport is a remarkable achievement; to be inducted into the shrines of *two* different sports is extraordinary, requiring an array of diverse talents.[1]

Robert Cal Hubbard, of Scotch-Irish descent, was born on October 31, 1900, in a small Keytesville, Missouri, farmhouse. One of six children born to Robert Porter Hubbard and Sarah "Sallie" (Ford) Hubbard,[2] he was always known by his middle name to distinguish him from his father.[3] His formative years featured family, fishing, farming, and football, all of which would remain important to him his entire life. Cal also always kept his country-boy roots, preferring the quiet charms of small-town living to any of the many bustling metropolises in which he would work.

At age 12, Hubbard smoked his first Camel cigarette behind the barn with a boyhood friend and became a chain-smoker for nearly the next five decades.[4] The bad habit certainly didn't stunt his growth. By age 14, he was a tall teenager, weighing a muscular 200 pounds. He discovered in his youth that he excelled at every sport; every sport, that is, except baseball. His bulk made him rather awkward on the diamond but he loved the game and would serve as umpire for his friends on the sandlot.[5] They nicknamed him "The Enforcer" because of the way he controlled the game.[6]

Football was an obsession with young Hubbard. He worshipped from afar Alvin "Bo" McMillin, the legendary college quarterback whose exploits Cal would faithfully follow by newspaper. Hubbard would travel to Glasgow, a town 15 miles away, because his hometown school did not have a football team. (He was back, however, at Keytesville High School for graduation.) His dreams of playing football for the United States Military Academy at West Point were dashed when he was denied acceptance after a physical exam revealed his flat feet.[7] So he enrolled in Chillicothe (Missouri) Business College because of its promising football program. He lasted only one year before returning home to work on the family farm.

In 1922 Hubbard enrolled in Centenary College in Shreveport, Louisiana, after his hero Bo McMillin became the school's head football coach. He joined the football, track, wrestling, boxing, and baseball teams. (He made the baseball team only because of the college's small enrollment.) Nobody had ever seen anyone quite like him before on a football field—a player with such an awesome combination of size and speed. Able to run the 100-yard dash in 11 seconds, Hubbard was a sensation on the gridiron. In addition to his girth and quickness, the fierce intensity with which Hubbard played made a durable impression. "I liked to hit people," Cal would say, so much so that coach McMillin would bar him from participating in team scrimmages for fear of injuring his teammates.[8]

Virtually every article ever written about Hubbard mentions his imposing physical stature, even those written when he was an elderly man in retirement.

Cal Hubbard.

Sportswriters would turn to their thesauruses to find new ways to describe his build—towering, enormous, massive, gigantic—but there was no consensus on how big he really was. He was variously listed as weighing anywhere from 220 to 280 pounds and standing between 6-feet-2 and 6-feet-5. Everyone agreed, however, that Hubbard had an intimidating physique, particularly for the era in which he played. (Actually, Cal stood 6-feet-3 and weighed 250 pounds, somewhat heavier in later life.)[9]

By leading Centenary College to three successful seasons, Hubbard earned acclaim as its menacing tackle. Meanwhile, coach McMillin came under heavy criticism from school administrators for placing too much emphasis on athletics over education. Professors complained that his football players were missing too many classes because of practices and long road trips.[10] When the controversy became heated, McMillin quit and became head coach at

Geneva College in Beaver Falls, Pennsylvania. And he took Cal Hubbard with him.

Under Geneva's eligibility rules for switching schools, Cal had to sit out the 1925 football season. On the plus side, Geneva was where he met his future wife. Their college courtship reads as if it were taken from a screenplay for a romantic comedy. One day, while strolling on the campus grounds with McMillin, Hubbard saw a pretty coed walk by with an armful of books. Transfixed, he stood silent until she passed out of sight. "There goes the future Mrs. Cal Hubbard," he said to his flabbergasted coach.[11] Catching up to the young woman, he bluntly asked her, "What's your name?" She replied "Ruth Frishkorn." Cal's comeback: "That name's too hard to pronounce. I'm going to change it to Hubbard."[12] Following the movie-script theme, he asked her for a date, was predictably turned down, he persisted, a college romance blossomed, and he eventually won her heart.

During his year away from football, Hubbard worked in the local steel mill and kept in shape by joining Geneva's track team. He set the school record in the discus throw at 142 feet, 8 inches. Returning to the gridiron in 1926, he earned national attention as a virtual one-man team when Geneva defeated powerful Harvard—a classic contest that remains one of the most stunning upsets in college football history. Cal's roommate Paul "Pip" Booth never forgot him: "[Hubbard] moved like a cat and always smashed into the ball carrier with his face or chest. Once I saw him smash down the whole side of a defensive line by himself. He was six to eight years older than most of us, and we looked up to him more as a father than as a teammate."[13]

Hubbard was admired as much for his character as for his athletic ability. He helped his coach maintain discipline on the squad, making sure his teammates followed McMillin's strict rules of no smoking, no drinking and no card playing. Booth said, "No man had clearer living habits [than Hubbard]. His only bad one was sitting up all night to drink coffee and talk sports. Baseball and football rules were his hobby; he spent days and nights studying them and drinking coffee."[14] The contrast in Cal's Jekyll-and-Hyde personalities was striking. On the football field he was brutal, mean, and intimidating; elsewhere, he was congenial, amiable, and friendly, a gentle giant replacing a scowl with a smile. A college professor who knew him said, "Big Cal was as kind and generous a man off the field as he was an untamed savage on it."[15]

For Hubbard 1927 was a landmark year, in which he earned his bachelor's degree, began his fabled career in the National Football League, and married his sweetheart, Ruth. When it was pointed out that it took him three colleges and seven years to obtain his degree, Cal joked that he was not exactly "what you would call a professional student."[16] After completing his college education, Hubbard was bombarded with offers from every NFL team. He signed with the New York Giants, teaming up with tackle Steve Owens to turn a good defensive team into a great one. By shutting out their opponents 10 times in 13 games and allowing in the entire season an absurdly low 20 points, the Giants won their first NFL championship. Hubbard kept up his ruthless, hard-nosed style of play from his college days—explaining to teammates "the fine art of using an opponent's helmet ear holes to improve your grip in preparation for smashing the opponent's head on your knee."[17]

Not only was Hubbard a star player, he was an influential one. He revolutionized NFL defensive tactics by creating the linebacker position. Cal realized that if he stayed anchored on one side of the scrimmage line, the opposing team would just run the other way to avoid his shattering tackles. Hub was missing out on all the fun. So he began roaming the backfield and with his amazing speed was able to plug up any hole to crash into opponents. "What was really scary for quarterbacks and blockers was that on any given play, they couldn't be sure where Cal would line up," wrote football historian Murray Greenberg. "Sometimes he'd play up on the line, but just as often he'd back off the line and freelance … and when he reached the ball carriers, it wasn't for a social visit."[18]

In those days of leather helmets and one-platoon teams, Hubbard usually played all 60 minutes of the game, roaring into the enemy line as an end on offense and creating havoc as linebacker on defense. In his later years, as retired athletes are prone to do, Cal commented on how much tougher you had to be in the old days: "I can't imagine playing less than half a game. We had to be in shape, and we were—or we'd have been killed."[19]

Professional sports a century ago paid relatively meager salaries, requiring players to seek employment in the offseason. Although Hubbard had one of the highest salaries of any NFL player, he needed something to supplement his income. A friend suggested that he write to the head of the minor leagues, Judge William G. Bramham, and apply to be a professional umpire between football seasons.[20] Although Hubbard had not umpired since he was a teenager on the sandlots, he thought the suggestion intriguing; it turned out to be a life-changing decision. He met personally with Bramham, who was so impressed with Cal's quiet confidence, style, and knowledge of the rules that he hired him immediately. For the next eight springs and summers Cal would gain experience as a minor-league umpire while in the fall and winter he continued his stellar career in football.

Hubbard was back with the Giants in 1928 but with his lifelong distaste for big cities he wanted out of New York. After the season, he demanded to be traded to Green Bay and a deal was made. Playing for Earl "Curly" Lambeau, Hubbard helped create pro football's first dynasty with the Packers winning three straight NFL championships (1929-1931), going undefeated the first year.[21] To improve their chances of beating Green Bay, opposing teams would provoke fights with Hubbard to get him ejected from the game. In one notable contest, Chicago Cardinals substitute Phil Handler persistently taunted Hubbard but the big guy did not fall for the scheme. "Get away from me, small change," he yelled at his tormenter. "I'm not getting tossed out for the likes of you."[22] A major brawl broke out between the two teams near the end of the game. After the players were separated and order restored, Handler was found lying unconscious in the end zone and Hubbard standing off to the side with bruised knuckles and an innocent smile.

On the gridiron, Hubbard left a lasting impression on the minds and bodies of every opponent he would come in contact with. "Green Bay had the most brutal lineman in the game—Cal Hubbard," said quarterback Harry Newman decades after their clashes. "He played with the intensity that Dick Butkus did later. We used to say of Cal that even if he missed you, he hurt you. When he tackled you, you remembered it. I do to this day."[23]

In 1934 Hubbard left the professional ranks and returned to college to serve as line coach at Texas A&M. The following year he was back playing for the Packers, after which he told his wife, Ruth, that he was retiring from football for good. She laughed because for years, after each battering season, he had said the same thing. It had become a running joke in the Hubbard household with Cal saying he was going to retire only to be back on the field each October smashing heads.[24] Sure enough, in 1936 Cal was playing football for the Pittsburgh Pirates (later renamed the Steelers) and then for the Giants, now coached by old friend Steve Owens.

During the last game of New York's 1936 season, with just over a minute left to play, several Boston Redskins players crashed into Giants halfback Les "Red" Corzine. The play had a profound effect on Hubbard. He heard the sharp crack of his teammate's leg being snapped in three places. He watched Corzine being placed on a stretcher and carried off the muddy field of the Polo Grounds. It got him thinking. When play resumed, Cal suddenly announced in a booming voice to the opposing team, "If any of you guys has a grudge against me, get it out of your system in the next minute and five seconds. This is your last shot at me. Come and get me because I'm through after this game."[25] Reportedly nobody was foolish enough to take him up on the offer. And, with that, Hubbard was out of football and this time he meant it. "I've taken enough beatings for one man," he later explained. "Not that I couldn't take some more, it's not fat nor age that's driving me out. … I've just had enough shoving and kicking around."[26]

After the game Hubbard returned home to his family in Zelienople, Pennsylvania (his wife's home-

town). By then, Ruth had become Mother Hubbard, having given birth to Robert Cal Jr. in 1929 and to a second son, William, in 1935.[27]

Already firmly established in his second sports career, Hubbard felt secure enough to retire from football. For the past eight years he had been toiling in baseball's minor leagues, traveling to towns and cities in 17 states and 2 Canadian provinces. He began in the North Carolina Piedmont League (Class C), calling balls and strikes for such teams as the High Point Pointers and the Henderson Bunnies. Being promoted to the Southeast and South Atlantic Leagues (Class B) meant umpiring in larger locales, including working Selma Cloverleafs and Charlotte Hornets games. And then up to the Western League (Class A) with teams like the Des Moines Demons and the Tulsa Oilers. Eventually, he was working International League games, one step below the majors, for teams representing larger cities like Baltimore and Toronto.[28] Hubbard still did not care for the noise and congestion of big-city life, but it meant he was advancing in his umpiring career; it also offered an opportunity for him to attend the opera, for which, probably surprising to his friends, he had developed a fondness.

Early in his umpiring career, Hubbard had a hostile relationship with the Macon Peaches fans of the Southeast League. Although recognizing that umpires are the natural enemy of many rabid baseball fans, Cal could not understand the particular hatred Georgia fans had toward him. Whenever he worked a Peaches game, the heckling and objects thrown in his direction were excessive. After one rambunctious game, Cal had to jump on a train and sneak out of town to escape a mob.[29] In an attempt to earn their respect, Hubbard agreed to be one of the fighters in a local boxing event. On Labor Day 1929, the Macon venue was filled to capacity with Peaches fans excited to see their nemesis take a beating. Cal's opponent was Spike Webb, a young heavyweight with about 40 bouts to his credit. Hubbard's battle plan was to forgo any finesse and just swing his massive fists at a furious pace until Webb fell to the canvas. For three rounds the plan worked. Webb was barely able to lay a glove on Hubbard, who relentlessly assaulted the veteran boxer with a barrage of blows. Ultimately, the strategy backfired. By neglecting to employ the finer points of boxing, Cal became completely exhausted and physically unable to rise from his stool for the fourth round. Although there was not a scratch on him, Hubbard threw in the towel, admitting later that he was so fatigued he would have fallen flat on his face if anybody had just given him "a harsh look."[30] As for Webb, the battered boxer stood wobbly and surprised when he learned that he had won. (It was said that had Webb received only one more punch, he would have collapsed.) Hubbard had lost the bout but had won the admiration of the Macon fans, who never again heckled him. The fans may not have liked Hubbard but they now respected him, which is all an umpire wants.

What separated Hubbard from other minor-league umpires was his encyclopedic knowledge of the rules, a reputation he took with him to the big leagues. Bo McMillin said that as a football player Hubbard would often hold up games to correct the rulings of referees, even if it went against his own team. Perfectionist Cal insisted that every call be the correct one. "He was born to be an official," said McMillin. "(As a player), he knew more about the rules than the officials! He spent more time studying them. He was a fanatic on rules."[31]

When asked what the greatest thrill of his umpiring career was, Hubbard found it difficult to name just one but said it might have been when he first learned he would be working in the major leagues. "Every time I walked out on the field of the American League, it was a thrill as it was a new challenge and it kept me always striving to do a perfect job," he said.[32] Hubbard's umpiring philosophy was simple: "You really have to understand only two things and that's maintaining discipline and knowing the rule book."[33]

It was apparent even as a rookie major-league umpire that Hubbard was something special; veteran umpires would praise him as the best newcomer they had ever seen.[34] Several attributes combined to make Hubbard exceptional; in addition to his vast knowledge of the rules, his imposing presence, cool manner in controlling a game, and sense of humor and professionalism all contributed to the package.

"What made him a great umpire?" said umpire Joe Paparella. "He carried the respect of the ballplayers, carried the respect of the management, and he knew how to handle the ballgame. He was rough, tough and fair. … And he was a good ball-and-strike umpire. I mean *real* good."[35] It was Hubbard's uncanny ability to call pitches that was truly astonishing, made possible by his extraordinary eyesight. Examined at Boston's American Optical Laboratory, Hubbard was found to have 20-10 vision, the strongest they had ever recorded and keener than that of Ted Williams, who also was tested at the lab. When told of this, Cal modestly said, "But I didn't have to call many strikes on Williams. If it was a strike, he hit it."[36]

In only his third year as a big-league umpire, Hubbard was assigned to work the 1938 World Series, indicative of how highly regarded he was as an arbiter. Even more remarkably, he had been initially selected to umpire the fall classic a year earlier but Commissioner Kenesaw Landis, fanatical about gambling, rejected Cal's assignment after learning that Hubbard had visited a racetrack. Hubbard, who rarely gambled, had gone just as a lark after being invited by two other umpires. Although disappointed at the time, he would laugh about it later, saying "Did the horse win? I don't even remember, only bet five bucks."[37]

Hubbard would be assigned to work three other World Series—1942, 1946, and 1949—and also the 1939, 1944, and 1949 All-Star Games. He was especially proud to have been chosen to umpire the last game of the 1949 season between the Red Sox and Yankees. The winner of that game would advance to the World Series, the loser would go home. Although a regular-season game, it was deemed important enough to have six umpires assigned with Hubbard behind the plate. After the game, losing Boston catcher Birdie Tebbetts approached him and said, "Hub, you worked a perfect game." It meant a lot to Cal, who said, "It is always easy for a catcher to tell you how well you've done, if his team had won."[38]

Though extremely confident in his umpiring abilities, Hubbard was humble enough to admit that he was seldom perfect but always strived to be. This was a departure from many headstrong umpires of an earlier era, who would never confess to being anything less than infallible. Bill Klem was noted for proclaiming, "I never called one wrong." Hubbard would say to players, "Boys, I'm one of those umpires that can make a mistake on the close ones. So, if it's close, you'd better hit it."[39] One game in which Hubbard would have acted differently in hindsight took place on September 12, 1939, when partner Lou Kolls misinterpreted a rule. American League President Will Harridge sustained the protest waged by Washington and ordered that the game against Chicago be replayed in its entirety. Although Kolls was an older and more seasoned veteran umpire than Hubbard, Cal should have conferred with him and insisted that he change his call when the protest was made.[40]

Sportswriters are apt to tag prominent athletic figures with catchy nicknames and it was no different in Hubbard's case. In his football days, he was called "The Mammoth Missourian," "Big Cal," or "The Human Bowling Ball" for his ability to bowl down opposing lines (and not leave many spares).[41] As an umpire he was dubbed "His Majesty" because of his regal manner on the field.[42] In any case, he was usually called simply "Hub," "Cal," or "Mr. Hubbard."

Hubbard's daunting physical presence earned him a reputation as one with whom players rarely argued and he thus had fewer ejections than other umpires. It is true that several of his ejections did involve players fighting among themselves and not for directly arguing with Hubbard, but he did have his share of confrontations with players. "I always hated to throw a guy out of a game, but sometimes it was necessary to keep order," he said. "When it was time for a player to go, he went."[43] Sometimes Hubbard was troubled to have to eject a player, such as when he had to toss Mike Guerra after a call of catcher's interference. The catcher never argued or swore but refused to get back behind the plate to continue the game. "I have to wind up throwing him out, but it had been bothering

me ever since," said Hubbard, "How can you throw out of a game a player who's refusing to stay in it?"[44]

Relationships that develop between home-plate umpires and catchers are intriguing and the one between Hubbard and Yogi Berra especially so. On June 11, 1948, Berra was ejected for the first time in his major-league career for repeatedly arguing Hubbard's pitch calls. When the popular rookie was sent to the showers, the Yankee crowd responded by showering the field with newspapers, cans, and bottles. One fan ran onto the field and threw a beer can directly at Hubbard, barely missing him. To his credit, Berra found Hubbard after the game and apologized, beginning an ongoing amusing rapport between the two. When upset about one of Hubbard's calls, Yogi would refer to the umpire's football days by saying, "I think you got hit in the head once too much."[45] During one blistering hot game in Boston, Berra swore at Hubbard in hopes that he would be ejected and escape the suffocating heat, but the umpire didn't fall for it, saying, "Yogi, you could call me anything you want. If I'm going to suffer, you're going to suffer with me."[46]

The most famous of Hubbard's ejections took place on July 20, 1944. The rule prohibiting the throwing of a spitball was introduced in 1920 with a penalty of ejection and 10 days' suspension. It took 24 years for the rule to be enforced and Hubbard was the first umpire to do so. After St. Louis pitcher Nelson Potter ignored the umpire's repeated warnings not to lick his fingers while on the mound or rubber, Hubbard gave him the thumb. "I made out a report to the league, and they suspended Nellie for 10 days," said Cal. Potter missed his next two starts when he went home and did some fishing, as well as some other pleasurable activities. "They said his wife gave birth to a child nine months later," said the umpire. Hubbard took some pride in giving Potter a vacation and the "chance to be home" with his wife. The pitcher acknowledged that the story was true but said, "We did not name the baby Cal Hubbard Potter."[47]

Hubbard thoroughly enjoyed all aspects of his profession except for the traveling that included riding in boiling Pullman railroad cars, lugging two large bags of clothing and equipment, and staying in hotels before the day of air-conditioning. "You'd almost smother to death," he recalled. "I would get so hot I'd soak a sheet of ice water and lay it on top of me in bed. Did that a million times."[48] Hubbard disagreed with American League President Will Harridge, his boss and close friend, about the umpires' travel arrangements. Harridge had an abnormal aversion to air travel, insisting that his umpires travel by rail even after airplanes had become the preferred mode of transportation for major-league teams. Whenever an emergency arose and his umpires had to travel by air to work a game, Harridge would have the three arbiters take three separate airplanes. "Before we got on the plane," said Hubbard, "we also had to sign a release to the effect that the American League wouldn't be responsible for anything that might happen."[49]

Hubbard made certain he always kept his cool and sense of humor on the field. He would tell his partners, "If you can't control yourself, you can't control a ball game."[50] One day while Cal was working an exhibition game in Houston, the fans suddenly burst into laughter. Base umpire Joe Rue had no idea what was going on until a giggling Hubbard came out to him, gave him his mask and chest protector, and told him to take over behind the plate because he had just split his pants wide open. The only problem for Rue was that Cal's huge mask kept wobbling, providing inadequate protection. "If a foul ball would have hit me," said Rue, "I would have been killed."[51]

Not only was Hubbard a revered partner to his fellow umpires, he was also their friend and mentor. In a September 1945 game, Cal saved the umpiring career of Joe Rue and possibly the life of a player. When Philadelphia A's catcher Charlie "Greek" George sucker-punched Rue during an argument, Cal quickly prevented his partner from retaliating. "Hubbard wrapped those large arms around me," said Rue, adding that it was a good thing he did because "I might have killed [George]."[52] Hubbard yelled at the player, "You'll never play another game in the big leagues!"[53] Cal was true to his word because George never did.

Hubbard was admired by his colleagues because he made them better umpires. "Hubbard would do anything he could to help you on the field," said umpire Bill McKinley.[54] Joe Paparella said, "He taught me more about umpiring in one year that I had ever dreamed there was to learn. If I wasn't in the right position, he'd move me over, and if I was calling pitches too quick, he'd flash me a sign. … I don't know if I would have made it if it wasn't for him."[55] Paparella said that when he became a veteran and had the opportunity to break in younger umpires, "I tried to teach them the same things that Cal Hubbard taught me, to work with them the same way he worked with me. Hubbard did so much for me that I wanted to pass it on to the guys who really wanted to be good umpires."[56]

Hubbard could be outspoken in his opinion of other baseball men but always mixed compliments with criticism. Cal said that Chicago White Sox manager Jimmy Dykes "was the only guy I couldn't stand. He was profane, foul-mouthed, and his voice irritated me." But Hubbard also said that he admired Dykes as a manager because he "got more out of humpty-dumpty players than anyone I ever saw."[57] Hubbard called fellow Hall of Famer Bill McGowan "a super umpire" but said, "I hope Bill never gets into arguments over the rules, because I don't think he owns a rule book—but he gets by because his instincts are great."[58]

Every offseason Hubbard traveled to small-town Milan in northern Missouri, which he called "God's Country," to walk the woods with his hunting gun and bird dogs. (The one year he did not, 1941, he returned to his first love, football, to serve as head coach for his alma mater Geneva College, recording a respectable 6-3 record.) In the late 1940s Cal was ecstatic when Ruth agreed to move their home from Pennsylvania to Milan, where they purchased a 300-acre farm. (For a while the couple operated a dry-cleaning store in town.)[59]

At the end of the 1951 season, Hubbard could not have been happier. He had just completed his 16th year as a major-league umpire, one featuring the thrill of working behind the plate in Yankee

Stadium for Allie Reynolds's no-hitter.[60] By this stage in his career, Cal was already recognized as "one of the most respected and authoritative umpires in baseball history" by no less an authority than Larry Gerlach, baseball's foremost umpire historian.[61] A few years earlier, his big mug had even graced the cover of *Newsweek*.[62] Hubbard looked forward to working several more years in a profession he cherished. Then tragedy struck.

On December 10, 1951, Hubbard went quail and rabbit hunting in the prairies near his home with a group of friends, including fellow umpire Al Barlick. While the group was taking a break with Cal sitting in the front seat of his truck, a neighbor boy took a shot at a passing rabbit. The bullet ricocheted and a small pellet, no larger than the head of a pin, entered Hubbard's left eye just above the pupil. After a local doctor superficially treated the delicate wound, Cal traveled to St. Louis, where the doctors were leery of risking further damage to his eyesight with an operation. He could still see out of the eye but his vision had been affected. Hubbard visited eye specialists in the East, including ones in Pittsburgh with experience in removing metal slivers from steelworkers' eyes, but none of the doctors would risk an operation. Cal had a trial run to see if he could still call balls and strikes with his sons playing pitcher and catcher. After a few pitches, his heart sank when he realized that he had no depth perception. The doctors had said that with proper rest his vision might recover completely, but it was not to be.[63]

Considering Hubbard's profession and the particular injury he suffered, the accident was as poignant and tragic as Beethoven losing his hearing. Realizing that he could no longer continue his career as an umpire, Cal sank into a deep depression and spent his time just staring off into space. Friends from town attempted to cheer him up with visits and talk about football, but to no avail. The Hubbards had regularly played bridge with their close friends Robert and Mildred Freeman but Cal was no longer interested. Ruth felt helpless seeing her husband so disheartened; a sharp change from his usual blissful nature. It was a difficult period for Hubbard, made tougher

when he learned that his old friend Bo McMillin had died.[64] With each passing day, Cal became more saddened.

When Opening Day of the 1952 baseball season arrived, Cal wept. Shortly thereafter, a phone call from Will Harridge triggered more tears from Hubbard but this time they were tears of joy. Harridge offered Cal the position as assistant to Tommy Connolly, supervisor of American League umpires. Cal readily accepted, saying, "It would have broken my heart to be forced out of baseball. … This is wonderful and thank you a million."[65]

When Hubbard began his third sports career, this one as an executive, it was a particularly opportune time for baseball because the major leagues had just introduced the four-man umpire crew for regular-season games. Cal immediately devised new mechanics and supplied charts outlining various rotations, clearly defined duties, and the positioning the four arbiters should take on the field to cover every possible play, basically the same system that is used today.

When Connolly retired in 1954, Hubbard was promoted to his position as American League umpire supervisor. Cal was frequently on the road touring AL ballparks to observe and assist his umpires, as well as visiting minor-league parks to scout and support their umpires. Hubbard served as a goodwill ambassador for baseball, representing his league as a speaker at winter high-school athletic banquets in towns across America, beginning each speech by saying, "I can speak on only three subjects, football, baseball, and bird dogs."[66]

In 1959, Joe Cronin replaced Will Harridge as AL president and kept Hubbard as his umpire supervisor. Cronin's ascension left a void on the major-league Rules Committee, of which he had a member, and Hubbard became his logical replacement; for years, Cal had served as consultant for the committee even as an active umpire. As a committee member, Hubbard was instrumental in the introduction, rewriting, and establishing the proper interpretation of several baseball rules. Considering the focus of baseball today to improve the "pace of game" and introduce speed-up rules, it is interesting that this was also a concern of Hubbard in his day. As highly respected as he was as a Rules Committee member, Cal did not always get his way in this regard and was also unsuccessful in his efforts to legalize the spitball, called the existing rule "unenforceable."[67] Hubbard would joke that baseball instead should ban another pitch, saying, "They outlawed the spitter, Christ, they ought to outlaw that knuckle ball," he said. "You don't know where the hell it's going. … To umpire knuckle ball pitchers, you've got to wait because if you call it too quick, hell, you're liable to miss it a mile."[68]

In hiring new umpires, Hubbard preferred the "strong, silent type," big men like himself who had a "low-key demeanor and made calls with understated gestures."[69] Joe Paparella said, "He hated what he called showboating. … When Cal took over as supervisor, he toned us down quite a bit. 'I don't want your sacrificing judgment for color'—those were his famous words."[70] When Hubbard (and Joe Cronin) hired Emmett Ashford in 1966 as the first African-American umpire in major-league history, it may have been a surprise to many because Ashford was one of the most flamboyant arbiters in history in both attire and gestures. After Ashford's historic first game behind the plate, Cal gave him a big hug. "Cal and I became good friends," said Ashford. "Later, when some of the umpires were getting set to organize against me, he quelled the uprising."[71]

Hub's dual positions as AL umpire supervisor and rules-committee member meant more travel—from one minor-league city to another to scout another umpire, to Florida to conduct another clinic, to Oakland to approve the A's wearing white shoes, and to Chicago to investigate charges that the White Sox were using frozen baseballs. If he wasn't busy enough, in the late 1960s, he wrote a nationally syndicated feature called "Cal's Column" on baseball rule interpretations.[72]

When the Pro Football Hall of Fame was established in 1963, Cal was among the first group enshrined, bringing back memories of his exceptional gridiron career. Fellow inductee George Halas, Chicago Bears coach, commented, "There never was a better lineman than that big umpire."[73]

Hubbard retired from baseball in 1969, ending 18 years of service as executive. He might have served longer if not for a major controversy. In September 1968 Joe Cronin had fired umpires Al Salerno and Bill Valentine, supposedly for incompetence but patently for spearheading an effort to organize a union for American League umpires. (National League umpires had been unionized for years and received much higher salaries and better benefits than their AL counterparts.) Several managers and sportswriters expressed their outrage at the unfair firings. The two umpires sued "Major League Baseball, Joe Cronin, and the American League alleging federal antitrust violations."[74] Cronin stubbornly maintained that he was totally unaware of their union activities and that they were dismissed solely because of their ineptitude as umpires. Salerno swore that shortly after Hubbard learned that Salerno and Valentine were unionizing, Cronin fired them.[75]

It was an agonizing situation for Hubbard, torn between allegiance to his umpires and to Cronin, his boss, who he said was "one of the finest men I ever met in baseball."[76] Wanting to avoid the entire mess, Hubbard responded by giving some tepid support to Cronin and then retiring. The National Labor Relations Board held a nine-day hearing on the case in July 1970. Cronin testified for almost two days, stuck to his story that Salerno and Valentine were incompetent, and related how both he and Hubbard had heard repeated complaints about the two umpires. Hubbard briefly testified and corroborated Cronin.[77] The board eventually ruled against the two umpires.[78]

It was probably best that Hubbard retired when he did because his big body was beginning to break down. In 1972 he collapsed in his home and recovered nicely but his decades of smoking had taken its toll. Cal had given up cigarettes in the late 1950s only to switch to inhaling cigars and then quitting smoking entirely in 1966. "I didn't do it soon enough," he would mutter and then chuckle and say, "If I'd known I was going to live as long as I have I'd have taken better care of myself."[79] On the advice of his doctors,

Hubbard began spending the colder months living in Florida.

When he retired, Cal had returned to his farm in Milan, became active in local youth sports, and spent his time fishing. When Ruth died in 1964, his friends Robert and Mildred Freeman were there to comfort him; when Robert died soon after, Cal was there to comfort Mildred. The friendship between the widow and widower flourished into romance and Cal and Mildred were married in 1966.[80]

In 1976 Hubbard received the news that he had been elected to the Baseball Hall of Fame.[81] Although suffering from emphysema, he made the trip to Cooperstown to attend the induction ceremony, the first one ever held indoors because of inclement weather. The rain didn't dampen Cal's spirits on his big day. Walking onto the stage using a cane and breathing heavily, he still projected a formidable figure, beaming with a broad, proud smile, as he acknowledged his family and bowed graciously.[82]

On October 17, 1977, two weeks shy of his 77th birthday, Cal died of cancer in St. Petersburg, Florida. His body was brought home to Milan for burial.

Hubbard has been enshrined in at least eight Halls of Fame.[83] The high-school football field in Milan and the high-school baseball field in his hometown Keytesville have been named in his honor. An impressive bronze and marble historical marker erected in Milan depicts Hubbard in a three-point stance and outlines his many achievements and honors.

Cal was proud of his sports careers and the many tributes bestowed upon him, yet he remained modest. He had devoted his life's work to games; albeit important because they provide an escape for many from society's ills, he recognized that sports stars are not the world's true champions. Late in life, Hub said: "Sports heroes are glamorized because they are constantly in the lime-light, but as I look back over the years that have brought honor to me, I realize that I fall short of the dimensions of many of the nation's unsung heroes — the Veterans of Foreign Wars. ... In their presence I stand in awe."[84]

NOTES

1   Other members of national halls of fame of two different sports are Jim Brown (football and lacrosse), Ted Williams (baseball and fishing), and Cumberland Posey (basketball and baseball).

2   Sadly, as was commonplace for many people a century ago, death was a recurring presence in Hubbard's life. He was 11 when his 16-year-old brother John died. Two unnamed brothers did not survive infancy. Cal was still a teenager when his father died. He was at the deathbed of his widowed mother (1935), as well as his younger brother Thomas (1954), with whom he was particularly close. Older sister Mary outlived Cal. (Mary Bell Hubbard, *Strike Three! and You're Out: The Cal Hubbard Story* [Marceline, Missouri: Walsworth, n.d.], 67, 71, 96; and family member grave markers found on Cal Hubbard Memorial page, Find a Grave website.)

3   Several sources contend that Hubbard's middle name is Calvin and not simply Cal. The Baseball Hall of Fame website has it both ways with Calvin being listed on his biography page and Cal embossed on his bronze plaque. To add to the confusion, his name is written as Calvin in the Hubbard family Bible yet he always insisted it was Cal. Larry R. Gerlach, Cal Hubbard entry, John Arthur Garraty et al, eds., *American National Biography*, Volume 11, (New York: Oxford University Press, 1999), 379.

4   Gary Ronberg, "Pigskins and Horsehides," Bears-Packers Game Program, November 28, 1976.

5   Martin Appel and Burt Goldblatt, *Baseball's Best: The Hall of Fame Gallery* (New York: McGraw-Hill Book Company, 1977), 216.

6   Bob Broeg, "Hubbard in Reminiscent Mood," *The Sporting News*, April 10, 1976: 6.

7   State Historical Society of Missouri website, Cal Hubbard entry under "Historic Missourians."

8   Ronberg, "Pigskins and Horsehides."

9   Hubbard said he never weighed more than 250 during his playing days. John Maxymuk, *Packers By the Numbers: Jersey Numbers and the Players who Wore Them* (Boulder, Colorado: Big Earth Publishing, 2003), 165. He is listed as 6-feet-3 and 260 pounds on his *Sporting News* umpire card, found on the Retrosheet website.

10 Mary Hubbard, *Strike Three!*, 55. After three years at Centenary College, Hubbard had earned only 32 credits. Cal Hubbard page on Louisiana Sports Hall of Fame website.

11 Hubbard, *Strike Three!*, 58.

12 Dan Jenkins, "A Lot Packed in a Little," *Sports Illustrated*, September 20, 1965: 82.

13 Ibid.

14 Ibid. Hubbard never drank hard liquor in his life and rarely drank beer or gambled, but he must have kept hidden from his teammates his smoking vice.

15 John Mosedale, *Football: A Hall of Fame Book* (New York: World Pub., 1972), 105.

16 Cal Hubbard obituary, *The Sporting News*, November 5, 1977: 41. Centenary and Geneva are strict Christian colleges, respectively affiliated with the United Methodist Church and the Reformed Presbyterian Church. Geneva College has "Pro Christo et Patria" (For Christ and Country) as its motto and an open Bible displayed on its logo. In March 2015, Geneva College proudly announced that its alumnus Hubbard had been selected as one of the "Top 25 All-Time Best Athletes from Christian Colleges" (news release found on Geneva College website). All of which makes it interesting that Hubbard's sister described Cal as "agnostic." (Mary Hubbard, *Strike Three!*, 57.) Hubbard did not attend these two colleges for their religious philosophy but simply because Bo McMillin was their football coach.

17 Murray Greenberg, *Passing Game: Benny Friedman and the Transformation of Football* (New York: Public Affairs, 2008), 199.

18 Ibid.

19 Lew Freedman, *The Packers Experience: A Year-by-Year Chronicle of the Green Bay Packers* (Minneapolis: MBI Publishing Company, 2013), 22.

20 Who was the friend who first suggested to Hubbard that he become an umpire? According to his sister Mary, it was Ed Holly, whom Hubbard had met through Giants teammate Steve Owens. (Mary Hubbard, *Strike Three!*. 69.) Holly was a long-time baseball man then serving as a New York Yankees scout. A sportswriter who interviewed Hubbard said the friend was Charlie Moran, a veteran major-league umpire who had met Cal through coach Bo McMillin (Stanley Frank, "Strong Silent Man," *Collier's Weekly*, April 15, 1939: 57).

21 Hubbard respected Curly Lambeau professionally, but not personally. "They won't be able to find six men to bury the so-and-so, but he got the job done," he said. "To be frank, Curly didn't know that much about football," adding that Lambeau would design plays "we just knew wouldn't work, and one of the veteran players would go right up to the blackboard and change it around." Rob Reischel, *100 Things Packer Fans Should Know & Do Before They Die* (Chicago: Triumph Books, 2010), 92-93.

22 Hubbard, *Strike Three!*, 66.

23 Richard Whittingham, *What a Game They Played* (New York: Harper & Row, 1974), 113.

24 Frank, *Collier's Weekly*: 55.

25 Ibid. The quote varies somewhat depending on the source but it all meant the same thing, the big boy was retiring and this time he meant it.

26 Pro Football Hall of Fame website, Cal Hubbard page. There is little doubt that Hubbard, as tough as he was, could have played a few more years in the NFL. A trainer once examined Hubbard and discovered that Cal had played an entire game with a broken foot. (Louisiana Hall of Fame website, Cal Hubbard page.)

27 Robert C. Hubbard Jr. became a prominent physician in St. Petersburg, Florida (one of the last doctors in the area to still make house calls), and died in 2013. (A.T. Still University website

memorial page.) William Hubbard, who died in 2014, was a Korean War veteran, owner of a gun shop in Milan, Missouri, for 50 years, and active in the Boy Scouts, Special Olympics, the American Legion, and local Democratic politics. (Obituary found on Tributes.com website).

28 Cal Hubbard's *Sporting News* umpire card, Retrosheet website.

29 Appel and Goldblatt, *Baseball's Best*, 216.

30 Frank, *Collier's Weekly*: 56.

31 "Hubbard Fanatic on Rules Even When Playing Football," *The Sporting News*, March 31, 1954: 22. Hubbard even tried his hand officiating basketball games, with Bo McMillin saying, "After (working) a few games, he was qualified to rewrite the rules."

32 Hubbard, *Strike Three!*, 93.

33 Cal Hubbard obituary, *The Sporting News*, November 5, 1977: 41.

34 Gerlach, Hubbard entry, *American National Biography*, 379.

35 Larry R. Gerlach, *The Men in Blue: Conversations with Umpires* (Lincoln: University of Nebraska Press, 1994), 134-135.

36 Ronberg, "Pigskins and Horsehides."

37 William B. Mead, *Baseball Goes to War* (Washington: Broadcast Interview Source Book, Inc., 1968), 59-60.

38 Hubbard, *Strike Three!*, 94.

39 Wayne Stewart and Roger Kahn, *The Little Red Book of Baseball Wisdom* (New York: Skyhorse Publishing Inc., 2012), 29.

40 For a more complete account, see David Nemec and Eric Miklich, *Forfeits and Successfully Protested Games in Major League Baseball* (Jefferson, North Carolina: McFarland Publishers, 2014), 215-216.

41 Lee Freedman, *New York Giants: The Complete Illustrated History* (Minneapolis: MBI Publishing Company, 2009), 19.

42 Appel and Goldblatt, *Baseball's Best*, 218.

43 Hubbard obituary, *The Sporting News*. In the 2,467 regular-season games that Hubbard worked, he had 64 ejections. Is this a particularly low number for his era? A study was conducted to determine the rate of ejections of the 38 major-league umpires who had worked at least 1,000 games and had worked at some point during the years 1936-1951 (Hubbard's career). Frank Dascoli has the highest rate with an ejection every 18.2 games; Harry Geisel has the lowest, every 134.4 games. Hubbard ejected a player or manager every 38.6 games, placing him near the bottom of the top third for the lowest ejection rate. Twenty-four of his contemporaries had a higher rate of ejections than Hubbard and 13 were lower. (Umpire games worked and ejections from Retrosheet website.)

44 Bill Nowlin, Mike Guerra biography, SABR website.

45 Carlo DeVito, *Yogi: The Life and Times of an American Original* (Chicago: Triumph Books, 2014), 92.

46 Ibid.

47 William B. Mead, *Baseball Goes to War*, 157-158. After the ejection, Potter's main concern was that he would be labeled a cheater and insisted he never threw a spitball in his life. He said he just had a habit of going to his mouth and then to the rosin bag. "[Hubbard's] report never mentioned the spitter," said Potter. (Frank Bilovsky, "Spitball Charge was a Phony, Potter Claims," *The Sporting News*, August 28, 1965: 14.) Hubbard agreed, saying, "I never said he was throwing spitters. I just said he was violating pitching rules." (Mead, 159). It should be noted that other pitchers before Potter had been ejected for cutting or discoloring baseballs.

48 Ronberg, "Pigskins and Horsehides."

49 Ibid.

50 Gerlach, *Men in Blue*, 138. Hubbard's Hall of Fame plaque includes the passage: "Gentle giant boasted special knack for dealing with situations on field."

51 Gerlach, *Men in Blue*, 63.

52 Gerlach, *Men in Blue*, 66-67.

53 Norman L. Macht, *The Grand Old Man of Baseball: Connie Mack in His Final Years 1932-1956* (Lincoln: University of Nebraska Press, 2015), 323.

54 Gerlach, *Men in Blue*, 161.

55 Gerlach, *Men in Blue*, 135.

56 Ibid.

57 Broeg, "Hubbard in Reminiscent Mood."

58 Bob Luke, *Dean of Umpires: A Biography of Bill McGowan* (Jefferson, North Carolina: McFarland Publishers, 2005), 127.

59 Hubbard, *Strike Three!*, 75.

60 Hubbard also was behind the plate for Bob Lemon's no-hitter on June 30, 1948.

61 Gerlach, *American National Biography*, 378.

62 *Newsweek*, April 14, 1947. The magazine cover, promoting an article entitled "Baseball: The Year of Decision," features Hubbard with his mouth wide open making a call while holding his mask.

63 Hubbard, *Strike Three!*: 78-79; Ronberg, "Pigskins and Horsehides."

64 In an interview shortly before his death, Bo McMillin said, "The greatest football player who ever lived was Cal Hubbard, lineman or back, college or professional." (Jenkins, "A Lot Packed in a Little," Sports Illustrated: 82.) McMillin was inducted as a player into the College Football Hall of Fame, in its inaugural 1951 class.

65 Hubbard, *Strike Three!*, 79-80.

66 Ibid.

67 Appel and Goldblatt, *Baseball's Best*, 218. Hubbard also wanted to eliminate all batting out-of-order incidents by permitting umpires and the official scorer to correct mistakes before they occur instead of the opposing manager having to appeal. Dan Daniel, "Harridge Denies A.L. Rule to Bar Batting Mixups," *The Sporting News*, March 25, 1953: 21.

68 Mead, *Baseball Goes to War*, 228-229.

69 Gerlach, *American National Biography*, 379.

70 Gerlach, *Men in Blue*, 161.

71 Gerlach, *Men in Blue*, 278.

72 Gerlach, *American National Biography*, 379.

73 Tom Barnidge and Joe Hoppel, *Football Hall of Fame Fact Book* (St. Louis: Sporting News Publication, 1983), 47. Hubbard was subsequently selected as the all-time greatest tackle of the NFL's first 50 years and, 25 years later, as a member of the NFL's 75th Anniversary All-Time Two-Way Team.

74 For a full and outstanding account, see Mark Armour, "A Tale of Two Umpires," *The Baseball Research Journal*, Society for American Baseball Research, Volume 38, Number 2, 2009: 126-130.

75 John Bacchia, *Augie: Stalag Luft VI to the Major Leagues* (iUniverse Publishing, 2011). 200.

76 Hubbard, *Strike Three!*, 85.

77 Bob Ryan, "Fired Umps, A.L. Awaiting Verdict," *The Sporting News*, August 8, 1970: 13.

78 "The NLRB ruled in favor of the American League, claiming that the umpires had not adequately proven that they were fired for their union activities," wrote baseball historian Armour. "The decision read that, although many umpires backed Salerno and Valentine in contending that the union activities were well known, no umpire would admit to telling Cronin or Hubbard." (Armour, "Tale of Two Umpires"; 129.) The active umpires who failed to testify on their colleagues' behalf were likely fearful of repercussions.

79 Ronberg, "Pigskins and Horsehides."

80 "Caught on the Fly," *The Sporting News*, March 5, 1966: 29. In an article written by sportswriter Gary Ronberg ("Pigskins and Horsehides"), for which he had interviewed Hubbard and his wife, Mildred, he states that their marriage began in 1970.

81 Hubbard worked the fewest major-league games (2,467) of any of the 10 umpires who have been elected to the Hall of Fame, 852 fewer than the next lowest on the list (Billy Evans). As outstanding as Hubbard was as an umpire, it is unlikely that he would have been made it to Cooperstown had it not been for his additional contributions to the game as American League supervisor and Rules Committee member. The executive positions also kept him known in baseball circles.

82 Bob Broeg, "Lemon Steals Show at Hall of Fame Induction," *The Sporting News*, August 21, 1976: 5.

83 In addition to the National Baseball, Pro Football and College Football Halls of Fame, Hubbard is a member of Missouri, Louisiana, Centenary College, Helms Foundation, and Green Bay Packers Halls of Fame.

84 Hubbard, *Strike Three!*, 102-104.

Bill Klem

By David W. Anderson and Dennis Bingham

Born on Washington's Birthday in 1874 in Rochester, New York, William Joseph "Bill" Klem became one of the greatest umpires to ever take the field. "I was born of German parents in the Irish section near 'Dutchtown' in Rochester, New York," Klem later said.[1] Both father Michael Klimm and mother Elizabeth were from Bavaria. Bill was their eighth child. Michael Klimm worked as a wagonmaker. Bill himself, at the time of the 1892 New York State census, was 18 and working as a shoemaker.

Bill Klimm followed his uncle's footsteps and changed his name to Klem ("I thought Klem had a firmer sound and was a better name for an arbiter.") He went on to fame on the diamond in a profession that was hardly respectable when he entered it. Elected to the Hall of Fame in 1953, Klem is credited with helping upgrade dignity and respect for umpiring during a major-league career that spanned 37 years (1905-1941).

As with many of his umpire contemporaries, Klem first tried to be a professional ball player. In 1896 he tried out for catcher for the Hamilton, Ontario team of the Canadian League[2], but a bum arm ended that hope. For the next few years Klem played semipro ball in New York and Pennsylvania and supported himself by taking construction jobs.[3]

His life took a turn in 1902 in Berwick, Pennsylvania when he tried his hand at umpiring a game between the New York Cuban Giants and a semipro team from Berwick. He was paid $5 for his efforts.[4] While in Berwick, Klem read a newspaper account about Frank "Silk" O'Loughlin, a hometown friend, and how he was faring as a National League umpire.[5] Reading about O'Loughlin influenced Klem to consider umpiring as a career, despite O'Loughlin's trying to discourage him by saying, "This is a rotten business."[6] Indeed, Klem said that O'Loughlin introduced him to umpire Hank O'Day and said that he was an example of how the profession had turned O'Day into a "misanthropic" loner.

Nonetheless, Klem contacted "baseball man and old friend" Dan Shannon, who suggested that he talk to Sydney Challenger, in charge of hiring umpires for the Connecticut League. It was on Shannon's recommendation that Challenger hired Klem. Two years later, in the spring of 1904, Klem ran into Hank O'Day again in New York. O'Day brought Klem to National League headquarters and introduced him to President Harry Pulliam. This led to Pulliam later hiring Klem as a major-league umpire. Klem put in three years in the minors, where he learned important lessons each step up the ladder.

Semipro work aside, Klem's professional umpiring career began in 1902 in the Class-D Connecticut League. The pay was $7.50 for a single game and $10.50 for a doubleheader. Klem recalled it was a tough league and, "if the home team lost you got an awful amount of abuse with your money."[7] Here he began to develop his reputation for toughness on the field along with determination and a sense of fair play. The money must have offset the abuse because he took on the challenge of umpiring in the Class-B New York State League in 1903.

Klem found himself in hot water with team owners and fans on a number of occasions because of his enforcement of a new league policy of fining players on the spot for using abusive language toward umpires. Klem often defied owners who tried to keep him from officiating; this defiance was illustrated years later when Giants manager John McGraw told Klem he would have his job. Klem's reply was if McGraw could have his job, then he did not want it.[8]

The 1903 season was not easy for Klem; he was the only New York State League umpire hired at the beginning of the year to last the entire season.[9] His tenacity and courage were tested on an almost daily basis in a league, which refused to hire more than one umpire for a game.

Bill Klem.

Klem moved his services to the Class-A American Association in 1904, and immediately applied what he had learned and developed what umpire historian Larry Gerlach called the tough cop approach to umpiring. It was in the AA that Klem first drew a line in the dirt and told irate players and managers, "Do not cross the Rio Grande." Those who did were immediately ejected.[10]

Automatic ejection was also Klem's response to the nickname "Catfish." The term was first used in the American Association as a commentary on Klem's piscine appearing mouth. Klem hated the nickname and the mere use of the word within his earshot bought the offending party an early exit from the ballpark.[11]

During his year in the American Association Klem started getting attention from the big leagues. In the spring of 1904, Hank O'Day had introduced Klem to National League President Henry Pulliam.[12] Learning he'd be working in the AA, Pulliam said, "I'm going to keep my eye on you, Klem."[13] Pulliam hired Klem to umpire a postseason National League exhibition game between Cleveland and Pittsburgh.[14] It was this gesture that made Klem a loyal National Leaguer.

In 1905 Klem was offered $2,100 to umpire in the American League through the efforts of O'Loughlin. Although Klem wanted to umpire in the majors, he resisted the urging of other American League umpires and held out.

American League president Ban Johnson had the reputation of strongly supporting his umpires and trying to eliminate rowdy behavior, and one might have thought Klem would find the AL more hospitable. But both Johnson and Klem were strong, autocratic personalities who probably would have clashed both on and off the field.[15]

Klem was waiting for word from Pulliam, the man who gave him his first major-league assignment. His patience and loyalty paid off. Pulliam offered Klem a job and matched the American League offer. Klem remained a loyal National Leaguer for his entire career, referring to the Junior Circuit as "the hucksters of the big leagues."[16]

Klem wasn't a large man. He stood 5-feet-7 1/2 and is listed at 157 pounds. Klem's first major-league game was on April 14, 1905 in Cincinnati as the Reds played the Pirates. He faced challenges establishing himself, as witness the 25 ejections in his first year in the league. In fact, he averaged more than 19 ejections over the course of his first seven seasons. In all, Klem ejected 279 persons during the course of his career, but after the 1915 season he only reached double digits once, in 1920.

In 1910, Klem married Marie Kranz, who he credited with helping him handle the stress of umpiring. With the couple being childless, Marie often traveled with her husband on the road. Regardless of any comfort Marie might have provided, Klem still developed a recurring skin condition attributed to the pressures of his profession.[17]

Klem's last full year as umpire was 1940, but he worked 11 games in August and September 1941 as the National League experimented with four-man crews. Age was beginning to get to him. Late in 1940 he was hit by a ground ball in the infield and realized that he was slowing down at the age of 66. He umpired those 11 games in 1941 in his role of Chief of the National League umpire staff. Klem knew he was done when in a St. Louis-Brooklyn game he missed a tag. Klem said that was the first time he only thought, not knew, that a man was out.[18]

He remained head of National League umpires until his death in 1951. During his career he umpired in 18 World Series, taking part in 103 Series games, both all-time records.[19] Klem called five no-hitters from behind the plate. He was the home-plate umpire in the first All-Star Game, in Chicago in 1933. He also worked the plate in the 1938 game.

He is credited with developing the inside chest protector, but Klem said that idea came from others. [20] He did claim credit for teaching umpires to work the "slot," which he claimed gave umpires a better look at the strike zone by looking between the catcher and batter. [21] He is also among those given credit for developing a system of signals for safe, out, strike, fair, or foul ball. Klem himself took credit for developing a fair-foul signal during his 1904 stint in the American Association.[22]

Many histories say Klem was so good at calling balls and strikes that he was plate umpire for the first 16 years of his career. This is not entirely accurate, but for those 16 years (1905-1920), Klem worked behind the plate a remarkable 88.8% of his games, many of them solo. It was this impressive record that led to the myth that he worked exclusively behind the plate his first 16 years. Even after the two-umpire rule was introduced in 1911, Klem continued to work almost exclusively behind the plate for more than a decade. While many other umpires were rotating between working the plate and bases, Klem mainly worked behind the plate. He only began to take his regular turn on the bases in 1921. The major leagues did not hire enough umpires to guarantee two-man crews until the 1911 season.[23] Hank O'Day has an even higher percentage (68%) of career games worked behind the plate than Klem (66%). Throughout his entire career, Klem would often work the plate when paired with a rookie umpire early in the season until the beginner gained experience.[24]

This one flaw in the historical record should not detract from a career that will probably be unmatched in baseball history. Anyone who umpires baseball at any level owes a debt to Bill Klem for his work in making umpiring an honorable profession.

NOTES

1   William J. Klem and William J. Slocum, "Umpire Bill Klem's Own Story," *Collier's Weekly*, March 31, 1951: 30.

2   Klem also "had trials with professional teams in … Springfield, Massachusetts and Augusta, Maine, during the 1896-1897 seasons." See Martin Appel and Burt Goldblatt, *Baseball's Best: The Hall of Fame Gallery* (New York: McGraw-Hill Book Company, 1977), 250. In the first part of the Klem series in *Collier's Weekly* (March 31, 1951), Klem says he tried out for the Hamilton, Springfield, and Augusta professional baseball teams.

3   Klem also worked as a painter, steelworker, construction foreman, bookmaker, and bartender. William J. Klem and William J. Slocum. "I Never Missed One in My Heart," *Collier's Weekly*, March 31, 1951: 30, 31.

4   *Collier's Weekly*, March 31, 1951: 59.

5   See David L. Fleitz. *The Irish in Baseball: An Early History* (Jefferson, North Carolina: McFarland Publishers, 2009), 119.

6   *Collier's Weekly*, March 31, 1951: 59.

7   *Collier's Weekly*, March 31, 1951: 62, 64.

8   Source for this is from "Jousting With McGraw," the second part of the *Collier's Weekly* "Bill Klem's Own Story" series, April 7, 1951: 50. The exact quote: "Mr. Manager, if it's possible for you to take my job away from me, I don't want the job." In the first part of the *Collier's* series, Klem related another story in which he had a somewhat similar retort as a rookie umpire (1902). When manager Jim O'Rourke was fined by rookie umpire Klem, O'Rourke yelled, "You will never umpire another game in the Connecticut League." Klem said, "All right, Mr. Manager. But I'll umpire this one." O'Rourke was also owner of the team.

9   *Collier's Weekly*, March 31, 1951: 62. Klem states: "There were never more than four umpires on the New York State payroll at any time, but to complete the 1903 season 35 had to be hired. I was the only arbiter to start and finish the season."

10   *Collier's Weekly*, March 31, 1951: 64.

11   Ibid.

12   *Collier's Weekly*, March, 1951: 64.

13   Ibid.

14   *Collier's Weekly*, March, 1951: 65.

15   Although Klem praised Johnson for his support of umpires as American League president, he referred to him as a "screaming harridan" and criticized Johnson's "domineering personality," "arrogance," and "domineering tactics." See part four of "Umpire Bill Klem's Own Story," *Collier's Weekly*, April 21, 1951: 73.

16   Ibid. "I liked Mr. Pulliam," said Klem. In 1905, the American League made an aggressive campaign to sign Klem. League President Johnson and veteran AL umpires Tom Connolly, Jack Sheridan, and Silk O'Loughlin sent letters and telegrams to Klem encouraging him to sign with the American League. Klem ignored the correspondence. "I felt I had given (NL President) Mr. Pulliam a promise and waited to hear from him," said Klem. *Collier's Weekly*, March 31, 1951: 64-65.

17   David L. Porter, ed., *Biographical Dictionary of American Sports: G-P* (Westport, Connecticut: Greenwood Publishing Group, 1987), Klem entry, p. 820; Frank Fitzpatrick, "Klem, the Old Arbitrator, was Father of Umpiring," *Philadelphia Inquirer*, September 2, 1999.

18   In later describing the play that prompted his retirement, Klem was incorrect in the details. Here's how Klem tells it: "A St. Louis man attempted to steal second. Billy Herman took the throw and put the ball on the runner. I called him out. The runner jumped up and protested. I walked away from the beefing player, saying to myself, 'I'm almost certain Herman tagged him.' Then it came to me and I almost wept. For the first time in all my career, I only 'thought' a man was tagged." (*Collier's Weekly*, April 25, 1951: 74).

On September 13, 1941, the Cardinals played the Dodgers in St. Louis and it was Klem's last major league game. The play-by-play account, however, reveals that there were no attempted steals during the game. Klem called out one runner at second base during the game and it was not a St. Louis runner. When Brooklyn's Lew Riggs attempted to stretch a single into a double, Cardinals shortstop Marty Marion "tagged" him and Klem called him out. This was likely the play that Klem was recalling a decade later that convinced him to finally retire. (Box score and play-by-play account for September 13, 1941 game between Cardinals and Dodgers from Retrosheet.org.) Actually, the game involving the possible "missed tag" was the last regular season major-league game Klem ever worked. Four years later, in 1945, he worked some spring training games despite being blind in one eye.

19   "Umpire Records," MLB.com website.

20   "I am frequently called the inventor of the umpire's chest protector. I am not. I merely resurrected it and basically followed the design originated by the first King of the Umpires, John Gaffney." See "Diamond Rhubarbs," part three of the *Collier's Weekly* series, April 14. 1951: 31.

21   Ibid. "Another innovation—this one *is* mine—scorned by the American League is the system we use to work behind the catcher."

22   *Collier's Weekly*, March 31, 1951: 64. Further confirmation is Klem stating: "I have already explained how I invented the 'fair' and 'foul' semaphores." (*Collier's Weekly*, April 14, 1951: 31). Klem, not a modest man, proudly said that he was responsible for several umpiring advancements, proclaiming that the fair-foul signal was just "the first of many innovations in umpire technique" that he had introduced. These other claims include: "I had the distinction of being the first umpire to put a fan out of the ballpark." *Collier's Weekly*, April 7, 1951: 30. (Unlikely, in that the major-league rule giving the umpire the authority to eject a fan had been introduced back in 1882. Dennis Bingham and Thomas R. Heitz, "Rules and Scoring," in *Total Baseball* (New York: HarperPerennial, 1993), 2280.

"Many of these innovations are mine, and all of them helped baseball grow from a county fair attraction to the great, beloved spectacle it is today." *Collier's Weekly,* April 14, 1951: 31.

In talking about the plate umpire's signals for balls and strikes, Klem said: "I originated that system in 1906 when my voice went bad and I could no longer follow the custom of bellowing each decision. I (also) invented the standard 'safe' and 'out' signals used today by umpires." *Collier's Weekly,* April 14, 1951: 31.

Klem may have helped popularize the ball-strike signals, but he was not the first to employ them. Baseball historian Peter Morris states: "Bill Klem is sometimes credited with pioneering umpire signals. While I have found no evidence to support that contention, it does appear that Klem was among the first to give added emphasis to his signals." Morris gives a detailed description of how the ball-strike signals developed in *A Game of Inches: The Stories Behind the Innovations that Shaped Baseball* (Ivan R. Dee, 2006), 385-391.

23 "It was not until 1911 that the second umpire was required by the rulebook," states baseball historian Peter Morris, *A Game of Inches,* 373.

24 Bill Klem's daily career umpiring log, Retrosheet.org. Working the plate when partnered with a rookie umpire was a common practice for other veteran umpires as well, such as O'Day, Billy Evans, and Tom Connolly.

Bill McGowan

By Bob Luke

"Superstar" is a superlative usually reserved for players. However, fellow umpire Jim Honochick used it to describe Bill McGowan.[1] Universally respected for his work behind the plate and on the bases, William Aloysius "Bill" McGowan umpired in the American League from 1925 to 1954. "He was one of the sharpest guys with balls and strikes I ever saw. I'd say he was probably 99.9 percent right," recalled Ted Williams.[2] Longtime New York Yankees manager Joe McCarthy agreed. He told his players not to ride McGowan "because he's the best ball and strike man there is."[3] His signature strike motion consisted of a clenched fist held about four inches above his head.[4]

McGowan himself had no doubts about his ability. When asked by Washington Senators first baseman Mickey Vernon, "How could you call [the runner] safe?" McGowan shot back "because I'm the best umpire in the business, I'm number one."[5] After a runner complained that McGowan had called him out at second before the play was over, McGowan replied, "That's right. Any umpire can call a play after it happens. Only the great ones like me can call 'em before they happen."[6] This, and similar assertions, led to the nicknames "Chesty," "No. 1," "Wild Willie of Wilmington," and "Hot Shot," often spoken with equal parts praise and scorn.

While it is often said that a good umpire is an invisible umpire, such cannot be said about McGowan. He gave his personality free range on the field. He would call a ball a strike to speed up a game or a strike a ball as a favor to a batter. To the astonishment and consternation of managers and coaches, he advised players during a game on their swing, attitude, or what a pitcher might throw them. He received three suspensions, once in the minors and twice in the majors, for displays of temper. McGowan was a tour de force, durable, calling 2,451 games from 1925 to 1940,[7] and, in spite of his suspensions, well thought of

in the commissioner's office, earning assignments to eight World Series and four All-Star Games including the first in 1933.

McGowan's contributions to the game went beyond umpiring. Acting as an unofficial scout during his minor-league career, he recommended players, notably Goose Goslin and Bucky Harris, to Washington Senators owner Clark Griffith and others, including Jimmy Dykes, to Philadelphia Athletics owner Connie Mack. Once in the majors, his contract forbade such activities, but, as he told *Washington Post* sportswriter Shirley Povich, "back in my International League days they didn't care what we did, and I was always placing young ballplayers. I got a kick out of it."[8] Known for his hilarious sense of humor, he was in demand on the rubber-chicken circuit. He wrote numerous newspaper and magazine articles. Toward the end of his career he founded a school for umpires that endures today. Baseball's Hall of Fame belatedly welcomed him to its membership in 1992.

McGowan was born on January 18, 1896, and baptized Catholic in Wilmington, Delaware, a month later. His parents, John Aloysius and Catharine McGowan, with his aunt Elizabeth, emigrated from England in 1883. His father operated three beer and whiskey stores in Wilmington before becoming a hotel manager until his death from pneumonia in 1909. Bill never took to beer or spirits. If he invited you for a drink it would be for a milkshake. He took up boxing in high school but lost his first professional bout on a first-round knockout. He told the story often, prompting players including White Sox pitcher Johnny Rigney to call him "canvasback" or "K.O."[9]

McGowan's brother John, chief clerk in the Wilmington fire department, introduced him to umpiring. At 16 in 1912, Bill reluctantly agreed to sub for his brother at a semipro game in Newark, Delaware.

It took the rookie ump four innings "before I contrived to keep my eyes open with the pitch and had no trouble for the rest of the game."[10]

To McGowan's surprise, the experience agreed with him to the extent that he gave up aspirations to play second base in the majors in favor of umpiring full time. Misrepresenting his age to Tri-State League President George M. Graham, McGowan worked a few games in that league in 1913. The next year he alternated between the Delaware County (Pennsylvania) League and the University of Pennsylvania. On Graham's recommendation, he landed a position in the Virginia League in 1915 but only after convincing the league president that at 135 pounds he was big enough for the job. Ed Barrow, president of the International League and later general manager of the New York Yankees, offered McGowan a job as a substitute umpire in the International League in 1916. McGowan also worked in the New York State League that year. From there he moved to the Blue Ridge League in 1917, sat out umpiring in 1918, and returned in 1919 to the International League, where he stayed until 1922.

McGowan earned his first suspension during a Sunday game in Baltimore in August 1922 by decking Baltimore Orioles second baseman Harry McCurdy, who had objected to being ejected by landing a punch on McGowan's chin. McGowan then landed a right jab to the jaw of a policeman who had stepped between the two. Fined and fired, he got a reprieve several months later from Southern Association President John D. Martin, who had confidence that the arbiter's skill would win out over his temper.[11]

After McGowan umpired two years in the Southern Association, American League President Ban Johnson offered him a job in the majors, where he made his debut in Philadelphia's Shibe Park on Opening Day, April 14, 1925.[12]

Starting in 1918, McGowan worked in the room where gunpowder was made at the DuPont Corporation for six years. He met his wife, Magdalein P. "Madge" Ferry, in 1918 after a basketball game that he won in overtime with a jump shot. They married that year at the Church of the Immaculate Conception in Elkton, Maryland. The couple had one son, Bill Jr., born in 1919, and raised two children of Madge's brother Bradford after he was killed at a gas station in Elkton when a man carelessly dropped a lighted match into a can of gasoline.[13] Once in the majors, the McGowans made their home in the Washington, D.C., area, living first in the city before buying their first house in Chevy Chase, Maryland, and their second in Silver Spring, Maryland.

An umpire's primary responsibility is twofold—maintaining control of the game and enforcing the rules fairly. McGowan did so with equal parts intimidation, firmness, and humor flavored with an occasional dash of favoritism and flashes of anger.

A player's status made no difference to him. Established stars like Babe Ruth and Ted Williams received the same treatment as did the rawest rookie. As a 29-year-old rookie major-league umpire in 1925 calling New York Yankees games in spring training, he tossed Babe Ruth, who complained mightily. "I know who you are and all about your reputation," McGowan replied, "but when I'm wearing this blue suit, you're just another ballplayer. Get out."[14] Ted Williams, in a game at Fenway Park in 1942, decided to strike out in response to boos from spectators. After he took two lazy swings, McGowan told him that after a third such swing "you'll be thrown out of the game, fined, and probably suspended." The Splendid Splinter managed a bloop single.[15] Rookies appearing before McGowan for the first time heard themselves called "Bush" or "Busher" accompanied by a lesson about who was in charge. After calling rookie Tommy Umphlett out on strikes, McGowan stepped in front of Umphlett and pumped his fist in the rookie's face so there would be no doubt about was in charge. "Yes sir," Umphlett answered.[16]

For all his aggressiveness, McGowan was not above admitting mistakes, as he did with infielder Joe Sewell. After bellowing, "Strike three, you're out!" on a ball that crossed the plate at cap level, "No. 1" said in the same sentence, "Oh my God, I missed that." He apologized to Sewell the next day.[17] Admitting a mistake never meant changing his call, as he explained to a runner he had wrongly called out at first base. Both agreed it had been the wrong call. "But," McGowan informed him, "after my hand went up, 35,000 people in the stands know you're out."[18]

If a player heckled McGowan from the bench, he whipped his mask off, stared into the dugout, and, if he could identify the player, gave him the heave-ho. Players who heckled other players also earned his ire. After hearing Yankees rookie pitcher Tommy Byrne direct some choice comments from his dugout seat to Red Sox infielders in a 1943 game, McGowan yelled "Shut up, Bush." Byrne did, but in his next at-bat McGowan called him out on strikes on a pitch well wide of the strike zone, adding, "How do you like that, you left-handed son of a bitch?"[19]

So sensitive was McGowan to anyone questioning a call that he once ejected a player before any words had been exchanged. Just as Washington Senators catcher Roy Spencer turned toward him to question a called ball on Ben Chapman during a game with the Yankees in 1931, McGowan snapped, "You're outta here." "You can't do that," Spencer protested. "I ain't done nothing yet." "You're outta the game," McGowan explained, "for what you were intending to say."[20]

Players' protests didn't always result in their removal from the game. McGowan sprinkled his iron-man persona with an occasional dose of tact, humor, leniency, and giving as good as he got. Red Sox pitcher Sid Hudson recalled flipping the bird to McGowan over a ball-four call that walked in a run and that Hudson thought surely had been a strike. In a move that today would be the lead story on ESPN and result in fines and suspensions, McGowan simply returned the gesture and said, "OK Sid, now let's play ball."[21] When Cleveland Indians pitcher Jim Bagby Jr. offered him the left-handed compliment during a 1945 game, "Good day for you. You only missed two on the last batter," McGowan responded with, "Miss that junk you throw? Anytime I can't count the stitches on your fastball, I'll give up."[22] When Jimmy Dykes protested being picked off second base, yelling, "Out? I made it. I got back," McGowan benignly replied, "Yes you did, James, you made it, but what detained you?"[23] Yankees third-base coach Earle Combs

always signaled a Yankee runner safe, extending his palms downward, after McGowan had called him out. Rather than toss Combs, McGowan promised him, "You'll be on our staff if you keep improving on those close decisions." A laugh and an apology from Combs usually followed.[24] McGowan gave Senators third baseman Buddy Lewis a rare gift on Lewis's first at-bat after returning from World War II by calling two pitches that were clearly strikes ball one and ball two. "What's going on?" demanded White Sox pitcher Earl Caldwell. "Don't you know who this is?" McGowan answered. "This is Buddy Lewis. It's his first day back. Ain't no way I'm calling a strike on him his first at-bat." Caldwell then issued an intentional walk to Lewis.[25]

McGowan twice overstepped his bounds to earn suspensions from American League President Will Harridge. After exchanges of unprintable names with Senators pitcher Ray Scarborough over the course of several games during the spring of 1948, McGowan took his frustration out on Senators outfielder Ed Stewart. He threw a ball at him while the outfielder argued with umpire Joe Paparella about a close call at second and then showered Stewart with profanity as Stewart ran by him to his position in the outfield. Harridge issued a fine of $500 and a 10-day suspension without pay. The episode did not, however, prevent Harridge from naming McGowan as the umpire-in-chief for the first-ever American League playoff game, a contest between the Indians and the Red Sox at the end of that season. The selection signaled that Harridge considered McGowan the junior circuit's best umpire. McGowan considered the game the highlight of his career. "Never had a guy turn his head on me all day. It was the only time both clubs congratulated me after the game," McGowan told a reporter.[26]

McGowan's second misstep came in a game between the St. Louis Browns and the Tigers in 1952 in Sportsman's Park. When a called third strike on Detroit outfielder Cliff Mapes brought jeers from the Tigers' dugout, McGowan promptly turned toward the dugout and ejected one of the occupants. When a writer in the press box passed a note to

Bill McGowan.

the field asking whom he had ejected, McGowan told the writers "it was none of their _____ business" and he threatened to write them up. Taunted by writer Ellie Veech who yelled down to the field from the press box, "Hey, McGowan can you write?" McGowan, by now an accomplished writer of magazine and newspaper articles, "made an offensive gesture toward the press box" and yelled back, "If you could write you'd be in New York." He repeated his gesture but with more gusto than the first. This time Harridge levied a $650 fine, the largest to date for an umpire, and an indefinite suspension that wound up lasting only four games.[27]

Though he could be quick to eject a player who he felt threatened his control of the game, McGowan would, with equal ease, offer advice to players. When

Philadelphia Athletics catcher Frankie Hayes told Ted Williams at his first at-bat during the last game of the 1941 season as Williams, with a .398 average, was striving to became the first player to hit .400 since Bill Terry hit .401 in 1930, "We're not giving you a damn thing today." McGowan called time out, walked around Williams, bent down to brush off the plate, and said, without looking up, "To hit .400 a batter has got to be loose. He has got to be loose."[28] The advice took. Williams finished the season at .406. McGowan advised Hank Greenberg, Hall of Fame first baseman for the Detroit Tigers, to shorten up on his swing. "You don't have to knock those homers into the 20th row," he told Greenberg, the first row is far enough." Greenberg credited the advice with helping him raise his homer production to 58 and acquire a

$70,000 salary the next year.[29] "Bushers" as well as established stars benefited. Irv Noren, just recalled from the Pacific Coast League by the Washington Senators in 1950, swung and missed at a borderline high fastball. "That's a Coast League strike, kid," McGowan told him. "In the majors it's a ball." Noren thanked McGowan for the tip.[30] McGowan even went as far as to alert rookie Senators outfielder Gil Coan what to expect from opposing pitchers. "He always encouraged the young ballplayers," Coan recalled in a 2004 interview.[31]

Off the field McGowan had two pursuits that kept him busy during the winter months, writing and speaking. "He'd sit there from sunup to sundown and bang away at that Smith-Corona," Bill Jr. recalled.[32] His articles, largely human-interest stories about players, managers, coaches, and, of course, umpires, appeared in *The Sporting News*, *Liberty*, and *Esquire*. For a number of years he wrote a syndicated column, "Three and Tuh," that ran in 30 newspapers. He traveled the Mid-Atlantic States to speak at dinners, banquets, award ceremonies, and, during World War II, at military camps and installations. When home he was often the keynote speaker at the Washington Touchdown Club. During one such appearance in 1944 the club presented him with a plaque for his outstanding work during the 1944 World Series. A reporter for the *Washington Post-Times Herald* judged his acceptance speech to be "one of the most entertaining after-lunch speeches ever given," adding, "Time and again the capacity crowd interrupted McGowan with prolonged laughter and applause."[33] McGowan was no stranger to radio and television, often appearing as a guest of Senators play-by-play announcer Arch McDonald's radio program and as a guest on Washington sportswriter Morrie Siegel's weekly TV program.[34]

McGowan's lasting legacy to the game came in the form of a school for umpires he started in 1938 working out of his home in Chevy Chase, Maryland. He conducted classes and practice sessions at the nearby University of Maryland. In 1939 he teamed with fellow umpire Emmitt Thomas "Red" Ormsby to establish a school in Jackson, Mississippi, that they

moved later to Florida. The school operated for about one month between January and March of each year in various Florida locations. Thanks to the G.I. Bill of Rights, enrollment swelled to 251 in 1947 with 95 percent of the students being veterans. Many graduates of the school found work in the minor leagues and a few, including John Rice, made it to the majors. The school continues today, after several changes in ownership, as the Harry Wendelstedt Umpire School in Ormand Beach, Florida, offering instruction to women as well as men.

McGowan died at his home in Silver Spring on December 9, 1954, of a heart attack brought on from complications in his struggle with diabetes. At his funeral Mass in Silver Spring, conducted by a nephew, Rev. William Buckley, all major-league umpires attended as did American League President Will Harridge, Senators owner Clark Griffith, Senators manager Bucky Harris, former Senators players Joe Judge, Sam Rice, and Ossie Bluege, and active Senators player Jim Busby. Burial was in the family plot in Cathedral Cemetery in Wilmington.

Eight months before McGowan's death, sportswriter Francis Stann spoke for many who knew and worked with him: "McGowan may be the last [of the umpires] who made his name strictly off his umpiring. He has that touch of personality that sets him apart from the others. It never hurt an umpire to flash a little pomp and strut as long as he knew his business, which McGowan did and does."[35]

NOTES

1   Honochick called McGowan "the very best umpire that I ever worked with." Larry Gerlach, *The Men in Blue: Conversations with Umpires* (Lincoln: University of Nebraska Press, 1994), 183. On page 184 Honochick used the word "superstar." For an in-depth discussion of McGowan's life and career, see Bob Luke, *Dean of Umpires: A Biography of Bill McGowan, 1896-1954* (Jefferson, North Carolina: McFarland & Co., 2005).

2   baseballhall.org/hof/mcgowan-bill.

3   Bob Luke, "Hall of Famer Bill McGowan Umpired With Vigor and Style," *Baseball Digest*, February 2002: 72-75.

4   Bill McGowan, *Text Book: Bill McGowan's School for Umpires* (Cocoa, Florida: privately published, January-February 1947), 5.

5   Mickey Vernon, author interview, February 2003.

6   Shirley Povich, "This Morning," *Washington Post*, May 30, 1958.

7   baseballhall.org/hof/mcgowan-bill.

8   Shirley Povich, "This Morning," *Washington Post*, May 13, 1938.

9   Newspaper clipping in McGowan's Hall of Fame file.

10 Don E. Basenfelder, "McGowan, Players' Choice as Leading A.L. Umpire," *The Sporting News*, January 23, 1936: 5.

11 J.G. Taylor Spink, "Series Tops in Thrills, Low in Kicks—McGowan," *The Sporting News*, October 14, 1947: 11.

12 Fred Sawyer, "Sox Unable to Hold Big League," *Boston Globe*, April 15, 1925.

13 Bill McGowan Jr. author interview, November 22, 2003.

14 Shirley Povich, "McGowan Walked Right In, Threw Ruth Out," *Washington Post*, December 10, 1954.

15 Ed Linn, *Hitter: The Life and Turmoil of Ted Williams* (New York: Harcourt Brace, 1993), 128.

16 Shirley Povich, *Baseball Digest*, April, 1954: 35.

17 Donald Honig, *The October Heroes* (New York: Simon and Schuster, 1979), 252.

18 Povich, "This Morning," *Washington Post*, May 30, 1958.

19 David Halberstam, *Summer of '49* (Scranton, Pennsylvania: William Morrow & Co., 1991), 217.

20 Lawrence Keating, "Baseball's Daffy Day," *Coronet*, June 1957: 73.

21 Sid Hudson, author telephone interview, February 22, 2003.

22 Doug Gilbert, *The Great Delaware Sports Book* (Montcharin, Delaware: Manatee Books, 1995), 100.

23 James Carmichael, "Dean of the Men in Blue," *The Sporting News*, December 22, 1954: 14.

24 Bill McGowan, *Text Book*, 13.

25 Bill Gilbert, Buddy Lewis, author telephone interviews, December 15, 2002.

26 Unidentified newspaper article in McGowan's Hall of Fame file.

27 Oscar Ruhl, "From the Ruhl Book," *The Sporting News*, November 5, 1952: 13.

28 Ted Williams as told to John Underwood, *My Turn at Bat: The Story of My Life* (New York: Simon and Schuster, 1969), 85-86.

29 Shirley Povich, *Morning Line*, December 10, 1954.

30 Irv Noren, author telephone interview, May 19, 2004.

31 Gil Coan, author interview, March 8, 2004.

32 Bill McGowan Jr., author interview, January 20, 2003.

33 Frank "Buck" O'Neill, "McQuinn, Case Face Operations to Save Careers," *Washington Post-Times Herald*, October 17, 1944.

34 "Sports on Television," *Washington Post*, October 24, 1954.

35 Francis Stann, "Connolly's Motionless Call: Old-Time Umps Would Have Been TV Naturals," *Baseball Digest*, April, 1954: 63.

Hank O'Day

The Courageous Curmudgeon

By Dennis Bingham

Hank O'Day is one of the few men to have played, umpired, and managed at the major-league level. He was a World Series pitching hero. He had one of the greatest starts of any rookie manager in history. He was the home-plate umpire for 23 World Series games, as well as for four no-hitters in four different decades.[1] He was called "about as odd a character as the game ever produced."[2] He was the driving force behind rule changes that have dramatically transformed baseball. Yet, for all his influence in a remarkable career that spanned nearly half a century, O'Day is principally remembered for only one play.

Granted, that one play was indeed a biggie, in what has been characterized as "the most celebrated, most widely discussed, most controversial contest in the history of American sports."[3] O'Day was the home-plate umpire in the famous (or infamous) game in 1908 when Fred Merkle neglected to run to second base. Hank's historic ruling in nullifying the apparent winning run sent a shock wave through the baseball world, turning what was already the most exciting race of all time into the most tumultuous. That one decision became O'Day's legacy, defining his entire lengthy baseball career. It is even embossed on his Hall of Fame plaque.

Henry Francis O'Day was born in Chicago on July 8, 1859, the middle child of seven born to deaf parents James and Margaret (Loftus) O'Day, Irish immigrants.[4] His father operated a small farm, worked as a plumber, and then served as an engineer at a school. Hank grew to a height of 6 feet, weighed a hefty 180 pounds, sported a fashionable mustache, and probably spoke with a brogue.[5] Hank and his two older brothers spent their formative years playing baseball on the many open fields of Chicago in the city's thriving semipro leagues. Charles Comiskey,

the same age as Hank, was a teammate. The O'Day brothers played under the name "Day" because their father disapproved of his sons playing the "frivolous pastime" of baseball.[6] For a while, Hank was a steamfitter's apprentice before giving it up and traveling to faraway California to play ball for St. Mary's College for three years.[7]

At age 22, in 1883, O'Day became a professional ballplayer when he joined the Bay City, Michigan, team of the Northwestern League as pitcher and center fielder for $125 a month. During that season, management of the financially strapped team realized it had to reduce its roster. They drew his name out of a hat and he was released, despite being the team's leading batter.[8] It was an appropriate beginning for Hank's career as a well-traveled journeyman pitcher.

The Toledo Blue Stockings, of the same minor league, picked up O'Day. At about the same time the team also signed catcher Moses Fleetwood Walker, who would later become the first African American in major-league history, 63 years before Jackie Robinson. *Sporting Life*, baseball's leading publication, was soon proclaiming O'Day and Walker as "one of the most remarkable batteries in the country."[9] With the addition of the talented twosome, Toledo quickly rose from fifth place to win the league championship. The team also fared quite well in exhibition games against major-league competition.

In 1884 O'Day became a major leaguer when the Blue Stockings, brimming with confidence after their great success, joined the American Association. Alas, when Toledo finished in eighth place, the team was dropped from the majors and O'Day was once again looking for another team. In his rookie big-league season, he pitched 326 innings, posting a 9-28 record and 3.75 ERA. He also displayed his versatility by playing 28 games at other positions. (In his major-league career, O'Day had spot starts at every position except catcher and second base.)

Veteran major-league catcher Deacon McGuire described O'Day's pitching style: "He was crafty and had a world of stuff, but he threw the heaviest and hardest ball I ever caught. It was like lead and it came at me like a shell from a cannon." To protect his hand whenever he caught O'Day, McGuire would insert a slab of raw meat into his thin catcher's glove.[10]

The year 1885 was a distressing one for O'Day personally. He was able to stay in the majors by signing with the AA's Pittsburg Alleghenys, but after missing several starts while visiting his dying father back in Chicago, he was released in midseason.[11] Unable to hook up with a major-league club after his father's death, O'Day pitched for Washington's minor-league club in the Eastern League. He rebounded with a sparkling 13-2 record and 0.74 ERA. This success was tempered with news that his 16-year-old brother Joseph had died after fracturing his skull in a fall from an amusement-park roller coaster in Chicago.[12]

In 1886 O'Day had an excellent year with Savannah (26-11, 1.03 ERA), prompting the Detroit Wolverines, hot contenders for the National League pennant, to pick him up late in the season. O'Day was overjoyed until he learned that Detroit had immediately sold him to the last-place Washington Nationals. He finally found some stability and remained with the Nationals for two full seasons, but it was a struggle pitching for a team with the worst hitting in the league. He started the 1888 season with a 0-9 record and one tie, thanks to his teammates scoring a total of nine runs in his first 10 starts. He was able to lead the league in a statistical category for the first and only time in his major-league career, but it was a dubious one –the most hit batsmen. O'Day was the team's workhorse with a combined 24-49 record, 657⅔ innings pitched, and a 3.52 ERA for the two seasons.[13] During his years with Washington, O'Day's catcher was the venerable Connie Mack.

O'Day would long remember the 1889 season, the most thrilling and satisfying of his playing career. He began the year still laboring for last-place Washington and at midseason had a 4.33 ERA and a 2-10 record. The New York Giants, fighting for the pennant, saw something special in O'Day and purchased him, with O'Day receiving a $200 cut. Being supported by a solid offense was a new experience. The Giants had four future Hall of Famers in their lineup, as well as two in their rotation.[14] However, it was O'Day who proved the difference by winning nine games down the stretch and leading the Giants franchise to their first NL championship. Baseball experts said that if the Giants "had not purchased O'Day from Washington at a critical period," New York would not have won the pennant.[15]

The Giants faced the Brooklyn Bridegrooms, winners of the American Association pennant, in a best-of-11 World Series to determine the best team in baseball. The Giants hitters were outstanding but their two aces, Tim Keefe and Mickey Welch, were pounded and New York found itself behind early in the Series. Giants manager Jim Mutrie turned to his two backup hurlers, Cannonball Crane and Hank O'Day, to pitch the rest of the games. They responded with a combined six consecutive wins to capture the crown for New York. "It was difficult to isolate a single hero in the Series," wrote author Jerry Lansche, "but the logical choice was pitcher Hank O'Day."[16] He was dazzling in the pitcher's box. O'Day won the only two low-scoring games, one to tie the Series and the other the deciding contest, by limiting Brooklyn to three earned runs in 23 innings and holding their hitters to a microscopic .135 batting average.

There was a revolution in baseball in 1890. More than 150 players, finally fed up with their treatment by management over the years, formed their own major league, the Players League. Twelve members of the 1889 Giants, including Hank O'Day, became the nucleus of a "new" New York Giants team. O'Day finished the year with a 22-13 record, 329 innings pitched, and a 4.21 ERA. The Players League folded after only one season and the circuit's players scattered, most of them returning to their big-league club of the previous year. O'Day was not so lucky. It was his last major-league season as a player. The many innings he had hurled over the years had taken their toll and his right arm was dead.

HANK O'DAY

Back of the platter the umpire stands,
With his stodgy frame and his pudgy hands,
　His bloodhound bay and his upraised mitt,
　His suit of blue and his working kit;
And day after day, year after year,
In the same old place you will see appear
　The guy who held the same old job
　While the game was making a Wagner
　or Cobb,
　Fashioning hero and mutt and slob,
To sink to the depths or rise to fame
In the onward rush of the baseball game.
　Little he reeks what time or change
　May work in the far-flung baseball range.
What pitchers star, what teams may come
To figure high in the pastime's hum;
　All he knows in the din and shout
　Is "Strike!" and "Ball!" and "Safe!" and "Out!"
The great teams come and the great teams go
In the game's unceasing ebb and flow,
　But come as they may and go as they will,
　The old fellow in blue is out there still,
Back of the plate, while they smash their way
To a waiting pennant, play by play.
　He is there when up with the great they ride
　As a winning club in their day of pride;
And he's out there yet when the hour glass
takes
The speed of youth and their luck forsakes
And a new club comes as the old team breaks,
　He welcomes the kid from the nether bush
　And watches him win to a place in the push
　Till the headline trumpets afar his name
　As a wonderful star and a king of the game;
And day by day he watches him slip
Till he marks the start on the downward trip.
　Glory is fleeting, transient is fame
　On the dizzy heights of the national game.
Ah, stodgy man in the suit of blue,
Naught else is permanent – only you!

　　　William B. Ruggles
　　　The Sporting News, October 19, 1916: 4.

Determined to extend his baseball life, O'Day toiled for four different teams in four minor leagues over the next three years (1891-1893).[17] In 1892 he suffered another personal tragedy when he learned of the death of his older brother James, 38, with whom he had played ball on the sandlots of Chicago. James was working for the Pinkerton Detective Agency when he suffered severe head injuries protecting Pennsylvania coal miners during a labor strike battle. Shortly thereafter, in a state of delirium, James committed suicide by jumping to his death from a moving train.[18]

In 1894 O'Day was at a crossroads in his life. A year earlier, baseball had increased its pitching distance to 60 feet 6 inches. He knew his playing career was over—nobody was looking for a has-been 35-year-old hurler with an ailing right arm—but he wanted to remain in the game he loved. He decided to take a crack at being an umpire (of which he had a little prior experience) and went to the Northwestern League to work some games. It would prove to be the wisest decision he ever made because it was a role he was born to perform.

A decade earlier, on September 11, 1884, while a rookie major-league pitcher with Toledo, O'Day had been selected to serve as the umpire when the regular arbiter had failed to show up. Despite having never done it before, O'Day performed his duties behind the plate "very acceptably."[19] He was a natural and would serve as a substitute umpire in another six games during his playing career. In O'Day's era, it was not unusual for an active player to serve as an umpire.[20] However, it is testament to his honesty, integrity, and talent that during his playing career no other active player was called upon to serve as "player-umpire" more than him.[21]

O'Day became an umpire during the profession's worst period. "It was hell to be an umpire in the 1890's; it's a wonder anyone would do it," wrote historian Bill James.[22] Larry Gerlach, the foremost umpire historian, aptly described the life of an arbiter during this violent decade on the diamond: "Umpires were routinely spiked, kicked, sworn at and spit upon by players, while fans hurled curses, bottles and all manner of organic and inorganic debris at the arbiters. Mobbings and physical assaults by players and patrons alike became commonplace; police escorts were familiar and welcome sights to the men in blue. … In short, a rough-and-tumble, no-holds-barred mentality dominated the game in the last past part of the 19th century."[23]

O'Day did not last long initially in the profession. In 1895 he quit umpiring, returned to Chicago, and took a job as a clerk in the City Recorder's Office. By taking his first job outside baseball, it is probable that he at that time had entirely given up the idea of remaining in the game in any capacity.[24] Fortunately for baseball, O'Day remained passionate about the game and would visit the old ballpark as often as he could.

On the overcast Sunday afternoon of July 7, 1895, Hank O'Day was sitting in the grandstand in a crowd of 9,000 awaiting the start of the game between the Chicago Colts and Cleveland Spiders. Chicago team owner James Hart noticed O'Day, approached him, explained that the regular umpire had not arrived, and pressed O'Day to take his place. O'Day agreed and the rest, in the oft-repeated cliché, is history. During the spirited contest, "not even the semblance of a kick was registered by either team." Sitting in the stands with Hart were Spiders owner Frank Robison and New York Giants owner Andrew Freedman. The three magnates were so impressed with O'Day's work that they prevailed upon National League President Nick Young to immediately hire him as a full-time major-league umpire.[25]

O'Day quit his clerk position, signed a National League umpire contract, and two days later was calling balls and strikes for the Colts-Giants game in Chicago. For the remainder of the season, he traveled around the NL circuit, umpiring almost every day for a total 75 games.

One game illustrates what O'Day had to endure during his rookie season as a major-league umpire. "O'Day probably never had as narrow an escape from serious or death" as in the Cleveland-Washington game of August 20, reported the *Washington Post*. After the Nationals had lost the close contest, a crowd of about 1,000 irate fans surrounded O'Day,

who "was so badly frightened … that his face blanched and his teeth chattered with a noise like castanets." Washington manager Gus Schmelz (for whom O'Day had once played for in the minors) pulled O'Day to safety into a dressing room, where he was guarded by a squad of police officers. When he later left with an armed escort, he was greeted by a shower of bricks. Hustled into a nearby hotel, he remained guarded by armed police until the outraged mob dwindled.[26] The next day the fearless O'Day was back at the same ballpark working a doubleheader behind the plate.

O'Day's first ejection involved Connie Mack, his old friend and former batterymate. Working alone, O'Day had hustled out to second base from behind home plate to make a close call of "safe" on a New York Giants batter-runner. Mack, manager of the Pittsburgh Pirates, uncharacteristically let loose a string of profanity that could be heard way up in the press box. O'Day ignored it until Mack "applied a name to him that was unprintable." O'Day walked up to the dugout and levied a fine of $100 on Connie, later upheld by the league president. Mack continued his tirade by "lashing him with language which could not be repeated in polite society." O'Day tossed Mack from the game and, when Mack refused to leave, summoned uniformed patrol officers to escort him from the park.[27] It was the first and only ejection of Mack's 66-year major-league career as a player and manager.

Needing more experience, O'Day spent the 1896 season umpiring in the Western League.[28] Ban Johnson, the minor league's imperious president, understood that baseball's frequent fistfights were eroding attendance and that if left unchecked would not only hinder the game's growth but might ultimately destroy it. Johnson insisted that strong security measures be employed in all his ballparks; that no profanity be allowed on the field or in the stands; and that players engaging in brawls be promptly suspended. Most importantly, Johnson gave his umpires total authority and supported them completely. Working full-time in the Western League was an epiphany for

O'Day—this was the way baseball should and could be conducted.

Returning to the National League as a full-time umpire in 1897, O'Day was determined to do his part to reduce the game's excessive violence. It would prove to be one of his most immense contributions to baseball.[29] Employing full use of all the weapons an umpire has in enforcing discipline—warnings, imposing fines, ejections, threat of forfeit, and recommending suspensions—O'Day remained resolute, sending the clear message that he would not tolerate any disrespect of the game or his authority. In 1897 he ejected players and managers at a steady clip, mainly for fighting and bench-jockeying. The following season he even ejected a Chicago fan for using profane language.[30]

O'Day has the third highest ejection rate of any veteran umpire in major-league history.[31] Hall of Fame pitcher Christy Mathewson said, "It is as dangerous to argue with him as it is to try to ascertain how much gasoline is in the tank of an automobile by sticking down the lighted end of a cigar."[32] Although O'Day had a high ejection rate, he was not known to have a quick trigger. Being a former player himself, he understood that in the heat of competition tempers can flare. He would let players blow off a little steam, as long as they didn't go too far. "That is why I consider Hank O'Day the best in the business," wrote F.C. Lane. "He makes allowances for a man. … Hank gives some leeway unless a player exceeds his bounds."[33]

"It is most important that an umpire not lose his temper," said O'Day. "As a matter of fact, he should not have a temper at all. He must not notice the little slurs." Nonetheless, when a player cheated or engaged in acts of unsportsmanlike conduct, "I order a player from the field promptly."[34] Stone-faced Hank O'Day, forever stoic, became known for never losing his cool. He also was recognized for never holding a grudge. O'Day would preach to young umpires the importance of having a short memory, to always strive to "forget all the little unpleasantness that has occurred on the field as soon as the game is over."[35]

When ejections weren't enough to restore order, O'Day would resort to forfeit. On June 22, 1900, in Philadelphia, the losing Phillies began making a mockery of the game by purposely walking batters and refusing to tag out runners in hopes that O'Day would call the game on account of darkness and have the score revert to the earlier inning. After several warnings, he forfeited the game to Brooklyn and was "nearly mobbed afterwards" by the enraged hometown fans.[36] A year later, on May 13, 1901, O'Day awarded another forfeit, this time against Brooklyn. In the top of the ninth with two outs, Brooklyn thought it had taken the lead when Bill Dahlen singled to left with the bags loaded, apparently driving in two runners. O'Day, however, would not allow the second run. He had noticed that the runner from second base had not crossed the plate before the runner from first had been thrown out at third base. It was a "time play," meaning the second run did not count. The Brooklyn players surrounded him, screaming in protest. An ejection, several warnings, and O'Day pulling out his watch and waiting three minutes did not restore the peace, so he awarded a forfeit win to New York.[37]

"During the formative era of major-league umpiring, no National League umpire was held in greater esteem for integrity and the ability to 'run the game' than O'Day," said Professor Larry Gerlach.[38] Far too often more than a few umpires of the era would make close calls in favor of the home team to avoid abuse from the local crowd. O'Day refused to be intimidated and continually made the right call as he saw it, regardless of the color of the player's uniform. Teams hated to see O'Day at their home games because they knew they would get no added advantage, but were delighted when he was assigned to their road games.[39]

Sportswriters, accustomed to bashing officials in their game accounts, praised O'Day for having the courage to make the right call, no matter how unpopular. One writer called him "the premier ump of all ages."[40] Another appreciated O'Day's talent of having "that wonderful knack of gauging that hairline width that separates a strike from a ball."[41] The words integrity, honor, and honesty became synonymous with the name Hank O'Day long before they were cemented by the call that would define his life.

On September 23, 1908, during the heat of a passionate pennant race, the Cubs and Giants were engaged in an intense game in New York's Polo Grounds. The umpires were Hank O'Day behind the plate and Bob Emslie on the bases. The score was tied in the bottom of the ninth with two outs and runners on first and third. The Giants' Al Bridwell hit a solid single to the outfield and Moose McCormick "scored" easily from third base. Hundreds of New York fans, believing their Giants had a walk-off victory, charged onto the field in celebration. However, rookie Fred Merkle, the baserunner on first base, had stopped halfway to second before running to the Giants' outfield clubhouse. It was a common practice of the day for players to run off the field to avoid fans entering the playing field after a game.

What followed next was pure pandemonium. As the fans swarmed the field, Cubs center fielder Solly Hofman continued to run after the batted ball. Johnny Evers, Cubs second baseman, stood on the bag screaming for Hofman to throw him the ball. Under the rules, if Merkle was forced out at second, the run would not count. Hofman threw the ball off the mark into the infield, where a Cubs player picked it up. Seeing what was happening, New York's Joe McGinnity wrested the ball from the player and threw it into a crowd of fans behind third base. Evers eventually got a baseball—if it was the actual game ball, nobody will ever know for sure—and stood on second base, declaring a force out.[42] Cubs shortstop Joe Tinker pleaded with base umpire Emslie to call the out; but Emslie said that in the chaos he did not see if Merkle had touched second base. O'Day, however, was watching everything. Hank conferred with his partner, told him that Merkle did not touch second base, and Emslie called the force out. O'Day then nullified the "winning" run and proclaimed the game a tie. The game did not continue into extra innings because O'Day determined that by the time the grounds were cleared of fans, it would have been too dark for further play.

Hank O'Day.

The riotous mob of fans surrounding O'Day in the middle of the diamond "began pounding him on all available parts not covered by the protector, while the unfortunate attackers on the outside began sending messages by way of cushions, newspapers, and other missiles."[43] Police officers rushed in to rescue the umpires and escort them to the safety of their dressing room. National League President Harry Pulliam later denied all protests and upheld O'Day's decision. Despite scathing editorials and extreme pressure for O'Day and Pulliam to change their decision and award the win to New York, the two remained steadfast. O'Day's call was crucial because the Giants and Cubs finished the season in a dead heat with records of 98-55. The "Merkle Game" had to be replayed and the Cubs won, giving them the pennant by one game.

Merkle was saddled with the nickname "Bonehead" for the rest of his life. Pulliam committed suicide by shooting a bullet into his head. And O'Day umpired another 17 years, abuse being heaped upon him every time he entered the Polo Grounds by fans who believed he had robbed them of a championship.

The manner in which league presidents assigned O'Day to games is illustrative of how highly regarded he was as an umpire. O'Day usually worked alone but when he was a member of a two-man crew, he was generally assigned the more demanding plate position. In his first 1,000 games as a major-league umpire, he was behind the plate 90.4 percent of the time. A rookie umpire was often assigned to work with him so that the neophyte could learn from the master. When there was a particularly important series between contending teams, ones involving great pressure and large riotous crowds, O'Day was the man selected to work the games.

As durable as O'Day was, there are several gaps in his career explained by the many illnesses and injuries he suffered while umpiring. There were the many bruises and beatings he sustained from irate fans charging onto the field after one of his calls. Foul balls were particularly treacherous: One broke his toe, requiring two players to take his place as umpire; another one smashed through his mask, producing a nasty gash on his cheek and severely injuring his jaw; and yet another inflicted a head wound requiring an operation for removal of a piece of bone from behind his ear. He was seriously ill one entire season with recurring stomach problems brought on by stress. In other seasons, a robust case of influenza knocked him out for several weeks and an attack of appendicitis in St. Louis meant an ambulance trip to the hospital.

"World Series assignments clearly reveal the greatest umpires in any given era, as well as in baseball history," wrote Larry Gerlach.[44] And Hank O'Day's World Series record is truly astounding. When the first modern World Series was established in 1903, the two leagues were asked to send their best umpire to work the best-of-nine Series. The National League selected O'Day; the American League chose Tommy Connolly. What is extraordinary is that the two umpires did not alternate their positions during the Series. O'Day worked the plate for the first four games, with Connolly serving as the base umpire. O'Day's reputation was so great, he was so highly acclaimed for his ability to call balls and strikes, and he was so noted for his integrity, that the AL had no problem having the NL umpire working extra games behind the plate. For six of the first eight World Series games ever played, O'Day was the plate umpire.

O'Day was assigned to umpire four of the first five World Series (1903, 1905, 1907, and 1908), always working more plate games than his partner. When the World Series expanded to a four-man umpire crew in 1910, Hank was one of the two NL umpires selected. He would be chosen to umpire five more fall classics later in his career (1916, 1918, 1920, 1923, and 1926) for a total of 10 World Series, tied with Cy Rigler for the second-most ever behind Bill Klem. (O'Day would have had more World Series assignments had he not taken a break from umpiring to become a manager a couple of seasons.)

O'Day had other notable World Series "firsts" other than being the first plate umpire. In Game Two of the 1907 Series, he alertly called out Chicago Cub Jimmy Slagle, the only player in World Series history to become victim of the hidden-ball trick.[45] In that same game, Tigers manager Hughie Jennings was the first ever to be ejected from a World Series game—courtesy of Mr. O'Day. In Game Five of the 1920 Series, Bill Wambsganss executed the only unassisted triple play in the postseason; Hank was the second-base umpire making the three "out" calls in quick succession. (O'Day also worked the pressure-packed Game Seven of the 1920 World Series.)

One of the more intriguing periods of O'Day's long baseball career was his two stints as a National League manager. When O'Day was announced as the new skipper for the 1912 Cincinnati Reds, the baseball world was stunned. Even more surprising was when the rookie manager led the team to "one of the most sensational starts in major league history."[46] On May 12 the Reds were in first place with a 22-7 record, an amazing improvement from the team's sixth-place finish the year before. The Reds then slumped badly before making a surge toward the end to finish in fourth place with a 75-78 record. When O'Day heard that the Reds were going to replace him as manager with Joe Tinker, he quit before he was fired. The *New York Times* reported that "President Thomas J. Lynch and the National League Club owners would undoubtedly welcome O'Day back as an umpire."[47] The newspaper was correct; O'Day was back holding the indicator for the 1913 season.

O'Day then pulled off another surprise by agreeing to be the Chicago Cubs' new manager for the 1914 season. Although he did a decent job by leading the injury-riddled team to a winning record and a third-place finish, he was fired after the season. This time a sportswriter questioned whether O'Day would return to the NL as an umpire because he would be "no fit person to give unbiased decisions" to two teams he had once managed.[48] Ban Johnson attempted to sign baseball's best umpire for his American League, but O'Day remained loyal to the NL and was back behind the plate during the 1915 season. "That he was rehired twice after managing two National League teams speaks volumes as to his talent and integrity," said Larry Gerlach.[49]

As the game's dean of umpires, O'Day was instrumental in firmly establishing the use of umpire hand signals to communicate calls to fans and players, and improving mechanics for better officiating. At first he was opposed to umpires using signals because he believed an umpire should not be demonstrative. He soon came around because it was in the best interests of baseball. Surprisingly, the usually progressive O'Day also initially opposed the two-umpire system. He said an umpire "has more trouble working double than single, as in many cases he not only has to make his own decisions, but sometimes his mate's as well."[50] He said this not long after he had to help his partner make the call in the Merkle incident. O'Day, of course, understood that two umpires can cover and control a game much better than one and quickly became an avid supporter of the double-umpire system. He umpired long enough to see three and even four arbiters being assigned to regular-season games.

As influential as O'Day was in other areas, his most far-reaching impact concerned baseball rules. His contributions in the development of baseball have significantly helped the sport evolve into the great game it is today. Hank O'Day was the most prominent member of baseball's Joint Rules Committee in his time, with his vote and opinion carrying considerable weight. Whenever a new playing or scoring rule was proposed, or a question arose on how an established rule should be interpreted, baseball authorities would first turn to O'Day for advice and counsel. "His brain is an encyclopedia of all the rules of the game," said longtime baseball man Ted Sullivan.[51]

Hank was the originator of the "foul-strike rule," in which the first two foul balls struck by a batter are strikes; previously, an uncaught foul was essentially a "no pitch."[52] The rule, still in use today, has had a massive impact on the game. O'Day pushed for the rule requiring the catcher to remain directly behind the plate throughout an at-bat because it made for better officiating in the fair/foul and ball/strike calls. Previously, the catcher would stand far behind home plate when there were runners on base. (This rule also helped advance the development of safety equipment for catchers and umpires.) In 1910 baseball officials, concerned about the lack of offense in the game, were about to pass a new rule allowing four strikes for a strikeout until O'Day objected. Instead, he supported the introduction of a "lively ball" with a cork center. As a former pitcher, O'Day initially opposed the proposal to ban the spitball but, to provide needed offense to the game, he endorsed rules prohibiting the spitter and other "freak pitches." Throughout his career, O'Day pushed for the uniformity of the rules and regulations in both major leagues. He also helped quicken the game by allowing on-deck batters on the field.[53]

One scoring rule in which O'Day did not get his way is one we take for granted today. In 1920 sportswriter Fred Lieb proposed that whenever a player hits a game-winning home run out of the park (what we call a "walk-off" today), he should get credit for the home run and all the RBIs for any runners on base. Previously, for example, in a tie game in the bottom of the ninth with a runner on third base, a batter hitting a home run got credit for only a single on the theory that the game ended as soon as the baserunner from third scored. O'Day vociferously argued against this proposal, stating that the rule is "sacred and untouchable" that no run can be scored after the winning run has crossed the plate. When the measure was passed 5-1 by the Joint Rules Committee, he pounded on the table, shouting, "I'm telling you, it's illegal. You can't score runs after a game is over!"[54]

O'Day was renowned for his moral character as well as for being an odd character. "He was an umpire and nothing else," said NL President John Heydler.[55] Baseball consumed every fiber of his being, leaving little time for anything else. O'Day was described as "this strange character who lived in a shell, emerging only when he visited the field to render his decisions."[56] With no interest in anything but baseball, he rarely attended parties, the theater, movie houses, or any social event. He had no hobbies, other than relaxing at the race track.[57]

You could count the number of O'Day's friends on Mordecai Brown's right hand. "He preferred his own company," said Lieb. "He minded his own business and expected others to do the same."[58] One offseason, O'Day traveled from Chicago to Ontario to visit fellow umpire Bob Emslie, but O'Day's "idea of a good time was to sit for hours on Emslie's front porch in complete silence.[59]

A lifelong bachelor, O'Day never owned a home. He preferred to live in solitude in hotels and dine alone in restaurants. He would spend his winters working out so that he would be in proper shape to meet the demands of the long baseball season. In his off-hours he sat by himself in hotel lobbies reading nothing but baseball publications and the rulebook. If a player, fan, or sportswriter approached, he would wave them away unless they were there to talk baseball. A cheerful greeting from others would be met with a grumble.

O'Day's lack of a sense of humor contrasted equally to his towering sense of honor. "It is a National League tradition that Henry has never yet been known to smile," commented a *Baseball Magazine* reporter.[60] Christy Mathewson claimed to have seen O'Day laugh once, explaining that his "face acted as if it wasn't accustomed to the experience and broke out in funny new wrinkles."[61] Even some of his

fellow umpires referred to him as "Groucho" behind his back.[62] Bill Klem called O'Day a "misanthropic Irishman" who "wouldn't speak a civil word to anybody."[63] O'Day's somber unsmiling face earned him the nickname "The Reverend."[64]

During an interview, NL President John Heydler talked about what it takes to be a great umpire: "The successful umpire must live the life of a hermit, apart from the friendships of the player and fans. He must be a man without a country, home or haunt in the world of baseball. He must be alone on the train. He must stay in a different hotel. He must keep aloof while in the baseball park and avoid all baseball assemblies. … Strength of character, courage of conviction, fixity of purpose and intelligence are necessary requisites for a successful umpire."[65] Although Heydler didn't mention Hank O'Day by name, everybody knew whom he was referring to.

It would take a skilled psychologist to determine why O'Day became such a sullen, secretive man both on and off the field. One explanation is that it was simply his nature, that "O'Day was born not liking people."[66] But accounts of his dour personality do not appear until after he became a full-time major-league umpire. A fan recalled that when O'Day was a pitcher in 1886, he was "a good-natured happy-go-lucky boy from the North, as full of fun as any other youngster on the Savannah team."[67] It is curious that the few friends O'Day had were all baseball men he had met as a younger man.[68] The many personal tragedies of his life may also have triggered the profound change in his personality.[69] There is yet another reason he was so unsociable: O'Day was so concerned that his integrity was beyond reproach that he had taken it to a ridiculous extreme. Fearful that even the slightest personal relationship might influence his calls on the field, he refused to get close to anyone.

All these factors no doubt contributed to O'Day's being so miserable, but the main one was likely the burden of being an umpire during his era. Umpire Silk O'Loughlin tried to persuade a young Bill Klem not to become an umpire by using O'Day as an example. "Look at O'Day," O'Loughlin told Klem. "One of the best umpires. Maybe the best today. But he's sour.

Umpiring does that to you. The abuse you get from the players, the insults from the crowds, and the awful things they write about you in the newspapers."[70]

"O'Day served as a model to young umpires for courage, loyalty and a deep ingrained honesty," wrote Fred Leib.[71] O'Day encouraged Klem to make umpiring a career and, in 1904, introduced and recommended him to NL President Harry Pulliam.[72] When Klem made it to the majors, O'Day tutored and guided him. During his long career, O'Day was a mentor for countless umpires. "He told me a lot about umpiring, things to look for," said 24-year major-league veteran umpire Beans Reardon. "He was big and tough; guys didn't fool around with him. … And he told me, 'Hustle all the time. Be on top of every play, so you're in position to make the decision.' … He recommended me to the National League. I was very fortunate to learn from a great umpire like Hank O'Day. He was the best."[73]

On October 2, 1927, O'Day worked the Cubs-Cardinals game as the third-base umpire in a four-man crew. Nobody knew it at the time but the game featured the oldest man to ever umpire a major-league game. O'Day was 68 years and 86 days old. During the 1927 season, he had been behind the plate only a dozen times out of 147 games, quite a contrast to his younger days. At the end of the season, Heydler took O'Day off active duty, conferred him the title "umpire emeritus," and offered him a job as umpire scout. Grumbling, O'Day accepted it "with regret" because, in his heart, he wanted to continue umpiring.[74] He spent the next few years touring baseball's sandlots and minor-league parks, instructing and developing young umpires. O'Day umpired in 35 major-league seasons, particularly notable in an era when there were no unions and umpires signed one-year contracts.

In the early months of 1935, baseball fans read various reports of O'Day being seriously ill. In his final days, he was delirious, muttering about games he had umpired years earlier. He could go through a catalog of more than 4,000 games, each one with a different story, some thrilling, many routine, others amusing or trivial, and more than a few dangerous.

There was that game in 1898 when a fast-burning fire destroyed the old wooden Sportsman's Park in St. Louis. O'Day and players from both teams were heroes by creating a makeshift chute from the dugout benches for fans to slide down to the field to escape the burning grandstand, and then leading them to safety through an exit untouched by the flames.[75] Or that game when Luther Taylor, a deaf-mute, swore at O'Day with sign language only to be surprised when O'Day signaled back that he was ejected from the game. Taylor was unaware that O'Day, having had deaf parents, was fluent in American Sign Language. Maybe, as O'Day lay dying, he remembered his extended work on October 2, 1920, when he umpired the only twentieth-century major-league tripleheader with partner Peter Harrison.[76] O'Day may have recalled that time he learned that Giants shortstop Bill Dahlen was purposely getting ejected from games so that he could leave early and go to the race track, so O'Day refused to toss him despite being called "a big beer-soaked, fat-headed loafer and thief."[77] And, of course, there was that game when the zany Rabbit Maranville humiliated him when he stole second base by sliding between the umpire's legs.

On July 2, 1935, Hank O'Day died in Chicago of bronchial pneumonia, six days shy of his 76th birthday. To the end, he was still drawing pay as a NL "advisory umpire."[78] His funeral service, held in St. Jariath Catholic Church, was attended by many baseball dignitaries with major-league umpires serving as pallbearers.[79] He left no will; his sole heir was Henry McNamara, a nephew who had been named after him. O'Day was buried in Calvary Cemetery in Evanston, Illinois.

The *Chicago Tribune* ran a feature on the venerated arbiter, saying O'Day was "one of those blunt, rugged characters who seldom allowed his crusty exterior to reveal the really warm heart beneath. Hank O'Day's bark was worse than his bite. He was a great umpire, one of the game's greatest, courageous, honest, and with a thorough knowledge of the rule subtleties."[80]

In announcing O'Day's death, virtually every newspaper included in its headline the name Merkle. In one obituary, it was stated: "Hank is gone, but he'll not be forgotten."[81] Sadly, he would be forgotten for years when it came to being bestowed baseball's highest honor.

On July 28, 2013, Hank O'Day was inducted into the National Baseball Hall of Fame, 78 years after his death and 86 years after he had umpired his last ballgame.[82]

Why did it take so long for such an influential baseball figure to make it to Cooperstown?

The Hall of Fame held its first election in 1936 and, in the years following, many of the game's great players were properly honored, along with influential pioneers, executives, and managers. But what about the umpires, those dedicated men in blue who have had such a positive image on the game? It wasn't until Bill Klem died in 1951 that attention was brought to the fact that no umpire had ever been inducted. Two years later the legendary Klem was honored along with Tommy Connolly, the first umpires enshrined in the Hall of Fame. Why Connolly over O'Day? As fine an arbiter as Connolly was, O'Day had always been considered the greater umpire and more influential. Simply put, Connolly was an American League umpire while O'Day was a National League umpire. When the electors honored NL umpire Klem, they wanted an umpire representing the AL in the Hall of Fame.[83]

After Klem and Connolly, it would be another 20 years before another umpire was elected. Subsequently, six other outstanding umpires were inducted. O'Day, arguably the best of them all, was always overlooked. Baseball historian David Anderson endorsed O'Day and wondered why he had not already been bequeathed the big honor. "That he is not in the Hall of Fame is an oversight," Anderson wrote. "This is partly a function of the fact that he never married; baseball was his love, and he had no family to lobby for him. Conspiracy buffs may believe the oversight to be a measure of revenge by New York sportswriters for O'Day's decision in the infamous Merkle game, but more likely it is because O'Day was not known to be a particularly friendly person."[84]

Anderson is correct but ironically, the explanations for O'Day *not* having been honored are reasons why

he *should* be honored. For O'Day, baseball was indeed his love, which came at the expense of not having the comfort of family and friends. He was also not "a particularly friendly person," but this was because he did not want to get close to anyone to ensure that his integrity as an umpire was never compromised. O'Day's credo was "I know no friends nor enemies on the field," an attitude that extended to his private life.[85] Nonetheless, it was through his forceful will and personality, at great personal sacrifice to him, that the game was enriched.

As for the Merkle incident, there is no better demonstration of O'Day's integrity, one of the criteria for the Hall of Fame.[86] That fateful day, it would have been easier to have just walked off the field when the "winning" run scored, but that would not have been the ethical thing to do.

Bill Klem's remarks also did not help O'Day's chances of reaching Cooperstown. He called the Merkle ruling "the rottenest decision in the history of baseball. … It was bad umpiring."[87] On the contrary, it was a courageous decision and excellent umpiring. It was a betrayal by Klem of his former partner and the man who helped Klem become a major-league umpire. Of course, Klem waited until O'Day had been dead for 16 years before making his craven criticism.

Klem is universally recognized as "the greatest umpire in baseball history" and is much more celebrated than his contemporary Hank O'Day.[88] The two men had quite different philosophies regarding their profession. Klem was a showman and self-promoter; O'Day eschewed publicity. Klem enjoyed drinking and dining with players and managers; O'Day avoided all off-field contact with baseball people. Klem would make up his own baseball rules; O'Day insisted on the enforcement of the rules as written.[89] One could argue that O'Day, rather than Klem, should have been the first umpire inducted into the Baseball Hall of Fame.

Dennis McNamara, a retired Chicago police officer and O'Day's grandnephew, gave the induction speech at the posthumous Hall of Fame induction of the great umpire. "Uncle Hank was almost a mythic figure in our family and his example guided me as a policeman," McNamara said. "The lesson of Hank O'Day is: Do your best with honesty and integrity."[90]

NOTES

1   When Ted Breitenstein (1898), Johnny Lush (1906), Hod Eller (1919), and Jesse Haines (1924) tossed their no-hit gems, Hank O'Day was calling the balls and strikes.

2   Lee Allen, *The Cincinnati Reds* (New York: G.P. Putnam's Sons, 1948), 99.

3   G.H. Fleming, *The Unforgettable Season* (New York: Holt, Rinehart and Winston, 1981), 243.

4   Personal information about Hank O'Day often conflicts because he always refused to talk about his private life. He was particularly thick-lipped about his age. Depending on the obituary or biography, his birth year varies widely. On his *Sporting News* umpire card, the year 1861 is crossed off and replaced with the handwritten "July 8, 1862." O'Day's birth certificate was lost in the Great Chicago Fire; however, census reports confirm that he was born in 1859. Hank's siblings were named Daniel, James Jr., Catherine (Kate), Margaret, Mary, and Joseph. His mother's name is often reported as Mary but it was actually Margaret. (Death notice, *Chicago Tribune*, March 14, 1895). Most sources contend that O'Day's middle initial is "M," including the National Baseball Hall of Fame; but prominent baseball historians, including Larry Gerlach, Norman Macht, and David Nemec, state that it is "F" for Francis. Dennis McNamara, O'Day's grandnephew, said Hank's parents were deaf. (YouTube website video entitled "Umpire O'Day Inducted Into Hall of Fame," posted December 11, 2013).

5   By the time O'Day became a full-time major-league umpire; he was much heavier and had shaved off his mustache. Hank would begin each baseball season weighing about 205 pounds, only to lose 30 pounds by October after hustling around the diamond in the hot sun all summer. "Not So Easy," *Sporting Life*, November 10, 1900: 5.

6   G.W. Axelson, *Commy: The Life Story of Charles A. Comiskey* (Chicago: Reilly & Lee Co., 1919), 21. The O'Day brothers, all pitchers, played for the semipro Libertys. Hank also played for the Spaldings, a team sponsored by Al Spalding. Publisher Alfred Spink was a teammate of the O'Day brothers, serving as their bare-handed catcher. Spink wrote: "The O'Day boys were all fine, brave fellows and Hank … is perhaps the bravest and best of the lot." Alfred H. Spink, *The National Game* (St. Louis: The National Game Publishing Co. 1911), 371.

7   Chris Goode, *California Baseball: From the Pioneers to the Glory Years* (self-published, 2009), 17-18. Whether O'Day actually attended any classes at St. Mary or just played baseball is a good question. At the time there was an intense athletic rivalry between California colleges and many schools recruited ballplayers to serve as ringers. St. Mary's College must have had an excellent team in 1881-1883, when O'Day was a member, because the team had six players who would later become major leaguers.

8   "Hank O'Day, Picturesque Figure in National League History, Retires," *Pittsburgh Post-Gazette*, December 14, 1927. Although it was reported that O'Day was Bay City's best hitter and fielder, few statistics survive from this minor league to confirm this. In any case, it most have been an aberration, because O'Day's hitting statistics for the rest of his career are not impressive.

9   David W. Zang, *Fleet Walker's Divided Heart: The Life of Baseball's First Black Major Leaguer* (Lincoln: University of Nebraska Press, 1995), 39. During his baseball career, Walker suffered much racial abuse from both teammates and opponents. Tony Mullane, self-admitted racist, and Curt Welch, open segregationist, were Walker's teammates. What was O'Day's relationship with Walker? Esteemed baseball historian Lee Allen wrote, "Neither O'Day nor Mullane liked Walker, and each did his best to throw the ball so hard the catcher would be injured, but they never succeeded in forcing him off the job." (Allen, *The Cincinnati Reds*, 100). If accurate, this is a large stain on O'Day's character. Allen is one whose view must be respected; however, his account is the only source that asserts that O'Day had any prejudicial tendencies. In his extensive research, David Nemec, the foremost authority on nineteenth-century baseball, "found nothing negative about (O'Day's) relationship with Walker" nor did he find "any reported derogatory incidents." (Email correspondence with author, January 2017) Additionally, according to Zang's well-researched biography, Walker had a cordial and successful partnership with O'Day.

10   Norman L. Macht, "Henry Francis 'Hank' O'Day," *Baseball's First Stars* (Cleveland: Society for American Baseball Research, 1996), 123.

11   "O'Day of the Pittsburgs Is in Chicago Attending a Very Sick Father," *Sporting Life*, July 7, 1885: 7.

12   "City Items," *Chicago Tribune*, September 4, 1885: 3.

13   Statistics are from Hank O'Day's minor-league page on Baseball-Reference.com. Typical of O'Day's hard-luck 1887 season was when he smashed a triple, "the longest hit of his career," and then scored on a wild pitch only to have the game called on account of darkness. The score reverted to the previous inning and Hank was deprived of his mighty hit and run scored. (Wm. A. Phelon, "Baseball Customs Past and Present," *Baseball Magazine*, October 1915: 55.)

14   O'Day's teammates and future Hall of Famers were Roger Connor, Buck Ewing, Jim O'Rourke, Monte Ward, Tim Keefe, and Mickey Welch.

15   "Championship vs. Exhibition Games," *Sporting Life*, November 6, 1889: 4.

16   Jerry Lansche, *Glory Fades Away: The Nineteenth-Century World Series Rediscovered* (Dallas: Taylor Publishing, 1991), 177.

17   In 1891-93, O'Day pitched for the Lincoln Rustlers, Columbus Reds, Marinette Badgers, and Erie Blackbirds, respectively in the Western Association, Western League, Wisconsin-Michigan

League, and Eastern League. In leagues for which we have statistics, O'Day had a losing record every year despite recording decent earned-run averages.

18 David Nemec, *Major League Baseball Profiles, 1871-1900*, Vol. 1 (Lincoln: University of Nebraska Press, 2011), 145-146.

19 Ibid.

20 During this era and into the early years of the twentieth century, usually only one umpire was scheduled to work major-league games. Quite often he would fail to show up by game time because of travel disruptions, illness, or the fact that he had simply quit. Whenever this occurred, the two managers would each select one of their players to umpire the game, usually a pitcher on his offday or a catcher needing a day off. The selected player would have to be agreed upon by the opposing manager. The players would umpire the game in their baseball uniforms.

21 No fewer than 135 active players served as emergency substitute umpires during O'Day's seven-year major-league playing career (1884-1890), the vast majority of them umpiring only one game their entire career. O'Day was the exception. While an active player, Hank was called upon to serve as umpire for seven major-league games (three behind the plate), tied with pitcher Mickey Welch for the most during this period. While he served as a substitute umpire, O'Day's "team" lost four times; it is likely his teammates had some choice words for him in the clubhouse afterward.

22 Bill James, *The New Bill James Historical Baseball Abstract* (New York: Free Press, 2001), 53.

23 Larry R. Gerlach, "Umpire Honor Rolls," *Baseball Research Journal* (Cooperstown: Society for American Baseball Research, 1979): 82.

24 Before taking the job with the city, O'Day umpired some games in the Western League. Hank returned to Chicago in 1895 not only to find employment but also because his mother had died that year and his sister Margaret had died not much earlier ("Deaths," *Chicago Tribune*, March 14, 1895: 7). It is not known exactly why Hank, at this point, had foregone baseball as a career and had taken the security of a government job. It may have been because of the low salary of a minor-league umpire. As tough as O'Day was, it is unlikely that he gave up umpiring because of the profession's harsh demands.

25 Addie Joss, "Hank O'Day Got Job by Accident," *Pittsburgh Post-Gazette*, January 7, 1910: 7. Some details of Joss's account are inaccurate, such as stating that Thomas Lynch was the absent umpire. Joss wrote the article on the occasion of Lynch being appointed National League president in 1910, when O'Day was baseball's most famous umpire. It made for a good story that Lynch, O'Day's new boss, was the tardy umpire responsible for Hank becoming a major-league umpire 15 years earlier. Although Lynch was an NL umpire from 1888 to 1894, returning in 1896, he was not a full-time umpire in 1895. Research reveals that the absent umpire was likely Miah Murray, who worked the Giants-Cubs game on July 8, the day after O'Day had come to the rescue as arbiter. (Umpire pages for 1895, Retrosheet.org) Joss mentions that "there were three or four baseball magnates in the stands" that game; although unusual, this rings true. The July 7 game was a makeup, with Cleveland traveling to Chicago for that one game. The Giants had played the Colts the previous day and would play them the next day, meaning the team (and their owner) were also in Chicago on July 7. Stanley Robison, part-owner of the Spiders, may also have been in the ballpark that day.

26 "Umpire's Close Call," *Washington Post*, August 21, 1895: 4.

27 Norman L. Macht, *Connie Mack and the Early Days of Baseball* (Lincoln: University of Nebraska Press, 2007), 118-119. Mack's ejection occurred on September 6, 1895; afterward, Connie still remained friends with O'Day.

28 On July 26, 1896, O'Day was called up from the minors to umpire one major-league game in Chicago that season.

29 Besides O'Day's strong actions, another influential factor in reducing the violence in baseball was Ban Johnson's minor league reaching major-league status in 1901 as the American League. Nonetheless, even with the forceful personalities of Johnson and O'Day, the game's culture of rowdiness was so embedded that it took several years before the problem was effectively curtailed. Meanwhile, the NL lost some excellent arbiters, like Jack Sheridan and Tommy Connelly, who jumped the senior circuit to umpire in the AL for its better working conditions. O'Day remained loyal to the NL, steadfastly working to rid the game of its violence. When the AL, in only its second season, outdrew the National League and continued to so for the rest of the decade, the older league eventually realized the importance of strict discipline and the wisdom of greater support of its umpires.

30 "Notes and Comments," *Sporting Life*, June 5, 1898.

31 Of the 81 major-league umpires who have worked more than 3,000 games (through 2017), the three with the highest rate of ejections are all National League umpires from the early twentieth century. Cy Rigler has the highest rate (an ejection every 17.2 games), followed by Bill Klem (17.9) and Hank O'Day (18.7).

32 Christy Mathewson, *Pitching in a Pinch* (New York: Grosset & Dunlap Publishers, 1912), 175.

33 F.C. Lane, "The Gamest Player in Baseball," *Baseball Magazine*, September 1913: 58.

34 "Live Talk About the Baseball Players," *St. Louis Republic*, March 20, 1904.

35 Ibid.

36 David Nemec and Eric Miklich, *Forfeits and Successfully Protested Games in Major League Baseball* (Jefferson, North Carolina: McFarland Publishers: 2014), 97.

37 Nemec and Miklich, 102.

38 E-mail correspondence with umpire historian Larry R. Gerlach, November 2012.

39 "Close Decisions: An Inside Study of the Life, the Work, the Difficulties and the Humor of a Baseball Umpire," *The American Magazine*, Volume 72 (New York: Crowell Publishing Company, 1911): 210.

40 "Notes of the Cubs," *Chicago Tribune*, July 16, 1909: 18.

41 Frederick G. Lieb, "Late Hank O'Day, Sphinx-Like, Fearless and Honest, Defied Wrath of McGraw in Merkle Decision," *The Sporting News*, July 11, 1935: 2.

42 As for the argument that Merkle should not have been called out because Evers did not have the right ball, O'Day later said the out would have been called regardless of what ball Evers was holding because of McGinnity's interference. "The Merkle Play," *Sporting Life*, October 24, 1914: 19.

43 *New York Herald*, September 24, 1908, account of game found in Fleming's *The Unforgettable Season*, 245.

44 E-mail correspondence with Gerlach.

45 John Snyder, *Cubs Journal* (Cincinnati: Clerisy Press: 2008), 141.

46 "Hank O'Day Resigns," *New York Times*, November 7, 1912. The Reds were so successful that a sportswriter joked that even their manager "Hank O'Day can smile these days without hurting his face." ("Around the Bases," *Chicago Defender*, May 18, 1912: 6).

47 "Hank O'Day Resigns."

48 "O'Day to Umpire American League," *Providence Evening News*, November 24, 1914: 4.

49 E-mail correspondence with Gerlach.

50 "Hank O'Day Is Unalterably Opposed to Proposed Double-Umpire System," *Pittsburgh Press*, October 16, 1908: 22.

51 Spink, 370.

52 For a fine description of the evolution of the foul-strike rule, see Peter Morris, *A Game of Inches: The Stories Behind the Innovations That Shaped Baseball* (Chicago: Ivan R. Dee, 2006), 84-89.

53 One of O'Day's rule proposals that never made the rulebook was actually not a bad idea. Hank wanted to install white rubber strips for the batter's box to prevent players from wiping away the chalk lines. ("Ump O'Day's Idea," *Sporting Life*, December 29, 1906).

54 Fred Lieb, *Baseball As I Have Known It* (New York: Coward, McCann & Geoghegan, 1977), 74-75.

55 David W. Anderson, *You Can't Beat the Hours: Umpires in the Deadball Era From 1901-1909* (North Charleston, South Carolina: CreateSpace Independent Publishing: 2013), 78.

56 Lieb, "Late Hank O'Day."

57 In honor of the great umpire, a thoroughbred race horse was named Hank O'Day. Dorothy Ours, *Man of War: A Legend Like Lightning* (New York: Macmillan Publishers: 2006), 77.

58 Lieb, "Late Hank O'Day."

59 Ibid.

60 "Short Lengths," *Baseball Magazine*, August 1913: 76.

61 Mathewson, 168.

62 Lieb, "Late Hank O'Day."

63 William J. Klem and William J. Slocum, "I Never Missed One in My Heart," *Collier's Weekly*, March 31, 1951: 59.

64 Associated Press, "Umpire Hank O'Day Dies at Age of 74," *Boston Herald*, July 3, 1935: 17.

65 Associated Press, "To Be Successful Umpire, Official Must Be a Pariah," *Ludington* (Michigan) *Daily News*, April 9, 1924: 3.

66 Cait Murphy, *Crazy '08* (Washington: Smithsonian Books: 2008), 185. Murphy's work is a wildly entertaining account of the exciting 1908 season and the Merkle incident.

67 Lieb, "Late Hank O'Day."

68 O'Day played ball with Charlie Comiskey as a teenager; Connie Mack was a teammate; Bob Emslie was an opposing pitcher in Hank's playing days; and John Heydler was a fellow umpire in the early years. To psychoanalyze, socializing with these men may have brought back memories of happier times for O'Day.

69 When Hank was 12 years old, the Great Chicago Fire ignited about a block north of the O'Day home in 1871, a catastrophe he refused to ever talk about. Hank outlived his six siblings; all dying at relatively young ages, one by suicide and another in a tragic accident. He may have been closest to his younger sister Mary, with whom he had lived with for a short time. When Mary gave birth to a son on Hank's 40th birthday, she named the baby after her brother. Mary's death in 1924 must have hit Hank hard. ("Deaths," *Chicago Tribune*, February 18, 1924: 10).

70 Klem, "I Never Missed One in My Heart," 61.

71 Lieb, "Late Hank O'Day."

72 Bob Considine, "Foghorn," *Collier's Weekly*, April 13, 1940: 76.

73 Larry R. Gerlach, *The Men in Blue: Conversations With Umpires* (New York: Viking Press, 1980), 9-10.

74 *Pittsburgh Press*, December 16, 1927.

75 "Fire Ends the Game," *Chicago Tribune*, April 17, 1898. Hank lost clothes and personal effects when the umpire's dressing room burned down.

76 A.D. Suehsdorf, "The Last Triple-Header," *Baseball Research Journal* (Cooperstown: Society for American Baseball Research, 1980): 30-33.

77 "Close Decisions," *The American Magazine*.

78 George Kirksey, "Hank O'Day is Near Death; Merkle Boner Recalled," *Pittsburgh Press*, February 22, 1935: 39.

79 "Many Baseball Notables Attend O'Day Funeral," *Chicago Tribune*, July 6, 1935: 17. Among those in attendance were Commissioner Kenesaw Landis; Tom Connolly, supervisor of American League umpires; his protégé Bill Klem; and Bill Emslie and John Heydler, Hank's greatest admirers and closest friends.

80 "In the Wake of the News," *Chicago Tribune*, July 11, 1935: 21.

81 "Hank O'Day, Picturesque Figure," *Pittsburgh Post-Gazette*.

82 O'Day received 93.8 percent of the vote from the Hall of Fame's Pre-Integration Committee to earn induction. The 16-member committee consisted of Hall of Famers Bert Blyleven, Pat Gillick, Phil Niekro, and Don Sutton; baseball executives Roland Hemond, Bill DeWitt, Gary Hughes, and Bob Watson; and sportswriters and historians Jim Henneman, Steve Hirdt, Peter Morris, Phil Pepe, Tom Simon, Claire Smith, T.R. Sullivan, and Mark Whicker. They deserve praise for bestowing on O'Day the honor he had long deserved.

83 Another reason Connolly was elected to the Hall of Fame before O'Day was that his name was much better known at the time. In 1953 Connolly was still actively serving as the American League umpire supervisor at age 82; O'Day had been dead for 18 years. It was not the first time the Hall of Fame Veterans Committee had selected the wrong man. Years earlier, it had inducted the worthy Ban Johnson, the first American League president; at the same election, as a counterpart, the electors honored the forgettable Morgan Bulkeley, the first National League president, rather than the influential William Hulbert, the second NL president.

84 David W. Anderson, *More Than Merkle: A History of the Best and Most Exciting Baseball Season in Human History* (Lincoln: University of Nebraska Press, 2000), 98.

85 Lieb, "Late Hank O'Day."

86 Evidence that the Merkle decision was indeed a reason O'Day had not been inducted earlier is the newspaper headline reading: "Despite Call, O'Day Gets Call" (David Briggs, *Toledo Blade*, July 28, 2013).

87 William J. Klem and William J. Slocum, "Jousting With McGraw," *Collier's Weekly*, April 7, 1951: 31.

88 David Pietrusza, Matthew Silverman, and Michael Gershman, eds., *Baseball: The Biographical Encyclopedia* (New York: Total Sports Publishing, 2000), 613.

89 "Klem was a czar on the field. He made up his own rules," said veteran NL umpire Lee Ballanfant. (Gerlach, *Men In Blue*, 9). Authors David Nemec and Eric Miklich wrote, "Klem's infallibility is not even remotely true. Klem, in actuality, may have been involved in more overturned and controversial contests than any other umpire in history." (*Forfeits and Successfully Protested Games*, 212).

90 YouTube website video "Umpire O'Day Inducted Into Hall of Fame," posted December 11, 2013.

Emmett Ashford

By Mark Armour

He spent 20 years as a professional umpire, baseball's loneliest profession, passing judgment on the performances of the game's great athletes and egos. Many people have pursued this particular job, but Emmett Ashford had the added burden of breaking racial barriers throughout his career, as a black man whose job required maintaining authority over white men. Doing his work with disarming charm, quick wit, and irreproachable dignity, he won over fans, players, and even his fellow umpires, leaving the game with countless friends and admirers.

Emmett Littleton Ashford was born on November 23, 1914 in Los Angeles. His father Littleton, a police officer, soon abandoned the family, and Emmett and brother Wilbur were raised by their mother. His mother Adele was a highly motivated and ambitious woman, who worked as a secretary for the *California Eagle*, a black newspaper. Ashford himself earned money selling *Liberty* magazine, building his route up to 300 customers, and later was a cashier in a supermarket.

Ashford excelled at Jefferson High School, rising to co-editor of the school paper, *The Jeffersonian*, and becoming a teen journalist for the *California Eagle*. He also played baseball and ran sprints for the track team. When he graduated in 1933 he was the senior class president, the first black student so honored, and a member of the scholarship club. Ashford then attended Los Angeles Junior College and Chapman College, where he played baseball.

About 1936 Ashford scored well on a civil service exam and landed a coveted job as a clerk with the post office, a position he held for 15 years. In the late 1930s he had a brief career as a semipro baseball player before turning to officiating. According to Ashford, he played on a white team called the Mystery Nine, who wore uniforms with question marks on the fronts. One day the umpire didn't show up, and Emmett (who rarely played) was called into

emergency service. He was soon busy officiating recreational baseball and softball in southern California.

In 1937 Ashford married Willa Gene Fort, and the couple had two daughters, Adrienne and Antoinette. It was not his only marriage; like many people his personal family life was complicated and private with much of it unknown. The next several years were taken up with family, post office work, and umpiring. Soon after he finished a three-year stint in the United States Navy during World War II, Emmett and Willa divorced. He continued to umpire, moving up to major college baseball, working regularly. He often officiated with Bill Stewart who had umped in the American League in the 1940s. Ashford credits Stewart for teaching him the major-league strike zone.

In 1951 Ashford took a leave of absence from his post office job for a two-month trial in the Southwestern International League, becoming the first black umpire in organized baseball. Les Powers, the league president, claimed that "Ashford has the making of a big league umpire." After the season, Ashford was offered a full-season job, so he resigned from the postal service, leaving behind 15 years towards his pension.

The following offseason, the Southwestern International League announced plans to field an "all-Negro" club, to play only road games. Ashford was named general manager and asked to put together a team. Two days later Chet Brewer, former Negro League star, was hired as the club's manager. Ultimately the team had a series of "homes" during the season, including Ensenada, Mexico; Riverside, California; and Porterville, California. The team did not remain all-black, though many former Negro Leaguers did play for them (including Brewer), as did two future major leaguers (Tom Alston and Dave Roberts).

As for our hero, Ashford relinquished his role with the club before the season began, and returned

Emmett Ashford.

to umpiring. By mid-summer the league folded and he hooked on with the Arizona-Texas League. In December 1952, *The Sporting News* first suggested that Ashford might be destined for the major leagues. "I know that the road to the big leagues will be a hard one," said Ashford, "but most of my biggest obstacles are behind me now."[1] He moved up to the Western International League in 1953, before a promotion to the Pacific Coast League in 1954.

During his 12 years in the PCL, Ashford became the best-known umpire in the minor leagues. "He was a showman, exuberant, strong, alert, loud and expressive," recalled Paul Wysard of Ashford's' days in the PCL. "He was constantly in motion, full of nervous energy and obviously delighted to be out there in front of everybody."[2] Between innings he often sprinted down the right field line to keep his legs loose. He constantly interacted with the crowd, doffing his cap and giving little speeches.

Ashford spent most of his time during the season alone, not hanging out with his fellow umpires. As he later related to Larry Gerlach, "I didn't come to town and have to go to the ghetto to enjoy myself. I stayed

downtown and went to the theater and the opera. I just love some opera—know the librettos of a few. … I made a host of friends; many of them were attorneys and doctors who invited me to their homes and nice functions. I'd meet with the lawyers for lunch in Spokane, and, shoot, in Vancouver, I think I could have run for office."[3] In the offseasons, Ashford refereed Pac-8 basketball and small college football. As early as the fall of 1958 he umpired in the Caribbean winter leagues. He was also a constant after-dinner speaker on the west coast, and ran several umpiring clinics.

In 1963 PCL president Dewey Soriano named Ashford the league's umpire-in-chief, making him responsible for the organization and training of the crews, and for advising the league on disputed games or rules. In June 1963, the league hired its second black umpire, Osibee Jelks, from the Northwest League. On July 4, a game in San Diego was officiated by Ashford and Jelks (the third crew member was ill), the first all-black umpiring crew in a minor-league game.

By the early 1960s, writers on the west coast began clamoring for Ashford's promotion to the majors. A.S. Young also took up the cause in the *Chicago Defender*, suggesting of major-league presidents Joe Cronin and Warren Giles, "Whereas they hire, and approve the hiring of Caucasian umpires solely on the basis of qualifications, they refuse to act on the Ashford case—and probably won't until the Ashford campaign, which should be unnecessary, becomes embarrassing."[4] In 1965 Cronin was considered the leading contender to replace the retiring Ford Frick as baseball's commissioner, but Jim Murray supported Bill Veeck for the top job, with Ashford as his umpire-in-chief. Both endorsements were due to Cronin's foot-dragging on Ashford.[5]

Ashford's most famous on-field incident took place during the 1964 playoffs in the Dominican Republic. After a strike call on Julian Javier met with prolonged disapproval, Ashford motioned the pitcher to continue, and rung up strike three. Javier reacted by slugging Ashford in the mouth, cutting the umpire's lip open and swelling his jaw. Ashford retaliated by hitting the Cardinal infielder with his mask, temporarily forgetting that Javier was a local hero. Ashford finished the game, applying ice packs to his mouth between innings. Javier received a three-game suspension, and Ashford had to be talked out of resigning from the league after the weak penalty.

Despite whatever frustrations he must have felt in the minor leagues for 15 years, he remained a cheerful and optimistic man his entire life, a disposition which stood out in his profession. He charmed his critics and admirers alike, relying on his quick wit and intelligence to get him through a crisis. In one southwest city early in his career Ashford needed to find a place a black man could sleep. He went to the best hotel in town and approached the desk. "Sir," he explained, "I am that barefoot, and uncultured Negro man you have been reading about. I wish to seek lodging in your handsome establishment."[6] He got the room, and his charm would get him many other rooms, and many meals in restaurants.

In mid-September 1965 he got a long-awaited phone call. The voice on the telephone was Dewey Soriano, telling Ashford that he had sold his contract to the American League. "That was the last thing I remembered for the next several days," recalled Emmett.[7] He always spoke fondly of Soriano's support throughout his years in the PCL, and for helping him get to the majors.

The nation's press was thrilled, though not willing to give baseball too much credit for its tardy step. Melvin Durslag figured that Emmett was "bound to raise the game to his refined level."[8] Bill Slocum wondered, "If corporate Baseball has joined the 20th Century, can Mississippi be far behind?"[9]

After his protégé's promotion, Soriano claimed, "The only reason he [Emmett] was not brought up to the majors sooner was because he was colored." Soriano later elaborated: "Emmett was very popular wherever he went, with the players and the fans. I've known him since 1953 and it is an all-out total effort—not showboating. With more Emmett Ashfords, baseball games would be better run and a lot more fun for the fans. I didn't make him umpire-in-chief his last three years out here for comedy."[10]

Ashford had a high-pitched voice that he utilized like a megaphone, keeping the fans aware of where he was and what he was doing. During his first spring training in the majors he interrupted an Angels-Indians game in Tucson to explain to the crowd a recent discussion with the Indians' manager. Removing his cap, he bowed to the throng behind home, loudly intoning, "Ladies and Gentleman... Mr. Tebbetts was merely questioning the strategy of the opposing manager... I thank you."[11] Putting his mask back on, he resumed the game. His fellow umpires soon realized what they were up against. The next day, home-plate umpire Bill Valentine turned to the crowd himself: "Ladies and gentlemen, I'm sorry to inform you that the eminent Emmett Ashford will be at third base and not behind the plate today..."[12]

Prior to his first season, Ashford reflected, "I feel proud being an umpire in the big leagues. Not because I am the first Negro, but because umpires in the major leagues are very select people. Right now, I just want to vindicate Mr. Cronin's faith in me... But first, I've got to buy me a pair of eye glasses," he added, his sense of humor ever present, ready to strike.[13]

Emmett Ashford's regular-season debut took place on April 9, 1966, in Washington's D.C. Stadium, the traditional American League opener. His first major-league hurdle was getting into the ballpark. Vice-President Hubert Humphrey was in attendance to throw out the ceremonial first ball, and the Secret Service needed to be convinced that a black man was there to umpire the game. Humphrey later kidded Ashford, who had worked at third base, that he hadn't had any plays to call. "No plays, no boots," responded Ashford, "but it was the greatest day of my life." Joe Cronin told his new employee, "Emmett, today you made history. I'm proud of you."[14]

Ashford was a sensation right away, but not principally because of his race. His style, well-known on the west coast, took the conservative major leagues by a storm. The stocky (5-foot-7, 185 pounds) Ashford sprinted to his position between innings, stepping on the bases or leaping the pitcher's mound, and raced around the field after foul balls or plays on the bases. *The Sporting News* was impressed enough to claim,

"For the first time in the history of the grand old American game, baseball fans may buy a ticket to watch an umpire perform."[15] The fans did not always need to watch Ashford, they could just listen to his high-pitched cannon of a voice, as he called out a batter or runner.

On a strike call, Ashford jerked his right arm first to the side, then up, then down like a karate chop. That completed, he would then reach either up as if twice yanking a train whistle, or to the right as if opening a car door. Even while dusting the plate he knew every eye in the house was on him, and he behaved accordingly, pirouetting on one foot and hopping back to his position. Emmett would say, "I never went to an umpiring school because they didn't accept blacks in those days, so I developed my own style of officiating."[16] Ashford was also known for his natty attire on and off the field. While umpiring he wore polished shoes, a freshly pressed uniform, cuff-links, and a handkerchief in his suit pocket.

In his first game behind the plate, Andy Etchebarren, the Orioles' catcher, recalled diving into the stands after a foul ball: "I knew I couldn't reach the ball, but I dove into the seats thinking a fan would put the ball in my glove or I could grab it off the floor. But while I was reaching I looked around, and who was in the seats with me but Emmett. I couldn't believe it."[17] In a later Baltimore game, Frank Robinson quipped, "That Ashford gets a better jump on the ball than Paul Blair [the Orioles' fleet-footed center fielder]."[18]

Though he was generally well-liked and admired by the people in the game, the open question was always whether he was a good umpire—whether his style came at the expense of substance. His flamboyance certainly left himself open for abuse, as he was generally the center of attention even when everyone agreed with his calls. Red Sox manager Dick Williams, after a controversial Ashford call in 1969, called the arbiter "a little clown." Joe Pepitone and Pete Ward, in separate incidents, had to be restrained from going after Ashford. "When he calls you out on a third strike," complained one player after a typically emotive Ashford punch-out, "you feel like he's sending you to the electric chair."[19]

Ashford toned down some of his mannerisms as his big-league career progressed. "Sure, I was a showboat," he told the *Boston Globe*'s Ray Fitzgerald. "For 12 years, that was my routine in the Coast League. I couldn't change overnight, but I'm different now. I've toned myself way down." But still, "I'm not exactly without color," he said, using a favorite double entendre.[20]

In 1967, Ashford was named to work the All-Star Game in Anaheim, though he saw little action working the left-field foul line. Ashford realized another dream in 1970 when he umpired the World Series. Unfortunately for Ashford, and for baseball fans, he was slated to work the plate in the sixth game, but his turn never came: the Orioles beat the Reds in five. "Maybe it's just as well it didn't happen—the World Series would never have been the same."[21]

When Ashford turned 55 in December 1969, he had reached the American League's retirement age of 55 for its umpires, a rule occasionally bent. He was given one additional year, but after the 1970 season Ashford announced his retirement. "I'm afraid that by continuing I would only dilute the thrills of the last five years and especially those I received by umpiring in the 1970 World Series," Ashford said.[22]

An unwritten baseball credo suggests that a well-officiated game is one in which the umpire is unnoticed. By that standard, Emmett Ashford was not a good umpire. Not surprisingly, his fellow umpires were the hardest people to win over.

Bill Kinnamon worked on the same crew with Ashford in 1969, and later recalled to Larry Gerlach, "I think he was a good umpire. On the bases and behind the plate he was no better or worse than the rest of us, but it is no secret that his eyes weren't too good when it came to balls hit into the outfield at night. The man was about fifty years old when he came into the league, and I think Emmett would be the first to say that he came up after the peak of his career. If he had come up ten, fifteen, twenty years earlier, he would have been one hell of an umpire."[23]

Speaking of Ashford's impact on the game, Kinnamon said, "He was good for baseball. I never saw him do anything detrimental to baseball. No one ever found any fault with his deportment off the field. He was a gentleman. And the people absolutely dearly loved him. One night, as we were leaving Yankee Stadium together, some kid all of a sudden yelled, 'Emmett!' The next thing I knew, he was standing there talking and signing autographs for a couple of hundred kids. Nobody recognized me; I just sat there on a railing and waited. He signed an autograph for every last kid. That's the kind of man he was, and that's the kind of feeling there was for him."[24]

As Ashford often said, he did not go through the traditional umpire training, and therefore that particular doctrine was not instilled. Kinnamon further explains some of the tension: "There was resentment toward him among the umpires. Everybody knows there was. Emmett knew it, but he shrugged it off. Many guys simply didn't accept Emmett. Politics or pull had nothing to do with it. Some questioned his umpiring ability. And Emmett had his idiosyncrasies—the cuff links, jumping over the mound on his way to second base, his showmanship, things like that. But mostly I think it was the publicity Emmett got. … It's also natural for there to be resentment when there were five reporters around Emmett's cubicle and none around anybody else's. Everywhere Emmett went he was news, good copy. Emmett got more ink in one year than the top five umpires in our league got in their whole career."[25]

It probably didn't help when teams would ask the league for Ashford to umpire their games. In 1968, Athletics owner Charlie Finley wanted Ashford to umpire his home opener—the inaugural game at the new Oakland Coliseum. Umpire crews generally rotate their roles from game to game—from third base, to second, first, and home. For this game Ashford was due to ump second base, but at Finley's urging he got the more visible home plate assignment.

In early 1971 Ashford was hired by Commissioner Bowie Kuhn as a public relations adviser, a role which allowed him to speak and hold clinics on the west coast, and as far away as Korea. He also umpired the occasional minor-league or college game, old-timers games in Dodger Stadium, pleasing the crowd as always. He was umpire-in-chief for the Alaskan summer league for three years. Ashford earned money doing TV commercials (he played a cashier in an ad for the A&P grocery chain), film (as an umpire in *The Bingo Long Traveling All-Stars & Motor Kings*), and television (episodes of *Ironside* and *The Jacksons*). He was also on *What's My Line* during his first year in the major leagues.

Ashford died at Marina Mercy Hospital in Marina Del Ray, California, on March 1, 1980, of a heart attack. At his funeral, he was eulogized by Commissioner Kuhn and Rod Dedeaux, longtime USC baseball coach. He was cremated, and his ashes are interred in Cooperstown, New York.

In looking back on his career, the ever-positive Ashford focused on his good fortune: "Think of all the people who live an entire life and do not accomplish one thing they really wanted to do. I have done something I wanted to do. I have that satisfaction."[26] This is only fitting, as Ashford's class and style provided so much satisfaction to others.

Note: This biography originally appeared in SABR's 2007 edition of *The National Pastime*, edited by Jim Charlton.

SOURCES

In researching this article, I made use of Ashford's extensive clipping file at the National Baseball Library and articles published in *The Sporting News* throughout his career. Larry Gerlach's *The Men In Blue* (Viking, 1980) includes interviews with Ashford and several of his contemporaries. Robert C. Hoie's article in the 1979 *Baseball Research Journal* ("Riverside-Ensenada-Porterville, An All-Negro Minor League Team") outlines Ashford's affiliation with the 1952 club. Ashford's daughter, Adrienne Cherie Ashford wrote a short book *Strrr-ike!!*, which outlines his early life. Bob Sudyk's article in *The Sporting News* ("Emmett Ashford: Only His Suit Is Blue," April 23, 1966) provided the backdrop to Ashford's debut in the major leagues and his first game. Retrosheet's essential website includes detailed game logs for umpires.

NOTES

1   Hugh Keyes, "Only Negro Ump in O.B. Sets Sights on Berth in Majors," *The Sporting News*, December 24, 1952: 9.

2   David Driver, "Umpire Ashford Crossed Different Color Line," *Baseball America*, March 2, 1997.

3   Larry R. Gerlach, *The Men in Blue—Conversations with Umpires* (New York: Viking, 1980), 274.

4   A. S. "Doc" Young, "Will Major Leagues Get Their First Negro Umpire?" *Chicago Defender*, May 28, 1963.

5   Jim Murray, "It Was A Strike," *Los Angeles Times*, February 17, 1965.

6   Gerlach, *The Men in Blue*, 270.

7   Bob Sudyk, "New A.L. Ump Keeps Fans, Players in Jovial Spirits," *The Sporting News*, April 23, 1966: 6.

8   Melvin Durslag, "Emmett Will Give 'Em Class," *Los Angeles Herald-Examiner*, October 2, 1965.

9   Bill Slocum, "Baseball Joins 20th Century," *New York Journal-American*, April 14, 1966: 19.

10 Sudyk, "New A.L. Ump," 6.

11 Sudyk, "New A.L. Ump," 3.

12 Sudyk, "New A.L. Ump," 3.

13 Sudyk, "New A.L. Ump," 6.

14 Bob Sudyk, "On His Biggest Day, Emmett Gets Thumb From Secret Service, *The Sporting News*, April 23, 1966: 6.

15 Sudyk, "New A.L. Ump," 3.

16 Gerlach, *The Men in Blue*, 278.

17 Ray Fitzgerald, "Ashford Stuck It Out," *Boston Globe*, August 16, 1970: 82.

18 Jim Ogle, "Inside Pitch—Ashford Career In Majors Brief But Flashy One," *Newark Star Ledger*, 1970 (exact date unknown—clipping from Ashford's Hall of Fame File).

19 Joe McGuff, "Ebullient Ashford Hid Wounds—He was Courageous Warrior," *Kansas City Star*, March 7, 1980: 19.

20 Fitzgerald, "Ashford Stuck It Out."

21 Gerlach, *The Men in Blue*, 286.

22 Office of the Commissioner, Press Release, April 1, 1971.

23 Gerlach, *The Men in Blue*, 261.

24 Gerlach, *The Men in Blue*, 261.

25 Gerlach, *The Men in Blue*, 261-262.

26 Paul Corcoran, "One of Baseball's Best Ambassadors," source unknown (clipping from Ashford's Hall of Fame File), February 7, 1971.

Charlie Berry

By Stephen Johnson III

Charles Francis "Charlie" Berry had one of the most extraordinary sports careers of the 20th century. He was a two-sport athlete who plied his craft as a player and official for more than 40 years. He was a National Football League end, a major-league baseball catcher, a college football coach, a minor-league baseball manager, an NFL head linesman, and a major-league baseball umpire. These dual sports put Berry in contact with the greatest sportsmen of his time and he earned the respect of everyone he met.

The Berry family story in America starts with Thomas Berry, Charlie's grandfather, who was born in Ireland about 1820. Thomas married and emigrated to the United States sometime before 1855, working as a laborer, teamster, and lineman. He and his wife, Catherine, settled in Camden County, New Jersey, before moving to Elizabeth, New Jersey, where they raised five children.[1]

The third child, Charles Joseph Berry, was born in 1860. He grew up to be a machinist. He and his wife, Ada "Addie" (née Bartch), lived for a time in Pennsylvania before moving to Phillipsburg, New Jersey.[2] As a young man, Charles played baseball well enough to play one professional season, 1884, for three teams in the Union Association. Playing second base for Altoona and Pittsburgh and second base and outfield for Kansas City, he batted .224 in 43 games. In the field he was less than stellar, committing 27 errors.

Berry and his wife had three children, Addie C., Lucy E., and Charles Francis. Charles F. was born on October 18, 1902, in Phillipsburg. His father put a baseball glove on his son's hand "when I could just about hold one," he said.[3]

Charlie inherited his father's love for sports and his athletic skills. At Phillipsburg High School he made the varsity team in football, basketball, and baseball. He received 11 varsity letters in his four years there. As a sophomore, Berry helped lead the football team to the New Jersey championship. When he was a senior, he was elected captain of the football, basketball, and baseball teams.[4] A local newspaper article declared Berry "the greatest athlete that ever wore a Garnet and Grey uniform."[5] In the summers he worked at a local foundry, and after hours played catcher and outfield for the company baseball team in the Ingersoll-Rand League, an industrial league.[6]

Berry was courted by several Eastern colleges. and ultimately entered Lafayette College in Easton, Pennsylvania, after high school.[7] As a freshman he was the starting left end on the football team and proved to be an excellent receiver. He also played defensive end. The 1921 team was undefeated, outscoring its eight opponents 239-26, and won a consensus national championship.[8] In the spring of 1922, Berry joined the baseball team, earning the starting catcher job and helping the team to a 14-8 record.

The 1922 football team went 7-2. In the spring of 1923 the baseball team went 17-6. Berry hit over .300 and had a game-winning three-run homer against the University of Pennsylvania.[9]

In his senior year, Berry was elected class president and named captain of both the football and baseball teams. In January 1925 Walter Camp named Berry to his 1924 All-American football team as first-string left end.[10]

After graduating in June 1925 with a degree in economics, Berry signed a contract with Philadelphia A's scout Mike Drennan.[11] He reported immediately to Connie Mack's Athletics, his major-league debut coming against the Cleveland Indians on June 15, 1925. Berry entered the game in the top of the sixth inning at catcher with the A's losing, 12-2. He had an inauspicious beginning as he made an error with an errant throw that allowed Freddy Spurgeon, who had stolen second, to continue to third. In the seventh inning Berry got his first hit, singling off Indians pitcher Jake Miller. Down 15-4 in the eighth, the A's scored 13 runs to win the game. During the rally Berry got his second hit of the day and his first RBI,

L to R: Bill Summers, Bill McGowan, Charlie Berry, Joe Rue, at Briggs Stadium, September 19, 1944.

and scored his first run. At the end of his first major-league game, he was batting 1.000.

Berry played in only 10 games for the Athletics in 1925, but was soon to find glory with the Pottsville (Pennsylvania) Maroons of the fledgling National Football League.[12] The Maroons were a collection of all-stars. Berry, despite never having played a down of professional football and being the youngest member of the squad, was named the team captain.[13] He more than proved himself as a leader and a player. Against the Green Bay Packers Berry scored three touchdowns and four extra points, and kicked a field goal. He led the NFL in scoring. Pottstown won the 1925 league championship, but the NFL stripped the Maroons of the title for playing an unauthorized game against the University of Notre Dame featuring the Four Horsemen.

In February 2006 the Athletics optioned Berry to the Portland (Oregon) Beavers of the Pacific Coast League. Two momentous events happened that summer. On June 30 in Portland Charlie married his high-school sweetheart, Helen S. Smith. During the season he suffered the first serious injury of his fledgling career, a broken wrist. He recovered before the end of the season, in all playing in 99 games.

After the season Berry resumed his football career with the Maroons, who won 10 games, lost 2, and had 2 ties, finishing in third place in the NFL. It was Berry's last stint as a professional football player.

Apparently the Athletics had doubts about Berry's wrist, for in the spring of 1927 they sent him outright to the Dallas Steers of the Texas League.[14] There he was the number-one catcher, and hit .330.[15]

When the baseball season ended, Berry took a job as head football coach at Grove City College in western Pennsylvania. He returned to the Wolverines each year through the 1931 season, compiling a five-year record of 27 wins, 7 losses, and 8 ties. The Wolverines won the Tri-Conference title in three of those years.[16]

After the 1927 football season, Berry was sold to the Boston Red Sox. The 1928 Red Sox (53-96) were a last-place team. Berry played in 80 games as a catcher and a pinch-hitter, batting .260 and recording his first major-league home run, off Jack Ogden of the St. Louis Browns. He showed a bit of temper, as he received his first two of three ejections as a player, one for arguing balls and strikes and the other for arguing a close play at the plate.

Over the next two seasons, the Red Sox remained mired in last place. Berry's batting average dipped in 1929, but bounced back in 1930 when he hit .289 in 88 games. He was proving himself to be a dependable man behind the plate.

Berry enjoyed a banner year in 1931. He appeared in the most games (111), batted .283, and had the most at-bats (357), most hits (101), and most runs scored (41) of his career. The season was memorable for a play involving Berry on April 22. When Babe Ruth tried to score after a fly out to center field, catcher Berry, the former football player, put a shoulder into the Yankees star and threw him skyward. Ruth came down in a heap safe at home plate."[17] Ruth took his position in left field in the bottom of the inning, but his left leg gave way and he collapsed. Ruth was carried from the field by his teammates and was taken to a hospital where he was diagnosed with a severe Charley horse in his left thigh.[18] Ruth, unable to return to action for two weeks, did not blame Berry, saying, "It's all part of the game and that was what he was paid to do. I'd have done the same thing in his place. Baseball isn't ladies ping-pong. It's a game played by men who want to win."[19]

In 1932 Berry got off to a dismal start. In the first month he played in only 10 games and batted a paltry .188. On April 29 the Red Sox traded him to the Chicago White Sox. The trade apparently motivated Berry, as for the rest of the year he batted .305. His slugging percentage for the White Sox was the highest of his career at .478 (.453 when combined with Boston for the season).

On Memorial Day, May 30, Berry was involved in a bizarre incident. The White Sox were in Cleveland for a doubleheader. The first game, which the Indians won, 12-6, was contentious, with near fisticuffs between opposing players and between the White Sox and umpire George Moriarty.

The tension poured over into the second game, and bickering between the White Sox and Moriarty intensified as the game went along.

After the game, which the Indians won, 12-11, the White Sox accused Moriarty of challenging the entire team to a fight. Berry said Moriarty challenged him in the players' tunnel. No matter the reason, the fracas started, with Moriarty punching pitcher Milt Gaston. Berry, Lew Fonseca, and catcher Frank Grube (Berry's friend from Lafayette College days) all jumped on Moriarty and gave him a good pummeling. Indians players and coaches arrived and rescued Moriarty, who went to the hospital to be treated for bruises, spike wounds, and a broken right hand. American League President Will Harridge issued fines and suspensions to the White Sox who had participated. Berry got off relatively easily with a $250 fine. Moriarty was only reprimanded.[20]

Berry continued with the White Sox in 1933, then was traded back to the Athletics after the season. Installed as the first-string catcher, he got off to an unfortunate start when on Opening Day, April 17, he was hit by a foul ball; the injury to the little finger on his throwing hand kept him out for two weeks.[21] Berry played in 99 games, batting .268. On July 21 in Detroit, his line drive to first base resulted in a triple play.

After the season Connie Mack invited Berry to join a barnstorming team for a trip to Japan.[22] However, Berry missed the trip as he was stricken by appendicitis in Valley City, North Dakota, and was hospitalized.[23]

In 1935 Berry played in 62 games and hit the last of his 23 major-league home runs. On May 22 he was involved in a bizarre incident involving an umpire. In the first inning of a game against Detroit, the A's Bob Johnson attempted to steal but was called out by umpire Charles Donnelly. Berry was one of several A's who left the bench to protest to the umpire. Berry returned to the bench, where he remained until he pinch-hit in the ninth inning. After Tigers pitcher Elden Auker threw a pitch to Berry, Donnelly came forward to say he had ejected Berry during the first-inning argument. Berry said he did not remember being ejected and his manager, Connie Mack, said he had never been informed. Even Donnelly's partner umpires did not know Berry had been banished. In the end, Berry was removed from the game. League President William Harridge investigated and determined that Donnelly was at fault and declined to reprimand Berry.[24]

On June 9, 1936, Berry was released by the Athletics as a player and hired as a coach. He remained in that position through the first half of the 1940 season. Berry not only helped the catchers, but he also instructed the pitchers. During spring training he would hold regular classes with the pitching staff.[25] Berry had one last hurrah as a player. On September 8, 1938, he replaced Hal Wagner at catcher and made two plate appearances, going 0-for-2. In 1939 Berry was ejected from games twice, his only ejections as a coach. On July 15, Bill Summers tossed Berry for arguing a call at third base and on August 6, Harry Geisel gave him the thumb for protesting a home-run call.

At the midpoint of the 1940 season, Connie Mack asked Berry to take over as manager of an A's farm team, the Wilmington (Delaware) Blue Rocks of the Interstate League. Berry took over a 28-29 team and piloted it to an overall 68-52 record, good enough for second place in the league.

Berry had continued to be involved with football, first as a scout and then as an official. He spent several years refereeing high-school and college games.

In January 1941 he was hired by the National Football League as a head linesman for the coming season.[26] At about the same time, Berry resigned as manager at Wilmington and became an umpire in the Eastern League.[27] He had worked only a few spring-training games when the International League president, Frank Shaughnessy, saw Berry's work and purchased his contract.[28] Explaining his switch to officiating, Berry quipped, "I found out that the umpires win every argument so I decided to go over to their side."[29]

Berry's rise through the ranks was meteoric. In football, he was the head linesman for the 1942 NFL championship game in only his second season on the field. He was the head linesman in 11 more NFL championship games before his career was over.

In baseball, Berry spent less than two seasons in the International League before being hired to umpire in the American League. He made his major-league umpiring debut on September 10, 1942, in Chicago in a doubleheader between the Senators and White Sox. Working in a three-man crew with Bill Summers and Art Passarella, Berry covered third base, then moved to first base in the nightcap. Although he umpired in only seven games that September, he had proven himself. For the next 20 years, he was a full-time umpire.

In his second full year as a major-league umpire, Berry umpired in the 1944 All-Star Game. He worked the bases starting at first base and moving to second in the fifth inning. It was the first of five All-Star Games Berry umpired. (The others were in 1948, 1952, 1956, and the second All-Star Game of 1959.)

In 1945 Berry joined the US Army special services and made a goodwill trip to Greenland and Iceland to entertain the troops stationed there and to give clinics on officiating.[30] After the war he continued to make trips at the behest of the US military. In the 1950s and early 1960s, he made four trips to Germany and three trips to Japan.[31]

Berry umpired four no-hitters and was at a different base for each one. He was at first base for Bo Belinsky's no-hitter in 1962, second base for Allie Reynolds' second no-hitter in 1951, third base for Jack Kralick's gem in 1962, and home plate for Bob Feller's third and last no-hitter in 1951. Berry was almost part of a perfect game. On July 27, 1958, Billy Pierce of the White Sox had one going with two outs in the ninth inning before the Senators' Ed Fitz Gerald lined a ball down the first-base line. Berry, umpiring at first, called it fair and the perfect game was gone.

Berry took time off from umpiring to serve as head linesman at the 1949 College All-Star Game, at Chicago's Soldier Field, which featured the best college football players against the previous year's NFL champion. That left a three-man umpiring crew for the White Sox-Indians game and when Cleveland lost on a disputed play, Bill Veeck, owner of the Indians, protested the game on the grounds that Berry should have been at the game. AL President Will Harridge disallowed the protest.[32] Berry also worked the 1951 College All-Star Game, after working both games of a doubleheader between Cleveland and Chicago.

During his 21 years as a major-league umpire, Berry ejected 55 players.[33] His ejections ranged from eight in 1956 to none in 1945 and 1959. Berry sent four future Hall of Famers packing: Casey Stengel, Lou Boudreau (three times), his old White Sox batterymate Ted Lyons, and Al Lopez. (Lopez was Berry's last career ejection.) Manager Paul Richards was thumbed by Berry the most times, four. The most men Berry ejected during one game was three and he did that twice, in 1952 and 1962.

Berry umpired in five World Series, 1946, 1950, 1954, 1958, and 1962. In 1958 Berry was the head linesman for the NFL title game, becoming the only man to officiate both major championships in the same year.

The 1962 World Series was Berry's swan song. In December 1962, after 21 years of wearing the blue suit, he called it quits. He had appeared in 3,079 regular-season games, 29 World Series games, and five All-Star Games as well as countless spring-training and exhibition games. He retired as one of the most respected umpires in the game. In 1960 and 1961 *The Sporting News* conducted a poll of writers, managers, and coaches to evaluate the major-league umpires.

In both polls, Berry was named the number-one American League umpire.[34]

Berry went to work for the American League as an assistant to the supervisor of umpires. He did some scouting of umpires and inspected field conditions at major-league ballparks. He also worked for the National Football League observing and evaluating officials. Twice he traveled to Mexico to give clinics on umpiring at the behest of major-league baseball. He also gave officiating clinics in the Pennsylvania area. Berry also kept busy on the banquet circuit. His gift of gab and storytelling ability made him a much sought-after guest speaker. He also participated as an umpire in a few Old-Timer's games. Berry kept his hand in umpiring by twice calling the plays at the NCAA College World Series.

In the fall of 1970, just before the League Championship Series, major-league umpires went on strike, demanding more pay for postseason assignments. For the American League Championship Series between the Orioles and Twins, the league office put together a replacement umpiring crew consisting of two minor-league umpires and two retired umpires, John Stevens and Berry. On October 3 Berry traveled to Minnesota and, in his last major-league umpiring assignment, took his position at third base. At the age of 67 years and 350 days, he was the second oldest umpire ever to appear in a box score. (The record lasted until 2007 when Bruce Froemming moved into the second spot and Berry moved to third oldest.) The strike ended the next day and Berry returned to his retired life.

Through the years, Berry received many honors. He received one vote in 1955 and three votes in 1958 for induction to the National Baseball Hall of Fame. In 1966, the Eastern Pennsylvania Chapter of the Pennsylvania Intercollegiate Athletic Association recognized him for his contribution to football officiating. Also in 1966, he was inducted into the Pennsylvania Sports Hall of Fame. His alma mater honored him in 1977, inducting him into the Lafayette College Maroon Club Athletic Hall of Fame and in 2000 named him as one of Lafayette College's 15

Charlie Berry.

Greatest Athletes of the 20th Century. In 1980 Berry was inducted into the College Football Hall of Fame.

In interviews Berry would often explain what makes a good official and the keys to his success on the field. Berry wrote, "With me, studying and reading the rules is a daily routine. I would feel I wasn't doing my job if I didn't look at the rulebook every day. Once you get the wording you get the feeling you're never in doubt. I feel that an umpire should know the rules so well that he could recite every rule in the whole book word for word."[35] Talking about on-the-field necessities he explained, "The main things to remember are these: you must know the rules; you must know where you should be on the field, and you must be there to call the play."[36] He added, "One qualification for a good sports official is that he does not call plays too quickly. Instead of anticipating the play, let it happen, follow it intently to its completion and THEN make the call quickly. I think that's a rule which can be followed in all ways of life."[37]

Summarizing his career, Berry said, "I got just as much kick out of officiating as I did out of playing. It was never an effort, never a burden."[38] He also said, "I think I am a lucky guy. I like my jobs. The pay is good. I wouldn't change places with any man."[39]

In June 1972, Berry suffered a stroke at his home in Phillipsburg. In late July he was transferred to a hospital in Evanston, Illinois to be nearer his oldest daughter. After an operation, and subsequent physical therapy, Berry suffered a massive heart attack and died on September 6, 1972. He was buried in Belvidere Cemetery, Belvidere, New Jersey. He was survived by his wife, Helen, and his three daughters, Helen, Charlé, and Lynn.[40]

On December 28, 1958, the New York Giants and the Baltimore Colts met in the NFL championship game. It has been called the "Greatest Game Ever Played." Late in the fourth quarter, the Giants had the ball. If they could get a first down, they could run out the clock and win the game. They gave the ball to Frank Gifford who charged into the line. After the play, Berry, the head linesman, spotted the ball short of the first down and the Giants had to turn the ball over. The Colts ended up tying the game and went on to win in overtime. Berry's call drew protests from the Giants and was second-guessed for years afterward. In 2008, on the 50th anniversary of that momentous game, the ESPN television network produced a two-hour documentary about it. They examined the disputed play and through forensic analysis of photographs and film determined that Berry's decision was, indeed, correct. But of course Charlie knew that the moment he made the call.

NOTES

1   1860, 1870, and 1880 US Federal Census.

2   1900, 1910, 1920, and 1930 US Federal Census.

3   Gilbert Millstein, "They Don't Build Monuments to Umpires," *New York Times Magazine*, September 14, 1952: 19, 64, 65.

4   "Phillipsburg at Allentown" and "Captain Berry on Side Lines," unidentified newspaper articles, Charlé Berry Reiber collection.

5   "Berry Greatest P.H.S. Athlete," unidentified newspaper article, Charlé Berry Reiber collection.

6   "Hammer Drill and S. Smith vs. Office and Foundry," unidentified newspaper article, Charlé Berry Reiber collection. (One of several box scores showing Berry on the Foundry team.)

7   Chester L. Smith, "Berry's Long Career Like Fictional Tale With Happy Ending," *Pittsburgh Post-Gazette*, December 16, 1962: 2, Sect. 4.

8   1922 *Melange* (Lafayette College yearbook), 256, 257.
    "A Man for All Seasons," *The Express-Times*, Easton, Pennsylvania, September 17, 2000.

9   1923 *Melange*, 276.

10 "Camp Picks Berry as All-American in 1924 Selection," *The Lafayette*, January 7, 1925.

11 Don Basenfelder (of the *Philadelphia Record*), unidentified newspaper article, National Baseball Hall of Fame clipping file.

12 David Fleming, *Breaker Boys* (New York: ESPN Books, 2007), 50.

13 Fleming, 110-111.

14 Clifford Bloodgood, "A Catcher With Plenty of Nerve," unknown source (probably *Baseball Magazine*), 412, date stamped August 25, 1932, National Baseball Hall of Fame clipping file.

15 Ibid.

16 Grove City College website: gcc.edu/sports/New/Football/fbyby.htm (accessed April 9, 2015) American League of Professional Base Ball Clubs, press release, June 6, 1950. Text from letter to Mr. John Hoffman dated September 17, 1942.

17 "Milestones," *Time Magazine*, September 18, 1972.

18 Associated Press, "Bambino Faces Month Lay-Off," *Los Angeles Times*, April 23, 1931.

19 Bloodgood.

20 Mike Lynch, "The Memorial Day Brawl of 1932," seamheads.com/2011/05/29/the-memorial-day-brawl-of-1932/, (accessed November 18, 2014).

21 "Mack Given Treat by Added Starters," *The Sporting News*, April 26, 1934: 2.

22 Associated Press, "Connie Mack Names Team for Tour of Japan," *Chicago Tribune*, September 9, 1934.

23 "The Old Sport's Musings" column, source unknown, hand-dated February 27, 1935. National Baseball Hall of Fame clipping file.

24 Al Horwits, "Protest Dropped by Connie Mack," unidentified newspaper article plus original correspondence (telegrams and letters dated May 22 through May 31) between Donnelly and Harridge in ejection file at National Baseball Hall of Fame Library and Archive. The ejection was nullified.

25 Bill Dooly, "Mack's 'Staff of the Future' Picking Up Advanced Technique In Post-Graduate Course Under Prof. Berry," *The Sporting News*, August 12, 1937.

26 Al Hailey, "National League Signs 6 College Grid Officials," *Washington Post*, January 7, 1941: 18; "Six Officials Named By Football League," *New York Times*, January 7, 1941: 27.

27 Arch Ward, "In the Wake of the News," *Chicago Tribune*, January 6, 1941: 19.

28 "Charlie Berry Now International Umpire," *Pittsburgh Press*, April 15, 1941: 26.

29 Sam Greene, "Umpire's Top Thrill," unidentified newspaper article (probably *Detroit News*), hand-dated May 1943, National Baseball Hall of Fame clipping file.

30 "Headed for Iceland," *Mediterranean Stars and Stripes*, January 15, 1945: 7.

31 *Stars and Stripes*, Mediterranean and Pacific editions.

32 "Veeck Charges Absence of Ump Costly to Tribe," *Cleveland Press*, August 13, 1949. See also "Umps' Calls Stir Squawks at Brooklyn and Cleveland," *The Sporting News*, August 24, 1949: 2.

33 retrosheet.org; Charles Francis Berry.

34 "Poll Tabs Barlick and Berry Top Umps," *The Sporting News*, October 5, 1960: 1-2; "Barlick Rated No. 1 Umpire in Poll of N.L.," *The Sporting News*, July 26, 1961: 1-2.

35 Harold Rosenthal, ed., *Baseball Is Their Business* (New York: Random House, 1952), 126.

36 Ed Pollock, "Enjoyed Every Minute, Ump Says, After Calling 'Em for 22 Years," unknown source (probably *Philadelphia Evening Bulletin*), hand dated February 1963, National Baseball Hall of Fame clipping file.

37 Hugh Bradley, "'Wouldn't Change Places With Any Man,' Says Ump," *The Sporting News*, July 26, 1961: 4.

38 Pollock.

39 Bradley.

40 "Charlie Berry, Big League Official," *Easton* (Pennsylvania) *Express*, September 7, 1972.

Augie Donatelli

Umpire And Union Organizer

By Larry R. Gerlach

During 24 years in the National League, August John Donatelli was one of major-league baseball's most respected umpires. He worked four All-Star games (1953, 1959, 1962, 1969), five World Series (1955, 1957, 1961, 1967, 1973), and two League Championship Series (1969, 1972). Moreover, he was the home-plate umpire for four no-hitters: Warren Spahn (1961), Carl Erskine (1956), Ken Johnson (1964), and Bob Moose (1969). In 1955, his fifth year in the majors, Donatelli was voted "the best National League umpire on the bases" by baseball writers. In February 1973 he received the Al Somers award as the Outstanding Major League Umpire of 1972; that the first two Somers awards, voted on by umpires, went to Al Barlick and Nestor Chylak, universally regarded as the premier arbiters in the National and American Leagues respectively, indicates Donatelli's recognized stature within the umpiring profession.

In some ways Augie Donatelli was a typical umpire of the post-World War II era. He was a second-generation, working-class American who successfully used sport as a vehicle for socioeconomic mobility, part of a group of Italian-Americans—Babe Pinelli, Art Passarella, Joe Paparella, Frank Dascoli, Augie Guglielmo, Joe Linsalata, and Alex Salerno—whose presence was conspicuous for the first time in ranks of umpires in the 1940s and 1950s. He was an ex-player who turned to officiating as a way of continuing his involvement with the game. And he was among the numerous war-hardened veterans who dominated college and professional sport after 1945.

In other ways, Donatelli was atypical. The peculiar circumstances of his family life and experiences as a prisoner of war forged a distinctive personality—forceful, determined, and tough-minded with a strong sense of fairness and camaraderie. As a rapid ascent through the minor leagues suggested, he was a "born" umpire, possessing that unusual combination of skill, judgment, and demeanor that marks the truly exemplary umpire. Most important, as the "founder" of the Major League Umpires Association, Augie Donatelli is one of the few men in blue to make historically important contributions to the umpiring profession as well as major-league baseball.

The following "oral autobiography" is a composite excerpt of an extended personal interview with Donatelli. It originally was to be included in the book *The Men in Blue: Conversations with Umpires* (1980), but was withheld because of his consternation that a contemporary National League arbiter would be included in the book. The interview is offered at this time for two reasons: 1) Donatelli's "story" should be a matter of record because of his demonstrable importance in baseball and umpiring history, and 2) it is an unusually comprehensive personal exegesis from an intensely private man who, like most umpires, had not sought the "limelight" and thus had not had his views widely recorded.

Although the material has been reorganized to present a coherent "life story" and the repetitious and incomplete statements characteristic of oral communication have been eliminated, I have tried scrupulously to preserve Donatelli's language and modes of expression in order to convey accurately a sense of the man as well as his remembrances. Excluded are his comments about memorable players, managers, and games, as they conform in all essentials to what has been said ad nauseam on those subjects. We have ample testimony, for example, that Jackie Robinson was "a terrific basestealer and a great hitter." What is emphasized here is unique information pertaining to Donatelli's personal life, his umpiring career, his thoughts on the art of umpiring, and his role in organizing the umpires union.

Augie Donatelli:

I spent most of my life in coal mining towns of Cambria County in western Pennsylvania. I was born in the small town of Heilwood on August 22, 1914. When I was about two months old, my family moved over to Bakerton, where I grew up, went to high school, and joined the service during World War II. After I got married, my wife, Mary Lou, and I moved to Ebensburg, the county seat, where we raised our four children, two girls and two boys. I lived in Ebensburg even after I got to the majors, and for 16 years worked during the offseason as a good-will representative for National Distilleries (even though I never drank whiskey). We moved to Florida a few years before I retired in 1973.

My parents were from Italy. They immigrated over here around 1900, and my father, Tony, went to work in the coal mines. There were eight children in our family; I was number five. The oldest and youngest were girls; the rest boys. All the boys worked in the mines. It was dangerous and hard work, but what else were you going to do? I started even before graduating from high school. Times were tough then because of the Depression. Jobs were scarce, so I was glad to have the work. I did everything—worked outside as a coal dumper and inside as a loader and a spragger.[1]

Sports was our main recreation. Two of my brothers were pretty good boxers, one was a Golden Gloves champ and the other had about 50 professional fights. I played football and basketball and ran track in high school. There was no baseball team, but we played pickup games and after graduation I played in an industrial league while working in the mines. I was a decent, scrappy shortstop, so decided to give pro baseball a try. My father was very encouraging as a way of getting out of the mines. Tom Monaghan, the famous scout, signed me with the St. Louis Browns. I started out in the local Penn State League [Class D Pennsylvania Association], but it folded financially. Then I played in the Kitty League [Class D Kentucky-Illinois-Tennessee], and was sent back to the Penn State League with Beaver Falls. I only played 14 games [batting .266] when the league folded again in 1938, so I went back to the mines.

I was loading coal when World War II broke out. Being single, I figured I was near to being drafted, so I enlisted in the Air Force. Like a lot of young guys, I felt it was something I had to do, not to escape the mines but because you just felt it was up to you to get into it. My basic training was at Lowry Field near Denver, Colorado. When they found out I was a ballplayer, they offered me the rank of staff sergeant if I would play for the base team. So I played ball while going to armor and gunnery school. I went into combat in October 1943 and flew 18 missions as a tail gunner on a B-17 before getting shot down. I'll never forget it. We were shot down before the [June 6, 1944, D-Day] invasion, on the first daylight bomber raid on Berlin [March 6, 1944]. It was a rough mission—fighters diving at us, 20-millimeter shells exploding all around. We flew into the clouds to hide. What action! That day 68 bombers were shot down. We got hit, so the crew bailed out. I got captured and taken to Frankfurt. I spent about 15 months in prison camps. We changed camps three times; the Germans kept moving us around so the Russians couldn't liberate us.

Early in the winter we marched from Frankfurt to the first camp, Heydekrug, about 40 miles south of Memel, Lithuania. It was no picnic. Sixty men to a barracks, 10 men to a table. No food, no clothes, cold in the winter, and wait, wait, wait. Being a noncom[missioned officer], I didn't have to work. You just sat around and waited for the next meal—if you got it. We were supposed to get a slice of bread a day; sometimes we would, sometimes we wouldn't. There was no coffee, just something black like coffee made of boiled weeds of some kind. Occasionally we would get some soup with wheat and whatever vegetables the Germans could find. Turnips mostly; lots of diced turnips. Potatoes occasionally. Horsemeat if they had it. We'd fill a bucket with water, toss in the vegetables, cook it for a while, and had a water bucket of soup. It was pretty bad, but, what the hell, you ate it to keep from starving. The Germans couldn't give us much because they didn't have anything themselves. After about six months, we started getting Red Cross parcels once a week. There was supposed

Augie Donatelli.

to be one parcel per man, but there was never enough so we shared—one package for four men. We got cigarettes, but that's when I quit smoking. I'd trade my cigarettes for food. Cliff Barker, who was later an All-American basketball player at the University of Kentucky, was in our group. He smoked, and would trade me bread for my cigarettes. He still owes me about half a loaf.

Believe it or not, I started umpiring in the prison camp at Heydekrug. When I bailed out, I broke a bone in my ankle and couldn't do anything for a time. The guys played softball for recreation. There were lots of English POWs in the camp; some of them had been there for three years. They had a few softballs and bats, but almost no other equipment. Each of the barracks had a team, so there were games going on all the time. I would sit on the sidelines and watch the games—good gosh, what unbelievable rhubarbs they had over rules and judgment calls. They couldn't find any good umpires. Some of the guys found out that I had played ball and asked me if I had ever umpired. I had never umpired before and it didn't strike me that I should umpire. But I wanted to see

that the games were run right and by the rules, so I started umpiring and was put on the rules committee. When you are behind the plate, they find out if you could really umpire. I must have done okay, because pretty soon the whole compound was coming after me. There was no way I could get out of it, so I umpired one game after another.

Toward late summer my leg started healing, and I wanted to get out there and play. The guys in my barracks wanted to win the championship, so they decided we needed a manager. I took over as manager, held tryouts, and let the best guys play. There was some dissension over that, but I told them that's what we had to do to win. Barker pitched and played first base, and we won the championship. About two days after we won the championship, the Russians started a major offensive [September 1944] and the Germans started marching us again. Those who couldn't walk, the sick and wounded, were loaded into boxcars.

They took us to Stettin, a port on the North Sea, and crammed us into the hold of a ship for two days. There must have been 2,500 of us in there—hot as hell, no water, no toilet. You had to go on deck to take a leak, but no way you could have a bowel movement. When they took us off the ship, they chained two guys together at the wrists, and ran us about three miles to a place called Griefenhagen. As we went through this little town, the guards were hitting us with bayonets, the people were chasing us, the dogs were barking and chasing us—what a mess that was. After a few months, they started walking us again, this time to Neubrandenburg, north of Berlin.

On the march to Neubrandenburg, another prisoner and I escaped. It was his idea. He said it would be easy to sneak away, and it was. On the march we were herded into barns every night. The guards couldn't take a count of prisoners because we were all split up, and guys were always going in and out of the barns because there was so much dysentery. It got dark real early, so about 6:30 one night we knocked on the barn door, went outside acting like we were going to the latrine, and took off into the woods. We were so afraid of being caught, we kept running almost all night. The next morning we were tired and cold, so we dug about 6-8 feet into a frozen haystack and tried to sleep. We slept for a while, but it was so cold in there that we had to crawl out and start walking again. We headed east, hoping to run into the Russians. They had started an offensive all right, but had been stopped by the Germans.

We survived for about 10 days before being re-captured. Most of the farms in the area were worked by Polish or Russian labor and my partner, who was Polish, could speak both languages. We would approach people working on the outskirts of the farm and find out if they were being guarded or not. At one farm, two of the Polish laborers were ex-soldiers, so they let us sleep in the barn and fed us. One day we went down to where the people were working in the field, we ran into the overseer. No one told us that he would be there; it was an unpleasant surprise. He immediately recognized us as air corpsmen because of our clothes, so he pulled a gun, and took us to his home. He put us into the cellar, which was made into a jail, and called the Germans. Three or four hours later two guards picked us up and started hiking us toward Neubrandenburg.

Neubrandenburg was a huge camp with maybe 15,000 prisoners of all the nationalities in the war. The war was coming to an end, and the Germans were rounding up prisoners from all over. Only privates, not officers, were supposed to work, but my penalty for escaping was to work for a week cutting timber for fortifications, digging trenches and burial pits, and stuff like that. The burial pits were for the Russians, who didn't get a military burial like the Allies under the Geneva Convention; they were just dumped into the pit. After about three months, the Russians liberated us [April 1945].

When I got back home, I thought about umpiring. I was 29 years old and knew the chance of making it as a player was gone. I didn't want to go back to the mines, so I thought maybe if I was lucky I could make it to the Big Time as an umpire. I talked with Elmer Daily, the president of the Penn State League about it, and he recommended that I go to the Bill McGowan Umpire School in Cocoa Beach, Florida.

My family encouraged me. You had to do something to get out of the mines, so away I went.

I went down to McGowan's that winter on the GI Bill. It was the only umpire school at that time, and there were maybe 100 guys at the school—big guys and small guys, young guys and old guys.[2] Most of them were umpires and four or five already had professional contracts. During the day we umpired games to learn proper mechanics and apply the rules. At night we had "skull" classes where McGowan would give us some pointers and tell us about umpiring in the majors. You worshipped a guy like that who was in the majors.

I never thought I would get a job, but I got a lucky break. After about four weeks, during one of the camp games, I handled the call on a steal at second base. Al Somers, a professional umpire who was the only instructor at the school, happened to see the play and immediately went to McGowan and said, "I think the little Italian kid is a prospect. Keep your eye on him." (I found this out later.)

The next day McGowan came out to watch to students, and it was my turn on the field again. That night during class McGowan called Al over and said, "Hey, what's that guy's name?" Al didn't know my name, so he points and says, "That's him back there." We were all looking around because we didn't know who in the hell he's pointing to. So McGowan says: "I have something I have to tell you. We have a fellow in here that is going to be in the major leagues in four years." We were all wondering, "Who in the hell is this?" McGowan kept on with his little speech: "I watched him out there and he's doing a hell of a job. He is the most outstanding student we have." And then he points at me. I thought, "Jesus, he doesn't mean me." I looked around behind me. He said, "No, no. You. You!" I couldn't believe it: "Me?" "That's right, you. You've got it kid. We feel that you will be in the majors in four years." I couldn't sleep that night. Here I was, just out of the service, at loose ends, going to umpire school on the GI Bill just hoping to get a job, and the man says I can be a major leaguer someday. It was one of my biggest thrills in baseball, I'll tell you!

So I came out of the school pretty highly rated. My first contract, 1946, was with the Pioneer League [Class C] for $150 a month and no expenses. A fellow from Pittsburgh, Pete Donett, and myself were teamed up as partners. We didn't have a car, so we rode the buses on those long trips through Idaho and Utah — Boise, Pocatello, Idaho Falls, Twin Falls, Ogden, Salt Lake City. It was pretty rough in the low minors — all kinds of rhubarbs, guys coming down to the edge of the screen and yelling and challenging you to fight them, police escorts to get you out of the ballpark, things like that. When I got back home, the family didn't know what kind of a year I had. I told them, "When you're umpiring, you're lucky if you last a season. They fire you."

In January I went back to the school. I couldn't believe it, but McGowan made me an instructor. The minor leagues were booming after the war, and lots of veterans on the GI Bill started showing up at the school. McGowan had to form two classes of about five weeks each; there must have been 300 men in both classes. After a few years it started to slack off. The boys thought it would be easy to get to the majors, but a lot of them got fired and a lot of them quit because it was hard work and no money in the minors.

In 1947, my second year, I was promoted to the Sally League [the South Atlantic League, Class A], with a raise to $300 a month plus $6 or $7 a day for expenses. In midseason the National League bought my contract for $2,000 and farmed me [August 15, 1947] to the International League [Triple A]. Now I'm getting $600 a month — $350 salary and $250 expenses. There was better organization and more police protection in (Triple A), and the rhubarbs weren't as bad as in the low minors. But you didn't have any smooth sailing, that's for sure. It is very difficult in the minors because there are only two umpires. On the other hand, there is no better place than the minors to be scouted because there *are* only two umpires. Class will quickly show, no question about it.

In my case, I was told that Branch Rickey was at a game one night when I was behind the plate and that he recommended somebody come down to see

me. Bingo! Bill Klem got a hold of me. He saw me work a game and afterward called me into his office. "Look," he said, "you use the inside protector."[3] I had been using the outside protector, but said, "All right. I can do that." And I did. I was in the International League for two years. I was supposed to go up the second year, but Ford Frick [president of the National League] called me into his office and told me they were bringing up Lon Warneke, the great pitcher, instead of me. But, he said, I would get the starting major-league salary of $5,000. When I hit the majors in 1950 — four years, just like McGowan said — I got a salary of $5,500 plus $15 a day expenses and free transportation. That was big money then.

I broke in at the Polo Grounds with the Giants and the [Boston] Braves. Leo Durocher and Billy Southworth. My first game behind the plate was in Brooklyn: Giants and the Dodgers. It was a hell of a thrill being in the major leagues. I was hoping and praying that I'd get everything right, give all the ability that I could put together. My first crew was Al Barlick and Lee Ballanfant. There were three-man crews in the major leagues at the time, but in a few years they went to four umpires. It was difficult to cover plays even with three men. Hellsfire, if you couldn't move, man, you had problems. I worked with Barlick off and on for six, seven years, then worked with Jocko Conlan, and then I became a crew chief myself in 1962.

I was the first guy to come into the National League from an umpire school, and the older guys took me a little lightly at first, but there was no animosity at all.[4] When they found out that you are a decent guy and that you intended to run the game, they worked with you. They had to. After all, there are three of you out there, and if one of you is in trouble, the three of you are in trouble. Barlick and Ballanfant were real good in helping me break in. Ballanfant was the best for breaking in young fellows because he was such a nice guy — you had to like him and feel welcome on the crew. They gave me pointers, discussed the rules, and helped with mechanics a little bit. I'd also learn just by watching them. Sometimes I followed their advice and examples, sometimes I'd decide to do it another way. Actually, being at the school was an advantage. You were ahead of the other fellows because you were alert on all the rules. Most umpires would read the rule book once or twice and then put it away. But when you are at the school for six weeks, you learned the rules and then applied them on the field so that they would stay with you. Umpiring is not a matter of quoting a rule, but applying it on the field.

The best umpires I worked with were Al Barlick, Larry Goetz, and Jocko Conlan. They had what it takes to be a good umpire. First, they had the respect of the ballplayers, which is very important. They could make calls and get away with it, when another guy would get hell for the same thing. They were feared, in a way; players knew they were running the game and would toss them if they got too nasty. The more ability you had and the meaner you were, the more respect you got on the field. Also, they had very good judgment—about 1-2-3 in that respect. (I never understood how ballplayers, fans, or anyone else could question my judgment. All they had to do is look at my wife, Mary Lou, and they'd know I didn't make mistakes.) Other umpires might have judgment just as good, but didn't run the game or—I don't like to admit it—worked the political end of it. You must have respect and run the game; if you don't, when the time comes the ballplayers will cut you to pieces.

The worst situation I was ever in happened a few years after I got to the majors. I almost got into a fight with Leo Durocher, who was managing the [New York] Giants. It was the first game of a Sunday doubleheader at the Polo Grounds [August 17, 1952]. Max Surkont was pitching for the [Boston] Braves. The whole game Durocher was screaming at Al Barlick, who was behind the plate, that Surkont was marking up the ball, spitting in his glove, and stuff like that. (At that time there weren't too many spitballs being thrown; the rules weren't relaxed as much as they have been recently.) Barlick ignored him, and Surkont kept getting them out and Durocher kept beefing. Then, in the top of the ninth, with the Braves leading [7-3], Durocher started raising hell. While waiting for his relief pitcher [Hal Gregg] to come in

from the bullpen, he knelt right down on the mound, covered the ball with dirt, and started roughing it up. You can't let a man show up an umpire like that, so I ran right in from second base and asked to see the ball. But he tossed it to the pitcher instead. I said something, he said something, and I chased him. He went berserk, probably because he didn't expect it. He hadn't been into an argument with an umpire, yet I chased him. He got so mad that a couple of players and coaches grabbed him to keep him from charging me. I was waiting for him. I wasn't going to run from him; you can't be run out of the ballpark. Besides, he wasn't that strong a guy, a man who couldn't be beat with fists. I knew a little bit about fighting; maybe he did too. While he was trying to get loose from the players, he was yelling some beautiful names at me. So I yelled some back at him and said, "Let him go. Let the man go." Fortunately, they didn't let him go; he actually had to be dragged off the field. That's the closest I ever came to protecting myself. In my report I told the league president [Warren Giles] what I said to Durocher and what he said to me. Leo got fined [$100] and suspended [five days].

Umpiring is more than applying the rules and handling situations: You must be alert mechanically be in the right position. That's important: You've got to be in the right position to call a tough play. If you're not in the right position and you guess at it, that is not good and you'll really catch hell.

There is also a timing element involved here. You've got to wait that split-second and then make the call. A split-second. You can't call it too quick or too slow. You'll be wrong or look bad if your timing is bad, especially behind the plate where there are so many decisions to make. When I was working, Chris Pelekoudas was one of the best umpires—in the top ten, maybe one of the top five. Some of the boys don't want to hear that, but it's so just the same. But he waited too long. He waited so long that sometimes the broadcaster would say a pitch was a "strike" and then he would signal "ball." It was so noticeable, even the other umpires didn't like his timing. Still, he seemed to be getting the calls right.

The mechanics in making a call are also important. You have to be decisive, and I always made a simple but very decisive motion. But no gestures, no dancing or jumping around. Toward the end of my career, some of the boys started "showboating." To me, showboating is out because you start taking your eyes off the ball and thinking more about how you make a particular call than the play itself. For example, Ed Sudol had the mannerisms of an acrobat; there's no room for it, no time for it. It's absolutely wrong. I don't know why he did it. Now take Ron Luciano over in the other [American] league. It appeared that he was showboating, but he was as serious as he could be. He applied a few more gestures on a call, but he was not really showboating. He was that way, so that's the way he umpired. It was natural; he never took his eye off the play or went into a dance or something like that.

Of course, experience is the big thing. When an umpire gets to the big leagues, he is sure he knows all there is about baseball. But an umpire should improve each year. First, you learn the importance of timing on your calls. Second, you get better at running the game. Third, you can handle the difficult situations more smoothly. Fourth, constant repetition as a pitch-caller or a play-caller automatically improves a man if he keeps hustling. Fifth, you're supposed to know all the rules—and keep them in your head—but after so many years you really acquire knowledge of the laws of the game. Sixth, with greater experience comes greater execution of the rules.

When I broke into the majors racial integration was still under way. The Dodgers had the most Negroes, with Jackie Robinson, Roy Campanella, Don Newcombe, and Dan Bankhead, but there were other colored boys coming in. There weren't any real problems with Negroes coming into the majors. Of course, in spring training down South there was still the Negro section of the bleachers and separate restrooms, things like that. What I remember most is how the Negroes would flock to the games to watch the Dodgers. There would be more Negroes than whites. Wherever Jackie Robinson was, boy, how they

would draw them. They used to get 10,000 people, easy, in Miami with Robinson.

The biggest thing that happened during my career was the Major League Umpires Association, and I am proud that I helped get it organized. I started out in the majors making a pretty good salary—at least it seemed like it to me, a young guy from the coal mines. But then the cost of things kept getting higher and higher, and we weren't making a salary you could brag about. Also, some of the boys weren't getting raises. It wasn't right: You've got to give a major leaguer a raise to keep with the economy. Then of course there wasn't much of a pension—$100 for every year in the majors [with 15 years' minimum service]. Maybe that seemed like a lot of money back when it was started in the 1930s, but didn't seem like much now. And we didn't get medical insurance or benefits like that.

Anyway, I started talking to Jocko Conlan about it. I knew that he would be retiring pretty soon. I'd call him aside and tell him that he wasn't going to have anything after he retired except his home. Jocko was always bragging because he was the highest paid umpire in the league, but I knew he didn't have much money in the bank because he was a high liver. I told him I was also thinking about myself and the other umpires, too. Several times I said: "Look, Jock. We can do something. You and me, we can do something about this." I had an ace in the hole—Al Barlick, another boy from the coal mines. Barlick, like Jocko, was well respected. They were the top umpires in the league, so they were the guys I had to go to right away. I knew I couldn't go to everybody. Some of the boys were afraid of losing their jobs if they spoke up for something, and some of them were, well, liked by the league more than some of the others.

All of a sudden, during the 1963 season, Jocko says, "All right. What do you want me to do?" So I told him. He said, "What the hell are you talking about? You can't do that!" I said, "The hell we can't. We can do it. We can form an association." Jocko was interested, but worried. "Half of these guys won't go along with it," he said. I told him: "That's right. We don't need half of them. All we need is half a dozen." Then

I went to Barlick, who said, "Anything you do is all right with me." Bingo!

We started with telephone calls to every umpire in the league. Jocko, who was from Chicago, was supposed to get this judge to be our representative, but he retired or something and we couldn't get him. So Jocko got what he thought was the next best thing, his attorney, John Reynolds. We got the boys together in Chicago on an offday and discussed an association. Barlick, Jocko, Tom Gorman, Shag Crawford, and I were elected to the board of directors. We had two or three meetings in all, and of the 24 umpires in the league, maybe 8 or 10 would go against us in the meetings. I remember every one of them.

The last meeting was in May 1964, another layover day in Chicago. Reynolds did all the legal paperwork for us, and all of a sudden we have to get the guys to sign the papers forming the association. When it got down to the last day, when we wanted to meet with the owners and get them to recognize us as an association, the other guys had gone on to their games and there was only four of us left, Al Barlick's crew—Barlick, Stan Landes, Mel Steiner, and myself. Reynolds met with us at our hotel at 10:00 in the morning. We were supposed to be at the ballpark at 11:30 for a game. "I'll tell you, fellows," he said, "they will fire you if you don't go along with the president of the league [Warren Giles] because the other fellows are done with it." I thought about it, and decided that I had gone this far and was going to go the rest of the way. So, I said: "John, I'm speaking for myself. I'm going the rest of the way. If we don't have an association, I'm going to go right to the first reporters I see and tell them what happened. That's the only way, because if I get fired, they will want to know why I got fired and I'm going to tell them."

I was hoping one or two of the other guys would speak up and do the same thing. Barlick spoke up first: "Augie, I'm with you." The other two guys came along too. So we told Reynolds, "Go ahead and tell Giles we are standing for our rights. We are going to hold the fort. If the rest don't do it, the heck with it. Let Giles do whatever he wants." Then we went on to the ballpark and worked the game. Maybe our

last one, who knows? What do you think happened? I don't know whether the owners called Giles, or Giles was approached by somebody else, or if Giles came to a decision on his own. Anyway, he told our attorney that he would meet with us umpires the following week. The following week we met with him and started not asking for things but *demanding* things that were right for us. We wanted a better pension, higher salaries, regular raises, fringe benefits, and more expense money. They finally agreed to all those things. That's how we started the association [National League Umpires Association].[5]

Of course the owners and the league president, Warren Giles, didn't like it. And Giles certainly was not happy with me for getting the thing going. I had some discussions with him that he didn't like. He had just given us a raise in pension before the association came together, but I had to tell him the truth, that he wasn't helping us enough. Maybe he felt he was, but he sure wasn't generous enough. But let's face it: Giles had a job to do. He had to protect the league and his job. He was against our organizing and so was his assistant, Fred Fleig. We got a lot of bad publicity in the press. The league wouldn't talk to us about it; hell, at first Giles wouldn't even meet with us. But eventually they came around.

I don't know why Giles didn't just fire me. He could have. Maybe he respected me in a way. And I never missed a day's work—that helped a heck of a lot. But I was demoted from crew chief and assigned to Barlick's crew for the 1964 season. In fact, Giles put the four of us together because he thought we were instigators. I guess he thought he was punishing us, but actually it was the best thing he could have done for us because it kept us together all the time. Maybe he would have been better off putting each one of us on a different crew.

The American League umpires didn't form an association at the time, so they fell far behind us in salaries, pensions, and fringe benefits. We wanted them to join the association so major-league umpires would all be the same with regard to salaries and benefits. We promised that we would back them if they wanted to join us, but they were afraid of getting fired.[6] Their league president, Joe Cronin, had them all tied up. They couldn't voice their opinion on anything. Finally, two of them, Al Salerno and Bill Valentine, tried to organize the American League umpires and got fired [September 16, 1968] for it.[7]

That got the American League boys organized and they joined our association. But then Salerno and Valentine asked us to back them in suing the league. That was their downfall. We did back them, but not enough of us. We had a meeting, and about a quarter or a third of the umpires walked out when Salerno and Valentine started demanding that we should back them. I agreed with them. I got up and made a speech saying the same thing. "Yes," I said, "they made a grave mistake. Sure they did. But we promised to back them and we have got to back these boys. We ought to have a vote on it." We had a vote and there only maybe nine or ten of us left—only six or seven in the National League and two or three in the American League stood up for backing them.

Cronin later agreed to hire them back, but he wanted them to go down to the minors for a couple of months to get sharpened up or whatever, and even said they would get their major-league salaries and benefits. But they wouldn't do it. I know how they felt. After all, it was embarrassing to be fired. Still, umpiring isn't too bad. I was a coal miner, and I always thought about the mines when things got tough.

Two years later I was involved in the first umpires strike. It was for the same thing—more money. The association was trying to negotiate a raise for the playoffs and the World Series, but the league presidents [Charles "Chub" Feeney and Joe Cronin] wouldn't see eye-to-eye on that. So we went on strike [October 3, 1970] for the first game of the championship playoffs. I was in Pittsburgh, and instead of working the game I was pounding the cement walks with picket signs.

I wasn't worried about losing my job that time, but I was worried about the public. After all, the fans pay all of us, even the league presidents and the commissioner. I didn't want to hurt the feelings of the people who went to the park that day to see the game.

We got blamed because four minor-league umpires were out there in our place. None of us umpires liked that; none of us wanted to be on strike. The strike only lasted one day. I was on the board of directors of the association, and the next morning we met with Feeney. A few days later, we got our raises. (The minor leaguers thought they would go to the majors because they worked out of turn. One of them [Hank Morgenweck] was brought up, but he didn't last.)[8]

I had a great career. Twenty-four years. I am proud of the fact that I missed only one game in 24 years. I had lots of thrills, especially All-Star Games and the World Series. You can't describe the feeling of excitement that pervades a World Series game. Sure, I felt the butterflies and the pressure and the responsibility. I worked with lots of great ballplayers—Stan Musial, Steve Garvey, Gil Hodges, Willie Mays; pitchers like Warren Spahn, Robin Roberts, Sandy Koufax, Bob Gibson. I have so many special memories: I was behind the plate [October 8, 1961] when Whitey Ford set the record for scoreless innings [32] in the World Series,[9] when Don Drysdale got the record [June 8, 1968] for the most consecutive shutout innings [58] in a season, when Stan Musial hit five homers in a doubleheader [May 2, 1954], and when he got his 3,000th base hit, and when Nate Colbert hit five homers and had the most RBIs [13] in a doubleheader [August 1, 1972]. I'll never forget Elroy Face winning about 20 games and losing only three or four [18-1] as a relief pitcher [1959]; even though the Pirates had a lot of power and could come from behind, that was really unusual.

After I umpired my last game, I thought, well, I'm glad to be going home. I had a good career with lots of wonderful memories. But I missed my friends, the profession itself, and baseball—my number-one game. I also missed the competitiveness. And it was hard to lose the money—hey, I was dragging down a pretty good salary when I left. I still think about it every now and then. I hope I'm remembered as a just, fair, honest umpire who called them as they were and as he saw them. And the Association was damn important to me. It went through, and it certainly is helping the boys who are in there now. It helped us a lot too, but it is too bad that we couldn't have been of the age where we could have enjoyed it more. I wanted to include the old fellows already on pension, but the boys wouldn't go for it. Today the Umpires Association is very powerful. Now the boys get just about whatever they ask for. But then we were risking our jobs just to get it organized. Things are so much better now—pension, working conditions, everything. And the boys are getting the salary. Even though they have to pay a lot of income tax, they are getting the salary. That's the important thing, isn't it?

Augie Donatelli died peacefully in his sleep on May 24, 1990, at St. Petersburg, Florida. He was cremated and is buried at Bay Pines (Florida) National Cemetery.

"Augie Donatelli: Umpire and Union Organizer" appeared in the long defunct *Baseball History: An Annual of Original Baseball Research* (1989), 1-11.

NOTES

1   A "spragger" controlled the speed of coal cars in mines by inserting or removing a metal rod called a "sprag" between the spokes of its wheels. Along steep sections of track the speed of the cars was slowed by inserting sprags to "lock" the wheel so that it slid instead of rolled along the track; the subsequent removal of sprags had the effect of speeding up the cars.

2   National League umpire George Barr established the first umpire school, in Arkansas in 1935; American League umpire McGowan opened the second school in 1939 in Mississippi. Barr's school closed during World War II, while McGowan moved his operation to Florida.

3   Upon retiring in 1941 from long service as a National League umpire, Klem, "The Old Arbitrator," served to his death in 1951

as the chief of umpires (i.e., supervisor and head scout) for the senior circuit. He made his preference for wearing a lightweight chest protector inside the jacket when umpiring behind home plate virtually mandatory for National League umpires, while his counterpart in the American League, Tommy Connolly, made the use of the large, inflated "balloon" protector held in front of the chest synonymous with junior circuit umpires. The distinction between the two leagues persisted until the 1970s, when the inside protector earned universal adoption.

4   William F. "Bill" McKinley, who attended both the Barr and McGowan schools, was the first graduate of an umpire school in the majors, being called up to the American League in August 1946.

5   When Ford Frick was named commissioner of baseball in 1951, Giles, then president of the Cincinnati Reds, replaced him as president of the National League. In his first year in office he increased the pension for umpires from $100 to $150 per year, and in May 1964 raised it to $200; the initial agreement with the Umpires Association increased it to $300.

6   American League umpires were hesitant to unionize in part because President Will Harridge had summarily fired umpire Ernest D. Stewart in 1945 for alleged unionizing activities. See Larry R. Gerlach, *The Men in Blue: Conversations with Umpires* (Lincoln: University of Nebraska Press, 1994), 123-26.

7   Ostensibly fired for alleged "incompetence," both were veteran American League umpires—Salerno since 1961 and Valentine since 1962.

8   Although the strike affected both the Baltimore-Minnesota and the Cincinnati-Pittsburgh championship playoff games, umpires picketed only the National League park. Negotiations resulted in new pay scales for both league playoffs (from $2,500 to $4,000) and the World Series (from $6500 to $8,000). One of the Triple-A arbiters who worked the Reds-Pirates game, Henry C. Morgenweck, later umpired in the American League, 1972-75.

9   Ford, who left the game in the sixth inning with a sore foot, extended the record on October 4, 1962, to 33 innings; he had broken Babe Ruth's mark of 29⅔ scoreless innings set in 1918.

Tom Gorman

By Bob Hurte

"When I go, I want to be buried in my umpiring suit, holding my indicator."[1]

When Tom Gorman died, his children carried out their father's final desire. Gorman was dressed in his suit, which was meticulously buttoned, and wore his blue cap with the white "NL" embroidered on the front of it. He also held his indicator in his hand. It was set at "3 and 2." Just like the title of their father's memoir.

Thomas David Gorman was born on March 16, 1919, in New York City. He grew up in the Hell's Kitchen neighborhood, at that time considered the bastion of poor, working-class Irish. The neighborhood is mentioned prominently by Damon Runyon in his stories. Gorman was of Irish heritage and was actually born an hour before St. Patrick's Day.

Hell's Kitchen was considered a rough neighborhood, but Tom felt that it was a nice place to grow up. The Gormans were from County Cork, as Irish as a family could get. Both of his grandfathers emigrated from Ireland. His grandfather, Francis O'Gorman, and two of his sons were police officers. Francis, at the age of 47, died falling off a roof while chasing a prowler. Francis had three sons, Tom, David Francis (Tom's father), and Vinnie. (O'Gorman was the original family name; the "O" was lost along the way.) Tom's mother was Katherine (Moran) Gorman; her family came from County Mayo. Tom had two sisters, Helen, and Mary.

Tom's father, David Francis, was a huge baseball fan, especially of the New York Giants. He gave his son his first glove, a Carl Hubbell model with short fingers. David Francis took his son to watch the Giants, and the Yankees. Tom's favorite player was Lou Gehrig, while Bill Terry was his dad's.

Tom's baseball career road map developed early. He loved sports but his allegiance was divided between baseball and basketball. Tom was 6-feet-2 and played center in basketball at Power Memorial High School, just like a later graduate, Lou Alcindor, who was later known as Kareem Abdul Jabbar. Gorman went on to play 13 years of professional basketball, in the Pennsylvania State Pro League, the New York State Pro League, and half a season for the Toronto Huskies of the Basketball Association of America, one of the forerunners of the NBA.[2]

Gorman was fond of basketball. Aside from playing, he also coached and refereed. Although he loved basketball, some of his biggest successes were on the diamond during high school. Tom pitched on Power Memorial's city championship teams in 1936 and 1937. Along with teammate Pancho Snyder, he threw batting practice for the Giants at the Polo Grounds.[3]

Gorman impressed Bill Terry and the Giants manager wanted to sign him. He could not wait to tell his father because his dad was a big fan of the former Giants great.

"Well," Tom told his father, "Bill Terry would like to see you tomorrow morning around ten, ten thirty." Terry gave Tom's father a cigar and told him how fine a boy his son was, and a good athletic specimen. Tom's father told Terry that he was a fan of his, and agreed to let Tom sign with the Giants.[4] The Giants gave him a signing bonus of for $500. After two years in the minor leagues, Gorman's major-league playing career consisted of five innings over four games at the end of the 1939 season as a 20-year-old. He gave up four runs, walked one, struck out two, and threw one wild pitch. He was hitless in his one at-bat; he handled his two fielding chances successfully.

Gorman was back in the minors in 1940. He was drafted into the US Army in 1941 and didn't return to professional baseball for four years. Gorman underwent training at Fort Dix, New Jersey, and Fort Meade, Virginia, before ending up at Camp Stoneham in San Diego. Unlike many other former players, he did not play baseball while in the service. Gorman was a sergeant in the 16th Infantry Regiment of the 1st Division, and fought in the North African campaign. Before being discharged, he organized service teams. On September 17, 1945, Gorman's father died suddenly.

Gorman proposed to Margaret Fay during a game between the Giants and Cincinnati Reds at the Polo Grounds. They were married in October 1945.

In 1946, while Gorman was in Winter Haven, Florida, for spring training, calcium deposits were discovered, and he developed a sore shoulder. He tried to keep it a secret, but because of his ineffectiveness the Giants traded Gorman to the Boston Braves.

Boston Braves manager Billy Southworth told him, "The way you're throwing right now, well, maybe your arm will come around. You've got a chance. Maybe we'll send you to the Eastern League."[5] The Braves management did decide to send him to the Eastern League.

Around this time Gorman was approached by the Pasquel brothers, who were raiding the major leagues for talent for the Mexican League. They offered him $8,000 to sign, and a contract for $12,000 over three years. He discussed his situation with Billy Southworth; the Braves agreed to give him his release.

Gorman, the only American on his team, experienced some success in Mexico. He had a 7-3 record his first year. But the Pasquels lost a lot of money that first season. They cut players' contracts in half and made players had to pay their own expenses for the 1947 season. Gorman got $6,000 for his second season. He lost his first two starts, his shoulder began to feel worse, and he returned to the United States.

Once back, Gorman coached, officiated, and played basketball. He did not return to playing baseball. He did not even consider himself to be Class-D material.

One night after he refereed a basketball game between St. John's and Holy Cross at Madison Square Garden, Neil Mahoney, a scout for the Red Sox, came into Gorman's dressing room and made him two job offers: to either manage one of Boston's farm teams or to umpire in the New England League. Gorman

Tom Gorman.

did not feel like umpire material. Mahoney disagreed; he felt that Gorman was the right size, possessed the right temperament, and knew the game. Although Gorman turned Mahoney down, the idea intrigued him. After thinking it over, Gorman informed Mahoney that he was interested.

Gorman met Claude Davidson, the president of the New England League, who told him that if he had a car, the job was his for $180 a month. Gorman was not exactly excited; he replied that it was not a lot of money. Gorman felt that he could make more selling newspapers. Neil Mahoney told Gorman that all of the leagues started their umpires out this way. Gorman's wife asked him to try it for a year. He agreed and soon he signed a contract for $180 a month and $55 in expenses for the 1947 season.

Gorman's first partner was Dave Clary, from Brockton, Massachusetts. Their first game was in Nashua, New Hampshire, where Walter Alston was the manager of the Nashua Dodgers and Don Newcombe, Roy Campanella, and Joe Black were players. Clary worked the plate, Gorman the bases.

Clary gave positioning advice to his partner; he asked Gorman where he umpired last.

"Dave, I'll tell you the truth. I've never umpired a game in my life."[6]

Gorman was behind the plate for his second game, with Don Newcombe pitching. It was a quiet night for both sides. So Clary, his partner, asked, "You sure you never umpired before?"[7]

Gorman's first rhubarb was with George Kissell, the manager at Lawrence. By the original account, the game was Gorman's first ejection as an umpire.

It did not take long for Gorman to make the major leagues. The National League purchased his contract from the International League and he made his debut on September 11, 1951, in Chicago. He was the third-base umpire that day, working with Al Barlick, Lee Ballanfant, and Augie Donatelli. He thought they were three of the best.

Gorman made his first mistake during that first big-league game. A batter popped up near the Cubs dugout and the third baseman made the catch on a slab of concrete next to the bat rack. Gorman signaled no catch. In the International League, concrete was not a part of the playing field; this was not the case in the majors and Ballanfant corrected him.

Throughout Gorman's career he often was associated with Leo Durocher. He first met Durocher during the 1951 season when Leo was managing the Giants. Their introduction was initiated by a play at second base. Gorman called a baserunner out. Durocher came charging out to argue the call. Gorman, who had a propensity to embellish the truth in order to make a story entertaining, said this is what happened next: Durocher said, "Hey kid, I want to tell you something. You called the play too quick."[8] Gorman stood his ground and informed Leo that the runner was out. Durocher walked back to the dugout for about five or six steps and then made a U-turn. He got into rhubarb with Gorman, calling him a SOB, but since he did not get in the umpire's face, Gorman would not eject him. In *Three and Two*, his memoir, Gorman recalled that a week or so later, his crew was in Brooklyn for a series between the Dodgers and Giants. According to Retrosheet, Gorman's crew never went to Brooklyn until May 4, 1952. Gorman tossed Durocher out of the game at Ebbets Field. He told Durocher it was retribution for the game in the Polo Grounds. Gorman said Durocher became his first ejection in the majors. In reality, Durocher was not one of Gorman's 27 career ejections. Durocher enjoyed getting into rhubarbs before a sellout crowd, especially a nationally televised game, and he played to the fans, which they loved. Gorman played along, although he did not throw out a lot of guys. The Durocher/Gorman routine later became popular in Miller Lite beer commercials and on the banquet circuit. Gorman's 27 career ejections are the least of any umpire who has worked at least 3,000 major-league games.[9] (His last ejection was Ron Cey of the Dodgers, for arguing a third strike.)

Gorman retired as an umpire in 1976, and worked for a while as an umpire supervisor for the National League. Someone once asked him if he was ever wrong. "No, I'm never wrong. I can't be wrong on my job," he replied. "But I've made mistakes. I am a human being. I could be wrong, but when I call a play that's the way I see it."[10]

If one umpires in the National League for 25-plus years, as Gorman did, one undoubtedly officiates in many meaningful games. Gorman umpired in five World Series: 1956, 1958, 1963, 1968, and 1974. He was stationed on the left-field line during Don Larsen's perfect game against Brooklyn in the 1956 World Series, and he was behind the plate when Bob Gibson struck out 17 Detroit Tigers during the first game of the 1968 World Series.

Gorman worked the 1971 and 1975 NLCS. He was the crew chief in 1971. He umpired the playoff between the Los Angeles Dodgers and Milwaukee Braves in 1959 to determine who was going to the World Series. He umpired in five All-Star Games: 1954, 1958, both games of 1960, and 1969.

Gorman umpired nine no-hitters, tying a NL record. He was behind the plate for Warren Spahn's no-hitter in 1960 and Bill Stoneman's in 1969.

Among Gorman's honors were being named the Outstanding Umpire of 1974 and the Umpire of the Half Century by the Al Somers Umpire School. In

1970 he received the Bill Slocum Award from the New York chapter of the Baseball Writers Association of America.

Gorman enjoyed being an umpire, but there were difficult managers. Leo Durocher and Fred Hutchinson were two who he felt were the most difficult. Bobby Bragan was always looking for loopholes in the rule book. There were several good-guy managers in his opinion, like Gil Hodges, Walt Alston, and Danny Murtaugh. He particularly appreciated ballplayers Bill Mazeroski, Roberto Clemente, Pee Wee Reese, and Dick Allen.

Gorman and his wife, Margaret, had three sons, Tommy, Brian, and Kevin, and a daughter, Patty Ellen. (Brian also became a major-league umpire, starting in the National League in 1991 and still active in 2016.) Margaret died in 1968. In July of 1986 Gorman remarried. His time with his new wife, Olga, was brief. He died of a heart attack on August 11, 1986, in Closter, New Jersey, at the age of 67. He is buried in the George Washington Memorial Park in Paramus, New Jersey.

In his acceptance speech for being named Outstanding Umpire of 1974 by the Al Somers Umpire School, Tom Gorman said, "People may come to see ballplayers, but there'd be no baseball without good umpires."[11]

SOURCES

In addition to the sources cited in the Notes, the author also consulted:

Holtzman, Jerome. "Never Missed a Call," *Chicago Tribune*, August 17, 1986.

O'Connell, Jack. "Umpire Gorman to Make Shea History," MLB.com, September 28, 2008.

NOTES

1   Ira Berkow, "Tom Gorman's Final Call," *New York Times* August 17, 1986.

2   "Queen city cagers set for pro debut," *Montreal Gazette*, October 31, 1946.

3   Tom Gorman and Jerome Holtzman, *Three and Two!* (New York: Charles Scribner's Sons, 1979), 8.

4   *Gorman and Holtzman*, 9-10.

5   *Gorman and Holtzman*, 21.

6   *Gorman and Holtzman*, 35.

7   *Gorman and Holtzman*, 36.

8   *Gorman and Holtzman*, 40.

9   Calculations performed by Dennis Bingham, using data on umpire ejections on Retrosheet.org.

10 *Gorman and Holtzman*, 60.

11 Brad Wilson, "Gorman, Umpire of the Year starting his 25th season in NL," *The Sporting News*, March 15, 1975: 39.

Steve Palermo

By Bill Nowlin

Steve Palermo thought about becoming a French interpreter at the United Nations. But he got into umpiring instead, paid $2 per game in his first professional job as a baseball umpire at age 13.

Oxford, Massachusetts was a small town of around 11,000 people, not that far from Worcester, where Palermo had been born on October 9, 1949. He spent his first nine years in Worcester, but his father was principal of an elementary school in Oxford and when the town mandated that principals were residents of the town, the family made the move and Steve became a third-grade student in the school where his father was principal. Steve's mother was a "professional homemaker…the consummate house-wife and mother. She's done this job 24/7 and she's 90 years old and she's still doing it."[1] It was indeed a fulltime job; Steve had two sisters and three brothers. Sisters Linda and Ann, and brother Jim, became teachers. Brothers Michael and Jim became invest-ment bankers. Linda was first born, Steve was the oldest boy.

Steve himself expected to become a teacher, ma-joring in education with a minor in French. His freshman year was at Norwich University, transferred to Leicester Junior College, and then to Worcester State. He was a year and a few credits from gradu-ating when he decided he wanted to go to umpire school.

Both Palermo parents promoted the kids going into athletics. Linda was a very good athlete, and played both basketball and softball. Steve played Little League, Babe Ruth League, high-school ball, American Legion, and even some baseball and bas-ketball at Norwich. It was basketball that interested him most there. At baseball, he started out at short-stop, and some second base, though at one time or another played every position on the field. The Little League program in Oxford was a successful one, play-ing in state finals for a shot at going to Williamsport.

How did he get his first paid job umpiring? "I el-evated to the Babe Ruth League when I was 13 years old but my brother was still playing Little League, so I still had some fascination with that. Somebody said, 'Why don't you start to try umpiring, Steve? It's two dollars a game.' It was a way of making a little bit of pocket money. Monday through Saturdays. Stan Johnson, who was the administrator for District 5 Little League, was very instrumental in making sure that the Little League ran and that it ran well. He made sure the kids had rides to the ballpark so they could make their practices. He was a great promoter of Little League Baseball, to try and help the kids."

After he was old enough, Palermo started working construction at age 16, for the next four years, "build-ing bridges and roads here in Massachusetts. I put money away because I was going to college. We had a rather large family. My dad, being a principal, there wasn't a ton of money coming in. We weren't poor, but by no means were we wealthy." For the next four years, he worked construction while going to school and over the summers, until a day when Stan Johnson called him and said he was in a bind and needed someone to work home plate at a Little League all-star game.

It was quite an active game with some unusual plays at the plate. Watching the game, by happen-stance after his nephew urged him to go to the game, was Barney Deary, administrator of Baseball Umpire Development, and he was in the area looking over a couple of umpires. Deary gave his card to Palermo. The card sat on Palermo's dressed for a year until August 1971 when he suddenly decided to go to umpire school in February, even at the expense of not completing college. His parents were not at all pleased, but figured he'd get it out of his system and finish his schooling. "Five years later, my first game's at Fenway Park and my mom and dad are sitting three rows behind home plate. My mom turned to my dad and said, 'You know, this isn't that bad a job, really.'"

First, though, there was umpire school and years in the minor leagues.

Umpire school was a six or seven-week program in St. Petersburg. It was a relatively new program, just started a couple of years earlier.[2] His first assignment was to work spring training games, based at the Cincinnati Reds camp in Tampa. His class was a productive one—"I believe this class of 1972 had more students who became major-league umpires than any other umpire class to date. That is what I have been told: Eddie Montague, Durwood Merrill, Mike Reilly, Al Clark, and Steve Palermo."

Palermo said that the most influential men at umpire school were Frank Pulli, Rich Garcia, John McSherry, Larry Napp, Barney Deary, and Joe Linsalata.[3]

After spring training, he worked for a couple of months in a Spring rookie league in Florida and then was assigned to the New York-Penn League starting in June. He worked the season, then went to the Florida Instructional League in mid-September for a couple of months. "It was a great learning experience in the instructional league and every day we had a supervisor there that we'd talk baseball with for an hour, hour and a half after the ballgame. He resided at the same place we did so we'd all congregate in either his room or some room and everybody would talk about the plays that they had in their particular games that day. We all learned from that. It was very advanced training and I was very fortunate to be able to do that."

He started 1973 working in the Carolina League, "a very, very tough league…a very advanced A-ball league at the time. I worked a half a year there and there just happened to be an opening in the Eastern League and I got promoted to the Eastern League in mid-1973. I worked there for a year and a half. After that, I got assigned to the American Association."

Palermo worked the A.A. for the 1975 and 1976 seasons and the beginning of 1977. In October 1975, he married Andrea Lee Giannotta, a flight attendant for United he had met while working winter ball that January. The marriage lasted eight years.

In 1976, he'd worked the Triple-A playoffs and a little while after his postseason was done, he got a call asking him if he could come to Boston. He'd worked with Nestor Chylak, the Hall of Fame umpire, in spring training both in '75 and '76. "He was a mentor to me. He was a very demanding taskmaster. You just thought he was tough, but you come to realize later on that it was tough love. He was tough on me for my benefit although I thought he was doing it just because he could yell at me and scream at me about everything. He was one of the biggest influences on my umpiring career. He approached Mr. Butler—Dick Butler, who was the supervisor of umpires in the American League—in 1976, and said, 'Stevie's home. He's worked his playoffs in Triple-A and he's got time. Would you allow him to come up and work with my crew the last couple of days with Baltimore and Boston at the end of the season? There's a good chance he'll be here in '77, so let's let him get some dirt on his shoes.'"

Butler called Palermo and asked him if he could come to Boston. "I had no idea or inkling. 'How'd you like to go up to Boston for a couple of days?' 'You want me to come up and sit with you, kind of just visit?'

"He said, 'No, you won't be sitting. You'll be standing the entire game.' I said, 'Really?' I'm thinking, is it so crowded we're just going to have standing room only? He said, 'No, you're going to be standing at third and second base.' I said, 'REALLY?' I said, 'Yes, sir!' And so I just packed everything up and I got to Boston way before they needed me."

Both leagues had been interested in him—they were not yet united in Major League Baseball –but the American League had acted quicker and bought his option.

Chylak sat out the October 2, 1976 game and sat in the stands grading the umpires—Jim Evans at home plate, Greg Kosc at first, Joe Brinkman at second, and Palermo at third. It was a 1-0 game, Reggie Cleveland and two relievers each getting one out for the Red Sox over Dennis Martinez of the Baltimore Orioles.

Steve Palermo.

Chylak worked the plate the next day, and Palermo worked second base. The game went 15 innings, a 3-2 Red Sox win.

Palermo was signed to a league contract starting in 1977 — "the first game I ever worked under contract, they wouldn't let me open in this country; I had to go to Toronto." It was the first game the Blue Jays ever played in the major leagues, a 9 — 5 win over the White Sox.

It had been fast advancement to the major leagues. Most first-year umpires at the time were in their early 30s. "Here I was a baby-faced 26-year-old kid and I'm up in the big leagues. It just didn't happen all that often. I was very fortunate, to have very good instructors and very good instruction. It's not a political thing. You are out there. You are exposed. You have to be very productive and you have to be very good at what you do…The only way you get to the big leagues is you earn it…You either do the job or the job won't be there for you to do."

It helped that Chylak, a senior umpire with 24 years in the big leagues and one who had basically been self-taught, liked his work. Palermo was eager to

learn. "I have cocktail napkins — after games — after games, we'd go have a beer or grab something to eat and I used to stuff all these cocktail napkins in my pockets. He'd grab another napkin and diagram where I should be on a particular play when a throw comes in from right field versus center field versus left field. He'd draw a circle around a base and say, 'Never get inside the circle. You always stay outside the circle. This way you have a wider perspective of the play and the play won't explode on you.' All these great little catch phrases and advice that he gave me, I followed to the letter. All it was going to do was enhance my umpiring and make me better. That's what he was all about. He was all about teaching you things. You'd learn great life lessons with him, and great umpiring lessons with him."

Life in the majors was a quantum step up from working the minor leagues — new cities, meeting people who knew the crew he was assigned to — Chylak, Richie Garcia, and Joe Brinkman. "There really are three teams out there on the field. There's that home team, the visiting team, and the third team is that crew of umpires.

"And they work as a team. Being familiar with everybody and their personalities and what they're going to do on the field. When a ball is hit, in a certain situation, depending on how many runners are on, you know exactly what your responsibilities are, your crewmate knows what responsibilities are his. Everybody knows what to do, and so you know you have to operate like a team and be very well-coordinated in order to be able to cover any and all plays that could possibly happen."

As of 2016, Palermo works as Major League Supervisor of Umpires. The philosophy regarding an umpire crew remains the same as when he broke in.

"The way we have it set up, we hope the same crew will stay together. Because of the Collective Bargaining Agreement, umpires are granted this time off now and after X amount of days on the road…. Mark Wegner should be on this crew right now, but his vacation slot is now and that's why Tom Woodring is in here. He's filling in. Mike Winters was off last week and so Tom was also working for

Mike last week, so he just remained with this crew from last week to this week. We like to keep guys on a crew for as long a period of time as we can, with guys' vacations, because we want everybody to be familiar with each other instead of shuttling guys in and out."

The core of the crew might be together the whole season, with one person coming and going now and again. And then, beginning with the 2014 season, that same crew will rotate in to New York as a group to work on replay. "Yes, they'll go into New York a week at a time and all four guys will go in as a crew, and there will also be another crew of four guys in there. There are time slots when they are to report in to the Command Center—I call it the ROC. It's the Replay Operations Center. It's in Chelsea."

After getting that little bit of dirt on his shoes at the end of 1976, Palermo worked as a major-league umpire from 1977 into 1991, when a very unfortunate incident ended his time on the field. Naturally, he had the opportunity to work some key games, including the 1978 single-game playoff to determine the winner of the American League pennant, one ALDS and three ALCS, Dave Righetti's no-hitter, the 1983 World Series, and the 1986 All-Star Game.

The 1978 playoff was between the Red Sox and the Yankees at Fenway Park, the so-called "Bucky Dent game," named after the Yankees shortstop whose wholly unexpected three-run homer in the top of the seventh carried the day. Palermo was the third-base umpire and thus the one who called the ball fair and signaled it was a home run.

Palermo's father was still working as school principal. "I called my dad up over that weekend and told him that if there was a playoff game, I'd be coming into Boston Sunday night and do you want to come to the game that afternoon? It was a Monday afternoon. I think it was a 2:30 start. He played hooky from school that day. He and I went to the umpires' room and I grabbed a sandwich and he had a Coke, and he was like a kid in a candy store. He just sat there and listened to everybody as we talked. After the game, he came back up. We used to dress above the Red Sox clubhouse. He knows never to mention anything about the game or what we do. It was just

small talk. He just sat there quiet. We all showered and everybody wished everybody well for the off-season. Guys were talking about we got golf games tomorrow, 9 o'clock. Everybody's excited to get home and get to their families and everything. I jumped in the car with my dad—my mom sat in the back and we got on Storrow Drive and then got on the Mass Pike to get out to Oxford. For the first 15 minutes, I'm playing this game over in my head and trying to wrap my head around its historical meaning in all of baseball. I don't know whether my mom and dad were talking together or not, because I was just…

"Finally I turned to my dad and then it just popped out of my head, 'That was a hell of a game, wasn't it?' He turned to me and said, 'You couldn't have called that ball foul?' I said, 'What?' He said, 'Bucky's home run. You couldn't have called that foul?' I said, 'Pop, that ball was 15 feet to the right of the foul pole!' He said, 'So what? You're in Boston. Nobody would have said a word.' Well…there are some far-reaching circumstances that reach far beyond Boston. I said, 'Pop, I'd be looking for a recommendation from you because I wouldn't be doing this very much longer if I did that.' When I talk to people, I say, 'You have no idea what internal pressure is, until your parents might be rooting for a team.'

"It's funny. I walk off a field and we'll go to a restaurant and know somebody there who'll ask, 'What was the score of the game?' and I'll say, 'I don't know. I think it was 5-4, but I don't know who won.' You don't care who wins or loses. You just make sure that you keep that playing field level all the time."

Truly? He worked the whole game and didn't really know who won or lost? "Yeah. If you stop and think for a second. Come August, you've been to all these different towns and sometimes you wake up in a hotel…these Hyatt rooms all look the same or these Marriott rooms all look the same, and you'll call the hotel operator and say, 'Can you tell me what town this is?' She'll say, 'Yes, sir. You're in Chicago, Illinois.' 'OK, thank you. Good night.' It happens. You wake up and you go, 'Where am I today? Is this Chicago or are we in Milwaukee?' That isn't the importance of your job."

The importance of the job is to make the calls correctly and tunnel focus can be key in doing so. Umpires don't care about how the official scorer may rule on certain plays. The difference isn't taught in umpire school. "We don't want to know if it's a base hit or an error. We don't know if that run is scored as an earned run or an unearned run. If you asked an umpire, 'How would you rule that?'—they probably don't know how to score a game, because it is not taught to them. They don't want to learn it, and the people who teach don't want that to be an influence on an umpire's decision…All the subtleties of official scoring, I have no idea. And even now, even though I am not on the field umpiring, I still don't, because I want to look at the game as objectively as possible." Official scorers, of course, can change their determination after the game, the next day, or even later. Umpires don't have that leeway.

Working another Red Sox/Yankees game, on the Fourth of July 1983, Palermo was the home-plate umpire—and perhaps the only one at Yankee Stadium who didn't know until the ninth inning that Dave Righetti was pitching a no-hitter. He was focused on calling the balls and strikes correctly, and in position and ready to make any other call he might need to.

There was one call in that game he should have made, but could not. It was 94 degrees and a pretty close game, 2-0 in favor of the Yankees after 7 ½ innings. Righetti hadn't given up a hit. With the Yankees batting in the bottom of the eighth, Lou Piniella hit a foul popup over by the seats on the first-base side. Just as Boston catcher Jeff Newman started to reach into the stands, Palermo blew out his knee. "It felt like somebody took a boat oar and just knocked my left knee out from underneath me and I went flying toward the crash pad." First-base umpire Rick Reed was in position to make the call. Though the injury cost Palermo six weeks after surgery, the severity was not so certain at the time and he finished the game.

After eight full, with only three outs standing between Righetti and a no-hitter, the 41,077 at Yankee Stadium gave the Yankees pitcher a standing ovation

as he walked out to the mound. Palermo thought, "That's nice. They're giving him a nice round of applause. The kid didn't get selected to the All-Star Game and these people are kind of sending him off after the first half of the season with good thoughts." As Righetti was taking his warmup pitches, Palermo glanced up at the scoreboard and saw no runs, no hits, and one Red Sox error. He thought maybe the scoreboard was broken and told Yankees catcher Butch Wynegar that he wanted to talk to him after the game. Wynegar said, "Steve, I might be jumping up and down when this game's over. Whatever you've gotta ask me, ask me now." Palermo thought to himself, heck, he didn't believe in superstition and so said, "I didn't know this guy had a no-hitter going." Wynegar was taken aback and laughed, "That's what makes you the wizard. You just stay right in the moment."[4] Palermo was so focused on one play at a time, he hadn't realized there was a no-hitter in progress.

He still remembers the final at-bat. On a 1-2 count —one strike away—"Righetti threw a pitch on the outside part of the plate, that was just off the plate, outside down and away, and I called it a ball and everybody at Yankee Stadium booed like hell. I thought they were going to come over the wall after me. I remember that pitch."[5] There was no debate about strike three; Boggs swung and missed. Palermo never said, "Strike three!" He says he just turned and walked away, and headed to the umpires' room. "Jerry Neudecker had worked Catfish Hunter's perfect game so he knew what it was like to work a no-hitter. He said, 'They aren't easy, are they, Kid?' I said, 'No, they're not.' Then I said, 'I'm glad I didn't know it until the ninth inning.' He said, 'What????' I told him."

His first postseason was in 1980, when the Royals swept the Yankees in the ALCS. It was his fourth year. At that time it was kind of an unwritten rule that a young umpire won't work the postseason until at least their sixth year. I was in my fourth year and I got assigned and in my first game, I 'm working home plate. That is rare, that you put a first-time umpire working in postseason, that his first game is behind home plate. It's funny. I was picking up somebody at the airport and Mr. Butler just happened to be at that terminal. He got off the plane and said, 'When are you playing?' I said, 'Tomorrow. I'm pumped up about working. Where are you going to put me?' He said, 'Make sure your plate shoes are shined.'"

And he was the home-plate umpire for the final game of the 1983 World Series where Baltimore's Scott McGregor shut out the Phillies, 5-0. He knew who won that game. "Yeah, you see one team congratulating one another and jumping up and down and the other team walking toward the dugout with their heads down. You knew it was over. And I know that Eddie Murray hit two home runs in that game."

But for the most part, it's the plays that would stand out in his memory. "I appreciate the playing of the game and playing the game the right way. A spectacular play? Now, that's a big-league play. Like that kid catching the ball over the bullpen wall last night and the other kid in center field reaching over the Red Sox bullpen and pulling a home run back off the field. You appreciate those plays and it makes you pay attention to that kid the next time he's playing, too. I've seen this kid do something special and he's got the potential ability to do something special again. Like this kid Trout, when he walks on the field every day. He's got the potential to do something that you might not have seen. He plays the game the right way. Robin Yount did it and George Brett did it. Ripken did it. Kirby Puckett did.

"People have asked me, as you did, do you have any kids? I said no, but if I had a son, I would definitely get a video of George Brett or Cal Ripken or Kirby Puckett or Paul Molitor or Robin Yount and I would sit him in a chair and put that videotape on and say, 'Here. This is how you're supposed to play the game of baseball.'"

Palermo remarried in 1985 to Debbie Aaron, who worked for a property tax consulting firm.

He worked a total of 1,871 regular-season games, the last being on July 6, 1991 at Arlington Stadium. The Rangers beat the Angels, 4-3, and after the game Palermo stopped by to have dinner at Corky Campisi's restaurant before returning to the Hyatt. A couple of the waitresses left to go home, and then another restaurant employee shouted out that they'd run into trouble. They were being beaten to the ground in a purse-snatching. Palermo and Terrence Mann ran outside and ended up chasing and catching one of the thieves, but there was a fourth man in a getaway car who circled back and fired five shots, hitting both Mann and Palermo.

"The first three bullets hit T-Mann—one in the throat that entered and exited from right side to left side. The second one hit him in the bicep of his right arm and then the third one hit him in his thigh. The fourth bullet missed all of us and it hit a brick wall behind us—Mrs. Baird's Bakery. The fifth one hit me at belt level and took a path through my body, hit my left kidney and bounced off the kidney, hit the abdomen, and then went straight down and struck my spinal cord and then went out my left side. It hit what they call the cauda equine, the peripheral nerves that come out the bottom of your spinal cord that enervate your muscles in your lower extremities. I was paralyzed immediately."

The police had already been called and they caught the shooter, who was sentenced to 75 years in prison.

Palermo was treated at Parkland Hospital in Dallas, the same hospital to which President John F. Kennedy had been taken after he was shot. It was a long, very difficult, and never-ending rehabilitation, and more than a dozen years later, Palermo still walks with supports. But he put in the months and months of work, and was eventually able to be assigned new responsibilities.

In 1994, he was asked to prepare a report on the pace of the game and presented it in June 1995 at the owners' meeting in Minneapolis. In 1999, he started working for Sandy Alderson and in 2000 in Baseball Operations. Palermo now reports to Chief Baseball Officer Joe Torre.

"I've become basically a supervisor and instructor, where I supervise stuff and evaluate umpires. We kind of handle everything that takes place as far as on field. We give a talk to the teams during the course of spring training. We go to visit with all the managers, coaches, and general managers. Tell them of the new procedures, if there are any. There's a host of duties. I also go out to the Fall League for seven weeks. We get 12 umpires to find out if they have the…to become major-league umpires.

"Frank Pulli was the first one named. Frank and I for a few years were the only two that worked for Major League Baseball. We started to add as time went on and as we implemented more and more things, the staff grew."

Asked to describe his work as Major League Supervisor of Umpires, "To describe the position, I'd like to think of it as either a liaison or a conduit between management and umpires, so that you can bring the mentality of management to the umpires and let them understand it and try to bring the mentality of the umpire to management so that management can understand it. It's a two-way street.

"This program all started after the breakup of the union in 1999 and the formation of another union. We were brought on board, starting in 2000, and even though I hadn't umpired since 1991—I'd been off the field for 10 years—you have to build up this trust. Through time. This is very new. They only had one supervisor in each league. Now we have five or six guys going around the big leagues, and four or five guys in the minor leagues.

"I don't like to think of it as constructive criticism. It's not tearing you down. It isn't criticism. It's constructive advice. Try not to commit a mistake that I made. You're doing this and I made a mistake because of that. I'm trying to be proactive rather than reactive. That's what teaching umpiring is all about. You teach them as much as they can possibly take it. I've had people tell me, 'Steve, we're trying to teach them math and you're trying to teach them trigonometry.' How do you know they can't do trigonometry? Unless you're talking with them, you don't know. And if you see they can't do trigonometry, you can go back to basic math. I believe you keep putting more and more and more out there, and then you find out where's their threshold. Once you know that, then

you understand and then you work with them. Then you can formulate a really good umpire regardless."

The umpire observers file their reports, for every game, submitting four reports—one for each umpire. "I get to see everybody's evaluations and they get to see mine. They go through Major League Baseball."

And he'll supply feedback directly to the umpires. "I let them decompress after a game. Give them a day to think about it. The only time you usually don't have a chance is on getaway day. There might be a phone call, once they arrive in their next city. I might give a call and let them know. Generally, what I'll do is I'll deal with the crew chief and say, 'Tell Tom this, tell Bill this, tell Dick this…This was excellent. He might need work on this….' Whatever it might be. Generally, that's what we do. We go through the crew chief and then the crew chief—being in that position—he's going to let it all filter down. That's part of his job. That's part of his crew chief responsibility. It's not only himself, but he's got three other people. We give it to them, because we know that they can handle it."

NOTES

1 Unless otherwise indicated, all quotations from Steve Palermo come from interviews with the author on August 20 and 21, 2014.

2 His employer during his years in the minor leagues was Baseball Umpire Development—"the minor-league arm of Major League Baseball. They're the ones who provided, or assigned, umpires to the Triple-A leagues, the Double-A leagues, the A+, rookie ball. I think they started the school in 1970. It was two years before I got down, when Baseball invested all this money. They basically subsidized umpire school at that time. It cost me $300 to go down, but Baseball picked up the rest of it. They said, 'We have training for all the players, but for umpires we have nothing. We just go kind of searching for them and then try to train and develop them, stick them in the minor leagues.' We did have the Al Somers School, which became the Harry Wendelstedt School. The only other thing was Baseball Umpire Development, and that was directly supported by the major-league teams that said, 'Let's develop the umpires, too.'"

3 E-mail to author, September 21, 2014.

4 Author interview with Steve Palermo, January 15, 2015.

5 Ibid.

Babe Pinelli

By Larry R. Gerlach

At approximately 3:15 P.M. on Monday, October 8, 1956, Babe Pinelli's right arm shot upward, ending Game Five of the World Series. Pinelli did more than punch out Brooklyn Dodgers pinch-hitter Dale Mitchell to conclude a 2-0 New York Yankees victory; his called third strike completed Don Larsen's perfect game, the only one in World Series history. It was also the culmination of Pinelli's umpiring career and a moment that fixed his—and Larsen's—place in baseball history. After the game the 61-year-old Pinelli sat in the umpires' dressing room tearfully reflecting upon both his career and the magnitude of the historic last game that he regarded "my greatest thrill in 40 years of baseball."[1] But not a single reporter or baseball official appeared to ask his thoughts about the game or to congratulate him on his 22 years as a highly respected National League umpire. Crew member Tom Gorman later recalled: "Nobody showed, not the commissioner [Ford Frick], not the president of the National League [Warren Giles]. I thought it was a disgrace."[2] Regarding the historic game as the capstone of his career, Pinelli retired after the final two games of the Series: "Why go on? I won't see a better pitched game. It's a perfect time to retire."[3]

Sports officials normally fade into historical oblivion, but Pinelli remains widely known because of the belief that he kicked the call. Second-guessers continue to contend that Larsen's final pitch was really low and outside the strike zone. Babe, whose vision tested 20/20 immediately after the Series, later recalled that Larsen had "the greatest pin-point control I've ever seen" and that "there was no doubt in my mind" about the pitch: "Larsen hit the corner of the plate with a beautiful fast ball" that was "just high enough. It was easy to call—and I called it."[4]

If "just high enough" is taken as the operative phrase implying that the pitch may have been beyond the precise parameters of the official strike zone, then

Pinelli's call was both correct and courageous. Aware since the sixth inning that no Dodger had reached base, he knew the unwritten rules of the game held that a batter shall not take a close pitch with two strikes in the bottom of the ninth with a perfect game on the line. Babe Pinelli made the right call, a gutsy call, just as he had done throughout his life.

Rinaldo Angelo Paolinelli debuted in the Western Addition section of San Francisco on October 18, 1895, the second of four children born to Rafael and Ermida Silvestri Paolinelli, immigrants from Lucca, Italy. When his father, who owned a produce market, was killed by a falling telephone pole during the devastating 1906 earthquake, Pinelli, age 10, left the fourth grade to help support the family. He sold newspapers until he was old enough at 12 to get a regular job, first separating nuts and bolts at Dyer Brothers' Steel Works, then as an errand boy, and finally as a commercial sign painter. (Inexplicably, he painted with his left hand but was right-handed in all other activities.)

Pinelli, who said he was "born with firecrackers in my blood," used his fiery temper and fistic prowess to survive on the mean streets around Bush and Steiner. Hauled to the police station at least seven times for fighting, the brash and belligerent, yet likable, youngster was a West Coast version of a Dead End Kid. "He'd take no lip from anybody," a childhood pal recalled. "He'd fight at the drop of a hat if he thought he was right."[5] Pinelli loved sports, especially baseball. Initially, the older kids chased him away when he wanted to play ball and called him "Baby" when he cried; however, his skills soon brought notoriety on the Hamilton Park diamonds and his nickname became "Babe" as he played with older boys. Pinelli briefly thought about becoming a professional boxer after winning (as Battling Joe Welch) a two-round amateur bout in his late teens, but Spike Hennessy, the legendary high-school and sandlot baseball coach who served as Babe's surrogate father, encouraged him to give up boxing and concentrate on baseball, starring on the aptly named North Beach Outlaws. Along with eight other youths, he played as a member of the Boston Bloomer Girls in 1912 after shaving his head and donning a wig; they defeated the Oakland Oaks of the Pacific Coast League, 3-2.

By 1916 Pinelli had demonstrated sufficient skills as a third baseman in semipro leagues in Oregon (1913), Utah (1915), and San Francisco to earn a trial with Portland of the Pacific Coast League. Released by the Beavers before the season began, he signed that summer to play the following year with the Salt Lake City Bees of the PCL. With a professional career in the offing, he married his childhood sweetheart, Mabel "Mae" Genevieve McKee, on December 2, 1916.

Following the advice of *San Francisco News* sportswriter Tommy Laird, Pinelli signed a second contract to play with Portland in 1917, disingenuously obtained his release from the Bees, anglicized his name to Ralph Arthur Pinelli, and joined the Beavers. Despite hitting a meager .199 in 79 games, the 5-foot-9, 165-pound Pinelli impressed manager Wilbur "Raw Meat" Rodgers with his scrappy style of play and remained with the club when it moved the next season to Sacramento. As a former teammate noted: "Babe was a hustler. He couldn't tolerate anybody who didn't go 100 percent."[6]

When the PCL suspended play on July 14, 1918, because of World War I, Pinelli, who had hit .267 in 94 contests with the Solons, was sold to the Chicago White Sox as a wartime replacement. He debuted on August 3 against the Philadelphia Athletics, playing third base and hitting 1-for-3 in the cleanup slot. He was used sparingly thereafter, and his first tour in the majors was unimpressive as he hit a mere .231 and committed 11 errors (.847) in 24 games at third base.

Back with Sacramento in 1919, Pinelli hit a modest .252 but stole 51 bases, 22 percent of the team's total. He also continued to display a combative attitude and hair-trigger temper. Angered when Rodgers docked him $50 for not playing him while recovering from a foot injury, Pinelli on August 1 badly beat the skipper in a closed-door clubhouse fight. Both men considered the incident a "family feud," and Babe got his money back.[7]

Acquired by the Detroit Tigers in 1920 to shore up their leaky infield, Pinelli displayed versatility by playing third base (74 games), shortstop (18), and second (1). He also revealed mastery of the hidden-ball trick, pulling it off twice in four days by catching Stuffy McInnis of the Boston Red Sox on June 19 and Sam Rice of the Washington Senators on June 22. His cockiness and resentment of the ethnic taunts directed to the second Italian-American in the league produced frequent "flare-ups," and a misinterpreted clubhouse comment led to a prolonged falling-out with Ty Cobb. Sold to Oakland after the season, he blamed, mistakenly, the Georgia Peach in the press for his departure; it was instead due to his hitting .229 with no home runs in 102 games.

Thanks to batting tips from teammate and former major leaguer Denney Wilie, Pinelli enjoyed a banner year with the Oaks in 1921, batting .339, scoring 127 runs, and pilfering 47 hassocks. But the "firecrackers" again threatened his career. On May 21 in Sacramento, ex-National League umpire Bill Byron, the so-called "Singing Umpire," ejected Babe for protesting a called strike. During the ensuing argument, Byron ripped off his mask, accidentally hitting Pinelli on the jaw. Babe forthwith punched "Lord Byron" in the eye, knocking him to the ground. When Byron (and Al Jolson who was in the stands) described Pinelli's action as "instinctive," PCL President William McCarthy imposed a $50 fine and a five-day suspension instead of banishment.[8]

The Cincinnati Reds then purchased Pinelli for $350,000 and three players to replace Heinie Groh in 1922. (Ever cocky, Babe returned his first contract for $10,500 unsigned, as he did each year of his major-league playing career.) On Opening Day against Grover Cleveland Alexander of the Chicago Cubs, he went 2-for-4 with a triple and stole a base; he also struck out twice with men on base and made "a serious error." In his first full major-league season, he led the league's third basemen in putouts (204), assists (350), and errors (32).

Don Larsen, Babe Pinelli, Yogi Berra. Undated photograph.

A fixture at third base during the next three seasons, Pinelli was part of the Reds' all-Bay Area infield with fellow San Franciscans Ike Caveney at short and Sammy Bohne at second and Oakland-born Lou Fonseca at first base. A good contact hitter with little power, he hit .305 in 1922, slipped to .277 in 1923, but rebounded in 1924 to enjoy his finest season hitting .306 with 70 RBIs, stealing 23 bases, posting a .956 fielding average — all personal bests in the majors — and again led third sackers in in putouts (182) and assists (318).

The "firecrackers" kept exploding as he admittedly had "no trouble finding trouble." Numerous fights with opponents stemmed from their resentment at his "bush-league" needling and use of the hidden-ball trick (he hid the ball in his right armpit), and Babe's "fist cocked" response to the bench-jockeying directed at the first Italian-American in the league.

The most ignominious incident occurred on July 25, 1926. Boston Braves coach Art Devlin and Pinelli had been jawing for weeks, and as the Reds left the field in the third inning, Babe recalled: "I bumped into Devlin on the coaching lines — and stepped all over his feet with my spikes. He howled like a coyote — and of, of course, started swinging."[9] One of the greatest bench-clearing brawls in baseball history ensued with order restored only by police intervention. Pinelli was ejected, fined $100, and sat out the next day's game because of a sore hand.

He also fought with teammates. His criticism of Rube Bressler led to a clubhouse fight, and Dolf Luque, also a hothead, chased after Pinelli once with a baseball bat and again with an ice pick. Another time Luque shouted: "We go outside. We get two taxicabs. You get in one, I get in one. We get guns. We go away. We fight duel."[10]

In 1924 Pinelli began thinking about umpiring as a way to stay in baseball. Unable to play in spring training because of injury, he volunteered to umpire an intrasquad game. He had always considered the umpire "as a necessary evil, possibly as a natural enemy," but confessed that "before the day was over, I'd changed my mind. The umpire was as necessary a part of baseball as the players."[11] Senior National League umpire Bill Klem and George Moriarty, the American League umpire who had been Babe's teammate in Detroit, encouraged his interest, but both advised him to learn to control his temper. In preparation for a post-playing career, he studied umpires, talked with them about their work, and continued to umpire intrasquad games. He also greatly reduced his umpire-baiting and was infrequently thumbed for arguing with an arbiter.

Babe's fielding and batting dropped off badly after 1925, and he became a utility player. In late June 1927 the Reds sold Pinelli, then hitting a paltry .197 in 30 games, to San Francisco for $17,500. He did not go quietly. Upon being told the news, he attempted to kill the messenger by charging after manager Jack Hendricks, who locked himself in his room while an irate Pinelli pounded on the door.

His major-league playing days were over. In eight seasons, Pinelli appeared in 774 games, batted .276, hit 5 homers, drove in 298 runs, and swiped 71 bases. A bit error-prone but with above-average range, he posted a good career .947 fielding average.

Pinelli flourished upon returning to the PCL. He hit .324 in 49 games for Nick Williams's Seals in 1927, and during next three years batted .310, .311, and .313 as San Francisco, led by the likes of Ike Boone, Smead Jolley, Lefty O'Doul, and Earl Sheely, pounded PCL pitching. He had learned to curb his fiery temper on the field, although a Seals teammate recalled: "When the fans would get on him at old Recreation Park, he had to be restrained from going into the stands after them."[12]

On July 4, 1929, Babe displayed fireworks of a different kind against the Seattle Indians at Recreation Park. Exploding for the best offensive game of his playing career, he went 6-for-6, hit three home runs

(two grand slams, one inside-the-park), and drove in 12 runs to tie the minor-league record. He said: "It wasn't that I'd improved as a hitter. I was stealing the signals of the Seattle catcher." Alertly noticing that Seattle's catcher, Charlie Borreani, held his glove straight up for fastballs and down in a scoop position for curves, Pinelli recalled he was "never fooled by a pitch."[13]

Released by the Seals in midseason 1931, Pinelli, then 35, signed with the Oakland Oaks. He hit .307 in 1932 but was released after the season due to declining fielding skills and an absence of power (no homers in 554 at-bats). During 10 PCL seasons he had batted a respectable .295, but hit only 13 homers. Babe went out on a low note: On September 30 he called umpire Forrest Cady a "blind bat" while arguing a strike call and was tossed from his final game. (Babe later said the umpire was Bill Burnside, but the box score lists Cady as the plate ump.)

An unceremonious departure as a player notwithstanding, Pinelli, armed with recommendations from sportswriters Tom Laird and Abe Kemp and several PCL club officials, after the season asked league President Hiland L. "Hi" Baggerly for a job as an umpire. Advised to get experience, Babe bought an umpiring outfit and during the winter and early spring worked college, semipro, and major-league exhibition games in the Bay Area. To the great surprise of many, he was hired in 1933 as a PCL umpire without any professional experience and despite a deserved reputation as a hothead. "I'll be a credit to you in a couple of months," Babe told Baggerly, and predicted: "I'll be with one of the major leagues inside of two years."[14]

Thus Pinelli began his professional umpiring career, as he had his professional playing career, in the Pacific Coast League, the "third major league." He worked in 1933 with veteran arbiter Perle Casey, who Pinelli thought was "the best at handling players I've ever seen." The consummate diplomat, Casey advised: "I don't want to see you get mad, Babe, until I do. When I burn up, you come over and cool me down." Once a two-fisted hothead, Pinelli learned an important lesson: "The toughest battle anyone can fight is the silent one he fights within himself."¹⁵ In 1934 he teamed with ex-major-league umpire Bill Guthrie, an aggressive arbiter who taught him how to take charge of ballgames.

The National League bought Pinelli's contract for $1,500, and in 1935 he became the first Italian-American hired as a regular umpire in the major leagues. Assigned to work with veterans Albert "Dolly" Stark and crew chief Charles "Cy" Rigler, he debuted at third base on April 16 in Boston as the Braves won the season opener, 4-2, over the New York Giants. Three days later he worked the plate for the first time, proving his mettle by twice calling third strikes on the legendary Babe Ruth and not backing down from the Bambino's beefing. Ruth complained: "There's forty thousand people in this park that know that was a ball, tomato-head!" Pinelli confidently replied: "Perhaps—but mine is the only opinion that counts."¹⁶

A dapper dresser, Pinelli soon became one of the most respected umpires in the senior circuit. Unlike his behavior as a player, his deportment as an umpire was even-handed and even-tempered. In an August 1955 *Sport* magazine article, "The Press Box Rates the Umpires," National League beat writers identified Pinelli as the arbiter who was "coolest in crisis" and "most cooperative with writers." Ironically, he enjoyed a better reputation with players and managers than with some umpires who felt he went too far in placating players and readily admitting wrong calls.

Nicknamed "The Soft Thumb" because of his reluctance to eject players and managers, perhaps because of his own feistiness, he averaged about three ejections per season during the heyday of Frankie Frisch's St. Louis Gas House Gang and Leo Durocher's Dodgers. Leo the Lip, a notorious umpire baiter, said "Pinelli never took me seriously. There were times when he knew I would be out there complaining, so he always stood there and let me have my say."¹⁷ Babe and Leo clashed a number of times, and on September 6, 1953, when Carl Furillo of the Dodgers and Durocher, then manager of the Giants, were grappling on the ground, Pinelli could be heard yelling: "Kill him, Carl, kill him!"¹⁸

During 22 years in the majors Pinelli, who became a crew chief in 1950, umpired four All-Star games (1937, 1941, 1950, 1956) and six World Series (1939, 1941, 1947, 1948, 1952, 1956), and called four no-hitters (Ed Head, 1946; Rex Barney, 1948; Jimmy Wilson, 1954; and Larsen).

He also umpired numerous historic games. Pinelli was at third base at Crosley Field in Cincinnati on May 24, 1935, for the first night game in major-league history, and at Forbes Field on June 4, 1940, for the first night game in Pittsburgh. He was at second base on October 5, 1941, when Mickey Owen of the Dodgers dropped the third strike on Tommy Henrich with two outs in the ninth inning, thereby sparking a game-winning Yankees rally, and on October 3, 1947, when Dodgers pinch-hitter Cookie Lavagetto doubled home two runs with two out in the bottom of the ninth to ruin Yankee Bill Bevens's no-hitter and give Brooklyn a 3-2 victory. Assigned in 1946 to the first playoff in National League history, he was the home-plate umpire for the second and concluding game of the Cardinals' sweep of the Dodgers. And on April 15, 1947, he was behind the plate at Ebbets Field when Jackie Robinson broke the color barrier with the Brooklyn Dodgers.

When St. Louis manager Eddie Stanky engaged in obvious stalling tactics hoping to reach the hometown curfew on July 18, 1954, Pinelli as crew chief demonstrated his courage and respect for the integrity of the game by awarding the game to the visiting Phillies—the last National League forfeit until August 10, 1995.

On May 8, 1948, at Sportsman's Park in St. Louis, a moment of umpiring irony occurred as Harry "The Cat" Brecheen of the Cardinals lost a perfect game when Johnny Blatnik, the Phillies' lone baserunner, was called safe on a bang-bang play at first—by Babe Pinelli.

As a former player, Pinelli appreciated the performances of outstanding players. From his perspective behind the plate, Stan Musial, Willie Mays, and Ted Kluszewski were the best hitters; Don Newcombe, Bob Friend, Robin Roberts, and Ewell Blackwell were the best pitchers. But Ty Cobb, he maintained, was the greatest player he ever saw.

Called "the Lou Gehrig of the umpires, our Iron Man" by Tom Gorman, Pinelli claimed he never missed a game in 22 seasons, a span of some 3,400 games. Luck preserved the skein on two occasions. On April 17, 1945, he was bedridden with the flu when rain washed out the season opener in Brooklyn. On June 28, 1941, Pinelli radioed Boston manager Casey Stengel that the boat his umpiring crew was taking from New York to Boston had become fogbound off Cape Cod; Babe, Al Barlick, and Lee Ballanfant arrived in the second inning and replaced the two players (Johnny Cooney and Freddie Fitzsimmons) chosen to call the game. Thereafter, whenever Stengel thought Pinelli missed a call, he'd shout: "You're still fogbound."[19]

Mae Pinelli never missed a game during Babe's playing career, but refused to watch him umpire regular-season games. She did, however, attend World Series games and root for the National League. Once, when asked if she ever got angry when people disputed Babe's decisions, she replied like an umpire's wife: "No, I don't get angry. I just figure, well, they saw it that way and Babe saw it right!"[20]

Babe Pinelli retired in 1956 after 22 years of callin' 'em with a pre-union pension of $187 a month. He and Mae moved from San Francisco to Sonoma County, and for several years Babe was a scout for the Cincinnati Reds. Reflecting upon his career, he said: "All told I was in baseball 40 [42] years, 16 [18] as a player. If I had to do it all over again, I'd concentrate on umpiring. It's the best job in baseball. You have no worries about streaks or slumps. You don't care who wins. I worried much more as a player than as an umpire."[21]

In 1953 Pinelli published with Joe King *Mr. Ump*, the first commercially published umpire's autobiography. He hoped the book, aimed at young teenagers, would "show youngsters interested in sports that their ambitions can be fulfilled regardless of obstacles."[22] Babe Pinelli, whose life was a testimonial to determination, died on October 22, 1984, at age 89 in a convalescent home in Daly City, California. He is buried in Holy Cross Cemetery in San Francisco

beside his beloved wife of 67 years, with whom he had two sons.

SOURCES

Portions of this essay are drawn from Larry R. Gerlach, "Ralph Arthur 'Babe' Pinelli" in David L. Porter, ed., *Biographical Dictionary of American Sports: 1992-1994 Supplement* (Westport, Connecticut: Greenwood Press, 1995), 168-169, and "Babe Pinelli: Mr. Ump" in Doug McWilliams, ed., *Northern California Baseball History* (Cleveland: Society for American Baseball Research, 1998), 43-45.

NOTES

1   *San Francisco Examiner*, October 23, 1984.

2   Tom Gorman, *Three and Two!* (New York: Charles Scribner's, 1979), 2.

3   *San Francisco Examiner*, October 24, 1984; Babe Pinelli, "I Umpired Baseball's Greatest Game," *This Week Magazine*, April 14, 1957: 45-47.

4   Unidentified newspaper clipping, Babe Pinelli file, National Baseball Library, Cooperstown, New York.

5   *San Francisco Examiner*, October 23, 1984.

6   Unidentified clipping, Pinelli file.

7   Babe Pinelli as told to Joe King, *Mr. Ump* (Philadelphia: Westminster Press, 1953), 42-44.

8   *Mr. Ump*, 45-49.

9   Unidentified clipping, Pinelli file.

10 *Mr. Ump*, 65-66.

11 *Mr. Ump*, 72.

12 *San Francisco Examiner*, October 25, 1984.

13 *San Francisco Examiner*, October 24, 1984.

14 . Unidentified clipping, Pinelli file.

15 *Mr. Ump*, 98.

16 Babe Pinelli, "Kill the Umpire? Don't Make Me Laugh!" *This Week Magazine*, April 7, 1957: 10, 12, 15-16, 17.

17 *The Sporting News*, November 5, 1984.

18 Carl Prince, *Brooklyn's Dodgers: The Bums, the Borough, and the Best of Baseball, 1947-1957* (New York: Oxford University Press, 1996), 45.

19 "Babe Pinelli" in John E. Spalding, *Pacific Coast League Stars, Vol. II* (Manhattan, Kansas: Ag Press, 1994), 70.

20 Unidentified clipping, Pinelli file.

21 Ibid.

22 *Mr. Ump*, endpaper comment.

Ernie Quigley
Arbiter Extraordinaire

By Larry R. Gerlach

Before the age of television, umpires worked in anonymity, only a handful of dominant personalities gaining widespread recognition. Among the virtually unknown arbiters is Ernest Cosmos Quigley, an outstanding and influential umpire who also was the greatest sports official in history. Indicative of how overlooked he has been is the fact that even a fairly comprehensive listing of Canadian-born major-league players, coaches, managers, and umpires, the latter including arbiters Jim McKean and Paul Runge, omits Quigley.[1]

For 31 years, 1913-1944, "Quig" served the National League with distinction as a field umpire, supervisor of officials, and public relations director. And for 26 of those years, he not only umpired major-league baseball, but also gained national prominence officiating major-college football and basketball, in all some 250 games a year. (It was then possible to combine major-league umpiring with officiating other sports because college schedules were more seasonal and limited in number—typically eight football and 18 basketball games in the 1920s.) In over 40 years of officiating, Quigley estimated working some 5,400 baseball, 1,500 basketball, and 400 football games logging 100,000 miles a year in coast-to-coast travel.[2] When baseball commissioner Kenesaw Mountain Landis wondered how his wife liked her husband being gone 325 nights a year, Quigley quipped: "Mrs. Quigley likes it fine. We're constantly getting reacquainted."[3]

Ernie was born on March 22, 1880, in Newcastle, New Brunswick, Canada, to Lawrence B. Quigley, an Irish immigrant, and Mary J. (Weir) Quigley, of Saint John, New Brunswick. His father, a salesman, sought greater opportunities by moving the family to Concordia, Kansas, in the 1880s. Quigley was an all-around athlete at the University of Kansas, but baseball was his favorite sport. He turned profes-sional in 1905 as a shortstop with Topeka in the newly formed Class-C Western Association. His professional career, which included occasional stints as a manager, took an abrupt turn in 1910 when, sidelined by a broken hand, he agreed to replace an umpire who had quit the Class-C Wisconsin-Illinois League. Quigley was a natural: Three years later he reached the major leagues.

A National League umpire for 26 years, he umpired 3,351 games, the seventh most in major-league history at the time. His career highlight was umpiring 38 games in six World Series including the infamous 1919 "Black Sox" series between Chicago and Cincinnati in which he worked home plate in Games Three and Seven. Shocked to learn that eight White Sox players had thrown the Series, Quigley said he "never saw a team try harder to win, and that they were beaten on the square by the superior strength of the Reds."[4] He was also behind the plate on June 1, 1923, when the New York Giants beat Philadelphia 22-8, setting a modern league record by scoring in all nine innings. He achieved another distinction when he and Charley Rigler in 1920 became the first National League umpires ever to "hold out" for more money before eventually signing their contracts.

Quigley experienced the physical dangers of umpiring home plate. On July 11, 1923, he was hospitalized for several days after being knocked unconscious by a foul ball to the left temple in the first game of a doubleheader. Cy Pfirman had to work the second game alone, making Quigley indirectly responsible for the last major-league game officiated by a single umpire.[5] In 1934 another foul ball hit him on the jaw; temporarily unable to speak, he had to communicate for days with pencil and paper. And in August 1934 he was overcome with heat exhaustion after the first game of a doubleheader in Philadelphia.

Sometimes Quigley just had a bad day. One such occurred while umpiring behind home plate in the 1935 World Series. In the fourth inning, while racing toward the Detroit dugout to track a foul popup, he "slipped in a puddle and was like to bust his neck falling into the Tigers dugout."[6] Another unfortunate occurrence came after a game at Wrigley Field in 1933, when Quigley suddenly collapsed unconscious in the umpire's dressing room. Taken to a hospital, he had not suffered a stroke as feared, but instead had been severely shocked after backing into an exposed electrical wire while exiting the shower. Contrary to doctor's orders, he returned to the diamond the next day.

As with all umpires, Quigley's decisions occasionally prompted arguments from players and managers as well as boos and even barrages of pop bottles from fans. On balance, however, he reportedly had good relations with players and managers owing to his diplomatic posture, decisiveness in upholding decisions, and total command of the rulebook. Casey Stengel thought him "a splendid man who knew all the rules."[7]

He repeatedly demonstrated knowledge of the most intricate applications of both playing and scoring rules and adamantly refused to tolerate verbal abuse. Instead of debating decisions, Quigley turned challengers away by sternly asking: "Now just what was it you said?" Continuing the discussion resulted in ejection from the game. He lost control once, early in his career on July 22, 1915, when he punched Johnny Evers, claiming that the Boston second baseman had stepped on his foot during an argument. Umpire and player were each fined $100.

Quigley enjoyed universal respect for his demeanor as well as his umpiring ability. At a time when players and managers like John McGraw were openly combative and profoundly profane, some umpires retaliated in kind with vulgarities and insults. Not Quigley, who had taught history, English, mathematics, and physical education at St. Mary's College in Kansas. Fred Lieb, the most prominent baseball writer of his day, who covered baseball for three New York City newspapers from 1909 to 1934, recalled that Quigley was "strictly high class" and "spoke with the diction and proficiency of a college professor." When McGraw once shouted, "Don't put on any airs with me," Quig replied: "One doesn't put on airs by speaking good English." To a player's uncomplimentary comment, he once responded: "Sarcasm, sir, is the weapon of the weak-minded." He enjoyed the respect of adversaries. He regarded Boston's Tony Boeckel, with whom he had numerous run-ins, as "the most pestiferous player in uniform," but when a serious illness sent Quigley to the hospital, Boeckel sent flowers.[8]

Quigley's contributions to umpiring extended abroad. After the 1928 season, the second most senior National League umpire to Bill Klem spent three months on an instructional mission to Japan with three recently retired ballplayers, including Ty Cobb. Treated "like royalty," he traveled throughout the country umpiring ballgames, lecturing, and conducting clinics, and even establishing schools for baseball umpires and basketball referees.

When Quigley retired at the end of the 1936 season, National League President Ford Frick appointed him the league's first supervisor of umpires. (The administrative appointment theoretically ended Quigley's on-field duties, but he returned to the diamond as a replacement umpire for several games in April and May 1937 and again in July and September 1938.) His duties as umpire-in-chief were to supervise the current umpire staff, review complaints of their decisions and performances, adjudicate fines levied for confrontations with umpires, and interpret rules for Frick and the teams. In this capacity Quigley's legendary knowledge of the rules was put to good use. Asked by Frick to facilitate the creation of a uniform code for both the major and minor leagues, he called senior circuit umpires to a three-day meeting to review "every word of every rule," posing questions about the formal rules as well as unusual situations and vague applications. The undisputed authority on baseball rules, he routinely received inquiries about interpretations from across the country and from as far away as Australia and Japan.

In December 1940 Ford Frick designated Quigley the league's first full-time director of public relations, a position he held until July 1944. The reassignment was both political and practical. The National League's Bill Klem, the most famous and respected major-league umpire, had retired in November 1940. When Tommy Connolly, Klem's famous counterpart in the American League, retired in 1931, he became major-league baseball's first umpire supervisor, so the National League followed suit by appointing Klem, "the King of Umpires," to the like position. Because Quigley had served concurrently as the voice of the league and umpire supervisor, the expansion of his public relations functions was apt. And in recognition of his skill in identifying new talent, he continued to be in charge of scouting for new umpires.

Ever the ambassador for sports, Quigley taught from 1938 to 1940 a summer-school course at Columbia University. To facilitate instruction on baseball rules in his course on Techniques and Mechanics of Umpiring, he invented Magnetic Baseball, a magnetized "blackboard" featuring the outline of a baseball diamond. By using a series of colored magnetized rings to represent players and umpires, he was able quickly and clearly to diagram positioning on various plays.[9] In the early 1940s, Quigley joined with fellow National League umpire Charley Moran, a former football player and coach, to publish "educational" pamphlets on "All phases of Foot Ball, Basket Ball and Base Ball."

No less significant was his public persona: The highly visible, personable, and outgoing Ernie Quigley did much to put a "human face" on umpires, thereby countering the conventional negative attitudes toward baseball's men in blue serge suits. It was commonplace for baseball players to endorse a variety of commercial products, but Quigley was the first sports official known to do so, pictured and identified as the umpire supervisor in a newspaper advertisement: "We solved the timing problems of baseball when we adopted Longines Watches for the use of all umpires."[10]

Sensitive to verbal abuse from fans and press coverage that called attention to controversies, umpires

Ernie Quigley.

typically were reticent and inconspicuous off the field. Quigley, however, relished the spotlight. He eagerly made a well-publicized appearance on a WEAF radio sports interview program in New York explaining how umpires dealt with difficult and unexpected situations, and regularly joined civic leaders at a variety of celebratory community affairs ranging from the annual Brooklyn Dodgers Knot-Hole Club fete to a joint Sportsmanship Brotherhood–New York City Baseball Federation dinner honoring Connie Mack, the 78-year-old owner-manager of the Philadelphia Athletics.[11] And he occasionally returned to the field as a celebrity umpire, as for the annual Army-Navy Day game at West Point and benefit games between teams from two New York military bases.[12] Perhaps his most effective outreach activity was the thrice-weekly evening radio program he hosted on station WIBW in Topeka for 17 years, from the late 1920s to the mid-1940s, talking about sports in general but mostly baseball, answering questions from listeners.

Although overshadowed in the minds of fans and historians by some of his more flamboyant contemporary National League umpires, Quigley's on-field reputation and administrative contributions following retirement testify to a long, distinguished, and influential career as a major-league umpire. In 1960, looking back over a half-century of covering baseball, Fred Lieb in his weekly column for *The Sporting News*, declared: "It is doubtful if any man ever had the rules of baseball, football and basketball at his finger tips as did Quigley. Unless it was Bill Klem, no National League umpire of his day commanded as much respect as did Quigley."[13]

The baseball diamond provided Quigley with his greatest officiating success, but football and basketball brought even more widespread recognition. For 40 years, 1904 to 1943, Quigley worked college football games, for most of his career serving as the referee, the head crew official. (He missed two seasons: 1928 because of the baseball trip to Japan and 1938 due to a severe ankle injury in September that kept him on crutches until the start of the 1939 baseball season.) He thought refereeing football was easier than umpiring baseball in one fundamental respect: Football players "usually vent their enthusiasm on their adversaries instead of taking it out on the officials."[14] Quigley was in demand for "big games" across the country including three Rose Bowls, and as with baseball, his command of football's rulebook was unrivaled; after retiring from the gridiron, he served as the ranking member of the NCAA Football Rules Committee from 1946 to 1954.

Quigley refereed college basketball from 1906 to 1942, rising to the top of basketball officialdom in the United States. In addition to a full slate of regional college games each year, he was selected to work premier national contests and officiated more national tournaments than any other referee. He was the second referee to be enshrined in the National Basketball Hall of Fame. Departing from the customary staid demeanor of sports officials, Quigley became the first flamboyant, "colorful" official, famous for exaggerated verbal and physical gestures as well an unorthodox behavior. To Quigley, the whistle was merely a device to announce a referee's presence. His trademark call became world renown. Upon detecting

a violation, Quigley pointed an accusing finger at the offending player and in a stentorian voice shouted: "YOU can't D-O-O-O that!"—a call invariably echoed by the spectators. His trademark call was so well known that in 1945 he received in Lawrence, Kansas, a letter from Europe addressed only as "You Can't Do That! U.S.A."[15]

His officiating career finally over, Quigley returned in 1944 to his alma mater, the University of Kansas, as the athletic director. He promptly retired the department's debt and launched a major resurgence in its athletics program by reinstituting five sports canceled during World War II and hiring superb coaches who elevated football, basketball, and track to championship levels. After he retired in 1950, the school's first baseball field, built in 1958, was named Quigley Field in his honor, the first and only ballpark named after an umpire.

Ernest C. Quigley underwent extensive cancer surgery in September 1958, and finally succumbed to the disease on December 10, 1960, age 81. He is interred in Mount Calvary Cemetery in Lawrence. Perhaps the best epitaph for the unique one-of-a-kind official came from his alma mater's student newspaper: "The most famous man in the field of sports."[16]

NOTES

1 William Humber, *Cheering for the Home Team: The Story of Baseball in Canada* (Erin, Ontario: Boston Mills Press, 1983), 149.

2 This essay is extracted with revisions from my comprehensive account of Quigley's career. See Larry R. Gerlach, "Ernie Quigley: An Official for All Seasons," *Kansas History* vol. 33, no. 4 (Winter 2010-2011): 218-239.

3 Ibid.

4 *The Sporting News*, October 7, 1920.

5 John Schwartz, "From One Ump to Two," *SABR Baseball Research Journal 2001*: 85-86.

6 *Chicago Daily News* and *New York World Telegram*, October 7, 1935.

7 Joseph Vecchione, ed., *The New York Times Book of Sports Legends* (New York: Simon & Schuster, 1992), 332.

8 *The Sporting News*, July 29, 1915; *New York Times*, January 9, 1927, December 5, 1929, and December 11, 1960.

9   "Magnetic Baseball á la Quigley," August 1941 press release, Ernie Quigley File, National Baseball Library, Cooperstown, New York. See also *New York Times*, July 30, August 3, and August 11, 1941; *Topeka Capital*, August 3, 1941.

10 *New York Times*, July 4, 1937; unidentified newspaper advertisement, September 29, 1940, Quigley File, National Baseball Library.

11 *New York Times*, July 31 and August 1, 1937; April 13 and 15, 1940; October 4, 1941.

12 *New York Times*, June 1 and 13, 1941.

13 *The Sporting News*, December 21, 1960.

14 *Sporting Life*, December 12, 1914.

15 University of Kansas Sports Bureau News Release, August 2, 1945. Ernest C. Quigley Collection, Spencer Research Library, University of Kansas, Lawrence, Kansas.

16 *University Daily Kansan*, December 12, 1960.

Beans Reardon

By Bob LeMoine

"When Mr. Reardon speaks you are under the impression that he has just spit out a hand grenade."

Harry A. Williams, *Los Angeles Times*[1]

Beans Reardon learned a lot about umpiring at the age of 16 when he worked as a riveter's assistant. "Riveting was good education for umpiring," he recalled. "If I didn't make the rivet hot enough the riveter would cuff me over the face with his leather glove and cuss me out. As a result, I was pretty good with those cuss words and rough work when I decided to try umpiring."[2]

The self-proclaimed "last of the cussin' umpires," Beans Reardon led a remarkable life both inside and outside of the baseball diamond. He was a small but scrappy Irish kid from the Boston area who learned never to back down from a fight. His grittiness carried him through the tough neighborhoods of Los Angeles and his days constructing boilers and swinging a pickaxe. He found his place in the sandlots around Los Angeles, where his tough but fair demeanor was discovered as the stuff umpires were made of. Reardon had a right arm that would call players out, or throw a fist when needed in the days when donnybrooks were common. With his distinctive polka-dot bow tie, he became one of the most visible and respected umpires over his 24-year National League career. Reardon also had cameo appearances in the early years of Hollywood, befriended celebrities, and was featured in a Norman Rockwell painting that placed him on the cover of the *Saturday Evening Post*. He left umpiring at an early age because he could make more money selling beer, but treasured his surplus of umpiring stories, which he was delighted to share for the rest of his life. He followed his own advice: "Hustle, be on top of plays, know the rules, and be honest with yourself."[3]

John Edward Reardon was born on November 23, 1897, in Taunton, Massachusetts, the son of William F. and Margaret (Ennis) Reardon. Both paternal and maternal grandparents had emigrated from Ireland. William Reardon was a dyer and foreman in a cotton mill, and the part-owner of a saloon. William was injured as a catcher in a 1910 semipro game when, not wearing a chest protector, was hit by a foul ball above his heart. His injuries led to his death from a "tumor of mediastinum" in 1913 when John was a child.[4] John's older brother, Bill, attended college, but John did not. "I never graduated from any place but grammar school. … I wasn't the best scholar who ever lived," Reardon said.[5]

Reardon learned his brute honesty from his mother, who impressed upon him not to tell a lie. "I've always been a little thickheaded and quick to tell somebody to go to hell. I got sent home from school one time for calling a nun an SOB. I don't know why I'm like that. Maybe I'm just honest," Reardon said.[6] At 14 he worked at the Reed & Barton silversmith shop in Taunton.[7] He loved baseball, but was undersized. "I had to stand twice in the same spot to make a shadow," he wisecracked.[8] He attended baseball games in Boston, and played for the Young Red Wings youth team in Taunton, which won the 1912 city championship. Squeaky, as he was called, played right field.[9] Reardon made up for his small size by being a solid, speedy fielder. He was not content playing in games with kids his own age, so he played on semipro teams when he was 15. Reardon's mother remarried and the family moved to Los Angeles when he was 16.[10] By the time he was 17, he had thrown his arm out, and from then on concentrated on being an umpire.[11]

"We lived in Boyle Heights, which was a pretty rough section of the city," Reardon said. "I went to work as a messenger boy, riding a bicycle. When I turned 18, I went to work as a boilermaker's apprentice in the Southern Pacific Railroad shops."[12] This neighborhood toughened Reardon even more for a future umpiring career. "It was on the East Side and there was a mixed population of Irish and Jews … and it was plenty tough. … You had to either fight or at least be willing to fight. If you didn't you'd just have to move, that's all."[13] He started umpiring games for his church team at St. Benedict's. Soon, he was umpiring in sandlots all over Los Angeles. He would umpire and play in the railroad league games held over the noon lunch break.[14] This was where he acquired his nickname of Beans.

"Whenever people asked me where I was from, I told them Boston because I figured nobody in California knew where Taunton was. So one day, when I came up to bat, Lee Allen, a fancy Pullman car painter, yelled, 'Come on, Baked Beans, old boy, hit one now!' The crowd picked it up, and from then on everybody called me Beans."[15]

Reardon was befriended by Harry Hammer, a blacksmith who was a catcher on a semipro team, and soon Reardon was traveling with the team, helping wherever needed. One Sunday in Pasadena, California, an umpire was needed. Hammer suggested Reardon, saying, "That kid can umpire." Reardon umpired the game, and then was offered a job umpiring every Sunday for $3 per game. Reardon demanded another quarter for carfare. "Every Sunday he'd put six half-dollars right in the middle of my locker, and I'd say, 'Another quarter,'" Reardon recalled. "I always had to battle him for the other quarter."[16]

Players often found Reardon jobs in the semipro leagues, saying, "Take care of the kid; the little SOB can umpire."[17] Eventually, he was making more money as an umpire than as a boilermaker. During World War I, Reardon went to the San Pedro shipyards as a boilermaker's apprentice, and also umpired games there. In 1918 he umpired in the War Service League for $7.50 per game, with an $11 outfit, his first umpire uniform.[18]

Reardon moved to Bisbee, Arizona, in 1919, being promised he could find umpiring jobs while working a "soft" job in the copper mines. "Soft job, hell!" he recalled. "They put me to work 'mucking' on a 'slope' 1,400 feet underground. We'd dig out the ore

with a pickaxe and shovel it into a big shaft close by. The boss told us to be careful not to step in that hole because it was 200 feet deep. It was damned hard work. … Had to string our lunches over a beam in the shaft to keep the rats from eating them. The rats were big as tomcats. … After three or four days I wondered what the hell I was doing there."[19] The Sporting News mentions Reardon umpiring in Bisbee for a weekend old-timers' league.[20] Reardon returned to Los Angeles shortly thereafter.

Reardon was umpiring a game in Pasadena involving the Los Angeles Angels of the Pacific Coast League. Angels manager Wade "Red" Killefer encouraged him to think about a career in umpiring. "You've got the ability and if you've got the courage, you don't need anything else," Killefer said.[21] They contacted Sammy Beer, a former Angels pitcher who was in Saskatoon, Saskatchewan. Beer found Reardon an umpiring job in the Class-B Western Canada League, making $250 a month plus expenses. "But that was better than swinging a 16-pound sledgehammer in the boiler shop 54 hours a week for 25 cents an hour."[22] Reardon was 22, and now a professional umpire. Reardon was extremely frugal, and saved $750 out of his total $1,000 salary for the four months. The league president asked him what he had been living on. Reardon winked and said, "On my good looks."[23]

Reardon's Calgary days were tough, with few amenities. "You had to dress in the groundkeeper's shack, where he kept his equipment," he recalled. "There was no shower, either. You just put your good clothes on over the dirt and sweat till you got back to the hotel. … In my day, you got no cab money. You had to wrestle your bag on a streetcar, dress in a shack that looked like an outhouse, umpire yourself with probably only a six-inch flag as a foul marker 450 feet from the plate."[24] There was also the rowdiness of the fans who "would follow you down the street and yell at you. … I had several street fights because I couldn't tolerate the names they were calling me."[25]

"You didn't have enough money for food, so you just hustled, that's all," Reardon said. "I stayed in a place in Moose Jaw across the street from the railroad

Boston Braves coach Casey Stengel arguing with umpire Beans Reardon in 1941 at Ebbets Field. Reardon called out Buddy Hassett at home plate standing up. Casey claimed Hassett had not been tagged. Reardon won the argument.

station; had to run down the hallway to the bathroom. Umpires didn't get enough money in those leagues to rent a place with a toilet in your room. ... You had to be tough to survive."[26] Because many umpires quit after just a few games, Reardon's fare home was guaranteed only if he lasted the entire season. After one game, policemen offered to escort him through a back way in the park to avoid the ferocious fans waiting for him at the gate. Reardon rejected the offer, saying, "I didn't sneak in, and I won't sneak out."[27] "I came in the front gate and that's the way I'm going out, and if one of those fresh thugs makes a move at me, I'll flatten him. If you want to come with me, all right. But I don't need you," Reardon told the gendarmes.[28]

Reardon never backed down from a fight. Back in California, he umpired a Winter League game on November 21, 1920, between the Los Angeles White Sox and an all-star team. "Umpire Beans Reardon put down a slight demonstration of Bolshevism in the

first of the sixth inning, when he called Boeckel out at the plate on Moore's throw to Ray," the *Los Angeles Times* reported. "Irish Meusel dissented, whereupon Beans pulled off his mask and chest protector and did a Jack Dempsey that made Irish wince with envy. About 25 cops intervened and pressed all the bellicose disposition out of both Meusel and Reardon and the game went merrily on."[29]

Reardon returned to Canada in 1921, and met New York Yankees scout Bob Connery, who was traveling through Canada looking for prospects. Connery recommended Reardon to PCL President William H. McCarthy, who hired him in 1922, telling him, "Now, I'm going to tell you something, Beans. We want umpires in this league, we don't want fighters."[30] Reardon did have a fistfight in San Francisco with player Paddy Siglin,[31] and newspapers carried pictures of the encounter. He also fought with manager Charlie Pick of Sacramento, who, after Reardon had thrown a player out, "came charging out of the dugout after me," Reardon recalled. "He threw a punch at me, but I was ready for him and we tangled. ... It was a better fight than many a one I've paid money to see since. We both got in some pretty good licks."[32] "Yes, I had a reputation as a fighter. But I really wasn't a fighter. I had some fights, but I didn't enjoy them. They just couldn't be avoided."[33]

In Portland, Oregon, fans would regularly throw seat cushions at Reardon at the end of the game. When asked if they ever threw the cushions before the game, Reardon joked, "Naw. Those fans up there wouldn't throw away a cushion they paid a nickel for until they had gotten their money's worth out of it."[34]

Reardon befriended major-league umpire Hank O'Day, and they would travel to the racetrack in Tijuana, Mexico, on Sundays in Reardon's Hudson Speedster. O'Day recommended Reardon to National League President John Heydler, and Beans was hired in November of 1925, after four years in the PCL.[35] Heydler warned him to never be in any fights. Reardon objected, saying that being about 5-feet-6 and 130 pounds, you have to be prepared. Heydler responded, "Okay, but promise me you won't throw the first punch."[36]

At the train station on April 9, 1926, Reardon waved to the crowd that came to see him off. "I'll sure do my darnedest to make good back there," he yelled. The train was heading to St. Louis, and Reardon's major-league umpiring career had begun.[37]

"Reardon has curly brown hair, blue eyes, and a square cut chin. He speaks with a nasal twang, which is his birthright. He comes from Massachusetts—from Taunton," wrote Damon Runyon.[38] Reardon's career could have ended early when a play in Pittsburgh led to Brooklyn's Chick Fewster having some unkind words for him. The umpire spun him around and would have hit him if Rabbit Maranville hadn't grabbed his arm. "Rab probably saved my job," Reardon gratefully acknowledged.[39] On a return trip to Boston, a delegation from Taunton came to Braves Field to welcome "Squeaky" home, including Mayor Andrew J. McGraw, Police Chief John P. Duffy, and former teammates from the Young Red Wings, who made a presentation on "Reardon Day."[40]

One memorable game in Reardon's rookie year occurred on August 15, 1926. Brooklyn loaded the bases when Babe Herman hit a fly ball off the fence in right field. One run scored, but runners Dazzy Vance, Chick Fewster, and Herman all wound up on third base. "Damn it, wait a minute. I got to figure this out," Reardon yelled. He awarded the base to Vance and called Fewster and Herman out. "That's it. The side's out. Let's play ball, fellas." Herman doubled into a double play.[41]

Reardon never got along with Bill Klem, chief of the National League umpires. He disregarded Klem's order for NL umpires to wear a chest protector under their coat. Reardon wore the outside inflated protector used by American League umpires. Reardon said he promised his mother he would never get hurt or suffer an injury due to a lack of protection.[42] National League umpires were also asked to wear a four-in-hand tie, but Reardon wore a blue and white polka-dot bow tie for his entire career.[43]

In 1927 Reardon had a cameo in the MGM silent film *Slide, Kelly, Slide*, along with players Bob Meusel and Tony Lazzeri.[44] In 1928 he was cast as an umpire in the Richard Dix film *Warming Up*, which included several major leaguers. *Warming Up* was Paramount's first film with sound. In the transition between silent films and talkies, production companies were experimenting with synchronizing sound into the film. While there was no dialogue in the film, post-production editing added the crack of the bat and the roar of the crowd to the action on the field.[45] This film is in the category of "goat-gland films."[46] No copy of the film is known to exist.

In August 1929 Reardon had surgery for appendicitis. Under spinal anesthesia, he was able to watch the operation as it took place. Before it concluded, Reardon wisecracked, "Doc, you'd better take a good look around in there and if you see anything else I don't need, take it out, too."[47] Reardon missed the rest of the season and a chance to umpire in the 1929 World Series.[48] He recovered, and got married in Los Angeles on November 23, 1929, to Marie Lillian Schofield.[49] The couple settled in Los Angeles.[50]

Reardon umpired in the 1930 World Series, and considered it his biggest thrill in baseball. It was the first World Series he had ever seen, and he wore the commemorative ring for the rest of his life.[51] He joined a group of major leaguers in a tour of Japan in October of 1931.[52] "No Japanese player ever talks back, none ever disputes a decision and not even the spectators razz the umpire," he said.[53] Reardon lost 10 pounds, however, not stomaching the raw fish and eels.[54]

Reardon umpired the 1934 World Series as "a man with the poise of a Supreme Court judge. ... He will jerk his thumb with the austere finality of a Nero."[55] He felt anxiety before a World Series game. "I don't say I never called a wrong one—maybe plenty of 'em wrong. But I'd hate to call one in the Series when so much is riding on every pitch and every slide. ... The night before the big game always gives me the jitters."[56] Reardon was umpiring first base in Game Seven when Ducky Medwick's hard slide into Marv Owen at third base led to a brawl and fans throwing debris on the field. Commissioner Kenesaw Mountain Landis removed Medwick from the game.

Reardon was also remembered for his wit and humor. Philadelphia Phillies manager Jimmie Wilson argued with him on a caught-stealing call, yelling, "You know something, Beans. There are fifty thousand people in the ballpark and you're the only SOB who thinks he's out." Reardon replied, "Yes, but I'm the only SOB who counts." Wilson returned to the dugout laughing.[57] A disgusted Hack Wilson once threw his bat up into the air after striking out. "If that bat comes down, Hack, you're outta the game," Reardon bellowed.[58] National League players often referred to Reardon as having "rabbit ears," claiming that you could whisper something at the Polo Grounds in New York and he would hear it while working a game in Boston.[59] Casey Stengel was managing in Boston and took exception to Reardon's ball-and-strike calls. Making his way up two of the three dugout steps, Stengel debated whether to come out and argue. Reardon warned him to stay right where he was. Finally, Stengel remarked, "I quit. You're the only bloke I've ever seen who can umpire and argue at the same time."[60]

Reardon was being accosted by a loudmouth fan one day, and looked into the crowd to identify him. As fate would have it, the fan was Reardon's waiter at a restaurant that night. He sheepishly took his order, and was extremely courteous to the umpire. Reardon asked the man why he, a total stranger, had been called such terrible names. "Well," the fan muttered, "I am an old man and I have slaved all my life. My bunions burn my feet. I am browbeat 12 hours a day. The chef curses me at one end; the customers throw scorched eggs in my face at the other. I go crazy. My only relief is to go to the ballpark and holler at you."[61]

Reardon's reputation for a no-nonsense, profanity-laced style became legendary. A player once asked NL President Ford Frick, "Mr. Frick, a ballplayer gets fined $50 for swearing at an umpire, right?" Ford concurred, and when the player said Reardon had sworn at *him*, Frick remarked, "Don't be mad. Consider it a compliment. That's like having anyone else say 'hello' to you."[62]

Reardon enjoyed the conflicts. "I never liked to toss 'em out of the game. If I had, there wouldn't have been anybody left to cuss at."[63] "If a player swore at me, I'd swear back at him. It was either that or

chase him out of the game. And if I did that, I had to make out a report, and I'd rather leave him in."[64] Bob Broeg wrote in *The Sporting News* that Reardon would "rather exchange sulphuric insults than pull his rank. Reardon's four-letter forensics were never more eloquent than when he and Frank Frisch were raising their penetrating pipes in cheek-to-jowl arguments which were classical."[65] Frisch was once ejected by Reardon and fined $50. Later that night, Frisch phoned Reardon and invited him to the bar. Reardon recalled, "It not only cost him $50 and five rounds of beer, but I borrowed his car for the evening and then told him to phone the garage and tell 'em to fill 'er up."[66]

Reardon appeared in the 1935 Mae West film *Goin' to Town*,[67] and also received $50 a day "as technical advisor when they were shooting baseball films."[68]

Fans in Cincinnati showered Reardon with pop bottles after he made a call against the home team on July 17, 1935. "The shower of glassware from the right field pavillion furnished the most exciting interlude in the long game which was marked by much bickering on both sides. The missiles were aimed at Umpire Beans Reardon because of his ruling in the seventh inning…" wrote the Associated Press.[69] NL President Ford Frick fined umpires Reardon and John "Ziggy" Sears for inciting the crowd.[70]

Still, Reardon was grateful he hadn't been working in the copper mines all those years. "Pretty soft job you have at that, Beans," someone yelled to him on the New York subway. "Yeah!" Reardon hollered back. "Let 'em yell at me for two hours every day, and I have the rest of the time to myself."[71]

Reardon was behind the plate for Babe Ruth's "last hurrah" on May 25, 1935, when the Bambino, now with the Boston Braves, hit his final three home runs in a game at Pittsburgh. He also ejected Ruth in 1938, when he was coaching at first base for Brooklyn.[72]

Reardon would attend horse-racing events at Santa Anita, California, with celebrity friend Al Jolson, who could rarely match Reardon's knack for betting on the photo-finish winner. "I love to bet on what the photo will show on a photo-finish horse race," Reardon boasted. "I'll give any odds to any takers. But I don't get many takers. Guess people know I spent a lot of years calling quick decisions on fast action. … I can pick the winner by a whisker!"[73] However, Commissioner Kenesaw Mountain Landis prohibited Reardon from gambling.

Reardon stayed busy in the 1935 offseason. "Now I had two weeks' work with Mae West on that new one that's coming out, *Klondike Lou*, or something like that. I had another two weeks in that grand opera thing with Gladys Swarthout and Jan Kiepura, acting like a stagehand or an electrician. It was easy for me."[74] The Mae West feature was eventually titled *Klondike Annie*, and also included an appearance by Jim Thorpe.[75]

"You would have been a fine asset to baseball if you had stayed in the movies," Brooklyn manager Casey Stengel remarked to Reardon in 1936.[76]

Reardon suffered two sunstrokes during the 1936 season, and was ordered by doctors to take the rest of the year off. "I wasn't feeling very good about it," he remembered, "until I saw the paper the next day. There I read that the same day I collapsed a camel of Barnum and Bailey's circus passed out while they were taking it to a train. … It died two days later. I knew then that if the heat killed off a camel, maybe I could take it better than I thought."[77]

Reardon appeared in the 1937 film *Internes Can't Take Money*, starring Barbara Stanwyck and Joel McCrea.[78]

Apparently Reardon was also a landlord in the Los Angeles area; *The Sporting News* wrote that tenants of his apartment building were suffering from the unusually cold winter and "have demanded that Beans install bathtubs before another winter rolls around. They say they have no place to store their coal."[79]

Reardon umpired in the 1943 World Series. On a train trip from New York to St. Louis, a thief reached under the pillow on his Pullman berth and swiped his wallet, containing $300. Reardon saw the intruder slipping away and cornered him, leading to a scuffle in which he sprained his finger, but got his wallet back. The man locked himself into a lavatory, and then jumped out a window while the train sped along. "I had a heck of a time," Reardon recalled. "I was trying to get my money back and hold up my pajamas at the same time."[80]

In late 1944 Reardon joined a USO baseball tour to the South Pacific to entertain servicemen in World War II. "We'd put in 16 hours a day talking baseball to servicemen and answering questions. They just couldn't get enough," Reardon said. He stole the show with his tales of umpiring.[81] He returned in January of 1945 and traveled to Chicago to speak to owners of major war plants in the city.[82] "Before I started on the trip (to the Pacific) I thought I was tough," Reardon told his audience. "Now I know I'm not tough at all. How anybody can think he is tough, after seeing what those kids in the South Pacific are going through every day, stops me. I have seen kids without eyes, without arms, without legs—and without life. Just looking in on their courage makes me blush that I ever thought I was tough, but mighty proud that I was born in the same country from which they sprang."[83]

Reardon was an alternate umpire for the 1946 World Series, which paid him $750 plus expenses. He arrived mere moments before Game Six in St. Louis as his train was either delayed or broke down (according to two different reports) and he took a 100-mile cab ride from Effingham, Illinois, which cost him $25.[84]

Reardon loved to have a good beer, and would walk out of a bar if they didn't have Budweiser. His brand loyalty led to a second career for him. Budweiser offered him a job making advertisements and sharing his baseball stories in talks. In 1946, Reardon bought the Budweiser distributorship in Long Beach, California.[85]

On July 20, 1947, at Ebbets Field in Brooklyn, St. Louis led Brooklyn 2-0 entering the ninth inning. Ron Northey of the Cardinals hit a long fly ball to center field that hit the top of the wall. As Northey approached third base, Reardon signaled home run, which slowed Northey's pace and led to his being thrown out at the plate. The Cardinals protested the game, claiming deception by Reardon.[86] Brooklyn scored three in the bottom of the ninth to win the game, 3-2, but NL President Frick ruled the game a tie, despite the fact there was only one out recorded in the bottom of the ninth, "in the name of common sense and sportsmanship." Brooklyn won the makeup game on August 18.[87]

A fight broke out on Opening Day in Cincinnati, April 19, 1948, after a play at second base. A fan tussled with Reardon, while fellow umpire Jocko Conlan wrestled with a photographer.[88] In October of 1948, Reardon's souvenir warehouse was robbed — the burglar stealing five autographed baseballs. "The only baseballs they didn't take were the ones with my autograph," he reported.[89]

Also in 1948 a photographer appeared at Ebbets Field and took pictures of Reardon and fellow umpires Larry Goetz and Lou Jorda, as well as Brooklyn coach Clyde Sukeforth and Pittsburgh manager Bill Meyer. These were reference photographs Norman Rockwell would use to paint the cover of the *Saturday Evening Post* for April 23, 1949.[90] The painting, named *Tough Call, Game Called Because of Rain*, or *Bottom of the Sixth Inning*, depicts three umpires eyeing the rainfall. Lauren Applebaum writes, "Rockwell pays tribute to baseball's uncelebrated heroes, the umpires, who dwarf the ballplayers during a game. …"[91] Reardon stands in the center, holding his chest protector and mask in one hand, and holding his other hand palm-up, catching raindrops.

In July of 1949, Marie Reardon was robbed in their home in Long Beach, California. She was bound and gagged in a closet while the robbers made off with $4,200 in jewelry. She was able to keep her wedding band when she pleaded, "It has never been off my finger."[92]

The 1949 season was Reardon's last as an umpire and he would now devote himself totally to his beer distributorship. "I'm getting out of umpiring. … Umpiring is a good job and I'd do it again if I had my life to live over. I have to get up at 7 A.M. to take care of my business here. When I'm umpiring, I get out of bed at 10 A.M. and work a couple of hours a day. You can't beat those hours. And my salary comes in five figures."[93] Reardon retired after the 1949 World Series, but umpired at the Latin Olympics in Guatemala in late 1949 and some spring training games in the spring of 1950.[94]

Reardon appeared on NBC Radio in an episode of Ralph Edwards' *This Is Your Life* on April 19, 1950.[95] In his post-umpiring years he also wrote a column called "The Umpire" for the Newspaper Enterprise Association, which was carried in newspapers across the country. The Q&A style included random baseball trivia and umpiring questions sent in by readers.[96]

Marie Reardon died of a heart attack on March 9, 1953, at the age of 57. The couple had no children, but Marie had a grown son, Stanley Schofield, from a previous marriage.[97] Reardon continued to run his beer-distribution business, which was reported to be profiting $2 million yearly in 1953.[98] On July 31, 1953, Twentieth Century-Fox Films released the motion picture *The Kid From Left Field*," starring Dan Dailey and Anne Bancroft. Reardon portrayed an umpire.[99]

On June 28, 1954, Reardon married Nell Eugenia Schooler, who owned an aluminum-window business that provided windows for the United Nations building. She was an avid painter who had studied art in the Netherlands, and she painted a portrait of Nancy Reagan that hung in the White House.[100] Along with her paintings, the Reardons' den included Beans' whiskbroom, polka-dot bow ties, the Rockwell painting, and pictures with Gary Cooper and other movie stars. There was also a large picture of a nude Mae West. "She always sent him a copy of that picture every Christmas," Eugenia said. "No, I was never jealous."[101]

Reardon appeared on the November 14, 1954, episode of *The Jack Benny Show* entitled "The Giant Mutiny." The episode was a spoof on *The Caine Mutiny* and also included baseball managers Leo Durocher, Fred Haney, and Chuck Dressen, and pitcher Bob Lemon.[102] Reardon sponsored a youth baseball team in the Long Beach Police League called the "Little Beans."[103] He sold the Budweiser distributorship in 1967 to Frank Sinatra for around $1 million but continued to work for Budweiser, making speaking appearances around the country. "Everyplace I go I run into someone I've known in baseball," Reardon said.[104]

One of his stories involved the time he called baserunner Granny Hamner safe, but inadvertently gave the out sign. He asked Hamner if he had heard him call safe, and Hamner said yes. "I know," Reardon told him, "but only you and the second baseman heard it and 8,000 people saw me call you out. Granny, it's 8,000 to 3, and you're out." Another favorite story included a baserunning blunder by Tommy Henrich, who was tagged out. Henrich asked Reardon to let him stand there pointing his finger at the ump for a couple of minutes so fans would boo Reardon and forget Henrich's boneheaded play.[105]

Eugenia Reardon traveled with her husband, calling on customers at the local taverns. "The people loved to see Beans," she recalled. "He never tired of going out. He loved to talk. He was very witty about this funny business called baseball."[106] Beans and Eugenia frequently attended Dodgers and Angels home games. The Reardons loved art, and would often visit Paris, Eugenia's birthplace, and she would point out historic buildings to him. The very vocal Reardon would be humbled watching his favorite artist. "He'd come out and sit three or four hours in the studio and watch me paint. He never talked at all, just watched me," Eugenia fondly remembered.[107]

In 1970 Reardon was presented the Bill Klem Award for meritorious service to baseball. In response he said, "I'm very glad to receive the Klem Award, but I'll tell you the truth. Klem hated my guts and I hated his."[108] Reardon also sent a get-well card to old nemesis Frankie Frisch, who was hospitalized after a car accident. "When you get prayers from the bottom of the cold heart of an umpire, you should have quick results and a speedy recovery," Reardon wrote.[109]

Reardon died on July 31, 1984, at the age of 86, at his home in Long Beach, after suffering from arteriosclerosis and two strokes. He is buried with his first wife, Marie, at Calvary Cemetery in Los Angeles. While he has never been inducted into the Baseball Hall of Fame, there is a part of him there. "I loved my little blue and white polka-dot bow tie," Reardon said. "That tie is more famous than I am; it's in the Hall of Fame."[110]

That tie could tell a lot of stories, too.

SOURCES

Besides the references cited in the Notes, the author consulted the following sources:

Ancestry.com

Beans Reardon file at the Baseball Hall of Fame, Cooperstown, New York.

Familysearch.org

Gerlach, Larry R. "Reardon, John Edward 'Jack,' 'Beans,'" in David L. Porter, ed., *Biographical Dictionary of American Sports: Q-Z* (Westport, Connecticut: Greenwood Press, 2000), 1257-1258.

NOTES

1   Harry A. Williams, "Bengals Belt Bees Blithely," *Los Angeles Times*, September 25, 1921: 19.

2   J.G. Taylor Spink, "Beans Calls Himself Out as Umpire," *The Sporting News*, October 12, 1949: 8.

3   Frank Graham, "Beans—the Vet Bluecoat Who Never Grew Up," *The Sporting News*, December 20, 1945: 2.

4   Tom Wall, *Augusta Chronicle*, May 16, 1941, notes that this information was contained in a Cincinnati baseball publication.

5   Larry R. Gerlach, *The Men in Blue: Conversations With Umpires* (New York: Viking Press, 1980), 4.

6   Ibid.

7   Gerlach, 23. The Reed & Barton silversmith shop began in Taunton in 1824. Taunton was nicknamed the Silver City because of its many silver-industry businesses. Reed & Barton, the last remaining silversmith company in Taunton, filed for Chapter 11 Bankruptcy in February of 2015. Charles Winokoor, "Silver City No More? Taunton's Reed & Barton Files for Bankruptcy," *Taunton Gazette*, February 19, 2015, tauntongazette.com/article/20150219/NEWS/150216074/13406/NEWS/?Start=1. Retrieved April 1, 2015.

8   Gerlach, 5.

9   Kerry Keene, "Taunton Native Donned Ump's Mask in Majors for 24 Years," *Taunton Gazette*, May 21, 1994: 7.

10 Some accounts say age 14 or 15. Reardon stated 16.

11 Graham.

12 Gerlach, 5.

13 Jack Diamond, "Play 'Em Safe, Call 'Em Safe, Says 'Beans,'" *San Francisco Chronicle*, January 14, 1936: 21.

14 Ibid.

15 Gerlach, 5.

16 Gerlach, 6.

17 Ibid.

18 Ralph S. Davis, "Reardon Became Ump, Without Being Player," article of unknown origin dated April 21, 1932, in Reardon's Hall

of Fame file; "Beans' First Job Behind Plate Paid Him Just $3," *The Sporting News*, October 12, 1949: 8.

19 Gerlach, 6.

20 Edgar Munzel, "25 Years Lower Beans' Boiling Point," *The Sporting News*, August 31, 1944: 7.

21 Gerlach, 6-7.

22 Gerlach, 7.

23 Spink.

24 Munzel.

25 Ibid.

26 Gerlach, 7.

27 Gerlach, 8.

28 Graham,

29 Ed O'Malley, "Walter Mails Gets Jarring," *Los Angeles Times*, November 22, 1920: 119.

30 Gerlach, 8.

31 "Paddy Siglin Loses to 'Beans' Reardon," *Los Angeles Times*, August 19, 1922: 112.

32 Munzel.

33 Gerlach, 9.

34 "Baseball Pick-Ups Gathered From Hither and Thither," *Los Angeles Times*, November 30, 1924: A6.

35 " 'Beans' Reardon Goes to National League," *Los Angeles Times*, November 6, 1925: B1.

36 Gerlach, 9. Reardon's *Sporting News* umpire card on the Retrosheet website lists him as 5-feet-9 and 190 pounds. Other sources, including Baseball-Reference.com, and the Internet Movie Database list him as 6 feet tall.

37 "Gene Tunney Arrives; Dempsey's Challenger Blows in as Kearns, Dorval, and 'Beans' Reardon Pull Out for East," *Los Angeles Times*, April 10, 1926: 11.

38 Damon Runyon, "Runyon Says," International Feature Service, in the *Harrisburg Evening News*, April 29, 1926: 19.

39 Gerlach, 9.

40 "Taunton Fans Coming Tomorrow to Do Honor to Reardon, Umpire in National League," article of unknown origin dated May 26 in Reardon's Hall of Fame file. The Braves hosted the Giants on May 28, 1926, in Reardon's first year, and he is listed in the box scores as umpiring that series.

41 Gerlach, 21; "Three Men on Third," research.sabr.org/journals/online/39-brj-1977/197-three-men-on-third.

42 Michael Gavin, "Wind Bags Again Vogue With NL Umps," *Boston Record American*, August 31, 1952, 18.

43 Associated Press, "Reardon to Retire as Umpire," *The Advocate* (Baton Rouge, Louisiana), October 4, 1949: 14.

44 Dan Thomas, "Big League Players in Hollywood," *Springfield (Missouri) Leader*, January 30, 1927: 28.

45 "Paramount's First Sound Film: A Newspaper Picture," *New York Times*, July 22, 1928: 93. Richard Dix, the male lead, portrayed Bert Tulliver, a baseball pitcher who tries out for the Yankees. He doesn't win a job in spring training, and endures the wrath of the team's star hitter and villain. He works at a carnival and draws the attention of Mary Post, daughter of the Yankees' owner, portrayed by Jean Arthur. She gets him another tryout with the Yankees, and he winds up in the "world's series." When the Yankees' starting pitcher is injured, Tulliver comes on to pitch, predictably with the bases loaded and no outs. Tulliver is also distressed in believing Mary will wed someone else. But then Mary nods to Tulliver that she will marry him, which is all the motivation he needs to strike out the side, the last of which was the villain who was now playing for Pittsburgh. Tulliver was the hero and Reardon was the home-plate umpire who called the villain out on strikes. The reviewer for the *New York Times*, however, was not impressed. "Paramount's first synchronized picture—'Warming Up'—appears to have been done in a little too much of a hurry. The synchronization is faulty in spots, the acting is not particularly good, and the plot reads like a success story from one of the lesser magazines." Another review from the *New York Times* concluded, "The synchronizing is such, however, that the smack of a ball against a bat is heard some time before Lucas (the pitcher) has finished winding up. ... There is plenty of noise in the exciting parts, and music when it isn't so exciting." ("The Screen: The Great American Game," *New York Times*, July 16, 1928: 27).

46 Goat-gland films were attempts to add sound to already completed silent films. The term came from a surgical technique developed by John R. Brinkley in which he transplanted testicles from male goats into men suffering from low libido. Movie critics used the term for describing desperate attempts to bring new life into dead films. Despite the poor review, *Warming Up* was popular with the public, and New York's Paramount Theater broke existing house records. See "Grift, Goats, and Gonads: Historians Ponder the Colorful Career of John Brinkley, American Quack," *The Chronicle of Higher Education* No. 16 (2002), accessed March 13, 2015; Debra Ann Pawlak, *Bringing Up Oscar: The Story of the Men and Women Who Founded the Academy* (New York: Pegasus Books), 2011, Anthony Slide, *Silent Topics: Essays on Undocumented Areas of Silent Film* (Lanham, Maryland: Scarecrow Press (2005), 79.

47 From an article of unknown origin in Reardon's Hall of Fame file.

48 "Umpire 'Beans' Reardon Must Go Under Knife," *Boston Herald*, August 11, 1929: 13; "Augie Walsh Sold to Chicago," *Los Angeles Times*, September 14, 1929: 9.

49 "Did You Know That," *State Times Advocate* (Baton Rouge, Louisiana), December 7, 1929: 10.

50 "Umpire Reardon Weds Coast Girl," article of unknown origin in Reardon's Hall of Fame file.

51   Keene.

52   "1931 Tour of Japan," vintageball.com/1931Tour.html, retrieved April 12, 2015.

53   Japan Umpire's Eden, Says 'Beans' Reardon," *Evening Tribune*, San Diego, January 6, 1932: 16.

54   L.H. Gregory, "Gregory's Sports Gossip," *The Oregonian* (Portland, Oregon), January 6, 1932: 18.

55   Henry McLemore, United Press, "Night Before the Series Plain Hell on the Umps," *Omaha World Herald*, October 3, 1934: 18.

56   McLemore, 19.

57   Gerlach, 17.

58   Bob Broeg, "Beans Reardon Makes Himself Heard," *The Sporting News*, February 17, 1973: 40.

59   *Boston Herald*, May 21, 1931: 29.

60   Newspaper Enterprise Association, "Interference of Owners Blamed for Poor Umpiring," *Daily Illinois State Journal* (Springfield, Illinois), October 4, 1953: 21.

61   Jimmy Powers, "Rassle Riots Beneficial," *Omaha World Herald*, October 17, 1934: 13.

62   Newspaper Enterprise Association, "Reardon Still the Ump," *State Times Advocate* (Baton Rouge, Louisiana), May 18, 1967: 39.

63   Newspaper Enterprise Association, "Interference of Owners Blamed for Poor Umpiring," *Daily Illinois State Journal* (Springfield, Illinois), October 4, 1953: 21.

64   Jeane Hoffman, "Reardon Was Cussinest Ump in National Loop," *Los Angeles Times*, May 3, 1957: C3.

65   Broeg, "Beans Reardon Makes Himself Heard," 40.

66   Ibid.

67   " 'Beans' in West Film," *San Diego Union*, January 20, 1935: 32.

68   "Umps Reardon in Movies," *Richmond Times Dispatch*, May 26, 1935: 22.

69   "Fans Throw Pop Bottles as Giants Defeat Redlegs: Umpire Angers Paying Guests," *Lexington* (Kentucky) *Herald*, July 18, 1935: 6.

70   "Umpires Given Fines by League President for Cincinnati Row," *Greensboro* (North Carolina) *Daily News*, August 24, 1935: 10; Wilbur Fogleman, "On the Rebound," *Riverside* (California) *Daily Press*, July 30, 1935: 11. Reardon challenged "the grandstand, bleachers and box-seat holders to come out collectively or in a single line of march to face him following that pop bottle shower…"

71   Harold Parrott, "Beans on the Pan!" *Brooklyn Daily Eagle*, April 25, 1935.

72   "Ruth and Grimes Put Out of Game," *Greensboro* (North Carolina) *Daily News,* August 8, 1938: 6.

73   Tex McCrary and Jinx Falkenburg, "It's Toughest Behind the Plate, Says Beans Reardon, on Last Job," *Boston Globe*, October 8, 1949: 13.

74   Jack Diamond.

75   "Mae West as 'Klondike Annie' at Roosevelt," *Seattle Daily Times*, May 18, 1936, 4; "Klondike Annie," Turner Classic Movies. tcm.com/tcmdb/title/80451/Klondike-Annie. Also in the film were boxers Ellsworth "Hank" Hankinson and Billy McGowan, as well as football player Dink Templeton.

76   Eddie Brietz, Associated Press, "Stengel and Ump Swap Fire Throughout Series," *Washington Evening Star,* April 17, 1936: 49.

77   Munzel.

78   imdb.com/title/tt0029050/?ref_=ttfc_fc_tt, retrieved April 12, 2015.

79   J.G. Taylor Spink, "Three and One," *The Sporting News*, April 29, 1937: 4.

80   Associated Press, "Beans Reardon 'Pins' Thief, Sprains Finger, but Gets $300 Back," *Boston Globe*, October 9, 1943: 5.

81   Charles C. Spink, "Beans Steals the Show at Base in New Guinea," *The Sporting News*, January 11, 1945: 4.

82   "Servicemen Want Major Baseball," *Rockford* (Illinois) *Morning Star*, January 13, 1945: 6; Walter Byers, "Aid of Sports is Sought to Speed Up War Production," *Daily Illinois State Journal* (Springfield, Illinois), January 19, 1945: 10.

83   Ed Burns, "Umpire Stirs Workers with Tearful Profanity," *The Sporting News*, February 8, 1945.

84   Will Cloney, "Sox 'Baby' Set for Big Test," *Boston Herald*, October 15, 1946: 17; "World Series Notes," *Rockford* (Illinois) *Morning Star*, October 15, 1946: 12. Reardon was seated next to NL President Ford Frick in the stadium for Game Seven in St. Louis. As Enos Slaughter scampered home from first base on a single in the eighth inning, sealing the championship for the Cardinals, Reardon began yelling, "Stop! Stop! Stop!" He later explained, "I didn't think he had a chance to score." Daniel W. Scism, "Sew It Seems," *Evansville* (Indiana) *Courier and Press*, October 17, 1946: 14.

85   L.H. Gregory, "Greg's Gossip," *The Oregonian* (Portland, Oregon), December 9, 1946: 2. Some even claimed Reardon told Northey to slow down, to which he responded "I was umpiring on third and when Northey thought it had gone into the stands for a home run … I was waving my arms in a circle, signaling a home run. However, I did not speak to Northey. … I want to get one thing clear and that is I didn't tell him to slow down."

86   Some even claimed Reardon told Northey to slow down, to which he responded "I was waving my arms in a circle, signaling a home run. However, I did not speak to Northey…I want to get one thing clear and that is I didn't tell him to slow down." Associated Press, Reardon Denies 'Slow Down,' Yell," *Evansville* (Indiana) *Courier and Press*, July 27, 1947: 20.

87 Associated Press, "Frick Orders Replay of Card-Dodger Game," *Dallas Morning News*, July 26, 1947: 10. See also David W. Smith, "The Protested Game of July 20, 1947," in Lyle Spatz, ed., *The Team That Forever Changed Baseball and America: the 1947 Brooklyn Dodgers* (Lincoln: University of Nebraska Press, 2012), 201-202.

88 Associated Press, "Scuffle Spices Reds' Win," *Boston Herald*, April 20, 1948: 18. Later in the season, the umpiring crew of Conlan and Reardon had to be broken up due to the two arbiters not getting along with each other, "Umpires Troubles Increase," *Daily Illinois State Journal* (Springfield, Illinois), July 11, 1948: 18.

89 International News Service, "Nobody Wants His Autograph," *The Oregonian* (Portland, Oregon), October 16, 1948: 16.

90 "Game Called Because of Rain," Rockwell Center for American Visual Studies. rockwell-center.org/exploring-illustration/game-called-because-of-rain/. Retrieved April 4, 2015.

91 Lauren Applebaum, "Rockwell, Norman (1894-1978)," in Murray R. Nelson, ed., *American Sports: A History of Icons, Idols, and Ideas* (Santa Barbara, California: Greenwood, 2013), 1093-1094. Applebaum writes, "(W)hile the scenario depicted in *Tough Call* is just a game, the uncertainty of the outcome between these opponents relates to more serious political and economic uncertainties in America at the dawn of the Cold War. As weather is an uncontrollable force that can determine the future of the game, the image is juxtaposed with a headline on the magazine cover, which reads, 'What of Our Future?' by American financier and political consultant Bernard Baruch. … Thus, baseball performs in a covert fashion the conflicts of our world, providing an outlet to collectively confront tension under the guise of participating in an American tradition."

92 Associated Press, "Mrs. Beans Reardon Robbed of $4200," *Boston Traveler*, July 18, 1949: 21.

93 United Press, "Reardon Undecided Whether to Quit," *Riverside* (California) *Daily Press*, February 11, 1949: 12.

94 "Reardon, Although Retired, Goes on Emergency Duty," *The Sporting News*, March 29, 1950: 9.

95 UCLA Film & Television Archive — Ralph Edwards Collection. cinema.ucla.edu/sites/default/files/REmasterlist.pdf. Retrieved March 29, 2015.

96 For instance, in one such column Reardon answered questions on how many at-bats a batting champion needs to have, how an earned run is determined, and what constitutes a wild pitch and sacrifice hit. *Canton* (Ohio) *Repository*, July 12, 1952: 7.

97 Associated Press, "Umpire's Wife Dies," *San Diego Union*, March 11, 1953: 16; "Beans Reardon's Wife Dies in Long Beach," *Fresno Bee*, March 11, 1953: 7C.

98 Newspaper Enterprise Association, "Interference of Owners Blamed for Poor Umpiring," *Daily Illinois State Journal* (Springfield, Illinois), October 4, 1953: 21.

99 "The Kid From Left Field" overview. tcm.com/tcmdb/title/80194/The-Kid-from-Left-Field/. Retrieved March 30, 2015.

100 Dick Wagner, "Umpire's Wife Lives With Memories of Beans and Baseball," *Los Angeles Times*, January 14, 1988: SE10.

101 Wagner.

102 Jack Benny Program Season Five, Episode Four. tv.com/shows/the-jack-benny-program/the-giant-mutiny-126554. Retrieved March 30, 2015. William Buchanan of the *Boston Herald* was less than awed by the episode, writing, "Benny, Durocher, and Umpire Beans Reardon hit singles, but not enough runs were scored to call this show a real winner." William Buchanan, "Benny Scores Too Few Runs," *Boston Herald*, November 15, 1954: 27. Benny enjoyed the episode and praised the performances of Durocher and Reardon, saying that "Beans Reardon is another good one who would make a good actor." Wayne Oliver, Associated Press, "Benny Enthuses Over Durocher's TV Skit," *Aberdeen* (South Dakota) *Daily News*, November 19, 1954: 9.

103 Bob Van Scotter, " 'Miss Game?' 'No,' Answers Former Ump," *Rockford Morning Star* (Rockford, Illinois), April 15, 1959: C1.

104 Earl Gustkey, "Beans Reardon Still Calls 'Em as He Sees 'Em," *Los Angeles Times*, August 3, 1973: D14. Reardon claimed the $1 million selling price, although other accounts vary. Gerlach, 23.

105 Lynn Mucken, "Beans' Story String Relates Funny Side of Gentlemen in Blue," *The Oregonian* (Portland, Oregon), July 26, 1972: 6.

106 Wagner.

107 Wagner.

108 Chauncey Durden, "Sportview," *Richmond Times Dispatch*, February 18, 1970: 24; Sports *Illustrated*, November 15, 1989. si.com/vault/1989/11/15/121035/1970. Retrieved February 25, 2015.

109 Bob Broeg, "An Old Friend's Letter to Frisch," *The Sporting News*, March 31, 1973: 34.

110 Gerlach, 13.

Rev. Dr. Crew Chief Ted Barrett

By Bill Nowlin

During an interview with Ted Barrett and his crew during their July 2015 visit to officiate a series between the Seattle Mariners and Boston Red Sox, it came out that Barrett was one of a select number of umpires who have earned advanced degrees.

Dan Bellino is another; he is a Doctor of Jurisprudence, a graduate of John Marshall Law School who has served as an aide to a federal judge in Chicago. Umpiring was suggested to Barrett by one of his law school professors.

"So you're Dr. Barrett?"

"Reverend Doctor—the guys call me Reverend Doctor Crew Chief."

Indeed, Dr. Barrett is also an ordained minister. In the most recent offseason—2015/16—he and fellow umpire Angel Hernandez traveled with others on a mission to Cuba. "This was my third year going. Angel went with me in December, which was really cool because, like he said, it was his first time back. He met his cousin for the first time. It was very emotional. We went and did missionary work."

"I was ordained in the Southern Baptists, but I'm in a non-denominational church right now. In Arizona. I live in Gilbert. My undergrad was in kinesiology; that was in '88. Then after a few years I decided it was time to go back to school and get a theological degree and I got my master's degree in Biblical Studies [in 2007], from Trinity, which is a seminary in Newburgh, Indiana. It's a four-year college as well as a seminary—Trinity University as well as Trinity Theological Seminary. They were big in the early days of distance learning. They also do regional seminars and I was able to go during the winter. You could go for a four-day thing and meet the professor, which was great then as we talked back and forth."

There have been umpires who went into the ministry later in life, just as there are former ballplayers (Billy Sunday comes to mind) who later became ministers, but Teddy Barrett is the only one known to be a minister while an active umpire.

Dr. Barrett received his degree in 2013. The title of his dissertation for Trinity is *An Investigation of Faith As A Life Principle in the Lives of Major League Umpires.* [1] Barrett is also a co-founder of Calling for Christ, an organization created in 2003 to "love, encourage, and disciple umpires in their relationships with Jesus." The board of directors of Calling for Christ (CFC) is comprised of MLB umpires Rob Drake, Mike Everett, Chris Guccione, Marvin Hudson, Alfonso Marquez, and Dave Rackley. [2]

Writer Jon Mooallem wrote a piece for *ESPN The Magazine* in which he gives some of the background to Barrett's interest. "Barrett broke into the majors full time in 1999 and, having grown up in a religious family in upstate New York, was deeply unsettled by what he saw when he arrived. 'How can I put this delicately?' he says. 'It was a devil's playground. It was a dark, dark time.'" [3]

When one stops and thinks about it a bit, umpires do not just come emerge from nowhere and return to anonymity. They are real people with real lives. As Barrett wrote in his dissertation, "When a major league umpire speaks at a fundraiser dinner, classroom, church group, or some other event, he will inevitably receive the usual questions. What team do you ump for? What base do you work? Who is your favorite player? What is your favorite team? It is almost is if people, even the die-hard baseball fan, is under the impression that umpires appear from out of the ground underneath the stadium and work the game. Many people think umpires live in a city with a major league team and only work that game. Perhaps the umpires are so maligned because they are largely misunderstood."[4]

To provide grounding for his dissertation, Barrett began with the words "It is said the job of the umpire is to start out perfect and get better." And yet, under all the stresses of the job, it is not surprising that in their personal lives "some umpires fall into destructive behavior patterns."

In order to better understand the experiences and concerns of his fellow umpires, rather than simply relying on conversations and anecdotal evidence, he distributed a confidential survey to every one of the 68 serving umpires in Major League Baseball during the annual meeting of World Umpires Association, the union which represents major league umpires, after the 2011 season. Removing himself from the research process, Barrett received completed surveys from 37 of the other 67 umpires. Their written responses were illuminating and exceptionally candid.

The pressures of the job are intense, first to advance up the ladder and then to continue to undergo public and professional scrutiny even when established as a major-league umpire. To make it to the top is, in the words of former minor-league umpire Rick Roder, to progress through "baseball's narrowest door."[5] By way of some perspective, there are 100 United States Senators and there are 76 major-league umpires (a total of eight more were added in 2014 and 2015.)

There are only 76 major-league umpires and once one makes it, the rewards of the job are substantial—starting pay of $140,000 increasing to $400,000 in 2012, first-class travel, a $400 per diem, and—recently—even vacation time during the season.[6] There remains a downside, however. Umpires are rarely home, missing milestone events in the lives of their children, hoping to hold together a relationship with a spouse who must inevitably be exceptionally understanding and capable of running a household. They do not travel with a baseball team, but in a very small group of four who must work together effectively on the field and who typically spend many of their non-working hours together as well. There is not only the strain on family life, but also the need to build productive working relationships while performing that work in an intensely competitive environment which inevitably pits one umpire against another, as it has throughout their entire professional development.

Very few people make it to the top. Every year about 300 people attend one of the two umpire schools recognized by MLB. Twenty-five from each school will go on to an evaluation course, from which some will become minor-league umpires. If hired, they are ranked at the end of every season in the minors and they will either be retained or released. There are 293 minor-league umpires, Barrett writes. In an average year, there might be one or two openings in the ranks of major-league umpiring. That math alone would be discouraging, but there is also the process of getting there for those who have, often a process that takes eight or nine years working for one-tenth the pay and with few of the amenities available at the top. The minor-league umpires do often work in the majors as fill-ins, and receive big-league pay during that time, but without the benefits or protection of the union. Rob Drake worked 1,218 games over 11 seasons as a Triple-A fill-in before being hired as an MLB umpire. Chris Guccione worked 1,250 over nine seasons.

All the while, every call of the umpires in every game is subject to reaction from ballplayers whose very livelihood can be affected by a safe-out call. And their calls are studied minutely by umpire observers, umpire supervisors, and by a general public which doesn't hesitate to spew out abuse when they (rightly or wrongly) disagree with a call.

Like any employee in any field of work, umpires make mistakes. When a file clerk misplaces a dossier, he/she will never have 35,000 people booing at them for their mistake. They won't be blasted through social media; their children will not receive abuse back in their hometowns. Barrett reminds us of one of the worst cases, after umpire Jim Joyce missed a very important call at the end of what would have been a perfect game for Armando Galarraga on June 2, 2010. Umpires take their mistakes to heart, and often can lose sleep to a bad call in a routine game. But, Barrett writes, "When Jim Joyce had the missed

Ted Barrett works second base at Fenway Park.

call in Detroit in 2010, his children received instant death threats on Facebook." He adds, "One need to only do an engine search by typing in the name of any major league umpire, the vulgarity and hatred the reader would discover is hard to believe."[7]

No one in the world felt worse than Joyce. A 20-year veteran umpire at the time, he'd made a mistake, but this was a mistake that deprived Galarraga of baseball immortality.[8] The players had just voted Joyce best umpire in the game the year before. And at the time of the call, he was suffering a profound loss. "His father had recently passed away and this would be the first time he stayed in the home he was raised in without his father being there."[9]

Umpires Larry Barnett and Don Denkinger are among others who received death threats that were taken seriously enough to result in a degree of mobilization by police and/or the FBI.[10]

It's not surprising that umpires overwhelmingly value the implementation of replay—it helps them ensure that the call is right.

This is not to say that most umpires don't find their work satisfying. Of the 34 umpires who re-

sponded to the question in Barrett's survey, 33 said they were happy in the jobs. "Many used the term 'very happy' or 'extremely happy.' Some of them went as far to say they 'love' their job."[11] They are the elite who made it to the very top, and do have significant job security—though even umpire supervisors are not exempt from termination. Barrett wrote, "Two supervisors were fired following the 2009 postseason in which there were several high-profile umpiring mistakes."[12]

Competition between umpires can be intense. Indeed, Barrett writes, "From the first day of umpire school the students are fully aware that they will be in direct competition with each other…The entire process from day one is a competition among umpires for progression."[13] Even after working as a fill-in for years, and being hired as a major-league umpire, there is a four-year probationary period. Perhaps it isn't a stretch to learn that "Of the thirty-seven umpires who responded, thirty-six of them say there are umpires they do not trust. Many men simply stated that there are those they do not trust and many added that they constantly watch what they say in front of others. Some men pointed out that while it is a problem in the umpiring profession, it is also a problem in society as a whole."[14]

Barrett had earlier mentioned finding a "devil's playground" when he first arrived in the majors. And indeed, there is politicking and back-stabbing in many workplaces. Umpires are susceptible to the same crutches and temptations that others fall victim to. It is unrealistic to think that because baseball is a game with some glamour attached to it, somehow umpires are immune. That is not the case. Barrett talks about the extra responsibility of the crew chief, to keep his men working together effectively: "There are members of the staff, who have manipulative behavior, and they need to be called on it or they will shatter the crew dynamic. There are members of the staff who are in the midst of full blown addiction; their behavior can be detrimental to the crew. There are members of the staff who suffer from severe psychiatric disorders, a crew chief must be able to navigate all of these problems and keeps the crew functioning as a cohesive unit….There have been situations in the major leagues where men have worked side by side with functioning alcoholics."[15] That this is true in many workplaces does not mean it is less challenging to professional umpires and those who care about them. And umpires are indeed subject to random breathalyzer tests and other drug tests during the season, before they walk on the field of play. But such a test cannot pick up other forms of substance abuse, and cannot determine the mental health of the umpire. One of the motivations behind Baseball Chapel and a baseball ministry such as Calling for Christ is to help the crew confront such problems.

There is already a great deal of stress with which umpires must cope, but a crew which harbors someone struggling with serious issues "can add a great deal of stress to an umpire's life, an umpires' locker room should be an inner sanctum, a refuge from the bedlam that is a professional baseball game. Instead, it can be a place of bitterness, anger, jealousy, tears, rage, and fistfights. It can also be a place full of despair, despondency, loneliness and depression."[16]

Divorce is not uncommon, but is not dramatically different than that in the population at large. And fully half the respondents said they have remained faithful and never engaged in "chasing." Of those who have entered second marriages, the divorce rate is much, much lower than in the general population.

Nonetheless, among the respondents there were four who admitted to some form of sexual addiction. Pornography is among the problems they face. Three admitted to tobacco addiction and two to alcohol addiction. Several acknowledged problems with food addiction. Some had multiple addictions.

"Umpires wear masks when they work home plate," writes Barrett in his dissertation. "This is something they become very adept at, wearing masks. Many of them know they need to keep a certain persona on the field as they do their jobs. Some of them feel the need to play the role of umpire off of the field as well. Many umpires emulate the veteran arbiters they look up to. They adopt their persona both on and off the field. As their career passes, they never take a good look at their own lives. They get so caught up in trying to emulate their idols they never take the time to discover their own personalities."[17]

The situation appears to be improving, unfortunately accelerated by the 1996 death on the field of umpire John McSherry. Major League Baseball hired a full-time medical consultant, and a nutritionist. Several have sought counseling, though often outside baseball's employee assistance program, in order to avoid unfortunate concerns regarding confidentiality. Barrett is optimistic: "I believe the umpires of the present are more mature, more aware of their surroundings, and make better decisions than umpires of the past."[18]

Ted Barrett also found work, earlier in his career, as a sparring partner for professional boxers, and has indeed sparred with seven world champions: George Foreman, Evander Holyfield, Greg Page, Razor Ruddick, Obed Sullivan, Tony Tucker, and Mike Tyson. "They put 'Everlast' on me and then hung me from the ceiling and punched me."

More seriously, he elaborated, "I wore head gear and everything. I got punched a lot. I had to have my

Prayer meeting before the August 14, 2016 game, Fenway Park. HP: Lance Barksdale, 1B: Angel Hernandez, 2B: Will Little, 3B: Ted Barrett.

nose fixed and this tooth. I've had a few scars. I kind of was in demand for a while because there aren't too many heavyweight sparring partners. I'd promise my wife that I'd stop and then I'd get a phone call, and when I was in the minor leagues, I needed the money so I'd go.

"There's an etiquette to it. You need someone you can trust. When you've got a fighter in there that they've got a lot of money invested in, they don't want someone sparring with him who's trying to hurt him or trying for a cheap shot. The first world champ I sparred with was Greg Page. He was a champ in the mid-1980s. He told me, 'You could make a lot of money sparring, but you've got to do it right. You've got to know the business. You've got to know what you're doing.' He taught me the sparring partners' creed and everything, and I became in demand."

The sparring is behind him now. Umpiring pays well enough to take care of his family. A son, Andrew Barrett, has entered the ranks of professional umpiring. "He went to umpire school in January of '15. He worked the '15 season in the Arizona League. Arizona rookie league. Then he worked Instruction League

in Florida. He worked minor-league spring training this year. He's in extended spring training now [April 2016], waiting for the season to start. He'll probably be in the Northwest or Pioneer League.

"I wouldn't let him go to umpire school out of high school. His buddy did, and his buddy is now in Triple A. But I told him he had to get a college degree or join the military. So he did four years in the Air Force. When he got out, that's when he went to umpire school.

"I never encouraged it. I never discouraged it. He always followed in my footsteps a little bit, other than he didn't play football. He played one year but it wasn't his cup of tea. He played baseball. He boxed a little. He kind of grew up in the gym, so it was kind of natural. That I did try to discourage, but….

"He was nuclear weapons maintenance. The sad thing is, he really wanted to travel. He joined the Air Force and he did four years in Albuquerque. It was 45 minutes for him to go through security and then go underground. I said, 'Man, it sounds awesome.' He goes, 'It sounds awesome, but it's not. It's pretty boring.' He and his wife have got a young baby and they've got another one on the way. It's going to be a challenge, like I had, with young kids.

"I've got a daughter. She's going to college. My youngest son's in the Army. He just got back from Kuwait. He's in Colorado Springs now. He's on a tank crew. He's only 20. They're talking about Eastern Europe right now, in February. I saw on Fox News they're sending 240 tanks to Poland in February."

For all the varied life Ted Barrett has enjoyed, it comes as no surprise that his work in the ministry is what he feels gives his life the most meaning.

SOURCES

This article began with a conversation in the umpires room at Fenway Park on July 11, 2015 and another on April 18, 2016. It was furthered by a reading of Dr. Barrett's dissertation, and subsequent communications.

NOTES

1 A copy of Edward G. Barrett's dissertation was supplied by Trinity, courtesy of Sheryle Knight of Trinity Theological Seminary.

2 The Calling for Christ website may be found at: www.calling-forchrist.com

3 Jon Mooallem, "Lest Ye Be Judged," *ESPN The Magazine*, June 20, 2014. Available online at: http://espn.go.com/espn/feature/story/_/id/11107264/mlb-umpires-flock-pastor-dean-baptized-espn-magazine

4 Edward G. Barrett, *An Investigation of Faith As A Life Principle in the Lives of Major League Umpires* (Newburgh: Indiana: Trinity Theological Seminary, 2013), 45, 46.

5 Rick Roder, *Baseball's Narrowest Door, How to Become a Professional Umpire*, 3rd ed. (Remsen, Iowa: by the author, 2003).

6 In the environment where they work, even the highest-paid umpire makes less than the minimum wage of the lowest-paid player, which in 2015 was $507,500. The highest-paid players earn more in a year than do all 76 major-league umpires together. Nonetheless, at one point, Barrett writes, "Umpiring at the big league level is a Peter Pan existence. You never have to make your bed because the hotel maid will do that for you. You never have to do your laundry because your clubbie will do it. You never have to do dishes because you are eating in a restaurant." (p. 82) And it falls on the wives to do most of the work in the household.

7 Barrett, 65, 66.

8 See the book which pitcher and umpire wrote together. Armando Galarraga, Jim Joyce, and Daniel Paisner. *Nobody's Perfect: Two Men, One Call, and A Game for Baseball History* (New York: Atlantic Monthly Press, 2011).

9 Barrett, 55.

10 See, for instance, Durwood Merrill and Jim Dent, *You're Out and You're Ugly Too! Confessions of an Umpire with Attitude* (New York: St. Martin's Press, 1998), 96, 97.

11 Barrett, 47.

12 Ibid., 38.

13 Ibid., 70-71.

14 Ibid., 72.

15 Ibid., 75-76. "Of the thirty-seven umpires in the survey, only three claim they have never abused alcohol and have never been drunk since they were members of the major league staff." (p. 79)

16 Ibid., 75.

17 Ibid., 112.

18 Ibid., 85. Calling for Christ holds an annual retreat for umpires and their families each winter, and Barrett reports that 11 major-league umpires have attended, while several others have participated in the other activities the ministry offers.

Chris Guccione

By Bill Nowlin

Chris Guccione has been a major-league umpire for eight full seasons, 2009 through 2016. Before that, he was an "up and down" umpire, for the eight prior seasons (2000 through 2008), and he had worked five years in the minor leagues, from 1995 through 1999. Like most umpires, he had to work many years before becoming hired as a major-league umpire. But he holds a record that may never be broken—having worked 1,255 games as a "fill-in" umpire before finally getting the promotion to the big leagues.

In October 2016, Guccione worked his first World Series and not only did he work one of the most exciting World Series in baseball history, it was his distinction to call the final out in the bottom of the 10th inning in Game Seven.

Christopher Gene Guccione (widely known as "Gooch" among his fellow umpires) was born in Salida, Colorado, on June 24, 1974. Salida is a small town in the "Heart of the Rockies" on the Arkansas River about 140 miles south and west of Denver, a couple of hours more or less west of Colorado Springs. Its population is a stable one, currently a little over 5,000, only about 600 or 700 more than it had been in 1920.[1] His father's aunt Rose was the first member of the family to emigrate from Italy to Salida, in the 1920s. Chris's father, Geno Luigi, emigrated considerably later, in 1958 at the age of 12. He came with his mother, two of his sisters, and one brother. The family came from the small village of Gesuiti, in Calabria.

The railroad ran through Salida, but it was perhaps the mining work that attracted so many southern Italians to the area. Word had spread, of course, from one family to another that there was work to be found, and the town—despite its Spanish name—was home to a large number of southern Italians.[2]

Geno Guccione came to America at the time the New York Yankees were riding high, and he became a huge fan of the Yankees, and of baseball in general. He was only 5-feet-8, but he was a very good pitcher and Salida had a very good team. Geno learned how to pitch from throwing thousands of times through an old tire. "They had an incredible team," Chris said. "He's got this trophy that they won when he was maybe 16 years old. They won third place in the state tournament in 1963."

Strange as it may seem, Salida nearly hosted a Boston Red Sox baseball game once upon a time. There was a game scheduled in Salida itself on March 30, 1911, as the team worked its way back east from spring training in California. The game had to be called because another train had been involved in a wreck and the line was blocked. The Red Sox went on to play in Pueblo on March 31.[3]

Chris was told that his father had gone to a tryout for the Pittsburgh Pirates at a minicamp held at Runyon Park in Pueblo. The love of baseball was passed down from father to son, to Chris and his younger brother, Stephen.

Geno Guccione had become a naturalized United States citizen, finished high school, and then served in the Army during the Vietnam War. His experience and talent with mechanical things stood him well after he arrived in Da Nang. That first night, there were nighttime mortar attacks on the American base there, but the real fighting was farther north, on the front lines. "They were sending guys up north, to go fight. They were just going down the line—'OK, you up north. You stay here. You up north ...' They were just picking guys. When they got near my dad, someone said, 'Hey, we need a mechanic to work around here'—and my dad's arm went up. They said, 'All right, you're staying here. You're working on the trucks and all the vehicles.'" He was thus spared a more active combat role.

Chris Guccione, Umpires room, Fenway Park, July 5, 2015.

After a year or year and a half in Vietnam, Geno returned Stateside and took up work mining for CFI Steel Corporation. [Colorado Fuel & Iron]. "He was mining limestone up at Monarch Mountain; at the time they used limestone to harden and purify the steel. He worked there all through the '80s, but then once steel production started going overseas to China and all that, they shut down the mine. Really, my dad was a handyman. Small motors, a mechanic, working on cars, trucks, and small engines like lawnmowers and all that. Real handy as a guy."

Geno Guccione married Suzanne Corinne Sparks, a blonde-haired, blue-eyed woman of Dutch descent. They divorced when Chris was in the sixth grade.

During the winters, when the mines were shut, Geno drove a school bus in Salida. After the mine closed for good, he worked at the school district for nearly 30 years, doing all the maintenance work for the Salida High School and becoming head of maintenance for the district. "He retired from that but to keep busy, he does lawn jobs. He's got like a lawn service and does that in the summer. He still gets to tinker with motors. He loves doing that stuff."

Chris started with baseball early. Claiming to be a year older than he actually was, he began playing Babe Ruth Baseball at the age of 5, on the Marvin Park baseball field. "I was usually an infielder. I was a second baseman for most of the time. Once I got older, I played center field, like during that 13-, 14-, 15-year-old league. I pitched some, too. My dad taught me what he knew about pitching. He loved

pitching, so he taught me little tricks about pitching. So at that same age, 13, 14, 15, I was a pitcher as well."

Their home had a backyard, and beyond that a field with cows and horses. In a vacant lot, Chris and a friend fashioned a pitcher's mound from dirt they took off the side of a mountain. They put some 2-by-4's together and buried those in the mound to serve as a pitcher's rubber, and they built a backstop, creating their own pitching area.

There was no high-school baseball at Salida back then, nor were there more than four or five interested in starting an American Legion team. When he turned 15, and was no longer eligible for Babe Ruth Baseball, Chris became devoted to the track team, throwing the shotput and the discus, and remained so when baseball was finally belatedly offered during his senior year.

However, Chris had already started umpiring at the age of 12. When he didn't have a game, chances were that Stephen did. "I was at the ballpark, regardless," he said. "I just started umpiring games. I was getting five bucks a game and I'd go and buy all the fishing lures I could muster up with five bucks."[4]

A very good friend in junior-high and high school was Chris Clarkson. "We started umpiring about the same time, and we did that for a year or two, and then his dad—John Clarkson—started like a small umpire organization. It was me, it was Chris, he had a brother C.P., and then his dad. There might have been a couple of other guys in there. We did that for a couple of years. And then when I was 18 or 19, he said, 'You guys got to think about going to umpire school.' I had never heard of umpire school. I had no idea what umpire school even was."

Umpire school was relatively expensive, about $3,000 per person, but Chris and the Clarkson boys held some fundraisers in town and some people helped financially, including the two families. In 1995, when Chris was 20 years old, the three of them went to umpire school.

That in itself was a haul. Chris's girlfriend, Amy Lynn Wyble, dropped him off at the Greyhound bus station. "That was the only thing we could afford. It took us 52 hours from Salida to Kissimmee, Florida, and we spent five weeks down there at the Jim Evans School. Out of there, we all ended up getting jobs. All three of us ended up getting placed in pro ball."

Guccione's first assignment was to rookie ball, to the Pioneer League in 1995. Chris Clarkson worked two, three, or four years. C.P. worked for a year. Chris Guccione is still at it.[5]

The Pioneer League had teams in Billings, Medicine Hat, Great Falls, Helena, Butte, Idaho Falls, Ogden, and Lethbridge, Alberta. The Helena Brewers, with a record of 49-22, won the South standings and also both rounds of the playoffs.

After the Pioneer League, it was one assignment after another, working his way up the ladder. In 1996 Guccione was assigned to the Class-A Midwest League, where he partnered with current major-league umpire Brian Knight. The Midwest League had three divisions, and it was the West Michigan Whitecaps that won the finals. Among the states represented were Wisconsin, Illinois, and Iowa, as well as Michigan.

Guccione says, "Between rookie ball and all the A leagues, it was all two-man. Once you get to Double A, it's three-man, and Triple A is three or four. First of all, hopefully you have a person you can get along with. Your partner. If not, it's a long season. At the time, we had to share rooms. These days, you get your own room. But you had to basically live with the guy for six months. You knew him better than you did your family, at times. You would talk about everything.

"I was 20 years old, so this was all new, exciting, and fun."

In 1997 he was assigned to the California League, again Class-A ball. San Bernardino, Bakersfield, Modesto, Stockton, and San Jose were among the cities fielding teams. The High Desert Mavericks won the playoffs in 1977. The accommodations were typically of the Motel 6 variety, two beds to a room, but the team would pay for the hotel. Having a good partner was essential. "You usually stayed pretty close. You usually had lunch together. You worked out together. You really did everything together. The team

would pay for the hotel, but you'd have to use your own car. That was kind of a sticking point."

Per diems were, to the best of his memory, $15 a day. "I ate a lot of Taco Bell, McDonald's, Arby's."

Guccione's partner in the California League was Brian Runge, of the famous umpiring Runge family. (Ed Runge was an American League umpire from 1954 to 1970 and his son Paul was a National League umpire from 1973-97.) Paul's son Brian had to work his way up, too. There was no limousine service provided. "I was the driver," Guccione remembers. "I had a 1988 Toyota pickup. We drove that thing up and down California the whole time. I had to replace a clutch, but it got us around, got us through. I actually still own the Toyota pickup. It's got a couple of hundred thousand miles on it. A new motor and everything else. My dad drives it now. I gave it to him."

Had he been paired with anyone who proved difficult? "You know, I was lucky. Every partner I ever had, we got along great. I never had any problem with league presidents, I never had a league I didn't like, but I'm a kind of easygoing guy. I consider myself easygoing. I can get along with just about anybody."

In both 1998 and 1999, he was assigned to the Texas League. This was Double-A baseball, an eight-team league with a 140-game season. Texas teams included El Paso, San Antonio, and Midland; also Wichita and one from Little Rock; and there were teams from Tulsa (Oklahoma), Shreveport (Louisiana), and Jackson (Mississippi).

The distances between parks could be considerable. "It depends, of course. In the Texas League, you're talking 15, 16 hours sometimes. You could go from El Paso to Jackson, Mississippi. You'd have to leave right after the game and get to the next city just before the next game. It was brutal. On average, it was like four, five hours between cities. The Southern League, you've got some long drives, too, but the Texas League, I think the shortest drive was four to five hours. All the rest of the trips were 8, 10, 12, 15 hours." That said, Guccione never missed a game, due to a breakdown or otherwise.

And for that matter, there weren't many days off. "You got a few days off. Not many in the minor leagues. You got a monthly salary. You only got paid for when you worked. You were probably at the poverty level."

It was difficult to maintain a relationship, too. Guccione recalls a time that first year he worked in the Texas League. Amy drove out to Wichita to see him at some point in May. She was graduating from the University of Colorado a little later; he wasn't going to be able to attend the graduation. "We were sitting at breakfast and I told her I was ready to call it quits. I was ready to come home. She basically told me to 'suck it up' and 'I've/we've put in too much to quit now.' It would have been real easy for her to agree. It was the only time the entire baseball season that I saw her.

"You have to come home after the season and hope that … that's the hard thing: You'd only get paid for April, May, June, July, August, and September. You'd get six months' salary. You'd make like $18,000 in that whole time. And then you'd come home, try to find a job. Hopefully, you wouldn't have to lie to the employer—saying you would keep working. I was kind of lucky. My cousin Pete had a painting business and for many, many years, the day I got home I'd be painting houses with him. Commercial, interior, exterior, anything. That was good.

"Amy was a nurse at the Veterans Hospital at the time. An RN. Then she went to the Tri-County Health Department. She worked and with what we could save from my salary during the season, we also had her salary." Amy and Chris married in 1998.

In 2000 Guccione was invited to big-league spring training and promoted to the Pacific Coast League. That was Triple-A baseball, the level just below the big leagues. But it was only a matter of a few weeks before he was asked to work his first major-league game. That first game was on April 25, 2000, in Atlanta, working with crew chief Tim Tschida. Guccione worked third base in a tight 1-0 game at Turner Field, Tom Glavine of the Braves shutting out the Dodgers.

At this point, he was "up" in the "up and down" cycle that would last through the 2008 season. And Guccione was up more than he was down. He

worked 106 games that first year. In 2001 Guccione worked 132 games, and then in 2002 he worked an almost difficult-to-fathom 156 games. There are only 162 games on the major-league schedule. That means that he was essentially asked to work all but six games that year.

With vacations and time assigned to work at replay, the average major-league umpire now works about 120-130 games a year. Guccione was still a Triple-A umpire, but was filling in working big-league games. "I was working probably 20 or 30 more games than most of the staff. The older staff, guys that had vacation time, they were working about 130 games and I was working closer to 160 in those years. I remember one year, between the All-Star break and the last day of the season, I had one day off. "

The good news was that he was being paid the same daily salary (if not accruing all the pension time) that a major-league umpire was making, so the money was good. Hoping to one day be hired as a major-league umpire, you wouldn't want to turn down an assignment. "They tell you where to go and you want to say, 'Yes sir, I'll be there tomorrow.' I'd be on a crew and I'd be with them for a month or whatever. Then they'd get their one week off, but because I wasn't on staff, I didn't fall under that umbrella. They'd say, 'OK, now you're going to go to this crew.' Well, that crew didn't have any days off. Then you're working another 10 days, and then they go on vacation. Then you've gotta go to another crew and they didn't have any days off, either. Just bad luck, I guess."

Over the course of the nine years he worked as a fill-in umpire, the fewest games Guccione worked was 128 games in 2005. In the back-to-back seasons of 2007 and 2008, he once again worked 156 games.

The extra pay was very helpful. Amy had been working at the Veterans Hospital for a number of years, but now she was able to take two years off from the VA and focus on her master's degree on a full-time basis, and the couple was able to buy their first house.

Despite being used so frequently and for so many years, there was a stressful aspect to it, in a way, year in and year out, never knowing for sure if you'd get the call or not. One does develop a sense as to where they stand, and whether there might open up a slot for them in the majors. But another year might go by without getting the call. "When you're going up and down as an umpire, you never really know where you stand. If you do something on the field they dislike … you just never know. … It's eight years of not knowing where you stand and where your future's going to be, how many games you're going to work that year."

You do develop a sense of when the time might be approaching. "At the time, Rob Drake and I were kind of in the same position. It was either/or. He was up around the same number of games I'd worked. You knew it was going to be either one of us. That's kind of what you speculate anyway. You don't really know for sure. We were all waiting for the call. There was a couple of years prior to that and maybe I thought I was in the mix and they hired somebody else."[6]

March 2009 was ending and April beginning, and there was no call. Chris and Amy were wanting to sell their home and move to another one. "It was the first house that we'd purchased. We were just waiting to see what my future was going to hold. We didn't want to sell until we knew what was going on."

He was in Tucson, working a spring-training game the Rockies were in. "It was actually my last plate job of spring training. I was working with Tony Randazzo, Lance Barrett, and Brian Knight. Anyway, I walked off the field and I didn't even have my chest protector off. I looked at my phone and it was Cris Jones. I was like, 'Hey, guys, look. Cris Jones called.' They were like, 'Call him back! Call him back!' I was like, 'All right.' So I called him. I think he was at the minor-league minicamp.

"He gave me the runaround. 'Hey, Gooch. You know, we're sorry. It was between a couple of guys. …' Kind of one of those deals. He was going on about this and that, and then he said, 'We're hiring you.'

"We all jumped. We screamed and yelled. They ended up getting beers and doing the old thing like we'd just won the World Series and were pouring beer over my head. It was pretty cool."

Then he called his wife. "The first thing I said when I called was, 'Hey, babe. What're you doing?'

Various ticket stubs from Chris Guccione's minor-league days.

'Oh, I'm doing this and that, or whatever.' I said, 'Well, go ahead and get that For Sale sign up.' She was kind of like, 'Huh?' Kind of confused. I said, 'I just got hired. Get that For Sale sign up on the house.'"

Needless to say, Chris' father was pumped, too.

The timing was nice. He was told he could skip the last four or five games of spring training and go home. There was a routine physical he had to take, and then he had to make his way to Toronto for the April 6 game hosting the Detroit Tigers. It was just another game, but it was the first game he had worked as a full member of the major-league staff. Ed Montague was the crew chief.

From 2009 through the 2016 season, Guccione has worked 1,032 games. Though he says he was a little more fiery earlier in his career, you wouldn't know it from looking at his record of ejections. There was one year (2005) when he threw out nine players, but five of them all revolved around a throwing incident involving an intentional hit by pitch. Over the four seasons from 2013 through 2016, he's ejected only six players.

Off the field, working with Associate Pastors Ted Barrett and Tom Drake, Guccione is one of six major-league umpires of the board of Calling for Christ.[7] The organization is made up of umpires of all levels of professional baseball, and their families.

Guccione's first postseason assignment was in 2010 to the American League Division Series (Yankees vs. Twins). He worked the All-Star Game in 2011 and the NLDS (Phillies vs. Cardinals) that year. And after the season was over, he served as grand marshal at the Parade of Lights in Salida that November.

He worked the American League wild card game in 2012, and the National League Championship Series, then worked Division Series in 2013, 2014, and 2015.

Then Joe Torre called, with an invitation to work the 2016 World Series.

"We kind of have an idea when they're going to make the phone calls. Not who they're going to call, but when they're going to call. If you've worked the Divisions and you've got so many years working the Divisions, and you've kind of met this criteria—you've worked an LCS, you've got some Divisions, and you've got some time working—like plate jobs in Game One, Game Two, Game Threes, Game Fours in the Divisions, you kind of have an idea like who might get it. Maybe. 'Well, I've got an outside chance. … Maybe. It'd be great.'

"We're waiting for the phone call. Well, nothing happened in the morning. People are texting me—'Hey, have you heard anything?' Then the afternoon comes and everybody's saying, 'Well, they must be making the phone calls tomorrow, or a couple of days from now.'

"I'm in the living room. I was playing with my daughter, Gemma, just kind of rolling around on the floor. Just having a good time, and I hear the phone ring. I could tell somebody left a voicemail. I thought, 'Huh. Well … let me go check it.' Sure enough. Joe Torre. It was from Joe. So I called him right back. He said, 'You're one of our guys.' We were pretty excited. In shock, and excited at the same time." Gemma was just under a year old at the time.

"My wife did an incredible job, getting everything packed up and ready. There's a lot to do for just a 1-year-old. Clothes, food, formula. … Talk about being lucky with the travel, though. Cleveland and Chicago. We got her all packed up and got her there. She didn't go to any of the games. My wife would put her down for bed around 6:30 or so. We had like a worldwide nanny service and we just hired a babysitter to come and watch her in the hotel room. Amy was able to get to the game around the third or fourth inning. So it worked out.

"We're actually high-school sweethearts so we've been through this roller coaster of baseball since Day One. She put me on the bus to go to Florida for umpire school and she's still taking me to the plane."

What was it like to work the World Series for the first time?

Guccione had worked two no-hitters—first base when the Florida Marlins' Henderson Alvarez no-hit the Detroit Tigers at Marlins Park on September 29, 2013, and second base at Safeco Field when Seattle's Hisashi Iwakuma no-hit the Orioles on August 12, 2015. "What was great about Alvarez's no-hitter is that it went to the bottom of the ninth inning and it was tied. Ron Kulpa had the plate. Alvarez is on deck. There were two outs and runners on second and third. Then there was a wild pitch that scored the winning run. 1-0."

But in 2016, this was the World Series, and it was a historic one, pitting the Chicago Cubs (who hadn't won a world championship since 1908) against the Cleveland Indians (who had been without a world championship since 1948.)

"It's a strange thing. Before Game One, I was like super amped-up. I just wanted the game to get started. There were butterflies. I was anxious to get out there. Sitting around all day, the game starting late. I kept telling myself, 'Yes, it's the World Series but it's the game of baseball you've been umpiring for many, many, many years. It hasn't changed. The game hasn't changed. It's just on a bigger scale.' You have to just do your job. I kept telling myself, 'I'm just going to treat this like any other day. I'm going to work out.' My wife and I had our daughter with us. We're going to hang out. But inside I was feeling, 'Oh, man, I just want to get out there.'

"You usually try to eat something before the game, but I didn't really want to eat anything. My stomach was tied up or whatever. So the minute I hit the grass in Cleveland … I'm telling you, the minute I hit the grass, I was like, 'I've done this. This is just baseball. I'm going to do my job. I'm going to do the best I can. And just do it.' Really, all the games, all the way to the last out, it was the same. It was just, 'I'm working.'"

Game Seven lasted 4 hours and 28 minutes. The Cubs had a 5-1 lead after 4½, but a three-run bottom of the eighth by the Indians tied the game, and it ultimately went into extra innings. Guccione had worked the plate in Game Two. He was working first base in Game Seven. The Cubs scored twice in the top of the 10th, but the Indians scored once and had a runner on first base with two outs. The batter was Michael Martinez. He hit the ball to Cubs third baseman Kris Bryant.

"That last play, the way it ended, the last out—Kris Byrant slips. I'm sitting at first base watching all this and there's this little chopper in the infield. 'Oh, this is going to be a tough play.' As an umpire, you always are trying to be ahead of the play. So I'm thinking, 'This is going to be a tough play for him.' And then I see him slip and I think, 'Oh, boy. He's going to overthrow it.' All this is like racing through your head. But obviously he made the right throw. As an umpire, you're thinking, 'He slipped. OK, now I've got to make sure that Rizzo stays on the bag.' There could be a swipe tag. Something goofy happens. All this stuff is going through your head. Rizzo caught it right at his chin basically. It ended up being a good throw."

"It wasn't until about a week or two after when you go, 'Man! We just got to experience one of the greatest World Series of our time!' That's when it hit you, when you have time to unwind. I was getting text messages from my family, 'Oh my gosh, you just called the last out of the World Series!'"

SOURCES

The primary information for Chris Guccione's family background and his experiences becoming a major-league umpire came from interviews conducted on July 3 and 5, 2015; May 9 and October 2, 2016; and January 5, 2017, with a number of exchanges by email. The author also relied on the remarkable umpire database at Retrosheet. org for information regarding major-league games.

NOTES

1   The 2010 census enumerated 5,236 inhabitants. In 1920, the figure was 4,689.

2   The 2000 census showed 12.8 percent of the town's population claimed Italian ancestry. See salidaarchive.info/wp-content/uploads/2014/12/Salida-in-English-October-2016-4th-edition.pdf.

3   The full story of the unusual 1911 preseason is told in Bill Nowlin, *The Great Red Sox Spring Training Tour of 1911: Sixty-three Games, Coast to Coast* (Jefferson, North Carolina: McFarland & Co., 2010).

4   Stephen Guccione works today as a teacher, or "a teacher-slash-coach." He teaches elementary physical education and also coaches as the defensive coordinator for the Brighton High School football team in Colorado.

5   Guccione said, "C.P. works in one of the correctional facilities up in Sterling, Colorado. Chris (Clarkson) is a pastor of a church. He was transferred—he's been kind of nomadic—he lives down in Florida now. He's been all over the place. His dad, John, he's also a preacher, but has also worked for the Department of Corrections as well."

6   Rob Drake was hired as a major-league umpire the following year, in 2010.

7   The others are Rob Drake, Mike Everitt, Marvin Hudson, Alfonso Marquez, and David Rackley.

Retired (and un-retired) Uniform Numbers

Most major-league teams have retired one or more numbers worn by the best players in franchise history. The New York Yankees have retired 19 numbers, the Cardinals 12, and the White Sox, Braves, and Dodgers have each retired 10. Only the Seattle Mariners are yet to retire a number. The Marlins retired the "number" of their first president, Dave Barger, but not one of an actual player.

Major League Baseball retired player #42 across baseball in 1997. Several umpires elected to wear #42 on Jackie Robinson Day in 2007 and 2008, and effective 2009 all umpires also wear #42 that day.

When the two leagues were separate, the National League and American League had each retired three numbers. When the two leagues merged, the retired numbers were, in effect, un-retired. Current major-league umpires wear each of the previously-retired numbers (though Major League Baseball recognizes the umpires whose numbers had previously been retired by presenting them with a page in its annual Media Guide.

National League

1 — Bill Klem
Nicknamed "The Old Arbitrator." Umpired from 1905 to 1940 and then served as chief of National League umpires. Holds the record for World Series appearances with 18 and consecutive appearances with five. Originated arm signals to coincide with verbal calls. In a rare tribute to an umpire, he was honored with gifts on "Bill Klem Night," September 2, 1949 at the Polo Grounds. He is a member of the National Baseball Hall of Fame.

2 — Jocko Conlan
Umpired in the National League for 24 years (1941-64). Umpired four World Series and six All-Star Games. Played in 128 major-league games as a member of the Chicago White Sox (1934-35). Became the fifth umpire elected into the National Baseball Hall of Fame. Conlan on umpiring: "You've got to have thick skin and a strong heart. You've got to have and command respect. Without them, you're nothing."

3 — Al Barlick
Umpired at the major-league level for 33 years (1940-72). Worked a record seven All-Star Games. At age 25, he became one of the youngest umpires to reach the major leagues. Known for his booming calls and distinctive hand signals. Started umpiring sandlot games after a coal mining strike forced him to earn extra money. Was a World War II Coast Guard veteran. Became the sixth umpire inducted into the National Baseball Hall of Fame in 1989.

Major League Baseball's Vice President for Communications Mike Teevan explained the retirement of the three National League umpires: "Umpires did not wear numbers in the era of Klem, Conlan, and Barlick, but in 1995, National League President Leonard Coleman took the step of honoring them - posthumously for Klem and Conlan, while Barlick passed away later that year. The ceremony was held at Wrigley Field on September 10, 1995. Conlan was born in Chicago, while Barlick was an Illinois resident after his career."[1]

American League

2 — Nick Bremigan
Umpired in the American League from 1974 to 1989. He tragically died of a heart attack on March 28, 1989 at the age of 43. He was a member of the AL umpire staff when he passed away. Worked the Florida State, Eastern, International, Florida Winter Instructional, and Puerto Rican Winter Leagues before joining the

AL. Called the 1980 World Series, four AL playoffs, and two Midsummer Classics.

9 — Bill Kunkel

Became an American League umpire in 1968 and served for a time as referee for the National Basketball Association. Also a pitcher for the New York Yankees and Kansas City Athletics, where he compiled a life-time record of 6-6. Died in 1988 at the age of 48, after a long battle with cancer. His son Jeff was an infielder with the Texas Rangers (1984-92).

16 — Lou DiMuro

Umpired in the American League from 1963-82. Worked two World Series, three League Championship Series, and four All-Star Games. His son Mike is currently a major-league baseball umpire. Died tragically on June 8, 1982, at the age of 51, when he was struck by a car as he was crossing a street in Arlington, Texas.

The write-ups for the above umpires are as written for the 2015 *MLB Umpire Media Guide*, edited by Michael Teevan and Don Muller.

NOTES

1   Mike Teevan e-mail August 31, 2015.

Honor Rolls of Baseball

By Larry R. Gerlach

In 1946 the Hall of Fame created "Honor Rolls of Baseball" to recognize the significant contributions of non-players then not eligible for formal induction to the Hall. Thirty-nine men were so named—5 managers, 11 executives, 12 sportswriters and 11 umpires.

Tom Connolly
Bill Dinneen
Bob Emslie
John Gaffney
Tim Hurst
Kick [John O.] Kelly
Bill Klem
Thomas Lynch
Silk O'Loughlin
Jack Sheridan

Subsequently, Connolly and Klem in 1953, Evans in 1973, were officially inducted into the Hall of Fame.

It is interesting that Kelly and O'Loughlin are identified by nickname.

While not enshrined, the other eight men recognized for their outstanding contributions as umpires also deserve special attention in the annals of baseball history.

Umpires Who Played and/or Managed in the Major Leagues

By Larry R. Gerlach

While it often noted that catchers make good managers, 19 of the 37 umpires were pitchers. Except for Conlan, Emslie, Hildebrand and Scott, umpires played and umpired in the same league. Dinneen, Moriarty, Pinelli, Orth, and Wallace played in both leagues. The National League hired the majority (25) of the former players.

Not included are the numerous players who umpired as substitutes for a game for a few games. For example, Cy Young in 1903 umpired at the start of a game on July 4 and a complete game on July 8.

Name	Played	Umpired
Charles (Charlie) Berry	C AL 1925, 1928-1936, 1938	AL 1942-1962
William "Kitty" Bransfield	INF NL 1898, 1901-1911	NL 1917
William (Ken) Burkhart	P NL 1945-1949	NL 1957-1973
Robert Caruthers	P NL 1884-1892	NL 1888, 1891, 1893; AL 1902-1903
John (Jocko) Conlan	OF AL 1934-1935	NL 1941-1964
E. Ellsworth "Bert" Cunningham	P & OF AA 1887-1889, 1891; PL 1890, NL 1895-1901	NL 1901
William (Big Bill) Dinneen	P NL 1898-1901, AL 1902-1909	AL 1909-1937
John "Jack" Doyle	C, INF, OF AA 1889-1890; NL 1891-1905	NL 1911
J. Francis "Frank" Dwyer	P NL 1888-1889; PL 1890; NL 1892-1899	NL 1899, 1901, AL 1904
Malcolm (Mal) Eason	P NL 1900-1902, 1904-1906, AL 1903	NL 1901-1902, 1910-1915
Robert Emslie	P AA 1885-1888	NL 1891-1924
William Friel	IN, OF AL 1901-1903	AL 1920
Thomas Gorman	P NL 1939	NL 1951-1976
William Hart	P NL 1886-1901	NL 1913-1915
Walter (Butch) Henline	C NL 1921-1931	NL 1945-1948
George Hildebrand	OF NL 1902	AL 1912-1934
William Kunkle	P AL 1961-1963	AL 1968-1984
Sherwood (Sherry) Magee	OF NL 1904-1919	NL 1928
Frederick (Firpo) Marberry	P AL 1923-1936	AL 1935.
William "Barry" McCormick	IF NL 1895-1901, AL 1902-1904	NL 1901-1904, 1917, 1919-1929
Charles (Uncle Charlie) Moran	P NL 1903	NL 1917-1939
George Moriarty	INF NL 1903-1904, AL 1906-1916	AL 1917-1926, 1929-1940.

Henry (Hank) O'Day	P AA 1884-1885, NL 1886-1890	NL 1895, 1897-1911, 1913, 1915-1927
Albert (Al) Orth	P NL 1895-1901, AL 1902-1909	NL 1901, 1912-1917
Ralph (Babe) Pinelli	INF AL 1918, 1920, NL 1922-1927	NL 1935-1956
George Pipgras	P AL 1923-1935	AL 1938-1946
Edwin (Eddie) Rommel	P AL 1920-1932	AL 1938-1959
James Scott	P AL 1909-1917	NL 1930-1931
Frank Secory	OF AL 1940, NL 1942-1946	NL 1952-1970
Leopold "Paul" Sentell	IF NL 1906-1907	NL 1922-1923
William "Spike" Shannon	OF NL 1904-1908	FL 1914-1915
Vincent (Vinnie) Smith	C NL 1941, 1946	NL 1957-1965
Cyrus (Ed) Swartwood	P AA 1884-1885	NL 1894-1900
Roderick "Bobby" Wallace	INF NL 1894-1901, 1917-1918, AL 1902-1916	AL 1915
Edward "Big Ed" Walsh	P AL 1904-1916, NL 1917	AL 1922
Lonnie Warneke	P NL 1930-1945	NL 1949-1955
Charles (Chief) Zimmer	C NL 1884-1903	NL 1889, 1904-1905

Six men played, umpired, and managed:

Name	Team Managed
George Moriarty	Detroit 1927
Henry O'Day	Cincinnati 1912, Chicago (NL) 1914
Roderick Wallace	St. Louis (AL) 1912-1913, Cincinnati 1937
Edward Walsh	Chicago (AL) 1924
Charles Zimmer	Philadelphia (NL) 1903
Frank Dwyer	Detroit 1902

Clarence "Pants" Rowland, AL umpire 1923-1927, managed Chicago (AL) 1915-1918

Umpire Records

By David Vincent

(all figures through 2016)

All-Star Game

Most ASG Appearances: 7, Al Barlick & Bill Summers

Most Consecutive ASG Appearances: 2, accomplished eight times (last: Doug Harvey, 1963-64)

World Series

Most World Series Appearances: 18, Bill Klem
Most World Series Games: 103, Bill Klem
Most Consecutive World Series Appearances: 5, Bill Klem (1911-15)

League Championship Series

Most LCS Appearances: MLB — 12, Jerry Crawford; NL — 10, Jerry Crawford & Bruce Froemming; AL — 7, Larry Barnett & Jim Evans

Most LCS Games: 64, Jerry Crawford

Division Series

Most Division Series Appearances: MLB — 12, by Gerry Davis; NL — 8, Bruce Froemming & Jerry Layne; AL — 7, Tim Tschida & Tim Welke

Most Division Series Games: 50, Gerry Davis.

Miscellaneous

Most Years Umpired: 39, Joe West (1976-99; 2002-16)

Most Games Umpired: 5,375, Bill Klem. (With 5,163 games, Bruce Froemming is the only other major-league umpire with more than 5,000 games.)

Longest Game by Plate Umpire by Time: 8 hours, 6 minutes, Jim Evans (May 8-9, 1984, Milwaukee Brewers at Chicago White Sox; 25 innings).

Gerry Davis has worked a record 12 Division Series and 50 Division Series games. In addition, Davis ranks first with 133 career postseason games umpired and 10th all-time with 4,467 games umpired.

Historical Umpiring Statistics

Most Years Umpired, Major Leagues

(Most years in which an umpire worked at least one major-league game)
39 Joe West
37 Bruce Froemming
37 Bill Klem
35 Joe Brinkman
35 Tommy Connolly
35 Jerry Crawford
35 Gerry Davis
35 Bob Emslie
35 Ed Montague
35 Hank O'Day
34 Derryl Cousins
34 Dana DeMuth
34 Mike Reilly
33 Tim McClelland
33 Tim Welke
33 Harry Wendelstedt
32 John Hirschbeck
32 Dale Scott

Most Games Umpired, Major Leagues

5,375 Bill Klem
5,163 Bruce Froemming
4,942 Joe West
4,769 Tommy Connolly
4,673 Doug Harvey
4,505 Joe Brinkman
4,500 Harry Wendelstedt
4,496 Derryl Cousins

4,491 Mike Reilly
4,467 Gerry Davis
4,425 Bill McGowan
4,371 Jerry Crawford
4,369 Ed Montague
4,281 Larry Barnett
4,236 Tim McClelland
4,231 Al Barlick
4,230 Bob Emslie
4,218 Bill Dinneen
4,216 Tim Welke
4,142 Cy Rigler
4,122 Bill Summers
4,098 Dana DeMuth
4,023 Larry McCoy

Most World Series Games Umpired

103 Bill Klem
62 Cy Rigler
57 Hank O'Day
47 Bill Summers
45 Tommy Connolly
45 Bill Dinneen
43 Bill McGowan
42 Al Barlick
42 Jim Honochick
38 Billy Evans
38 Ernie Quigley

Most Postseason Games Umpired

133 Gerry Davis
122 Joe West
111 Bruce Froemming
111 Jerry Crawford
103 Bill Klem
100 Jeff Kellogg
99 Ed Montague
98 Tim Welke
96 Dana DeMuth
95 Ted Barrett
94 Tim McClelland
94 Mike Winters
93 John Hirschbeck
92 Randy Marsh
91 Mike Reilly
91 Dale Scott

Prior to the Red Sox/Braves game on April 28, 2016, baseball fan Shawn Gibbons — a student at the University of Massachusetts Lowell — spotted crew chief Joe West headed to the Fenway Park umpires room and asked him to pose for a photograph.

Most World Series Games Umpired, Umpires Active in 2016

33 Joe West
29 Dana DeMuth
28 John Hirschbeck
28 Jeff Kellogg
24 Gerry Davis
22 Mike Winters
18 Ted Barrett
17 Jim Joyce
17 Alfonso Marquez
16 Gary Cederstrom
15 Dale Scott
15 Jeff Nelson

Most Games Worked as Crew Partners

2,123 Joe Brinkman & Derryl Cousins
1,913 Larry Goetz & Beans Reardon
1,634 Lee Ballanfant & Al Barlick
1,493 Bob Engel & Paul Runge
1,491 Larry Barnett & Greg Kosc
1,455 Larry Napp & Johnny Stevens
1,436 Ed Montague & Lee Weyer
1,399 Jim Evans & Ted Hendry
1,398 Larry Napp & John Rice
1,326 Shag Crawford & Doug Harvey

Umpires and No-Hitters

By David Vincent

Bruce Froemming, who umpired in the major leagues from 1971 through 2007, was on the field for the most no-hitters ever—11. Froemming was the home-plate umpire four times for a no-no. He called Milt Pappas's in 1972, Ed Halicki's in 1975, Nolan Ryan's in 1981, and Jose Jimenez's in 1999. In addition, Froemming worked on the bases for Burt Hooten's in 1972 (second base), Phil Niekro's in 1973 (third base), Bob Forsch's in 1983 (third base), Dennis Martinez' perfecto in 1991 (first base), Kevin Gross's in 1992 (first base), Darryl Kile's in 1993 (second base), and Bud Smith's in 2001 (second base). Silk O'Loughlin, Paul Pryor, and Jim McKean each worked 10 no-hitters. Tom Hallion has been on the field in some capacity for seven no-hitters, the most among umpires active in 2016.

Silk O'Loughlin, an American League umpire from 1902 through 1918, was behind the plate for six no-hitters in his career, the most called by an umpire behind the plate. His first and second no-hit games were both in 1905, within 45 days of each other. He followed with no-nos in 1908, 1911, 1912, and 1917. Bill Dineen, Bill Klem, and Harry Wendelstedt called five no-hitters apiece while behind the plate.

Ted Barrett is the only umpire to have been behind the plate for two perfect games. Barrett called David Cone's on July 18, 1999, and Matt Cain's on June 13, 2012. Barrett was also on the field at third base for Philip Humber's perfecto on April 21, 2012, making Barrett the only umpire to work three perfect games in his career.

Bill Dineen pitched in the majors from 1898 through 1909. On September 27, 1905, Dineen threw a no-hitter for the Red Sox against the White Sox. After his playing career ended, Dineen was an American League umpire from 1909 through 1937. He was behind the plate for five no-nos: Chief Bender in 1910, George Mullin in 1912, Dutch Leonard in 1918, Sam Jones in 1923, and Howard Ehmke, also in 1923.

Dineen is the only person to throw a no-hitter and call one as an umpire in the major leagues.

Bill Klem, a National League umpire from 1905 through 1941, called his first no-hitter on September 20, 1907. Twenty-seven years and one day later, on September 21, 1934, Klem called his fifth and last, making him the umpire with the longest gap between his first no-hitter behind the plate and his last. Joe Brinkman called two no-nos from behind the plate, on June 19, 1974, and May 12, 2001, 26 years and 327 days apart. Bruce Froemming called four no-hitters. The first was on September 2, 1972, and the last on June 25, 1999, a period of 26 years and 296 days.

Many umpires have called no-hitters or perfect games on more than one occasion. Ten umpires active in 2016 have called multiple no-hit games:

- Ted Barrett (3): David Cone's 1999 perfect game, Ervin Santana's 2011 no-hitter, and Matt Cain's 2012 perfect game.
- Eric Cooper (3): Hideo Nomo's 2001 no-hitter, Mark Buehrle's 2007 no-hitter, and Buehrle's 2009 perfect game.
- Phil Cuzzi (2): Bud Smith's in 2001 and Cole Hamels' in 2015.
- Rob Drake (2): Felix Hernandez' perfecto in 2012 and Chris Heston's no-hitter in 2015.
- Greg Gibson (2): Randy Johnson's perfect game in 2004 and Clayton Kershaw's 2014 no-hitter, in which an error cost Kershaw a perfect game.
- Ed Hickox (2): Matt Garza's in 2010 and Homer Bailey's in 2012.
- Adrian Johnson (2): Edwin Jackson's in 2010 and Homer Bailey's in 2013.
- Jeff Kellogg (2): Anibal Sanchez's in 2006 and Ubaldo Jimenez's in 2010.
- Brian Knight (2): Jon Lester's in 2008 and Josh Beckett's in 2014.
- Ron Kulpa (2): Justin Verlander's in 2007 and Henderson Alvarez's in 2013.

The following umpires have been behind the plate for multiple no-hitters in the same season.

- Foghorn Bradley, 1880
- Mike Walsh, 1882
- Billy McLean, 1884
- John Valentine, 1884
- John Gaffney, 1888
- Tom Lynch, 1892
- Silk O'Loughlin, 1905
- Tommy Connolly, 1908
- Bill Brennan, 1915
- Dick Nallin, 1917
- Bill Dinneen, 1923
- Harry Schwarts, 1962
- Harry Wendelstedt, 1968
- Bill Deegan, 1977
- Drew Coble, 1990
- Brian Runge, 2012

Lou DiMuro and his son, Mike, are the only father-son tandem to have both been behind the plate for no-hitters (Mike for Roy Halladay's 2010 perfect game, and Lou for Jim Palmer's 1969 no-hitter). Ed Runge was the home-plate umpire on September 16, 1965, for Dave Morehead's gem. His grandson, Brian, worked the plate for three no-hitters. The younger Runge called Jonathan Sanchez's game on July 10, 2009, in which an error cost the hurler a perfect game. Runge also called Philip Humber's perfect game on April 21, 2012, and Seattle's six-pitcher no-hitter on June 8, 2012. Brian's dad, Paul, was on the field for six no-hitters but never behind the dish.

Ed Vargo, a National League umpire from 1960 through 1983, was the first major-league umpire to call two no-hitters for the same pitcher. Vargo was behind home plate for Sandy Koufax's no-hitter on June 4, 1964, and his perfect game on September 9, 1965. Eric Cooper is the only other umpire to achieve this feat, by working Mark Buehrle's no-hitter on April 18, 2007, and his July 23, 2009, perfect game.

Dick Nallin is the only umpire to call two no-hitters on back-to-back days. On May 5, 1917, he called Ernie Koob's game for the St. Louis Browns and the next day, Nallin was behind the plate for Bob Groom's no-hit game. Both these games were

Tim Tschida, June 1, 2011.

played at Sportsman's Park in St. Louis. Bill Dinneen called two no-hitters within three days. He umpired the gems by Sam Jones on September 4, 1923, and Howard Ehmke on September 7, 1923. Since umpires no longer work the plate on consecutive days, Nallin's record seems secure.

There have been 11 no-hitters with multiple pitchers. Mike Fichter was the home-plate umpire on June 11, 2003, when a record six Houston Astros pitchers combined to no-hit the New York Yankees at Yankee Stadium. Fichter called balls and strikes as Roy Oswalt, Peter Munro, Kirk Saarloos, Brad Lidge, Octavio Dotel, and Billy Wagner held New York hitless in an 8-0 victory. This feat was matched by the Seattle Mariners on June 8, 2012, when Kevin Millwood, Charlie Furbush, Stephen Pryor, Lucas Luetge, Brandon League, and Tom Wilhelmsen combined on a no-hitter with Brian Runge behind the plate. Three no-hitters have featured four pitchers each. On September 28, 1975, Bill Kunkel called the gem by Oakland hurlers Vida Blue, Glenn Abbott, Paul Lindblad, and Rollie Fingers against the California Angels. On July 13, 1991, Chuck Meriwether called the game by Orioles pitchers Bob Milacki, Mike Flanagan, Mark Williamson, and Gregg Olson at Oakland. Jordan Baker was the home-plate umpire on September 1, 2014, when Cole Hamels, Jake Diekman, Ken Giles, and Jonathan Papelbon of the Phillies blanked the Braves in Atlanta.

Tim Tschida called balls and strikes on September 14, 2008, for Carlos Zambrano's no-hitter against the

Astros. The 5-0 Cubs win, the team's first no-no in 36 years, was relocated from Houston to Milwaukee's Miller Park because of Hurricane Ike. It was the second no-hitter in which Tschida was the home-plate umpire, having called Nolan Ryan's record seventh no-hitter on May 1, 1991.

Two no-hitters have been thrown in the postseason. On October 8, 1956, Don Larsen of the Yankees threw a gem against the Brooklyn Dodgers at Yankee

Stadium. The home-plate umpire that day was Babe Pinelli, working behind the plate for the last time in his 22-year umpiring career. On October 6, 2010, John Hirschbeck called the no-no by Roy Halladay of the Phillies against the Reds in the National League Division Series.

Table 1 contains a list of perfect games while Table 2 shows all other no-hitters.

Date	Pitcher	Team	Opponent	League	HP Umpire
6/12/1880	Lee Richmond	Worcester	Cleveland	NL	Foghorn Bradley
6/17/1880	Monte Ward	Providence	Buffalo	NL	Charles Daniels
5/5/1904	Cy Young	Boston	Philadelphia	AL	Frank Dwyer
10/2/1908	Addie Joss	Cleveland	Chicago	AL	Tommy Connolly
4/30/1922	Charlie Robertson	Chicago	Detroit	AL	Dick Nallin
10/8/1956	Don Larsen	New York	Brooklyn	NL	Babe Pinelli
6/21/1964	Jim Bunning	Philadelphia	New York	NL	Ed Sudol
9/9/1965	Sandy Koufax	Los Angeles	Chicago	NL	Ed Vargo
5/8/1968	Catfish Hunter	Oakland	Minnesota	AL	Jerry Neudecker
5/15/1981	Len Barker	Cleveland	Toronto	AL	Rich Garcia
9/30/1984	Mike Witt	California	Texas	AL	Greg Kosc
9/16/1988	Tom Browning	Cincinnati	Los Angeles	NL	Jim Quick
7/28/1991	Dennis Martinez	Montreal	Los Angeles	NL	Larry Poncino
7/28/1994	Kenny Rogers	Texas	California	AL	Ed Bean
5/17/1998	David Wells	New York	Minnesota	AL	Tim McClelland
7/18/1999	David Cone	New York	Montreal	NL	Ted Barrett
5/18/2004	Randy Johnson	Arizona	Atlanta	NL	Greg Gibson
7/23/2009	Mark Buehrle	Chicago	Tampa Bay	AL	Eric Cooper
5/9/2010	Dallas Braden	Oakland	Tampa Bay	AL	Jim Wolf
5/29/2010	Roy Halladay	Philadelphia	Florida	NL	Mike DiMuro
4/21/2012	Philip Humber	Chicago	Seattle	AL	Brian Runge
6/13/2012	Matt Cain	San Francisco	Houston	NL	Ted Barrett
8/15/2012	Felix Hernandez	Seattle	Tampa Bay	AL	Rob Drake

Table 1 — Perfect Games

Date	Pitcher	Team	Opponent	League	HP Umpire
7/28/1875	Joe Borden	Philadelphia	Chicago	NA	Nick Young
7/15/1876	George Bradley	St. Louis	Hartford	NL	Charles Daniels
8/19/1880	Larry Corcoran	Chicago	Boston	NL	Herm Doscher
8/20/1880	Pud Galvin	Buffalo	Worcester	NL	Foghorn Bradley

Date	Pitcher	Team	Opponent	League	HP Umpire
9/11/1882	Tony Mullane	Louisville	Cincinnati	AA	Mike Walsh
9/19/1882	Guy Hecker	Louisville	Pittsburgh	AA	Mike Walsh
9/20/1882	Larry Corcoran	Chicago	Worcester	NL	Kick Kelly
7/25/1883	Hoss Radbourn	Providence	Cleveland	NL	George Burnham
9/13/1883	Hugh Daily	Cleveland	Philadelphia	NL	Billy McLean
5/24/1884	Al Atkinson	Philadelphia	Pittsburgh	AA	Jack Brennan
5/29/1884	Ed Morris	Columbus	Pittsburgh	AA	John Valentine
6/05/1884	Frank Mountain	Columbus	Washington	AA	John Valentine
6/27/1884	Larry Corcoran	Chicago	Providence	NL	Billy McLean
8/04/1884	Pud Galvin	Buffalo	Detroit	NL	Billy McLean
8/26/1884	Dick Burns	Cincinnati	Kansas City	UA	George Seward
9/28/1884	Ed Cushman	Milwaukee	Washington	UA	Bill McGunnigle
10/04/1884	Sam Kimber	Brooklyn	Toledo	AA	John Valentine
7/27/1885	John Clarkson	Chicago	Providence	NL	Tommy Bond
8/29/1885	Charlie Ferguson	Philadelphia	Providence	NL	Wes Curry
5/01/1886	Al Atkinson	Philadelphia	New York	AA	Billy Carlin
7/24/1886	Adonis Terry	Brooklyn	St. Louis	AA	Mike Walsh
10/06/1886	Matt Kilroy	Baltimore	Pittsburgh	AA	Tom York
5/27/1888	Adonis Terry	Brooklyn	Louisville	AA	Herm Doscher
6/06/1888	Henry Porter	Kansas City	Baltimore	AA	Jack McQuaid
7/26/1888	Ed Seward	Philadelphia	Cincinnati	AA	John Gaffney
7/31/1888	Gus Weyhing	Philadelphia	Kansas City	AA	John Gaffney
9/15/1890	Ledell Titcomb	Rochester	Syracuse	AA	Walter Taylor
6/22/1891	Tom Lovett	Brooklyn	New York	NL	Jack McQuaid
7/31/1891	Amos Rusie	New York	Brooklyn	NL	Phil Powers
10/04/1891	Ted Breitenstein	St. Louis	Louisville	AA	Tom Dolan
8/06/1892	Jack Stivetts	Boston	Brooklyn	NL	Tom Lynch
8/22/1892	Ben Sanders	Louisville	Baltimore	NL	Tom Lynch
10/15/1892	Bumpus Jones	Cincinnati	Pittsburgh	NL	Jack McQuaid
8/16/1893	Bill Hawke	Baltimore	Washington	NL	Bob Emslie
9/18/1897	Cy Young	Cleveland	Cincinnati	NL	Kick Kelly
4/22/1898	Ted Breitenstein	Cincinnati	Pittsburgh	NL	Hank O'Day
4/22/1898	Jim Hughes	Baltimore	Boston	NL	Tom Lynch
7/08/1898	Red Donahue	Philadelphia	Boston	NL	John Gaffney
8/21/1898	Walter Thornton	Chicago	Brooklyn	NL	James McDonald
5/25/1899	Deacon Phillippe	Louisville	New York	NL	Bob Emslie
8/07/1899	Vic Willis	Boston	Washington	NL	Tom Lynch
7/12/1900	Noodles Hahn	Cincinnati	Philadelphia	NL	Adonis Terry
7/15/1901	Christy Mathewson	New York	St. Louis	NL	Frank Dwyer

Date	Pitcher	Team	Opponent	League	HP Umpire
9/20/1902	Nixey Callahan	Chicago	Detroit	AL	Bob Caruthers
9/18/1903	Chick Fraser	Philadelphia	Chicago	NL	Bob Emslie
8/17/1904	Jesse Tannehill	Boston	Chicago	AL	Jack Sheridan
6/13/1905	Christy Mathewson	New York	Chicago	NL	George Bausewine
7/22/1905	Weldon Henley	Philadelphia	St. Louis	AL	Silk O'Loughlin
9/6/1905	Frank Smith	Chicago	Detroit	AL	Silk O'Loughlin
9/27/1905	Bill Dinneen	Boston	Chicago	AL	Tom Connor
5/1/1906	Johnny Lush	Philadelphia	Brooklyn	NL	Hank O'Day
7/20/1906	Mal Eason	Brooklyn	St. Louis	NL	Bill Carpenter
5/8/1907	Big Jeff Pfeffer	Boston	Cincinnati	NL	Bob Emslie
9/20/1907	Nick Maddox	Pittsburgh	Brooklyn	NL	Bill Klem
6/30/1908	Cy Young	Boston	New York	AL	Silk O'Loughlin
7/4/1908	Hooks Wiltse	New York	Philadelphia	NL	Cy Rigler
9/5/1908	Nap Rucker	Brooklyn	Boston	NL	Jim Johnstone
9/18/1908	Bob Rhoads	Cleveland	Boston	AL	Tommy Connolly
9/20/1908	Frank Smith	Chicago	Philadelphia	AL	Rip Egan
4/20/1910	Addie Joss	Cleveland	Chicago	AL	Bull Perrine
5/12/1910	Chief Bender	Philadelphia	Cleveland	AL	Bill Dinneen
7/29/1911	Smoky Joe Wood	Boston	St. Louis	AL	Silk O'Loughlin
8/27/1911	Ed Walsh	Chicago	Boston	AL	Billy Evans
7/4/1912	George Mullin	Detroit	St. Louis	AL	Bill Dinneen
8/30/1912	Earl Hamilton	St. Louis	Detroit	AL	Silk O'Loughlin
9/6/1912	Jeff Tesreau	New York	Philadelphia	NL	Bill Klem
5/31/1914	Joe Benz	Chicago	Cleveland	AL	Rip Egan
9/9/1914	Iron Davis	Boston	Philadelphia	NL	Mal Eason
9/19/1914	Ed Lafitte	Brooklyn	Kansas City	FL	Spike Shannon
4/15/1915	Rube Marquard	New York	Brooklyn	NL	Cy Rigler
4/24/1915	Frank Allen	Pittsburgh	St. Louis	FL	Bill Brennan
5/15/1915	Claude Hendrix	Chicago	Pittsburgh	FL	Barry McCormick
8/16/1915	Alex Main	Kansas City	Buffalo	FL	Bill Brennan
8/31/1915	Jimmy Lavender	Chicago	New York	NL	Bill Klem
9/7/1915	Dave Davenport	St. Louis	Chicago	FL	Joe O'Brien
6/16/1916	Tom Hughes	Boston	Pittsburgh	NL	Bill Klem
6/21/1916	Rube Foster	Boston	New York	AL	George Hildebrand
8/26/1916	Bullet Joe Bush	Philadelphia	Cleveland	AL	Tommy Connolly
8/30/1916	Dutch Leonard	Boston	St. Louis	AL	Brick Owens
4/14/1917	Eddie Cicotte	Chicago	St. Louis	AL	Silk O'Loughlin
4/24/1917	George Mogridge	New York	Boston	AL	Tommy Connolly
5/2/1917	Fred Toney	Cincinnati	Chicago	NL	Al Orth

Date	Pitcher	Team	Opponent	League	HP Umpire
5/5/1917	Ernie Koob	St. Louis	Chicago	AL	Dick Nallin
5/6/1917	Bob Groom	St. Louis	Chicago	AL	Dick Nallin
6/23/1917	Babe Ruth (0 IP), Ernie Shore (9)	Boston	Washington	AL	Brick Owens
6/3/1918	Dutch Leonard	Boston	Detroit	AL	Bill Dinneen
5/11/1919	Hod Eller	Cincinnati	St. Louis	NL	Hank O'Day
9/10/1919	Ray Caldwell	Cleveland	New York	AL	Billy Evans
7/1/1920	Walter Johnson	Washington	Boston	AL	Ollie Chill
5/7/1922	Jesse Barnes	New York	Philadelphia	NL	Bob Hart
9/4/1923	Sad Sam Jones	New York	Philadelphia	AL	Bill Dinneen
9/7/1923	Howard Ehmke	Boston	Philadelphia	AL	Bill Dinneen
7/17/1924	Jesse Haines	St. Louis	Boston	NL	Hank O'Day
9/13/1925	Dazzy Vance	Brooklyn	Philadelphia	NL	Cy Pfirman
8/21/1926	Ted Lyons	Chicago	Boston	AL	Bill McGowan
5/8/1929	Carl Hubbell	New York	Pittsburgh	NL	Charlie Moran
4/29/1931	Wes Ferrell	Cleveland	St. Louis	AL	Harry Geisel
8/8/1931	Bobby Burke	Washington	Boston	AL	George Moriarty
9/21/1934	Paul Dean	St. Louis	Brooklyn	NL	Bill Klem
8/31/1935	Vern Kennedy	Chicago	Cleveland	AL	Bill Summers
6/1/1937	Bill Dietrich	Chicago	St. Louis	AL	Cal Hubbard
6/11/1938	Johnny Vander Meer	Cincinnati	Boston	NL	George Magerkurth
6/15/1938	Johnny Vander Meer	Cincinnati	Brooklyn	NL	Bill Stewart
8/27/1938	Monte Pearson	New York	Cleveland	AL	Lou Kolls
4/16/1940	Bob Feller	Cleveland	Chicago	AL	Harry Geisel
4/30/1940	Tex Carleton	Brooklyn	Cincinnati	NL	Bill Stewart
8/30/1941	Lon Warneke	St. Louis	Cincinnati	NL	Jocko Conlan
4/27/1944	Jim Tobin	Boston	Brooklyn	NL	Bill Stewart
5/15/1944	Clyde Shoun	Cincinnati	Boston	NL	Beans Reardon
9/9/1945	Dick Fowler	Philadelphia	St. Louis	AL	George Pipgras
4/23/1946	Ed Head	Brooklyn	Boston	NL	Babe Pinelli
4/30/1946	Bob Feller	Cleveland	New York	AL	Eddie Rommel
6/18/1947	Ewell Blackwell	Cincinnati	Boston	NL	Al Barlick
7/10/1947	Don Black	Cleveland	Philadelphia	AL	Eddie Rommel
9/3/1947	Bill McCahan	Philadelphia	Washington	AL	Art Passarella
6/30/1948	Bob Lemon	Cleveland	Detroit	AL	Cal Hubbard
9/9/1948	Rex Barney	Brooklyn	New York	NL	Babe Pinelli
8/11/1950	Vern Bickford	Boston	Brooklyn	NL	Larry Goetz
5/6/1951	Cliff Chambers	Pittsburgh	Boston	NL	Frank Dascoli
7/1/1951	Bob Feller	Cleveland	Detroit	AL	Charlie Berry
7/12/1951	Allie Reynolds	New York	Cleveland	AL	Bill McGowan

Date	Pitcher	Team	Opponent	League	HP Umpire
9/28/1951	Allie Reynolds	New York	Boston	AL	Cal Hubbard
5/15/1952	Virgil Trucks	Detroit	Washington	AL	Jim Honochick
6/19/1952	Carl Erskine	Brooklyn	Chicago	NL	Jocko Conlan
8/25/1952	Virgil Trucks	Detroit	New York	AL	Scotty Robb
5/6/1953	Bobo Holloman	St. Louis	Philadelphia	AL	Jim Duffy
6/12/1954	Jim Wilson	Milwaukee	Philadelphia	NL	Babe Pinelli
5/12/1955	Sam Jones	Chicago	Pittsburgh	NL	Artie Gore
5/12/1956	Carl Erskine	Brooklyn	New York	NL	Augie Donatelli
7/14/1956	Mel Parnell	Boston	Chicago	AL	Bill Summers
9/25/1956	Sal Maglie	Brooklyn	Philadelphia	NL	Hal Dixon
8/20/1957	Bob Keegan	Chicago	Washington	AL	Johnny Stevens
7/20/1958	Jim Bunning	Detroit	Boston	AL	Frank Umont
9/20/1958	Hoyt Wilhelm	Baltimore	New York	AL	Joe Paparella
5/15/1960	Don Cardwell	Chicago	St. Louis	NL	Tony Venzon
8/18/1960	Lew Burdette	Milwaukee	Philadelphia	NL	Bill Jackowski
9/16/1960	Warren Spahn	Milwaukee	Philadelphia	NL	Tom Gorman
4/28/1961	Warren Spahn	Milwaukee	San Francisco	NL	Augie Donatelli
5/5/1962	Bo Belinsky	Los Angeles	Baltimore	AL	Harry Schwarts
6/26/1962	Earl Wilson	Boston	Los Angeles	AL	Harry Schwarts
6/30/1962	Sandy Koufax	Los Angeles	New York	NL	Mel Steiner
8/1/1962	Bill Monbouquette	Boston	Chicago	AL	Bill McKinley
8/26/1962	Jack Kralick	Minnesota	Kansas City	AL	Jim Honochick
5/11/1963	Sandy Koufax	Los Angeles	San Francisco	NL	Frank Walsh
5/17/1963	Don Nottebart	Houston	Philadelphia	NL	Ed Vargo
6/15/1963	Juan Marichal	San Francisco	Houston	NL	Ed Sudol
4/23/1964	Ken Johnson	Houston	Cincinnati	NL	Augie Donatelli
6/4/1964	Sandy Koufax	Los Angeles	Philadelphia	NL	Ed Vargo
8/19/1965	Jim Maloney	Cincinnati	Chicago	NL	Mel Steiner
9/16/1965	Dave Morehead	Boston	Cleveland	AL	Ed Runge
6/10/1966	Sonny Siebert	Cleveland	Washington	AL	Jim Honochick
4/30/1967	Steve Barber (8⅔ IP), Stu Miller (⅓)	Baltimore	Detroit	AL	Bill Valentine
6/18/1967	Don Wilson	Houston	Atlanta	NL	Bill Williams
8/25/1967	Dean Chance	Minnesota	Cleveland	AL	Larry Napp
9/10/1967	Joe Horlen	Chicago	Detroit	AL	Jerry Neudecker
4/27/1968	Tom Phoebus	Baltimore	Boston	AL	Frank Umont
7/29/1968	George Culver	Cincinnati	Philadelphia	NL	Harry Wendelstedt
9/17/1968	Gaylord Perry	San Francisco	St. Louis	NL	Harry Wendelstedt
9/18/1968	Ray Washburn	St. Louis	San Francisco	NL	Bill Jackowski
4/17/1969	Bill Stoneman	Montreal	Philadelphia	NL	Tom Gorman

Date	Pitcher	Team	Opponent	League	HP Umpire
4/30/1969	Jim Maloney	Cincinnati	Houston	NL	Frank Secory
5/1/1969	Don Wilson	Houston	Cincinnati	NL	Satch Davidson
8/13/1969	Jim Palmer	Baltimore	Oakland	AL	Lou DiMuro
8/19/1969	Ken Holtzman	Chicago	Atlanta	NL	Dick Stello
9/20/1969	Bob Moose	Pittsburgh	New York	NL	Augie Donatelli
6/12/1970	Dock Ellis	Pittsburgh	San Diego	NL	Tony Venzon
7/3/1970	Clyde Wright	California	Oakland	AL	Marty Springstead
7/20/1970	Bill Singer	Los Angeles	Philadelphia	NL	Ed Sudol
9/21/1970	Vida Blue	Oakland	Minnesota	AL	Larry Barnett
6/3/1971	Ken Holtzman	Chicago	Cincinnati	NL	Satch Davidson
6/23/1971	Rick Wise	Philadelphia	Cincinnati	NL	Jerry Dale
8/14/1971	Bob Gibson	St. Louis	Pittsburgh	NL	Harry Wendelstedt
4/16/1972	Burt Hooton	Chicago	Philadelphia	NL	Paul Pryor
9/2/1972	Milt Pappas	Chicago	San Diego	NL	Bruce Froemming
10/2/1972	Bill Stoneman	Montreal	New York	NL	John McSherry
4/27/1973	Steve Busby	Kansas City	Detroit	AL	John Rice
5/15/1973	Nolan Ryan	California	Kansas City	AL	Jim Evans
7/15/1973	Nolan Ryan	California	Detroit	AL	Ron Luciano
7/30/1973	Jim Bibby	Texas	Oakland	AL	Art Frantz
8/5/1973	Phil Niekro	Atlanta	San Diego	NL	Terry Tata
6/19/1974	Steve Busby	Kansas City	Milwaukee	AL	Joe Brinkman
7/19/1974	Dick Bosman	Cleveland	Oakland	AL	Hank Morgenweck
9/28/1974	Nolan Ryan	California	Minnesota	AL	Art Frantz
6/1/1975	Nolan Ryan	California	Baltimore	AL	Hank Morgenweck
8/24/1975	Ed Halicki	San Francisco	New York	NL	Bruce Froemming
9/28/1975	Vida Blue (5 IP), Glenn Abbott (1), Paul Lindblad (1), Rollie Fingers (2)	Oakland	California	AL	Bill Kunkel
7/9/1976	Larry Dierker	Houston	Montreal	NL	John McSherry
7/28/1976	Blue Moon Odom (5 IP), Francisco Barrios (4)	Chicago	Oakland	AL	Russ Goetz
8/9/1976	John Candelaria	Pittsburgh	Los Angeles	NL	Nick Colosi
9/29/1976	John Montefusco	San Francisco	Atlanta	NL	Paul Pryor
5/14/1977	Jim Colborn	Kansas City	Texas	AL	Bill Deegan
5/30/1977	Dennis Eckersley	Cleveland	California	AL	Bill Deegan
9/22/1977	Bert Blyleven	Texas	California	AL	Fred Spenn
4/16/1978	Bob Forsch	St. Louis	Philadelphia	NL	Lee Weyer
6/16/1978	Tom Seaver	Cincinnati	St. Louis	NL	Terry Tata

Date	Pitcher	Team	Opponent	League	HP Umpire
4/7/1979	Ken Forsch	Houston	Atlanta	NL	Murray Strey
6/27/1980	Jerry Reuss	Los Angeles	San Francisco	NL	Jim Quick
5/10/1981	Charlie Lea	Montreal	San Francisco	NL	Jim Quick
9/26/1981	Nolan Ryan	Houston	Los Angeles	NL	Bruce Froemming
7/4/1983	Dave Righetti	New York	Boston	AL	Steve Palermo
9/26/1983	Bob Forsch	St. Louis	Montreal	NL	Harry Wendelstedt
9/29/1983	Mike Warren	Oakland	Chicago	AL	Marty Springstead
4/7/1984	Jack Morris	Detroit	Chicago	AL	Durwood Merrill
9/19/1986	Joe Cowley	Chicago	California	AL	Rick Reed
9/25/1986	Mike Scott	Houston	San Francisco	NL	Bob Engel
4/15/1987	Juan Nieves	Milwaukee	Baltimore	AL	Jim Evans
4/11/1990	Mark Langston (7 IP), Mike Witt (2)	California	Seattle	AL	Vic Voltaggio
6/2/1990	Randy Johnson	Seattle	Detroit	AL	Al Clark
6/11/1990	Nolan Ryan	Texas	Oakland	AL	Don Denkinger
6/29/1990	Dave Stewart	Oakland	Toronto	AL	Drew Coble
6/29/1990	Fernando Valenzuela	Los Angeles	St. Louis	NL	Jerry Layne
8/15/1990	Terry Mulholland	Philadelphia	San Francisco	NL	Eric Gregg
9/2/1990	Dave Stieb	Toronto	Cleveland	AL	Drew Coble
5/1/1991	Nolan Ryan	Texas	Toronto	AL	Tim Tschida
5/23/1991	Tommy Greene	Philadelphia	Montreal	NL	Jim Quick
7/13/1991	Bob Milacki (6 IP), Mike Flanagan (1), Mark Williamson (1), Gregg Olson (1)	Baltimore	Oakland	AL	Chuck Meriwether
8/11/1991	Wilson Alvarez	Chicago	Baltimore	AL	Don Denkinger
8/26/1991	Bret Saberhagen	Kansas City	Chicago	AL	Ted Hendry
9/11/1991	Kent Mercker (6 IP), Mark Wohlers (2), Alejandro Pena (1)	Atlanta	San Diego	NL	Harry Wendelstedt
8/17/1992	Kevin Gross	Los Angeles	San Francisco	NL	Mike Winters
4/22/1993	Chris Bosio	Seattle	Boston	AL	Vic Voltaggio
9/4/1993	Jim Abbott	New York	Cleveland	AL	Ted Hendry
9/8/1993	Darryl Kile	Houston	New York	NL	Ed Montague
4/8/1994	Kent Mercker	Atlanta	Los Angeles	NL	Ed Rapuano
4/27/1994	Scott Erickson	Minnesota	Milwaukee	AL	Dale Scott
7/14/1995	Ramon Martinez	Los Angeles	Florida	NL	Eric Gregg
5/11/1996	Al Leiter	Florida	Colorado	NL	Steve Rippley
5/14/1996	Dwight Gooden	New York	Seattle	AL	Dan Morrison
9/17/1996	Hideo Nomo	Los Angeles	Colorado	NL	Bill Hohn

Date	Pitcher	Team	Opponent	League	HP Umpire
6/10/1997	Kevin Brown	Florida	San Francisco	NL	Bob Davidson
7/12/1997	Francisco Cordova (9 IP), Ricardo Rincon (1)	Pittsburgh	Houston	NL	Tom Hallion
6/25/1999	Jose Jimenez	St. Louis	Arizona	NL	Bruce Froemming
9/11/1999	Eric Milton	Minnesota	Anaheim	AL	Tim Welke
4/4/2001	Hideo Nomo	Boston	Baltimore	AL	Eric Cooper
5/12/2001	A.J. Burnett	Florida	San Diego	NL	Joe Brinkman
9/3/2001	Bud Smith	St. Louis	San Diego	NL	Phil Cuzzi
4/27/2002	Derek Lowe	Boston	Tampa Bay	AL	Steve Rippley
4/27/2003	Kevin Millwood	Philadelphia	San Francisco	NL	Mike Everitt
6/11/2003	Roy Oswalt (2 IP), Peter Munro (2), Kirk Saarloos (1), Brad Lidge (2), Octavio Dotel (1), Billy Wagner (1)	Houston	New York	IL	Mike Fichter
9/6/2006	Anibal Sanchez	Florida	Arizona	NL	Jeff Kellogg
4/18/2007	Mark Buehrle	Chicago	Texas	AL	Eric Cooper
6/12/2007	Justin Verlander	Detroit	Milwaukee	IL	Ron Kulpa
9/1/2007	Clay Buchholz	Boston	Baltimore	AL	Joe West
5/19/2008	Jon Lester	Boston	Kansas City	AL	Brian Knight
9/14/2008	Carlos Zambrano	Chicago	Houston	NL	Tim Tschida
7/10/2009	Jonathan Sanchez	San Francisco	San Diego	NL	Brian Runge
4/17/2010	Ubaldo Jimenez	Colorado	Atlanta	NL	Jeff Kellogg
6/25/2010	Edwin Jackson	Arizona	Tampa Bay	IL	Adrian Johnson
7/26/2010	Matt Garza	Tampa Bay	Detroit	AL	Ed Hickox
10/6/2010	Roy Halladay	Philadelphia	Cincinnati	NLDS	John Hirschbeck
5/3/2011	Francisco Liriano	Minnesota	Chicago	AL	Bruce Dreckman
5/7/2011	Justin Verlander	Detroit	Toronto	AL	Jerry Meals
7/27/2011	Ervin Santana	Anaheim	Cleveland	AL	Ted Barrett
5/2/2012	Jered Weaver	Anaheim	Minnesota	AL	Mark Carlson
6/1/2012	Johan Santana	New York	St. Louis	NL	Gary Cederstrom
6/8/2012	Kevin Millwood (6 IP), Charlie Furbush (0.2), Stephen Pryor (0.1), Lucas Luetge (0.1), Brandon League (0.2), Tom Wilhelmson (1)	Seattle	Los Angeles	IL	Brian Runge

Date	Pitcher	Team	Opponent	League	HP Umpire
9/28/2012	Homer Bailey	Cincinnati	Pittsburgh	NL	Ed Hickox
7/2/2013	Homer Bailey	Cincinnati	San Francisco	NL	Adrian Johnson
7/13/2013	Tim Lincecum	San Francisco	San Diego	NL	Mark Wegner
9/29/2013	Henderson Alvarez	Miami	Detroit	IL	Ron Kulpa
5/25/2014	Josh Beckett	Los Angeles	Philadelphia	NL	Brian Knight
6/18/2014	Clayton Kershaw	Los Angeles	Colorado	NL	Greg Gibson
6/25/2014	Tim Lincecum	San Francisco	San Diego	NL	Adam Hamari
9/1/2014	Cole Hamels (6 IP), Jake Diekman (1), Ken Giles (1), Jonathan Papelbon (1)	Philadelphia	Atlanta	NL	Jordan Baker
9/28/2014	Jordan Zimmermann	Washington	Miami	NL	Alan Porter
6/9/2015	Chris Heston	San Francisco	New York	NL	Rob Drake
6/20/2015	Max Scherzer	Washington	Pittsburgh	NL	Mike Muchlinski
7/25/2015	Cole Hamels	Philadelphia	Chicago	NL	Phil Cuzzi
8/12/2015	Hisashi Iwakuma	Seattle	Baltimore	AL	Jeff Nelson
8/21/2015	Michael Fiers	Houston	Los Angeles	NL	John Tumpane
8/30/2015	Jake Arrieta	Chicago	Los Angeles	NL	Pat Hoberg
10/3/2015	Max Scherzer	Washington	New York	NL	Tony Randazzo
4/21/2016	Jake Arrieta	Chicago	Cincinnati	NL	Dana DeMuth

Table 2 — No-hitters

Historical Timeline of Major League Umpiring

1876 — William McLean, from Philadelphia, became the first professional umpire when he umpired the first game in National League history between Boston and Philadelphia on April 22.

1878 — The National League instructed home teams to pay umpires $5 per game.

1879 — National League president William A. Hulbert appointed a group of 20 men from which teams could choose an umpire, therefore becoming baseball's first umpiring staff.

1879 — Umpires were given the authority to impose fines for illegal acts.

1882 — The American Association is the majors' first league to hire a full-time staff of permanent umpires. They would begin work the next year.

1882 — National League umpire Richard Higham, the first to wear a mask, became the only major-league umpire ever expelled from the game after the league judged him guilty of collusion with gamblers.

1885 — Umpires began wearing chest protectors for the first time.

1888 — The American Association's John Gaffney alters the way umpires work games. Previously, an umpire worked behind either the pitcher or catcher. Gaffney moved behind the plate for all calls except with runners on base, when he moves behind the pitcher.

1901 — Thomas Connolly umpired the first game in the American League between Cleveland and Chicago on April 24.

1903 — Hank O'Day and Thomas Connolly worked the first modern World Series between the Boston Americans and Pittsburg Pirates.

1906 — William Evans, at 22 years old, became the youngest umpire in major-league history.

1909 — The four-umpire system was employed for the first time in the World Series.

1910 — The umpire organizational chart was established. The plate umpire was appointed the umpire-in-chief and the others were field umpires.

1910 — Chicago Cubs manager Frank Chance became the first person ejected from a World Series game when umpire Thomas Connolly threw him out for protesting a home run call.

1911 — Bill Dinneen worked as an umpire in the World Series and became the first person to play and umpire in the Fall Classic. Dinneen played for the Boston Americans in the 1903 Series.

1912 — Both the American and National Leagues had 10-person umpiring staffs with two umpires being used in games and two reserves.

1921 — Umpires in both leagues began the practice of rubbing mud into the balls prior to each game in order to remove the gloss.

1933 — Bill Dinneen, Bill Klem, Bill McGowan, and Cy Rigler umpired the first All-Star Game at Comiskey Park in Chicago.

1935 — George Barr of the National League opened the first umpire training school in Hot Springs, Arkansas.

1939 — The Bill McGowan School for Umpires opened.

1941 — Bill Klem, the oldest umpire in major-league history at 68, retired from umpiring after working a record 37 seasons and became the National League's first modern chief of umpires.

1946 — Bill McKinley became the first graduate of an umpiring training school to reach the major leagues.

1947 — In the 1947 World Series, featuring the Brooklyn Dodgers and New York Yankees, the current six-man crew was established as an alternate umpire was stationed along each foul line.

1950 — Umpires were no longer allowed to levy fines for illegal acts, as they were instead to be handled by each league president.

1951 — Emmett Ashford became an umpire in the Southwestern International League and became the first black professional umpire.

1952 — The four-man umpiring crew was instituted for all regular season games.

1953 — Thomas Connolly and Bill Klem became the first umpires inducted into the National Baseball Hall of Fame.

1956 — Ed Rommel and Frank Umont broke a long-standing taboo by becoming the first umpires to wear eyeglasses on the field.

1961 — Emmett Ashford became the first black umpire in the major leagues when he was hired by the American League to call games. At 46, Ashford worked the Pacific Coast, Southwest International, Arizona-Texas and Western International Leagues. He became a full-time AL umpire in 1966.

1970 — The first strike by umpires in major-league history lasted one day during the League Championship Series, an action prompting both the American League and National League presidents to recognize the newly-formed Major League Umpires Association and negotiatea labor contract with them.

1972 — Bernice Gera became the first woman to umpire a professional baseball game when she worked a Class-A New York-Penn League game.

1973 — Art Williams became the first black umpire to reach the National League staff.

1974 — Armando Rodriguez became the first Hispanic umpire to work in the major leagues as he joined the American League staff.

1978 — Major-league umpires strike for better benefits. Amateur crews call 13 games before a judge issues a restraining order and sends the regular umpires back to work.

1979 — Major-league umpires went on strike for the third time in history from Opening Day until May 18. Replacement umpires were used during this strike.

1984 — Because of a strike, Game One of the NLCS is called by college umpires.

1991 — Steve Palermo, an AL umpire, suffered a gunshot wound while attempting to prevent the robbery of two women. (Palermo continues to serve as an MLB umpire supervisor.)

1996 — National League umpire John McSherry collapsed during an Opening Day game in Cincinnati and, tragically, passed away after being rushed to a nearby hospital.

1997 — Mike DiMuro became the first American umpire to work a regular-season game in Japan's Central League.

1998 — Harry and Hunter Wendelstedt became the first father-son umpire combination to work a major-league game together.

1999 — Alfonso Marquez became the first-ever Mexican-born, full-time Major League Baseball umpire.

2000 — On February 24, the World Umpires Association ("WUA") was certified as the exclusive collective bargaining agent for all regular full-time major-league umpires.

2005 — Major League Baseball and the World Umpires Association ratified a new collective bargaining agreement extending through December 31, 2009.

2006 — Bruce Froemming worked his 5,000th career game on August 16 at Fenway Park.

2008 — On August 26, Commissioner Allan H. (Bud) Selig announced that Major League Baseball would implement a system of limited instant replay, applying only to home run calls—whether they are fair or foul, whether they have left the playing field, or whether they have been subject to fan interference. Instant replay was available for the first time in the three new series that began on Thursday, August 28 and in all ensuing games.

2008 — On September 3, a home run by Alex Rodriguez of the New York Yankees at Tropicana Field in St. Petersburg was upheld in the first use of instant replay in Major League Baseball history.

2009 — On October 31, in the first use of instant replay in MLB postseason history, a ball hit in play by New York's Alex Rodriguez during Game Three of the World Series was reviewed at Philadelphia's Citizens Bank Park. The subsequent reversal results in a home run for Rodriguez, who had also hit the ball that led to the first regular season use of instant replay on September 3, 2008.

2009 — On December 23, Major League Baseball and the World Umpires Association announced a tentative five-year collective bargaining agreement through December 31, 2014. The major-league clubs and the membership of the World Umpires Association ratified the agreement in January 2010.

2014 — On January 16, Commissioner Allan H. (Bud) Selig announced that Major League Baseball would expand instant replay for the 2014 regular season, with the consent of the MLB Players Association and the World Umpires Association.

2015 — On January 21, Major League Baseball and the World Umpires Association officially ratified a five-year labor agreement, covering the 2015-2019 seasons.

Umpires in Postseason

David Vincent

Playing in postseason is a special time for players. It is also special for umpires who are assigned to officiate.

The first modern World Series in 1903 was umpired by two men: Hank O'Day and Tommy Connolly. O'Day, a retired player, had been a member of the National League staff since 1897, but had umpired some games in the American Association, Players League, and the NL as early as 1884. Connolly represented the American League in this Series. He had worked some games in the AA and NL before joining the NL staff in 1898 and moving to the AL in 1901. O'Day went on to umpire 57 games in 10 World Series assignments while Connolly worked eight Series, encompassing 45 games. Both men are Hall of Fame umpires.

On October 9, 1907, the Tigers were playing the Cubs in Game Two of the Series at Chicago. In the top of the third inning, Germany Schaefer was called out at second on a steal attempt. Tigers manager Hughie Jennings argued the call and was ejected by Hank O'Day. This was the first ejection in a postseason contest. In 1972, Sparky Anderson became the first person to be tossed from a post-season game that was not the World Series. In the first game of the National League Championship Series, Cesar Geronimo hit a line drive in the top of the fourth frame that struck first-base umpire Ken Burkhart. Burkhart ruled it a foul ball and then ejected Anderson for arguing the call. Bobby Cox is the only person to be ejected more than once in postseason. He was tossed three times, twice in the World Series (1992, 1996) and once in the NL Division Series (2010). A complete list of postseason ejections can be found at the end of this article.

The umpire with the most World Series ejections is George Moriarty (3). For all of postseason, the leader, in addition to Moriarty, is Vic Carapazza (3 in the Division Series). Of note is the fact that both Harry and Hunter Wendelstedt have ejected someone in postseason. Commissioner Kenesaw Landis pulled Joe Medwick of the Cardinals from the seventh and final game of the 1934 World Series. Medwick and Mickey Owen tangled in the sixth inning and Medwick was pelted with fruit and bottles by Tigers fans. Landis decided to remove Medwick from the contest for Medwick's safety.

Bill Klem appeared in the World Series for the first time in 1908. "The Old Arbitrator," who made his National League debut in 1905, worked 103 Series games in 18 Series assignments through 1940. Both of these figures are records for an umpire in the World Series. Klem is the only umpire to work more than two consecutive Series, having umpired in five consecutive seasons from 1911 through 1915. Cy Rigler is a distant second in games worked in the Series with 62. Refer to lists at the end of the article for more information.

In the 1908 Series, four different umpires worked games. Jack Sheridan (AL) and Hank O'Day (NL) alternated with Bill Klem (NL) and Tommy Connolly (AL). This was the first time that more than two umpires worked in one Series. In 1909, the same alternation of assignments was used to start the Series. Jim Johnstone (NL) and Silk O'Loughlin (AL) umpired Games One and Three while Klem and Billy Evans were on the field for Game Two. All four umpires worked on the field for the first time in Game Four, with Klem behind the plate and Evans on the bases. O'Loughlin and Johnstone were positioned on the outfield lines. This change of umpire assignments occurred due to a controversial foul call in Game Two of the Series.

The assignments with two arbiters in the outfield lasted though the 1916 Series. In 1917, the four umpires all stood in the infield. The home plate and first base umpires still acted as a pair and they moved to second and third for Game Two. In 1918, the four umpires worked a rotation around the infield as we see now: home plate to third base to second base to first base. This method continued through 1946, but more on that later.

The 1911 Series featured umpire Bill Dinneen, a former big-league pitcher. Dinneen had pitched in the 1903 World Series for the Boston Americans and became the first person to both play and umpire in the World Series. Dinneen went on to umpire in eight Series (45 total games).

The people who have played and umpired in the World Series are listed in Table 1 in alphabetical order. No one has played in a League Championship or Division Series and also umpired in postseason.

Player/Umpire	Played	Umpired
Bill Dinneen	1903	1911, 1914, 1916, 1920, 1924, 1926, 1929, 1932
George Moriarty	1909	1921, 1925, 1930, 1933, 1935
George Pipgras	1927-28, 1932	1944
Eddie Rommel	1921, 1931	1943, 1947
Frank Secory	1945	1957, 1959, 1964, 1969
Lon Warneke	1932, 1935	1954

Table 1 — People Who Played and Umpired in Postseason

The first time six umpires worked in a postseason game was in the 1947 World Series. The lineup for game 1 at Yankee Stadium was Bill McGowan (AL, HP), Babe Pinelli (NL, 1B), Eddie Rommell (AL, 2B), Larry Goetz (NL, 3B), George Magerkurth (NL, LF), and Jim Boyer (AL, RF). Magerkurth and Boyer worked only in the outfield for the seven-game series. This practice continued through the 1963 World Series. Starting in 1964, all six arbiters rotated through all six positions, which is the current practice.

In 1984, staff umpires went on strike and all except one game of the two League Championship Series were worked by college umpires. In the American League, retired arbiter Bill Deegan worked behind home plate for all three games. Jon Bible, a veteran of four College World Series, umpired at first in the series while Randy Christal, also a four-time College World Series veteran who also had umpired in the

1984 Olympics, worked at second. Nine other umpires worked the other positions in the three-game series, with no one umpiring more than one contest. These were the only major-league games umpired by Bible and Christal.

In the National League Championship Series, four men worked the first two games in Chicago and four new umpires worked the next two games in San Diego. The strike was settled after Game Four and a four-man crew of veteran staff umpires worked the deciding Game Five in San Diego: John Kibler, Paul Runge, John McSherry, and Doug Harvey.

In 1990, Gerry Davis, then a nine-year veteran in the majors, worked as the junior man on the crew for the National League Championship Series. This was Davis' first postseason experience but certainly not his last. Through the 2016 season, Davis has umpired more postseason games than any other person in history, with 133 (24 in the World Series, 57 in the League Championship Series, 50 in the Division Series, and 2 Wild Card games). He has had more opportunities to do so with extra rounds having been added in 1995 (Division Series) and 2012 (Wild Card Play-in games). However, Davis is at least 11 games ahead of his contemporaries, who have had equal opportunity to umpire in the postseason.

In 2009, there was a series of incorrect calls in early rounds of the playoffs, which led to a reassessment of how umpires are chosen for the World Series. That year, three umpires with at least 25 years in the majors and three World Series assignments each (Gerry Davis, Dana DeMuth, and Joe West) were selected along with three umpires with at least 11 years on staff and one Series assignment each. This was a major change from recent practice. From 1983 through 2008, only one World Series did not have an umpire working his first Series assignment (1997).

More recently, the initial positioning of umpires to start a series has changed. The tradition was that the crew chief would umpire at home plate in Game One, but, more recently, the crew chief has started in right field with another experienced umpire at the plate for Game One. This change places two experienced umpires who are highly-rated calling balls and

Umpires Ernie Quigley, Tom Connolly, Hank O'Day, and Bill Dinneen at the 1916 World Series. Braves Field, Boston, October 7, 1916.

strikes behind home plate for Games Six and Seven. In the LCS, the crew chief starts at second base. In the five-game Division Series, the chief starts in left field.

When the expanded replay system was put in place for the 2014 season, a small change was made to umpiring assignments for the postseason. An umpire was tasked as the replay official in New York during games for each series. The home plate umpire for Game One of each series worked two games on the field and then switched with the replay official for the rest of the series. This system is in place for the Division, League, and World Series. There is also a replay official for the Wild Card games. With the addition of one more umpire to a seven-game series, the starting rotation changed again. The crew chief started at second base and the umpire who was to leave after two games was the home plate umpire for Game One.

Most Games Umpired in the World Series

103 Bill Klem
62 Cy Rigler
57 Hank O'Day
47 Bill Summers
45 Tommy Connolly
45 Bill Dinneen
43 Bill McGowan
42 Al Barlick
42 Jim Honochick
38 Billy Evans
38 Ernie Quigley
36 Babe Pinelli
34 Ed Montague
33 Augie Donatelli
33 Harry Wendelstedt
33 Joe West

Most World Series Appearances

18 Bill Klem
10 Hank O'Day
10 Cy Rigler
8 Tommy Connolly
8 Bill Dinneen
8 Bill McGowan
8 Bill Summers

7 Al Barlick
6 Billy Evans
6 Jim Honochick
6 Ed Montague
6 Babe Pinelli
6 Ernie Quigley
6 Joe West

10 John Hirschbeck
10 Jim Joyce
10 Mike Winters
9 Eric Cooper
9 Paul Emmel
9 Bruce Froemming
9 Greg Gibson
9 Jeff Kellogg
9 Ron Kulpa
9 Jerry Layne
9 Tim Tschida

Most League Championship Series Appearances

12 Jerry Crawford
10 Gerry Davis
10 Bruce Froemming
9 Doug Harvey
9 Randy Marsh
9 Tim McClelland
9 Mike Reilly
9 Paul Runge
9 Joe West
8 Ted Barrett
8 Angel Hernandez
8 John McSherry

Most Games Umpired in Postseason

133 Gerry Davis
122 Joe West
111 Bruce Froemming
111 Jerry Crawford
103 Bill Klem
100 Jeff Kellogg
99 Ed Montague
98 Tim Welke
96 Dana DeMuth
95 Ted Barrett
94 Tim McClelland
94 Mike Winters
93 John Hirschbeck
92 Randy Marsh
91 Mike Reilly
91 Dale Scott

Most Division Series Appearances

12 Gerry Davis
11 Dale Scott
10 Gary Darling
10 Dana DeMuth
10 Brian Gorman

Postseason Ejections

Date	Series	Ejectee	Umpire	Reason
10/09/1907	WS	Hughie Jennings	Hank O'Day	Call at 2B
10/12/1909	WS	Bill Donovan	Bill Klem	Refusing to end conf. with 3B coach
10/20/1910	WS	Frank Chance	Tommy Connolly	Home run call
10/22/1910	WS	Tom Needham	Tommy Connolly	Bench jockeying
10/06/1919	WS	Ray Schalk	Cy Rigler	Call at HP
10/06/1919	WS	Jimmy Smith	Cy Rigler	Bench jockeying
10/10/1923	WS	Bullet Joe Bush	Hank O'Day	Call at 1B
10/06/1933	WS	Heinie Manush	Charlie Moran	Call at 1B (Bumped umpire)
10/09/1934	WS	Joe Medwick	Kenesaw Landis	Disruption after fight at 3B
10/04/1935	WS	Woody English	George Moriarty	Bench jockeying

Date		Argued	Umpire	Reason
10/04/1935	WS	Charlie Grimm	George Moriarty	Bench jockeying
10/04/1935	WS	Tuck Stainback	George Moriarty	Bench jockeying
10/04/1935	WS	Del Baker	Ernie Quigley	Call at 3B
10/07/1952	WS	Ralph Branca	Larry Goetz	Bench jockeying
10/08/1959	WS	Chuck Dressen	Eddie Hurley	Balls and strikes
10/15/1969	WS	Earl Weaver	Shag Crawford	Balls and strikes
10/07/1972	LCS	Sparky Anderson	Ken Burkhart	Fair/foul call
10/08/1972	LCS	Lerrin LaGrow	Nestor Chylak	Intentional HBP
10/08/1972	LCS	Bert Campaneris	Nestor Chylak	Fighting (Threw bat)
10/12/1972	LCS	Frank Howard	John Rice	Call at 1B
10/21/1976	WS	Billy Martin	Bruce Froemming	Throwing baseball onto field
10/27/1985	WS	Joaquin Andujar	Don Denkinger	Balls and strikes
10/27/1985	WS	Whitey Herzog	Don Denkinger	Balls and strikes
10/10/1986	LCS	Gene Mauch	Nick Bremigan	Call at HP (Reversed)
10/25/1987	WS	Danny Cox	Dave Phillips	Balls and strikes
10/08/1988	LCS	Bruce Hurst	Ken Kaiser	Interference call
10/08/1988	LCS	Jay Howell	Harry Wendelstedt	Doctored ball (Pine tar)
10/10/1990	LCS	Marty Barrett	Terry Cooney	Balls and strikes (Threw equipment)
10/10/1990	LCS	Roger Clemens	Terry Cooney	Balls and strikes
10/13/1991	LCS	Cito Gaston	Mike Reilly	Balls and strikes
10/20/1992	WS	Bobby Cox	Joe West	Checked swing (Threw helmet)
10/04/1995	LDS	Raul Mondesi	Bob Davidson	Balls and strikes
10/17/1995	LCS	Luis Sojo	Drew Coble	Called third strike
10/09/1996	LCS	Davey Johnson	Rich Garcia	Fan interference non-call
10/26/1996	WS	Bobby Cox	Tim Welke	Call at 2B
09/30/1998	LDS	Dwight Gooden	Joe Brinkman	Call at HP
09/30/1998	LDS	Mike Hargrove	Joe Brinkman	Call at HP
10/09/1999	LDS	Cookie Rojas	Charlie Williams	Fair/foul call (Bumped umpire)
10/17/1999	LCS	Jimy Williams	Dale Scott	Call at 1B
10/15/2000	LCS	Dave Duncan	Steve Rippley	Balls and strikes
10/16/2005	LCS	Tony LaRussa	Phil Cuzzi	Balls and strikes
10/16/2005	LCS	Jim Edmonds	Phil Cuzzi	Balls and strikes
10/11/2008	LCS	John Farrell	Sam Holbrook	Balls and strikes
10/07/2010	LDS	Joe Maddon	Jim Wolf	Checked swing
10/07/2010	LDS	Ron Gardenhire	Hunter Wendelstedt	Balls and strikes
10/08/2010	LDS	Bobby Cox	Paul Emmel	Call at 1B (Threw hat)
10/14/2012	LCS	Joe Girardi	Jeff Nelson	Call at 2B
10/04/2014	LDS	Asdrubal Cabrera	Vic Carapazza	Called third strike (Threw bat)
10/04/2014	LDS	Matt Williams	Vic Carapazza	Called third strike

10/07/2015	WC	Sean Rodriguez	Jeff Nelson	Fighting
10/14/2015	LDS	Mark Buehrle	Dale Scott	Coming onto the field (not on roster)
10/14/2015	LDS	Michael Saunders	Vic Carapazza	Bench jockeying
10/19/2015	LCS	Troy Tulowitzki	John Hirschbeck	Called third strike

Umpires In The Negro Leagues

By Leslie Heaphy

What about our Negro baseball umpires? They are cussed, discussed, made the subject of all sorts of fuss. They are reviled and often as not, riled as they go about their highly-sensitive calling of calling 'em right, knowing that the fans in the stands are prejudicing them from the start, and that the players are the greatest umpire "riders" in the business. … All together, the life of the Negro umpire isn't cheese and cherries by any means.[1]

Information about various aspects of black baseball can be difficult to find, and there are still lots of gaps in the story that need to be filled in—none more so than the role of umpires. Few stories in the newspapers ever said much about the umpires beyond their names unless something happened involving a bad call or a brawl. Some fans are familiar with the name Emmett Ashford as the first black umpire in the major leagues, but what about all the men who came before him? Who were these individuals who toiled in the shadows and never got any recognition for the difficult job they had on and off the field? Why did the leagues employ white and black umpires? How much of a difference did it make to have umpires who were white rather than black?

When the Negro National League (NNL) was created in 1920, one of the most important issues to be figured out was the way umpires would be chosen and paid. League President Rube Foster believed that the umpire needed to be in charge and provide order to every game. The umpire could maintain the legitimacy of the new league if he knew the rules and could command respect. There were mixed feelings among the owners about whether the umpires should be white or black. In 1920 most games had

only two umpires rather than the four we see today. This made the role of the umpires even harder and more important. It was not until 1923 that the NNL owners voted to hire the first all-black crew for the league. Prior to that umpires were generally provided by the home team and were often white.

One of the earliest recorded stories of a black umpire involves Jacob Francis, who was chosen to represent Syracuse as one of the official umpires in the newly formed New York State League. In the census records of 1870 and 1880, Francis is listed as "mulatto." He umpired at Stars Park throughout 1885 as one member of a three-man crew, becoming the first black umpire for an all-white league. In addition to umpiring, Francis managed the Syracuse Pastimes, a local black team. Francis first appeared in the 1870 census in Syracuse with his wife, Sarah, having come from Virginia. Fans generally supported Francis and even booed another umpire when he subbed for Francis. One news reporter said Francis "is one of the most popular men that ever officiated as an umpire before a Syracuse audience. An instance cannot be recalled where there was any trouble or delay in a game in which Mr. Francis officiated. He possesses an excellent judgment, is quick on his feet and gives his decisions promptly."[2]

A 1909 Seattle article talked about Pete Johnson, a black umpire in the Jacksonville area during the late 19th century. Johnson appeared to be a fan favorite and well respected for his calls. Reporting on one game, a writer commented that "all the hotel guests were desirous of seeing Pete Johnson umpire as they were to witness the game itself." He had a unique way of calling the game, deciding a runner who was out on the bases was "cancelled." When a runner refused to leave the field after Johnson called him out Johnson simply said the player would be a "ghost runner."[3]

Francis and Johnson were rarities: Most games involving black teams always had white umpires before 1923. That was partly due to the lack of trained black umpires, but more importantly most teams were owned by white men. They had control of the resources and therefore black men did not get the chance to umpire.[4] Given the nature of race relations in the 1900s and 1910s, the idea that decisions by whites would be more accepted than those by blacks was not a stretch, and provided an additional rationale for the owners to justify using white umpires.

As early as 1910 the question of umpires for a proposed all-black league was being discussed. When Chicagoan Beauregard Moseley wrote about his proposed league, he noted many decisions that had to be made, but one he seemed to be adamant about was paid umpires. He said the umpires should receive $5 a game and be paid by the home team. Moseley did not comment on whether the umpires would be "race umps" or white arbiters but his proposal matched the pattern most often used by later leagues, with umpires provided by the home team. That added an extra burden to the men in black, who had to work harder to prove their impartiality.[5]

Foster did use black umpires for exhibition and benefit games. In 1910 he hired boxer Jack Johnson and vaudeville performer S.H. Dudley to work a benefit for Provident Hospital, a black-owned institution. The use of such stars gave the black community figures to look up to as role models. Foster himself umpired a benefit game in 1913, but for regular Chicago American Giants contests he used white umpires like Goeckel.[6] With the creation of the NNL in 1920, Foster recognized the importance of umpires, writing in a 1921 column, "Future of Race Umps Depends on Men of Today." He used this column to explain why the new league would be using white umpires rather than black. Foster's basic explanation was simply that black men lacked knowledge of the rules. Opportunities were just not present, but the NNL was not a charity; it was business.[7]

Since there were no professional schools for black umpires, many of the best African American umps were former players who relied on their knowledge

Umpires "Bullet" Rogan, Robert Boone, and Hurley McNair, Ruppert Stadium, May 2, 1940.

of the game from personal experience. For example, Newark Eagles first baseman-outfielder Mule Suttles umpired after he retired in the late 1940s. Pitcher Billy Donaldson turned to umpiring in the 1920s and 1930s, while second baseman Mo Harris umpired from the 1930s through the 1940s after his career with the Homestead Grays ended. Local Cleveland sports star Harry Walker umpired for the Cleveland Bears in 1939 to try to help support black baseball in his community. Cincinnati native Percy Reed played second base for a local athletic club and the Lincoln Giants. He started umpiring in 1929 and from 1935 to 1947 he called every Sunday game played by black teams in Cincinnati. Reed worked as part of a local two-umpire team with Harry Ward, known locally and in the papers as Wu-fang. Reed learned his trade from Bill Carpenter, who was an umpire in the International League.[8] Hurley McNair, a pitcher and outfielder for a number of Negro League clubs, umpired after he retired as a player in 1937. He traveled for league games until his death in December 1948.[9]

The Baltimore Black Sox employed black umpires as early as 1917 when Charles Cromwell was hired by owner Charles Spedden. Cromwell umpired in the Negro Leagues through the 1947 season. In 1923 Rube Foster tried to hire Cromwell as part of a new team of African American umpires for the NNL. Foster wanted the best umpires and felt that white umpires had provided that in the first years of the league. With the creation of the Eastern Colored League (ECL) in 1923, Foster felt the time was right to find the best black umpires he could. His first hire was Billy Donaldson from the Pacific Coast League, and then he went after Cromwell. Cromwell turned Foster down to stay with the Black Sox after Spedden hired Henry "Spike" Spencer from Washington, D.C., to join him as the team's umpires.

Spedden proved he wanted the Black Sox to succeed by spending money on the team, and so Cromwell opted to stay and umpire at the Maryland Baseball Park. By 1924 Spedden vowed to use all black umpires for Black Sox games, a move some said "is bound to meet with favor."[10] Cromwell's choice did not turn out to be the best when the ECL decided in 1925 that teams should not hire their own umpires as had been the practice. This put Cromwell and Spencer out of work. Cromwell came back in 1926 when the ECL gave back the hiring of umpires to the teams. In 1927, when George Rossiter took over operations for the Black Sox, he fired Cromwell and Spencer. Rossiter felt that black umpires were not yet competent and that he would use white umpires until they were. Cromwell found work in a minor black league in the South before returning to umpire for the Baltimore Elite Giants through 1947. Cromwell's career was like that of so many of the other black umpires, who always had to fight to prove they were as worthy as white umpires.[11]

When the Negro National League was being formed, Rube Foster talked with the press about a variety of subjects vital to the league's success. One of those topics was umpires, who Foster stated needed to be totally in charge. Their decisions would be final and then needed to be supported by the league. Foster wanted "utmost good order on the ball field." He saw the league as an investment, a business venture, and so the right arbiters would be essential to the success

of the league. Foster commented, "I think an ump should be pacific but firm, positive but polite, quick but unshoddy, strict but reasonable."[12] On the question of the use of white versus black umpires, Foster wanted to use African American men but believed that there were not enough available and that anyway many people would accept the decisions of white umpires more readily. Reporter Charles Marshall thought colored umpires should be given a chance but agreed with Foster about white umpires. He wrote, "Of course we know that some players as well as some managers and fans alike feel that the white umpire's decision carries more weight and generally comes closer to the right decision than the colored official. In most cases just because he is white."[13]

With the creation of the Eastern Colored League (ECL) in 1923, the leagues continued serious discussions, deciding to hire all black umpires for the NNL. Reporter Frank Young began a campaign to hire black umpires in 1922. He called for training of black men and at the same time criticized the mistakes of white umpires. He tried to counter Foster's concern that black umpires would be swayed by the cheering of black fans rather than engage in good decision-making. Young used his column to highlight the work of men like Jamison in Baltimore and Donaldson in California to show that there were African American men capable of umpiring for the league.[14] Kansas City was the first of the cities to use two black umpires, Billy Donaldson and Bert Gholston.

Foster hired six black umpires for the league, with two-man crews responsible for different cities. Leon Augustine and Lucian Snaer worked around the Milwaukee area while Caesar Jamison and William Embry worked the Indianapolis region. When Foster failed to hire Charley Cromwell, he had to look harder for qualified men. Tom Johnson was the last of the original hires, being used as a rotating umpire.[15]

Finding arbiters with the necessary qualifications and abilities to control the game and the situations that could arise proved difficult from the beginning to the demise of the Negro Leagues. While owners like Foster and Kansas City's J.L. Wilkinson favored all-race crews, they also knew having qualified umpires was even more important. Foster would not even use black umpires for Chicago American Giants games, preferring to pay white umpires while black umpires sat idle.[16] By the end of the 1925 season, Foster released the black umpires who had been hired by the league and went back to the practice of the home team providing the umpires.[17] At the end of the season the other owners hired back four of the six men who had been let go. These men continued to work for the league through the 1927 season without significant incident.

After Foster left the NNL in 1926, black umpires still had a difficult time being hired. However, when the short-lived American Negro League was created in 1929, it hired black umpires led by former players Bill Gatewood, Judy Gans, and former umpire Frank Forbes. Because of the Great Depression, pressure on the owners increased to give black men a chance. Unfortunately, the ANL collapsed after the 1929 season, ending one of the best opportunities for black umpires to be hired. *Chicago Defender* reporter Al Monroe stated in more than one column that black umpires needed to take better control of the game, they need to be less tentative and show control if they wanted respect. Without control they would never find regular employment.[18]

Umpires always had a tough time with players and fans who did not want to listen, but Negro League umpires often had a tougher time without much league support. Bert Gholston believed that the umpires always worked with the fear that they would be attacked and the league would not support them. He stated, "Several of the teams of the Negro National League are still under the impression that they shouldn't take orders from the colored umpires. Several of them were threatening to jump on the umpires."[19]

In 1934 NNL Commissioner Rollo Wilson tried to improve the situation by imposing fines and suspensions. One particular target was Jud Wilson, who had a temper and a reputation for attacking umpires. Wilson's $10 fine was not much of a deterrent. By 1936 things had gotten so bad that $25 became the fine with a 10-day suspension for assaulting an umpire. New

league secretary John L. Clark created a schedule for the three league umpires, Ray "Mo" Harris, John Craig, and Pete Cleague. The other umpires would still be chosen by the home team, which encouraged charges of favoritism. Unfortunately for the umpires, without strong support from league officials, they were pretty much on their own. Longtime umpire Virgil Blueitt stated, "If the club owners would order their managers and players to abide by the umpires' rulings, much of this trouble could be avoided."[20]

Another veteran umpire, Frank Forbes, was attacked on June 5, 1937, by New York Black Yankees players, and just a few games later he got into an altercation with Newark manager Tex Burnett. A month later Forbes and fellow umpire Jasper "Jap" Washington were attacked in their dressing room by Baltimore Elite Giants players. Washington resigned when nothing happened to the players involved. League honchos Gus Greenlee and Cum Posey finally responded with tougher policies, but the enforcement was lax depending on how a team's players were affected. For example, when umpire James Crump forfeited a game, manager George Scales attacked him and the league let Crump go without any hearing at all. The lack of official support made an already hard job even more difficult for umpires, who earned no real respect for just doing their job.[21]

A reporter for the *Kansas Whip* stated that the "weakest link in a game is found in the set-up of umpires, which is limited to three." He included a variety of criticism from around the league about the umpires not being harsh enough in their actions towards players who broke the rules.[22]

In 1944 Dan Burley wrote about the abuse umpires took for little pay. He reprinted a letter he received from Fred McCrary, a longtime umpire in the NNL. McCrary was upset at the lack of attention paid to umpires. For example, he worked in every East-West game from 1938 through 1944 and all the umpires got for each game was $10 and expenses. When McCrary asked for more money, the owners told him the umpire was not important for the game.[23] Not all agreed with that assessment, as there were owners and players who treated umpires

Bob Motley, umpiring in 1950 at Blues Stadium, Kansas City, Missouri.

respectfully. By the 1940s some were also concerned about improving the respect because they feared the violence on and off the field might hurt the increasing push for integration.

In 1945 umpire Jimmy Thompson had his nose broken by player Piper Davis and pursued legal action against him since the league did little. Thompson won his case, though Davis only paid $230 in court costs. Later, President J.B. Martin added a league fine of $250 and indefinite suspension when the true story of the fight came out. Sometimes things got so bad that the police had to be called in to restore order. While police help was necessary it did not help the umpires exercise true authority. Sadly, it happened with both white and black umpires, as evidenced by Goose Curry harassing white umpire Pete Strauch until the police escorted Curry off the field. The Chicago Cubs finally raised the rent on Wrigley Field to keep black teams from using it if they could not control their players.[24]

Even the minor Negro Leagues had regular discussions about umpires and their roles. The Texas-Oklahoma-Louisiana League (TOL) decided in 1929 to hire four umpires who would be paid by the league. The league officials hoped this would give the umpires more authority and lessen incidents on the field. The Florida State Negro League in 1949 followed the pattern of having the home teams provide the umpires. But at the winter meetings before the 1950 season, discussion about the umpires' situation dominated the talks. The league decided to hire two umpires, Williams Washington and Archie Colbert, and have the "balls and strikes" umpires travel around the league. At the same time, league President Skipper Holbert let two other umpires, Gus Daniels and Charles Merrit, go for inefficiency and misconduct.[25]

At the annual East-West Classic the leagues often used both Negro League and white minor-league umpires for the contest. Having a bigger pool to draw from allowed the Classic to have four umpires which often meant better control and legitimacy for the game. The only real difference in rules for the minor-league umpires was the fact that the spitball was legal in the Negro Leagues.[26]

The best-known black umpire from the Negro Leagues is Bob Motley, who in 2016 was the last living umpire from the leagues. Motley was born in Autaugaville, Alabama, in 1923, the sixth of eight children born to parents who were sharecroppers. Motley's father died when he was 4, making it even tougher on the family to survive. Motley served in the US Marine Corps during World War II, earning a Purple Heart for a wound. While serving in the Marines, Motley umpired a few pickup games and discovered a career that would take off after the war. He umpired for over 25 years in the Negro Leagues and white minors. Umpiring from 1949 to 1956 in the Negro Leagues, Motley got to see some of the best players of the day and even umpired the 1953 and 1954 East-West Classics. Motley commented on umpiring, "An umpire has got to have guts. And force right; an ump can count on being no one's friend—at least while on the diamond."[27]

Motley attended the Al Somers Umpire School twice and graduated at the top of the class each time. His high scores did not help in the face of segregation; he never umpired above the Pacific Coast League.[28] Motley recognized that umpires were not treated well by anyone. For example, he commented, "It was pretty common in the Negro Leagues, that if the catcher didn't like the way an umpire was calling balls and strikes, he would purposely let a pitch go by and let it smack the umpire right in the facemask.

That happened to me at least a half a dozen times."[29] After he called Hank Bayliss out on strikes and threw him out of the game, Bayliss came after Motley with a butcher knife on the bus home. The fans were even worse than the players in their continual comments. Motley said most fans had a favorite chant, *"Kill the umpire, Kill the umpire!"* You heard the chant so often you just expected it. Fans loved to blame the umpire when their team lost.[30]

While Motley has received some attention in his later years and Emmett Ashford is known because he was the first African American umpire in the majors, Julian Osibee Jelks never really got a shot. Jelks umpired for four years in the Pacific Coast League but never got a call to the majors. Before umpiring in the minors, Jelks was discovered by Alex Pompez when he came to New Orleans with his barnstorming Negro League teams. Pompez was so impressed with Jelks that he hired him to travel with his clubs in the mid-1950s. By 1956 Jelks got his first chance in the white professional leagues and began his climb to Triple A. Jelks umpired until the assassination of Dr. Martin Luther King Jr. and then he stopped, fearing he or his family might become targets. In 2008 Jelks was invited as a guest to the major-league draft where teams symbolically selected a former player from the Negro Leagues.[31]

Throughout the history of black baseball and the Negro Leagues, the issue of who would act as arbiters for their games was always a concern. While Rube Foster and other owners might have favored in principle hiring black men as umpires, they were businessmen first and needed to put the best product on the field. This led to decisions to hire white umpires most of the time based on the beliefs that they knew the rules better and could control the behavior of players and fans. With that said there were still many fine black umpires, from Jacob Francis to Julian Jelks. Sadly, good umpires rarely get noticed and their stories are not told, making it hard to track them down and give them credit for their contributions.

NOTES

1   Dan Burley, "Chicken-feed for Negro Umpires," in James Reisler, *Black Writers/Black Baseball: An Anthology of Articles From Black Sportswriters Who Covered the Negro Leagues* (Jefferson, North Carolina: McFarland and Company, 2007), 136.

2   Sean Kirst, "In Syracuse, A Groundbreaking Umpire Finds Himself Called Out," syracuse.com, February 17, 2011.

3   "Black Umpire Springs New One in Ball Game," *Seattle Times*, January 31, 1909: 14.

4   Scott C. Hindman, "Blacks in Blue: The Saga of Black Baseball's Umpires, 1885-1951," Bachelor's Thesis, Princeton University, 2003, 18-19.

5   "Tentative Plan National Negro Baseball League of America," *Chicago Broad Ax*, November 26, 1910.

6   "Diamond Dashes," *Indianapolis Freemen*, August 6, 1910; "Benefit for the Old Folks Home," *Chicago Defender*, August 20, 1913.

7   Rube Foster, "Future of Race Umps Depends on Men of Today," *Chicago Defender*, December 31, 1921. Joe Rue, American League umpire 1938-1947, the only white NL umpire to advance to the majors, began his career calling Kansas City Monarchs games in 1920. Larry R. Gerlach, *The Men in Blue: Conversations With Umpires* (New York: Viking Press, 1980): 52.

8   Brent Kelley, *The Negro Leagues Revisited* (Jefferson, North Carolina: McFarland, 2000), 32-35.

9   "Hurley McNair," pitchblackbaseball.com.

10 *Baltimore Afro-American*, January 1924; "Best in League," *Baltimore Afro-American*, September 11, 1926: 9.

11 Gary Cieradkowski, "Charles Cromwell," Infinitecardset. blogspot.com; "Black Sox Want Cromwell Here," *Baltimore Afro-American*, March 30, 1923: 14.

12 Dave Wyatt, "Chairman Foster's View on Grave Subjects," March 27, 1920, paper found on negroleagues.bravehost.com.

13 Charles D. Marshall, "Will Colored Umps Be Given a Tryout?" March 27, 1920 paper found on negroleagues.bravehost.com.

14 "Demand for Umpires of Color is Growing Among the Fans," *Chicago Defender*, October 9, 1920.

15 "Seven Colored Umps Signed for League," *Kansas City Call*, April 27, 1923.

16 "Rube Foster's Sportsmanship," *Chicago Defender*, July 11, 1924.

17 "Kansas City the First City to Use Negro Umpires," *Kansas Advocate*, April 27, 1923; "Change the Umpires." *Chicago Defender*, August 19, 1922; "Foster Explains Action in Releasing Umpires," *Pittsburgh Courier*, August 22, 1925.

18 Al Monroe, "Speaking of Sports," *Chicago Defender*, July 21, 1934.

19 "Gholston Says It's Hard to Umpire in This League," *Chicago Defender*, August 28, 1925.

20 Neil Lanctot, *Fair Dealing and Clean Playing: The Hilldale Club and the Development of Black Professional Baseball, 1910-32* (Syracuse: Syracuse University Press, 2007), 176; Leslie Heaphy,

The Negro Leagues, 1869-1960 (Jefferson, North Carolina: McFarland and Company, 2003), 110.

21 Lanctot, 176-77.

22 "National Association of Negro Baseball Clubs," *Kansas Whip,* July 17, 1936.

23 Dan Burley, "Chicken Feed Pay for Negro Umpires," September 9, 1944, in Jim Reisler.

24 Lanctot, 180, 181.

25 E.H. McLin, "Official of Negro League Swinging Ax on Umps," *St. Petersburg Times,* May 30, 1950.

26 Dave Barr, "Monarchs to Grays to Crawfords," MLB.com/blogs; *Kansas Plain Dealer,* August 20, 1948.

27 Byron Motley, *Ruling Over Monarchs* (Champaign, Illinois: Sports Publishing, LLC, 2007), Introduction.

28 Sportscelebs.com.

29 Bob Motley as told to Byron Motley, " 'No, I'm a Spectator Just Like You': Umpire in the Negro American League," *Baseball Research Journal,* Fall 2010.

30 Bob Motley.

31 Bill Madden, "Black Umpire Missed his Calling in the 1960s," *New York Daily News,* February 10, 2007; Jay Levin, "Julian Osibee Jelks, 1930-2013: Pioneering Umpire Built a New Life Outside Baseball," NorthJersey.com, July 4, 2013.

Three Arizona League Umpires

By Chuck Johnson

As an official scorer for the Arizona Rookie League I have the opportunity to see first-hand the professional debuts of not only players, but umpires as well. For the players, their journey to pro ball commences with their selection in the June Amateur Draft or as an International Free Agent signing. For the umpires, it begins with a successful completion and graduation from an accredited Umpire Training and Development School.

The idea for this project began during the 2015 AZL season and I was fortunate to have three league umpires agree to be interviewed; Ben Phillips, Lorenz Evans, and James Folske. Phillips, the league designated Crew Chief, is a 32-year-old native of Cary, North Carolina. Evans is 25 and a native of Morton, Illinois, and Folske is 27 years of age from Big Rapids, Michigan.

The three men were not only willing talk about their baseball experiences which ultimately led them to make umpiring a career, but also shared it would not be possible without the support of their family and friends. Folske in particular was very candid in relating how his career choice cost him a relationship but pointed out in closing his story with "I surely won't ever forget the past but I now have new relationships that have become a priority in my life."

On with our questions:

First question is a two-parter: What was your baseball background before deciding on umpiring as a career, and what led you specifically to pursue Umpire School?

James Folske: I started umpiring amateur baseball at the age of 12 but never thought anything of pursuing umpiring as a professional career until my mid-20s at which point I hadn't umpired in years. I grew up around college athletics. Both of parents were college coaches for years; my father recently retired after 48 years of coaching college baseball. I played ever since I could remember, through college. I then did a few different career moves, including two years as a college baseball coach before ultimately deciding to look online what it took to become a MLB umpire.

Ben Phillips: Played in high school and started umpiring LL in college. Wanted to go to umpire school because I got tired of guys telling me, "Man, you're pretty good. Have you been to pro school?"

Lorenz Evans: I always dreamed of being in professional baseball, but I never imagined it would be as the guy who called balls and strikes. I played baseball from the time I was 4 years old and was a catcher through it all; two teams in the summer every year through high school, where I was on the varsity roster for three years. Senior year of high school I seriously injured the labrum in my right shoulder and had reconstructive surgery. That following summer I played for the Kenosha Kings (Wisconsin State League). After a rough summer of pain and heartbreak, I decided to give up my playing days and stay in the game solely as an umpire. I got my high school patch when I was 18 years old because my grandfather had umpired for 15+ years and told me to give it a shot. I set some serious umpiring goals of high school varsity, college, and then one day professional. I went to one college camp in Illinois called the Great Plains Baseball Alliance Umpire Camp; afterward, I was assigned college baseball regularly. There were three professional umpires also from the Peoria area who had helped me along the way and taken me under their wing to prepare me for my ultimate goal: umpire school and professional baseball. I worked a couple seasons in the low levels of college baseball before I decided it was my time to go to umpire school…and it paid off.

Arizona League umpire Ben Phillips, 2015.

What school did you attend and were you classmates of any other AZL crew member?

JF: I attended Wendelstedt Umpire School in 2014. There were other guys working the AZL that attended school with me.

BP: The Umpire School (Now called the Minor League Umpire Training Academy, located in the former Dodgertown at Vero Beach, Florida.) Classmates with Wilmes, Evans, Walsh, Larkin, Silverman, Burch.

LE: I attended The Umpire School in 2015 and was classmates with Randy Wilmes, Ben Phillips, Harrison Silverman, Sam Burch, Andrew Larkin, and Brian Walsh

How is it that you were assigned to the AZL this season?

JF: I was selected to go to the evaluation course with what was then called Professional Baseball Umpire Corporation (now Minor League Umpire Development). Was put on the reserve list after the evaluation course week. I went and attended an umpire camp and was offered a job working for an independent baseball league called the American Association. I worked that league for roughly a month before getting assigned to work the Coastal Plains League, where I worked the rest of the regular season and postseason, including the championship. Late 2014 I was called by Mr. Dusty Dellinger who congratulated me on a great Coastal Plains season and extended me an invitation back to the evaluation course in February 2015; I didn't have to go

back through school again and that entire selection process. I started the summer of 2015 working the Coastal Plains League again until I received the call of a lifetime from Mr. Dellinger and was promoted into Minor League Baseball and was told I would be traveling out from North Carolina in a couple days. I flew from North Carolina into Phoenix the day before the Arizona League meeting and the following day the season began.

BP: Got assigned to AZL because I live on the West Coast. East Coast guys get GCL. Midwest guys are split for the most part

LE: We as umpires don't have any say in where we are assigned. Personally, I received an email on May 1 that said I was being assigned to the Gulf Coast League, which is also a Rookie league located in Florida, and then a few weeks later I received another email that said I was being laterally transferred to the Arizona League. It's all the same game. We work hard and umpire baseball games using every situation to get better; they just tell us what part of the country we are going to do that in and hopefully we continue to advance

Do you think that your school prepared you for the season?

JF: Yes, umpire school was the first training or direction or teaching I had ever received in umpiring.

BP: School absolutely prepared me for the season. Gave me a ton of confidence

LE: I firmly believe that I received the best instruction available today. My umpire school gave me every tool needed to be successful in this game and helped me build on these tools. I am very grateful to have received such a world class experience.

A couple of things school can't prepare you for were travel and the downtime during the day. How did you adjust?

JF: I grew up traveling around for sports ever since I was a kid and have always enjoyed traveling as I have grown older. The adjustment wasn't that tough as far as travel and hotel living. I came to realize even more in my second year of umpiring that downtime is exactly what you make of it. I often tried to fill my days with working out with some of the guys or going out and doing different activities and trying my best to stay active and do stuff.

BP: The travel was really easy in AZL, obviously. The games all being night games is also a huge plus. Gives you the whole day to do whatever you want.

LE: Well, to be quite honest, we didn't have to. The Arizona League has every umpire in the same hotel for the summer and our longest drive with traffic was 45 minutes to and from games. We had the luxury of being with 11 other umpires who we shared this new experience with. We all stayed indoors most of the day because temperatures were around 114 degrees outside and we needed to be hydrated and at our best for the games which were at 7 PM. We would leave around 5 PM for the games and return between 10:30-11:30. Once we all got back we would play video games, go to a restaurant, or play cards which is what myself and three others did nightly. Spades was the game and we would play until around 3 AM every day. We even signed a deck of cards after the last night to remember the summer by.

How long was the Umpire School program, and could you describe a particular day that stands out for you in your memory?

JF: The umpire school program was about six weeks long and there wasn't really any particular day that stands out. It was the longest and most stressful time of my life but went by incredibly fast and was one of the greatest times of my life. The final day receiving the news of being chosen was obviously the greatest highlight of the program.

BP: School was January 3 to February 6. The last day was very memorable for me due to the fact that I was not taking for granted that I was going to make it to the Eval course. I ended up killing it all day until my very last field rep, but then totally screwed up a catcher's interference. There was a very bitter taste in my mouth for the rest of that day and night. It ended up working out.

LE: My umpire school was four weeks. After that we had two days off and then those of us selected to go to the evaluation course went for another week

of training to showcase our talents in hopes of being selected for MiLB. There was one day that sticks out with a rather neat memory. It was Super Bowl Sunday 2015 and I had gone to the laundromat on the other side of campus with a few close friends. As we were waiting for the laundry, we stopped into the tavern next door to play pool and watch the game. After about an hour, a retired MLB umpire walked in and shared old stories with us for a bit before we got our laundry and headed back to the rooms. We watched *Jeopardy* every day at 7 PM right after dinner, six or eight of us all in a room studying and watching.

It's been said one difference between a good player and a great player is anticipation. Since most people aren't familiar with two-man crews, can you explain how you learned to anticipate on the field, both individually and with your partner?

JF: Anticipation and baseball instincts have become as valuable and important as anything in today's umpiring world and often are what separate one umpire from another. A great crew is one where not only does each individual have great instincts for the game but also for one another. A great crew works so well each individual can anticipate where every other person will be at all times on the field.

BP: Having plus baseball instincts helps a lot as does time spent on the field. As for the partner, you just get to the point, quite quickly I might add, where you can just tell by body language what is likely about to happen.

LE: As a professionally-trained umpire, you know where you are supposed to be and where your partner is at all times. It makes it much easier when you don't have to worry if your partner will be in the correct spot because he will be. After you rid yourself of that worry, you just have to have instinct for the game. This is where those who played the game will use their years as a player to know where the ball is going and where the plays will happen. A rule of thumb for me is, "If you react, action has already happened. You need to act and make the play a reaction to you." This helps me stay one step ahead of the game and be prepared for anything.

What kind of signals do you use during the game to anticipate position on possible plays, etc.

JF: We are constantly using pre-pitch signals to just alert each other as far as possible plays that could be developing and reminding us how each of us will be reacting to those developing plays.

BP: The obvious ones are "infield fly" and "two-out timing play." There are some other things that you can communicate through signals such as potential trouble between players, whether the height of the zone is good, things like that.

LE: We use simple signals on the field that are the same as any other umpire: touch the bill of the cap to remind of a possible infield fly situation, signal the outs and where we are going on a batted ball, and touch our wrist to remind of a possible time play at the plate.

Beyond signals, how — in general — do you establish a rhythm with a new umpiring partner?

JF: Beyond signals so much of today's umpiring is taught to us to be the same and is very symmetric across the board so that general rhythm just comes when working with any other professionally-trained umpire. Real umpire chemistry and rhythm develops over time both on and off the field.

BP: Well, in pro ball I've only had one new partner so far but I think just being friends in general is the first step.

LE: Once you step onto that field in your uniform anything in the outside world just goes away. You two (three, or four depending on the level or game) are there to do a job and that's all that's on your mind. Be confident and quick on your feet, but slow enough to see everything and rule correctly. We are just out there to get the plays right and handle things as professionally as possible. When you both understand that, things just come naturally between partners and things off the field will fall into place.

I know the managers and coaches in Rookie ball understand the league is a starting point for umpires as well as players. Was there anyone who stood out to you as being most tolerant of mistakes and helpful in correcting them?

JF: No particular manager stood out as most tolerant. I would say that in general most managers were relatively the same in that they understood our development, along with the players, and they tolerated what they saw and your reasoning behind your ruling.

BP: Quite frankly all the managers treated us with a lot of respect. There was a situation in particular where my partner and I incorrectly ruled a home run a ground-rule double. I'll always remember how we handled that, learned from it, what we could have done better. Amazingly, the manager didn't really lose his cool at all even though in hindsight, we kicked that pretty bad.

The Road to the Show is much longer for an umpire than a player, so short term goals are sometimes easier to accomplish, to that end — where do you see yourself in five years?

JF: In five years, I see myself umpiring at the AA level and pushing the brink of working AAA.

BP: I see myself on the doorstep of, or in AAA

LE: I hope to be advancing my professional career as a Minor League Baseball umpire. Every journey in this game is different and sometimes it takes longer to develop skills from one umpire to the next, so I just hope to be fortunate enough that my hard work will continue to pay off and allow me this great opportunity I have been given. MLB umpire Ted Barrett said, "The pressure is a privilege," and I hope to enjoy that pressure for many years to come.

Now that your first season is under your belt, what did you like best about being an umpire? What did you like the least about being an umpire?

JF: I think the best part of umpiring is being part of a brotherhood and all the relationships developed around the game. The part I liked least about being an umpire was the general overall lack of knowledge of the rules by individuals involved in the game.

BP: Best: Being able to do a game every day with a good friend of mine. Least: Doing more laundry than I'd have liked to.

LE: Everything about my experience with Minor League Baseball has been very enjoyable. I took every situation, both on and off the field, as a learning experience and became a better man because of it. My personal life and my umpiring career have both benefitted from this experience and it will only get better the deeper and higher I go.

Do you know the process of being evaluated during the AZL, who does it and how it's done?

JF: We were evaluated for four games during the AZL season. It was done at two different points in the season on back to back days, once at each spot on the field. Two of our bosses from Minor League Baseball Umpire Development come into town and did the evaluations, one at each time.

BP: An evaluator from Umpire Development will come right at the beginning and in the middle of the season. You'll know they're in town so when they come to your game, they tape you on night one, say hello after the game, then meet with you in the locker room the next day, go over the previous night's game, tape game two, then go over that. That way they see each guy on both plate and bases.

LE: We were seen for a total of four games this summer by two different members of the Umpire Development staff. Once, in the beginning of the season, a member will come unannounced and show up at your game. No one knows he is there, but after your game you will get a knock on the door and he will come in and talk with you to make sure everything on and off the field is going okay before he talks briefly about your game. Either that night or the following he will take the camera footage he gathered of you and project it on the wall in your locker room. They do this to break down plays, stances, pitches, and anything else needed to help you become a better umpire. Since we only have two umpires per crew, you switch between plate and bases every night. The

Arizona League umpire Lorenz Evans, 2015.

evaluator will watch you at one position the first night and the other on the next night.

After this evaluation you won't see an evaluator sometimes for a month or more when the same thing happens with another member of the evaluation staff. I was very lucky in my first evaluation to be working the plate in a spring training stadium and just as I had returned to the locker room after the game and taken off my chest protector there was a knock at the door. I opened it and our evaluator was there. He sat down as we let our mind rest for a minute and then made casual conversation. After a few minutes of small talk there was another knock at the door and in walked an MLB umpire and his wife. They took time out of their personal life to come in and speak with my partner and me. This is something that will always stick with me because they showed me no matter who you are or what your job title is, you are just like everyone else and need to show compassion and help those who walk in your footprints like they did for me.

Managers' meetings at the plate aren't just about ground rules? What else do you talk about? Any good stories?

JF: To me, manager's meetings are very similar to the locker rooms, what happens in a meeting stays in a meeting and others involved in such type meetings.

BP: Pleasantries, the managers mostly talk to each other about who's in town (if there are any roving instructors there), why they can't catch the ball, why their team strikes out so much, etc. Always very self-deprecating. They were all cool with us.

LE: Some things in baseball are just best left unsaid and I believe this to be one of those things. If you ever have the privilege of attending a professional plate meeting, you will know what is said and maybe share a laugh or two.

For anyone who may have experienced an injury, especially a concussion; can you explain the concussion/medical process you go through in order to be allowed back on the field?

BP: The old man made it through season one unscathed, somehow!

LE: In my second week of the season I was struck in the face by a pitched ball that the catcher and pitcher got crossed up on. I remember the next inning writing down the incident on my lineup card and looking up to a massive headache from the bright stadium lights. I knew something may be wrong then, but I remembered everything that had happened and didn't feel as though I needed to be removed from the game or that I was in any danger if I continued. After the game I sat down in the locker room exhausted, put our Cryo Helmet on (ice helmet used to decrease brain swelling in potential concussion situations like this), and my partner noticed I may have been slightly out of it so he took the car keys and drove home that night. I filled out the mandatory form for any umpire who is struck in the head during a game and went to sleep. I awoke in the morning to a phone call from our Medical Coordinator. He asked how I was feeling and what happened. I just remember standing in the kitchen of my hotel room as if everything were cloudy and not quite right. He directed me to stay in the room and take two days off to ensure I was healthy enough to return to the field. Those two days were the worst days of my entire life. I wanted nothing more than to be back on the field getting better and working, but in order to do that as soon as possible I kept the lights & TV off and curtains closed. I laid down while wearing the ice helmet and waited two days until I was directed to take a concussion test and was cleared to return to work.

The offseason. What will you do to prepare for next year? Are there mandated programs you need to complete? Do you have Winter ball assignments? Will you head back to Umpire School as instructors?

JF: I applied for instructor positions with both umpire schools for this next year. I will prepare for next season personally by further developing myself physically through mountain and high elevation training. Mentally it is always important for us to stay in the rulebook throughout the entire calendar year. There are no specific mandated programs and I did not receive any winter ball assignments this year through Minor League Umpire Development.

BP: Thankfully for me I live in Southern California where it is always baseball season so I can work good games with good guys to keep my skills sharp. A couple of guys from our level usually get instructional league from 9/15 to 10/15. Winter ball is usually reserved for guys several levels ahead of us. I said I was available to be an instructor. There's basically a "check yes or no" box on our website for that. I wasn't selected. Hopefully before my career is over I will have the opportunity to do all those things.

LE: I just use my time in the offseason to work out and enjoy being with my family and friends. We miss a lot of birthdays, weddings, and family time we will never get back during the season, so when I get an opportunity to be with family I take advantage of it. I also officiate high school basketball and football to stay busy. I have one more year in college to earn my bachelor's degree, so I am taking classes on campus at Western Illinois University this Fall and next to complete my requirements. I am planning on taking a vacation this winter to relax my body and mind and prepare for another baseball season in just a few short months. There are no mandated programs we need to complete in the offseason and young umpires usually are not assigned to Winter ball. As far as heading back to Umpire School as instructors, that is all up to the Umpire Development Staff. They select about 10 umpires each year to go and instruct at each school and I just hope to be one of the few selected for that opportunity.

Once Upon a Blue Moon: A Love Affair with Umpiring

By Hank Levy

Foreword

Please do not tell my umpire assignor this: I conceived of the format of this memoir while I was doing the bases at a somewhat boring freshman high-school game last fall in California.

Actually, it was something called a "showcase." Parents of aspiring high schoolers who feel they can make college teams will know what this is. Anyway, my assignor would definitely not like the idea that I was thinking about anything but what might happen at the precise next moment in my game, and was I prepared for all the various possibilities? I probably wouldn't have done this while doing the plate. While doing the plate, I would never have another thought in my head. I would be single-focused, concentrating, ready for anything. Sounds like war!

No, baseball umpiring is not really that. There is a lot more to umpiring than being ready for the call on the next play. That's what I want to write about.

I have been a sports official in other sports, but baseball feels unique because of the way the game moves. It's like a wave. It moves slowly, slowly, slowly, and then all of a sudden something happens. What you DO, and how you PERFORM when the play happens is how you are judged as an umpire (by yourself, by others).

But what about all those in-between moments as you wait for the play? In fact, what about all the in-between moments elsewhere? Driving to the games? Getting ready? In fact, life in general is made up of those in-between moments. As I get older, I am learning to appreciate those in-between moments.

You won't hear much about this at umpire clinics. No one teaches what one is supposed to think about or feel about in those in-between moments. Umpire clinics train us to act correctly at the moment something happens and prepare us to be ready for those moments. But all those other mixed-up feelings are up to each of us to sort out.

That's what this memoir is all about. It will start out with my earliest feelings, but it is definitely not in chronological order.

Fear

I have three sons and a daughter. My oldest son oldest didn't play baseball at all; he wasn't interested, and I had myself temporarily lost my love for the game, so I didn't encourage him. My second oldest son was interested, and did play a bit; he only played Little League for two years, but his team managed to win his league's championship one year. I may have had some influence on this, as the Little League's registration process enforced its deadlines ultra-strictly; I was more attracted to the more friendly local soccer league, and probably encouraged my two older sons to play soccer more than baseball. I find this pretty ironic now. I was a "joiner," so I became a soccer official and joined the board of the Rockridge Soccer League as its treasurer.

By the time my daughter was born, I had fallen back in love with baseball, head over heels. I was playing on two softball teams (managing one); I was the organizer for a season-ticket-holder group for the Oakland A's. My daughter tried to play softball for one year, but it didn't suit her. She became a very good soccer player, and then a star All-American rugby player.

So this left one more child, my youngest child, and my third son. He was going to play baseball!! We all know how influential dads can be. And I made sure that his registration was on time! I guess I was ready to accept their rules.

As all parents of youth athletes know, the first thing that happens when teams are formed is the infamous "parent meeting." At this meeting, parents volunteer for various chores (uniforms, snack coordinator, "phone tree coordinator"—that was before emails—and lastly, umpires). The official Little League structure in this country has been built on volunteer umpires: adults and even youth umpires who receive a lot of training and are expected to umpire all the games. The league provides uniforms, equipment, anything needed. The youth umpires get paid a small stipend, the adults do not get paid. It is a credo of the Little League organization that adult umpires are unpaid volunteers.

Little League is unlike other youth baseball organizations, like the Pony and Cal Ripken leagues. Those organizations, at least in the Bay Area, make no attempt to train and use their parents to umpire games; they contract with umpire associations, who provide paid umpires. So you can see where this is about to take me, but more about that later.

Back to the parent meeting: So, still being a soccer referee, I readily volunteered to be one of the team's volunteer umpires. No problem, I thought. No problem, they said. I simply had to attend two clinics being put on by the league (one for rules, one for field mechanic training), and I would be good to go. I have been watching and playing baseball and softball most of my life. Baseball is inside of me. I know the rules, I know how to do this. This will be easy.

No way.

No fan or even player or (dare I say) even coach or manager of any sport can appreciate the difficulty of what a sport official has to learn. An official has to learn the rules of the game; an official has to learn how to be in the right position to make a call; an official has to learn how to look good, how to "sell a call" if the play is close; an official has to develop the confidence that he or she can make the call in front of fans and parents who have no appreciation for the first three things.

There are some sports where the play is continuous, like basketball, soccer, rugby, hockey. Some attention is put on the referee/official, but it is somewhat muted by the pace of play. Baseball, on the other hand, is a sport where the play ends and everyone looks at the umpire. Tennis comes to mind as the most similar, because the calls are very binary (the ball is either "in" or "out"); football is similar, but it has as many noncalls as it does actual calls.

But in baseball, when the play is over, the attention on the umpire is riveting. There are umpires who like this attention. For me, when I started out, it was nerve-racking.

So after my two clinics, I did one game. It didn't go well. I didn't know where to stand. I didn't think I made good calls. The parents were screaming at me. I felt as though I deserved it. I felt terrible.

So what did I do? Did I seek out a mentor? Did I get back on that field? Did I take more training clinics?

NO!

I didn't answer the telephone when the league called for me to umpire. I became an umpire coward. I told my wife to tell the league I wasn't home when she answered the phone. I was completely scared to try umpiring again. A colonoscopy was better than umpiring. I avoided umpiring the rest of that year.

Of course, I wouldn't be writing this memoir if I hadn't done something about my fear.

But fear does return, and now I have come to accept it, even enjoy it a little. And I invite it. It returns for "big" games like playoff games or games between rival teams. It also returns when I move to a higher level of baseball. In the summer of 2016 I worked my connections and pushed myself to umpire for a semipro league based in Eureka, California. Not so much my first game, umpiring at third base, but the following night, when I was the home-plate umpire, the butterflies were certainly alive and well. My plate job that night went superbly, and overcoming that fear with pride for myself was so pleasurable that putting myself in fearful situations almost became an addicting drug. I think this is something that performing artists may feel.

Also, I had to rebound from the previous evening, when truly disastrous things occurred: two umpires making the opposite call on the same play! I think

Gary Bonetti, South County Umpires Association, North Coast Conference playoff between Fremont Christian High School (red uniforms) and Redwood Christian High School (white uniforms). May 27, 2015.

that actually helped overcome the fear. I was either going to be great or die in a blazing fire of hell!!

The night before, when I was in the third-base umpire position, a batted ball was coming toward third base. I was about 15 feet from the ball, and I felt I had a good view of it as it just veered foul as it got to third base, so I yelled "Foul!" and put up my hands to designate the ball was foul. Then I looked up at the home-plate umpire, whom I had never worked with, who was coming up the line, but much farther from the play, who was pointing Fair. (When a ball is fair, an umpire only points, nothing is verbalized.) Well a foul-ball call trumps a fair-ball call, so the call I made was the one that stood. But we had two unhappy managers, not to mention a very, very angry plate umpire. When an umpire feels that the call is his, he pats his chest. Well, I think you would say he was patting his chest very heavily at me after that play. And then in the postgame meeting, he told me

a "bounding ball" up the line is always the home-plate umpire's call.

Umpires are trained to have both pregame and postgame meetings. At what's called the "pregames," umpires are supposed to go over basic, even advanced mechanics, imagine difficult situations, and discuss who will make the calls and how. What is interesting for us professional/amateur umpires is that the number of umpires may change for any particular level of baseball and for the importance of the particular game. All major-league fans know that every game has four umpires for regular-season games and six for playoff games. But for us there can be anywhere between one and six. In general, all youth games have two umpires; high-school varsity and community colleges have two umpires; minor leagues below the level of Triple A have two umpires. However, often the younger kids, high-school freshmen, and junior varsity will only have one umpire. In high-school playoffs, the early rounds have three umpires, but then jump to either four or six for the championship games. College Division I games have three umpires, and lately Division II have had three umpires.

So part of the pregame is to review the mechanics for the number of umpires doing that particular game. Who will cover catches in the outfield when the center fielder is moving toward his/her right? Who will make the call at second base when there is one out and runners at first and third and the ball is hit to shallow right field? So there are endless possibilities to discuss.

Unfortunately, that night we didn't discuss who would make the call on a batted ball going up the third-base line!

An umpire crew is itself a team (umpires say it's the third and best team on the field), but like any team, it needs practice. Baseball umpiring is like a language that can be learned. Not just the rules, but also the mechanics. But unless the team practices, it may make mistakes. Unlike major-league umpire crews, we pro/am umpires usually work with different partners every game we do. In my debut with the semipro team, I was working with two complete strangers.

In every game I often have a range of emotions about my partners, from deep respect and affection to complete dislike. I recall at one high-school game, as my partner and I walked off the field and attempted to do a postgame critique, as my (field) partner began criticizing me for not calling "ball four" loud enough so that he wouldn't look foolish when making a call on a steal of a runner from first base, I began shouting at him that it was his responsibility for knowing the count and watching my call. I recall another game when, as my partner and I started walking off the field at the completion of the game, he began yelling at me because he thought I was laughing at him with a coach for blowing a call. (He did blow the call, but I would never have laughed at him with a coach or even admitted to a coach that my partner had blown a call.)

Actually, umpires have to have solidarity with each other. Even if we think our partners have made a bad

call, we can never express that to anyone other than the umpire in a postgame meeting. This is a sacred time when you are supposed to say to your partner(s), "Do you have anything you want to tell me anything that you feel I could do better?" and assure them that no criticism they may give you will hurt your feelings.

Right.

In theory, this is a wonderful practice. It was the basis of Mao Tse-tung's "criticism/self-criticism" practice for his Communist Party members, but I doubt that many umpires understand they are practicing communism every game! Where else in anyone's lives is this truly practiced? Does anyone even ever say this to his/her spouse? ("Darling, please tell me how I can improve so that I can truly be a better husband?" My wife would love that, but let's face it, only a bad fight brings out this type of question.)

The postgame meetings don't actually happen after every game, but they are supposed to. Most of the time umpires are rushing off to beat the traffic; sometimes, the games go so smoothly and there are no close calls, so we get lazy and don't do it. But sometimes we are nervous about being really honest with our partner. It takes a lot of courage.

And a real thick skin. Developing a thick skin (also known as a hard shell) is something all umpires need to do. What a thick skin does is to allow an umpire to move on from a call that either was really blown or that the crowd thinks was blown. It allows an umpire to continue to gain confidence and to improve.

And it helps with the fear.

Luck

Many umpires, as well as others in my life, will deny that luck is ever a factor in performance. They will say that only preparation helps with performance.

But I think this is ridiculous. Even for an experienced umpire, if a close play occurs right at the beginning of a game before the umpire gets in the rhythm of the game, it can throw him off.

I had bad luck in that first Little League game, which caused me to hide out for a season. In the fall of that year, I decided that I was going to get some serious training. I had heard that our son's Little League would pay for any umpire who would really commit to games (now I had to choose!) to attend training in the Little League Western Regional San Bernardino facility. So I started planning to go; eventually five of us from the North/South Oakland Little League attended for one week in January.

I have never served in the military, but a week's training at the hands of the Little League trainer gave me a taste of what true boot camp is like. He was worse than the stereotype sadistic Army sergeants that you might see in the movies. He made fun of the two women who were there, for being female; he ridiculed one of my friends, a lawyer; he made jokes at the Canadians who were there. Luckily, I escaped this. Luck?

One of the most sadistic things happened on the field one day early in the week: It had to do with how an umpire makes an "out" call. It is a common mistake and misconception than an umpire makes an "out" call by moving his fist in a backward direction towards his shoulder with his thumb extended.

NO!!

The correct way to make an out call for most plays is to move the arm forward with a fist, like hammering on a wall. (On close plays, an umpire can move the arm forward with a closed fist more like a punch.) So a friend of mine from our Little League made an out call in the way an umpire is not supposed to do it. I don't know how the trainer saw him among 60 umpires on the field that day, but he did. He made him tape his thumb to his fist, and made him keep it taped all week.

The trainer, I later learned, was a dentist. I won't say anything about the stereotype of the sadistic dentist, but I have thought about him a lot for the past 15 years.

Although two of my colleagues chose to stay at nearby hotels and eat out at restaurants, three of us braved it out in the bunks (where 12-year-old ballplayers stay) and ate cafeteria food. We started our day around 6:30 A.M. and ended around 10 P.M. Classroom training would start right after breakfast, then on-field training, then lunch, and then start all

over again. We would take rule quizzes each night. We were videotaped. We were thrown a million different directions at once to see if our various body parts could figure out the right thing to do. The Mad Dentist used every opportunity he could to belittle you, trying to replicate what a coach/manager might do on the field to help begin to develop the thick skin we needed.

It was horrible, but it worked.

I came back from the training camp full of new confidence for the coming season. But I did one more important thing. Before I actually did a game that next season, I went to a game that was being umpired by one of the senior umpires in the league (whom I knew a little, because he had actually been one of the San Bernardino crew). I sat in the stands and simply watched him; (He was doing the plate.) I was completely focused on him, from his strike and ball calls to the way he moved around the field to the way he interacted with the players, coaches, and even the fans. I chose things to emulate (copy!) and things I decided I would do differently.

So my first game came (well, maybe it was my second game after that first horrible one from the prior year). And no one can tell me that luck didn't factor into it. The game went without a hitch. But there were no close plays, so there were no arguments. Sure, some of my ball and strike calls were questioned, but I don't recall that bothering me. I came home mostly thinking about how lucky I was, and although I knew I wouldn't always be this lucky, I could tackle more difficult situations as they came up. Some might say the camp gave me skills, and I am sure that was true. But I still like to think luck was a big part of it.

Every umpire develops his/her own style for dealing with conflict. The old style from a bygone era, that whatever the umpire thinks and says is right, is dead. No more. Now, it's about listening and showing that you as the umpire are "open" to hearing them. But briefly. And not for everything, including balls and strikes. Some umpires are more honest about their mistakes, and in many situations are allowed to ask their partner for "help." Partners are also taught how to silently communicate to the umpire who made the call that they have information which may explain why the coach is upset and why their partner may want to reconsider changing his/her call. Think about how difficult it is reading subtle eye and body signals, especially for two umpires who have never worked together, and who may or may not have discussed it in their pregame meeting.

And how about dealing with parents and other fans? This can be very tricky. Umpires are trained not to talk to fans, but depending on the situation, talking to fans can be satisfying, or even fun. I enjoy talking to fans, and I will even do it when the fans are arguing with me. Again, luckily, I usually don't get into trouble or make things worse. Mostly I will talk to fans and explain the rules, which I love to do, especially when I am sure I am right.

We all know the stereotype of the "too-invested" parent. My personal favorite story is actually one

that was somewhat horrifying. It took place while I was doing a one-man junior-varsity high-school game in Moraga, in Contra Costa County, which is a very un-diverse, mostly white suburb in the Bay Area. I was doing the plate, and a pitcher for the home team threw a pitch a bit too close to the batter, which caused the batter's father (how could I tell??) to yell something insulting about the pitcher. A few innings later, the same thing happened. I didn't think the pitch was close enough to have been done on purpose, but again the batter's father began yelling at the pitcher and suggest to me that I should eject him. I could tell the batter was embarrassed. Now, here is the key: The batter was not Caucasian (he appeared to be of Middle Eastern background) and his father's accent was clearly not that of a native-born person. I could hear the batter's father behind me, to the right, where the visiting team fans and parents were sitting. Then, from my left, I heard a father yell: "You don't

Hank Levy at Eureka, California, July 2016, working first base for the Humboldt B-52s.

know the rules, and you should go back to where you came from." At that point, I stopped the game. First, I went over to the dad on my left, who was of course white and I soon figured out was the pitcher's father, and told him, "The great thing about America is that people have the right to argue about the rules without being racially insulted." I am not sure he completely understood what I meant, but that seemed to stop him from further insults. (Of course, I then went over to the Middle Eastern dad and told him that he had the rule wrong.)

My wife thinks that I love umpiring because I can bring my own sense of justice to the field while I am in charge. Maybe that is true.

I have umpired games at locations that serve alcohol, which or course is taken for granted at professional and semipro games but seems wrong at youth-oriented fields. In Manteca, California, there is a field called Big League Dreams, where five fields surround a restaurant that serves beer. It is about 10 steps from the restaurant to the stands, so it is easy to get food and drink before, during, and after a game in which one's child is playing. These are often used for tournaments, so both the umpires and the parents are there all day long, from 7 A.M. until 8 P.M. One day when I was umpiring there, by the afternoon a number of parents were completely rude and completely drunk. I stopped the game until security came and escorted them away. Yes, my sense of justice!

I have had to use all my instincts to learn how to interact with coaches, players, and fans. As much as I would like them all to be reasonable, respectful, and rational, this isn't going to happen all the time. That's when I use my power.

I cannot remember when I have ever gotten into serious trouble; I know that some coaches don't like me, but that is part of the game. I have learned to avoid situations that could inflame tempers.

Some say that is the skills I have learned, not luck. But I like my story, and I am sticking to it.

Ambition and Lance Armstrong

You might think I am referring to what became of Lance Armstrong's downfall, that he was too ambi-

tious. Nope. As far as I know, Lance Armstrong has nothing to do with baseball and I am talking about my own ambition. Where Lance Armstrong comes into it is those silly rubber yellow wrist-bands that his foundation, Livestrong, were selling and giving to hundreds of thousands of people across the county.

At about the time I was now feeling more confident in my umpiring skills, and feeling I could possibly do high-school and even college ball, my wife had a recurrence of her cancer. Her cancer was a life-threatening cancer; she had read Armstrong's book, and had gotten courage out of it. I was terrified. Well, that damn little yellow rubber thing on my wrist really helped me through some dark times. It made me remember what was important in life (it wasn't whether that pitch really had been a strike or not), and it connected me to her as I did my umpiring.

Believe it or not, umpiring can be therapeutic in and of itself. I can't express how satisfying it feels to umpire a baseball game in a competent manner, where I felt I haven't missed a call, in a game that went really well. The highest compliment is when a losing player or coach congratulates you for a job well done. And, yes, whether you call it luck or skill, doing a good job is very gratifying.

But the game of baseball can help center you on the details of life. The tiniest things. And this exercise makes you appreciate the small things. It did it for me.

After a few years of umpiring at the Little League level, I moved up the levels of Little League as my son grew older and continued to play baseball (the levels in Little League are called Minors, Majors, Juniors and Seniors; the other youth organizations—Cal Ripken and Pony—have different terms for the same idea, as the kids get older). One of my Little League umpire buddies (in fact, the one who had had his hand taped up by the Mad Dentist) had joined a high-school baseball and softball association and urged me to join.

These umpire associations are private (or non-profit) organizations that contract with high schools to provide umpires for all the games. These associations also may provide umpires to other leagues as well. Because high schools may change their league configuration from time to time, this may cause an association to lose schools to another one, or gain them. This has happened to me now a few times in my high-school career.

I have risen and then fallen back and risen again. I umpired community-college games for a few years. The commitment to do these games is much greater than high school: These are nine-inning games (high school is seven); the assignors want the umpires at the games one hour before game time (for high school, the standard is 30 minutes). Also, community colleges can often be farther away, and take longer to get to. So umpiring a college game can easily be a five-hour commitment.

Also, while the baseball quality is usually very high, community-college baseball is more about careers than playing a game. This gets very serious. Many of the players are trying to "move up" to four-year colleges, where they are hoping to get noticed by major-league scouts. Even the managers and coaches may want to move up. So community-college baseball, even though it is the next level after high school, is actually much closer to making a living, more professional.

Umpires at the community level and above are terrific. That's what I witnessed, and was often the main motivation for me to stick with it. They all take those pre- and postgame meetings very seriously. My guess is that a large number of college umpires worked in the minor leagues but didn't make it to the major-league level, and are well-trained and extremely professional and skilled. However, I wasn't getting enough games to get the confidence I needed, so I gave up on that.

All associations begin to become activated in January for the coming season. I would often find myself thinking how much drive and ambition I had, and whether or not I really wanted to push myself to climb higher. After two seasons doing community-college ball, I decided that I wasn't getting what I wanted enough. Between my wife's cancer, the time it was taking to do the games, the fanatic coaches, and my assignors not being completely wowed by my performance, I decided not to keep pushing myself to higher and more difficult limits.

Then came the summer of 2016, when I had an opportunity to umpire in the semipro league in Eureka. On one hand it was daunting: a real stadium with paying (not much, only $5) customers who expected to see a good performance from the players/umpires/coaches, etc. But on the other hand, it was summer ball, where no championships really counted. I loved it.

Will I do it again? Probably. But baseball, like the seasons, allows its participants to re-evaluate every year. My wife's cancer is back, I am starting new business ventures, so we'll see. It means long weekends away from home.

I have learned about ambition, and what I have learned is that I am in control of it. I can move forward or back, and it will always be my decision.

Sport for Old Men

When I first started umpiring high school, I was in my early 50s, and I umpired with someone who was 74 years old and who had survived cancer. He moved really slowly, and probably was not in shape to perform at a high level anymore. But as I move closer to that age, I often think about him. I know a number of umpires who span from their late 60s into their 70s. I don't know anyone who is over 80 and still umpires, but maybe that will be me. Because being a baseball umpire doesn't involve so much athleticism, umpires can continue to work until they are fairly old. Their bodies may prevent them from getting super-close to plays; but their experience allows them to anticipate what may happen in any given situation.

I often umpire for older players. In the Bay Area there are different leagues for senior men, and often I am umpiring men who are my age and older. Older players have many limitations, and I am sad to admit that some younger umpires can be very judgmental about their skills. I am no saint, and I like better ball just like anyone; but when I umpire these older ballplayers, I have so much respect for someone in their 60s or 70s playing hardball that it almost makes me cry. I feel I am there with them, trying to figure out how to grow old together, and connecting around this wonderful sport we love so much.

A few years ago I was doing the plate for one of the older-aged teams, and a relief pitcher came to the mound. When I told him he had only eight warm-ups, he politely told me that he really needed at least 14 before his old arm would start working. I let him have as many warm-ups as he wanted, and no one complained.

Some of my fellow umpires, who have been doing umpiring longer than I have, are umpiring for the children of the players they umpired for 20 to 30 years ago. I haven't been umpiring that long, so that hasn't happened to me. But while umpiring, I often see old friends of my son's, or other people he played baseball with. Connecting to my son's friends is a connection with him, which I love. He is still playing ball in the Vintage League, but he has moved back east for a while, so it will be sad not to umpire his games.

Time Travel

Umpiring has taken me to prison and to the nineteenth century as well as other interesting places.

I have umpired many times at San Quentin prison in the Bay Area, with an outside men's team playing against prisoners. (There used to be two teams, but more recently there is only one; it is considered a privilege for a prisoner to be on the team.) In order to get into San Quentin, a visitor must be preapproved; the prison checked me through my Social Security number and my driver's-license number. San Quentin opened in 1852, and the way one enters feels as if you have gone back in time. They have their own umpires, but are happy to have an outside umpire. The fans, of course, are all prisoners, but the sportsmanship is outstanding. In one game, the team that brought me was arguing a lot more than the prisoner team. I think that they are told to be on their absolute best behavior; when you think about it, if a prisoner is disciplined by the prison authorities for bad behavior, it's likely a whole lot worse than whatever I could do.

I have very rarely ejected a player or a coach. I used to be more of a softie than I am now. But I do have

a few stories. When I first started umpiring, I was so proud that I wanted my family to come watch me; that weekend my in-laws were visiting, so I had a big cheering section. It was a high-school freshman scrimmage; something was very strange about the coaches of one of the teams, and during the game, he came behind the backstop (which was very close to where I was standing) and began to criticize my calling of strikes and balls. After a very short warning, not only did I eject him, but I really got angry at him for violating my space. After the game, parents from his team came up and congratulated me, and told me he was an alcoholic and often got ejected. It is important when you eject someone to do it "strategically," to make it look like they and not you are the bad person in the situation.

I do warn coaches and players often, and that is usually enough. I love all the ways that we are taught to give "warnings," from the glance to the dugout, to the casual taking off of the mask, to the more deliberate taking off the mask, to the making of a note while looking at the bench, to the step toward the bench, to the actual verbal warning.

I umpire in a league called Vintage Baseball. This is an adult baseball league played by 1886 rules, with a slightly softer ball, heavier wooden bats, and the old-style "mitts." In this league an umpire is called "Sir" and a player or a coach is always supposed to be super-polite. (I am still trying to find out when the negative attitude toward umpires began.) Every single player on every single team was polite to me.

Except for the Oakland team.

One game, their first baseman was giving me a hard time for what he thought was a bad call. When the inning was over, I told him that not only was he out of line based on modern baseball etiquette, but considering the culture of being super-polite to the "Sir," he should correct his behavior very quickly. But the trouble was that the whole team was led by a captain who either didn't communicate the proper cultural mood or at least didn't practice it himself. Almost every game I "sirred" the Oakland team, they were a problem. And in the championship game (which they won), I almost ejected their captain.

Aside from San Quentin prison and traveling back to the nineteenth century, I have also umpired in upstate New York at the Cooperstown Dreams Park, which is an extraordinary place with 22 fields for 1,000 kids and 100 umpires coming every week during the summer. And I almost went to Cuba to umpire. I know umpires who have umpired in Europe, Australia, and many other places around the world.

The Call

When umpires make a decision on a play, like "strike" or "ball" or "safe" or "out" or "fair" or "foul" or "catch" or "no-catch," that is called "THE CALL." On many of these, the umpire may make a combination of gestures and/or verbal sounds. Probably the most important thing I learned about being a good umpire was to not rush THE CALL. I learned how to take my time, to let my brain understand what my eyes had seen, and then to make THE CALL. Also, in some situations I learned how to wait to see if some subsequent event happened, say the ball falling out of a player's mitt before the play was completely finished.

An umpire can make a call too soon, either by rushing it or by not waiting to see if something else happens. It is actually pretty rare for an umpire to make a call too late. There are some umpires in the major leagues who get complaints from the sports announcers because they wait too long to make THE CALL, but at my level, this is rare.

While the training schools do not say calls have to be made in a certain prescribed way, I think one has to be brave to do things differently. Most of the umpires I know, including me, make calls in generally the same way, with the same pauses, cadences, voice style, etc. While I don't normally see or hear many umpires veer from the norm, I do think that in my high-school association the African-American umpires will often have a more distinct style than the white umpires. I appreciate that, and I often root for them.

There are other "calls" I remember that had nothing to do with what was happening on the playing field. I am not supposed to bring my cell phone onto the field. There have been a few times when my games went into extra innings and I know my wife would be looking for me, and I needed to tell her I would be late. I have actually been successful a number of times when I have asked an understanding fan (usually a mom) to call my wife and explain the situation.

Finally, I have to say that becoming an umpire was a Great Call on my part. I can't say I have loved every minute of it. I remember feeling terrible when after a game in which I had missed a call, I would feel absolutely terrible. Remember the story of Jim Joyce, the major-league umpire who blew a call to cause a pitcher to lose a perfect game. He cried. There were many games when I almost cried. Some of my worst calls were against my own son.

But umpiring has taught me to pick myself up and get back on my feet. It has helped me deal with the ups and downs of my wife's cancer. It has helped me in my professional career.

My day job is as a certified public accountant. I often appear in court as an expert witness. One day I was standing outside a courtroom in Marin County, and an angry lawyer who didn't appreciate the conclusions I had reached regarding her client began yelling at me and pointing her finger the exact same way that managers do it on the baseball field. For a brief moment, when I looked up at her, the hallway had disappeared behind her, and we were standing on a baseball field. I knew just how to act! The Mad Dentist had taught me.

I am very thankful that I have become part of what some people would call the best team in baseball, and others would call a "cult." It has filled up my life with memories, with stories and life lessons that I couldn't have gotten anywhere else.

The author wishes to thank his wife, Marcia Goodman, and his dear friend Larry Hendel, for editing and giving comments on this personal essay.

Around the World of Umpiring

By Clark G. "Red" Merchant

I worked as a sports official for more than 37 years, starting my career in California doing sandlot, little league and Division II college games. At one of those games I was introduced to the legendary umpire Shag Crawford, who had an umpire school in San Francisco for Triple-A umpires. He asked me if I would be interested in coming to his school and that I was good enough then, at age 20, to be accepted as an umpire in Triple-A baseball. What a thrill that would have been, but unfortunately I had just committed to re-enlist in the Air Force (eventually retiring after 26 years) and was waiting for an assignment, which I felt fairly certain would take me to Vietnam.

I also worked in Texas and Maine but the majority of my time, more than 18 years, was spent at overseas assignments. During that time I was either in charge of, or basically responsible for training, officials assigned to local associations. These associations provided officials not only for base-level sports, but also grade-school and high-school games, as well as local universities. University level in this case would have been equivalent to Division III or possibly II in the US. There were also instances, such as in Korea, where I officiated, and trained officials for the Korean Professional Baseball League, which at that time was basically equivalent to Double-A ball in the US.

For the most part, the local officials I worked with were college-aged, especially those in Europe: Germany, Italy, Austria. The hard thing about baseball here was that baseball being played was not on baseball fields, as we know it, but on makeshift, empty fields, with diamonds haphazardly laid out. No mound for the pitcher, in the case of school-aged ball [which as we see now may have been a good thing] and most times slightly less than 90 feet between bases; and less than 60 feet 6 inches from what would pass as a pitching rubber to the cardboard box cut

out to resemble home plate. Italy probably had the most well-defined baseball fields, even if some were laid in the middle of a soccer pitch! In Greece, on the island of Crete, it was US baseball almost exclusively, between the Air Force and the Navy.

In the Far East, Okinawa, which at that time was still under US jurisdiction, probably had the most regulation fields as the Okinawans followed Japanese and American professional baseball almost as fanatically as some of the servicemen stationed there. Vietnam provided spectators for baseball, but very few participants. In my time there I trained 15 officials, only one of whom umpired any of the service games (more about Captain Do later). The Philippines had one of the best structured associations I have worked with outside of the US, with professional level training facilities and staff that worked with all levels of officials year round. The baseball played there in the '70s was between Double-A and Triple-A level, and involved not only base teams from all the services, but Philippine teams as well, who were well coached, and motivated.

TRAINING OFFICIALS

The first thing in training any of the officials, in any region, was common language. It did no good if you could not communicate the intent of the rule. As both the Rulebook and the Umpire's Manual were written in English, and then translated into the native language, there was a loss of nuance, so to speak. For instance, when making a call on a very close play, the manual's intent of the rule was: "to be 'emphatic in the call, leaving no doubt as to your decision.'" For the Asian umpires this was extremely difficult to get across, as their culture was not one where you intentionally ever made someone "lose face." And to their way of thinking, that "emphatic call" was definitely a "loss" for the individual. It took much persuasion to bring them around to the idea of the correct way of doing it.

Another universal difficulty was going behind the plate and making the interpretation of the strike zone [not an uncommon factor in any league]. To tell them that the call is to be made on any ball that "passes over any part of the plate while being in a zone between the bottom of the letters/elbows, and the hollow of the knee, while the batter is in his regular stance …" took a considerable amount of time and effort. First of all one had to be able to tell what was a "regular stance" once the batter entered the box, whether it was a 6-foot-3 American, or a 5-foot-1 Asian. Also, about 99 percent of the trainees had never been hit: By a pitched ball, not to mention a foul ball, in their lives, and the first time this happened it was a complete shock! "Geez, that HURT!" or some form of that were the first words normally uttered; not "foul" as was required. We spent one entire week in this training alone; eventually it ended up that the Americans had to actually stand on the mound and throw hard balls at the trainees who stood on the plate and let the balls hit them. Of course the trainees all were protected with masks, chest protector, and shin guards, but it still took a great deal of courage on their part to stand on the plate and get plunked by baseballs; some of our guys could get the ball on the plate upwards of 90 mph.

Once we had gotten them over the stigma of being hit, then getting them to be able to stand in the proper position to call the pitch was paramount. The difference in size between umpiring behind an American catcher and an Asian was considerable and played a huge role. Eventually it came down to the Asian umpires almost having to stand side-saddle to the catcher on the inside of them between the batter and the catcher to get a decent view of the plate. We also tried having them stand on the opposite side of the batter, which worked fairly well, but did not "catch on" as a standard.

Another difficulty was getting equipment to fit. A standard mask was always too large, and getting Pony League type equipment took a while. Learning how to properly wear a cup was another shock for

the Asian men, except those who were martial-arts students, who were familiar with the practice. Most of the students could not understand why it was necessary, until we gave them a practical demonstration (which I shall leave to your imagination). Fitting the mask was the most difficult of the ensemble as the straps on most masks were just not long enough to be pulled tightly enough to fit properly; it was either too loose at the top or kept bouncing off the chin as the umpire moved. In some cases we had to take the mask to a local belt maker and have extra-long straps made.

THE "TORNADO"

Vietnam in 1967-68 was still quite new to American baseball. Having been a French colonial possession, the country's main passion was soccer. However, on the American bases, particularly in and around the Saigon area, service teams played baseball and softball on regulation fields over the weekends, and the Vietnamese service members and their families would come out to watch and cheer along with the rest of the crowd. I arrived in May of 1967 and started umpiring games in July. It was basically myself and three other Americans who could get the time off from our busy schedules (I was working as part of an Inspector General team at the time) to do games in what was considered III and IV Corps (military designated districts of South Vietnam) encompassing most of the area in the southern part of the country.

In early September, I was approached by the commander of the Vietnamese Air Force (VNAF), stationed in Saigon. He asked me if we would train some of his officers to be umpires so that his men could play "regular baseball" and possibly be able to compete with the American teams by the coming year. I was one of the trainers for our blossoming umpire program, which unfortunately was ended by the Tet campaign, and had not been resumed by the time I left in May of 1968. I told him we would be glad to have them, but they must remember that we were the instructors, and they were students, not "officers," and that our instructions were to be obeyed; questioned as necessary, but obeyed. He agreed to this, and the next night, fellow trainers and I were introduced to 15 VNAF personnel. Among them was one Tho Tran Do, a captain, and pilot.

Tho Tran Do stood all of 5-feet-3 in his stocking feet. I had met him previously as we had been ferried by him in his helicopter for a couple of missions. He had a specially designed helicopter, with wooden blocks on his anti-torque pedals so he could sit in the pilot's seat and see out of the wind screen!

Do took to the training with a will, and was especially delighted at the maneuver necessary to come in from the first-base line and pivot to make a call at a base on a ball hit into the outfield. As we basically worked only a two-man system, this required the first-base umpire to enter the field from his position on the foul line, keeping an eye on the batter/runner, as well as sighting the ultimate contact point of the fielder and the batted ball, all the while anticipating whether the batter/runner was going to make a turn at first and attempt second base, or just run out and then return to first.

Captain Do's approach was unique, to say the least, and thus earned him his well-deserved nickname. As a student of the martial arts, he was already quite fluid in his movements, and as a pilot his anticipatory powers were better than average.

With a ball hit into the outfield, Do would "launch" himself, literally, from the foul line into the field of play, sometimes by as much as three feet into the air. Landing in a full run, he would then proceed past the first baseman and, jumping in the air, complete a 180-degree pirouette, landing on his feet, with his back towards the plate, his head on a swivel looking at the batter/runner, and his body in a position to turn towards first, or to follow into second base! It was amazing to watch, and justly earned him the 'moniker' "Tornado"! He would have made an exceptional umpire in any league; his knowledge of the game was good, and his moves were up to our expectations. Unfortunately, he died in February 1968 during the Tet campaign when his helicopter went down near Saigon.

BEST EXPERIENCE

The best experience I ever had as an umpire occurred while I was in Korea. Some of the Korean air force personnel who worked for me at the time were going to Soul to see a Korean Professional Baseball League game. They asked me if I'd like to accompany them, and I said I'd be delighted. We boarded the bus outside the base, and an hour later arrived in front of the stadium in downtown Seoul. It was not impressive, massive concrete from the outside, and gray. But inside? Bells, whistles, cheering, and colorful costumes were the norm. The fans loved their baseball, and were there for the spectacle of the game, as well as to be seen and heard. It was wonderful, and exciting to be in the middle of it. About half an hour before the game was to start there was an announcement over the PA system. Since my Korean was rudimentary at best, I had no idea what was being said, but all of a sudden all my friends were jumping up in their seats, turning towards the press box, and waving their hands. I just sat there, wondering what was going on. Five minutes later one of the security officials came down to our row, and started talking with the "leader" of our group; he then turned to me and asked in English: "Are you an umpire?" Well! I told him I was and asked why. "The third umpire in this crew is sick and cannot get on the field, we would consider it an honor if you would take his place and help with umpiring this game." Not having a uniform or anything remotely resembling one I said, I'd love to help, but was not dressed for it. "No matter," he replied. "We keep umpire uniforms in all sizes on site."

Fifteen minutes later, to the cheers of my friends, I accompanied the other two Korean umpires on to the field, and assumed my position at third base. I had one call the entire game, a foul ball outside the foul pole.

In my experience, umpiring is how you were trained, and most of the world's umpires have, ultimately, been trained by American sources. It is fairly standard, with slight cultural differences in body posture and gestures being the only real modifications to an otherwise excellent system.

Larry Young and International Umpiring

By Bill Nowlin

Major League Baseball's point man for international umpiring is Larry Young. A veteran who umpired for 25 years at the big-league level highlighted by two World Series and All-Star games in addition to several Division and League Championships, Young has worked as a supervisor since the latter half of 2007 and represented MLB at each of the World Baseball Classics, enjoying a good working relationship with the International Baseball Federation (IBAF), and has worked in 17 countries hosting clinics and giving advice, and also conducted clinics for the U.S. Marine Corps and United States Air Force.[1] His titles are: Umpire Supervisor, Major League Baseball; Umpire Advisor, International Baseball Federation; and he is the Umpire Coordinator for the World Baseball Classic. His first experience umpiring began at the age of 13. It's been something of a lifelong calling.

"I started when I was really young," he said in a 2015 interview. "I was 13 years old. I lived in a small town in Illinois. It was one of those Mayberry-like towns. I could ride my bike anywhere. I rode my bike to a Little League field one day and it was a day game and there was a father doing the umpire; that's how they used to do it—volunteers. So I volunteered to umpire and I caught the bug. I've been doing it ever since."[2]

In 2014 alone, travel took him to Australia, Europe twice - to Prague and Amsterdam, Korea, Taiwan, Japan, Puerto Rico, the Dominican Republic, and Venezuela. He's both an ambassador for umpiring and helping bring about consistency in the profession.

His first professional work came about three years later. "When I turned 16 and was able to get a driver's license, then I was in business. I was doing baseball and softball in Oregon, riding my bike everywhere.

As soon as I got my own wheels, then I was in business. I did football, basketball, and baseball, year-round, for years and years and years."

Oregon, Illinois was the small town. Young was born in nearby Dixon on February 6, 1954. His father worked as a police officer in Oregon, retired, began work with the Post Office, and then retired from that. Larry himself worked in the Big Ten and the Alaskan Baseball League even before joining MLB, giving him an early taste of something different in baseball. He was a graduate of the Bill Kinnamon Umpire School in 1978; one of his classmates was Jim Joyce.

His first work after graduation was in winter ball in Puerto Rico for three years, 1980-82, and in the minor leagues. He says, "I was always interested in seeing different cultures in different parts of the world." In Puerto Rico, he even got introduced to another sport and wound up refereeing a little with World Wrestling. "That was kind of a lark. I didn't do a lot of it. I started doing that when I was in winter baseball in Puerto Rico. The umpires and the wrestlers were living in the same complex, so I got to be friends with them. I got a little bit of it in Puerto Rico and then I did a little bit of it here in the States. I just did a very little bit of that."

Young's first work in the majors was as an American League umpire, when the leagues hired separately, and the first game he worked was June 23, 1983, a Thursday afternoon game at Comiskey Park which saw the White Sox beat the Twins, 8-6. John Hirschbeck was the home-plate umpire, Young worked first base, George Maloney was at second, and Bill Kunkel at third. Young only worked seven games in 1983, upping that to 52 in 1984 and 86 in 1985. From 1986 through 2006, he worked more than 100 games each season. When the two leagues combined in 1999, he was promoted to crew chief and

Larry Young instructing in San Antonio.

worked as a Major League umpire until injury forced his retirement.

Young worked the All-Star Game in 1991 and 2003, in six Division Series, in three League Championship Series, and the World Series in both 1996 and 2003. In all, he worked 2,848 big-league games, plus 49 postseason games.

The day came in mid-July 2007 when he couldn't work on the field any longer. "After 24 years on the field, my knees gave out and I had to leave the field. I had been battling bad knees for a long time but I got hurt on the field in Chicago and that was just the last straw. The doctor said, 'No more,' so I had to move on. But you know, one door closes and another one opens. It's a cliché, but it's true."

"I became a supervisor almost immediately—about a month afterwards—and the World Baseball Classic was coming up. I told my boss at the time that I had an interest in working with umpires from the international aspect. That's how I got started with the World Baseball Classic."

It wasn't an easy transition, field umpire to supervisor. "It's difficult to go from being one of the guys to the boss. It's like going from being a teacher to being the principal. These are people you've worked with for a lot of years and all of a sudden you're their boss. It took me a while to realize that I wasn't an

umpire any more—because I'd been an umpire all my life. To this day, I still think like an umpire, which sometimes doesn't sit well with my bosses. They keep reminding me that I'm administration and I keep reminding them that I'm an umpire. But I think that there is kind of a wall now, after so many years. You have to relate to what they're doing, but you have to recognize that now you're in a position of authority. They don't think of me as an umpire anymore; they think of me as a supervisor. The last thing I want to do is forget that I umpired."

There was a bit of an eye-opening experience at the first WBC and it involved Miguel Cabrera. Young had experience working winter ball in Puerto Rico and working in the Caribbean World Series. He knew that ballplayers have a natural degree of nationalism, but some of the players he talked to at the WBC talked of their pride in playing for their national team. Cabrera told him that he was more excited to be playing for the Venezuelan national team in 2006 than he had been playing for the Florida Marlins in the 2003 World Series. Perhaps there was a little hyperbole involved, but there was also genuine patriotism as well.

After the WBC, the powers that were in baseball wanted to work to expand baseball's reach. "There was an interest in international baseball that came through the WBC and through some of the other programs like the Envoy program. The umpires just weren't developing like the coaches and the players. They got interested in sending people over in the Envoy program as coaches but in a lot of places—specifically, Europe—the umpires just weren't catching up. So they needed to have that dimension and that's where I came in."

There really aren't variations in rules from country to country, but—for instance—the IBAF has some rules for younger players that are safety-related. "Sliding, you have to slide; you can't barrel into anyone. There are some differences, but for the most part they use our rulebook." All the umpire schools reach the same techniques and the same rules—balls and strikes, safe and out. Rich Garcia, who was in charge of winter ball for many years, and Gus

Rodriguez, the supervisor of umpires for the IBAF, deserve credit for getting all international umpires to use the same system, in terms of rotation on balls in play and the like.

Regarding Rodriguez, Young says, "He and I have participated together in several clinics and several joint ventures. He went to WBC and I went to some of his tournaments. We work with umpires on a joint basis. We have a real good working relationship. In fact, we're going to Italy next month [March 2015] and doing a joint clinic together." A clinic in, say, Amsterdam, will draw umpires from several European countries. The Dutch city is where Young met the supervisor of umpires of the Israel Baseball Federation. "There's interest there [Israel] in doing a clinic. I probably will do something in the near future."

The real differences, Young says, come in handling situations. It's an old adage that no two games are alike and you never know when a game starts whether you're going to see something that has never happened before. That's one of the reasons they sent recent umpire school graduates to the Caribbean: "There's no shortage of situations. You get something virtually every day."

There can be language barriers as well. "We try to get the umpires that are bilingual. That's a big plus, but it's not a deal-breaker if they don't speak English or they don't speak several languages. In that case, we'll have interpreters and if there's an argument we'll have the interpreter come right on the field. They'll say *exactly* what the manager's saying and say *exactly* what the umpire's saying. Which has made for some interesting conversations. Some of our interpreters aren't real excited about using the language but...'You tell me exactly what he said.' Sometimes things get lost in translation.

"We try to get interpreters with a baseball background but sometimes we have to take who we can get. In Germany, we tried to find an interpreter from Germany who spoke English and Korean. That was a difficult task but we finally found one. That was hard to do."

Football—soccer—is, of course, a far more popular sport in Europe than baseball. "Cricket is huge in a number of places," Young adds. "I've run into a few umpires in Australia who do both cricket and baseball. One of the examples I was really surprised was South Africa. South Africa has virtually no baseball, yet they fielded a team for the World Baseball Classic. The baseball in South Africa is much like cricket is in the United States. We have some, but it's very, very little and it's a club sport. That's the same way that baseball is in South Africa."

There are minor variations here and there, but not as many as there used to be. "In the international tournaments, they stop the game after the fifth inning and take a break. It's kind of like a halftime, where everybody leaves the field and they drag the infield. The teams leave the field, the umpires leave the field. They take a little five-minute break and then

Larry Young.

they come back on. The first time I saw it, I wondered what was going on. I thought it was a rain situation. It's done in a lot of foreign countries.

"I go to the Dominican and Venezuela every year. Some of the most rabid fans around. It's interesting. Japan is probably the closest to us, in the form of an organized umpire system. They have professional umpires for whom that's their only job, and they have a minor-league system. Japan's very close to us.

"Korea has a professional staff and Taiwan has a professional staff. But for the most part every other country, they have to rely on some other occupation. Japan, Korea, and Taiwan are the only other countries with a fulltime professional staff. They have some very, very good umpires there. Their training is close to ours. In fact, a lot of the Japanese umpires come to our umpire schools. We've worked closely with them over the years to develop the same system as far as rotations go.

"There is very, very little difference between Japan and the U.S. I did notice a little bit of a difference with Korea. Those umpires—95% of those umpires are former players. The difference in pay between a player and an umpire is not that great in Korea, so it's kind of a logical progression to go from player to umpire in that country.

"I've seen a big change in Japan over the last 10 years. At one point, the umpires were treated horribly there. They were physically pushed. The money - their pay—was horrible. The conditions were horrible. They expected them to take the bus to the games. For a country that respected authority, that didn't translate into umpiring. Over the last 10 years, I've seen a real big difference. The pay has become better. The backing of the umpire has become better. The whole situation now is much better than it used to be.

"At one point several years ago, if an umpire missed a call, he was expected to get on the P.A. system in front of all of the fans and apologize. That was the custom, but that's gone. If he just missed it, and there was no way to look at it, he would have to apologize.

"I'd have been apologizing a lot over my career."

Umpires being pushed? "It was common. Normally, it was by the manager. We had a young umpire who was in the minor leagues and was sent over there to work for an entire year. Mike DiMuro, who's now a major-league umpire. He was part of that. The manager came out and instead of getting nose to nose, which is common here, he was pushed. It was very common for the managers to push the umpires. It's a huge difference between 10 or 20 years ago and how it is today, how they're respected and how much their profession has come, not only in terms of salary but in terms of training and their respect level."

There have been no umpires from Japan to work in the U.S. majors, but there have been some from other places. Armando Rodriguez was a Cuban native who worked 318 games in 1974 and 1975. Puerto Rico's Delfin Colon worked 46 big-league games in 2008 and 2009. Manny Gonzalez began working in 2010. Through the 2014 season, he's worked 408 games.

"He had to go through the same system. He umpired in Venezuela for several years and then went to umpire school and worked his way through the minors like everyone. That's the only way to get to the big leagues.

"He was a young man. He was 18 years old when he first started. I think he umpired four or five years exclusively in Venezuela and then came to the United States, still a young man. [Gonzalez was born in 1979.] There are eight or nine Venezuelan umpires now in the minor leagues. Dominican has, I think, two. And Puerto Rico has two. No one from the Dominican and no one from Puerto Rico has gotten to the big leagues yet.

"We had no one from Asia yet or from Europe. We have one Australian who worked his first major-league game this year. Jon Byrne. He has yet to make it on our staff, but he's on our call-up list. He worked a few games. [Byrne worked seven MLB games in 2014.] That was big news in Australia. Australia's baseball is probably Double-A level. They have a very organized league, but the umpires are part-time. They get paid $250 a game and have other jobs.

There may be a female umpire before there is one from Europe. Asked about Yanet Moreno in Cuba, Young said, "I'm interesting in seeing her work. It's time for us to bring a female umpire into the WBC this year. She's one of the candidates. I have one from Venezuela, one from Cuba, and one from Canada, and I'm thinking that after I've seen them work, I'm hoping that one of them can step up."

What does his schedule portend for 2015, going into 2016?

"I do about 80 games in the major leagues [as a supervisor] and I'm in replay once a month, in addition to my international duties. This year, I've already gone to Puerto Rico for the Caribbean Series. My next international trip will be to Toronto for the Pan Am Games in July. We have the Premier 21 tournament coming up in Japan in November. And I'll do another clinic for ISG sometime in the winter. Next year will be crazy again, because the qualifying rounds will begin. We'll probably have three qualifying rounds in March and then in September."

Young is a proud recipient of the National Association of Sports Officials Gold Whistle award, presented for community service.

Larry Young has been married to his wife Joan for 40 years. They have two daughters, Jessica and Darcy, and a grandson, Bo. Though Young has done clinics in 17 countries, and counting, he says, "There are a lot of countries on my list that I'd like to get to and conduct clinics. There's a lot of places that had never had an MLB presence." That's for sure, one of his daughters is quick to chime in, "You haven't done one in Antarctica yet."

NOTES

1   Other than the United States, Young has also instructed in Puerto Rico, Dominican Republic, Venezuela, Japan, South Africa, Panama, Taiwan, Germany, Spain, Australia, Canada, Korea, Italy, Mexico, Netherlands, and Czech Republic.

2   Author interview with Larry Young on February 10, 2015. All quotations from Young come from this interview or a follow-up interview on February 18, 2015.

Cuban Umpiring

By Reynaldo Cruz

Perhaps one of the most difficult umpiring jobs in the world is the one carried out in Cuba, where verbal abuse can come from the stands when a call is blown, or when a close play that has been called right negatively affects the home team. When taking on umpires, Cuban fans can be really virulent.

With a very modest salary and no union, umpires are prone to be constantly put under the microscope by the fans, the players, the managers, and the media. Since they do not have leadership separate from the Cuban Baseball Federation, they have exactly the same boss as the players, an almighty commissioner who makes decisions within games, stripping all authority from everyone, and creating a bad climate among the men in dark blue.

Cuban umpires have in Amado Maestri their most celebrated colleague, acknowledged more for his action in 1952 preventing a slaughter of university students protesting at Estadio del Cerro during the regime of dictator Fulgencio Batista. A group of students from the University of Havana, led by student leader José Antonio Hecheverría, jumped into the field on Estadio del Cerro (now Estadio Latinoamericano) during a game, protesting the Batista regime, just a few months after he had led a coup d'état on March 10. The police stormed onto the field with the clear intention of clubbing the students to death. Maestri stood in the middle, stating that he was in charge of whatever happened on the field, and even though the police took the students away, no fatal incident took place at the ballpark. That day transcended so much politically, that even today November 23 is celebrated in Cuban baseball as the day of Cuban umpiring.

Maestri was indeed known for his authority on the field. He even went as far as ejecting Mexican League President Jorge Pasquel (the guy who once intended to challenge the American major leagues) from a game in the Mexican League on June 5, 1945,

despite knowing that this could possibly come back to hurt him.

Another umpire embraced in Cuba for nonbaseball-related events during games was César Valdés. During the "friendship series" between Cuba and the Baltimore Orioles at Camden Yards in 1999, Valdés physically threw down a man who entered the field making noise and carrying a sign offensive to the Cuban Revolution

But more than those moments of praise, it has been the infamous moments surrounding umpires due to the lack of comprehension and the inborn hostility toward them that has marked them in Cuba.

There was a time in the mid-1960s when, after arguing a call, catcher Ramón Primelles punched umpire Alfredo Paz. This led to a one-year suspension for all-time great Manuel Alarcón (who retired at 27 holding almost every major pitching record in the National Series). And there were the recent unfortunate incidents of the 2012-2013 season, which may well stick in the fans' memory and haunt umpires for years to come.

The recent incidents started on Sunday, December 22, 2013, when Ciego de Avila's Vladimir García plunked Villa Clara's Ramón Lunar, who had been tormenting Ciego de Avila's pitching. Instantly after the beanball, home-plate umpire Lorién Lobaina ejected the hurler; he believed García had thrown at Lunar. Claiming that no warning notice had been issued, Ciego de Avila's manager, Roger Machado, withdrew his team from the field and refused to play. Rules state that when that happens, the umpires have a given time (not to exceed five minutes) to forfeit the game to the other team. Yet, an unprecedented occurrence took place, altering forever not only the outcome of that game, but also the way umpires would work for the rest of the season.

Cuban Baseball Federation President Higinio Vélez, then commissioner of Cuban baseball,[1] made a phone call and persuaded Machado to take the

Mid-game refreshment break for Cuban umpires. Mártires de Barbados Stadium, Granma, March 4, 2015.

field again, even though the time for forfeit had been long reached (28 minutes had passed since Machado had withdrawn his team). At the same time, he had umpire Lobaina removed from the game in one of the most disrespectful things ever to happen to a Cuban umpire in the long history of the game on the island.

The next time Lunar and García met was in the second round of that season. Machado's team had not made it to the Top Eight, and García was acting as a reinforcement for Pinar del Río.[2] The first pitch he threw to Lunar was a second straight plunking. This time the hitter jumped at the pitcher. Only Lunar was ejected, despite the earlier history, and Villa Clara's manager, Ramón Moré, then defending champion, didn't cause as much of a commotion as Machado had.

Cuban umpires felt caught in the middle of a very bad situation: ejecting a key pitcher of the national team (García had been a member of the World Baseball Classic team) would probably lead to a scene

by the manager, and then to a phone call that would end the umpire's night.

It all reached a low in the night of February 17, 2014, when an unusually wild Freddy Asiel Álvarez (from Villa Clara, coincidentally) got a piece of Matanzas's Yasiel Santoya, who had previously homered off him. In the heated environment, Álvarez delivered a brushback pitch against Víctor Mesa Jr., son of Víctor Mesa, manager of Matanzas and the Cuban team. Out of the dugout, bat in hand, came Demis Valdés, looking for Álvarez with the clear idea of murdering him. A melee ensued, and when the dust had settled, Ramón Lunar was lying face down with a serious blow to his mouth with the bat.

Umpire Osvaldo de Paula should have ejected the pitcher after the Santoya plunking. Yet, he was walking on thin ice given the fact that the previous similar incident had been costly for Lobaina. With no umpires' union, and with the obvious need the commission had to punish someone (one might have thought Vélez would present his resignation), de Paula could not find defense, and was given a treatment similar to that of the players: a suspension for not having proven his authority.

Such an event definitely threw light on the biggest complaint Cuban umpires have, aside from wages: There is no union for the umpires to respond to and to be represented by. The fact that someone with power but little umpiring knowledge makes a phone call and disposes of an umpire at will is a dangerous situation, one that can only lead to other unfortunate events.

Even though Cuban umpires are accorded the respectful treatment of being provided a glass of water and a cup of coffee on a tray by a very beautiful attendant during the fifth-inning stretch, the reality of their work is very rough, and most of the times they are the weakest link of the chain, depending on who the transgressor is. Make it Roger Machado or Víctor Mesa, and we'll have the umpire paying the price for it, since both are commission favorites.

Umpires are trained first in their province and later on in the national umpiring school, and they need to officiate many games at lower-level tournaments (Provincial and National School Games, Provincial Series, and so on) before making it to the National Series. Many of them begin as substitutes before getting a so-called full-time umpiring job, for 32.00 national pesos per game (the equivalent of $1.42 US). Even though many things in Cuba are subsidized, that is still a very low income. (On September 27, 2013, the Cuban government an-nounced a new system to pay athletes better, but did little for umpires.)

Umpires are closely evaluated. Every game is monitored and assessed by a technical commission, making sure that the umpires work properly and call the game the way it should be. That commission gives a game evaluation to every umpire, based on the accuracy of his calls and the control he kept of the game, and all that is kept in a file for the whole season.

The aggressiveness of players can also be a problem; there is often a tendency to protest every decision an umpire makes. We have even seen a hurler protesting a call and a hitter doing exactly the same thing on two different pitches during the same at-bat. Nevertheless, all these events could be prevented or stopped with an umpires' union that looked after their rights and protected their authority. Maestri's ejection of Pasquel some 70 years ago is not something that could happen in Cuba today.

NOTES

1   Right now, Cuban Baseball is divided into two: the Cuban Baseball Federation, which handles mainly issues regarding the Cuban National Team, contract signings, and relations with foreign bodies; and the Baseball National Direction, which handles the Cuban National Series and the rest of the domestic baseball activities.

2   After the 2012-2013 season, the Cuban Baseball National Series changed its format into a two-round tournament in which the top eight teams advance to the second round, each drafting five players from the remaining eight teams.

Umpire Elber Ibarra

By Reynaldo Cruz

Recognized as one of the top umpires in Cuba for the past five seasons, Elber Ibarra Santiesteban has the satisfaction (or the luck, as he puts it) of never having called a play that would not let him sleep that night.[1] Born in Tacajó, a settlement in the current municipality of Báguano, within the province of Holguin on September 11, 1958, the first son of Sótero "Bolinga" Ibarra and Eugenia's four children (one girl), Ibarra has come a long way to become Cuba's top umpire (as of 2015).

His father was a sugar mill worker who built his house and started a settlement that is now known as "el Barrio de Bolinga." He taught his children that hard work and family values and honesty were qualities that should be embedded in a person's character. "Bolinga" worked very hard his entire life, and all of his four children learned to do the same. Both parents raised their children and the family remained together the two parents passed away. Ibarra, his two brothers, and his sister remain very close.

Since his family was so humble, when he was a boy, Elber had to sell pasty baked by his mother while he was not at school.

A graduate with three diplomas (Elementary School Teacher, PT Professor, and Political Economy), Ibarra went to Primary School Julio Antonio Mella in Tacajó and then to Secondary School Julio Antonio Mella (both schools had the same name) in the same municipality, until ninth grade, when he was transferred to Secondary School Conrado Benítez in Banes.

He started playing baseball from a very early age, primarily playing third base and shortstop until becoming a junior, and representing the Banes region in all provincial school games from the earliest to the Junior level. One year, playing in the age 14-15 category, he had to switch to the outfield to accommodate shortstop Jorge Cruz, the first shortstop to hit 100 homers in the Cuban National Series, who had moved from Palma Soriano (Santiago de Cuba) to Banes.

After playing in the Juniors, Ibarra worked as a school teacher for three years, and first came across umpiring in 1980. Thirty-five years later, he is Cuba's top umpire and has been a crew chief for 16 years. As it happens, he worked as a volleyball referee in his early years.

Ibarra does not make a full living out of umpiring, since he is part of the *Combinado Deportivo*[2] of his native Tacajó, where he works as a professor, despite having a house in Holguin a few blocks from Calixto Garcia Stadium, where he lives with his wife, his daughter, his son-in-law, and his beloved grandson. The umpire's salary as of the end of 2015 is 32.00 CUP (Cuban National Pesos) per officiated game, meaning 1.28 CUC (Cuban Convertible Pesos), or what is to say the equivalent of 1.42 US dollars, so the job at the *Combinado* is what works best to make ends meet. Ibarra has enjoyed the opportunity of working abroad as an umpire or as an instructor.[3]

His international résumé includes the National Championship of El Salvador in 1996; the Italian National Championship in 1998; the Haarlem Baseball Week, in the Netherlands, in 2002; the first World University Championship in Messina, Italy, in 2002; the last-ever Intercontinental Cup in Taichung, Chinese Taipei, in 2010; the 2012 16U World Championship, the 2013 World Baseball Challenge in Prince George, Canada; the 2014 Caribbean Series in Margarita, Venezuela; the 2014 Central American and Caribbean Games in Veracruz, Mexico; and the 2015 Pan Am Games in Toronto, Canada.

For three years in a row (through the 2014-2015 season) he was chosen the most outstanding umpire in Cuban baseball.

When the Tampa Bay Rays visited Havana to play against the Cuban national team in March 2016, Ibarra served as the home plate umpire.

When and how did you become interested in umpiring?

In 1980, Norge García, an umpire in the Provincial Series from Báguano, encouraged me and started inviting me, playing in a second category game, he gave me a three-day seminary in Báguano, and we came to a provincial course, with a very large number of umpires from Holguín (there has always been good umpiring in Holguín). We had lessons with Ángel Hernández[4], who was the director and main professor of that course, and to whom I owe most of my umpiring knowledge. After the course, Norge was the first in the class and I came as the runner-up, and I started working right away. I never forget that my first game was in Mayarí, in Cerones, in a 13-14 category game. Before that I did not have any interest in umpiring: all I ever wanted was to play.

Tell us about your first National Series game.

Well, my first National Series game was in Puerto Padre (a municipality in Las Tunas), in a game of which I don't remember who Las Tunas was playing —that's why I am constantly telling young umpires that they need to write those things down and keep track of their work— in those three games. I do remember it was in the umpire crew led by Alfredo Paz. The Calixto García Stadium manager went to the boarding school where I worked in Tacajó, looking for me urgently, and told me I had been summoned to go to Puerto Padre. I took one of those bags they used to give to catchers to pack their gear and headed to the stadium. I slept in the dorms there, and took a bus to Puerto Padre in the early hours of the morning. Those were my first games, along with Paz (then crew chief), Omar Lucero, and Lázaro Ramírez.

What do you think is the hardest thing for umpires in terms of dealing with the crowd?

I personally don't pay attention to the crowd's reaction after a call, and I think the umpire should not listen to them; if you start listening and paying attention to what is happening in the stands, you can't work at all. Sometimes you can get really annoyed, but as an umpire your best reaction, and what is expected of you, is to remain concentrated on the ballgame. Fans will always scream; they scream at the ballplayers, at the managers, the umpires... But as an umpire you have to think they are in a different world.

What is the hardest thing for being an umpire in Cuba?

I believe that one of the most difficult umpiring jobs in the world is the Cuban. I have had the opportunity to officiate abroad, and it is another kind of baseball, another culture, another idiosyncrasy. When you go to soccer, there have been deaths in the stadiums, but that is not a common happening in baseball. Come to our area, Latin America, you hear some screaming towards the umpire, but it's also part of our culture as Latinos, and there is no offense. Our baseball is really rough, and our fanbase can get really verbally violent. In earlier days, it was not like that, but lately it has escalated. Our baseball is really rough in that aspect, and the fans are very demanding and knowledgeable.

What are the main characteristics you consider an umpire should have?

They must love this job, that is the first principle. Cuban umpiring is difficult, complex, because of many things we have—like we are directed by the same institution directing the ballplayers, and that is not the case in the rest of the world. In the rest of the world, umpiring is separated from the teams. Second, you have to study, you need to have courage, courage to make the right decision in the difficult moment, whether it is to make the right call affecting the outcome of the game or ejecting a player... and in order to do that, you need to have another characteristic: neutrality. You need to be impartial. You cannot start thinking of who is hitting, who is pitching or what team is playing in order to make a call. For me it is the same, whether the batter is Cuba's top slugger or a rookie out of the junior category. You do need to try to do your job better every day, especially when a championship is on the line, and be impartial. The whole world acknowledges that Cuban umpires are very impartial.

It is said that Cuban umpires have two big challenges: the strike zone and the calls on plays at third base. What can you tell us about it?

Sometimes people do not understand much about those two plays. Ever since I started playing and umpiring, the strike zone is only one, and varies according to the player who is hitting. When I started, it was said by rule that the strike zone went from the armpits to the lower part of the knees, at the moment when the hitter started swinging. Now the rule says the strike zone goes from a middle line between the shoulders and the waist of the hitter, what we call "to the letters," to the lower part of the knees, and seventeen inches in the width of the home plate. Every batter has his own strike zone, and you need to take into account that it is at the moment when he is about to swing, because there are hitters who look tall, but then crouch at the moment of swinging. The call must be made at that moment because that is the effective area for him to hit. What cannot happen, and it is the challenge you mentioned, is calling it a strike if it goes outside the seventeen inches of home plate. If it doesn't go over the plate, it cannot be a strike. We can always improve in that aspect (and I criticize myself along with my colleagues). We Cuban umpires also have to work on the lower part of the strike zone, because we often overlook that type of pitch (normally above the knees of the batter) and call them balls. When we watch the games on television we assess the work of our peers and we see that those pitches, normally called for balls, are strikes. That can create a problem when Cuban hitters play overseas, that they get those pitches called for strike, because they like working in the low area of the strike zone. I remember asking two Puerto Ricans in the 2014 Caribbean Series, and they preferred the low zone over the high zone. It is my personal opinion that the strike zone is established to be called properly, both high and low areas. If we don't do so, we are unfair to the pitchers.

Regarding the third-base plays, every time the umpire is positioned wrong, there can be a wrong call. Sometimes the umpire places himself where he should be, and there is a wide throw, or the baserunner slides awkwardly, and the umpire cannot see the play properly and then he will struggle to make a call. It is very hard, and sometimes the fans are cruel to third-base umpires. I have spoken to some fans and explained this point, and they have finally agreed with me, but in the heat of the game, they don't stop and think for a moment.

I remember, during a course given by an umpire from Puerto Rico, he said that "the umpire has to know how to 'read' the plays." By that, he meant that even when the umpire is positioned correctly, he needs to anticipate what can happen in order to avoid being surprised. You know, whenever there is a play, the umpire normally tends to position himself for a "perfect play," in other words, a good throw and a clean slide, but when one of those things is not like that, you as an umpire need to read the motion of the ball and the players in order to re-position yourself to make the right call. And even so, the call can be blown.

A difficult call you have had to make?

I remember a particular play in the final playoff of the 2009-2010 Cuban National Series between Villa Clara and Industriales, and I'm pretty sure you remember that play: the two consecutive outs made at the plate by Ariel Pestano. It was really tough, because it was a very heated playoff, and they came one after the other. When I looked over the left side and I saw Serguei Pérez rounding third with Rudy Reyes on his heels I told myself, "Oh, dear Lord." Then I had to follow the ball and at the same time follow up the runners. It was so fast! All I remember is the dust lifting, and Pestano blocking the plate, ball in hand, preventing Serguei from scoring and Rudy lying down there, then he tagged them both in the blink of an eye... I remember looking at the plate, looking at Pestano, then at Serguei and realizing there was no way Rudy would have gone under both of them to touch the plate, because Serguei himself hadn't been able to, and I called him out as well. This all happened much faster than I tell you and I had just seconds to make a call. Later on, I was told by a similar play made in the major leagues, but I have no information about another play like that in Cuba.[5]

That playoff had a particular play at second base, when Andy Sarduy tagged Alexander Malleta as he was running by trying to elude the tag and the umpire called the runner safe. It was actually the first time a manager (Eduardo Martin, in this case) called for replay to be used.

Yes, that was out... I cannot forget that play. That is one example of what I was telling you before: the umpire was positioned correctly, and then there was no way that he could have seen that play. He was in his right position, but when Malleta ran by, he blocked the umpire's view, so he didn't see whether Canto had tagged him or not and called him safe. That heated up the game and the situation went pretty difficult for us.

I remember umpiring the last game behind the plate, and Yandris Canto homered and tied things up when Industriales was about to celebrate. Imagine how I felt.

Elber Ibarra Santiesteban.

The last thing I want or like to do as an umpire is to work extra-innings, because you are normally walking on thin ice when it comes to fan and media criticism. You may have umpired a nice game, and made the right calls most of the time, and then, all of a sudden, you blow a call in the tenth inning that costs one team the game. That is one game I never forget, because by the ninth inning I had this feeling and was thinking "I'm doing a great job here," then comes Canto and ties the game, because no umpire wants to work extra innings. But when things are on the line, and a close play is the difference between ending the game and keeping it going, the umpire won't let this influence, even though it is a bang-bang play and he may be prone to miss a call later on. By that time, I want the game to end, but that is very different from ending it myself with an unfair call.

Let's talk about what was requested that day: the replay. What do you think of it?

I'm going to be straight honest with you. When I heard that they were using the replay in the majors and it was decided to use it in Cuba as well, I was very critical because I thought the umpire's work would become meaningless. But when I saw it for the first time I had to admit that things truly are fairer now... although there remain times when the calls are really hard even with replay. We Cubans don't have the technology we see in MLB Advanced Media, so sometimes the calls are still hard to make. The other day we had contact in Havana with the authorities, and I was asked the same question. I told them I liked it, because when the replay is available, the

umpire works without the pressure of having the possibility of deciding a ball game with a blown call. Now the umpires have more confidence, and they will be less prone to mistakes. You know what would be terrible? If they decided to disallow it after people have gotten used to it. Can you imagine?

Can you give us examples of how an umpire can anticipate?

The umpire should not be thinking about who's hitting or pitching or who's on base, but he needs to prepare for what can happen. When Luis Ulacia used to play, or now when you have guys like Julio Pablo Martínez or Yurisbel Gracial, you need to be ready, because you can allow your eyes to get caught up in a close play at first base with an apparently easy grounder, and you need to decide fast and properly. When one of these players hits a chopper, you know things are going to get messy at first, so the umpire needs to be prepared in order to make the right call. Of course, the most important anticipation is to know the umpiring job and to do everything possible to make the right call all the time. But as tension rises for the players, it rises for the umpires as well, and it is then that you need to avoid making the wrong call. We are human beings, thus subject to err, but even so, the umpires are not expected to, and when they do, they are seldom forgiven. There are moments, like a base- loaded situation on a full count and the tying run on third base... you see it wrong and call ball four, the hitter wins the game, if you see it wrong and call strike three, the hitter loses the game, so we need to double out concentration in moments like that. I daresay those tense moments are more tense and difficult for the umpire, because if the hitter strikes out, or hits a homer, it is part of the game... the umpire making the wrong call is not supposed to be part of the game, and the repercussions can last for days and days.

So, you would say that people are unfair to umpires?

I would say so. People are unfair to umpires without thinking that we are just as the players: human beings who can be wrong sometimes, but we always want to do things right. When a player makes an error that costs the game, what do you think happens? His world collapses around him, and he barely sleeps that night. We go through the same thing. The fielder misplays an easy grounder, or an easy fly ball, or the hitter swings at the wrong pitch, or the pitcher throws a pitch right up in the strike zone, good enough for a homer. None of them wants to mess things up. We are just the same. I would say that I am very fortunate that I haven't blown a call in a moment like that, but I have made mistakes too, and it feels really bad. There are those bang-bang plays that you can call right or wrong, but I have to say that I do believe in luck, because it has kept me from blowing a big call in a big moment.

Do you believe that the way catchers prepare and train can have any influence in the work of an umpire?

For sure. A catcher who doesn't work properly or doesn't keep good framing makes it very difficult for umpires to make the right call. And I will give you an example: Pedro Luis Rodríguez. Working with him was great, because he never stepped off the catcher's box and kept great framing on pitches. When catchers are good doing their job, the umpire finds it easier to do ours. Sometimes the catcher will even jump and stand up in front of the umpire at the moment of the delivery, thus blocking the umpire's view and making it impossible to make the right call. With the speed of pitches and the little time one has to decide, it is important that the umpire's view doesn't get disturbed. So, when there is a good catcher, the umpire calls strikes and balls with little problems, but when the catcher is not good enough, the umpire has to work twice as hard.

What do you think can be done to improve the work of Cuban umpires?

First, we have to be more demanding and critical of our own work. We also really need to be under the command of a different entity; today we are still being led by the same organization as the one leading the players. So we do not have an umpires' union, and we need an umpires' union that is independent from the baseball apparatus. Increasing the umpires' wages, in order to gain more motivation. One other thing that can make things better is the exchange with other leagues, both inward an outward. Bringing foreign umpires to work here and sending Cuban umpires to work in leagues overseas will widen the knowledge and experience of umpiring in Cuba. We once had an experience with Italian umpires

in Cuba, and right now they are discussing bringing some Panamanians to work in our league. Interacting with foreign umpires would give us the opportunity to exchange knowledge, tricks of the trade, and experience, and our going to their leagues would provide an opportunity to experience different levels of demand. It is nothing but the same as with the players: in order to increase the quality and professionalism of our players we need to let them go and play in other baseball leagues... well, umpires should have that opportunity, too, as should scorekeepers and everyone related to baseball, It will help make it better for the fans. We recently had a seminar with a Puerto Rican umpire and I would assess the experience as very fruitful. Now, those actions should be multiplied.

Who do you consider to be among the great umpires in Cuba? And the ones you have had the opportunity to work with?

Well, I never had the chance of seeing or working with the all-time great Amado Maestri, nor did I meet Rafael de la Paz, who was known as one of the top umpires. Yet, I have had the honor of working with the next generation of umpires. I started very young, at 31, which was considered such an earlier age at the time, that after starting in 1980 it took me four years to go to a national course. So, I worked with umpires who were extremely respected, such as Alfredo Paz, Manuel "El Chino" Hernández, Alejandro Montesinos, Ivan Davis, Orlando Valdés, and many others. Then came another generation, and I worked with Nelson Díaz, César Valdés, Omar Lucero, Melchor Fonseca, Javier Rodríguez... there have been very good umpires in Cuba.

We have a very unique case in Cuba, and that is Yanet Moreno, a female umpire in the Cuban National Series. What can you tell us about her?

Yanet is the only woman in Cuba working baseball as an umpire at the national level. There are other female umpires in Cuba, but those work mainly female baseball and males within their own provinces, and I heard (I don't know whether it is true or not) that she is the only female umpire in the world working in the top male league in her country. She has been working with me for two years, right now she is in my crew. She has come a long way, and has learned a lot. She has become a good umpire, and of course, she still has a lot to improve, like all of us do. She works pretty well as home plate umpire, and she makes very good calls on the bases. She likes the job very much and she is also very devoted to it.

It is nice to report that there has been no discrimination towards her by her peers (as far as I understand). We get along very well in our crew. All we do is help her, like trying to keep her from lifting heavy loads and stuff like that, mainly the young guys. We have a very good work relationship in our crew. She has been climbing due to her hard work and devotion, and due to her talent and the quality of her performance. She has not been given any special treatment in terms of reaching the position she holds now: it has been the result of her own effort.

NOTES

1 Author interview with Elber Ibarra was conducted in person on December 11, 2015.

2 Combinadodeportivo: In Cuba, every large area, part of People's Councils, have a similar to a sports academy, covering several sports, where different trainers coach kids and promote sports activities.

3 The average Cuban salary is around 600 CUP, which is the same as 24 CUC or 21.60 US dollars. In Cuba, most food, houding, medical care, education, and other things are provided free of charge.

4 This is not the same man as MLB umpire Ángel Hernández.

5 The reference is to the play in which umpire John Hirschbeck called out Jeff Kent and J.D. Drew during the second inning of Game One of the 2006 NLDS between the Los Angeles Dodgers and the New York Mets.

Umpiring In Korea

By John Behrend

In 2016 there were 46 umpires at the highest professional level in the Korean baseball league.

Most umpires in Korea have either played some type of baseball, in youth leagues, high school, college, or even in amateur ranks, but not many have played professional baseball in Korea with any of the KBO (Korean Baseball Organization) teams.

If you want to become a professional umpire in Korea, playing experience is not a requirement, but it does help. One can join the Korean Baseball Association (KBA), an umpire school run by the KBO. The school lasts about 45 days and anyone can attend—even this author. Those who earn the highest scores can get an opportunity to umpire in the Futures League (low minor-league baseball). If you make the cut, before you can call in the Korean professional league you will have to work at least five years in the Futures League. One umpire, Um Jae-gook, had no prior baseball-playing experience; he passed and joined the KBA/KBO umpires but retired after three years of Futures League ball. As of 2017 he worked as a freelance amateur-league umpire.

Some Korean umpires have attended the two professional umpire schools in the United States, run by former umpires Jim Evans and Hunter Wendelstedt. There are some female umpires in Korea in the amateur ranks and some are very good; one with whom I have worked in umpiring amateur ball is Munsook Jeon. Some have attended the school; some have passed all the requirements but were not eager enough to accept a position.

While the rules of game are the same, umpiring in Korea is unique. One difference is that in the Korean Baseball Organization, umpires work in a five-man crew instead of the standard four-man crew used in the US major leagues. So the rotation is a bit different. The home-plate umpire doesn't move to third base the next game as in the United States;

that umpire sits out the next game and is part of the instant-replay team. Only one umpire from the crew reviews the questioned call while the other three remain on the field. In the United States, of course, the umpire who made the call and the crew chief go to the headphones and are in contact with the umpires making the actual replay calls.

In Korea there is a fifth-inning stretch and the umpires leave the field, returning in about two minutes while the grounds crew drags the field and re-marks the home-plate area. The grounds crew also drags the infield after the third inning.

There is no pregame meeting at home plate. The batting orders of both teams are received by the plate umpire during batting practice. Five minutes before the game, the umpires enter the playing field together and jog straight to their positions on the field, and then the Korean National Anthem is played.

Umpires in the KBO have neither a union nor a retirement system. The retirement age is 57. They are independent contractors, hired from year to year. They are evaluated in listed categories. Plate umpires, for instance are rated on Body Head Positioning, Timing, Judgment/Consistency of Strike Zone, Use of Voice, and Positioning of Plays. All umpires are

Korean umpire Won Hyun-sik.

The unusual "gorilla" stance favored by many Korean umpires.

graded on Communication with Partner(s), and Knowledge of Four-umpire Mechanics system.

Pay for umpires in Korea is very low. Umpires almost went on strike one season for that reason. The starting pay for a rookie umpire is about 20 million won for a season, equal to about $17,590. A 20-year-veteran umpire gets up to 100 million won ($87,950), plus hotel and travel expenses. Because they have no union, if an umpire makes a serious mistake, he may be paid less. After a third serious mistake, he will be demoted to the Futures League. One umpire named Park was demoted in 2015 for making some serious mistakes such as in signaling safe and out and was sent down for six months to the Futures League.

Do players give the umpires a hard time in the Korean League? It is probably no different than in the US professional leagues. But sometimes the players can be punished for their actions. In one example from 2014, pitcher Charlie Shirek of the NC Dinos, a team that plays in the city of Changwon on South Korea's southeast coast, was fined 2 million won and had to perform 40 hours of community service as punishment for swearing at an umpire. He showered abuse on umpire Kim Jun-hee in the first inning of a game against the SK Wyverns. Shirek strongly complained about Kim's calls on his pitches. Despite repeated warnings from the plate umpire, Shirek continued to swear in both Korean and English and was soon ejected—or, as they say, ordered to leave the pitcher's mound.

Another odd practice: The pitcher can wear foreign objects attached to his body unless the opposing team appeals to the umpires. If they determine that it neither confuses the hitters nor affects the movement of his pitches, it will be allowed. An example would be the wearing of "health necklaces." If it doesn't affect the game and there is no intention to cheat, then it is permissible. The rules also allow taping, jewelry, and so on, quite different from US major-league standards.

Umpires are human, and that is part of the human element of the game. The statement that the best umpires in baseball are the ones the fans don't know is not necessarily true. Some of us do know their names.

Fans naturally hope for fewer missed calls from umpires. Complaints arose over a series of controversial calls by umpires, many of which were obviously incorrect. The KBO, which had long turned a deaf ear to outcries from fans, players, and coaches, finally decided to expand its replay system, which was not as accurate as that in the US major leagues.

At first, the system was only for home-run calls. The KBO had to amend its rules, which banned challenges to ball/strike, fair/foul, and safe/out calls. Managers can only challenge fair/foul and safe/out calls, or a questionable home-run call. Even this was a drastic change in the stance of the league, which had merely stressed that the umpire's authority should be respected. During replays, the stadium scoreboards do not show the play, but spectators can see them on their smartphones, even watching frame-by-frame. While the playing rules are universal, Korea illustrates that umpiring varies from country to country in terms of training, compensation, and on-field procedures.

Professional Woman Umpires

By Leslie Heaphy

"Are you blind?" is a familiar cry for fans sitting in the stands at any baseball diamond. Fans believe it is part of their job to harass the men in blue. But what happens when that man is a woman in blue? Do the insults change? Yes. Are fans so surprised some of them do not even know how to react? Yes. But baseball has been played professionally in the United States since the 1860s. Why are people still surprised by female umpires? Because they are absolutely still a novelty. Women have had limited success breaking in to the ranks of the arbiters of the game, though the few who have been allowed to participate have proved they know the rules and how to call a game. And why have both the NBA and professional football added female referees but not baseball?

Baseball made one concession to change in 2006 when the rules committee voted to acknowledge the presence of a female umpire. "An amendment to Rule 2.00 in the Definition of Terms reads: "Any reference in these Official Baseball Rules to 'he,' 'him,' or 'his' shall be deemed to be a reference to 'she,' 'her,' or 'hers,' as the case may be, when the person is female."

Veteran big-league umpire Larry Young, a member of the Playing Rules Committee, voted in favor of the wording."[1] Those who voted believed it needed to be done.

Where does the story begin for the seven US professional female umpires? One of the earliest women to be paid to umpire semipro games was Amanda Clement in the early 1900s. Her brother Hank helped get her started and people, while surprised, were impressed with her ability and knowledge. After Clement there was a long hiatus until Bernice Gera got her chance as the first professional. Gera was followed by Pam Postema and then there were Christine Wren and Theresa Cox. Ria Cortesio and Shanna Kook worked at the same time in 2003

and 2004. In addition to these ladies there is also Cuba's Yanet Moreno, who has been umpiring in the National Series since 2003. In 2015 Guam added a female umpire to its ranks with Jhen Senence Bennett. She umpired her first game with her father. And as recently as early 2016 Jen Pawol became the seventh after receiving a contract from the Gulf coast Leagueupon successful completion of umpire school.

Bernice Mary Shiner Gera was born on June 15, 1931, in Ernest, Pennsylvania but grew up in Erath, Louisiana. Gera graduated from high school in 1949, with a graduating class of three. She married Louis Thomas Jr. and after their divorce married freelance photographer Stephen Gera. She worked as a secretary before turning her hand to umpiring. A longtime baseball fan, Gera graduated in 1967 from the Jim Finley umpire school but no one came calling to give her a job professionally. Gera's experience came with local ballgames and semipro tournaments. Due to Organized Baseball's lack of acceptance Gera began a six-year battle to get a chance to umpire. She stated, "I was not out there fighting anybody's cause. I didn't do what I did because of women's liberation or anything like that. ... I just wanted to be affiliated with baseball."[2] She received a contract in 1969 but it was invalidated by NAPBL President Philip Piton before she even got an opportunity. She finally won her lawsuit in 1972 when the New York Court of Appeals ruled in her favor. Gera signed her first and only contract on April 12, 1972. Her only officiated game took place on June 24, 1972, a Class-A game in Geneva, New York. She was supposed to ump a doubleheader between Auburn and the Geneva Senators but she left after the first game and never looked back. She retired after that one game. It was a tough game with at least three disputed calls, one of which led to her ejecting Auburn manager Nolan Campbell. Campbell said, "She should be in the kitchen, peel-

Bernice Gera at the Jim Finley umpire school in 1967.

ing potatoes."[3] After leaving the field Gera went to work for the New York Mets in community relations and promotions. When Gera died on September 23, 1992, from kidney cancer, her tombstone read, "Pro Baseball's First Lady Umpire."[4] A historical marker was also placed at Blue Spruce Park near the ball field close to her home in Pennsylvania.[5] Her uniform and equipment are on display at the Bridgeton Hall of Fame All Sports Museum.

After Gera left the game, Christine Wren had a short career in the 1970s. Wren played softball growing up in Spokane, Washington. She spent about 13 years playing fast-pitch softball, usually as the catcher. After being called out on a play at second that was clearly wrong, she decided she could be an umpire too. She attended umpire school in Mission Hills, California. When she finally got her chance

to umpire, she commented, "I'm not a freak. I'm just somebody trying to do a job."[6] Wren umpired for two years in the Northwest League, in 1975 and 1976, and then in the Class-A Midwest League in 1977. In 1977 she made $250 a month plus $60 for travel expenses. Her most unusual experience came in an exhibition game when a Portland player came up to her and kissed her on the field. She gave him a warning and no one ever tried that again. Midwest League President Bill Walters was so impressed with Wren that he stated, "The girl is good and I want to convince Mr. (Bowie) Kuhn that she's good."[7] She managed the players on the field like any good umpire and ejected players only when needed. Her first ejection came in a Seattle Rainiers game against Boise. She ejected catcher Ron Gibson in the seventh inning over a pitch call.[8] Wren said she loved the work but hated the travel and the low pay. "The athlete in me, the ballplayer in me, always liked umpiring. It was something I always wanted to do."[9] After a few years Wren decided to call it quits and make her winter job a full-time one driving a delivery truck.[10]

After Gera and Wren left the game, Pam Postema was the next to try to break the barrier. Postema had the most success before Ria Cortesia made it to Triple A in the early 2000s.

Postema umpired for 13 years before filing a lawsuit against major-league baseball after her career stalled at the Triple-A level, following three years in the Pacific Coast League. Postema grew up in Willard, Ohio (born April 1954), playing softball and baseball with her brothers. She even played some football with her brothers growing up. Though she played the game she never thought about umpiring until she got older. She was waitressing at a Red Lobster when she read an ad about umpire school.

She started in the Gulf Coast League in 1977 after attending the Somers School in Daytona Beach, Florida, as one of 130 students. She wanted to be sure she made the cut because she was a good umpire and not because she was a woman. "And if I wasn't good enough I didn't want to make it then just because I was a woman."[11] Postema actually applied three times without ever getting even a reply. She decided to just show up and ask for a chance in person, which she got. After graduating 17th in her class, Postema got her first assignment in the Gulf Coast League. After her time in the Gulf Coast League Postema moved to the Class-A Florida State League and then the Double-A Texas League in 1991. By 1993 Postema found herself promoted to the Pacific Coast League, where she worked for four years before making her final move to the Triple-A American Association. Postema commented on her career saying, "I love every moment of my work."[12] No matter how much she loved her work, Postema still had to fight for everything she got. One of the more difficult things she had to deal with in many parks was the conditions in the locker rooms because they did not have accommodations for female umpires. At many parks the best that could be done was to hang a sheet to

give her some privacy while she changed to go out onto the field.

Postema got the chance to umpire a spring-training game between the Cleveland Indians and San Francisco Giants in 1982. For her the game was like any other for an umpire trying to earn a chance to move up to the next level. Postema was assigned to "B"-level spring-training games to get more experience after umpiring the previous fall in the Arizona Fall League. She was working to earn her dues like any other umpire. She said she took no more abuse than any other umpire. She stated, "I get the same amount of harassment as any ump, I think, and there's been no favoritism, no prejudice. I've been really lucky and worked with super umps. It's no big deal being a woman ump."[13] Postema also commented that any umpire who was the least bit different would take flak, if they were fat, or black, or a woman. Her answer was the same as any other umpire: If you get too much flak you throw them out.[14]

As expected, reaction to Postema's work was mixed. Manager Jim Fregosi said, "I hardly noticed her so I guess she did okay." Pitcher Tim Burke commented on her calling balls and strikes, saying, "She's just another mask behind the plate." When she tossed batboy Sam Morris for not retrieving a chair thrown onto the field by his manager, the reaction was loud and wide. Postema believed she did the right thing and maintained that if she had been a man no one would have said anything at all.[15] Red Sox superstar Wade Boggs said, "I have no objection if she can do a good job. If she's there as a publicity stunt; I don't agree with that."[16] The real compliment for Postema's skills came from Louisville outfielder Jack Ayer who said, "Tell you the truth, I don't really recognize that she's a woman. I don't have time for that."[17] Randy Kutcher, a utility infielder for the Boston Red Sox, commented, "She does a good job. She's as good as anybody." Kutcher had a unique perspective, having had the chance to see Postema umpire for five years at Double A and Triple A.[18] Catcher Ozzie Virgil thought she did a good job. "I had no complaints. I was really impressed with the way she handled all the stuff people in the stands were yelling at her."[19]

In contrast, Bob Knepper asserted that God did not like what she was doing in a man's job.[20] Toby Harrah, manager of the Oklahoma City 89ers, got thrown out by Postema and was not complimentary in his reactions. Harrah stated, "she just doesn't grasp the game of baseball. If you haven't played the game—and I'm sure she hasn't—you miss the grasp."[21] Postema's reaction was simply that she was trying to make the major leagues like any other umpire. Dick Butler, who scouted umpires for the American League, said she was there and so why not give her a chance.[22] Postema's best chance at making the majors was lost when Commissioner Bart Giamatti died. He had seemed receptive to the idea of a woman moving up to the highest level of baseball.

Postema also had to deal with those who only saw her as a woman and never as someone who could control a game. A reporter in Cuba simply referred to her as "un mujer muy bonita, por cierto (a very pretty woman, by the way)."[23]

Postema's real trouble developed because she never got a chance to move beyond Triple A. By Organized Baseball rules there was a limit to the years one could spend in the minors without being called up to the majors. If one did not get the call then they were let go, as Postema was. She believed that she was let go because of her gender and not because she was unqualified. The interesting issue for Postema was that previously she had been ranked at the top of the list for umpires moving up and then without any indications or written concerns she dropped from the top to out of contention for an opening,

Postema filed suit in Manhattan District Court in 1991 because the league did not promote her to the majors even though she had excellent performance reviews. She sued for damages, money, and a job. US District Judge Robert Patterson ruled that her case could go forward to trial.[24] Postema was able to bring suit against the National League but not the American because of the number of job openings each had and potential candidates for those jobs. After leaving baseball she went to work for Federal Express in San Clemente, California.[25]

After her career ended, Postema received a number of honors. In 2000 she was inducted into the Shrine of the Eternals. She also published a book about her experiences in 1992 entitled *You've Got to Have Balls to Make It in This League*. In the book she describes her view of why women have such a difficult time even getting a chance to umpire. "Almost all of the people in the baseball community don't want anyone interrupting their little male-dominated way of life. They want big, fat male umpires. They want those macho, tobacco-chewing, sleazy sort of borderline alcoholics."[26]

After attending the Wendelstedt umpire school in 1982, Perry Lee Barber began her still continuing (as of 2015) career; for her long and varied career, which included being assignor of umpires for the independent Atlantic League from 1998 to 2001, see her essay "The Stained Glass Window" in this book.

Theresa Cox of Ohio (later Cox-Fairlady) had a short career after Postema and together they paved the way for Ria Cortesio and Shanna Kook. Cox went to the Harry Wendelstedt School for umpires and graduated fifth out of a class of 180. Cox never really got a fair chance as she was told her voice was too high and she could not really wear the uniform. When she tried to change the tone she was told her voice now sounded fake. Since Cox umpired college and high-school games, her voice was simply an excuse for not wanting her on the diamond. Wendelstedt challenged that view when he claimed Cox was "… the best female candidate I've ever had."[27] He trained 28 women and 5,000 men so his view was certainly one to be taken seriously. In 1989 Cox worked two Double-A Southern League games before umpiring for two years, 1989-1990, in the Arizona Rookie League. She said that in her Arizona League season she walked 22 batters in her first game before the pitchers discovered her strike zone. Cox acknowledged that Postema's work helped her in trying to break into the game. "What she went through has made it easier for me, and if it's not me who is the first woman ump, then maybe I'll make it easier for somebody who follows after me. But we have to keep trying. It's like life, either you evolve or you die out."[28] In 2008 Cox-Fairlady had a chance to umpire a Mets spring-training exhibition game against the University of Michigan. The game was not that unusual but the umpiring crew was, since it included four women, one of whom was Cox-Fairlady. She was joined by Perry Barber, Ila Valcarcel, and Mona Osborne. When she was not umpiring Cox drove for UPS in Birmingham, Alabama, to supplement the money she made umpiring.[29]

Next in line was Ria Cortesio (real name Maria Papageorgiou), from Rock Island, Illinois, who got her start as a professional umpire in 1999. She decided to become an umpire when she was about 16, after talking with umpire Scott Higgins, who sat down with her and explained how the whole process worked.[30] Growing up she never got the chance to play since girls were expected to play softball and baseball was a boy's game. She played in her front yard with her cousins but never in organized ball. She graduated from the Jim Evans Umpire Academy in Kissimmee, Florida, after attending the five-week program in 1998 as her second try, having also attended in 1996. Cortesio was one of only two women each time she attended the school. In addition to umpire school, Cortesio was also a graduate of Rice University, graduating summa cum laude. Evans commented after her graduation from umpire school, "I don't think sex should be a criterion for umpiring in the big leagues."[31] Her goal was to work her way up through the ranks and win one of the 68 major-league umpiring jobs. She even cut her ponytail and lowered her voice so she would not stand out as much. But Cortesio was up against a large group of men working for the same goal. By 2006 she was umpiring the Futures game and home-run derby in Pittsburgh. In 2007 she got the opportunity to umpire a spring-training game between the Cubs and the Diamondbacks. Derek Lee, first baseman for the Cubs, stated, "It's awesome. I think it's about time. Female eyes are as good as male eyes. Why can't they be umpires?"[32]

During a 2007 Double-A game Cortesio received the ultimate compliment from a fan who said, "He might be young, but he looks like he's consistent. So

far, he's called a good game."[33] The fan had no idea the umpire was female and therefore he judged the performance solely on the quality and not the gender. One of her fellow umpires, Jason Stein, got a chance to work with her in the Futures game and continued to be impressed. "She's good enough to be here," said Stein, who worked in the Double-A Texas League. "She's just as good as we are. If she gets the opportunity to advance to the big leagues and be successful, it would be a great thing. I'm pulling hard for her."[34] "She has inconsistencies but she's just as good as any other umpire," said Suns pitcher Joel Hanrahan, who also saw Cortesio in the Pioneer League in 2000 and in the Florida State League in 2002.[35]

Not all reactions were positive to Cortesio's work. While she seemed to get less criticism than Postema and the other early pioneers, there were still critics of her as a female umpire. One of those was George Steinbrenner who expressed displeasure over her strike zone when she called a rehab game for Roger Clemens. Told that Cortesio had once umpired Clemens's boys in Little League in Texas, the New

Pam Postema.

York Yankees owner huffed: "Is that right? Well, that's good; I guess she'll go back there."[36]

Cortesio never really saw herself as a pioneer, just someone who wanted to umpire in the major leagues. "Until I work a regular-season major-league baseball game, I haven't done anything," Cortesio said. "I don't want to be a pioneer. I just want to do my job."[37] Another time, she said, "It never crossed my mind that because I was a female, I couldn't do this job. I was lucky to be raised by parents without barriers; that there is no difference between a male and female doing the same job. The guidelines should be equal for both as long as you can do the job."[38] At the same time Cortesio realized she could do a lot to get other women involved.

Cortesio got the call from Mike Fitzpatrick (executive director of the Professional Baseball Umpires Corporation, the umbrella organization for minor-league umpiring) telling her they were letting her go after the 2007 season. There were no openings at the Triple-A level and her ranking had fallen, making her ineligible for a promotion after nine years. Because there are few openings, senior umpires can be let go if they do not move up, to make room for new hires.[39]

Other major-league players and managers agreed with Derek Lee and thought Cortesio had earned her chance. Willie Randolph commented, "I hope she gets her shot, that's important." Felipe Alou believed a female umpire like Cortesio would be good for the game, claiming, "I believe a woman umpire would bring some good ingredients to the game and added interest."[40]

When asked in 2007 why baseball and not softball, Cortesio had the following to say,

> I bet you if you go to any high school or college softball team and ask any of the girls, probably most of them when they're growing up dreamed of playing major league baseball. You know, baseball is our national pastime, but for some reason half of the nation is shut out of it. There's this pretty ridiculous stereotype, I think, in this country that baseball is just for boys, and girls, go play with dolls or play softball or something.[41]

Cortesio, the last woman to rise through the minor-league ranks to the present day in 2016, helped mentor Canadian Shanna Kook; they were the only two ladies whose career overlapped.

In 2003 Torontoan Kook umpired in the Pioneer League (she spent two years there) after graduating from the Harry Wendelstedt Umpire School. Her first game she umpired behind home plate in a game between Provo and Casper. Provo manager Tom Kotchman said, "I'll give her credit. She was not tentative. It's tough to tell from the side but our catcher said she called a very good game."[42] Before taking up her place on the diamond, Kook attended Clinton Street Public School, where she excelled in the classroom and on the diamond. Kook joined the school baseball team and helped lead it to a championship during her senior year. Kook then enrolled at McGill University, where she majored in music and played the viola. She missed baseball and wanted to return to the game as an umpire.[43]

Kook's view on umpiring was best stated when she said, "I really don't care if people notice me. Really the more I'm anonymous, the better. If people don't know who I am, that's fine, because then I am doing my job."[44] She learned her craft on the diamonds in Canada starting at the age of 16 and by 2002 she was the crew chief for the Women's World Series. She attended a clinic to get started at the community center level. After starting college and realizing she needed more money, she returned to umpiring and eventually rose to umpiring higher-level games. From there she was invited to attend a women's umpire clinic in Canada and then she went for one week to the Jim Evans Academy of Professional Umpiring. Kook was hooked on umpiring and left school to pursue her chance. She joined the small rank of professional female umpires.[45]

After Cortesio was let go, Kate Sargeant tried to earn a spot, attending the Wendelstedt School in Florida in 2007 after umpiring with her dad in the Peninsula Umpires Association. She made it to the final selection process but was not picked for a position. She was the last umpire on the eligible list and she did not get a call. She also had previously attended the Jim Evans School twice. Her only shot came in the independent New York State League, where she spent two years umpiring (2007-2008).[46] Those who worked with her had no qualms about being on the field with Sargeant, saying she knew all the rules. After her failed attempt, league officials were asked when they thought a woman might get an opportunity. When MLB Vice President Mike Teevan was asked if it might be at least another six years before a woman could break into the majors, he said, "Basing on the roads that most [umpires] traveled, that's fair to say." He added, however, that the league "would love to see" a woman officiate one day.[47] Sargeant continued to umpire high-school games for a bit longer but finally gave up her dream and became a forest ranger with Canada's National Forest Service.[48]

One of the most successful female umpires in recent years has been working under the radar in Cuba, Yanet Moreno. Moreno loved baseball as a child but just like other women had trouble playing because others, like her father, thought baseball was for boys and not girls.[49]

In 2016 one more female umpire was added to the ranks of professional baseball. Jen Pawol graduated from Minor League Baseball's umpire camp along with Annie Monochello. While both graduated, only Pawol got an official assignment with the Gulf Coast League, making her the first female umpire at the professional level since 2007. Pawol brought a lot of umpiring experience from both baseball and softball. She played soccer and softball at West Milford High School (New Jersey) before getting a scholarship to play at Hofstra from 1995-1998. Pawol earned All-American honors as a catcher, hitting .332 with 102 RBIs. She umpired for fast-pitch softball as well as being an NCAA Division I postseason umpire. She also umpired in the Big Ten Conference from 2013 to 2015. In her first Gulf Coast League game Pawol umpired behind home plate. She worked a flawless game with the Blue Jays manager Cesar Martin saying, "She did a great job. Controlling the game, all these things. It was a nice game."[50]

Pawol is also an artist. She earned her BFA from the Pratt Institute and then an MFA from Hunter College. When she was not umpiring in previous years she also worked part-time as an eighth grade art teacher. Pawol sees a lot of correlations between painting and baseball, the sounds the rhythm of the game, the artistry of the players, etc…Pawol stated, "I don't really view umpiring as a gender job, I just view it as, if you're good at it, and you like it, you should do it."[51]

The path to becoming an umpire is a long and arduous journey for anyone but especially for a woman. After the establishment of an umpire school for the minor leagues in 2011, only one woman attended and graduated, Sarah Allerding, who then decided to become a deaconess in the Lutheran Church. She said she always felt welcome and simply made the choice to join the church. If she had made the cut and decided to pursue umpiring, it still would have been a minimum of six years before there could have been a female umpire, based on how promotions work. So there have been only six women in the professional ranks and we are still years away from possibly seeing that glass ceiling broken in the United States, even though the NBA and NFL have both employed female referees. Some make the claim that because women do not play baseball as much that is why there are fewer female umpires, but you do not have to play to know the rules.[52]

Writer Derek Crawford ended his article on the trials of female umpires saying, "Baseball truly is a fraternity and a brotherhood, but we live in a society in which a woman can run for President, sit on the Supreme Court, fight on the front lines in combat, but can't put on a chest protector and call balls and strikes in a Major League ballpark for a living."[53]

NOTES

1 Ben Walker, "Just One of the Umpires," *Seattle Times*, July 9, 2006.

2 Craig Davis, "She Never Wanted to Be a Pioneer," *Chicago Tribune*, October 8, 1989.

3 Lisa Winston, milb.com, June 22, 2007.

4 vrml.k12.la.us/ehs/history/berniceshiner.htm.

5   Edward J. Shiner obituary, *New York Times*, August 14, 2014.

6   "Woman Umpire Has a Single Goal," *The Oregonian* (Portland), July 1, 1976: C8.

7   Ibid.

8   "Christine Wren Uses Her Thumb," *Seattle Times*, June 27, 1975: C3.

9   Howie Stalwick, "Spokane Native Paved the Way for Postema," *Spokesman Review* (Spokane, Washington), March 8, 1988.

10 "Kill the Ump. If It's Christine Wren, Kiss Her," *People Magazine*, July 14, 1975.

11 Linda Lehrer, "Sporting Chance," *Chicago Tribune*, June 21, 1992.

12 Mal Bernstein, "Who Is That Woman Behind the Mask," *Christian Science Monitor*, July 29, 1985.

13 AP, "Female Umpire Inches Toward Major Leagues," *Dallas Morning News*, March 14, 1982: 47. 1982.

14 Robin Finn, "Female Umpire Aims for Majors," *Lakeland* (Florida) *Ledger*, July 28, 1987:16.

15 "Batboy Ejected for Disobedience," *Mobile Register*, May 27, 1984.

16 Stephen Harris, "Woman Behind the Plate No Threat," *Boston Herald*, March 15, 1988: 97.

17 "Umpire Pam Postema Is Fighting Tradition," *Mobile Register*, July 6, 1987: 4D.

18 Stephen Harris.

19 Jayson Stark, "She Awaits a Call From the Majors," philly.com, March 13, 1988.

20 Bernie Lincicome, "Woman Umpire Balks at Spotlight," *Chicago Tribune*, March 20, 1988.

21 *Mobile Register*, July 6, 1987: 4D.

22 Jerome Holtzman, "Lady Ump Could Find Home in Majors," *Chicago Tribune*, April 6, 1986.

23 Luis Perez Lopez, "No Maten al Umpire. Que es Una Mujer!" *El Miami Herald*, June 2, 1980: 9.

24 *Mobile Press Register*, July 14, 1992: 3C.

25 "Former Major League Umpire Pam Postema Sues Baseball," December 1991.

26 Pam Postema, *You've Got to Have Balls to Make It in This League* (New York: Simon and Schuster, 1992).

27 Anna Quindlen, "I Don't Know Why a Young Lady Would Want this Job," *Chicago Tribune*, September 3, 1991.

28 Robin Finn, "Ohioan on Deck," *New York Times*, December 25, 1989.

29 Perry Barber and Jean Ardell, "Women in Black," *Cooperstown Symposium*, 2011-2012, State University of New York, College of Oneonta, 2013, 55; Cox Hopes Her Fate as Umpire Turns Out Better Than Postema," *Spokesman Review*, December 25, 1989.

30 Michel Martin, "Baseball's Leading Lady," NPR, April 30, 1977.

31 Josh Robbins, "Female Umpire Hopes for Shot at Major Leagues," *Lawrence* (Kansas) *Journal-World*, May 12, 2007: 16.

32 Lisa Winston.

33 Josh Robbins.

34 Lyle Spencer, "Female Ump Gets Futures Game Nod," MLB.com, July 9, 2006.

35 Jeff Elliott, "Female Umpire Plays Out Dream," *Florida Times-Union* (Jacksonville), June 25, 2003.

36 Ben Walker, "Just One of the Umpires," *Seattle Times*, July 9, 2006.

37 Lyle Spencer.

38 Jeff Elliott.

39 Associated Press, "Baseball's Only Female Umpire Fired," *Houston Chronicle*, November 1, 2007.

40 AP story, "RI's Cortesio Is Hoping Not to Get Rung Up," *Quad-City Times*, September 8, 2005.

41 Michel Martin.

42 Jason Franchuk, "Umpire Story," *Daily Herald* (Provo, Utah), July 10, 2003.

43 Justin Skinner, "Clinton Street PS Looks for Past Grads to Celebrate 125 Years," InsideToronto.com, October 26, 2012.

44 Fran Chuck, "Umpire Story," *Toronto Daily Herald*, July 10, 2003.

45 Leslie Heaphy, ed. *Women in Baseball Encyclopedia* (Jefferson, North Carolina: McFarland Publishing Inc., 2006), 57-58.

46 Pat Borzi, "Woman Umpires Are Striking Out in MLB," ESPNW, August 9, 2011.

47 Lucy McCalmont, "MLB Probably Won't Have a Female Umpire for at Least Six Years," *Huffington Post*, April 16, 2015.

48 Terry Mosher, "Female NK Grad Sargeant Made Run at Umpiring in Pros," *Kitsap Sun* (Bremerton, Washington), April 12, 2014.

49 Shasta Darlington, "In Cuba's Male Baseball League, Female Umpire Calls 'Em Like She Sees 'Em," CNN.com, January 6, 2010.

50 Paul Hagan, "Female Umpire Calls Game in Rookie Ball," MLB.com, June 24, 2016.

51 David Dorsey, "Jen Pawol Travels Rare Baseball Path as an Umpire," News-Press.com, July 10, 2016; David Wilson, "Jen Pawol Ends Female Umpire Drought on Opening Day of GCL," *Bradenton-Herald*, June 24, 2016.

52 Lucy McCalmont. Of course, even fewer women play football.

53 Derek Crawford, "Behind the Mask: Where Are the Women?' baseballessential.com, April 4, 2015.

Amanda Clement

The Lady In Blue

By Leslie Heaphy

"Can you suggest a single reason why all the baseball umpires should not be women? Of course you can't. I mean just what I say, seriously, that all the official baseball umpires of the country should be women."[1] A statement that the baseball world has long disagreed with but was stated in 1906 by a young Amanda Clement, the first female to be paid to umpire. She "is an example of what a woman can do even in a sphere that seems to be entirely out of range of the fair sex."[2]

Amanda Clement was born on March 20, 1888, in Hudson, Dakota Territory, a year before South Dakota became a state. Growing up with her brother Allen (better known as Hank) gave Clement the chance to play sports and learn the rules. Her mother, Harriett, raised the two alone after Amanda's father died when she was a little girl. The family lived near the local ballpark and so Amanda and her brother spent a great deal of time there. Accompanying her brother to his games, Amanda often found herself umpiring the sandlot games, since girls did not play baseball with any regularity. However, when the boys asked her to fill in, she occasionally played a little first base, which helped her learn the game.

One day, after Amanda traveled with her mother to Harden, Iowa, to watch Hank's Renville team play a semipro game against Hawarden, history was made. The umpire did not show up for the preliminary game and her brother volunteered his sister. And when the umpire did not arrive for the scheduled contest, the teams accepted her after having seen her umpire. And so in 1904 Amanda Clement became the first woman paid to umpire a game. The teams actually had to persuade her mother to let her umpire since this was not something young ladies did. Clement put any doubts to rest immediately and began a successful career as an umpire for six years, traveling across the upper Midwest, umpiring about 50 games a summer. Earning between $15 and $25 a game, Clement earned enough money each summer to put herself through college. Baseball was hugely popular at the time; there was little else to draw away people's attention. Every small town had a ballclub and games were a constant with town pride at stake. Umpires were in demand and Clement benefited from that need. At this time umpires generally worked alone, calling balls and strikes from behind the pitching mound. This gave the umpire a better view of all the action on the bases as well. For Clement this also meant she was not as close to the fans as she would have been behind the plate.

Since this was a time when women were not encouraged in such public pursuits, Clement became a novelty during the six years she umpired. The woman's place was still at home, taking care of the household. Clement was so good at her job, however, that she got calls from all over the Midwest to umpire. One paper described her as "possessor of an eagle eye, seldom makes a mistake."[3] Promoters quickly came to realize that a young female umpire who was good at what she did would attract more fans and so Clement was in demand. One newspaper reporter claimed she even received more than 60 marriage proposals from across the country as her reputation grew. In response to one young man's overtures, Clement told him, "I'm wedded to baseball."[4]

Clement's reputation grew with each game she umpired. She was in such demand during the summers that she often had to make choices about which games she would umpire. Many communities invited her back after seeing her work. As one reporter said, "But see her once, mask on, behind the catcher and hear her call the balls and strikes, and at once you reach the conclusion that a young woman of skill, judgment and determination is performing with

Amanda Clement.

marked ability."[5] Clement did miss a few weeks in the summer of 1910 after she injured her left knee while playing catch. She had to wear a plaster cast and then walked with a cane for a few weeks.

On one occasion in South Dakota, Clement was introduced to President Teddy Roosevelt, who told her he had heard of her already. A local writer, Will Chamberlain, wrote a poem about the lady in blue in 1905. After a game between Gayville and Garretson, the local paper reported, "She umpired the game as quietly and easily as other young women would sweep a floor or make a cake."[6] Clement's umpiring took her all over the Midwest. One week might find her umpiring a game in Sioux City and the next in Elk Point, South Dakota, or Brookings, or Minneapolis. One of the most interesting games recorded that Clement umpired was one in Tekamah, Nebraska, between the White Sox and a colored team from Omaha called the Midway.[7]

Clement had few problems on the diamond or on the road as she traveled across the Midwest. A Congregationalist, she often stayed with local min-

isters' families and would not umpire on Sundays. Further supporting the idea that Clement did not compromise her femininity or her morals by working as an umpire, she was invited to speak from the pulpit at a local church in Rock Rapids, Iowa. Afterward she spoke at the high school on "The Value of Athletics." She even walked off the field once when one of the players, Toots Thompson, used profanity. She refused to umpire any games Thompson played in after that. She remained convinced that having female umpires would truly clean up the game since at that time it was unacceptable for a gentleman to publicly insult a lady. "Now if women were umpiring, none of this would happen," she said. "Do you suppose any ball player, in the country would step up to a good-looking girl and say to her, '[Y]ou color-blind, pickle-brained, cross-eyed idiot, if you don't stop throwing the soup into me, I will distribute your features all over this ground until the janitor will be compelled to soak you up with gasoline?' Of course, he wouldn't. Ball players aren't a bad lot. In fact, my experience is that they have more than the usual allowance of chivalry. And I don't believe there's anybody in the country that would speak rudely to a woman umpire, even if he thought his drive was 'safe by a mile' instead of a foul."[8] In fact, a friend said players were likely to say, "Beg your pardon, Miss Umpire, but wasn't that one a bit high"[9] She was also not afraid to eject a player in order to maintain control of the game. Clement believed she ejected about six players over the years.[10]

Clement also believed the fear that a female umpire was more likely to be assaulted or mistreated than a man was overplayed. "Then there's the crowd," she said. "There's a good deal of cowardice about the roasting of umpires by crowds, because hardly any of the fans that shout all sorts of insults from the bleachers would have the nerve to say anything of the kind to the umpire's face."[11]

Not all the teams or reporters were kind to Clement. Some of them clearly followed the attitude of the time, believing that women belonged at home and not out in public. One reporter made his feelings quite clear, stating, "The female umpire, the bloomer girl ballplayer and the dodo bird can be spared very nicely. A woman in bloomers isn't an inspiring sight, anyway."[12] Another individual, Brother Sturges of the *Bereford Republic*, chastised Clement for her athletic endeavors and claimed that the only thing anyone one cared about was her ability to make a proper meal or sew her own clothes. In other words, tasks accepted at the time as womanly. The people of Clement's hometown responded to this attack with great support, saying, "Miss Clement is not a paragon. She is simply a young woman who loves athletics and who is paying her way through college with what she earns during the summer working as an umpire, for she is not only perfecting herself in physical culture …but she is also desirous to perfect herself in the study of medicine, as it has ever been her ambition to become a doctor, and it costs money to go to college."[13]

From 1904 to 1911 Clement regularly umpired about 50 games a season in the Dakotas, Minnesota, Nebraska, and Iowa. Billed as "The World Champion Woman Umpire," she appeared on the diamond wearing "a full-length blue skirt, black necktie, white blouse with UMPS stenciled across the front of a peaked cap."[14]

Clement saved a portion of her umpiring earnings, $15 to $25 a game, to finance her education. She studied at Yankton Academy for two years, then Yankton College for two years and finally finished at the University of Nebraska, graduating in 1909. While in college Clement played basketball and tennis, ran track, and worked for the local newspaper. One game reported in the paper had Clement's Yankton Academy basketball team winning 15-1 while listing her as the star player. The college hired her to umpire the club team, hoping her presence would stop some of the "rowdyism" through her "good judgment and fine mind."[15] She also refereed local high-school basketball games. This has raised speculation that in addition to being the first paid female umpire, Clement might have also been the first female referee. There were also many stories published about records she set in different sports, most of which were more rumor and legend than fact. She did, however, set a national record for females throwing a baseball, 275 feet. She

broke the existing record, set by a young woman from Chicago, by five feet. She also won a vase in a "Carrie Nation Hatchet Throwing Contest."[16]

Clement's college degree in physical education let her work as a teacher and professor throughout her professional career. She taught for a time at the University of Wyoming as well as for four years at Jamestown, North Dakota, High School. In addition she also worked at the YWCA in La Crosse, Wisconsin. While in La Crosse one of Clement's projects was to show how the footwear forced on young ladies deformed their feet. Clement took photos of the feet of 75 young women with and without their shoes and put the pictures on display, hoping this might force some changes. She also gave swimming lessons and helped save a man's life after he nearly drowned in the local river. After he was pulled out of the river, Clement administered mouth-to-mouth resuscitation.[17] From her experience playing college basketball, she later coached an independent basketball team in Hudson and even refereed high-school basketball –perhaps the first woman to do so.[18]

Clement, who never married, moved home in 1929 to take care of her ill mother. She then moved to Sioux Falls in 1934 after her mother died and she worked as a social worker for 25 years, overseeing both the city and county welfare divisions, until her retirement in 1966. Until her death in Sioux Falls on July 20, 1971, she remained an ardent fan of the game that got her started in life, rooting for the Minnesota Twins.

In recognition of her many athletic accomplishments, Clement was elected to the South Dakota Sports Hall of Fame in 1964. In 2014 she was inducted into the Yankton College Alumni Hall of Fame. A children's book, *Umpire in a Skirt: The Amanda Clement Story* (2010), by Marilyn Kratz, tells her incredible story for the generations to come.[19] Clement loved the game and never saw umpiring as something ladies should not do. "There is no reason why a young woman cannot make a business of umpiring and be a perfect lady," she said. "I maintain that it is just as womanly as it is to play tennis."[20]

NOTES

1 "One Who Made a Big Success Tells of the Work," *Pittsburgh Press,* September 17, 1906.

2 Amanda Clement Hall of Fame File, National Baseball Hall of Fame, Cooperstown, New York. See also Sharon L. Roan, "No One Yelled "Kill The Ump" When Amanda Clement Was a Man in Blue, *Sports Illustrated,* April 5, 1982, and Colin Kapitan, "Nobody Yelled 'Kill the Umpire!'" *South Dakota Magazine,* July 1985.

3 "Woman as Umpire," *Meriden Daily Journal,* June 20, 1906.

4 "Players All in Love With Girl Umpire," *Reading Eagle,* August 26, 1906.

5 "Girl Baseball Ump," *Reading Eagle,* June 29, 1906.

6 Clement Scrapbook, National Baseball Hall of Fame, Cooperstown, New York.

7 Hall of Fame file.

8 *Pittsburgh Press,* September 17, 1906.

9 Kapitan, "Nobody Yelled 'Kill the Umpire!'"

10 "A Girl Umpire," *Sporting Life* (Vol. 46, No. 4), October 7, 1905: 8.

11 *Pittsburgh Press,* September 17, 1906.

12 *Pittsburgh Press,* January 22, 1906.

13 *Sioux City Journal,* n.d., Hall of Fame file.

14 Kapitan, "Nobody Yelled 'Kill the Umpire!'"

15 "Would Wed Ump," *Sporting Life,* Vol. 47, No. 20, 1906.

16 Will Talsey, "The Umpire Was a Lady," *Baseball Magazine,* October 1952: 31.

17 Clement Scrapbook, National Baseball Hall of Fame, Cooperstown, New York.

18 "South Dakota Woman Is Jack of All Trades," *Ludington* (Michigan) *Daily News,* April 7, 1929; "150 Feet to the Bad," *The Gazette Times,* June 10, 1913.

19 "Sioux Falls Woman Recognized in Yankton as Baseball's First Female Umpire," Associated Press, July 21, 2014.

20 Amanda Clement File, National Baseball Hall of Fame, Cooperstown, New York.

The Stained Grass Window

By Perry Barber

We shall not cease from exploration, and the end of all our exploring will be to arrive where we started and know the place for the first time.

— T.S. Eliot, *Little Gidding*, from *Four Quartets*

If it hadn't been for my mother Jaqueline's suggestion that I apply for a job as a Little League umpire when I was 28 years old, my life would be a lot different right now. To this day I wonder if umpiring is something I ever would have considered doing on my own. Sports officiating is not routinely presented to girls or women in the United States as an activity we might actually be good at or enjoy, and baseball, our beloved national pastime, lags far behind other sports, and other countries, in confirming what empirical evidence has already proved: that women can and do make excellent umpires.

Jack, as my mother liked to be called, cut out a notice one day from the *Desert Sun*, the local paper in Palm Springs, California, where she'd moved from New York after my twin sister and I graduated from high school. I was enjoying an extended visit with her in the late spring of 1981, riding shotgun in her '66 Chevy Malibu convertible almost every night while she would drive 200 miles round trip to take me to see either the Dodgers in LA or the Angels in Anaheim. I had fallen in love with baseball only a couple of years earlier, so we were bonding in a new and significant way as mother and daughter, but I couldn't figure out her motive for wanting me to see the notice that blared Indio Needs Umpires! at me in bold type from the ad she'd cut out of the newspaper and left on my pillow that fateful night. *Little League season starts soon*, it cooed alliteratively. I loved baseball with a passion by then, but my first thought upon seeing it was not, "What a great idea! I'll call first thing tomorrow." It was more along the lines of, "Why on earth did she leave that there for me?"

My identical twin sister, Warren, and I were products of an all-girls private school on the Upper East Side of Manhattan, former debutantes, and unlike our brainy Stanford graduate older brother Rocky, college dropouts. Since leaving Arizona State University in 1972 after two uninspired semesters, I'd become a traveling troubadour, playing guitar and singing self-penned songs of romantic quandary and betrayal in the bars and boîtes around New York. A decade later, I was an obscure musician/songwriter clinging to the vestiges of a fading career highlighted by gigs as the opening act for Bruce Springsteen, Billy Joel, Hall and Oates, and other rock luminaries. When money was tight I would apply to be a contestant on TV quiz shows, and in that way financed the more impecunious episodes in my life with cash and parting gifts earned on *Jeopardy!*, *Tic Tac Dough*, *The $128,000 Question*, and *The Challengers*, hosted by Dick Clark. Between the complimentary cases of Rice-a-Roni and Bon Ami scouring powder, I think I won enough food and cleaning supplies to last me a lifetime.

Basically, as a young adult I did everything I possibly could to avoid getting a real job. In 1978 practical considerations and an appealing offer from my friend Gloria Bell persuaded me to take a part-time position in the New York management offices of Gladys Knight & the Pips and B.B. King. My bosses let me set my own schedule, and granted me time off to stay with Jack after her husband, Norman Davies, died in 1979. That was the year I fell head over heels in love with baseball by reading about its history and lore in books after having been completely uninterested in it my entire life. By the spring of 1981 I was such a devotée that I took a two-month sabbatical to go on a baseball road trip out in California with my sister, who was living in Los Angeles by then, and Jack. I was a working stiff enjoying the game from

David Wright crushes one! Mets spring training 2008. Plate umpire Perry Barber.

the stands like millions of spectators, and gave no thought to donning a chest protector, shin guards, or face mask. But luckily for me, someone else did.

In early June of 1981, the threat of a major-league players' strike had been looming malevolently on the horizon for weeks. Although I viewed the impending work stoppage with a certain degree of fatalism, as the inevitable outcome of another of my doomed affairs, in truth I was devastated by the notion of not being able to go see the Dodgers or the Angels with my mother and sister. It had become our near-nightly ritual during my hiatus from the reality of work back in New York, and I dreaded losing the connection that baseball had so recently sparked among the three of us. I'd been in love with the game for only a couple of years, and the prospect of a divorce so soon after the first blush of romance was breaking my heart.

The morning after I found the notice from the paper on my pillow, I asked Jack why she'd left it there, and she reminded me that I'd written a song about umpires. This was true, but I'd composed an entire suite of songs about baseball, and "The Umpire Stands Alone" was just one of several I'd recorded and played for her. I shrugged, still mystified.

"I saw you reading a book about umpires," she added, a bit enigmatically, I thought, since she'd also seen me reading books about serial killers.

The one to which she alluded was *The Men in Blue: Conversations With Umpires* by Larry Gerlach, which I had indeed read, but only after exhausting the Palm

Springs Public Library of every other baseball-related book in the stacks. I had no idea then of the world-rocking, path-altering role that book would play in my life. It was Jack, not I, who connected the dots from my song to a book to a completely innocuous ad placed by a little league seeking umpires; Jack who understood the ad's significance as soon as she spotted it. She pointed me in the direction she sensed I would eventually wander anyway, as if umpiring had been my idea, my discovery, when right from the start it was hers. That was her gift to me, one she offered without judgment and with infinite love. She saw in me what I did not see in myself, set aside her own misgivings, then pushed me unceremoniously out of the nest, off the pedestal, straight onto the diamond. A ruder awakening, a former debutante never had.

The more I'd thought about Jack's suggestion, the more umpiring seemed a way for me to stay connected to baseball during the strike, so I'd called the number listed in the ad, amplified my nonexistent credentials, presented myself at the league office, and much to my surprise, got handed a beat-up old face mask, a pair of used shin guards, and an ancient balloon-style chest protector. I was then hustled off to confront my destiny with no training to speak of, very little idea about where to go or what to do on certain plays, barely even knowing what a force play was, or a foul ball. I could tell you who was on third in 1908 when Fred Merkle of the New York Giants ran to the clubhouse at the Polo Grounds instead of second base and was called out, famously nullifying Moose McCormick's winning run in the mishegoss that came to be known unjustly as "Merkle's Boner," but I had only a vague understanding of why an infielder would throw the ball to first base with two outs when a runner from third was heading home.

There I stood just a week later, on a dusty, nondescript diamond in Indio, California, surrounded by a band of unhappy 10-year-old boys, their even unhappier coaches, and a fidgety mob of fussy, disgruntled parents. My first game, needless to say, was a complete catastrophe. I was unprepared for the hostility emanating from the coaches and parents, and the eye-rolling, sneering derision aimed at me was a total shock. All my life I'd been petted and praised, convinced I was witty, charming, and irresistible, but this was far beyond my experience. The coaches got in my face, the parents screamed at me, and the kids took their cues from the adults. My mother, who had driven me to the game, witnessed the whole debacle in stoic silence. That's right, I was 28 years old and my mother drove me to my first Little League game. I'd learned to drive only the year before and didn't have a car since I'd never needed one in New York, so Jack, the architect of my new career, chauffeured me to my inaugural assignment and sat stalwartly in the stands while the menacing scrum of parents around her frothed and foamed with fury at my calls. My initial foray into umpiring proved so disastrous that the next day, the *Desert Sun* published several letters to the editor pleading for mercy, begging to please never let that woman ruin another game for anyone ever again.

I interpreted these comments not as an indication of any particular sexism or misogyny on the part of my detractors, but as an accurate, if somewhat harsh, assessment of my ineptitude. I actually felt the criticism was warranted because I knew I hadn't done a very good job. I didn't know the rules, had no clue about game management or how to deal with obtuse coaches, and though my intentions were noble, I had fallen far short of even a minimal proficiency out there. Yet somehow the ill treatment I received because of my poor performance did not deter me from wanting another chance to do better. All that bad behavior was a puzzle I wanted to solve; the mysteries of the darker side of human nature fascinated rather than frightened me.

Right away—the very next day, in fact—I sent out inquiries to the two professional umpire schools in Florida, and decided to attend the Harry Wendelstedt Umpire School the next January of 1982. My twin sister, Warren, and I were the only women in the class of more than 150 male students that year. I'd conscripted her as my partner in Indio the summer before when it became apparent that not a whole lot of other umpires were exactly leaping at the chance to work with me. To provide me with a partner, any

partner, the assignor threw caution to the winds and hired Warren at my request. Somehow the two of us managed to survive the season together, and I convinced her to go to umpire school with me the following January. Later on she would put herself through nursing school, earn a degree, get married, and raise two wonderful sons, but back then we were both still searching for something to satisfy the longing we'd felt ever since our father inexplicably vanished in 1959. We were 6 years old when he took a small watercraft out on the ocean off the coast of Atlantic City by himself and was never seen or heard from again. Neither of us had ever really gotten over the hurt and confusion caused by his sudden disappearance, but umpiring, strange as it sounds, helped us heal.

It was also strange that we would seek validation and happiness in an arena where positive feedback is rare, but that's one of baseball's beautiful paradoxes. Being an identical twin is the ultimate paradox: we are unique in all the world, yet we are one of two, part of a pair, our uniqueness dependent upon our sameness. Umpiring is paradoxical too: It requires us to have the heart of a warrior but to refrain from engaging in warfare. We're on the front lines, exposed and alone except for our partners, yet are expected to do our job so expertly that our presence goes completely unnoticed. Umpiring is a constant challenge for me even now, 35 years after my first little league game. Through observation and practice, I've learned that it's not about throwing my weight around, showing people who's boss, proving my balls are bigger than someone else's, or anything like that. It's about participating in a game I love, making sure everyone involved has a safe and welcoming place to play or watch, and providing a useful service as capably and courteously as I can.

Umpiring has never been easy for me, the way it is for someone born with natural ability or with a size and carriage that confer instant respect. I've had to work hard and deflect a lot of negativity to achieve whatever level of proficiency I've attained. A lot of things I learned to just let roll off my back like water. Earl Weaver used to stare at me as if I were a Martian

Perry Barber and colleagues, Cape Cod League.

when he'd see me every year at the Orioles fantasy camp in Sarasota. I would greet him with a pleasantry, and he would say the same thing every time: "Oh, you're still doing this?" As if umpiring were a little hobby of which I would soon grow weary and then slink back to doing regular woman-type things. When I started getting NCAA college assignments, I'd stop by the security gate at the campus entrances to announce myself, standard protocol for umpires. I can't tell you how many times I'd be given directions to the softball field instead of the baseball diamond in spite of my specific, repeated insistence that I was there to umpire the men's baseball game. A bizarre irony tinged the rare occasions I was offered any real respect, like the time I sang the National Anthem at Memorial Stadium in Baltimore before an Orioles game in 1986. I'd been invited to perform by someone in the front office who liked the job I'd done assigning and umpiring the fantasy camp in Florida enough that he asked me to join the campers on the field in Baltimore the day they were to be introduced to the crowd as part of the total camp package. I mentioned

that I was an experienced Anthem singer, which was true, and he was nice enough to approve me as the singer for the reunion game. I was given the choice of performing by home plate, close to the fans behind the backstop, from which vantage point I would be subject to the dreaded feedback, that weird delayed-echo effect that gives so many Anthem singers such problems staying on key and in cadence; or to perform way out in the outfield underneath the giant electronic scoreboard, from where my image would be projected on the big screen and there would be no feedback.

I chose the outfield. So there I stood that sultry summer night, underneath the scoreboard where I couldn't see it looming above and behind me, all dressed up in a sapphire blue silk dress and sparkly high-heeled sandals as I accompanied myself on my treasured 1953 Martin 00-18 acoustic guitar, singing my patriotic little baseball-loving heart out. Things went well, I thought. A few weeks later I got a nice note in the mail from one of the campers with a photograph enclosed, a picture he had taken of me from where he stood on the field way back by home plate with his teammates. When I looked at the photo, I couldn't believe it. I was a tiny blue shadow silhouetted against the distant scoreboard, my image displayed in gigantic detail, flowing silk dress, sparkly sandals, and all. The scoreboard operator had thought to provide a caption, so *this* is what 50,000 fans saw up in huge, flashing lights while I was humming and strumming away:

BALTIMORE ORIOLES THANK TONIGHT'S ANTHEM SINGER, PERRY LEE BARBER. HE WAS THE CHIEF UMPIRE FOR THE ORIOLES FANTASY CAMP LAST JANUARY.

Having a sense of humor and perspective has helped me maintain my equilibrium whenever I could have just as easily flown into a rage or spiraled into a depression about the unfairness of it all. I've learned to work with and get the most out of the tools I have, not the ones I wish I had but don't. To compensate for my petite stature, I've taught myself to walk tall and make human nature work for me so things turn out the way *I* want, not the way someone else does. This is an invaluable but invisible skill that most people don't see when they watch the umpires. Umpiring expertise is not just accuracy on the balls and strikes, safes and outs, fairs and fouls. It's much more than that, a lot of it undetectable by the naked eye, like keeping the pace of the game flowing smoothly over the blips and bumps that can intrude upon an intense, well-played contest and turn it into a nightmarish, draining experience. It's a thousand little things that go unnoticed and unappreciated, but that are at the heart and soul of what make a good umpire and a great partner. Not all great umpires make great partners, by the way. I always strive to be both.

During the decades I've been umpiring, fortune has been both cruel and kind to me. No woman has yet worked a major-league game during the regular season, but I call major-league ball every year during spring training down in Florida. In 2008, extremely obscure major-league history was made when Theresa Fairlady, Mona Osborne, Ila Valcarcel, and I became the first four-woman crew to umpire a New York Mets spring-training game. I've umpired major-league exhibitions in Japan too, and gone to Hong Kong, Taiwan, and Guam for international baseball tournaments. I umpired four years in the Atlantic League, one of the best independent circuits in the country. I'm the first and so far only woman to umpire in either the Cape Cod League or the Alaska League, a distinction I view with as much regret as I do pride since it means I'm still the only woman umpire in far too many of the leagues or associations I represent. Things are a lot better now than they were when I started, though. Women are playing, coaching, and umpiring baseball all over the globe these days, and I've been partners with dozens of excellent women umpires in my travels overseas and here at home. Our numbers are growing, but we still have a long way to go to keep the stained grass window of professional baseball cracked open wide enough for women to get through on a regular basis and start climbing the ladder that leads to jobs as major-league umpires. That means drawing women to the two professional

umpire schools in Florida, 10 or 20 in each class so several, not just one at a time, wind up earning jobs as minor-league umpires every year.

There is no fast track to the major leagues for an umpire. Six to eight minor-league seasons are the minimum necessary to gain enough experience to even be considered as a vacation umpire who fills in when the major-league umps take their union-authorized four weeks off during the regular season. The first woman or women to join the major-league umpiring staff will have to be resolute and durable enough to absorb the special punishments reserved for mold-breakers and history-makers, but I have no doubt anymore that it *will* happen, and in my lifetime. Thirty-five years ago, the prospects of a woman becoming a major-league umpire were bleak, and statistically speaking, nothing much has changed in all that time. There was one woman umpire in pro ball back then, and as of 2016 there is still only one. That's

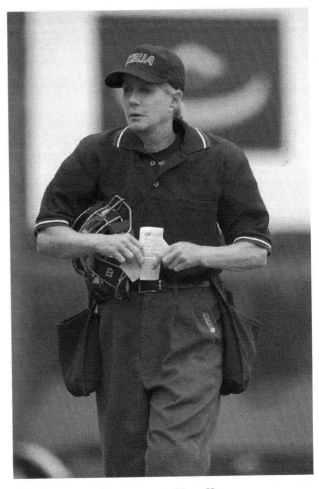

Perry Barber working a game in Hong Kong.

right, one. Our numbers have completely stagnated rather than risen.

There's no rational justification for this anymore, particularly since the NBA and now the NFL both employ women referees at the top echelons of their respective sports. Baseball has a lot of catching up to do, but there are positive signs, a growing awareness of the logic in expanding the annual pool of umpiring candidates to regularly include women, as well as of the marketing possibilities inherent in appealing to us as more than mere consumers. The institutional resistance that used to be such a huge impediment to our entry into the ranks of pro umpires has dissipated, but the messaging and branding have to change too if pro umpiring wants to attract women. Umpiring is *not* about being yelled at or publicly shamed; those are very brief, inconsequential elements of the big picture. It's about discovering the kind of person you are while working in the greatest office on the planet, beneath a sapphire blue sky, atop emerald green grass, on a diamond. It's the bling, baby! It's about giving back to the game and the community, about growing as a partner and a person whether you umpire little-league or major-league baseball.

I won't rest until there are enough women out there once I leave the field for the last time to feel confident we're moving forward instead of stagnating, or worse, slipping backward toward a time when women really weren't welcome on the diamond. It's not the bad attitudes we have to combat these days so much as a kind of inertia. "The One" or "The Ones" aren't just magically going to appear, all polished, poised, and ready to vault to the top of the umpiring firmament. A little time, effort, and a multi-pronged approach will be necessary to find, recruit, and train the women who possess the aptitude and skills to sparkle on the diamond. A few tweaks to the exist-

ing framework of minor-league umpire evaluations and promotions, and all it will take after that is sufficiently steadfast support from their supervisors and partners to help them progress upward through the ranks.

When I started umpiring in 1981, my focus was mostly on me, on my survival and upward mobility in a business that does not treat its distaff practitioners delicately. Now, it's about setting up a mechanism that will funnel women into the pipeline leading to jobs as minor- and major-league umpires on a regular basis, and helping other women grow and flourish through umpiring. Until the day one or more of us stand at home plate in a major-league ballpark and take the lineup cards from the managers for the first time, I'll be doing what I can to render "woman umpire" as redundant as "woman doctor" or "female astrophysicist," and to ensure that our participation in professional baseball is regarded not as a problem, but as a productive partnership. It will be at least eight years from the time a woman graduates from umpire school until she makes it to the major leagues, but make it she will. When she does, I'll be thinking of my sister, who was my first steady partner, and of my mother, watching over her daughter as she umpired her first baseball game on a dusty, windswept, nondescript little diamond in the desert such a long time ago. The best thing is, it feels like I'm really only now getting started. So much is still possible.

The Desert League, an independent fall league, will be using all female umpires for their 2017 season. The umpires will be under the direction of Perry Barber.

--Leslie Heaphy

Yanet Moreno, the First Woman Umpire in Any Country's Major League

By Reynaldo Cruz

Walking into the old-school-like surroundings of Estadio Changa Mederos in Havana's Ciudad Deportiva and running into umpire Yanet Moreno Mendinueta is an interesting experience in itself.[1] Off the field, the short and smiling umpire lacks the serious and stern look that she displays while wearing the black-and-blue outfit and calling the shots either behind the plate or at third base. At 43 (born on November 9, 1973, in Luyanó, Havana), she has 17 years of experience and 14 National Series seasons (13 of them as a regular umpire and one as a substitute) under her belt.

Everyone seems to know Yanet and love her, whether players, managers, or her peers, and they all greet her with respect and affection. With three siblings (two brothers and a sister), she is without question the most *sui generis* member of her family and perhaps one of the most appealing people in all of baseball.

Her resolve on the field, which turns into a constant smile off the field, has made her feel admired by everyone, including the overdemanding Víctor Mesa (manager of Matanzas), who, she says, has asked for her to be the home-plate umpire because "I like the way she handles the strike zone." Even with the microphone in front of her and an arsenal of questions in store, she still keeps her poise and humor, and answers with the same care and calmness with which she calls a runner safe or out at third base.

When and how did you get interested in baseball?

I would say basically since I was born. My father used to live just behind right field in Estadio del Cerro *and when I was in the first two years of my life it was very difficult for me to fall asleep, so my father used to take me*

there, with a feeding bottle of milk, and I would fall asleep in the game, in the middle of the crowd. Afterwards, you know, he didn't want me to be in the ballfield, but it was he who first got me into baseball, and then there was no way to take me out of the ballpark.

Did you play baseball at any stage during your childhood?

I started as a child, playing with the boys from the neighborhood. My father would lecture me, and even ground me when he caught me red-handed, because he didn't want people to say that I was a tomboy. I would tell the boys, "Guys, if you see that my father is coming, let me know so I can hide. Don't narc on me!" But they were just kids, and it happened that when my father was coming, driving the car, they would tell me:"Yanet! Your father's coming!" and I would run and hide (chuckles). But then there was always someone who would say: "Yanet, come on you're up!" and then my father would know that I was playing (chuckles).

When did you decide to become an umpire?

For several years, up to around 1997, I was a member of the Havana softball team, because we didn't yet have women's baseball. I was included in three pre-rosters of the Cuban National Softball Team, until I decided not to play softball anymore, because I didn't see myself as fully accomplished. When women's baseball started in 1998, I switched to baseball. I was the number three hitter of the Havana team, playing second base. But as a "new" sport, there were limitations. You could not be above 25 years old, and I was approaching that age. They told me that since I was that close, when the game fully developed in Cuba I was going to be well above the age limit.

However, since I had already become a national softball umpire, commissioner Margarita Malleta told me that since I liked baseball and being in the ballfield so much, it was a good idea for me to become a baseball umpire. That way, I would be able to stay on the field. I agreed and took a provincial course, which enabled me to go to the zonal [regional] course, due to my good grades. I placed in the top five in the Western Zone, and made the grade among the 20 students that were going to attend the national school.

I spent three years at Villa Clara, the regular venue for the national school. During those three years we got qualified to be umpires at any level or category, working with the youngest kids or in the National Series, the top league. I ranked second at school and made it to the National Series as a substitute.

Were there umpires whose example you followed?

Before I started with the idea of umpiring, I looked at umpires as an athlete did, not as role models. But when I started umpiring, I had an inspiring guide in the late Felipe Casañas; he took me under his wing when I was basically a child in umpiring terms, and it was near him that I took my first steps. When I started observing umpires during the National Series, I took special notice of César Valdés, and I owe a lot to him: he didn't see the fact that I was a woman as a shortcoming; instead, he saw that I was a capable umpire who could work in the Cuban National Series.

How was the level of acceptance?

At first, they saw me as a freak. They would say, "This woman is crazy!" "What is she doing on the field surrounded by men?" "She won't be able to handle it!" But when they saw me work and they saw how serious I was about my job, they said, "Okay, this girl does have a chance! She can make it!" and then everyone started helping me and encouraging me to be better each day, and that worked out pretty well for me. When they saw that I had no fear of taking the field, whether the stands were packed or empty, they gave me a lot of support. They saw that as courageous, because sometimes they felt pressure themselves in such situations. My mindset was: If I can work in the Provincial Series, why can't I work in the Zonal Championships? And if I can work in the Zonal Championship, why can't I work in the National Games in all categories? And so on, until I took the challenge. It was like climbing a ladder, from the youngest kids to the Junior Championships, Development Leagues, and then the National Series.

Do you remember your first game in the National Series?

My first game in the National Series was in Villa Clara, as a third-base umpire. Villa Clara vs. the defunct Havana Metropolitanos. When I took the field, it was the first game of the season, and the stands were crowded … and everyone stood up and gave me a standing ovation. That was the province where I went to umpiring school, many fans knew me from that time. My second game was in that very ballpark … behind the plate (chuckles).

What were the first challenges you had to face as an umpire and as a female umpire?

The first challenge was to be accepted by my peers, then by the players and managers. At first, when I took the field, they looked at me in disbelief and said: "A woman on the field? What the hell is this? This is a man's game!" but when I started working and they saw how confident I was, they used to say: "Okay, she's a woman, but she works pretty well! At least she is strong-willed." I made mistakes, like every umpire and every human being, and at first those mistakes were more frequent, but I stood by my calls. After that, everyone began to accept me and when they didn't see me they asked, "Where's the girl?"

So you established respect simply based on the seriousness of your work …

Umpiring is a very difficult job. First you have to learn the rulebook which is one of the biggest of any sport and which every year includes a lot of modifications. Then, you have to make athletes, managers, and fans believe in your calls. In order to do that, I had to work perhaps harder than any man. But working in the small categories, mainly in the 12U, you get to make calls on plays you probably won't see in years of National Series experience. I worked a lot in those categories, and it was there that I honed my skills, so when I took on older categories, the range of mistakes narrowed, and it was then that I made people believe in me.

Tell us about the time when a US media crew came to interview you … when you found out that you were the first female umpire in a high-level league in the world.

I had no clue I was the first. I was stunned and didn't even know how to react or what to say. When they got to the hotel where I was staying, they told me, "We had been trying to contact you because you are the only woman working in her country's major league. Do you know you're famous?" I had no clue. As a matter of fact, I thought there were other women working in other major leagues in the world. I had to ask them to give me a few minutes for the idea to sink in because I couldn't believe it myself.

What has been the most difficult call you have had to make?

Well, about three National Series ago, I had a very difficult call to make. It was on National Television, Matanzas playing against Las Tunas, and Yosvani Alarcón went off to try to steal home plate. I called him safe. That year replay had come into force, and Matanzas challenged the call on the field, which was confirmed by the replay. I was sure of what I had seen, but nobody thought I had made the right call. When the replay proved me right, I got even more confident behind the plate (chuckles), and it enabled me to finish the game with a lot more confidence.

How do you feel when you make a wrong call?

Just as I am proud and confident when I make a difficult call right, the world collapses around me when I'm wrong. We umpires don't ever want to blow a call, but sometimes poor positioning, or rushing too much, can make us blow the call. I always try to give it a little time before I decide, in order to have a smaller percentage chance of being wrong. But that's true: When I blow the call, I don't even want to be looked at and if I am at home, even my mom cannot talk to me.

What has been your best moment as an umpire?

My best moment was when I worked the playoffs for the first time, in the semifinals. It was the first of many postseason jobs. Also, when I went to the Women's World Championship, and in 2015, that I went to the Pan Am Games in Toronto. I have been to three World Championships and a Pan Am Games tournament, and in all three events I have been chosen the top umpire. They don't say so explicitly, but normally the one they choose is the one who officiates home plate in the Gold Medal Game, and that was my assignment in all three events.

Yanet Moreno, Havana 2017.

What do you consider to be today's top difficulties in Cuban umpiring?

If you had asked me two or three years ago, I would have answered differently, but today we are pleased in the sense that umpires come from abroad (mainly the World Baseball Softball Confederation) to give lectures and courses mainly on how to work in a way that we are similar to the Major League Baseball. These clinics take place twice a year, and that has helped us overcome certain doubts, mainly in terms of the strike zone. We have tried to unify the strike zone and have everyone call the low strike (which we had normally called balls), and to help us get rid of the trend of calling strikes horizontally and not vertically. We have learned that from them. Normally we would call a strike a ball going two or three inches from the plate, and that is not a strike. We have better awareness now that what we have to narrow the sides and widen in the height. Work remains to be done, though.

Are there others like you in Cuba?

There are three other girls who took the course, but they're working exclusively on women's baseball; they don't work with men. I am trying to encourage them to work in the provincial leagues among males, and make them start in the low categories. I would love to see another woman as my peer in the National Series.

So, you see a future for female umpiring in Cuba?

Yes, I do. I am working very hard with female umpires in Cuba. My biggest accomplishment would be to help these three girls (who are the most advanced) get to the National Series and obtain the international level as I have.

At some point, you must have had terrible moments as an umpire. What has been your worst experience so far?

As an umpire, you suffer a lot when you blow a call, when you make a mistake. You suffer a lot when you work a ballgame and perform below the level you know you have. I believe that is what hurts an umpire the most. We also don't like it when we have to eject someone because we have to; you can't allow a batter to throw a bat or a helmet in contempt, and you know that you're tossing a player needed by the team, but that it's something you have to do because it's in the rules.

How do you see the future of women in baseball, alongside men?

Things are very difficult in that aspect. Even though we have seen here in Cuba that women have been given many opportunities to exercise any profession, we can't take back the fact that this is a macho country. And I think that having, for instance, four female umpires in a National Series is a little close to fiction. It could be accomplished, but it's far from happening. Here in Havana we have female scorekeepers, but I think that getting to a point where four women got to be National Series umpires would be very difficult.

But you would love to see that?

Of course, and I'd love to be the crew chief there (chuckles).

NOTE

1   This interview was conducted by Reynaldo Cruz on January 11, 2017, in Changa Mederos Stadium, within the Ciudad Deportiva in Havana.

Umpire Schools: Training Grounds for the Guardians of the Game

By Bill Pruden

Introduction

In September 2005 the confirmation hearings of John Roberts as the nominee for chief justice of the United States included an unexpected but telling nod to the national pastime when Roberts observed, "Judges and justices are servants of the law, not the other way around. Judges are like umpires. Umpires don't make the rules; they apply them."[1] He went on to say, "The role of an umpire and a judge is critical. They make sure everybody plays by the rules. But it is a limited role. Nobody ever went to a ball game to see the umpire."[2]

While the analogy itself may be open to debate, Roberts' comments linked the two professions in an interesting way and, in fact, further investigation reveals that another similarity between the two roles is the way the formal preparation for them has evolved from the more practical, sometimes apprentice-like training that characterized the experience both of early American lawyers and umpires, to the more formalized, structured educational experience that is central to the training of their modern counterparts.

Preschool Days

The road that marked the transition of umpiring schools from curiosities to their establishment as the official gateway to umpiring in the minor and major leagues has been a long and sometimes meandering one. The end product is a result of individual initiative coupled with changing attitudes about the all-important role of the umpire in the game of baseball. Too, the development of the umpiring school as a required part of the career path that leads to the major leagues is an important part of the development and professionalization of baseball, one that brought a structure and consistency to a process previously characterized more often than not by human interaction and unplanned happenstance, where becoming a major-league umpire was more likely a happy accident than the final rung on a progressive career ladder. Indeed, the schools represented a significant change from a system that really was not systematic, with the path to becoming a major-league umpire more often than not being an uncharted and unscripted one. Sometimes it was a case of knowing someone who knew the right person who could open the appropriate door, while at other times it was all about being in the right place at the right time as an amateur or lower-level umpire was stumbled upon by a baseball-wise scout or executive who, looking for a potential player, could not help but notice the skill of the attendant umpire. He would then pass the word to the appropriate league officials and the rest would be history.[3]

The Development of the Umpire Schools

This began to change, however incrementally, in 1935 when the first umpire school was opened by George Barr, a National League umpire.[4] Ironically, what has become a required part of the path to becoming a major-league umpire began simply as an entrepreneurial enterprise at a time when a professional umpire underwent an apprenticeship-like experience, and not one that included a formalized educational component. Barr's establishment of the first umpiring school changed all that and when his effort was complemented in the winter of 1938-39 by the opening of another school by Bill McGowan, an American League umpire, the direction of umpire

1958 Sporting News ad for Bill McGowan's School for Umpires.

training, not to mention the road to the major leagues, began to change.[5] Mandatory attendance at an umpire school was still many years off, and in fact, when Bill McKinley, who attended both schools, joined the ranks of major-league umpires in 1946, it was the first time an umpire-school trainee had reached the major leagues. However, within a decade, school-trained umpires were common, and by the end of the 1960s it had become all but impossible to be hired as a professional umpire without formal school training. Indeed, Jim Evans, whose rookie major-league umpiring season was 1972, was the last major-league umpire to be hired without umpire-school training, and by the 1990s attendance at one of the approved schools had been added to the list of basic requirements for anyone aspiring to be a major- or minor-league umpire.[6]

Interestingly, unlike the other schools that would follow Barr and which operated out of Florida, from 1935 to 1940 the pioneering George Barr Umpire School was located in Hot Springs, Arkansas, where it operated in conjunction with the Ray Doan Baseball School.[7] However, in 1941 Barr moved his school to Florida, initially Orlando, where it would continue, except for a brief interlude in Tulsa, Oklahoma.[8] Meanwhile, McGowan never ventured away from

Florida and in fact took full advantage of the weather and other attractions that would lead Florida's tourism industry to explode in the aftermath of World War II. Indeed, such realities were particularly important in the early going, for while their dedication to the profession was clearly central to Barr and McGowan's early efforts, their schools were also entrepreneurial business ventures looking for customers and their early marketing efforts did not ignore those factors beyond the allure of the baseball diamond that might serve to enhance a prospective student's experience. Veteran major-league umpire Ed Sudol, who attended McGowan's school in the early 1950s after a lengthy minor-league playing career, recalled leafing through *The Sporting News* in the winter, at a point when his future in baseball, especially the likelihood of finally reaching the majors, was looking increasingly dim, and saw an ad that caught his eye. Featuring a picture of a bikini-clad beauty basking in the sun next to an oceanside palm tree, the advertisement touted Bill McGowan's Umpire School, declaring, "Enjoy the beautiful girls and the climate under a six week course of tutoring to become a professional umpire." While the motivations of the future umpire may not have been purely professional, Sudol nevertheless responded to the ad exactly as McGowan would have wanted, mailing a letter that night, that said simply, "Dear Bill: Count me in."[9] On such experiences were careers like Sudol's and the success of the schools based.

The Barr and McGowan schools continued operations during World War II and were thriving as baseball emerged from the global conflict more popular than ever. While Barr continued to run his camp until he retired in the mid-1960s, McGowan died in December 1954, and for two years veteran Pacific Coast League umpire Al Somers, who had long served as the chief instructor under McGowan, oversaw the operations of the school while McGowan's son handled the business side. After some often acrimonious negotiations between McGowan's widow and Somers, the school was ultimately sold to him, and beginning in 1957 it operated as the Al Somers Umpire School.[10]

After a successful two decades running what had become the preeminent umpire school in the nation, in 1977 Al Somers sold the school to veteran National League umpire Harry Wendelstedt. It was a fitting succession, for the Somers School had been central to the development of Wendelstedt's career, one that had been launched back in 1962, when Wendestedt, contemplating re-enlisting in the Marines, instead enrolled in Somers' school. That experience proved to be the launching pad for one of the most distinguished careers in umpiring, one which saw Wendelstedt, after only four years in the minors, reach the majors, where he would umpire for 33 years before retiring in 1998. Wendelstedt never forgot his professional roots, and after reaching the majors he returned to the Somers School annually to serve as an instructor. Wendelstedt died in 2012, but the school continued to thrive under the leadership of his son, Hunter, himself a major-league umpire.[11]

Meanwhile, looking for a way both to standardize the quality of work as well as oversee the development of umpires, in 1965 MLB initiated the Umpire Development Program (UDP), which for the most part was made up of a single supervisor whose job it was to travel around the country assessing the quality and progress of minor-league umpires. Using the UDP, Major League Baseball funded the oversight and development by the minor leagues of minor-league umpires until 1997. At that time it decided that what had become a $5 million annual cost was not worth the return, given that new umpires were hired at the rate of one every other year.[12]

In 1969 Organized Baseball made an effort to start its own instructional program, which it called an "umpire specialization course" for young umpires deemed to have major-league potential. But after five years it abandoned the scheme, selling it to umpire Bill Kinnamon, who operated it for about a decade before he sold it to Joe Brinkman.[13] By the early 1970s, the Somers Umpiring School was the established leader of the field, with the second spot filled by a succession of others, beginning with the long-established Barr School, then by the Umpire Development Program, which morphed into the

Umpire Development School, which in turn became the Bill Kinnamon Umpire School in 1971.

In 1982 major-league umpire Joe Brinkman bought the school from Kinnamon and gave it his own name. Like the transition from Somers to Wendelstedt, the move from Kinnamon to Brinkman was both a smooth and a fitting transition. Brinkman's major-league umpiring career began in September of 1972, following a short stint in the Somers School in 1967 as well as some time with the Umpire Development Program, with that training leading to an initial job in the Class-A Midwest League in 1968. As a young umpire living in St. Petersburg during the winters of the early 1970s, he checked in at the Umpire Development School, and in 1973, just as his major-league umpiring career was starting, he began serving as an instructor at the Bill Kinnamon Umpire School. In 1985 the Joe Brinkman Umpire School relocated to Cocoa, Florida, where Brinkman continued as the owner and an instructor until 1998. That year he sold it to Jim Evans, who folded it into his own operation.[14] Evans had, in fact, started his own school in 1990 after receiving permission from MLB. Seeking to provide a geographical alternative to the Florida-based Wendelstedt and Brinkman operations, he chose to run the school in Arizona, an effort that mirrored the shift of some major-league teams' spring-training operations from Florida to the Arizona desert. Then in 1993 he moved it to Kissimmee, Florida.[15]

Sign on classroom wall, Wendelstedt Umpire School, 2017.

Umpires in training at the Al Somers School. Undated photograph.

Beginning in the late 1990s, aspiring major-league umpires had to attend one of the two approved schools — Evans and Wendelstedt — who in turn annually recommended their top graduates to the Professional Baseball Umpiring Corporation (PBUC) which, with responsibility for the administration of minor-league umpires, would place them in the appropriate entry-level positions.[16]

As baseball moved into the twenty-first century, both schools were thriving when, in 2012, a new entry, The Umpire School, sponsored and underwritten by Minor League Baseball, opened its doors. The school held its sessions at the Vero Beach Athletic Complex, a storied baseball venue, familiarly known as Dodgertown, which had been the home of the Brooklyn and Los Angeles Dodgers' spring-training efforts from 1948 until 2008.[17] The Umpire School, which beginning in March 2015 began to operate under the name Minor League Baseball Umpire Training Academy, quickly became a well-regarded source of young umpires.[18] Its competitive position was strengthened when Minor League Baseball announced it was cutting its ties to the Jim Evans Academy in February 2012, in the aftermath of a racially charged incident at a staff party at the conclusion of a school session. While Evans himself made no excuses and condemned the actions of his employees, he also expressed his belief that the severance of ties between his school and Minor League

Baseball, a decision that meant that graduates of his school would no longer be sent to the PBUC, was an excessive punishment. He also raised questions about whether there was not a conflict of interest given that Minor League Baseball was running its own Umpire School as well as certifying the others, all while serving as the placement agency for the top graduates each year.[19]

Not surprisingly, Evans's objections fell on deaf ears. However, despite his lack of a formal connection to Minor and Major League Baseball, as of 2017 he continued his operation. The school's marketing made much of its long history and the accomplishments of alumni who have gone on to work in the major leagues, while also touting the high-quality preparation for professional umpiring positions that the school offered. However, it was also very careful to include a wide range of options under the label of professional umpiring, while scrupulously avoiding any direct connection to the current process through which the top graduates of the certified schools were being placed in minor-league jobs.[20] But while graduates of the Evans School can subsequently attend either of the certified schools as a next step on the path to the majors, such an option represents an added, expensive barrier and as baseball approached the 2016 season, the only approved options were the Wendelstedt School and the Minor League Umpire Training Academy.

Life in School

For all their history and the twists and turns that have led ultimately to the pair of schools that as of 2017 served as the gateway to a career umpiring in the minor and major leagues, it is the experience and the training that the aspiring umpires receive that is at the heart of the school experience, while making it a required part of any major-league umpire's professional journey. At the same time, the rules of baseball, as well as the very nature of the job, limit the individuality of any umpire's performances. In fact, so standard can the curriculum appear that Bill McKinley, who had attended both the Barr and McGowan schools on the way to becoming the first school-trained major-league umpire, once said that there was little real difference between the schools beyond the fact that Barr taught his students to use the inside chest protector (as used in the National League) while the American League's outside protector was the choice at the McGowan School.[21]

Regardless of the specific program, the curriculum and the practical instruction offered aspiring umpires by the schools were consistently rigorous and intense from the start. Each was pursuing the same goal. In the words of one veteran instructor, they wanted to make each student "think like an umpire, not like a player or a fan," adding that "Old habits must be broken."[22] From the start, the schools were intent on training and preparing prospective umpires for the harsh realities of the profession. Instruction was followed by tests, more instruction, and more tests. Meanwhile, out on the field every gesture was subject to being critiqued and assessed. It could leave even the best student fatigued and confused. As one instructor noted, "[We] spend the first 3½ weeks building people up, and we spend the last week and a half breaking them down to see if they can handle the pressure."[23] All of this not only served to prepare future umpires for the challenges of their chosen profession, but like schools that train other professionals, it also helped weed out those not fully equipped to handle the demanding, pressure-filled role.

At the same time, the experience has been at least a little different at each school, with those often subtle differences reflecting the distinctive approach, philosophy, and personality of their founders and directors. Not surprisingly, given his experience and his reputation, McGowan's school featured a textbook that he wrote. With a mixture of "Do's" and "Don'ts," the book offered directives and guidance on everything from equipment and personal appearance to proper hand signals and positioning. In addition to an extensive text, it also included position sketches and a number of practice tests. Instructions explained in the textbook, covered in the classroom, and then reinforced in the practical exercises on the field included everything from how to sweep off home plate to the proper way to indicate fair and foul balls as

well as the appropriate gestures to go with calling balls and strikes.[24] Drawing upon a wealth of personal, professional experience, McGowan tried to anticipate every question and situation. Meanwhile, Bill McKinnamon saw his mission as focusing on technique and mechanics. He noted that "[You] can't teach judgment," adding, "If a man has poor judgment he is not going to make it as an umpire anyway." He averred that "Good mechanics—position—is the only thing that will keep you out of trouble. Consequently, we try to give as much on-field instruction as possible—walking through play situations, footwork, timing, working actual games."[25] Al Somers shared this view, asserting, "You cannot teach someone judgment, just technique."[26] He added that he believed former players made "lousy" umpires because "[T]hey're used to applause, not boos," no small thing when training for the profession includes "creat[ing] rhubarbs just to see how [the] students will react."[27] Alternatively, from its beginnings in 1990, Jim Evans's school always prided itself on personalized instruction, promising a teacher/student ratio that would never exceed seven to one.[28] At the same time, Evans, seen as a rulebook expert, saw the rules as the foundation of the umpire's authority on the field. Consequently, students at his school historically spent more time on classroom coverage and discussion of rules.[29] The Wendelstedt School takes a different approach, believing that while the rules are obviously important, an umpire's strength and authority comes from game experience. As a result, students at the Wendelstedt School spend considerably more time in action, umpiring games between

Drill in progress, Wendelstedt School, January 2017.

Classroom, Wendelstedt School, January 2017

local high-school and college teams, opportunities that allow the students to get real experience and, especially importantly, "live pitching."[30] In contrast, Evans maintained that games actually limit what students see. Rather, believing that in reality most games are "parades of the run of the mill," the Evans school devoted large amounts of time to simulations, where the instructors created situations that the students must address.[31]

From the beginning with Barr's school, the basic session was five to six weeks long, always taking place in January and February. This remained the basic model, until the Minor League-sponsored Umpire School compressed its program into four weeks.[32] Meanwhile, regardless of the school, the daily program was pretty much the same with a full day beginning with a morning session in the classroom where the aspiring arbiters were drilled on the rules, rules interpretations, and proper positioning. They viewed and studied films illustrating the various situations they might encounter and then they were tested on all of it. The afternoon sessions featured hands-on instruction and workouts on the field. These workouts often included simulations that almost always use the two-man system that is standard in the minor leagues. These lessons included controlled games, simulated contests in which countless situations are presented and assessed.[33] In addition, the students also got game experience by working local high-school and college contests.[34] And while evenings were usually a time to relax, they also offered study time for the many tests the students took. There also were periodic evening Q&A sessions with major- and minor-league umpires. Meanwhile, occasional organized or informal social events helped begin to develop the camaraderie and sense of team that is no less important to being a successful umpire.[35]

More than Rules

Yet for all the formal instruction, all the schools' leaders have long recognized that there was more to being a successful umpire than knowing the rules and soaking up what was taught in the classroom and on the field. Rather, their many years of experience left Barr, McGowan, and company well aware that developing a certain type of personality and character was no less important to becoming a successful umpire than a mastery of the mechanics. Indeed, that was why Barr was known to levy a 10-cent fine on any student who asked a stupid question, made "bonehead" actions, or uttered a stupid comment. Too, with the money that was collected going to the waitresses in the hotel where the students ate, the practice not only made an impression on the students but also helped highlight the relationship between baseball and the local community.[36]

In that same vein, as part of their broad-based efforts to fully prepare and train their students for the rigors and realities of umpiring in the world of professional baseball, the school leaders would often get creative in their efforts to identify and help develop the more intangible professional talents, the character attributes, and attitudes that give one the ability to command the respect needed to control the game, things that cannot necessarily be taught but are critical to success as an umpires. Illustrative of that effort was a story Joe Brinkman told about a student at his school who had clearly been one of the top participants in his class but who, in the middle of the final exam, turned to him and made an obscene gesture. Brinkman was dumbfounded at witnessing such an unprecedented act of defiance. And yet he could not overlook the fact that the student was one of the very best prospects in the class. Events came to a head on the final night when the offending student was left off the list of those students who would be recommended for positions in minor-league baseball. As people congratulated each other, the forlorn rebel sat alone, unbelieving. But as people began to exit, Brinkman announced that he had left out a name, announcing that the offending party was also on the list of recommended aspirants. Brinkman recalled that he was sure the message had been received, noting that the humbled rookie went on to have a great year.[37]

Similarly, Brinkman also recounted another time when, in conjunction with the restaurant, he had an additional $10 put on each student's bill at the end of one dinner. Brinkman recalled that while there was lots of grumbling among the prospective umps, no one directly asked the waitress about the overcharge; Brinkman later said he thought that perhaps his charges did not want to make a scene for fear of embarrassing him, and admitted that he was not sure what kind of reaction he was expecting, but he did believe that such efforts helped the prospective umpires learn how to react appropriately to unexpected situations.[38] Such exercises and efforts were thought valuable in the never-ending efforts to help craft the attitude, approach, and demeanor necessary to handle a complaining player or maintain control of a game. In the heat of competition, those attributes were as important as a comprehensive command of the rules and the other technical aspects of the profession.

A Highly Competitive Process

Of course while the umpire schools provided the training, the process of becoming a major-league umpire is a highly competitive one, requiring skills and talents that oftentimes could not be taught. Consequently, attending a school has never guaranteed a career in umpiring and, in fact, in addition to their instructional role, the schools have long served as a winnowing process. Each year only the top students in each class at each school earn the opportunity to move on, starting at some level in the minor leagues, the only place where real attrition occurs as prospective big-league umpires' work is assessed, and they move up or, with insufficient progress, wash out.

Bill Kinnamon recalled that "McGowan made it clear the competition for advancement would be keen. He always said that if you weren't the best umpire in your league, you wouldn't move to a higher classification."[39] Indeed, there is no denying that the world of professional umpiring is highly competitive, with only a very few openings occurring each year. Former minor-league Umpire Development Director Mike Fitzpatrick noted that despite the fact that there are only 68 major-league umpires and around 225 in the minor leagues, and openings for new umpires are extremely limited, the two certified schools still enrolled approximately 300 aspiring umpires each year.[40] Quite simply, as Fitzpatrick noted candidly, "it's long odds."[41]

Many attendees have no intention of becoming a professional umpire, but instead want to prepare themselves for amateur baseball—for instance, youth, high-school, and college umpiring.

Beyond its role in developing new umpires, the schools do have one other, often overlooked role, one that, however unintentionally, helps fill their instructional staffs. And that is the way veteran umpires see the sessions as a way to sharpen their skills and prepare for the coming season. Notable among those who felt that way was Bill Kinnamon, who worked as an instructor under McGowan, his son, and Al Somers after he took over the school.[42] And of course school leaders like Brinkman and Wendelstedt also spent many years as instructors before they assumed ownership of their schools.

Instruction in progress at the Wendelstedt School, January 2017.

Impact of the Schools

With all modern umpires being graduates of the recognized umpiring schools, the question has arisen about the impact of the schools on the umpiring profession and the way modern umpires differ from their less formally trained predecessors. First and foremost, by all accounts the graduates of the schools have been far more knowledgeable about the rules of the game than their counterparts. At the same time, there has been an increased uniformity in their styles, as modern students, who have been taught, in some cases literally, "by the book," are less apt to develop a distinctive style. Indeed, the whole formalized educational process has served, however unintentionally, to tone down the potential big personalities and filter out those who might have been mavericks, a somewhat interesting irony given that for all his professionalism and the respect with which he was held, McGowan, an author of one of the "books," was certainly regarded as having a distinctive style and a personality that was as important to his ability to keep control of the game as his experience or his command of the rules.[43]

Another impact of the schools on the process has been the change in the prospective candidates. The formal training now required, coupled with the attendant career development, has given the profession a greater sheen of professionalism and as a result it has begun to attract a wider range of prospects. In transitioning from what was formerly viewed as an avocation into a vocation, a true profession, umpiring now attracts more middle-class candidates and college graduates, people who see umpiring as a distinctive and worthy career. This view represents a marked contrast to the previous view that saw umpiring as little more than a way for former players and others to simply remain involved with the sport.[44] Indeed, attendance at an approved umpire school is not only at the top of a list of requirements for aspiring umpires that also includes a high-school diploma or a GED, reasonable body weight, 20/20 vision with or without glasses, good communication skills, quick reflexes and good coordination, and basic athletic ability. It is also something that has clearly added to the stature and to the respect umpires are accorded by the public and members of the professional baseball community.[45]

Looking Ahead

No one would deny that the game of baseball is deeply rooted in history, but that has not prevented it from changing, however slow that change has sometimes been. Umpires are certainly not immune to those changes. Indeed, things like instant replay and other types of technology have become accepted parts of the game and their use is expanding. At the same time, the umpires union's ongoing efforts are impacting both working conditions and workloads. These newly achieved work rules have gone so far as to impact the culture of the game, disturbing some of the old umpire-team approach that added a certain stability, if one sometimes affected by fatigue. In the midst of all these changes, questions are sometimes raised about the education and training that umpires receive. But for now, the basic instructional approach pioneered by veteran umpires George Barr and Bill McGowan more than three-quarters of a century ago remain in place, offering a distinctive form of training for those who have been entrusted almost since the beginning with the oversight and the protection of the integrity of the game. Any changes to its approach must address the question of whether it will allow the umpires to better discharge their fundamental responsibility—the protection of the character and integrity of the game. In the end, it is that—the duty of the umpire to, as John Roberts put it, "make sure everybody plays by the rules"—to which everything pertaining to their training and responsibilities must point.[46]

NOTES

1 "Roberts: 'My job is to call balls and strikes and not to pitch or bat,'" CNN.com, September 12, 2005; cnn.com/2005/ POLITICS/09/12/roberts.statement/.

2 "Roberts.

3 Larry R. Gerlach, *Men in Blue, Conversations with Umpires* (New York: Viking Press, 1980); The portraits in Gerlach's book offer some interesting examples of the somewhat haphazard ways in

which pre-school umpires entered the profession and ultimately arrived in the major leagues.

4 "George Barr Umpire School," *Arkansas Baseball Encyclopedia*; arkbaseball.com/tiki-index.php?page=George+Barr+Umpire+School.

5 Bob Luke, *Dean of Umpires: A Biography of Bill McGowan, 1896-1954* (Jefferson, North Carolina: McFarland & Company, Inc. Publishers, 2005), 87-88. Many authorities date the start of McGowan's school to January 1939, but according to Luke, McGowan had conducted a short session in November 1938 with practical experience from umpiring University of Maryland games. In January he set up shop in Jackson, Mississippi, but after a couple weeks moved to Florida.

6 Bruce Weber, *As They See 'Em, A Fan's Travels in the Land of Umpires* (New York: Scribner, 2009), 50.

7 "George Barr Umpire School," *Arkansas Baseball Encyclopedia*.

8 Ryan Aber, "Part of Major League History Finds Home in Guthrie," NewsOK.com, May 6, 2013; newsok.com/article/3806892; Mark Blaeuer, "Reaching for the Brass Ring: A Portrait of Doan's 1937 Baseball School," Historic Baseball Trail, Hot Springs, Arkansas; hotspringsbaseballtrail.com/untold-stories/reaching-brass-ring-portrait-doans-1937-baseball-school/; "George Barr Umpire School," Tulsa Historical Society & Museum; tulsahistory.pastperfectonline.com/photo/C2D2A68F-C8B9-483A-A874-454432539760.

9 Gerlach, 219. While he initially settled in Orlando when he moved to Florida, at various points Barr's school operated out of Sanford and Longwood.

10 Luke, 103-106.

11 Bruce Weber, "Harry Wendelstedt, Umpire in Five World Series, Dies at 73," *New York Times*, March 9, 2012: D8.

12 Weber, 50.

13 Ibid.

14 Kevin Hennessy, "Joe Brinkman," SABR BioProject, sabr.org/bioproj/person/62a6e3cc.

15 Weber, 50.

16 Weber, 51.

17 Harold Uhlman, "Beating the Odds—An Umpire's Near Impossible Road to the Majors," ThinkBlueLA.com, November 19, 2015; thinkbluela.com/index.php/2015/11/19/beating-the-odds-an-umpires-near-impossible-road-to-the-majors-2/.

18 Minor League Baseball Umpire Training Academy; milbumpireacademy.com/default.aspx.

19 Andrew Keh, "For Umpiring School, a Staff Party Proves Costly," *New York Times*, February 9, 2012; nytimes.com/2012/02/10/sports/baseball/umpiring-school-loses-baseball-relationship-over-behavior-at-party.html.

20 "About the Academy," Jim Evans' Academy of Professional Umpiring; umpireacademy.com/aboutacademy.php.

21 Luke, 92-93.

22 Matt Schudel, "Life's a Pitch," *Sun-Sentinel* (Fort Lauderdale, Florida), March 26, 1989; articles.sun-sentinel.com/1989-03-26/features/8901160574_1_professional-umpire-two-umpires-umpire-development.

For some insight into how the game as seen by an umpire is different and what thinking like an umpire might really mean as they go they do their job, see Dan Boyle et al., "Observations of Umpires at Work," *The Baseball Research Journal* 40, no. 1 (Spring 2011): 77-87, an interesting article that recounts the results of an experiment conducted by seven SABR members who watched only the umpires during a game. The article offers some real insight into their work—and what they schools are preparing them for.

23 Schudel, "Life's a Pitch."

24 Luke, 135-187.

25 Gerlach, 253.

26 Martha Smilgis, "Act Up in Al Somers' Class and You Get Sent to the Shower," *People*, 9, No. 8 (February 27, 1978); people.com/people/archive/article/0,,20070277,00.html.

27 Ibid.

28 "About the Academy," Jim Evans' Academy of Professional Umpiring; umpireacademy.com/aboutacademy.php.

29 Weber, 51.

30 Ibid.

31 Weber, 50-51.

32 "How to Become an Umpire"; mlb.mlb.com/mlb/official_info/umpires/how_to_become.jsp.

33 Doug Miller, "Aspiring Umpires' Paths Start at Florida Schools," MLB.com; m.mlb.com/news/article/26485860/.

34 2013 Umpire School, 2013 Umpire School Experience, Day; 2013umpireschool.wordpress.com/.

35 Ibid.

36 "Student Umpires Fined for 'Boners,'" *Milwaukee Journal*, March 14, 1939; news.google.com/newspapers?id=-qVQAAAAIBAJ&sjid=MCIEAAAAIBAJ&pg=2739,4069523&dq=george+barr+umpire&hl=en.

37 Angelo Cataldi, "Aspiring Umps: Only the Strong Survive," *Philadelphia Inquirer*, February 19, 1989; articles.philly.com/1989-02-19/sports/26153452_1_professional-umpire-young-umpire-joe-brinkman-umpire-school.

38 Ibid.

39 Gerlach, 237.

40 "How to Become an Umpire"; mlb.mlb.com/mlb/official_info/umpires/how_to_become.jsp. With the advent of instant replay, the number of major-league umpires is now 76.

41 Mike Couzens, "Chasing A Dream: Being an Umpire in Minor League Baseball," August 26, 2013; mikecouzens.com/2013/08/26/chasing-a-dream-being-an-umpire-in-minor-league-baseball/.

42 Gerlach, 238.

43 "The History of Umpiring," Hernando Sumpter Umpires; hernandosumterumpire.com/HISTORY.html. For a full sense of the way Bill McGowan did his job, as well as his multifaceted influence on the umpiring profession, see Luke, *Dean of Umpires*.

44 Ibid.

45 "How to Become an Umpire."

46 "Roberts: 'My job is to call balls and strikes and not to pitch or bat.'"

An Umpire School Diary

By Shaun McCready

Shaun McCready, an amateur umpire in Pennsylvania, wrote a daily blog detailing his experience as a student at the Wendelstedt Umpire School in 2013. It is a superb account not only of the instruction he received, but also the about techniques and duties of an umpire. This edited version of the blog, about one-third of the original, is presented in chronological order to better convey the day-to-day progression at the school. To appreciate Shaun's full experience, readers are encouraged to consult the entire blog at https://2013umpireschool.wordpress.com/

January 1, 2013 — Arrival! Hey everyone, first of all I would like to start this by saying thanks to all of my family and friends, especially my wife who supported me in coming to school. I will not be here to compete for a pro job (discussed this with my wife and came to the conclusion she would kill me if I took it) but am here to do the best that I can and hopefully finish in the top of the class. Killer day today, got up at 545 AM, drove to Pittsburgh, flew out of Pittsburgh at 1230 PM and landed in Orlando at 305 PM. Went from 30 degree temps to 75! Sick of the snow too so the timing is pretty good. Hired a private car and got a ride to Daytona Beach. Got to the hotel about 530 PM. It has definitely seen better days, but the view out of the back window is stunning, full view of the Atlantic Ocean. Tomorrow is registration day and orientation.

January 2 — Registration/Orientation. Went through registration today. Met several of the instructors while registering, all of them are very friendly and seem more than willing to help out however possible. After filling out the paperwork, got assigned my meal plan card as well as a dinner menu. Food looks to be pretty good, a nice mix of several types of food. Then I was issued a small duffel bag with the Wendelstedt logo, four t-shirts with the logo (two white and two navy), and my baseball bible aka. the rulebook, and a hat with the logo. Then onto a one-on-one meeting with Hunter Wendelstedt and Jerry Layne. They were very nice and seemed to know a little bit about all of us, some things that we never told them. Seems like they check into you a little bit. After that it was free time until orientation.

At orientation I would estimate that there are around 130-150 people in the class. We had to stand up when our name was called and give our name, hometown, room number, and who were rooming with (I'm in my own room). Funny thing, I noticed that the instructor reading out our names at roll call when he came upon a difficult name would say, "Here's a whacker." For those who don't know, a whacker is a baseball term for a very close play, usually difficult to call. Wendelstedt and Layne gave their speeches, both very good speakers, going over some of the dos and don'ts. Then the lead instructor, Brent Rice, ran us through his welcome speech. They told us not to read anything in the rule book yet, but if we wanted a head start to read rule 2.00, which is definitions. They told us that the only thing we would need tomorrow for class is our rule book, hat, and mask. The next couple of days will be on very basic things, things that some of us with experience may already know.

January 3 — First day of class! The first day of class, up at 6:30 AM, showered and down for breakfast. Class started at 8:30 sharp and we have assigned seating alphabetically. The guys next to me are pretty good guys, one guy drove down from Connecticut so myself and two other guys are hitching rides with him to the field. Also found out there is one guy from Canada, one from Puerto Rico, and one from Japan. Class started with reading very simple rules, about the goals of the game and such, followed by general guidelines for umpires. Found out in MiLB you are not allowed to have any facial hair, or visible piercings or tattoos.

After the classroom work we went to the fields, about a 20-minute drive from here. There are three baseball fields, which are all very nice. We started out around home plate watching how to get hands on knees set (this is one phrase "hands on knees set" an umpiring position), call an out and a safe. They are VERY specific about how to make these calls, and they want you to yell LOUD! When you make the out call you yell "he's out" and that is all you are allowed to yell. When you call safe you can yell "safe" or "he's safe." We then learned about how to call balls, strikes, and get into the plate stance in the slot position, the proper way to clean off the plate, and how to start the game. You call a strike or ball by saying which one it is followed by what number is it e.g. "Ball 3" "Strike 2," etc. Once again, you are only allowed to work the slot, no other stances as that is what is required in MiLB. Then we formed up in lines in the outfield. We warmed up with some calisthenics and stretching and then we practiced all of the calls we learned. The instructors walked around and corrected whatever they saw that was wrong.

We then broke up into groups and practiced getting into the proper plate stance and tracking a slowly tossed ball with just our eyes and calling either ball or strike. They didn't care what we called they were just watching our stance, tracking the ball, and timing. We did that for quite some time and then ended the day again practicing the calls. We then broke around 5:30PM. It was a pretty long and action-packed day. I'm off to practice my calls in the mirror for a bit, read my assigned rulebook section.

January 4—TIME—Rain delay! Today was our first rainout, so it was a complete classroom day. We started by going over all of the rules and the measurements that are required by the rules. There are measurements for everything, from the dimension of the field, to the pitcher's mound, home plate, batter's box/catchers box, bases, walls, etc. Also the size requirements of bats, balls, gloves and mitts. Learned that the difference between a glove and mitt, that a mitt does not have fingers and a glove has fingers. Also that the catcher is required to wear a mitt, first baseman can wear a mitt or a glove, and everyone else has to wear a glove. We learned the specifications for uniforms, undershirts, and helmets.

We then learned about the different things that each umpire is in charge of, the difference between the crew chief and the umpire-in-chief and the responsibilities of each. We then got a long, two-hour lunch break, which was fine by me because I was sore from all of the drills we did yesterday. I do not kid, I probably got in and out of my plate stance about 200 times, and also made safe, out, strike, and ball calls about 50 to 100 times each. I ate my lunch and took advantage of the time to practice mechanics in the mirror, taking off my mask without knocking my hat off, and also to study as I believe we will have a test on Monday (we have 25 ten-question tests during out time here). We then returned to class and began two-man mechanics. We started learning about how to be positioned with no runners on base and where to go on ground balls to the infield and also base hits.

January 5—First full field day. We were able to hit the fields for our first full field day! We got a demo on how to drop step back from the catcher on a passed ball or on a pop fly to the catcher, calling catch or no catch, and how to call that the ball is still in play after a passed ball. After that we drilled for the first half of the day. We had to drop step and get distance from the catcher. This was difficult at first for me as I never got that much distance from the catcher before, but I know why now, you can see so much more without the play "exploding" on you as they say here. I must have gotten in and out of the slot stance several hundred more times. Then it was off to formation for calisthenics and to practice the mechanics that we learned yesterday, plus passed ball and pop flies. After lunch we had another demo about how to move down the first base line on a ground ball to the infield, and what to do if the hit would happen to get through for a single. We then broke again and drilled the same drills as earlier, but they added running down the base line. We then had formation again to work on mechanics and voice.

January 6—First day off! Today was our first day off, and I have to say it is welcome. Muscles are sore and trying to rest my voice as I am pretty hoarse from all of the yelling we do! Started my day by taking my laundry to the laundromat. They will wash and fold the items for you, plus the school worked out a 10 percent discount of that service, as well as some others around the town. They gave us a discount card to show to the businesses. Ate breakfast and about 10:30AM saw some guys down on the beach so I headed down. Took my hat, mask, and indicator and worked with the guys for about 2 hours on mechanics. It was great to work with the other students, everyone is trying to help each other out. Went to the store and got a sub as the only meal our plan does not cover is lunch on Sundays.

January 7 — No test yet... In class we went over fair/foul, and catch/no catch. There is a proper way to call and signal foul and fair. We also went over the definition of a catch and what is required to have a catch, then the definition of foul and fair territory and also how a ball can become foul (there are four ways), and learned what would cause the ball to become dead. Then we went over what we need to see on the field to start the game (there are five requirements) and to resume play (there are three requirements). They want us to use rule book terminology here so they were very specific in how we describe things that happen.

At the fields they demonstrated the proper footwork and mechanics for fair/foul and catch/no catch. We then broke off into formation to practice our mechanics. It is starting to take a little more work to concentrate and think about what you need to do for certain situations. By no means are any of us what I would call good, but you can tell that we are making progress as a group. Mechanics are looking sharper and we are moving with a little more confidence and purpose.

January 8 — Test day today...and a real baseball! Today we started class with our first two tests on field measurements, dimensions, and equipment regulations! I aced both of them as they were just straight memorization of the numbers, two tests down, 23 to go! After the tests we got down to Rule 6.00 and some others which cover the batter. We also learned that a batter cannot just leave the box and that a

Instructor Jason Visconti and student Shaun McCready, Wendelstedt School, 2013.

batter REQUESTS time, THEY **do not** call time, we do and we can tell them "no." We then went over when a batter CAN leave the batter's box (there are 8 times) and when he can actually leave the dirt circle (there are two times). One student asked what you would do if the count was 3 balls and 2 strikes and the pitcher delivered a ball, but the batter stepped out what you would do as he would technically have 4 balls and 3 strikes at that point. We stumped the instructors on that one, but they will find out for us and let us know. We also learned what to do on overthrows, bobbled balls, dropped balls, and when the first baseman pulls his foot off of the bag and how to properly call and signal these things.

Then we went to the fields and drills for the base umpire. When dealing with a ground ball, as soon as you get in and get set and see that the throw is true (which does not mean it is accurate, it just means it is not going to hit you) you quit watching the ball and turn immediately to the bag to make the call. Not watching it took some getting used to. We ended the day with a "whacker" drill.

January 9 — Balls flying everywhere. Today we took a break from rules and met Rich Rieker (director of MLB umpire development) and Bruce Froemming (Special assistant to MLB umpiring). We also got to have a Q and A session with one of our guest MLB instructors, Paul Nauert. It was very interesting to hear Nauert talk about his experience through the minors up until the big leagues. He went on to tell us that they are evaluated every game that they have, and the plate umpire gets a record of how well he did calling pitches. He also said that last year, as a group, MLB umpires got 95.7% of the called pitches correct. He also told us that MLB umpires get around $400 a day for per diem rates, but that they have to pay for their own lodging, as well as a rate for the "clubbie" (the guy who takes care of the umpires at the stadium), food, and also to hotel staff/wait staff/etc. so he said that per diem does not really go that far. He also told us that come tax time they are required to file a "jock tax" and file taxes in every city that they work in, which creates a large tax preparation bill for him.

Then we headed out to the fields and worked on our pause, read, react technique. Lot of quick decisions and also trying to work on mechanics and footwork, whew! Then after lunch we went to a drill about ground balls to all infielders. There are a lot of small things that can happen that can cause you to have to move differently, too many for me to get in to here.

January 10 — Confused is good? Then I'm great! Today another instructor arrived, MLB umpire Doug Eddings. In class we went over the definition of a bunt and a line drive, and the infield fly rule! Also the definition of ordinary effort, foul tip, and the ways a batter can be out. Then we went over pickoffs to first base, second base, runner on first stealing second base, and coverage of third base when a runner goes from first the third (the home plate umpire should take the call if he can, if he does not have other responsibilities).

Then off to the field for the footwork with pickoffs and stealing of second. First of all you have to position yourself in the infield in the correct position. Then when you are set there you have to watch the pitcher and step hard towards a point between the 45-foot line and first base, without getting hands on knees set. I screwed that up. The next time through I still did not step towards the right place, the last time I stepped well but went hands on knees set. Then we went onto pickoffs and steals of second base, you have to take a drop step towards second base then get set for the call as the ball passes you. Then we went onto first to third coverage. You have to communicate with your partner, stop and observe. Oh and by the way, remember that ball? Yeah you have to keep trying to find it and oh yeah those runners they are still moving around the bases. Oh my god, consider me confused! Well they say it's okay and that we should be completely lost by Saturday, so I guess I am excelling and somewhat ahead of schedule.

January 11 — Test day, and more footwork than a ballroom dancer! After two more tests, we went over a few rules where a batter is out for illegal actions and how to deal with illegal bats, and the definition of a force play. We then went over several ways a runner can be put out. At the fields we practiced mechanics again and then practiced the double play. It is frustrating in that I know the 2-man umpire system as far as where I need to go and what I need to look for, but adding all of this footwork in is frustrating to me. Tomorrow is Saturday, which means we get to sleep in some because we don't have to be there until 10AM. Maybe the rest will allow me to kick the rest of this cold that I have, a lot of guys are sick in this class so it's going around.

January 12 — Putting a puzzle together. We met at the fields and worked on fly balls to the outfield with one runner on. After that we did a fair/foul drill with base and plate umpires down the right field line with no runners on. We finished off the day with the whacker drill.

January 13 — Relaxing off day. I will be going to the fields with some guys to practice for a bit later today, and then I will just be relaxing and watching some playoff football.

January 14 — It's getting, it's getting, it's getting kind of hectic... They threw all kinds of information at us in class — base awards to runners for infractions that may occur, if a fielder hits a batted or thrown ball or pitched ball with any detached equipment (the award is different for all three), deflected balls out of play in fair or foul territory, kicked balls out of play, the definition of what a play is by an infielder, and the proper way to award bases. We also went over how a batter must still touch all of his bases in order even if they are awarded and what happens if a ball lodges in the umpire or player's equipment or uniform. The frustrating thing is the way the official rulebook is written, it says the same thing two or three times but just worded differently so there is a lot of repeating. I am officially in the camp now calling for a rewrite and update on the rulebook.

We are almost done with the two man umpire system. At the fields we went over base and plate umpire responsibilities with runners on first and second base and positioning for plays at the plate. When we went to the field for practice, it was on! They could throw us double plays, pickoffs, base hits, fly outs, fair/foul calls, all kinds of things. We finished up the day with a demonstration on how the pitching cages will work, where you get evaluated on working behind the plate. Evaluations will start next week, so instructors will be walking around with iPads making notations on us. I'm sure nerves will be shot then. We start control games (games where the instructors set up whatever scenario they want to), camp games (games where we play each other), and live games (high school and college teams play) this week.

January 15 — Finally some real action. We started off class today by going over interference, what happens if a ball hit a broken bat or a helmet in fair or foul territory, and a running lane violation. There are about five things that all need to happen for a running lane violation. Then we went out to the fields and covered how to deal with rundowns between first and second base and third base and home plate. We did that for half of the day and then after that we started control games. We finally got to put all of the stuff from the drills we have been doing into practice, and you know, working the two man system is so much easier now that things are live. My turn on the bases went fine. I then went to the plate, and things

didn't go quite as well, but they didn't go badly either. Hope I get to call some pitches tomorrow!

January 16 — Test double header. We started off with two more tests today, and I got a one hundred on both again. We went to the fields and had a demo on how to award bases. They are very specific about how they are awarded, and both umpires have to award bases simultaneously. We then broke off to control games where they added on overthrows and awards of bases to the situations along with everything else we already covered. My group got called for cage work. They use a pitching machine and the instructor sits and watches your plate stance, head height, if you move your head when the pitch comes in, if you are tracking the pitch the whole way into the glove with your eyes, your voice and mechanics. I didn't do too bad, head was locked in and tracked all the way with my eyes. The only thing that needs work is my slot foot getting up enough on a left handed batter, which apparently is a common problem, and he also said I have to explode up more with my mechanic and yell louder.

I'm off to go to a Q and A session tonight with Hickox, Eddings, and Knight. They will show the tapes they get after their games that show how accurate they were on their called pitches.

January 17 — Jumped the gun...NOW s*&t got real! Ok, first I would like to start out by telling you all about last night's session with Ed Hickox, who showed us the ZE system that grades all major league umpires on their plate work. I have to tell you that this system is amazing, it uses the same technology that the military uses to precision bomb targets to track pitches. There are three cameras in every major league ballpark. There is one in center field, and two on each side. There is about a 2-inch buffer zone around the entire strike zone, so if you call a pitch there they give you credit for you being right. So Hickox pulled up his score sheet from the last game that he called behind the plate. He had around 160 decision pitches (pitches that he actually had to call a strike or ball) and he only called 5 incorrect according to the system, so his percent correct right was around 96 percent. The average for all umpires this last season was 97.8 percent. There is also another system called BASES that grades them on all plays on the bases. On average every MLB umpire only missed three whackers each total for the whole season this last year. Oh and they went on to tell us how much BS the K-Zone that ESPN uses is. That box they use only gets extended a generic up or down for a taller or shorter batter.

Today we had two tests and I'm sad to say the streak has ended. Missed my first question on the second test, but I guess 79/80 on 8 tests is pretty good. At the fields we had a demonstration of interference by a base runner, by a batter runner and catcher's interference.

Then we broke off to control games. After that, we started our first live game with a college team inter-squad scrimmage. The way it works is you are assigned a half-inning. The first umpire works the plate and one base for a half inning. Then you go and change while two other students work the bottom half of the inning. Then you and your partner come back out to do the top of the next inning in the position that you have not worked.

January 18 — Strap it on boys! Game time. Class today covered appeals and apparent fourth outs, and let me tell you that stuff is enough to make your head spin. It's bad enough on a dry erase board trying to figure that stuff out, god be with me if I have to do that in a real game some day. At the end of class they gave assignments for innings during live games today. My half inning came up and I had the bases first. Had pretty routine stuff, the only thing I had a pop up to the infield with nobody on. After that half inning I ran in and put on the plate gear and took over behind the dish. Man, working behind the plate felt so smooth and natural now since I have had some instruction on how to do it. Had good pitch tracking, and I even took a foul ball off of my face mask and stayed locked in and didn't move! Finished my half inning with no major blunders, did a few things wrong but nothing horrible.

January 19 — Beautiful field day. Today we headed straight to the fields and we immediately started with live games with a high school team that played a scrimmage for us. I didn't have any innings today but I did have a good idea. One of the guys that I hang out with did have two innings today and I had an idea from our cage sessions. I whipped out my cell phone and took video of him at his time during the plate and the bases. I got with him afterwards and transferred the files to his computer so now he has film of himself at work that he can critique. He said he would use my phone and record me the next time I go so that will be really cool to have video of us working.

After the live games we started control games, but my cage group was called. I was in the cages for the rest of the afternoon. After that we had a demo about illegal pitching moves and balks that ran kind of late into the evening so we got out pretty late today.

January 20 — Finally, an off day. Boy, I tell you what, an off day is really something to look forward to around here. We are just so darn busy during the week that everyone is looking forward to Sunday to rest and recharge.

January 21 — That's a balk! In class we went over obstruction and how to enforce it, then to the fields for demonstrations on how to call and enforce balks and obstruction. After drills, we had control games, I think I did alright in my turns, messed up some small stuff but no major blunders. Also had my first one-on-one cage review session and was told that I looked pretty good behind the plate. I was locked in and comfortable; they just told me to relax my mechanic some.

January 22 - Cage match and live innings. Started off with two tests then headed to the fields. We did drills on pause, read, and react, while the other two fields did control games. After lunch my group got called for cage work. I went to the cages and didn't have really any bad critique other than my timing being quick at times. After that I had a live half- inning behind the plate and one on the bases. I called out a balk that my partner didn't see when I was on the bases so I felt pretty good about that.

January 23 — Punchouts and whacker mechanics?!?! I'm in!!! Today started in class with covering interference by authorized personnel and interference by spectators, then a crash course overview of two-man mechanics with a runner on first and runners on first and second base. Out to the field for control games, then demonstrations on called third strike and whacker mechanics. On the bases you still have to stay hands on knees set for the play, and stay square to the base. You can take one step forward and use your "punch out," but only on close plays. Also for the strike three mechanics there are rules. You have to stay looking forward at the ball, cannot take your eye off of it while doing your mechanic and are only allowed to take one step backwards on your mechanic. My group got called to the cages! Man I was pumped, got into the cages and "HIKE THREE!!!!" rung that sucker up sharp. Can't wait to ring my first batter up looking in a game, it's gonna be sweet!

January 24 — Cage session, control game, and live innings…one of each please! Today started with two tests, went over how to handle situations. Not necessarily ejections, but all situations. I got to go in the cages again, and had a good session. Then I got some innings in control games. I thought that I did pretty well with those as well. I was also assigned live innings today so I got a half inning on the bases and a half inning behind the plate.

January 25 — You're outta here! New instructors arrived today— Brian Gorman, Mike Winters, and Sam Holbrook. Tomorrow Randy Marsh, the director of MLB umpiring, will be in attendance. We went over more rules regarding ejections of players, managers, coaches, and other personnel. At the fields Layne, Gorman, and Winters had an hour-and-a-half long presentation about how to handle situations. We learned when it is appropriate to warn someone, and when to just toss them immediately. Then we were put into situations and the instructors played the managers and players. It was a really fun day, and it was funny to see how some people handled a little chirping. They are starting to evaluate us on our judgment on balls and strikes in the cages now. Some guys are really starting to stand out now as being very good umpires. I think we can already point to a few that are going to get selected to go to PBUC for MiLB evaluations.

January 26 — Early dismissal. We started with the class photo and individual photos with the staff if we wanted. After that we went straight to live innings, 18 innings to be exact. I got my turns in and did pretty well. They had a few things that I could have done better, but they said that it is obvious that I know the two-man umpire system and that I have good instincts. They left us go at 3:00 PM today so this is awesome! I think we could all use the break and get a little bit longer time off to help us recover and heal. Can't believe that it has been five weeks already, it is pretty cool to look back and see how far everyone has progressed. Off to enjoy my R&R!

January 27 — Another well-earned day off. Got up this morning and some friends and I decided to head to the Daytona International Speedway to catch the end of the Rolex 24-hour race. After that watched a little of the Pro Bowl and then got some studying done.

January 28 — Busy, busy day! We went over game preliminaries as well as how a pregame plate meeting works, what should be on a lineup card, how many baseballs the umpire is required to have in his possession at all times, how many need to be prepared before the game and how many trips per inning per pitcher the manager gets. Then we were given our inning assignments and cage groups. I didn't have any innings today but I did have a cage group. We were then given a scenario that we have to write an ejection report about this evening. The setup was given to us in class, about a batter grounding out to first base and the manager not liking that he was called out. Also, we were given our declaration forms as to whether or not we would accept a job in professional baseball. I know I came down here knowing I wouldn't take a job, but after these past four weeks I feel like I am doing pretty well. I know that I must refuse to accept a job because of my situation, but it is a sobering feeling knowing that by checking one box on a sheet of paper that I'm slamming that door shut permanently. Oh well, it is what is best for myself and my family, and I will still be one heck of a high school umpire and hopefully one day a college umpire as well!

We then broke for the ejection demo. They set the scenario up on the field and had the instructor playing the manager wearing a microphone. We watched the scenario unfold and tonight have to write two ejection reports from the viewpoint of the base umpire and the plate umpire. Then we broke for cage groups. It was a little unsettling in the cages with the instructor just staring at you the whole time and not offering any advice after getting nothing but advice for the past four weeks, but I think I did fine. Then I went to my field, where they had a double play drill set up. It is crazy to see 6 MLB umpires watching guys take their turns at the plate and bases and know they are deciding if you are good enough.

January 29 – Back in the saddle! We went over substitution rules and how the double switch works and when they are able to do the double switch, also when players are allowed to be substituted and how to signal them into the game. After that we headed to the fields to control games and then the cages. After lunch we had live games. I did get innings today, had the plate first and then the bases. I did ok on the plate, a few dumb mistakes. On the bases, my partner called a balk but I have no idea what for. Oh well, gotta back your partner, so I echoed his call and awarded the runner his base. There were guys from two independent baseball leagues here today that are looking for about 10 umpires each.

January 30 — Crunch time. Two tests and I aced them both again, 195/200, with five more tests to go, not bad. We then went over what makes a game a regulation game, when a game can be called, when a game can be suspended, and when a game is a "no game" which means it has to be played all over again. Let me tell you what, there is so much crazy information on these things it was making our heads spin. We are required to know the MLB as well as the MiLB rules regarding all of this stuff. Oh yeah, right before lunch we had another guest come to school, Joe West! It was awesome hearing him speak with us briefly. He told us he will be at our graduation banquet this Tuesday.

January 31 — Switch it up! We started class today by going over the rules for the designated hitter. We

are now assigned innings on different fields with different people than what we are used to working with. I had a control game on the bases, the only major thing that I messed up was that we had catcher's interference and then the ball was thrown out of play. I forgot that since the ball was thrown out of play that the batter/runner needed to be awarded second, I was still hung up on the catcher's interference being nullified because he reached first base safely. After that I had my turn at the plate and things didn't go that great. I was in position for everything, and I got to all of the places that I needed to be, but I screwed something small up on just about every play. Then I had another cage session, evaluation only. I watched the video when I got back and I was pretty upset that I saw my head move slightly on a couple of pitches. There are some very good umpires here, and I do not envy the instructors having to just pick a few guys to go to PBUC. From what I saw today it is going to be a tough decision.

February 1 — What a long day! After two tests to start the day, covered batting out of order, which can be quite confusing sometimes. At the fields we had another ejection scenario that we had to write a report on this evening. Then we broke and went straight to live innings. My first turn was at the plate. I should have gotten off of the line for some foul balls that were caught, and the pitcher asked for a new ball one time and I forgot to call time while replacing it. On the bases all went pretty well. I had to call obstruction on a runner rounding first base, but I called him out at second base because in my judgment he would have been out anyway had the obstruction not occurred. Well, I knew it was coming, so here comes the instructor out to play the part of the manager to argue the call. I told him to calm down and I would explain what I had to him. I explained about my judgment call and he proceeded to tell me that "You are $(*#&$#(*$&." Well, BOOM, threw him out of the game! Afterwards as I was coming off of the field one instructor told me that I nailed the obstruction call and the ejection so I was happy about that.

After dinner with some friends, went to class tonight at 8PM. We covered double header rules, forfeited games, and protest.

February 2 — Another really long day. We started the day out on the fields. Several high school teams were there and they played seven innings on all of the fields. I had a cage session during the high school games and then had innings later in the day. I had a few mistakes, but it was much better than the last two times. They told us if we give them a hard day's work on Monday that on our short day Tuesday we will have a camp game with us against each other. Everyone is tired but it is the last Saturday night here in Daytona and my buddies and I are going to go get dinner and go out tonight.

February 3 — Last Sunday in Daytona. Had a good time last night, the last Saturday night dinner and drinks down here with the friends that I have made. Just relaxing today, hoping to get my leg healed up for the last few days of class. Just laying low and looking over some stuff for our last three tests that are going to be given to us tomorrow morning. Going to order some pizza and wings, then go to a friend's room and watch the Super Bowl later tonight. Tomorrow is looking to be a good day, after our tests we get to roast the instructors so that should be a good time!

February 4 — Coming down the stretch. Today we had our last three tests and I finished the course with 242/250 questions correct. After that we had a session where the instructors ripped on all of us and then we had the chance to give it back to them, kind of an open mic forum. There was some pretty funny stuff said, and that is all I will go into about that, if you want to know more you gotta come to school! We also received our class photos and banquet tickets for tomorrow. Then we went to the fields for our last full day of work, cage sessions and live innings. After my last cage session we played 20 innings as to give everyone their chances to go and even up everyone's turn. They informed us that as a reward for hard work we are going to have a 7-inning camp game tomorrow. They divided the class up into AL and NL teams, with two instructors as managers. They

also said that everyone that is here from a foreign country has to sing their national anthem before the game. Tomorrow sounds like it will be a lot of fun.

February 5 — We are officially done! A short classroom session today on deportment and how our grades are going to be calculated. They told us that if we get a C on our evaluations, not to freak out a C means that your performance in the graded area is average with all other students, A's and B's are for doing something exceptionally well and above average. Two students got arrested last night for an alcohol-related incident, and that one of them was actually in the running for a job until that. I cannot imagine coming down here and throwing away five weeks and all that money over some stupid behavior due to alcohol. Then our camp game. What a fun time! Then we had lunch and were officially done! We have the banquet coming up in a few hours, and then evaluations are tomorrow! I cannot believe that the end is here, it doesn't seem like that long ago that I was just starting with all of this.

February 6 — Judgement day! Well, at long last we are at the end of school. Got up early and went in for evaluations. The head instructor, Brent Rice, asked me if he was correct that I did not want a job in professional baseball. After talking to him as to why I could not accept a job, he stated that he now understood. He said that the staff was actually puzzled as to why I checked the box about not wanting a job. He stated that I would not have been considered for professional baseball as I was not in the top 25, but that I would have been considered for placement into independent baseball had I chose to accept a job. He stated that they would have no problem writing a recommendation for me to any associations that I needed one for. I told them that I really wanted to get into college baseball and they told me that there is no reason, based upon my performance, why I could not have a successful career in college baseball. Here are my grades:

Attitude A (Excellent)
Coordination C (Average)
Instinct C (Average)
Mobility C (Average)

Hustle C (Average)
Timing C (Average)
Judgment C (Average)
Positioning C (Average)
Voice C (Average)
Rules Interpretation on the Field B (Above Average)
Final Test Score 242/250 96.8% (A)

I am completely satisfied with how I performed while I was down here. I know that I am 100 times the umpire that I was before, and that I can only get better with this behind me. I am a proud graduate of the Wendelstedt Professional Umpire School. One of my best friends down here made it to PBUC placement camp, and the one guy that I pegged from week one also made it. I am so excited for them and I know that I will be friends with these guys for life, and cannot wait to hear about their journey through the minor leagues. I have no doubt that my friend will make it into MiLB. I will leave you with a quote from the late founder of this school, Harry Wendelstedt: "Not everyone can be a major league umpire, but everyone can be a major league person."

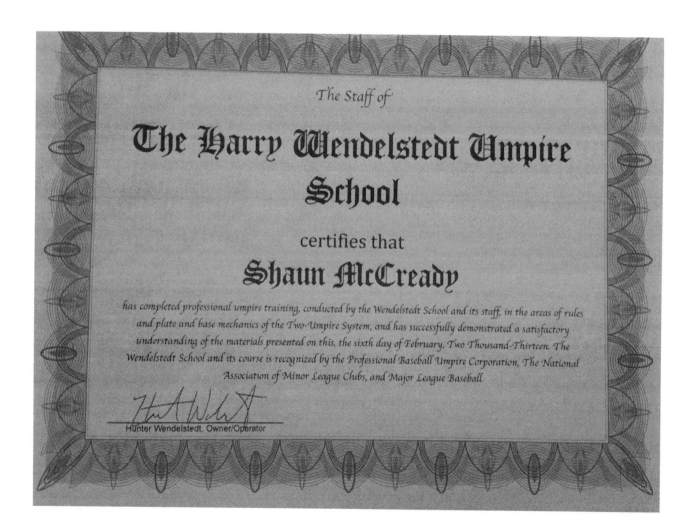

The Staff of

The Harry Wendelstedt Umpire School

certifies that

Shaun McCready

has completed professional umpire training, conducted by the Wendelstedt School and its staff, in the areas of rules and plate and base mechanics of the Two-Umpire System, and has successfully demonstrated a satisfactory understanding of the materials presented on this, the sixth day of February, Two Thousand-Thirteen. The Wendelstedt School and its course is recognized by the Professional Baseball Umpire Corporation, The National Association of Minor League Clubs, and Major League Baseball.

Hunter Wendelstedt, Owner/Operator

A Visit to the Wendelstedt Umpire School in 2017

By Bill Nowlin

After interviewing so many umpires, and hearing about their experiences in umpire school, and reading Shaun McCready's wonderful blog, I figured the final thing I needed to do to try to bring this SABR book on umpires and umpiring to completion was to see where modern professional umpiring all begins.

Hunter Wendelstedt invited me to visit after his umpire school began in January 2017, and I took him up on it, flying to Daytona Beach, Florida, and visiting the school for parts of three days from January 12-14. It was an enlightening experience.

The school has turned out umpires for all levels—some make it all the way to the big leagues, but of course there simply aren't that many openings. Others find slots in the minor leagues. Many go on to work in college or high-school ranks, some working in multiple sports. It was evident to me within just a couple of hours that a certificate of graduation from the school really meant something and would be an asset valued in many walks of life.

A quick count of today's 76 current major-league umpires shows that 39 of them are graduates of the Wendelstedt School or its predecessor Al Somers School.

This session had 139 students enrolled, 132 of them for the full course. (Two of them, including the only woman in the course, had signed up for two weeks.) There were three students from the Korean professional league. Six or seven were returning students, coming back for a second year. The students ranged in age from 16 to their early 60s. In the past, the school has had students as old as their early 70s. Almost every one of them—realistically or otherwise—declared they were seeking a position in professional baseball. There has been at least one student in recent years who was as old as 45, and ultimately hired by professional baseball.

The days are not easy. Classroom work on the 13th started at 9:00 A.M. and ran until nearly 1:00, with just over 30 minutes for lunch, and then fieldwork that ran until close to 6:00 P.M. Dinner is 7 to 8 and then most students join in study groups in the evenings. There is one day off, Sundays.

The cost to attend is $3,200 and you get a *lot* for your money. Even leaving aside the most important part—instruction and training by a dedicated, hard-working group of around 25 or 26 instructors—each student receives room and board, and umpire school gear—four shirts, a rule book, a tote bag. The school provides 20 meals a week for students (only Sunday lunch is not included in tuition) and 32 nights at the hotel. We stayed at the Best Western Castillo del Sol at Ormond Beach. You can look it up on the internet—this is indeed a beachfront hotel. Sometimes students hit the beach in the evenings, working on stances and the like.

It's about a 20-minute ride to the sports complex where the school is based. A classroom building and four baseball fields are utilized. The fields are for demonstrations and drills, and part of me was surprised to see the level of detail. Nearly an hour was

Working on mechanics, Wendelstedt School, January 2017.

spent on demonstrating the way an umpire should properly handle a discarded bat near the plate when runners are on the bases, and might come home to score—without taking your eye off the ball.

For 2016 the school added a doctor to the staff, Steven Dorsey. He took the course with his son, Harley Acosta, in 2016, and enjoyed the experience so much that he returned on staff in 2017. Harley was hired by Minor League Baseball. Steven wanted to come back. He'd seen a need—for students to improve their stretching and conditioning and for the occasional problem. Someone had collapsed on the field in 2016 and it took 20 minutes for EMS personnel to arrive. Steve told Wendelstedt, "If you will allow me to come here and lead a Bible study—that's the reason I got into medicine, to open that door for me—I will come here and help you with your medical needs." It's a win-win. He's a volunteer, the school covering his expenses. "I don't want a salary," he added, "This is just an extension of my missionary work."[1] Every day there are one or two things. The day I arrived, student Jeff Diosi suffered strained ligaments that put him on crutches. Another had very low blood pressure, with "complaints that were consistent with a neurologic deficit." Fortunately, he tested OK after being transported to the emergency room.

This is a school with a long tradition. Before it was the Wendelstedt School, it was the Al Somers School, and before that Bill McGowan's—started in 1938/39. Reverence for history was one thing that struck me right away. Students were told that their

first test was going to be at the end of the classwork on Friday the 13th. During the course, they were taught about the two-man system with a runner on second base. They were taught about the infield-fly rule, taught the discretion involved in how many pitches to allow a pitcher brought in unexpectedly (perhaps to replace an injured pitcher), taught about the 12-second rule, what constitutes a quick pitch, about the rosin bag, why an umpire's judgment call cannot be wrong (it's his judgment), and more. So what was the quiz about?

The students had all been assigned to 15 working groups for the course as a whole—the Chylak Group, the Froemming Group, Hubbard, Klem, etc.—each named after a noted past umpire. The quiz was, unexpectedly, for each group to get together and then identify images projected onto the screen at the front of the room. Each image was of a former umpire. There were five multiple-choice questions, and each group needed to come up with an answer and key it into an app on their phones. There were 10 images. The winning group was the McGowan Group, with a perfect 10-for-10. I didn't fare as well myself; I was only 8-for-10 (but plead interference in one of the two I got wrong—I couldn't see the fifth name at the bottom of the screen and that's who it was.)

Was there any reason that students planning to umpire contemporary ballgames in the twenty-first century should be able to pick out a face of an umpire who worked 80 or 100 years earlier? The reason I was given made perfect sense to me. Umpires need to stick together. They need first of all to respect the profession and each other, and a respect for those who came before and excelled is an important part of building on a tradition.

The chief of instruction at the school is Brent Rice, a former student at the school and someone who Hunter Wendelstedt said was "a real asset to the program, one of the best teachers of baseball I've ever seen."[2]

Brent Rice comes from Michigan and had been instructing at the Wendelstedt School for 17 years, the last eight of them as chief of instruction. He first attended the school at age 18, graduated, and put in his time in the minor leagues, getting as high as Double A. Much of his work is administrative and it's year-round work, though he does some forensic work for an accounting firm and a private investigation firm. He oversees the staff of 25 or so, several of whom are returnees. Junior Valentine was there, instructing for his sixth year. Brian Carnahan would be working Triple-A ball this year, in the International League; he's got a degree in environmental economics in case somehow umpiring doesn't work out.

Rice is, I observed, an exceptional teacher with a sense of perspective and good humor, and yet displays the clarity, certitude, and forcefulness it takes to command the attention of nearly 150 students for a couple of hours at a time, in the classroom or during demonstrations and drills on the fields, without allowing "drill-itis" to creep in. The demonstrative gestures we see umpires make are no accident; the students are taught to make calls loudly and aggressively—and to "sell the call." As he explained, "We're definitely a different group. A lot of Type-A personalities—and we're dealing with other Type-A personalities" in baseball's highly competitive ballplayers and managers.

Umpires are taught, though, to always keep their chest to the ball, and never to rush their mechanics.

I told him that most of the games I see are big-league games, and that it was an eye-opener to see the instruction for two-man crews, to see how much more work there seemed to be for umpires working (as all students initially will) in two-man crews.

Rice said, "Way more! Now, in some aspects, it's easier, though. You don't have a lot of gray areas. One umpire does *this*, and there's only one other umpire so that umpire does *that*. There are a lot of good things in the two-umpire system. We say that in the two-umpire system, a lot of it is just black and white. You do this; I do that. In the three-umpire system, it becomes a lot more about verbal communication. You're rotating, and you're covering up for another umpire, and so a lot of it's verbal communication. Yelling on the field and communicating with each other. With the four-umpire system, when they get there, there's

Brent Rice, Chief of Instruction, Wendelstedt School, January 2017.

obviously verbal communication involved, but it's a lot more visual communication."[3]

There are a lot more people in the stands in major-league ballparks. It's much louder.

"That's right. It's more of a looking at each other. Pre-pitch signals to determine what's going to happen. Four-man is more difficult in some ways, because you have a lot more things that you *could* end up doing. Your responsibilities change simply on where the ball is hit. In the two-umpire system, OK, it's hit there. This is where I go. But you're definitely covering a lot more of the field when you're in the two-umpire system."

The basics are the basics, though, and the class was building from the two-man system, on up. Major-league umpires Dana DeMuth and Ed Hickox were at school for the duration. Dana, who had first attended the school in 1976, the year before Al Somers sold it to Harry Wendelstedt, told me that what I was seeing was more or less akin to observing students finish elementary school. Were I to come back in three weeks, he said, I'd be impressed at the tremendous progress the students had made.[4]

Hunter Wendelstedt expressed his feelings that the Class of 2017 was one of the best he's seen, "a class like I've never seen in terms of their work ethic." That will just make it more difficult for the staff in the end. "Our evaluation day is the hardest day for us. You have to look somebody in the eye and say, 'Your highest level is going to be high school. You can work high school and you're going to do good but don't try and do college.' And that's really hard to do." And when it comes right down to it, there may be far more people truly qualified to start working in professional baseball—but only so many openings.

There's good news for some, though. In fact, just a day or so before I arrived, Wendelstedt explained,

"We have a couple of kids—instructors—who just found out they're getting big-league spring training. Rich Rieker and Ed Rapuano came and they told the kids they were going to big-league spring. They worked in the Fall League. They're going to get the opportunity to work spring-training games and then if they're successful, they might get the opportunity to fill in at the major-league level this year. So it's a pretty exciting time for them. Their dream started here, coming through these doors, and now there are big-league supervisors on these fields saying. 'You know what? We're going to give you a shot.' I find that pretty cool."

NOTES

1   Author interview with Dr. Steven Dorsey, January 13, 2017.

2   Author interview with Hunter Wendelstedt, January 12, 2017.

3   Author interview with Brent Rice, January 12, 2017.

4   Author interview with Dana DeMuth, January 13, 2017.

The Evolution of Umpires' Equipment and Uniforms

By Bob Webster

The evolution of umpires' equipment and uniforms began in the mid-nineteenth century when modern baseball under the New York Rules was introduced. Beginning in 1846 when the New York Rules came into effect and the popularity of baseball began to spread across the country, umpires had to enforce the rules of play. Since leagues were not yet created, the competing teams were likely from nearby towns and the umpires were selected by the home team. The umpires were supposedly well-known townspeople of high ethical standards, such as lawyers, merchants, and doctors.[1] They were the "representatives of authority." There were no regulations on the umpires' uniforms, but they were expected to be one of the most formally and conservatively dressed men at the grounds.[2] The early umpires were dressed in a "sober black suit, white linen shirt, black scarf ties, and a tall silk hat."[3]

Umpires' dress began to evolve about 20 years before they began using protective equipment.

One of the first "tools of the trade" was the ball-and-strike indicator, introduced in 1874. The home teams were required to furnish a device consisting of pieces of wood moving on a wire, like a billiard tally, to track balls and strikes. In 1875 Peck & Snyder Sporting Goods began selling an "Umpires Assistant," a ball-and-strike indicator made of black walnut with each ball and strike registered by turning the thumb screw. By 1885 the technology was improved to include a method for keeping track of runs scored in addition to the balls and strikes.[4]

In 1882 the American Association, organized as a major league the year before, became the first league to require umpires to wear a uniform, a blue wool suit. This was the first time umpires officiated in uniforms rather than their own clothes.[5] The Association decided that having the umpires wear the same uniform would make a statement about their authority to judge the action on the playing field as well as making the single umpire working the game more identifiable to players and spectators as he moved around the field to make a call.[6]

At first the umpire made calls from a stationary position behind the pitcher. Starting in the 1880s National League umpires worked from behind home plate, where they had a complete view of the field. The umpire could also move around the field to get the best view of a play in order to make the best call possible.[7]

The National League adopted umpires' uniforms in 1883, and the American League did when it was founded in 1901.[8]

There were only slight changes in the appearance of the umpires until the 1960s.

Umpires' protective equipment evolved just as did the catchers' equipment and the game itself. A rule change in 1880 required that the catchers had to catch the ball on a fly to record a strikeout.[9] The catchers thus had to move closer to the batter and home plate, making their job far more dangerous. As the catchers moved closer to the plate, so did the umpires. Both required protection.

The first form of protective equipment used by catchers and umpires was the face mask, in 1882.[10] Dick Higham is credited with being the first umpire to wear one.[11]

Top hats could no longer be worn with the face masks, and in the June 21, 1886, issue of *The Sporting News* the C.J. Chapin Arms Company, a dealer in firearms and sporting goods, advertised a new sunshade hat for $1. Wearing the hat allowed umpires to dispense with the umbrellas they held to ward off the sun's rays, an annoyance to catchers.[12] Eventually base umpires wore a "university style" of cap while the home plate umpire wore a shorter-billed "Boston style" cap that would fit under his mask.[13]

After the face mask was widely accepted and used throughout the umpiring community, the next piece of equipment introduced was the chest protector. The earliest chest protector was created by umpire John Gaffney, who in the 1888 season was reported to be wearing "an ingenious breast and stomach protector … made of pasteboard in sections, joined together with elastic, and made to fit tight around."[14] When Gaffney buttoned up his cardigan jacket, no one would know he was wearing a protector. He said he had been "hit so often in the chest and over his heart that he had to make some means to save his life."[15] By the end of the 1891 season most umpires were following Gaffney's lead by wearing cork chest protectors. In 1913 Bill Klem was credited with having invented the aluminum rib protector, which was worn inside the coat.[16] But Klem maintained that umpire Jack Sheridan invented the inside chest protector after suffering numerous injuries. Sheridan used a 20-by-10-inch hotel ledger which was worn inside his coat.[17]

Bill Klem also claimed that the inside protector gave him a better view of the ball. Before that, umpires used a "balloon," the name for the outside protector because it had an inflatable bladder that deflated for travel and was worn outside the coat. The outside protector evolved in design to where it could not be deflated. Therefore, two outside protectors were kept at each ballpark so that umpires did not have to travel with them.[18]

Following Klem's lead, the National League eventually made the inside chest protector mandatory for its The only exceptions were Lou Jorda and Beans Reardon, who were allowed to continue wearing the balloon, and Jocko Conlan, who was allowed to wear it for five more years because he had a throat problem and the outside protector offered greater protection.[19]

The next piece of protective gear to be introduced to the umpires was the shin guard. For years it was determined that since the umpire stood behind the catcher, they didn't need shin guards. The earliest reported use of shin guards by an umpire were by Bob Emslie in 1900, when he showed up wearing cricket pads.[20] By 1911 shin guards were in standard use, worn under the umpire's pants and slightly smaller than the catcher's shin guards.[21]

Changes in equipment have required changes in uniforms. Wearing shin guards under the pants, required that home-plate umpires' pants have larger legs. When the chest protector moved from the balloon style to being worn inside the coat, the coats became bigger.

Whisk brooms replaced the large brooms used in both the National and American Leagues after Chicago Cubs outfielder Jack McCarthy stepped on a broom and sprained his ankle in a game on May 14, 1904.

By 1906 umpires could buy a kit to screw in spiked plates to prevent slipping on the field.[22] Toe pads were introduced by umpire Jim Johnson in 1912.[23] Since the late 1930s, umpire shoes have been available with a steel toe. The Major League Umpires Association has its own shoe endorsement.[24]

After blue suits became the symbol of authority for major-league baseball, they remained so with slight variation until the 1960s.[25] The coat was modified over the years to keep up with changes in the game. As inside chest protectors became more common, the umpires wore jackets two sizes larger than usual to present a neatly tailored appearance.[26] After Ray Chapman was killed by a Carl Mays pitch in August 1920, presumably because he couldn't see the dirty ball as it came toward him, the "clean ball rule" was introduced, requiring the home-plate umpire to carry a supply of new balls. His suit jacket had larger pockets to carry the additional baseballs.[27]

In 1913 American League President Ban Johnson announced that an alternate white flannel suit would be worn on holidays and when the president of the United States attended a game.[28] That year he also decided that umpires would wear a row of braid on their coat sleeves for each year of service, to be replaced by a gold star after five years.[29]

The white flannel suits quickly went away, but in 1926 alternate colored suits were tried again, this time light brown khaki suits for summer games. On "gala days" umpires wore "peachy ice-cream outfits."[30] The umpires accepted these outfits enthusiastically, even placing carnations in the button holes on Mother's Day, the first day of wearing the new garb.[31] After hoots and catcalls greeted the umpires when they took the field, they went back to the traditional blue for the next 40 years.[32] A few years later the National League tried white trousers and blue blazers, but the players made a sport of kicking dirt on the white pants.[33]

During the last half of the nineteenth century and the first half of the twentieth, fans wore suits to games. By the 1960s they were wearing sport shirts, khaki pants, jeans, shorts, and T-shirts to games. The umpire's dress was way out of style. The days of attending a game in a suit were gone unless you came directly from work.[34] In the transformation to a more relaxed atmosphere at the ballpark, the umpires appeared to project a formal, stiff, undertaker image. They needed to look more modern and the traditional colors did not look good on television. Times were changing and baseball umpires had to adapt while continuing to project an authoritative image.[35]

On March 20, 1968, the American League announced the first change in umpires' attire in three decades. They began wearing blue blazer-style jackets and gray slacks with a white shirt. In hot weather the umpires could wear a blue shirt with the league's symbol on the breast pocket with gray slacks, and without a jacket.[36]

The National League retained the blue suits, but added patches on the breast pocket and sleeves. In 1970 the league permitted umpires to wear short-sleeved blue shirts.[37] The same year, the NL attached identification numbers to the umpires' right sleeve, moving the league patch to the chest.[38]

When the leagues relaxed their rules about wearing jackets, the umpires needed something to hold spare baseballs. Two ball bags hung from an umpire's belt and each held six balls.[39]

By the mid-'60s the American League was encouraging its umpires to use the inside protector, in part so they would look better on television. For the 1977 season, the inside chest protector was made mandatory for all new American League umpires.

The last umpire to wear the outside chest protector was Jerry Neudecker in 1985, his last year before retiring.[40]

The chest protector had an influence on how the umpires called strikes. National League umpires could squat lower while wearing the inside protector and see around the catcher, better enabling them to see low strikes. American league umpires stood more upright with the balloon protector, and called more high strikes.[41]

The leagues also started to pay for umpires' uniforms in the 1970s, a cost the umpires had to bear up to that point.[42]

This was the beginning of many slight changes to umpires' uniforms for years to come. Sometime in the early '70s, National League umpires were permitted to wear black turtlenecks under their blue suit jackets as well as a dark T-shirt under their uniform shirts, for a popular layered look.[43]

In 1975 the American League broke tradition by attiring the umpires in maroon suit jackets, the first deviation from blue since the 1920s. These maroon coats were worn with dark gray or black slacks, a white shirt, black tie, and a hat with a white shield.[44]

By 1980 both the American and National Leagues began to move more and more toward identical standards. Both leagues were now required to wear the inside chest protector (with the few specific exceptions), and umpires from both leagues came out of the same umpire schools and were governed by the Umpire Development Program.[45] Both leagues adopted the blue blazer and gray trouser combination with a white AL or NL on the dark blue cap. League emblems were located on the left jacket pocket. Turtlenecks and short-sleeved shirts continued to be worn.[46] The trend of slight color changes and shirt styles continued into the twenty-first century.

An interest in focusing on safety for both the players and the umpires brought many technology advancements to the game. Joe West, who umpired his first major-league game in 1976 at age 23, designed and patented the only umpire gear endorsed by Major League Baseball for use by its umpires.[47] The "West

Vest" line of umpires' equipment is made by Wilson Sporting Goods.

The "Pro Platinum Chest Protector" is manufactured for maximum protection. The reason is that it fits better. This chest protector conforms to the shoulders, and the enhanced side pads add comfort and protection. It has the most armor and fits the best, making it the most widely used chest protector today.

Joe West also designed a mask that is made with two single crossbars made of solid steel for strength. This style is an upgrade from the hinged masks that create a blind spot on balls hit up or down.[48] Today's masks are made with a variety of pads including deerskin and memory foam, which conforms to the face and are wrapped in a moisture wicking fabric.[49]

Innovations in the West Vest line of shin guards includes protecting one of the hardest areas to protect—the knees. Increased padding behind the knees absorbs the blows so the knees and legs don't need to. These shin guards are adjustable in many ways to help make the best fit for each umpire.[50]

West Vest supplies other umpire protection equipment like the biceps protectors and throat protector that hangs from the mask and protects the throat from foul tips.[51]

Toward the end of the twentieth century, some catchers and umpires began wearing hockey-style masks, which provide better visibility and protection from a hitter's backswing, but does not offer as much protection from foul tips as the conventional mask and skull caps from the past. Since concussions from foul tips are much more common than being hit in the back of the head with a backswing, many catchers and umpires who tried the hockey-style helmets have gone back to the conventional mask.

Former official Dick Honig started Honig's Whistle Stop in 1984, a supply house for officiating clothing and equipment which has expanded to eight branch offices in addition to the main office in Ann Arbor, Michigan.[52]

Honig's latest Pro-Elite Chest Protector key features include increased strength, rigidity, and hardness, as well as being lightweight. Removable Velcro pads on the backside provide extra protection while at

the same time creating a quarter-inch space between the protector and the torso for improved air flow and comfort. A vest style mesh harness replaces the typical "y-strap" harness for added comfort and ventilation. Additional waist and shoulder adjustment straps make this chest protector fit like a glove.[53]

As with the chest protectors, Honig's shin guards and face masks are designed to provide the greatest protection as well as comfort for today's umpires.

Recent advancements have allowed the umpires' uniforms to be more comfortable with variations for the weather, and technology advancements in equipment are providing the umpires with a safer and more comfortable environment.

NOTES

1   Elizabeth K. Martin, *The Development of Baseball Umpires' Uniforms, 1846-1996* (University of Rhode Island master's thesis, 1997), 6.

2   Martin, 1.

3   Matin, 5.

4   Peter Morris, *A Game of Inches* (Chicago: Ivan R. Dee Publisher, 2006), 391.

5   Martin, 2.

6   Ibid.

7   Martin, 4.

8   Martin, 13.

9   Martin, 64.

10 Morris, 391.

11 Jonathan Fraser Light, *The Cultural Encyclopedia of Baseball, 2nd Edition* (Jefferson, North Carolina: McFarland & Company, Inc., 2005), 970.

12 Morris, 391; *The Sporting News*, June 21, 1886.

13 Light, 970.

14 Morris, 391.

15 Ibid.

16 Ibid.

17 Light, 970.

18 Ibid.

19 Ibid.

20 Morris, 391.

21 Light, 970.

22 Light, 971.

23 Morris, 391; *The Sporting News*, June 15, 1912.

24 Light, 971.

25 Martin, 4.

26 Martin, 16.

27 Ibid.

28 Martin, 34.

29 Ibid.

30 Ibid.

31 Ibid.

32 Ibid.

33 Ibid.

34 Martin, 37.

35 Ibid.

36 Ibid., 39.

37 Ibid.

38 Martin, 40.

39 Light, 970.

40 Ibid.

41 Ibid.

42 Martin, 40.

43 Ibid.

44 Ibid.

45 Martin, 43.

46 Ibid.

47 Umpirejoewest.com/umpire_equipment.htm.

48 Ibid.

49 Ibid.

50 Ibid.

51 Ibid.

52 honigs.com/

53 Ibid.

Ted Barrett's Chest Protector and Plate Brush

Bill Nowlin: Bob Webster told me you have the same chest protector you've had since 1991?

Ted Barrett: 1992. My Carlucci.

BN: You never found a better one? Or is for good luck?

TB: No, it's good protection. He custom made them. If you look up Cecil Carlucci, he was one of those Coast League umpires. He was one of that group of Pacific Coast League umpires; they thought the PCL was going to be like a third big league. A bunch of them were offered major-league jobs and they didn't take them. He was one of them. I think he was the record holder for the number of games in the PCL. He was an older guy by the time I knew him, and he custom made these. He's passed away since, so they don't make them anymore. He made another one for me. I've got a black one. So I still have one in reserve, when this one goes.

BN: I guess this has taken a few hits over the years.

TB: Yeah, and I've had the straps re-done by a luggage guy. It's kind of distinctive when you see the blue, especially when I wear the plate coat where the blue's exposed.

BN: I think that's pretty cool that you've had the same protector for more than 25 years now.

TB: Yeah, and not only that. I've had a couple of things I've had even longer. This is my grandpa's belt. When my grandpa passed away, I got his belt. I wear it behind the plate, just to honor my grandpa. I'll be wearing it tonight.

I've had this brush since the day I got in the game.

From a conversation with Ted Barrett before the August 13, 2016 ballgame at Fenway Park.

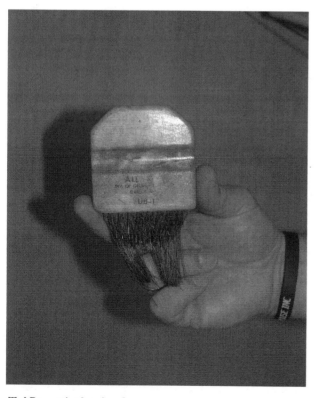

Ted Barrett's plate brush.

Ted Barrett with his 1992 Carlucci chest protector, August 14, 2016.

What Do Umpires Do Exactly?

By Al Piacente

With the advent of limited instant replay in MLB in 2008, its subsequent expansion in 2014,[1] and technological innovations like strike-zone automation on the horizon across baseball,[2] it makes sense for us to ask in a serious vein what has been asked before mostly tongue-in-cheek: What do umpires do exactly? Angry musing after a blown or controversial call, blown or controversial at least to the "experts" sitting in the dugouts, the stands, the press boxes, and/or behind their TV sets, laptops, and phones, has prompted and will continue to prompt the knee-jerk rhetorical question concerning what umpires do, e.g., "What do those bums do exactly?!" But ask the question seriously and not rhetorically, as we will here, and what becomes clear is that the frequent anger directed toward umpires, as well as the introduction of technology into umpiring, is based on the assumption that we all know precisely what umpires *do*, *should do*, and sometimes *fail to do*, and how technology can help.[3] What also becomes clear is that this conventional wisdom about umpiring, like so much conventional wisdom, is at best only partially correct; a view that its failings show the need for a better, more fully developed picture of what umpires do, but also a view that points us in the direction of that picture, one suggesting we may want to alter our too often negative view of umpiring and umpires and that can provide us with a sense of the role technology can (and cannot) play in umpiring.

The Assumed View

In his late-seventeenth-century *Second Treatise of Government*, John Locke, the godfather of what might be called today "classical liberalism"—as opposed to liberalism's twentieth-century counterpart championed by the likes of Franklin Roosevelt—speaks of sovereign authority in society as a form of authority where "all private judgement of every particular member being excluded, the community comes to be *umpire*, by settled standing rules, indifferent, and the same to all parties."[4] A view with roots deeper into history than even Locke, Locke nonetheless sums up in one fell swoop what he and most of us take to be the role of an umpire, whether that umpire is one responsible for officiating over society in general, or officiating over something as humble as a game of baseball: umpires must be, at base, *neutral or impartial in applying the rules*. They must manifest that ideal of blindfolded justice captured in the statues and paintings found in courtrooms the world over, an ideal that appears odd considering that one of the common insults hurled at umpires (in baseball at least) is the yet again rhetorical question "What are you ump, blind?" Umpires in baseball (and out) must manifest *blindness*.

But this long-standing view of umpires, now the conventional wisdom assumed true by most of us to the point that we can call it the Assumed View (AV), understands blindness in a peculiar way. Umpires in and out of baseball must keep their *eyes wide shut* when applying the rules to a particular situation, but they must keep their *eyes wide open* when ascertaining the facts of a particular situation, the facts in whose terms their judgment is rendered. Indeed, it is here that we find the source of the insult questioning a baseball umpire's ability to see, because unlike the umpires who happen to sit under or around those statues and paintings in courtrooms, umpires we otherwise know today mostly as "judges"—who stand in for the community according to Locke—umpires on the baseball diamond are expected not just to rule based on the facts, they are expected to gather the facts, gather them by way of being in a unique eyewitness position to the events in question.[5] Unlike judges, whom, on the AV, umpires might seem to mirror so closely and do mirror so closely at certain points, baseball umpires play the role of judges but also the roles of eyewitnesses and at time detectives (e.g., the appeal by the home-plate umpire to the third- or first-base umpire to determine if a batter checked their swing). Umpires are even required, according to the AV, to play the role of executive/punisher when their judgments are questioned too forcefully (e.g., throwing a player or manager out of a game), making umpires in baseball the embodiment of nothing more nor less than of the *entire criminal justice system.*

Baseball umpires, to be good umpires, therefore should and must, on the AV, manifest both blindness and not, in exactly the right measure at exactly the right time, with any act of umpiring involving at least the following: 1] accurately witnessing the event; 2] applying the relevant standing rule covering the event in an impartial fashion; 3] rendering judgment of the event accordingly; 4] preparing to execute 1, 2, and 3 again if and when necessary. And our anger, as well as the increasing reach for technology, is built around the fact that we often believe umpires fail at 1, 2, 3, or 4. We are angry because we believe the umpire either was blind when they shouldn't have been, or wasn't blind when they should have been, a failing in either case that an appropriately tuned bit of technology would seem to be able to avoid (the attention of a camera never wanders, and computer algorithms do not care at all what uniform you are wearing or how much money you might be willing to pay).

Problems for the AV

On the AV, umpires in baseball are like judges only more so, a point that might seem to settle exactly what umpires do and in fact should do, when our anger is appropriate and when it is not, and how we can keep umpires from falling short of what they should do (with technology and otherwise).[6] It might, until we notice a few problem cases.

Problem Case 1: Ruling when there is no rule

Wes Curry, while umpiring an 1887 American Association game between Louisville and Brooklyn, calls a Louisville player who crossed home plate out even though there was no force at home nor did the catcher make a tag with the ball. Curry does so

because a Louisville player who had crossed home plate immediately before had turned around and "interfered with" the Brooklyn catcher, impeding the catcher's ability to make a tag.[7] A reasonable enough call we might think, the problem is that at the time there was *only* a rule that prevented "baserunners" from interfering with play on the field and once the previous Louisville player had crossed home plate he was no longer, technically speaking, a baserunner. Not a baserunner at the point of interference; again technically speaking, no rule thus existed in terms of which that interference by a nonbaserunner could be viewed as an infraction allowing Wes Curry to call the next baserunner out. As such, if we accept the AV, which requires every act of umpiring to involve the above 1, 2, 3, and 4, Curry's call must be invalidated because 2 never occurred. There was no application of a rule based on the facts of the situation because there was no rule *at all*. Hence, either we invalidate Curry's call, or we admit that the AV is wrong because 2 is not a necessary condition for every act of umpiring.

Problem Case 2: Sticking too closely to a rule

In 1983, nearly 100 years after the call of Wes Curry, George Brett of the Kansas City Royals was called out after hitting a home run in a game against the New York Yankees. He was called out because Yankees manager Billy Martin, having noticed that Brett had used a bat with pine tar too high up on the handle, maintained that the use of that bat, which was an illegal bat as it was clearly altered contrary to the rules (the umpires actually measured how high the pine tar went), not only invalidated Brett's home run, but necessitated Brett's being called out because that is what the rules stipulate when an illegal bat is used. Though loath to do so, given that the infraction seemed irrelevant to the play in question, the umpires nonetheless agreed with Martin, including the lead umpire for the game Joe Brinkman. After all, Brett had contravened a standing rule against the use of an illegal bat, a rule that was clearly in place (it was rule 1.10 [b] at the time), and as Brinkman famously later commented in his handbook for umpires, "(R)ules are all an umpire has to work with." Operating under the AV's 2, the umpires thus called Brett out, the home run was voided, and the game was in turn lost by the Royals as Brett was the third out in the Royals' last at-bat. Until American League President Lee MacPhail intervened and overturned the umpires' decision, that is.

Arguing that "games should be won and lost on the playing field—not through technicalities of the rules,"[8] MacPhail thought the overuse of pine tar, while technically in violation of the rules governing bats, nonetheless did not rise to the level of subterfuge or cheating, especially given that pine tar too high up on a bat more likely impedes rather than aids batters. In other words, unlike the Wes Curry case, the umpires had been operating *exactly* as the AV would suggest they should, with each 1, 2, 3, and 4 taking place. But their decision did not, in fact, stick (apologies for the pine-tar pun). And it did not stick because according to MacPhail and ultimately to history, the umpires were overly strict when performing 2, possibly to the point of being martinets and committing the logical Fallacy of Accident.[9] Thus we are presented with the same choice as above only now arrived at from the opposite direction: Do we abandon MacPhail's reversal and side with the umpires on the field, or do we abandon the AV?

Problem Case 3: Not sticking to a rule closely enough

The calling of balls and strikes has a rather notorious history in baseball. Not only has the strike zone been redefined 12 times in baseball since 1876 (i.e., 1887, 1894, 1899, 1901, 1907, 1910, 1950, 1957, 1963, 1969, 1988, 1996),[10] but what *counts as* a strike in actual play is famously (infamously?) subject to the home-plate umpire's discretion and to this day rarely adheres to the strict definition of a strike—which stands at present as that space over home plate between a batter's armpits and the bottom of their knees.[11] Arguably the greatest area of discretion in umpiring, as well as the most active in terms of baseball's attempting to "refine" a rule—the rule has been changed on average nearly once every 12 years—what is odd is that through all the exercises of discretion and changes of the rule, batting averages have hovered in the mid- to high .200s during this roughly 130-140 year period,[12] with averages around .260 remaining the most con-

stant.[13] Such constancy and consistency in batting averages across so much time, through so many umpires exercising discretion and so many changes of the rule defining the strike zone would make it seem that when calling balls and strikes umpires have been and are operating according to some "rule" *other than* the rule defining balls and strikes as stated in the rulebook. Unlike the prior two cases, one where a call was made without there being an antecedent rule and one where there was an antecedent rule that was deemed to be followed too closely, here we have a case where a rule would seem not to be followed closely enough. No matter that a euphemism may be applied, namely "discretion," once again we seem to find ourselves in a dilemma where the actual world of umpiring must be abandoned, or the AV, and 2 in particular, must be called into question if not outright jettisoned.

The Good-of-the-Game View

Confronted in each case with the choice of either calling into question the legitimacy of actual umpiring and rules application in baseball or abandoning the long-standing AV, many of us might be willing to bite the bullet and opt for the former. (Though imagine the number of asterisks this means we would have to enter in to the record books!) But J.S. Russell, who first joined together these three cases in his widely read essay "Taking Umpiring Seriously," argues that it is the latter course we should follow. The AV, not umpiring history, must give way because contrary to conventional wisdom, the AV's account of umpiring as appropriate blindness and appropriate sightedness falls short of capturing the essence of umpiring. Actual umpiring shows that at times any one of the AV's 1, 2, 3, or 4 may be missing, or they may all be present, yet this does not tell us definitely about the legitimacy of the umpiring in question.

Citing the work of the late legal philosopher Ronald Dworkin, who saw exactly the same difficulties confronting those nonbaseball umpires we met while discussing Locke, i.e., judges, Russell argues that in baseball *"rules should be interpreted according to principles of fair play and sportsmanship, and so that the good conduct of games is maintained."*[14] Simply put, sound umpiring, like sound judicial reasoning, requires at times what Russell calls, following Dworkin, "hard cases"; that umpires, like judges, appeal to a broader set of rules than those actually present in the rule books of the game (or law books of society); a broader set in the case of baseball that Russell calls the *principles of fair play and sportsmanship*. The basic idea being that when the rules in the rulebook contradict in some way the principles of fair play and sportsmanship and hence the good conduct of games, umpires, or even a league president, *have, do, must, and should* rule according to the broader principles of fair play and sportsmanship. To put this in terms of the AV's four-part analysis of good umpiring, 2 is not always the straightforward act of rules ap-

plication it seems to be. Rules themselves, at times (in hard cases), butt up against a set of "meta-rules" that are the *principles of fair play and sportsmanship*, and when they do, the meta-rules should prevail. In other words 2, rather than being a one-step process of rules application, is (again in hard cases at least) a two-step process: 2a) interpret the rule (according to the principles of fair play and sportsmanship); 2b) apply the rule.

Using this "Good-of-the-Game View" (GGV) as we can call it, Russell attempts to absorb the AV, seeing the AV as the appropriate way to view umpiring when cases are *not* hard—as they mostly are not—yet with the GGV Russell can go beyond the AV to explain why Curry, MacPhail, a century or

THE UMPIRE

Tim Hurst carries around with him the following touching lines, which he received from an admiring Philadelphia poet:

Who enters meekly at the gate?
Who walks unnoticed to the plate?
Who cares not what will be his fate?
　　The Umpire.

Who's damned at once by all the throng?
Who gets abuse from weak and strong?
Who's never right and always wrong?
　　The Umpire.

Who's called by every nasty word
That's in the English language heard?
Who is a "lobster," yet a "bird?"
　　The Umpire.

Who takes his life within his hands,
When he as arbutrator stands,
Yet stolidly ignores commants?
　　The Umpire.

Who'll fight each "hoodlum" one by one,
Return for more when they are "done?"
Who from ten thousand will not run?
　　The Umpire.

Who really is a hero bold,
As great as any knight of old,
If half the truth were only told?
　　The Umpire.

Who stands out there upon the field
Like adamant, and will not yield?
Whose nerves by insult have been steeled?
　　The Umpire.

Who kicks when losing games just now,
And starts up each disgraceful row?
The "good old has-beens," they know how –
　　The Umpire.

Who, like us all, sometimes may err?
Who's only human, as it were,
Yet does his best, ignores each slur?
　　The Umpire.

Who some day will arise in might,
Assert his manhood – ruffians smite?
Who'll then be cheered from morn 'till night?
　　The Umpire.

Trenton Evening Times, May 12, 1907: 18.

more of umpires exercising discretion from behind home plate, and a host of other moments from the history of umpiring (we have hardly exhausted the sound decisions made in hard cases from the history of baseball) have all acted appropriately. That is, it becomes possible to account for many of the most controversial moments from the history of baseball umpiring by showing how those moments are, in point of fact, not that controversial when the AV is transcended in favor of the GGV. Returning to the three cases in front of us, through the GGV Wes Curry is vindicated when he calls the second Louisville player out in the absence of a rule because otherwise baseball would become "a nine-inning-long wrestling match."[15] Lee MacPhail is made clearly right in overturning the technically correct decision of Brinkman and his crew because had he not, the minutiae of the rules would have worked counter to Brett's superior play and athleticism. And home-plate umpires' use of discretion in calling balls and strikes is upheld because discretion (along with frequent rule changes) helps keep play between offense and defense in relative equilibrium across time.

But the GGV does more than just set the historical umpiring record straight. The GGV can, according to Russell, provide a fully general theory of umpiring through which it becomes possible to improve umpiring now and in the future—hence Russell's subtitle "How Philosophy Can Help Umpires Make the Right Calls." For instance, the GGV allows us to address present controversies such as those surrounding performance-enhancing drugs (PEDs) or the one with which we started this essay about ever-increasing amounts of technology entering umpiring. Clearly, on the GGV, umpires and leagues should act in every way to keep PEDs out of baseball, otherwise baseball is slated to become a contest between competing pharmaceutical companies, not competing athletes (hardly the point of athletic competition). And just as clearly, the GGV shows technology has a positive role to play in aiding baseball umpires to be appropriately blind and sighted in non-hard cases (which is what umpires confront 99.9 percent of the time), but has no role in *determining* hard cases, as

algorithms are quite poor at figuring out what is sportsmanlike, or at giving meaning to the first G in GGV. Technology has had and can continue to have a role in umpiring for the GGV, but the flesh-and-blood umpires we know and love to hate (and sometimes love, respect, and admire) nonetheless should have, and must continue to have, job security.

Problems for the GGV

By combining the AV's emphasis on good umpiring as appropriate blindness and sightedness with a more nuanced understanding of the nature of appropriate blindness in hard cases (turning the AV's 2 into 2a and 2b), the GGV gives us an alternative view of baseball umpiring with impact both rearward and forward-looking. Understanding blindness to mean in part what it does to the AV, namely impartial application of the rules (2b), nuance enters in that the rules in the rulebooks are themselves to be measured against the rules of a broader sporting ethic (2a), an ethic that must be in the "mind's eye" of those applying the rules (mostly umpires), especially when the rules in the rulebook contradict (at least in a particular instance) that ethic (creating a hard case). Giving us not only an alternative to the AV, the GGV allows us a way to see much actual umpiring as in line with umpiring's "best practices," relieving us of what the AV seemed to require, which was overturning what has happened in history, and continues to happen now, at many points. It also gives us a way of defining our anger as appropriate or not, and it gives us insight into how umpiring might need to change now and in the future, especially in regard to technology.

So, problem cases solved and our title question answered? Do we now know what umpires do exactly? Well, not so fast.

The GGV understands appropriate blindness and sightedness in umpiring as the AV's 2, but it breaks up the one-step 2 into the two-step 2a and 2b in hard cases. The GGV then requires that in such hard cases not only that 2a be performed but that it be performed in what we can call a "loose" manner, whereby the rule in question gets interpreted in light of the broader *principles of fair play and sportsmanship* and not by the "strict" definition of the rule (what might be called the "technical" definition following MacPhail in the Brett case). But this raises the question: how loose is too loose?

Take the example of arguably the most exciting time in recent baseball history—at least from the perspective of fans—when from the mid-1990s to the mid-2000s benchmark records in hitting, especially home-run hitting, were set.[16] As we know now, this same period happened to coincide with the heyday of PEDs in baseball, and, in fact, we now know that many of those who set the records were "juiced." According to the AV and its one-step 2, where rules are strictly understood and no separate act of interpretation takes place (there is only 2b not 2a, so to speak), it would seem that umpiring and rules application in baseball more generally would demand that no matter the excitement of those times, rules against PEDs were broken and therefore the records in question should not count, and had umpires known players on the field had broken the rules in relation to PEDs, they should have ejected them from play. A point with which the GGV would seem, on the surface, to agree because of the line of reasoning expressed above about competing pharmaceutical companies. PEDs do not constitute for the GGV a hard case and hence 2 alone is sufficient.

However, is 2 alone sufficient here for the GGV? If we define the "good of the game" not primarily in terms of the pursuit of some sort of "pure" athletic competition where PEDs and the "unfair" advantage they bring offend "sportsmanship," but instead as athletic activity focused upon the *excellence* produced in play, it appears clear the GGV can and should yield a very different result from the AV. Focus on that part of sportsmanship concerned with excellent performance and not purity of competition (as MacPhail did in the George Brett case), and the GGV apparently tells us that the batting records of the 1990s/2000s should stand and that umpires, leagues, and frankly all of us should be more "loose" in our interpretation of the injunction against using PEDs. We should, because now we confront a "hard case" where there is a contradiction between the rules and the principles of fair play and sportsmanship (remember we are understanding sportsmanship primarily in terms of the pursuit of athletic excellence) and thus there is a need for 2a and 2b, no longer just 2, with, according to the GGV, the fair play and sportsmanship "meta-rule" winning out in 2a. The point is that given that one of the central aspects of sportsmanship is the production of athletic excellence, one as important as and maybe more important than some longed-for purity in competition, there is no necessity to siding with purity. Indeed, "purity" itself seems subject to a "loose" interpretation as it isn't clear why cortisone injections and Tommy John surgery are qualitatively different than PEDs. Because one heals injury while the other just boosts performance? But why is that definitive?

The GGV, it seems, is caught in an infinite regress of interpretation, one we have just seen in operation as a matter of fact. Returning to our above case, when the rule against PEDs is to be understood against the meta-rule of fair play and sportsmanship, we confront the question of how best to interpret "sportsmanship" and "fair play"? Do we interpret *that* rule in a *strict* or *loose* fashion? Do they even have a *strict* and *loose* fashion of interpretation? We are now in need of a rule for interpreting the meta-rule, some now meta-meta-rule which tells us about how to understand fair play and sportsmanship, about just how loose is too loose. But this meta-meta-rule will in turn require its own interpretation, putting us in need of a meta-meta-meta-rule, and so on ad infinitum. The GGV, rather than addressing the problems confronting the AV, especially the all-important 2 of the AV's four-part analysis of good umpiring when it confronts actual umpiring history, instead just re-creates the problem at a higher level of analysis. 2 must ultimately yield to 2a and 2b in hard cases according to the GGV, but this means 2a must in turn yield to 2aa, which in turn must yield to 2aaa, etc. The GGV, for all its nuance, simply re-creates the same problem confronted by the AV only now at the meta-level, and thus, in the end of it all, we must wonder just how different are the AV and GGV?

The Common Law View

What all this tells us is two-fold. First, that the conventional wisdom of the AV has never been available to us. (There goes that possibility for those who a while back, in the face of the three cases raised by Russell, were ready to become bullet biters.) It has not, because the 2 in the AV's 1, 2, 3, and 4 is at base *always* what the GGV understands it to be in hard cases, namely 2a and 2b; hence, in answer to the question with which we ended the previous section, the AV and GGV are not different but only appear that way because the AV *assumes too much*. Second, the GGV's attempt to restrict the need to perform 2a only to "hard cases" fails because what constitutes a hard case is subject to the interpretation of the meta-rule. 2a thus enters the picture *in every instance* of umpiring and rules application and not just in so-called hard cases. Alternatively put, there is no such thing as a "strict" or "technical" interpretation of a rule, one that is literal or "uninterpreted." There is not because even the strict or technical interpretation *is an interpretation*. And when "strict" or "technical" go, so too goes "loose" (i.e., non-strict). We are thus left simply with interpretation *all the way down*!

Taken together, these two confront us with the fact that there is no act of umpiring where a rule is applied but not interpreted. There is no act of umpiring where the rule is applied "blindly." That is, the AV's 2 does not exist. Indeed, just the opposite. Each time an umpire performs 2 they are really performing both 2a and 2b. Each act of umpiring thus depends upon how the umpire "sees" the rule. An analysis that leads us, it would seem, to answer our title question "What do umpires do exactly?" with "Whatever they like!" because umpires appear constrained only by their own perspective on the rule—the sneaking suspicion of every fan in the stands at one moment or another and hence one reason for our anger! But this radical, even heretical, view of umpiring, where umpires are always ruling based on their "bias," turns out to be neither if we are willing to adopt a yet third view of umpiring which still sees umpires like judges, only judges as understood differently than Locke or Dworkin/Russell understand them.

Building on a line at the end of Russell's own "Taking Umpiring Seriously," where he says, "Umpires, like judges everywhere, are by nature conservative and will generally act with restraint,"[17] according to what we can call the Common Law View (CLV), umpires, like judges, show restraint and are constrained in the interpretation and then application of rules not by the meaning of rules, meta-rules, or what have you, but by *the practice of other umpires that have come before*. Rather than umpires applying rules through an act of deductive reasoning, moving from the rule to the specific case—which draws out the above infinite regress—instead the CLV tells us that umpires do and should compare specific cases in the present with *similar cases* in the past and make their call as closely as they can to that made in the past. (They make present umpiring practice conform with past umpiring practice.) In other words, umpires *are* and *should be* conservative in that they attempt to *conserve* the practice of the past, relying on an analogical form of reasoning that maintains a connection with previous umpiring not a deductive form of reasoning that attempts to maintain a connection with an abstract rule, meta-rule, etc. And while this conservatism leaves it always possible that a novel interpretation may present itself, in fact often does when prior umpiring is unclear in regard to some present case (the CLV's account of a hard case is one without obvious precedent, not the GGV's rules/meta-rules contradiction), it is also a conservatism that keeps umpiring remarkably consistent across umpires and time (witness the history of batting averages and the calling of balls and strikes).[18]

Simply put, tradition is what keeps umpires "in line" because without tradition, the very act of umpiring itself makes no sense. Umpires are not calculating machines that blindly apply the general to the specific, umpires are part of what the Austrian philosopher Ludwig Wittgenstein calls a "form of life,"[19] in this case a form of baseball life we call umpiring, where umpiring is a matter of doing what "we" do, with the "we" being all those men and women who have ever umpired. Therefore, what makes umpiring umpiring, and baseball baseball, for that matter, is its history, not its rules. Or better yet, it is the history of its rules viewed as actions, where the play and umpiring define the rules, the rules do not define the play and umpiring; a history that constrains umpires lest the very practice of umpiring itself disappear. And this is to say, in one very important way Locke is right about umpires. Not that they need to be blind because at base the CLV is telling us umpires do and should adopt a historical "sight," not strive after some oxymoronic "blind perspective" that strives to be no perspective at all. He is right in that the community is the ultimate umpire, and when a particular umpire stands in for *that* umpire, they also stand *in* that umpire, not above or outside it.

Conclusion

So, what do umpires do exactly? On the surface and day to day, it is clear that they do exactly what the conventional wisdom about umpiring, as captured by the AV and its four-part analysis of umpiring, tells us they do. Even the umps themselves would agree that they "call them as they see them," and they do so according to the rules. We can and should expect nothing less of umpires when we enter the stands or turn on our TVs.

But scratch that surface and a world of nuance and subtlety appears, one that throws us back on the simultaneously comfortable and uncomfortable truth that umpires in baseball are like the game itself: not just steeped in tradition but defined by it. Rather than reaching outside of umpiring to understand umpiring—in particular as per the GGV where umpires do and should step "outside" the rules and appeal to the baseball equivalent of Lincoln's "better angles of our nature"—instead we should see that it is further into umpiring and baseball itself that umpires always need to go. A trip which may, or may not, address every situation confronted by every particular umpire at every particular time, yet it is one that at least will show when an umpire, and in fact the game itself, needs to ask not so much what the rules require, but what baseball has been and wants to be.

Returning to where we started, with the AV and GGV each capturing something important about umpiring while in the end falling short of giving a full, sustainable account, they nonetheless helped point us toward the CLV, a view that puts tradition and practice at the heart of umpiring and hence quite clearly shows that the much debated and ballyhooed technology may be able to refine umpiring and the techniques of umpires, but technology will certainly *not* be able to become part of umpiring's essential "form of life" (any more than home-run hitting machines or cyborg players could be a part of baseball). Indeed, the only reason technology might seem to hold out the promise of doing more is that those holding out the promise are operating under views of umpiring, especially that of the AV, which do not see the complexity at work. And as to our anger at umpires, if what I have argued here is correct, umpiring is a good deal more sophisticated than it might have ever seemed, with appropriate blindness and sight only having meaning, as much as they have a meaning at all, against the backdrop of something that deserves far greater respect: *insight*. So, given the unbelievable difficulty of the job, let me end on a question that I ask entirely rhetorically: Why not cut umpires some slack?!

NOTES

1 Gil Imber, "Reviewing Instant Replay: Observation and Implications From Replay's Inaugural Season," *The Baseball Research Journal*, sabr.org/research/reviewing-instant-replay-observations-and-implications-replay-s-inaugural-season, Spring 2015 (accessed April 10, 2016).

2 Alex Shultz, "Rise of the machines? Baseball Weighs Use of Automated Strike Zone," *Los Angeles Times*, latimes.com/sports/la-sp-automated-strike-zone-20150810-story.html August 10, 2015 (accessed April 10, 2016).

3 espn.go.com/mlb/story/_/id/9278742/eight-ways-improve-umpiring-mlb. See 1.

4 John Locke, *Second Treatise of Government* (Indianapolis: Hackett Publishing Company, 1980), 46. Author's italics.

5 J.S. Russell, "Taking Umpiring Seriously: How Philosophy Can Help Umpires Make the Right Calls," in Eric Bronson, ed., *Baseball and Philosophy: Thinking Outside the Batter's Box* (Chicago: Open Court, 2004), 91.

6 espn.go.com/mlb/story/_/id/9278742/eight-ways-improve-umpiring-mlb. See 2-8.

7   David Nemec, *The Rules of Baseball: An Anecdotal Look at the Rules of Baseball and How They Came to Be* (New York: Lyons and Burnford, 1994), 174; J.S. Russell, 98-99.

8   J.S. Russell, 94-95.

9   As in your child telling his great-aunt that she looks bad in her new hat because you told her earlier in the day to "never tell a lie." logicallyfallacious.com/tools/lp/Bo/LogicalFallacies/2/Accident_Fallacy.

10 baseball-almanac.com/articles/strike_zone_rules_history.shtml.

11 mlb.mlb.com/mlb/official_info/umpires/strike_zone.jsp.

12 baseball-reference.com/leagues/MLB/bat.shtml.

13 J.S. Russell, 100.

14 J.S. Russell, 101. His italics.

15 J.S. Russell, 99.

16 baseball-almanac.com/feats/feats1.shtml; nytimes.com/2007/08/08/sports/baseball/08bonds.html?_r=0.

17 J.S. Russell, 102.

18 For an interesting account of how umpires call balls and strikes, one that works nicely in conjunction with overall view of umpiring expounded here, see sabr.org/latest/molyneux-umpires-arent-compassionate-theyre-bayesian.

19 Ludwig Wittgenstein, *Philosophical Investigations*, 3rd edition, trans. G.E.M. Anscombe (New York: Macmillan Publishing Co., 1989), passage 241.

When the Rules Aren't The Rules

By Dennis Goodman

Introduction

Somewhere in America on an April afternoon, there is a father being pelted by sideways drizzle, enduring brisk winds, and sitting on a set of cold metal bleachers. He is watching his son play high-school baseball. With runners on first and third, the pitcher lifts his foot, fakes to third base, and whirls back to first base.

The father screeches "BALK" as loud as his cold body allows. Umpires and coaches say nothing. Talking loudly so other fans can hear, the father tells of how this rule was recently changed. He continues making snarky comments about how the quality of high-school umpires is lacking.

The key question—is the umpire or the fan right? No surprise: The umpires are right, but the fan is not 100 percent wrong. This rule did change—in the major leagues. The fake-to-third-throw-to-first move is still perfectly legal in high school. To add more confusion, if this same dad has a child playing Babe Ruth/Cal Ripken baseball, it would be a balk.

Umpiring is a tough gig. In addition to having perfect judgment and stellar interpersonal skills, the umpire must memorize and master a dense, heavy rule book. Mastery of the rules brings about a couple of other interesting challenges—namely switching between levels where rules are different and knowing when to properly apply the rules.

Rule Differences

The first challenge might come as a surprise to many people. Aren't the rules of baseball the same everywhere? The answer to that question is tricky.

Yes, the core rules are the same everywhere. Three strikes is an out. Three outs is a half-inning, and four balls is a walk in any league. After that there are numerous differences. How many? There are enough differences between the three major rule sets (professional, college, and high school) that longtime umpire and prodigious author Carl Childress publishes a book every year focused only on these differences. The 32nd edition of *Baseball Rule Differences*, 400-plus pages of 200 official interpretations, is, according to *Referee Magazine*, "essential" for umpires.[1] Childress has also written numerous other books on umpiring and articles for leading officiating publications.

This book does not even cover the differences between the standard "big boy" ball and the various youth leagues. Youth leagues generally use professional rules as a baseline and make modifications.

Some of the differences are very basic. Youth baseball has shorter distances for bases and the pitching mound. This makes sense. A 12-year-old can hardly throw strikes from 45 feet, let alone 60. Some youth baseball does not allow leads off bases—again smart, as few people enjoy seeing a walk turn into a "triple."

The more nuanced differences fall into two buckets—those that make sense in the context of the league and those that appear to be different for the sake of being different.

All of these differences add complexity for not only umpires who work multiple levels, but the fans, coaches, and players participating. Conversations happen nightly in which a coach questions a ruling due to its difference from what was seen watching a major-league game.

The biggest difference in the core rules has to do with participation. As the players get older, making sure everyone plays becomes less important. Youth leagues have mandatory participation rules. Teams that don't fulfill them are subject to games being forfeited. Also, youth and high-school baseball leverage starting player re-entry and courtesy runners to boost participation. These rules certainly make sense for these levels.

The difference in the designated-hitter rules also helps spur participation. In college, the DH and pitcher can be the same player. This means that when the pitcher leaves the mound he can still bat. In high school the DH can bat for anyone and not only the pitcher. Oddly, youth baseball does not have a DH. Meaning the strange answer to the riddle "what two leagues don't use a DH?" is the National League and Little League.

Safety is a major concern for young players as well. This makes its way into rule differences. Youth and high-school baseball allow no malicious collisions at home plate. Even if the catcher is where he is not supposed to be, a player at this level cannot crash into him. The penalty is severe—an out and an ejection.

High-school baseball also dictates that a runner approaching second base on potential double plays has to slide directly into the base. In professional baseball, a slide is legal if the runner can reach the base with any part of his body. The penalty in high school is an out not only for the runner but for the batter as well.

Youth baseball has started to institute pitching maximums. Pitchers can pitch only so many pitches or innings at a time. Some state associations are also putting innings caps on high school pitchers. The intent of these rules revolves around player safety.

Participation and safety are good reasons for rule differences. Other differences make less sense. Here is a sampling of some of the major rule differences. Codifying these to one standard would make baseball less confusing for fans and make umpiring between levels much easier.

The strike zone in professional baseball is defined as the batter's position when he is prepared to hit. A batter is not ready to hit until he has taken his stride. Often taking a stride lowers the top part of the strike zone. In high-school baseball the zone is judged by his position while he is in his stance.

The strike zone also has the particular distinction of being different not only between leagues but within games. For simplification purposes, the strike zone is roughly from the letters to the knees. There is variation in the location of the knees and letters from batter to batter. This can make judging the strike zone more difficult. Proper mechanics and training aid in mastery of calling the zone.

College and professional baseball have two types of player obstruction. The penalty and procedure are different based upon whether a play is being made on the runner when the obstruction occurs. High-school baseball has only one type of obstruction. High school also has a minimum base award while the other leagues do not.

When a pitcher commits a balk in college or professional baseball, the play is not over. If the pitcher balks on a pitch but the batter hits a home run, the

Randy Marsh, inspecting fair/foul angles at Fenway Park's Pesky Pole on April 16, 2011, the day after a ball hit to the pole prompted some concern for a closer look.

Door to the umpires room, Fenway Park.

home run stands. If this happens in high-school baseball, the pitch is treated as if it never happened. The batter hit no home run. Most other balk rules are the same between codes—except, of course, for the example that started this article

In high-school baseball, the ball does not have to be in play for a coach or player to make an appeal. He can just call time and ask an umpire if a player missed a base. In professional baseball, the ball has to be put back in play with the ball thrown to the missed base for an appeal.

A ball that hits a sprinkler head in the grass in front of second base and bounces back into foul territory would be a foul ball in professional and college. But it would be a fair ball in high-school baseball.

The rule on whether a batter is out or the ball is foul if the ball strikes him after it is hit is different in all three rule sets. In professional ball, the batter is out if any part of a foot is not in the box. In college ball, the batter is out if a foot is on the ground completely outside the box. In high-school ball, the batter is out only if no foot is left in the batter's box.

Rules about managers visiting the mound are also different. In professional baseball, the second trip in an inning means the pitcher has to come out of the game. In high school, the manager gets three visits per game. He can use all three for the same pitcher in the same inning. Violation of the rule means the

pitcher has to come off the mound but can stay in the game.

This is just a sampling of the differences. There are many, many more. There are more than 150 rule differences between high-school and professional baseball. Granted, some of them are minor and may rarely occur. But when the difference between a good umpire and a great umpire is complete mastery of the rules, these differences makes working different levels challenging.

Game Management

These differences do highlight one thing. Sometimes the rules just aren't the rules. This can happen because a rule in one league is completely different in another. There are other instances when the rules aren't really the rules. Examples are due to game management. Much like a policeman who does not stop the driver going 57 mph in a 55-mph zone, there are instances where rules are broken, but it is in the best interest of all not to bring attention to them. The umpire has to choose between being right or being *right*.

Like the example of rule differences, many of these are dependent on the age of the participants. A major-league pitcher is held to a higher standard when it comes to procedural matters. A pitcher who starts to come set with a slight flinch will be called for a balk. Umpires of 12-year-olds will often and correctly let this slide unless the pitcher gained an advantage. If every small flinch was called at a youth level, the game would take a very long time.

Former major-league umpire Tim McClelland answered a question in this vein during an online chat posted on mlb.com. A man named Al Arellano wrote: "I'm an old catcher (78 years of age). Many years ago I was called for committing a 'Catcher's Balk.' I happened to move to the right of the plate just before the delivery of the pitch. Is this still in the rule book?"

McClelland replied: "It is a balk if the catcher doesn't stay in the catcher's box until the pitcher delivers the ball. If he were to step out of the catcher's box—the little box behind home plate—before the pitcher delivers the ball it would be called a catcher's balk. The runners would advance.

"As a matter of fact, I have never seen it called, it's one of those things you just kind of let slide. But it is in the rule book, we haven't updated the rule book in a long time. If it was called recently, it would be by an umpire taking the rule book to the letter of the law and sometimes we have to kind of overlook some things to make the game run smoother."[2]

This is a great example of game management trumping the exact wording of the book. Often umpires will subtly remind the catcher to stay in the box when a pitch is coming. This solves the issue.

Interestingly, McClelland was the umpire who famously called George Brett out for having too much pine tar on his bat. His ruling was ultimately overturned. The rule book now contains language that an out is never to be granted for this issue. Rather, the bat is to be taken out of play.

The "neighborhood" play at second used to be another instance where game play trumps the rule book. The book states that a player with possession of the ball must touch a base in order for an out to be recorded. Often on double plays, the pivot man would steal a step or two before making the return throw. Although he was in the "neighborhood" of the base, he actually never contacted it when having the ball. This play died before the 2016 season as Major League Baseball made this play subject to review.

Why did umpires grant this cheat step? It was again about player safety. When the pivot man is forced to stay on the base, he is more exposed to a chance of injury. The little cheat step on a clean double play eliminated the chance. Many amateur umpires will still grant a high school pivot man a little latitude in the name of safety.

The last example of umpires not interjecting themselves into games deals with foreign substances. Rarely, if ever, will an umpire go on his own accord to check a pitcher for the presence of a foreign substance. Instead, he will wait until the other team complains before checking. In early 2015, there were several occurrences of pitchers being ejected for having sticky substances on their arm.

Many opposing managers will not ask an umpire to search an opposing pitcher because they know their pitcher does the same thing. Not looking for issues, but ruling on them as they occur insulates umpires from unwanted confrontation. A basic tenet of good umpiring: "Use the rules to solve problems, not make them."

Umpires who never learn these lessons are nicely accused of being an "overly officiate official." In more sophomoric terms, they pick too many "boogers." The point is that often when an umpire does not call something, the context should be examined before rushing to judgment. What looks like a bad umpire might actually be a brilliant umpire due to the respect he garners from participants.

In fact, with enough time and hard work, anyone can learn the rule book. Anyone with enough training can learn the correct mechanics and timing. The thing that truly separates the greatest officials is the ability to manage the game. Knowing when to apply a rule and when to let the game breathe is paramount to excellent game management.

Final Thoughts

Baseball rules are a tricky subject essential to learn to be a good umpire. Numerous differences between rule sets add to the challenge. Most amateur umpires work multiple leagues making this a very real concern. After learning the rules, umpires must learn the right way to manage the game through the application of the rules. Regardless, whether watching a game on television or at the local high school, sometimes the rules just aren't the rules.

NOTES

1 See Carl Childress, *Baseball Rule Differences, 32nd Edition* (CreateSpace Independent Publishing Platform, 2014). The 436-page book has 578 "off interps" from recognized authorities in professional, college, and high-school rules.

2 mlb.mlb.com/mlb/official_info/umpires/feature.jsp?feature=mcclellandqa.

Baseball Q & A— Applying the Rules

It is the responsibility of umpires, of course, to apply the rules of the game. The rules are often far more complicated than most fans realize. These 11 situations, or questions, provide a bit of inside into some of what an umpire might face, or ponder.

They have been provided by a former minor-league umpire who preferred to remain anonymous.

1. How many legal outs can be made in one half-inning?

2. How wide is the strike zone?

3. Runner on third base, no outs. The batter hits a deep fly ball to right field. The ball is caught and the runner from third tags and scores with no play made on him. The batter's swing, however, hit the catcher's mitt. What is the ruling?

4. Runner on first base. No outs. A soft fly ball is hit to the second baseman. He acts as if he is going to catch the ball, but lets it fall to the ground untouched at the last minute. Is the ball dead or alive and in play?

5. The batter squared to bunt. The foot closest to home plate was both touching home plate and the inside line of the batter's box when he bunted the ball. His other foot was in the batter's box. What should the umpire rule?

    a. "Out" for stepping on home plate.

    b. Nothing, this is legal because both feet were in the batter's box.

6. With a runner on third base and one out, the offensive team tried a suicide squeeze and the ball was bunted down the third-base line. The catcher, trying to knock the ball foul, touched the ball with his mask while it was on the foul line. What should the umpires rule?

7. Can an outfielder catch an infield fly?

8. Match the correct penalty for each rule infraction:

    A. Fielder touches a batted ball with his hat, mask, or any part of his uniform detached from its proper place

    B. Fielder touches a pitched ball...

    C. Fielder touches a thrown ball...

    Penalty:

    1. one-base award

    2. two-base award

    3. three-base award

9. The count is 0-2. The batter swings at the pitch and foul-tips it. The ball hits the catcher in the chest protector and is then secured by the catcher before it hits the ground. Is the batter out?

10. It's a tie game, in the bottom of the ninth inning. There is one out and a runner on third base. The catcher goes after a foul popup that ranges toward the stands. He catches it, flips over the railing and falls into the seats, but holds onto the ball. Why would it have been better to just let the ball drop?

11. How can a team skip legally over one or more batters in the order?

ANSWERS

1. The answer is: 5. Bases loaded, one out. Batter flies out to deep right field: two outs. All three runners tag up, but all three leave early. The defense appeals at first base. The runner is out: three outs. The run would still score, so the defense then appeals second base. That runner is out, too: four outs. The run would still score. The defense then appeals third base. That runner is out: five outs, no run scores.

2. The plate is 17" wide. However, the baseball is approximately 3" across. If any part of the ball touches the inside or outside part of the plate, it is a strike. Therefore, the strike zone is actually approximately 23" wide (17" + 3" inside + 3" outside).

3. Manager's option. The manager can choose to have the catcher's interference enforced (batter is awarded first base and the runner on third is returned to third) OR the manager can opt to let the play stand (take the out and allow the run to score).

4. Alive. The ball is dead only if the fielder touches the ball before it touches the ground.

5. Answer – b.

6. The runner on third scores and the batter is awarded a three-base award (the ball is alive and in play, however). This is the penalty for a player touching a batted ball with detached equipment.

7. Yes, as long as, in the umpire's judgment, an infielder could have made the catch with ordinary effort.

8. Answers:

   A = three bases

   B = one base

   C = two bases

9. No, in order for that to be a legal catch by the catcher, the ball must first be touched by the catcher's mitt or his hand before being secured.

10. With less than two out, if a player makes a catch and falls into the stands, every runner is awarded a base. Therefore the runner is waved home from third base and wins the game...on a foul ball the catcher should have just let fall.

11. If a batter hits out of order, the "improper batter comes a proper batter because no appeal is made before the next pitch" and, in this situation, "the next batter shall be the batter whose name follows that of such legalized improper batter. The instant an improper batter's actions are legalized, the batting order picks up with the name following that of the legalized improper batter." One could theoretically skip over several batters in this fashion, whether intentionally or mistakenly.

Likely routine use of Braille on Dodger Stadium signage.

Umpire Mechanics

By David Vincent

All professional umpires use the same basic mechanics on the field, from rookie ball to the major leagues. This includes positioning behind home plate and on the bases, as well as how to indicate "out," "safe," "ball," and "strike." Fans are familiar with the signals for out and safe. However, most fans are not familiar with an important part of the umpire mechanics: how umpires move on the field during a play to provide good coverage of that play. One might use the term "choreography" to describe the movement on the field since it is a coordinated, prearranged sequence much like that of a ballet company.

The major leagues have developed a standard system of mechanics that are used to cover the field while the ball is in play. There are separate systems for a four-man, three-man, and two-man crew in use at various levels of pro ball. This article will discuss the four-man system, although some of the mechanics are used in all three crew types. But first a few other notes.

General Principles

There are a few general principles.

- With no runners on base, the first- and third-base umpires start a play with both feet in foul territory.
- One umpire will go into the outfield on all fly balls and line drives. This umpire should go out as far as possible but be stopped when making calls.
- An umpire who goes out into the outfield should not return to the infield until the play is completed.
- When there are runners on base (other than a runner only on third base), the second base umpire will be positioned between second base and the pitcher's mound. This umpire will set up to one side of the mound and will not go out on fly balls to the outfield.
- The home-plate umpire will stay at the plate when there are runners in scoring position.

A second-base umpire who is positioned in front of the second-base bag is said to be working the "inside" position. This term will be used in this article.

The system in which all umpires use the same mechanics is a recent change. Through 1999, each league had its own staff of umpires and each league's arbiters had different ways of working. The most obvious difference was the chest protector. American League umpires wore the outside "balloon" protector through the late 1970s, when new AL umpires were required to wear a protector inside the jacket. National League umpires had been wearing the inside protector for many years. The American League umpires at first base and third base would stand completely in foul territory but the NL umpire straddled the line. The second-base umpire would stand behind the bag at all times in the AL, while the NL umpires would move in front of the bag.

In the minor leagues, where umpires use the two-man and three-man systems, their position at the start of a play is with their hands on their knees. In the major leagues, it is up to the crew to decide if they will use that hand position or not. Many crews do use it in the big leagues.

On balls hit to the outfield, each base umpire has a responsibility on coverage, with the exception noted above for the second-base umpire who is working the inside position. These coverage areas are delineated in the Umpire Manual and are based on where the ball is hit. In general, the dimensions of a ballpark do not alter the outfield coverage areas for umpires. In a ballpark like Fenway Park, with its unusual outfield configuration, the umpire crew might temporarily alter its mechanics and coverages to fit the field. Severe weather conditions might also cause a temporary alteration of mechanics.

The Umpire Manual contains diagrams that show general movement and the base for which each umpire has responsibility on plays. Communication among members of a crew during a play is one of the essential tools to ensure that the umpires properly cover all bases.

When an umpire runs into the outfield on a play and another umpire has moved to cover a different base, that covering umpire stays with the runner in question at the end of the play and only releases once the umpire who went into the outfield returns and has assumed responsibility for the runner. This ensures proper coverage of each runner on base.

Professional umpires are taught not to watch a fly ball. Instead, they watch fielders. For example, on a popup in foul territory behind home plate, the plate umpire will watch and move with the catcher. The catcher will watch the baseball in flight and move according to the location of the ball. One of the key factors in this example is that the catcher usually throws his mask away before catching the ball. By watching the catcher, the umpire knows when and in which direction the mask flies and can avoid being struck by that mask. An obvious exception to this mechanic is a fly ball to the outfield that is a possible home run.

Umpires are also taught that their first responsibility on all batted balls is to determine if the ball is fair or foul. Many batted balls are easily judged, such as one hit to center field. However, many fly along one of the lines and must be judged by an umpire to be fair or foul. A batted ball in the infield is judged fair or foul by the home-plate umpire before it reaches the bag and by a base umpire once it reaches the bag and/or moves past it.

The first requisite of an umpire is to get all calls correct. An umpire is urged to seek help from a partner when that umpire's view is partly blocked on a play. It is the responsibility of the calling umpire to request help; a partner should not interject himself into a discussion without being asked to do so. The ultimate decision to change a call rests with the umpire who made the call. One example of a play in which the calling umpire might request help is on a foul ball that is caught or not by the catcher. In this situation, a base umpire might have a better look at the play and be able to determine if the ball was caught on the fly or not.

On a dropped third strike, plate umpires are instructed to signal that the pitch was a strike. When the batter has been put out by a tag by the catcher, the plate umpire then signals the out with a separate mechanic. If the batter is put out at first base on a throw, then the first-base umpire would signal the out.

Field coverage and movement

Here are some examples of field coverage and movement of umpires during a play as defined in the Umpire Manual. These examples are for the four-man system.

Coverage with no baserunners

With no runners on base, the second-base umpire covers more than half the outfield area. This is defined as all fly balls from the left fielder moving straight in or out to the right fielder moving straight in or out. The first-base umpire covers the area from the right fielder to the right-field line. The third-base umpire covers the area from the left fielder to the left-field line. Among other things, the second-base umpire watches for a catch/no catch on these plays.

If the second-base umpire goes out into the outfield, the third-base umpire is responsible for covering any possible play at second base, so he moves from his position to the second-base bag while the play is in progress. The home-plate umpire moves to third to cover any possible play there and the first-base umpire, after the batter/runner has reached second base, moves to home plate for any possible play.

Coverage with a runner on first only

When there are runners on base, the coverage changes depending on the initial position of the runners. With a runner only on first, the second-base umpire starts a play in the inside position. The first-base umpire covers the area defined as the center fielder straight in or out to the right-field line, while the third-base umpire has coverage on all fly balls that cause the center fielder

At Fenway Park, the umpires take the field through the same runway as used by the visiting team. On September 17, 2016 when the New York Yankees were in Boston, we see plate umpire Bill Welke (#52). On his way to the field, Welke is followed by #17, John Hirschbeck. John is followed by #19, Vic Carapazza, and then #70, D. J. Reyburn.

to move to his right all the way to the left-field line. Movement around the infield with runners on base varies slightly depending on where the runner started the play.

With a runner on first and a ball hit to left field, the third-base umpire goes out on coverage. The home-plate umpire moves toward third base for any play on the runner or batter/runner at third. The first-base umpire is responsible for any tag-up at first or any play on the runner or batter/runner at first. The first-base umpire releases to home plate once the runner from first commits to third base. The second-base umpire drifts between first and second. He is responsible for a play at second on the runner from first. Once that runner commits to third base, the second-base umpire releases from that runner and picks up the batter/runner.

Of course, this changes if the first-base umpire goes out on coverage. The plate umpire moves toward first base and has responsibility for any tag-up at first. The plate umpire also has responsibility for any play on the runner at first. If that runner commits to third base, the plate umpire returns to home plate for any possible play there. The last responsibility of the plate umpire when the first-base umpire goes out into the outfield is the touch of first by the batter/runner.

The second-base umpire has responsibility for any play on the runner or batter/runner at second. He also is responsible for the batter/runner back into first base after rounding the bag. The third-base umpire

has the runner from first into third base and the batter/runner at third. One variation on this choreography is that a crew may have the second-base umpire cover first base instead of the home-plate umpire.

Coverage with runners on second and third

Responsibilities get much more complicated if there are runners on second base and third base. One of the complications is whether the infield is playing in or not. If the infield is in, then the second-base umpire is positioned on the outside on the shortstop side. He should be far enough behind the infielders to clear them. In this situation, fly-ball coverage is basically the same as with no runners on, but if the infield is not playing in, the second-base umpire is positioned in front of the bag and the choreography changes to coverage with a runner on first base only, which was discussed above.

There are also mechanics for all other combinations of runners on base: second only, third only, first and second, first and third, and bases loaded.

Line drives to the infield with runners on base

This situation is less clearly delineated than most others because of the complexities of how and where the ball may be hit and where the infielders and umpires are positioned. The general rule is for the umpire to whom the glove is opening takes the ball. If there are any runners on base, the home-plate umpire takes all balls hit to the pitcher or an infielder who is charging in on the play. The first-base umpire generally takes any ball hit directly to the first baseman

or any ball that takes the first or second baseman to his left.

The second-base umpire would take any ball hit directly to the shortstop or second baseman, any ball that causes the first or second baseman to dive to his right or any ball that causes the shortstop or third baseman to dive to his left. The third-base umpire takes any ball hit directly at the third baseman or any ball that takes either the third baseman or shortstop to his right.

Mechanics for six umpires

Some of the four-man mechanics change if there are six umpires on the field, such as in postseason games. The two umpires positioned on the outfield lines are referred to as "line umpires" in the manual. If the second-base umpire goes out on coverage, the line umpire on the side on which the ball is hit drifts into the outfield. Umpires continue to rotate as they do with four umpires. However, the only time the home-plate umpire rotates to third base is with no runners on base and the second-base umpire goes out in coverage. In all other cases, the plate umpire stays home.

With runners on base and the second-base umpire on the inside, both line umpires go out in the direction in which the ball is hit. The line umpires make fair/foul calls only on balls that land behind them and line umpires do not rotate to cover a base.

Conclusion

This article discussed many of the umpire mechanics for the four-man umpiring system as defined by Major League Baseball. Should a crew work with fewer than four umpires due to injury or other reason, there are also defined mechanics for the three- and two-man umpiring system. The Umpire Manual also contains sections on "Conduct and Responsibility of Umpires" and "Rule Interpretations," neither of which are part of this article.

Umpire Changes During a Game

By David Vincent

In 1891, baseball rules were changed to allow unlimited player substitutions during games. It is common in the modern game to see pinch-hitters and relief pitchers during a contest, but it is uncommon to see an umpire leave a game once it has started. There are many reasons why a game would end with a different set of umpires on the field that from the start of the contest. This article will look at the most common reasons.

Suspended Games

From the early 1930s through the late 1950s, Sunday games in Pennsylvania could only be played between 2PM and 6PM. After that, the game would be suspended due to state law. This situation was exacerbated by the fact that teams often played double headers on Sundays, thus making the second game end later in the day. Those games would have to be completed on another day and that completion sometimes occurred weeks later when the two teams met again in the same city. In many cases, the original umpire crew would not complete the suspended game and another set of umpires would work the second part of the contest. The latest instance of this type of change occurred on July 12, 1959 in Pittsburgh. The game was completed on August 19 with a new crew. Suspended games were also an occasional occurrence at Wrigley Field in Chicago before the lights were installed in the stadium in 1988.

At other times, games were suspended due to weather and completed later. The most unusual instance of a weather-related umpire change came in 2009 in Washington. The Astros were in town for their one visit to the Nation's Capital that season. The last game of the series went into extra innings on May 5 and the game was stopped due to rain in the bottom of the 11th inning. After a 1:16 delay, the game was suspended. However, since the teams were not scheduled to meet again in D.C. and a compatible open date could not be found, the game was completed in Houston on July 9. In between, the Nationals had made roster changes, including a trade. Joel Hanrahan, the pitcher of record at the time of the delay, had been traded to the Pirates on June 30 and was in Philadelphia that day. Nyjer Morgan, part of that same trade, pinch-ran for Elijah Dukes, who had been demoted to the minors by the Nationals, and scored the game-ending run on a throwing error in the infield when Josh Bard pinch-hit for Hanrahan! A different umpire crew was assigned to the Houston series than had started the game and took the field for the two plays that completed the contest. The Washington Official Scorer, David Vincent, acted as scorer of record to complete the game, doing so from his house. A Houston Official Scorer sat in the Astros press box as the scorer in place for the remainder of the contest.

Injury and Illness

The most common cause for a change in umpires is an injury or illness suffered by one of the arbiters. Home Plate umpires are frequently struck by foul balls, errant pitches, and flying bats. Those events often lead to injuries. Umpires have suffered head, neck, chest, back, groin, hand, wrist, arm, leg, and knee injuries that have caused them to leave a game. The ball often strikes an umpire's mask and this can be debilitating, causing concussions and vertebrae issues in the neck. Umpires have left games with an imprint of the baseball stitches on a forearm, sometimes with broken bones included.

Flying bats can strike a home-plate umpire. Blows to the head can be dangerous and cause a lot of bleeding. Many umpires wear the full helmet first used by hockey goalies but not all umpires wear that protection, opting for the old-style mask. On June

23, 2016, Paul Emmel was struck by a flying bat on the top of his head. He was wearing a cap and mask and was bleeding profusely from the top of his head when he left the contest suffering from a concussion.

In Toronto on August 6, 2005, the Yankees were in town to play the Blue Jays. In the top of the second inning, Jason Giambi's bat broke and the heavy part struck home-plate umpire Marty Foster on the right knee. There was a 15-minute delay while he was attended to and eventually taken off the field on a cart. Foster suffered a bad bruise but no broken bones. Second-base umpire Laz Diaz moved behind the plate. Diaz had been scheduled for an off-day the next day and minor-league umpire Chad Fairchild had flown to Toronto to work in Diaz' place. He received a call once he arrived at the airport and went directly to the ballpark. Fairchild entered the field in the middle of the third inning and worked the rest of the contest at second base. Foster returned to work on August 13.

Often, these injuries are suffered by a base umpire, such as when Bill Brennan slipped on a wet field in 1912 and broke a kneecap and tore ligaments in his leg while running to view a play at second base. In that game in Pittsburgh on August 20, home-plate umpire Brick Owens (there were only two on the field in those days) was struck on the chest by a foul ball. He suffered a broken breast bone and rode to the hospital in the same ambulance as his partner. Players took over the umpiring duties for the rest of the day and a new pair of umpires was rushed to the Steel City for the next day's game. Both umpires worked next on August 26 in St. Louis.

Bats, balls and other player equipment are only part of the list of items that could injure an umpire. Many years ago, fans were given drinks in bottles instead of the modern plastic cups. These bottles often turned into missiles when fans were upset by an umpire's call on the field. In the bottom of the eighth inning in Chicago on July 26, 1936, Rip Radcliffe hit a grounder to Lou Gehrig, who tossed the ball to pitcher Pat Malone. First-base umpire Charles Johnston called Radcliffe out and then turned away from the bag. Malone dropped the ball in a colli-

sion with Radcliffe. Johnston consulted with third-base umpire Bill Summers, who ruled that Malone dropped the ball because of the collision after the play was over and that Radcliffe was out. Bottles, cans, and fruit were thrown at Summers. In the bottom of the ninth, Summers was struck on the groin by a bottle thrown from the stands and left the game. Summers missed one game due to the injury.

Another common reason for an umpire to leave a game is dehydration and/or heat exhaustion. On a hot summer day, the home-plate umpire is wearing a lot of extra gear and does not have the ability to sit in the dugout for a half-inning as does the catcher. Drinking water helps but a sunny day with a high temperature and humidity can still wear out a person. This is far less common than injuries but is still a factor in whether an arbiter finishes a game or not.

Umpires have suffered other sorts of injuries on the field. On July 31, 2009, home-plate umpire Charlie Reliford tore his right calf muscle during a play in the second inning of a game in a Tampa Bay game. Reliford left the contest in the seventh inning and the injury ended his career.

In Anaheim on August 15, 2012, Torii Hunter tried to dive around Indians catcher Carlos Santana to avoid a tag in the bottom of the fifth inning. As Hunter reached to touch the plate, his feet swung around and the cleat on the heel of his left shoe struck home-plate umpire Greg Gibson near the left eye. Gibson received stitches but suffered no more serious injuries. He left the contest and returned to the field on August 28.

Pirate Francisco Cervelli tried to score on an infield grounder on May 23, 2016. As he slid into the plate, dirt flew up and struck home-plate umpire Jeff Nelson on the eye. Nelson made the out call but left the game to be treated; he missed no further games.

On August 9, 1953, the Braves were entertaining the Pirates for two games. In the first inning of the second game, home-plate umpire Len Roberts, while watching a foul popup, crashed against the backstop. He suffered a back injury and left the contest. Roberts returned to work on August 15 and worked 43 games in his only year in the big leagues.

Umpires have certain positions from which they are supposed to adjudicate plays. There is choreography worked out for each umpiring position for most play situations but occasionally a player and umpire collide during a play. This can occur whether or not the umpire is in the correct spot. Some of these collisions have resulted in serious injuries to umpires. On June 29, 1987 in San Francisco, the Giants tried a squeeze play with Joel Youngblood on third and Matt Williams batting. Braves pitcher Zane Smith fielded the bunt and ran to the plate to tag Youngblood. Smith fell over the runner and collided with home-plate umpire Bill Williams. Williams suffered a broken right leg and was knocked out in the collision. This was the last game in Williams' career.

From the start of the 2000 season through 2016, 112 umpires have left a game due to injury and 24 have left due to an illness. Before 2000, the leagues had separate umpire staffs but they were combined into one by Major League Baseball for the 2000 season.

Travel Issues

In the 21st Century, travel is much faster than it was 100 years before. This does not mean that umpires do not have occasional glitches in their travels, though. On June, 28, 1941, the umpires failed to show up at Braves Field in Boston for the 2:00 PM start of the game between the Braves and the Dodgers. A telegram was sent to the Braves from Babe Pinelli stating that the arbiters were delayed by fog on the night boat from New York to Boston. Players made the calls for the first inning and the umpire crew, consisting of Pinelli, Lee Ballanfant, and Al Barlick, took the field to start the second frame.

Umpires in the twenty-first century are not immune to these sorts of issues. An umpire crew was late arriving at a game in Philadelphia due to a cancelled airline flight from Cleveland. On July 23, 2004, Joe West, Paul Emmel, and Mike DiMuro took a different flight to Baltimore and then rode to Philadelphia. Darren Spagnardi, a minor-league umpire scheduled to fill in for Terry Craft, had taken an earlier flight to Philadelphia and was scheduled to work at third base. Instead, Spagnardi worked behind home plate while three college umpires worked on the bases. The regulars walked onto the field in the middle of the second inning and finished the game.

Upheld Protests

Sometimes games appear to be over but are not. Managers are allowed to protest a decision that appears to be a misapplication of a rule but cannot protest a judgement call by an umpire. These protests are adjudicated by the league president or a designee for validity and if the protest is upheld, the game is resumed from the point of the protest. Perhaps the most famous upheld protest occurred in the Royals game at Yankee Stadium on July 24, 1983. With two out in the top of the ninth inning, the Yankees led, 4-3, when U. L. Washington singled. George Brett then homered to put the Royals in the lead. Yankees manager Billy Martin objected to the location of the pine tar on Brett's bat. The umpires huddled and home-plate umpire Tim McClelland measured the bat against the width of home plate and determined that the pine tar went further up the handle than allowed by the rules. He called Brett out because of illegal equipment and the home run was disallowed. Brett charged out of the dugout and was restrained. This out ended the game but the Royals protested the decision. American League President Lee MacPhail upheld the protest on July 28 and ordered the game be resumed after the homer. MacPhail stated that Brett's bat did not break the "spirit of the rules" as he was not trying to alter the bat to increase distance. On August 18, the teams met to finish the game. Martin, in a childish move, put left-hander Don Mattingly at second and pitcher Ron Guidry in center field. A new crew of umpires worked this part of the game. The Yankees appealed at first and second base that Brett has not touched those bags. When the appeals were denied, Martin came onto the field to argue. Crew chief Dave Phillips produced a notarized letter stating that both runners had touched all the bases and both runs counted. Hal McRae struck out and the Yankees were out 1-2-3 in the bottom of the ninth to end the game a second time.

THE SABR BOOK ON UMPIRES AND UMPIRING

Other

Two other causes of umpires leaving games many years ago may look a little odd to the modern fan. There have been occasions when an umpire and a player have fought on the field during a game, and several umpires have been arrested and taken to the police station during a game. In New York on July 7, 1903, the Yankees were entertaining the White Sox. In the seventh inning, umpire Jack Sheridan called out Danny Green of Chicago at first base to end the frame. Green yelled at the umpire as he left the field. Sheridan ran towards Green and struck the latter on the head with his mask and Green retaliated by punching Sheridan. The two were separated by players and the police. Sheridan was arrested. Green refused to make a complaint against the arbitrator although his head was bleeding from the assault. Sheridan was locked up for about an hour on a charge of disorderly conduct, but was released on bail provided by the President of the New York club, Joseph Gordon. Two players officiated the remainder of the contest.

Mention was made earlier of bottles flying from the stands. On August 4, 1897, the Pirates were in Cincinnati for a double header. The second game was called due to darkness in the sixth inning but finished without Umpire Tim Hurst. In the second, Hurst made a call against the home team that riled the fans. One rooter threw a beer glass onto the field. The arbiter picked up the glass and threw it back into the stand. The glass struck a patron over the right eye, causing an injury. The police were called and Hurst was arrested and charged with assault and battery. The game was finished with a former player as umpire.

Umpires spend a lot of time on the playing field during a game. Rarely does one leave the contest and not return. A list of all known instances of umpires leaving a game can be found on the Retrosheet web site, at http://www.retrosheet.org/umpgmchg.htm .

You're Out of Here—A History of Umpire Ejections

By Gil Imber

The theater of baseball contains many acts and scenes, from the overarching storyline of a masterful pitching performance or offensive feat to the intricate beauty of the pitcher-batter dialogue, yet no sideshow features more prominently in the baseball movie house than the ballad of the ejection. Throughout the years, arbiters from Adams to Zimmer ejected firecrackers from Aaron to Zupo for a variety of offenses, and in doing so provided fans with a brief intermission from baseball's expertly crafted feature presentation. As the game itself evolved, when the so-named Deadball Era rose to life, and the era of the pitcher gave way to the age of the batter, and back again, so too did the fine art of the umpire's practice of removal from the game.

Ejections throughout the years, much like home runs, strikeouts, or any other viable statistic, have waxed and waned, all the while remaining susceptible to their own trends. Unlike home runs, strikeouts, and the like, however, attitudes toward ejections and how umpires should make use of this disciplinary tool have also changed over the years.

Umpires eject players, coaches, and managers for a variety of reasons—abusive language when arguing the arbiter's decision, especially balls and strikes, pitchers intentionally throwing at a batter, brawling with an opponent, violating rules such as doctoring pitches or corking bats—but this essay is not about specific ejections. It is about reviewing the pattern of ejections that reflect distinct umpiring eras beginning in the late nineteenth and early twentieth centuries.

The umpire's authority to impose discipline for unsporting conduct initially took the form of fines, not ejections, beginning in 1879.[1] Indeed, umpires during the subsequent decade believed that fines were a more effective measure of discipline than ejections, as reflected by a late-century National League vote.[2]

When inappropriate behavior persisted, however, the ejection was born in 1889. As a result, explosive personalities like Baltimore/New York's John McGraw racked up ejections by the score: McGraw himself was ejected 132 times over the 1893-1931 seasons, including four years with at least 10 ejections each, and 10 seasons with at least five, all 10 ejection-heavy seasons taking place prior to 1917, a trend common to the first era of umpiring and men like baseball's "Old Arbiter," William Klem.[3]

Colloquially deemed the Father of Umpiring, or, as Arthur Daley wrote, "the foundation stone on which that foundation stone [of umpiring] rests," Klem began his 37-year National League career at a time when there was a distinct lack of respect for umpires, even the concept of the umpiring profession. Klem's magnificent reach in umpiring certainly extended into the realm of ejections To offset the amount of abuse umpires routinely took during that early era, Klem gained a reputation as a "tough cop" umpire: he was known for drawing a line in the dirt during an argument and using the expression, "Do not cross the Rio Grande." Those who did received an immediate ejection, as did any player/coach/manager who called Klem "Catfish," a nickname he detested.

Klem set a frenetic major-league record with 288 career ejections from that of Fred Clarke in April 1905 to pitcher Danny MacFayden in August of 1940, ejecting 26 players, managers, and coaches during his rookie season in 1905; he ejected fellow Hall of Famer John McGraw a record 15 times from 1905 to 1921 and with an MLB-most 5,375 regular-season games under his belt, averaged an ejection every 19 games worked.[4] That's a higher rate of ejection than that of all 76 umpires on the full-time MLB staff in August 2016 as well as all minor-league call-up umpires.[5]

Klem's repeated and religious use of the ejection was the tool that brought dignity and respect to the profession. Perhaps this is why Klem averaged 20.4 ejections per season from 1905 to 1911, but just 3.6 per season during his final five full years in the National League (1936-1940): He ejected over 20 players during a season four times (1905, 1907, 1910, 1911), but never hit the double-digit mark during any season after 1920. Klem's outlier year of eight ejections in 1935—which was significantly high for later in his career, but would have been significantly low early on in his career—was that high only because of an April brawl that produced four ejections.

Klem had so much work to do, in part, because umpiring was more or less an afterthought in early baseball culture. When National League President William A. Hulbert appointed the first umpiring staff of 20 men in 1879, he allowed teams to select their umpire from this roster. When NL umpire Richard Higham earned an expulsion in 1882 after reportedly colluding with gamblers, the reputation of umpiring—already weak—suffered.[66] Baseball officiating only received its first "umpire organizational chart" designating the plate umpire as umpire-in-chief in 1910. The fact that from 1901 through 1946 five managers and 31 players served as fill-in umpires when the regularly scheduled umpire was unable to make his assignment only served as reminders of early umpiring's transient state.[77]

Similarly, Klem's National League brethren tended to take a more abrasive approach than American League counterpart Tommy Connolly's diplomats. Whereas Klem and the NL staff tried to command respect through an "autocratic personality" that wasn't above the occasional show of force or ejection, American League President Ban Johnson tried to eliminate rowdy behavior from the administrative level. Consequently, the league's head umpire — the 5-foot-7, 170-pound Connolly—along with his AL staff, commanded respect through his rules knowledge, fairness, and "firm manner."[8]

In the late 1930s umpire history began to change dramatically with the advent of formal umpire training. George Barr founded the first School for Umpires in 1935 and Bill McGowan followed suit in 1939; his school subsequently fell into the care

Hillsboro Hops manager Shelley Duncan being ejected from the game against the Tri-City Dust Devils by short-season Single-A Northwest League umpire Joe Schwartz, August 26, 2015.

League during the first half of the twentieth century, not a single active player or manager has served as a major-league umpire since Bill Kunkel in the 1960s.

Professionalization of umpiring changed the attitudes toward and treatment of umpires, correspondingly impacting ejections. By the mid-twentieth century veteran umpires collectively tended to eject less and less frequently, from Jocko Conlan's once-per-32 games rate to Al Barlick's one-in-52 mark. Umpires embraced Conlan's words, "I demand respect on the field from managers and players. To me, that's 75 percent of umpiring."[10] During this era, an umpire like Marty Springstead could be described as someone who was "not shy about arguing with players and managers" because he led the league in ejections in 1971.[11] Yet Springstead never ejected more than six players during any one season (he ejected six twice:

once in 1971 and again in 1975), which is considerably less than the double-digit marks common to early-era umpires.[12] Springstead's 60 ejections over 3,010 games worked is a rate of approximately one ejection for every 50 games, about average for his time. Even Terry Cooney—who was lambasted for ejecting Red Sox pitcher Roger Clemens, alongside Marty Barrett, for multiple profanities regarding the strike zone during the 1990 American League Championship Series[13] — only ejected 40 people during his 2,232 regular-season games in the American League, a rate of one ejection for every 56 games worked.[14]

For Cooney and Springstead's era, perhaps the advent of televised games caused an overrepresentation of umpire aggression and ejection to give some umpires a hotheaded reputation—after all, the manager-ump rhubarbs were now broadcast visually and over the radio as well—but there is no denying that umpire ejections were trending downward. There is perhaps no umpire who epitomized the concept of the consistently rare ejection during this period more than "God" himself, Doug Harvey.

Harvey worked over 4,600 games during his 30-year career before retiring in 1992, and ejected just 56—with season highs of seven ejections apiece in 1963 and 1987.[15] Though Harvey's ejections total and one-per-82-plus rate were both lower than those of many earlier umpires, Harvey still entertained managers and players who wanted a good old fashioned argument (see Harvey's memoir *They Called Me God* for anecdotes of his favorite arguments) and earned the respect of many, including the major leagues' managerial ejection record-holder, Bobby Cox: "Doug's a real class guy. You feel good when he's working your game."[16] Another famous face with a low ejection rate during the 1970s, '80s, and '90s was Don Denkinger (1 per 83), as well as Hall of Famer Barlick, who, after ejecting a career-high 12 players and managers in 1951 and a total of 52 people from 1941 to 1951, ejected no more than three people per year for the final two decades of his illustrious career, or just 29 over the 1951-71 period (overall rate: 1 per 52; rate from 1951-71: 1 per 97).[17] In other words, Barlick himself could be considered a microcosm of the dif-

ference in the early vs. late twentieth century umpiring eras' approach to the ejection, similar in general trend to Klem's statistics, but with a turning point much closer to the beginning, as opposed to the end, of his time in the National League.

The era could also be categorized as more colorful or flamboyant with respect to umpiring mechanics and even uniforms, such as the American League's maroon blazers. Looking back on his career, NL veteran Dutch Rennert (21 ejections in 2,693 games—1 per 128) remembered the officiating philosophy of the late twentieth century: "You've got to add something to your work, you've got to be a little more colorful."[18] NL umpire Jerry Dale wrote a master's thesis on umpiring in the 1980s, noting that umpires must develop an "aggressive and volatile persona" in order to survive in the big leagues.[19] Players and managers responded to the added flair, and arguments could successfully subside without an ejection. The classic rhubarbs were spectacles in their own right, but those didn't come about every game.

Television in general helped popularize the sport as entertainment, though managers have long played to an in-stadium crowd; TV just made this crowd larger and faceless. Ted Barrett recalled one such ejection that, from the audience's perspective, would on its surface appear to be a contentious battle: "I started chuckling at him, and the guy gets up in my face and says, 'Don't you laugh. If you laugh, then they know this is all an act.' So I did everything I could just to bite my tongue."[20] Veteran Dale Scott summed it up thusly: "Sometimes you're going to be the prop for their little stage show." As journalist Jerome Holtzman noted in 1990 during one such ejection, "Durocher had no case and knew it, but the more he argued, the greater the cheers."[21]

Toward the later portion of this historical era, baseball as a whole solidified and expanded the scope of umpiring's organization. The Joe Brinkman Umpire School and Jim Evans Academy of Professional Umpiring provided an alternative for the McGowan/Somers/Wendelstedt training program, while baseball itself had founded the Umpire

Development Program in 1964 and the Professional Baseball Umpire Corp. (PBUC) by 1999.[22]

The Major League Umpires Association gained recognition by both the American and National Leagues in 1970, and thereafter won several significant pay raises for its umpire membership.[23]

Umpires during this era "controlled the game," were "very well respected," and got "the players [to] respond to [them]" in a way far different than the response Klem might have seen during his early seasons in the big leagues.[24] These contemporary umpires learned, possibly through McGowan/Somers' educational program alongside individual experimentation, ways to control the game that did not often need to result in an ejection. What worked for a Harvey may not have worked for a Rennert, and vice versa. "To each his own" seemed to work just fine during this evolving period.

The current era of umpiring comprises the twenty-first century: that which came after the merging of the American and National League staffs into one big Major League Baseball umpiring family.

In 1999, the Major League Umpires Association executed the controversial collective-bargaining strategy of mass resignation, due in part to a no-strike clause in the umpiring contract: Only some of its members submitted and maintained resignations while others did not or submitted and rescinded their resignations. According to union leader Richie Phillips, "(T)he relationship between Major League Baseball and umpires [was] at an all-time low," citing the tendency of league officials and team personnel to monitor, evaluate, critique, and ultimately decry umpire performance based on "amateur" analysis of television replays.[25]

In the aftermath, baseball accepted 22 resignations, leading to 22 lost jobs in 1999, umpires voted out Phillips as union chief, actually disbanded the 30-year-old union, and replaced it with the World Umpires Association.[26] The separate and distinct AL and NL staffs merged to form one major-league staff and the standardization of umpires was under way. As Rennert remarked, "We just had one league, National League, it was terrific. That was the only way; we took

pride in the National League staff. ... That's all gone now. They take away all the colorful umpires. They want them to work one way, all uniform, same way."[27]

On a related note, the burgundy red uniform jackets were retired and replaced by black jackets, the red shirts replaced by black ones, and the colorful NL and AL logo caps, along with the associated breast-pocket logo patches, were sent packing in favor of the generic black-and-white MLB graphic.

In 1999 NL umpires experienced 107 ejections while the AL staff generated 100 ejections for a grand total of 207. In 2000 the combined major-league staff threw out 228 players, managers and coaches, climbing to 242 ejections in 2001 before hitting a modern-era high of 282 heave-hos in 2003.

So what happened during the first few years of the new millennium that could possibly account for that spike in ejections?

First, getting rid of 22 umpires meant that MLB found itself in a hiring spree—prior to merging, the American and National Leagues hired a combined 25 minor-league umpires in the wake of the mass resignation—and statistics dating back to Klem indicate that umpires tend to eject more frequently earlier in their careers; this trend was much more pronounced back in Klem's day, but made another collective appearance with the mass hiring at the beginning of this umpiring era.[28]

Second, MLB in 2002 introduced a revolutionary new computerized pitch-mapping system known as QuesTec. The league office set goals for every umpire to maintain a certain minimum accuracy level in pitch calling (about 90 percent when introduced, and higher ever since), and umpires—a handful of them new to the full-time MLB level, and the rest of them new to either the AL or NL teams—felt the pressure. Speaking about the system in retrospect, then-crew chief and now Director of Umpires Randy Marsh recalled being thrown into the fire, only to gradually have cooled off ever since: "Guys have calmed down since then, partly because now a supervisor also looks over video of your calls."[29]

Though the modern era of umpiring may also be known for its breakneck pace of technological advances, the ability of MLB to forgo QuesTec in favor of the Pitch f/x and Zone Evaluation system effectively signified the league's acknowledgement that umpiring cannot be 100 percent automated: While QuesTec relied nearly fully on technology alone to evaluate an umpire's strike-zone performance, Zone Evaluation is a system that uses Pitch f/x data (essentially QuesTec's successor), *combined with* a supervisor's oversight and the ability to throw away bad pitches (such as those poorly caught by the catcher, missed when the catcher blocked out the umpire, etc.), to generate a pitch-calling report in addition to various evaluations for other elements of the umpires' game, such as the Supervisor Umpire Review and Evaluation (SURE) system.[30]

Even situation handling is reviewed—as Rennert noted, the "colorful" antics of the classic umpire-manager "rhubarb" found itself being taken out of baseball. For example, MLB suspended umpire Bob Davidson for violating the Office of the Commissioner's standards on situation handling after a 2012 rhubarb with Phillies skipper Charlie Manuel.[31] Thirty years before, that same argument would have been commonplace. As Randy Marsh explained, the modern umpire is one who can follow present-day officiating's golden rule: "Keeping yourself under control."

Situation handling and other similar duties have been standardized and placed in the Major League Baseball Umpire Manual (MLBUM), released annually to MLB umpires directly by MLB—not by an umpiring school or other third party. Umpires in the modern era are told that "over-elaborate, excessive signals [are not] an acceptable technique," and receive specific instructions related to character, dress code and appearance, fraternization, and other similar guidelines that follow umpires both on and off the field.[32] MLB looks for "staff uniformity in dealing with situations on the field" while stressing that its umpires shall "remain calm, confident, and non-confrontational."[33]

MLB and its minor-league PBUC (now called MiLB Umpire Development) counterpart began issuing "Standards for Removal from the Game" guidelines, which also appear in the MLBUM. These standards for ejection include the expected clauses regarding use of profanity directed at an umpire, vulgar insults, physical contact, histrionic gestures, and other similar unsporting conduct, along with instructions on the timing of certain ejections—eject a player/coach/manager who leaves his position to argue balls/strikes/warnings *after* warning him to immediately return. Put together, the MLBUM criteria or standards for removal further enforce the goal of "staff uniformity in dealing with situations" in the modern era.

In addition to the increased review and evaluation process, MLB developed a network and emails that have allowed baseball to effectively distribute "Heads Up" alerts to crews working games between two teams with bad blood. As major-league umpiring supervisor Steve Palermo explained in 2005, "We don't take any of this lightly."[34]

Does "Heads Up" lead to more ejections for intentional hit-by-pitches or fighting? In May 2004, MLB sent a "Heads Up" alert to Bruce Froemming's crew in Cleveland after a heated Twins-Indians series earlier in the year and, in lieu of officially warning the teams prior to the series, notified the two clubs that any intentional HBP or other retaliation would result in an immediate ejection. Over the four-game series, only one batter was hit and no ejections occurred.[35]

Former Washington Nationals manager Davey Johnson, for one, felt that umpires in the modern era overuse the warning allotted by Rule 6.02(c)(9)(B).[36] "What I grew up under, if somebody was intentionally plunked, very obviously and you knew it, 'Gone.'"[37] One theory regarding baseball's preference for the intentional-HBP warning over ejection posits that the league office itself is lenient in attitude toward the intentional hit-by-pitch through its lack of meaningful, strict punishment, thus implicitly encouraging the eons-old practice with, as Johnson states, more emphasis placed on the intermediate penalty of warnings, rather than on ejection: "By leaving ejections to the discretion of umpires, MLB creates a perverse incentive to strike first: The retaliatory hit-by-pitch is far more likely to warrant an ejection than the event that precedes it."[38]

In 2015 umpires ejected eight managers and coaches for arguing decisions related to warnings and similar non-ejections of pitchers; in several of these games, these actions nonetheless preceded a bench-clearing incident as the result of a later hit-by-pitch, which may both give credence to this theory and help to identify the prevailing subject of the modern baseball fight.[39] The misunderstanding that all hit-by-pitches after a warning is issued must be accompanied by ejection similarly perpetuates the theory, while the entire event of the post-warnings intentional HBP collaterally explains the presence of an extra ejection or two per fight-inclusive ballgame (since the manager/acting manager is ejected alongside the pitcher).[40]

Umpiring's modern era may be further divided into the following segments: one with no video instant replay, the second with limited replay, and the present with expanded replay. In the middle of the 2008 season, baseball adopted limited instant replay review specifically for home-run boundary calls—whether the hit was fair, foul, live, dead, or subject to spectator interference.[41]

From 2008 through 2013, baseball experienced 392 total replay reviews of home-run boundary calls, 132 of which (33.7 percent) were overturned.[42] A corresponding decline in ejections followed, bottoming out at 164 in 2009 and 179 in 2012.

When MLB expanded replay review to cover safe/out, catch/trap/transfer, select fair/foul, and HBP/foul/pitch calls for the 2014 season, some theorized that the more cordial process of asking an umpire for a replay review would drastically reduce if not wholly eliminate arguments and ejections from the game: "The advent of replay could spell the end of the flamboyant manager ejection."[43]

One of the reasons Hall of Famer Harvey cited as his opposition to expanded instant replay in 2014 was precisely the manager-umpire argument: "That's part of the game. That's getting fans into it. Now you're taking that away and saying, 'OK, we'll check with the replay.' Bull! Bull! That's not baseball."[44]

Fortunately for fans of the ejection, that ominous prediction has not come to fruition. Predictably, man-agers, coaches, and players were ejected 37 times for arguing a safe/out call in 2013 before a severe drop-off occurred thereafter when expanded replay took hold. In the replay-laden 2014 season, that figure had dropped to just five not-replayed safe/out ejections (32 fewer ejections), an 86 percent decline; there were also five safe/out ejections in 2015.[45] However, balls/strikes ejections grew from 83 in 2013 to 96 in 2014 (13, or 16 percent, more ejections) and 97 in 2015. MLB saw an additional 24 ejections for arguing a replay review in 2014, 15 replay review ejections in 2015, and 12 in 2016.[46]

In sum, it appears that the quantity of ejections since expanded replay came into existence has not decreased—to the contrary, it has increased—but instead simply has taken a different form or reason for ejection. Replay review ejections may be on the immediate decline following expanded replay's inaugural season, but MLB in 2015 also experienced the most regular-season ejections (212) since the pre-replay era (2007's 215 ejections).[47]

As far as ejection quality of correctness is concerned—whether the umpire made the correct or incorrect call on the play or pitch that was the subject of the ejection—statistics indicate that umpires were and continued to be correct a majority of the time, including a high of 72.3 percent ejections-specific accuracy in 2013.[48]

In the end, it appears that the umpire's accuracy or correctness seems to have little bearing on the ejection: What truly seems to matter is how the disagreeing or offended party/parties conduct themselves and whether their conduct violates the modern, uniform, and "colorless" umpire's standards for removal from the game.

As such, it appears that umpiring is set to cross a final threshold: Umpires in baseball's infancy were afterthoughts who struggled to establish their legitimacy as a working class within the game through frequent use of the ejection to establish their influence. This gave rise to arbiters who sought to preserve this legacy through individuation and vivacious distinctiveness during the latent era of the twentieth century's second half while resorting to ejection only when respectability and similar personality-based management failed. Finally, the modern umpire, burdened and pressured by a movement toward uniformity, systematically selects from his toolkit the hook of ejection only when appropriate, pursuant to a checklist of standards growing ever more uniform and, pursuant to league policy, unemotional in nature.

For more information and insight into the modern ejection, the website *Close Call Sports & The Umpire Ejection Fantasy League*, available at closecallsports. com, contains analysis of each ejection event, updated as such events occur. The data spreadsheet itself is available on the *UEFL Portal* section of the website.

NOTES

1 Josh Leventhal, *A History of Baseball in 100 Objects* (New York: Black Dog & Leventhal Publishers, 2015), 30.

2 James Charlton, *The Baseball Chronology* (New York: Macmillan, 1991), 106.

3 "John McGraw," retrosheet.org/boxesetc/M/Pmcgrj101.htm.

4 "Bill Klem," retrosheet.org/boxesetc/K/Pklem901.htm.

5 Gil Imber, "Polls: He Gone," *Close Call Sports/Umpire Ejection Fantasy League*, August 1, 2011, closecallsports.com/2011/08/polls-she-gone.html.

6 Harold Higham, "BioProject: Dick Higham," Society for American Baseball Research, sabr.org/bioproj/person/80be8b6b.

7 Major League Baseball, *2015 Umpire Media Guide*, ed. Michael Teevan and Donald Muller, 80.

8 David W. Anderson, "BioProject: Tommy Connolly," Society for American Baseball Research, sabr.org/bioproj/person/e99149e7.

9 Lee Lowenfish, "Dean of Umpires: Bill McGowan (review)," *NINE: A Journal of Baseball History and Culture*, 15 (2), Spring 2007: 142-144.

10 David H. Martinez, *The Book of Baseball Literacy*, 2nd ed. (Lincoln, Nebraska: Authors Choice Press, 2000), 120.

11 Bruce Weber, "Marty Springstead, Longtime Baseball Umpire and Supervisor, Dies at 74," *New York Times*, January 18, 2012, nytimes.com/2012/01/19/sports/baseball/marty-springstead-managers-bane-as-al-umpire-dies-at-74.html.

12 "Marty Springstead," retrosheet.org/boxesetc/S/Psprim901.htm.

13 Claire Smith, "Sox Complain as Clemens Is Biggest Out," *New York Times*, October 11, 1990, nytimes.com/1990/10/11/sports/the-playoffs-sox-complain-as-clemens-is-biggest-out.html.

14 "Terry Cooney," retrosheet.org/boxesetc/C/Pcoont901.htm.

15 "Doug Harvey," retrosheet.org/boxesetc/H/Pharvd901.htm.

16 *2015 Umpire Media Guide*: 17.

17 "Polls: He Gone."

18 "Rennert on His Umpiring Career," *Major League Baseball Advanced Media*, September 26, 2015, m.mlb.com/video/v503830783/atlmia-dutch-rennert-discusses-his-umpiring-career.

19 Jerome Holtzman, "Ump Earns a Major Cheer," *Chicago Tribune*, October 12, 1990, articles.chicagotribune.com/1990-10-12/sports/9003270572_1_augie-donatelli-umpire-diplomatic.

20 Zack Meisel, "Skipper vs. Ump Arguments Not Always as They Seem," Mlb.com, m.mlb.com/news/article/40650956/.

21 "Ump Earns a Major Cheer."

22 "Professional Baseball Umpire Corp.," SIC #8699, *Manta.com*.

23 "Stoic Men in Blue: Major League Umpires," *247baseball.com*. 247baseball.com/web/wp-content/uploads/2009/04/14-ban-bb2008-gp2.pdf.

24 *2015 Umpire Media Guide*: 17.

25 Murray Chass, "Baseball; Umpires Threaten to Quit on Sept. 2," *New York Times*, July 15, 1999, nytimes.com/1999/07/15/sports/baseball-umpires-threaten-to-quit-on-sept-2.html.

26 Tim Brown, "Umpires Replace Phillips, His Union," *Los Angeles Times*, December 1, 1999, articles.latimes.com/1999/dec/01/sports/sp-39263.

27 "Rennert on His Umpiring Career."

28 Murray Chass, "The Umpires Change Their Call: They No Longer Want to Resign," *New York Times*, July 28, 1999, nytimes.com/1999/07/28/sports/baseball-the-umpires-change-their-call-they-no-longer-want-to-resign.html.

29 Zev Borow, "Law & Order," ESPN, April 15, 2009, sports.espn.go.com/espnmag/story?id=3661613.

30 Evan Drellich, "Complex System in Place to Evaluate Umpires," MLB.com, m.mlb.com/news/article/37468304/.

31 Stephen Smith, "Umpire Bob Davidson Suspended One Game by MLB for Bad 'Situation Handling,'" *CBS News*, May 18, 2012, cbsnews.com/news/umpire-bob-davidson-suspended-one-game-by-mlb-for-bad-situation-handling/.

32 Tom Lepperd, *Major League Baseball Umpire Manual (MLBUM)* (USA: Major League Baseball, 2014), 5.

33 MLBUM, 1.

34 Mark Gonzalez, "Umps Give Peace a Chance," *Chicago Tribune*, June 22, 2005, articles.chicagotribune.com/2005-06-22/sports/0506220260_1_umpires-white-sox-cubs-cubs-dugout.

35 "Minnesota Twins vs. Cleveland Indians Box Score," Baseball Almanac, May 24, 2005, baseball-almanac.com/box-scores/box-score.php?boxid=200505240CLE.

36 "Official Baseball Rules," *Major League Baseball*, 2015, 75.

37 Patrick Reddington, "On the Nationals; Warnings After HBPs and MLB's Instructions to Umps," *Federal Baseball*, September 20, 2013, federalbaseball.com/2013/9/20/4752848/on-the-nationals-warnings-after-hbps-and-mlb-instructions-to-umps.

38 Adam Felder, "Battering the Batter," *The Atlantic*, May 5, 2015, theatlantic.com/entertainment/archive/2015/05/no-more-battering-the-batter/391991/.

39 Gil Imber, "Label: Warnings," *Close Call Sports/Umpire Ejection Fantasy League*, September 29, 2015, closecallsports.com/search/label/Warnings.

40 Eric Stephen, "Dodgers-Diamondbacks HBP Lead to Ejections, Managerial Hierarchy Lessons," *True Blue LA*, March 23, 2015, truebluela.com/2015/3/23/8280413/dodgers-diamondbacks-hbp-ejections.

41 Associated Press, "MLB Approves Replay in Series that Start Thursday," ESPN, August 27, 2008, sports.espn.go.com/mlb/news/story?id=3554357.

42 *2015 Umpire Media Guide*: 90.

43 Brendan Kennedy, "The Lost Art of the Ejection: Will MLB Replay Take Passion Out of the Game?" *TheStar*, April 8, 2014, thestar.com/sports/bluejays/2014/04/08/the_lost_art_of_the_ejection_will_mlb_replay_take_passion_out_of_game.html.

44 Daniel Brown, "Rewind This: Are Umpire-Manager Spats About to Become Extinct?" *San Jose Mercury News*, March 20, 2014, mercurynews.com/athletics/ci_25387123/rewind-this-are-umpire-manager-spats-about-become.

45 Gil Imber, "Historical Data," *Close Call Sports/Umpire Ejection Fantasy League*, portal.closecallsports.com/.

46 Gil Imber, "Reviewing Instant Replay: Observations and Implications from Replay's Inaugural Season," *Baseball Research Journal*, Spring 2015: 43-54.

47 "Historical Data."

48 "Historical Data."

Throwing Out 17 Players in One Game

By Bill Nowlin

The record for the largest number of participants ejected from one game is 17. The game was at Atlanta-Fulton County Stadium on August 12, 1984. The ejections were all made by home-plate umpire Steve Rippley, and one of the men he threw out was his current boss, Joe Torre.

In an early 2017 interview, Rippley recalled the game. "It was a beanball war. That was the gist of the whole thing. Remember Pascual Perez? He was a pitcher for Atlanta. The second baseman for San Diego was Alan Wiggins. The night before, Saturday night, Wiggins had laid down four bunts, two for base hits. I was working first base. Pascual Perez was sitting in the dugout charting and he was sitting at the first-base end of the dugout. After the third one, he started yelling at Wiggins. "Swing the bat ..." You know, baseball crap. They were yelling back and forth at each other, and then the fourth one they got on each other again, screaming.

"Well, the matchup the next day, the pitcher is Pascual and the first batter is Wiggins. First pitch of the game, he hits Wiggins. That started everything going. Then Pascual came up to bat and I believe Ed Whitson couldn't hit him. After I gave him three chances. It just escalated from there. Had he hit Pascual on the first pitch, everything would have been done. Eye for an eye. They got Wiggins, you got Pascual. OK, everything's done. Well, he couldn't hit Pascual and it escalated. I think I ran five sets of twos—managers and pitchers—and then we had seven guys that went in a brawl."[1]

Whitson had tried to hit Perez in the second but failed, and both teams were issued warnings. Perez struck out. In the fourth, Whitson tried to hit Perez with three consecutive pitches. Perez was dancing around with the bat in his hand, and looked menacing as Rippley kept approaching him to try to calm him. The benches cleared, but there was no further problem. The first two tossed were Whitson and his manager, Dick Williams.

The fifth passed without incident, but in the sixth inning both Williams's replacement, acting manager Ozzie Virgil Sr., and Padres pitcher Greg Booker were ejected. Greg Harris threw two innings for San Diego without incident, but with Craig Lefferts on the mound in the bottom of the eighth (the score was 5-1, Braves), Perez came up to bat again and Lefferts' first pitch hit him on the arm. Rippley threw out Lefferts and the third San Diego skipper, acting manager Jack Krol.

As described on Retrosheet, "both benches cleared and a 10-minute brawl ensued; Pascual Perez went to the Braves bench during the brawl but Champ Summers went after Perez there; Bob Horner blocked Summers from getting to Perez and the two fought; Rick Mahler, Steve Bedrosian, Gerald Perry, Summers, and Bobby Brown ejected as a result of the brawl." McSherry was knocked to the ground in the melee.

Rippley noted of Horner: "he was in the press box with a broken hand at the start of that game. As the game progressed, he went down and got in uniform and got in one of the fights." He wasn't thrown out of the game, because he wasn't in it. He was on the DL at the time. But after seeing Perez get thrown at a third time, he went downstairs. "You didn't have to be a brain surgeon to figure out what was going on."[2]

It still wasn't over. In the top of the ninth inning, Donnie Moore came on in relief. First batter up was Graig Nettles. Oops, hit by pitch. Rippley threw out Braves manager Torre and also Moore. But Nettles charged the mound, and four more Padres were ejected—Nettles, Kurt Bevacqua (who had been on the bench and was standing in the dugout; when hit by a beer, he charged into the stands), Tim Flannery, and Goose Gossage.

At this point, crew chief John McSherry (again, per Retrosheet) "ordered both benches cleared, sending the remaining players to their clubhouses; they were still available to play; McSherry thought about forfeiting the game but decided not to do so since the Braves had started the last brawl and McSherry did not want to give the game to the Padres, who were the instigators of the series of events."

"We started worrying about crowd control," McSherry said after the game. "That's the reason we cleared both benches."[3] Policemen were positioned on the tops of both dugouts, and police later said five fans had been arrested.[4]

After the game, McSherry said of the brawl, "I've never seen violence like that. It's a miracle somebody didn't get seriously hurt."[5] San Diego GM Jack McKeon accused the umpires of losing control of the game. McSherry retorted, "The guy who lost control was in their dugout," referring to Williams, who watched the last few rounds from the stands. *Atlanta Constitution* columnist John McGrath headed his admittedly biased column "Padres' Williams Wanted to Play Thug for a Day."[6]

Fourth on the Padres' managerial depth chart was bullpen coach Harry Dunlop. It was he who was acting manager when the game ended.

Torre called Dick Williams "an idiot and you can spell that with a capital I," and said, "He should be suspended for the rest of the season."[7] While he was at it, Torre added, "It was gutless. It stinks. It was Hitler-like action."[8] Dick Williams said the Braves started it, adding, "We will not be intimidated."[9] Bob Watson of the Braves declared, "It won't end here."

In all, five Braves were tossed and an even dozen Padres. Two guys who *didn't* get thrown out were Perez and Wiggins. In fact, Perez got the win, improving his record to 11-4.

Dick Williams was suspended for 10 days and fined $10,000, and Torre for three days, fined $1,000.[10] Five players were also suspended and fined, two from the Padres and three from the Braves. Seven other Padres players and the team's first two ejected acting managers were also fined.

Torre is, in 2017, chief baseball officer for Major League Baseball. Rippley has worked as an umpire observer since 2009.

Several videos made during the game are on YouTube, the longest of which appears to be at: youtube.com/watch?v=rlHJ9ZaREmc

NOTES

1   Author interview with Steve Rippley, January 10, 2017.

2   Steve Dolan, "14 Are Ejected as Beanball War Erupts in Atlanta," *Los Angeles Times*, August 13, 1984: C1. Different newspapers gave different numbers of how many had been ejected.

3   Gene Ballard, "Padres Go Down Fighting, Literally; Braves Win, 5-3," *Augusta* (Georgia) *Chronicle*, August 13, 1984: B5.

4   Associated Press, "Atlanta Tips Pads in Brawl-Marred Tilt," *The Oregonian* (Portland), August 13, 1984: 66.

5   Chris Mortensen, "McSherry Calls Brawls the Worst He Has Ever Seen," *Atlanta Constitution*, August 13, 1984: 3D.

6   John McGrath, "Padres' Williams Wanted to Play Thug for a Day," *Atlanta Constitution*, August 13, 1984: 3D.

7   Ballard.

8   "Braves, Padres Brawl, Then Say Wait 'Til Fall," *Seattle Daily Times*, August 13, 1984: 18.

9   Associated Press, "Atlanta Tips Pads in Brawl-Marred Tilt."

10 Associated Press, "NL Gives Suspensions to Williams, Torre," *Dallas Morning News*, August 17, 1984: 5B.

Dave Mellor, Director of Grounds, Fenway Park

I started here in the 2001 season. I grew up a Red Sox fanatic. Previously I worked for the Milwaukee Brewers for 16 years, from 1985. I also interned with the Angels and the Giants. The Green Bay Packers played half their home games in Milwaukee, so I also worked Packers games for eight years, too.

Safety and playability is our first priority. Certainly, if we have a big event, a concert, that could cause extra work for us to repair—if it's a major sod job or something—we'll certainly keep the umpire in the loop. We'll say, "Hey, if you notice something, let us know." But we wouldn't let a team go out there if we thought it might be in unsafe condition.

Most concerts are on the field five to seven days, and the length of time combined with the weather dictate a lot of how much wear and stress the grass gets. If it's hot and wet, there's potential for more stress on the grass. The Rolling Stones concert in 2005 was actually out there 13 days. We- re-sodded 40,000 square feet of the outfield. We did everything we could. We had guys on their hands and knees smoothing everything out. Just like we talk to the players—"Hey, there's new sod out there. If you need anything, let us know. If you notice anything, let us know." I think that communication both ways is important.

We hope for the best, but we plan for the worst. So we always have sod on call. Based on the size of the stage, what we think we might need. We have contractors on call for aerating and top dressing and sod if we need it. The sixth day of that concert, a roadie said to me, "Dude, do you smell rotting pumpkins?" And I said, "Yeah, I think that's the grass" because it had been really wet and hot. We had 30 hours from the time the stage came off to replace 40,000 square feet.

Most of my contact with umpires is weather-related. But my office is next door to the umpire's room, so I try to stop by and see them even if it's a dry homestand just to say hi and welcome them, let them know if they need anything to let me know. A lot of times, they'll stop in themselves. The relationship with the umpires is so important. A lot of them are good friends. I want them to know that they can trust me, that. I'm going to give them the accurate forecast and I'm going to be honest with them about how much water the field can take. That working relationship is so important.

If it looks like weather is going to be an issue, I talk with the crew chief. It's important that the umpires are in the loop with the percentage chance of rain, the timing of the rain, the duration, how heavy it could be, if there's wind involved—which can certainly affect the tarp, if there's lightning, which can certainly affect player safety but also the people in the stands. It's all-inclusive. Before the game, they may talk to the weather forecasters themselves. They have their own weather service but we share ours with them, too, if they want to see that everybody's on the same page. We want to be very open with our forecast. We wouldn't want them ever to think that they weren't getting the full picture.

The technology has improved so much. For a long time you didn't have radar at all. When I started 31 years ago, you watched the news in the morning and if they said there was a chance of rain this morning and you saw a black cloud roll in—which could just be a normal dark cloud with the sun behind it—everybody was on edge. "Oh, my gosh, it might rain." The boss would say, "Hey, get ready." There was a time in Milwaukee where groundskeepers would call the local airport for a forecast. In the late 80s and early 90s, private weather service contractors went to Congress and said you shouldn't be able to call the airport unless you're a pilot. So sports teams started doing private deals. We actually have two weather services, Telvent Weather, which is part of DTN, and Fox 25, which is here in Boston. Sometimes they have similar forecasts and sometimes they interpret things different, too. We provide all that information to the umpires so they can make the best decisions. The umpires have a separate service that they use, Accuweather.

Certainly now with the technology that we have with all the different weather apps, combined with the weather service that we can talk to, it's incredible. We can look at radar, but to have the weather service meteorologist be able to look at it and decipher how the winds are affecting it and the pressure and the temperature and the sea breeze and the ocean really is important, all of that. Weather changes so much. Boston has to be some of the most challenging to predict. The ocean's involved. The Worcester hills. Forecasts can change so rapidly.

If there's a potential weather situation, before the game, the umpires get on the phone, but after it starts they just go off of whatever information we provide them. During the game I try to be down the bottom of the runway so it's close proximity. If the weather's good, I can be in my office and then just go across the hall, come through that runway, see them, and then end up in our drying agent supply in a storage area over there and also down by Canvas Alley where there is literally tons of it. Then I'll go out every three outs and will take my phone with radar on it and show the umpire what's happening and what the weather service sees with that rain or arrival time, how heavy it could be, the duration, if there's wind, like I said. If it's a long inning, we try to give them the most up-to-date forecast that you can. With one out, I'll call, but if it's a long inning, I may call two or three times during an inning.

We do the tarp when the umpire wants it, just like we do drying agent when the umpire they want it. If a player says, "Hey, we want drying agent" or "Why don't you put the tarp on?" that's not our decision. It's up to the crew chief. So we work very closely with them. They are great to work with, because they respect what we know about our field—if the field can take more rain, what the crew can do. I'm very proud of how hard the crew works. They will sprint with 50-pound bags of drying agent, calcined clay that soaks up water for us on a wet day and holds water on a hot day. Guys have taken out five tons of Turface during a game, in a nine-inning game over three hours. There's 40 bags in a ton. That doubleheader a couple of years ago, 2011 at the end of August there was a doubleheader with tropical weather. The guys actually did 10 tons. Five tons per game. That communication with the umpires is huge.

It's always through the umpires. I'll usually work with the crew out of the dugout for home plate or the mound and Jason [Griffith, Assistant Director of Grounds] runs the Alley [Canvas Alley] and will do the skin, and he'll work with the umpires on the skin, where they want it.

My hat's off to the umpires. They are great to work with and the communication and respect that they have for what our guys can do is outstanding and greatly appreciated. It really makes a difference in how smooth things operate.

Interview with Dave Mellor by Bill Nowlin on August 16, 2015

Dave Mellor, head groundskeeper, Fenway Park.

Dean Lewis, Umpires Room Attendant

Dean Lewis has been with the Red Sox since 1980, when he was 16 years old, working in the Red Sox clubhouse with his twin brother Dan. Dan has gone on to other work as a VP in the hotel industry. Dean spent 25 years investigating insurance fraud, working both jobs, but has been exclusively with the Red Sox since 2005.

He started as the umpires room attendant in 1990, some 25 years as of the time of the interview.

Bill Nowlin: So you've been doing it from when the room used to be above the Red Sox clubhouse.

Dean Lewis: Yeah, that whole room was about as big as this room right here [the eating area]. That room had like six showers. They make this nice room, but here it's only one shower. The umpires are usually leaving right after the game. They always cut their flights close. They'll be like running back and forth—"keep the water running. Keep the water on"—and then they go flying out the door.

BN: You never know when you're going to have an extra-inning game.

DL: Exactly. Many times they miss their flights. I already asked them, "Are you leaving Sunday night after the game, or are you leaving Monday morning?" They said Sunday night. I always like that.

It's come a long way, the way the umpires are treated. They used to get eight cold sandwiches after the game and they'd have to ask for hot dogs before the game. Now I get everything. We've got deli meats, tuna, chicken. There's catered food that I start heating up right now so it will be done. Its fresh catered, not frozen.

BN: In the refrigerator there you've got about 10 kinds of drinks—ginger ale, Sprite…

DL: Then I record the game for them in case they want to see…Now with the replay on the field, they don't do this as much. But before replay, "Could you go back to the play in the fourth inning with Pedroia?"

BN: But you're video recording the whole game here? [Television and DVR on top of the refrigerator]

DL: Right.

BN: Did they ever come in during a game? Like if there's a delay or something?

DL: There's the home run thing, for the disputed home runs. [Points to closed door.] That's a replay box they can look at. They only use that for home runs and that was before they had the replay on the field, but I think they can still review home runs here. We haven't had one reviewed for quite a while. But they check that box every day; a rep from MLB comes in and checks the box. They open the top thing, they get on the phone, and the people in New York ask, "What do you see on the screen?" I'll hear them say, "I see stripes in right field. OK, it's red. It's green. OK."

And they come in during a rain delay.

BN: They usually get here about an hour and a half before the game?

DL: Yeah. Some are a little earlier, some are a little later, but that's probably the average.

BN: And how long after the game are they gone?

DL: It depends. The crew chief or whoever does home plate, I'll go, "Do you want a drink? Do you want a beer?" He'll go, "Oh, just throw me a Miller Lite or a water for now." Usually, they'll just want a water.

BN: Do you stay in the room here during the game in case they need something?

DL: No, I go back to the [Red Sox] clubhouse. I have to do laundry and towels.

BN: What if they need something?

DL: They'll call the batboy. If all of a sudden the temperature dropped or the sun started glaring, the batboy will say, "Dean, Laz Diaz says he needs his sunglasses. They're in the top right of his trunk." I'll come down and run them to the batboy on the visiting side. I'll say, "Here, just give these to Chris." Our batboy. He'll give them to the umpire.

BN: When they go to the field, they go from here over across the way to the visitors….

DL: Right. They're led by Security. There's a new rule - it's posted right here on the wall—that the visiting team can't go in the runway…. Official MLB Director of Security. The umpires had an incident this year. Doug Eddings. [There was a shoving incident during the April 29 game at Fenway, where Blue Jays hitting coach Brook Jacoby shoved umpire Eddings after the game. Jacoby was suspended for 14 games.]

BN: "Must wait until all the umpires are completely off the field and out of the visitor umpire tunnel before departing the…" So the visiting club has to stay in their dugout until after the umpires have left the field.

DL: It only takes a few seconds. I remember the umpire telling me, "I've been umpiring a long time and, including my minor-league career, I have never been pushed by a coach or a player."

BN: Back in the old days, 100 years ago….No umpire's going to linger on the field for very long anyhow. They have no reason to.

DL: You might see them get yelled at by players, and they'll yell back. I remember the old umpire room—Jim Leyritz, the catcher, yelling at Tom McLelland, who's like seven feet tall, about something, a call. And Tim McLelland was not taking it. I was midway on the stairs up to the room and I'm thinking, "Are they going to charge each other?" They didn't, but I was right in the middle on the staircase and I had nowhere to go.

DL: I've never had any bad [relationships with umpires]. Based on my job, we're all "yes men." Even with the ballplayers. I mean, if they asked for something illegal…Major League Baseball prohibits chewing tobacco. We're not allowed to get that.

DL: They get treated well now, the umpires. They didn't used to. They got treated like crap back in the day.

Dean Lewis.

BN: They were telling me the other day that DHL ships their trunks in. You're the one who opens them up.

DL: Yeah, I unpack them. It doesn't take long.

BN: They've got their dirty laundry in there from the night before.

DL: Right.

BN: So you have to take that for the four of them and get that all washed.

DL: Yeah, the laundry room is right there [across the way.]

BN: You wash it and dry it and hang it up in their lockers here.

DL: It's not a hard job. It beats insurance. I didn't sell insurance; I did claims. But this job beats that. I never went back.

BN: You get tips from them.

DL: Oh yeah. They take care of me. The Red Sox don't pay for this. They don't pay for the food. I pay for it out of the money they give me. I also do all the baseballs. Up until the mid-'90s, the umpires did the baseballs. One by one, the umpires would ask, "Do you mind doing the baseballs?" and next thing you know, I do them all the time. That's why they take care of me.

BN: You've got that Chesapeake mud.

DL: Yeah, here it is right here.

BN: Each crew comes through maybe twice a year?

DL: Some of these guys it seems like I see them three or four times a year and then I don't see them for a couple of years. I get the schedule at the beginning of the year.

BN: What is it that you're making there for them right now? You're cooking something for them?

DL: Today I'm making lasagna, ribs, chicken wings, and then there's a veggie. I usually get a pasta, two meat dishes, and a veggie dish.

BN: Do they tell you what they'd like to have?

DL: I just sort of mix it up. It's the caterer who used to do both clubhouses for 20 years.

BN: Oliva's?

DL: Right. I pick it up now. They don't deliver it. He's in Milford. He does a great job.

BN: So if there's a rain delay, you come whipping back over here to see if they need anything.

DL: If they're wearing their jackets, I'll ask if they want me to put them on a low heat. Maybe they'll say, "No, I have another one here."

BN: But for the most part if something happens in the middle of the game, like a piece of equipment…

DL: The batboy calls me. He doesn't have a key to get in here. They just call me. I'm in the clubhouse. Maybe the umpire brought out a heavy jacket and all of a sudden, the sun came out. Or he'll need his sunglasses.

BN: If they want a bottle of water during the game, the batboy….

DL: He has those. Mostly I'm in the clubhouse during the game.

BN: But as soon as you know the game's wrapping up, you're over here.

DL: Yeah, to finalize the DVR.

BN: And then you'll pack up their trunks?

DL: They'll pack up their trunks. Sometimes if they're running late at the end of a series, like if the game ends at 4 and they've got a flight at 5:15, they'll get a police escort. They'll say, "Dean, we're cutting it close. Do you mind packing our trunks?" I never say no. Or if they're going on vacation, I'll have the guy from DHL — there's tons of food left over every

night — I'll have him sit down and eat. "Do you want me to do your clothes for you so you don't have them stinking up your trunk for a week?" Usually, they say, "Oh, that would be great." Like I say, I try to help them out as much as I can.

It's a pretty simple job. It's just the hours. We're here a lot of hours. Twelve, 14, 16-hour day. I mean, I'm not complaining.

BN: You wouldn't have been doing it all these years if it was intolerable.

DL: Exactly. The players are good. The umpires treat me good. They never got any of this. Like I said, they used to get cold sandwiches. They used to stay at the old Howard Johnson's, right behind. Now they all stay at upscale hotels. The money's a lot better for them. The conditions are way better for them. They get a lot more than I get.

They get tickets to each game; they can upgrade their rooms. They can give tickets to hotel clerks and hotel general managers. "I can give you tickets tonight — Yankees/Red Sox."

BN: When you get into the postseason, is it much different for you?

DL: Well, there's six umpires. I get more food. A lot of people in and out. The Commissioner was here. Joe Torre, really nice guy. In fact, he had a really classy comment when the umps thanked me at the end of the 2013 World Series. The umpires said, "Dean, congratulations for winning the World Series." I looked at the umps and said, "Well, thank you, but I really didn't have anything to do with it. All I did was show up each day for work." Joe Torre — he was right here, and I was right here, finalizing the DVR — he goes, "Dean, that's what it's all about." I thought that was classy. I just said, "Thanks, Joe."

BN: Well, if you hadn't rubbed up the balls….

DL: Yeah, exactly. It was nice that somebody recognized me a little, being the peon that I am. Working in the back room.

BN: Joe Torre worked from the ground up. He was a catcher, had to go through the minor leagues before that.

How many balls do you do per game?

DL: Like 12, 14 dozen. It depends if it rains. Or if Pedro Martinez is pitching and they're fouling them off. Out it goes. Out it goes.

BN: Clint [Fagan] is a minor-league umpire now, filling in. I guess most crews usually come in together, but do you sometimes have guys that had never been here come wandering in on their own?

DL: That hasn't happened in a long time. Maybe once in a great while. They might be directed to the umpires room. They'd say, "He says he's umping the game, and it's his first time here." I'd say, "Oh, tell him I'll be right down." I'll unlock the door in two seconds. He'll say, "I just landed. They told me to meet them at the park." I'll say, "Well, just relax. Sit down and watch TV."

After a game, sometimes I'll pop in and they'll still be here. "Oh, sorry, Dean, we're leaving in a second." I'll say, "Guys, Gate D is open 24 hours. You stay as long as you want. I can always clean this tomorrow." They like when I say stuff like that. And I mean that. It's not bothering me. When I'm done in the clubhouse, if you're still here, shut the door on the way out.

BN: And these guys are probably not high-demand guys anyhow.

DL: No. They're umpires, not players.

Interview with Dean Lewis conducted by Bill Nowlin on July 4, 2015

There were nine photographs of umpires on the walls of the Fenway Park umpires room. Knowing that there were 10 umpires in the National Baseball Hall of Fame, it was easy enough to "poll the photos" and see that Hank O'Day was the one who was missing. O'Day was named to the Hall of Fame in 2013. Apparently his induction had not prompted an upgrade to the room. A quick email to Mike Ivins of the Red Sox resulted in him contacting Susan Perrin of the Sox, and within a matter of weeks, a photograph of O'Day had been affixed to the wall. --BN

Chris Cundiff, Batboy, Fenway Park

I started working as the Red Sox batboy in 1992. I used to help Dean [Lewis] wait on the umpires, so I know most of them. I'll stop down there and say hello. They're all pretty good. Always exceptions.

After Dean rubs up the balls and the umpires inspect them, the authenticator usually brings them to me. Sometimes a security guard brings them across the field to me. Once it got screwed up and nobody brought them to me, so there was a little bit of a panic.

I start with 60. Five dozen. Dean's also done maybe 10 or 12 extra dozen sitting around. We probably use 90, maybe 120 a game. Before the game, I keep the ball bag by the manager's bench in the Red Sox dugout. When the game starts, they're on the field with me the whole game. I probably sit them about five feet out from the wall. I've been using the same bag since the beginning, the original handles and everything. Had to have it get repaired a couple of times, but it's the very same bag.

I'm both batboy and ballboy. The umpire usually signals that he wants three balls. I keep a running tally. If they foul one off, it's four, so I usually go with one more, and I usually keep a couple in my pocket. If I run out to get a bat, and I know he needs two, I'll give them to him. The thing that throws you off is when it gets fouled off to the visitor's side and there's nobody there to get it, I've got to run over and get it and then I don't have the balls with me. So if I'm stuck over there and they need a couple, I can do something to keep the game moving along. I don't want to break the rhythm, whether it's the pitcher or the hitting. You just try to get in and out of there as quick as you can. There's always this weird dichotomy of what they throw out. If the ball is hit, they won't throw it out, but if it's fouled…it's weird, the same damage is done to the ball.

Recently, the ground crew started bringing water out to the umpires, which is great. You've got two minutes between innings so you've got to run it around and then get back around and collect the bottles, too. I always keep one behind the bag for the home-plate guy. Yesterday he needed water almost every half-inning. If the home-plate guy has to leave the field in between innings, I'll stand at the plate with some balls while they're warming up so if they throw it in the dirt, I'll have another ball. They're pretty quick about getting back after leaving.

I'll joke with them throughout the game. You've got nothing else to do when you're stuck out there for three hours. We usually have running jokes about the time of game. They don't care who wins, but—es-

Chris Cundiff.

Ball bag, Fenway Park.

pecially if we're [Red Sox] up, I'll go, "Can we have a couple of strikes so we can get out of here a little quicker?" I probably said stuff that could get me ejected, but they know I'm joking. If someone gets really mad at them, I'll say, "I don't think he agreed with your call there. I'm just going out on a limb with that one."

I interact with them more than I do with the players during the game. They'll ask how my kids are doing. You'll know some things about their family. When John Hirschbeck's son Michael died, he'd batboy'd with me a few times. He was a big Cleveland Indians fan, but he loved it here, too. He probably batboy'd about four times. I know where certain ones of them go drinking, where they hang out at, where they're going to go eat. I'm from Kentucky originally, and there's like seven umps from Kentucky so I'll talk to them about down there. I get along with most of them pretty well.

Interview with Chris Cundiff by Bill Nowlin on August 16, 2015.

Replay as an Umpiring Tool

By David Vincent

In 1955, a producer on Canadian television used a kinescope to show a replay during a Hockey Night in Canada telecast, the first time anyone had shown a play a second time on television. In the early 1960s, a director for CBS Sports invented a replay system using video tape that could be played immediately, unlike the kinescope. Tony Verna's invention, first used in the 1963 Army-Navy football game, has grown in scope and capability and has become one of the fundamental technologies in modern-day sports television.

This capability has crossed over into the world of sports officiating. As televised sports grew in popularity and capability, fans became more concerned with the accuracy of officials. The National Football League first used an "instant replay" system in 1986, allowing officials to review a play immediately after it occurred. The NFL's current system was instituted in 1999. The National Hockey League started using replay in 1991 with an off-ice official in the building. The system was centralized in 2003 with a crew watching every game from Toronto. Those replay officials discuss certain plays with the referee at the arena via telephone. The National Basketball Association started using a replay system in 2002.

Major League Baseball was slow to embrace the technology. As televised games became more popular and production companies expanded their camera coverage, fans got to see new and unfamiliar angles. This included a camera slightly offset in center field and the later addition of a strike zone outline. Fans could then judge the accuracy of an umpire's balls and strikes calls, although the box on the screen did not correctly show the zone. This technology later led to a series of systems used by MLB to judge an umpire's work behind the plate.

It was only after a series of questioned calls in a ten-day period during the 2008 season that MLB officials put a system in place to review home runs. The review system, instituted on August 28, 2008, could only be used to answer one of the following three questions:

Was the potential home run fair or foul?

Did a fan interfere with a potential home run?

Did a potential home run go over the fence?

The decision to use the new replay system could only be made by the umpire crew chief, who was also the person who determined whether or not a call should be reversed. All games are monitored at a central location in New York by a technician and an umpire (either a retired umpire or an umpire supervisor). A television monitor and phone were provided in each ballpark for the crew chief's use. The chief was required to check the equipment before the game by calling the technician who would send video to that monitor.

If the crew chief decided to review a play, he would speak with the technician. The umpire supervisor would not talk with the umpires at the game. One umpire always remains on the field while the others watch the replay. The chief would only reverse a call if there was clear and convincing evidence that the ruling on the field was incorrect.

Once the crew chief made a determination and announced it to the teams, neither team was allowed to argue the decision. Any such argument was grounds for ejection. Also, no one can request that the umpires review the call. Managers do ask about certain rulings and as they have done in the past but it is up to the chief to make the determination to actually watch the replay.

If a home run ruling is reversed to a ball in play, the crew chief must place runners where he believed they would have been had the call been made properly on the field.

Table 1 shows the yearly totals of review system usage. Since the implementation, about 33% of calls reviewed have been overturned. Table 2 shows the breakdown of calls by one of the three types allowed. Most calls that have been reviewed are to see if the ball went over the fence. The fair or foul reviews have been overturned about 33% of the time whereas the "over the fence" type has been overturned about 38% of the time.

Most of the new ballparks have seats that allow fans to reach over the fence and possibly interfere with a ball in play. Tropicana Field in St. Petersburg, AT&T Park in San Francisco and PNC Park in Pittsburgh are often quoted by umpires as particularly bad in this regard. The Trop also has a roof that makes tracking the ball difficult for players and umpires. Fenway Park in Boston (the oldest park in the majors) has many quirky configurations that keep umpires on their toes. The configuration of the relatively new Monster Seats above the left-field wall in Boston causes a lot of balls to carom back onto the field after flying over the top of the wall. This is a tough call for an umpire 37 feet lower than the top of the wall and a long distance from the wall. In Houston, Minute Maid Park has lots of lines in left-center field that can cause issues with rulings and Citi Field in New York has a set of painted lines on the outfield walls that cause issues for umpires when trying to decide where the ball struck the wall in relation to those lines.

The ballparks with the most replay uses are shown in Table 3. It is no surprise that most of the parks at the top of this list are the ones noted in the above paragraph. Table 4 shows the other end of this spectrum: the parks with the fewest uses of the replay system. The Marlins moved into the new stadium, Marlins Park, in 2012. There were six usages of the replay system in their former home and four through 2013 in the new home. Those parks are not listed in the chart.

The first use of the new system occurred on September 3, 2008, six days after it was put in place.[1] The Yankees were playing the Rays at Tropicana Field in St. Petersburg. With one runner on base in the top of the ninth inning, Alex Rodriguez hit a ball down the left-field line that cleared the wall just inside the pole but much higher than the top of the pole. After the ball was ruled fair by third-base umpire Brian Runge, Rays manager Joe Maddon came onto the field to ask about the call. Crew chief Charlie Reliford watched the replay and upheld the call.

Sixteen days later, the Twins were at The Trop. In the bottom of the fourth, Carlos Pena hit a fly ball to right-center field that was touched by a fan. The ball was ruled in play but crew chief Gerry Davis watched the replay and overturned the call to a three-run homer. This was the first time a call was reversed using the new system.

On September 26, 2008, the Dodgers were playing at AT&T Park in San Francisco. Bengie Molina batted in the bottom of the sixth frame and swatted a fly ball down the right-field line. The ball struck at the top of the wall a few feet to the left of the "Splash Hits" sign and was ruled in play. Giants manager Bruce Bochy had told Emmanuel Burriss to pinch run for Molina if he reached base, so Burriss ran onto the field and replaced Molina at first base. In the dugout, Omar Vizquel told Bochy that the ball struck the green metal roof on top of the wall, which is out of play and a homer. Vizquel handed Bochy the ball, which had green paint on it. Bochy showed the ball to crew chief Tim Welke and asked about the call. After a brief huddle with the other umpires, Welke watched the replay and reversed the call to a home run. Burriss (remember him—the pinch runner?) ran the bases from first to home to score the run on Molina's homer (remember him—the batter?). Bochy wanted the umpires to allow Molina back into the game and when they refused, Bochy protested the contest. Molina was credited with a home run and two runs batted in but no run scored since Burriss scored the run. When Burriss returned to the dugout with a big smile on his face, Molina greeted him by saying "Good swing!" The total delay was 12 minutes, including time discussing the pinch-runner situation. The Giants won the contest, 6-5, so the protest was not heard.

The first time a ball was ruled a home run on the field but overturned by replay occurred on May 13, 2009 in Pittsburgh. In the bottom of the first inning, Adam LaRoche hit a fly ball to right that struck either a railing or a screen above the 21-foot wall. Either object is in play but the ball was ruled a home run. LaRoche stopped at second base on the play but then went on to score on the initial call. Crew chief Randy Marsh watched the replay and put LaRoche back on second.

On June 19, 2009, the Brewers played the Tigers in Detroit, and, for the first time, two calls were reviewed in the same game. In the bottom of the third inning, Miguel Cabrera's hit went over the top of the fence, hit the roof of the bullpen dugout, and came back on the field. It was ruled in play but the Tigers argued the call so crew chief Dale Scott looked at the replay and overturned the call to a home run. Dusty Ryan's line drive down the left-field line in the bottom of the fourth was ruled a home run. Brewers manager Ken Macha objected to the call, so Scott watched the replay and reversed the call to in-play, awarding Ryan a double. Two calls were reviewed and both were changed, one to a home run and the other from a home run to a ball in play.

Through the 2013 season eight games have had more than one play reviewed. Three of those were at Citizens Bank Park in Philadelphia (7/11/2010, 5/5/2013, and 8/4/2013) and two of them at Citi Field in New York (9/22/2012 and 8/4/2013). All six calls in Philadelphia involved possible fan interference or whether the ball cleared the fence.

The Diamondbacks were in San Francisco on September 29, 2009. In the top of the fourth inning, immediately after a home run by Miguel Montero, Ryan Roberts hit a fly ball to left that Andres Torres jumped for and caught over the top of the wall. The ball flew up out of the glove as Torres started back to the ground, hit the top of the wall and bounced back onto the field, where Torres, while lying on the ground, caught it. Since the ball did not go over the fence, it was still in play. Since it hit the fence it was not a catch. The play was ruled a homer but crew

chief Dana DeMuth watched the replay and overturned it to a double.

On October 31, 2009, the replay system was used for the first time in postseason play. In the top of the fourth inning of Game Three of the World Series, Alex Rodriguez hit a fly ball down the right-field line just inside the pole. The ball struck a television camera and was called in play by RF umpire Jeff Nelson. Yankees manager Joe Girardi asked about the call, so crew chief Gerry Davis and three of the other five umpires watched the replay and overturned the call to a home run. Thus, ARod was the batter for the first usage of replay and the first usage in postseason.

The Nationals visited Citi Field in New York on April 11, 2010. In the top of the first, Josh Willingham hit a fly ball to center field that struck the wall just to the right of the vertical line indicating a home run. The ball was called in play and three runs scored on the triple. The third runner, Adam Dunn, ran over the Mets catcher, Rod Barajas, and the ball rolled towards the backstop. Willingham tried to score on the misplay but was tagged out by Barajas. The umpires huddled on the field and then crew chief Derryl Cousins watched the replay and overturned the call to a grand slam home run, thus negating the out call at the plate on Willingham.

The Minnesota Twins opened a new ballpark, Target Field, on April 12, 2010. In that first game, Mike Cameron of the Red Sox hit a fly ball down the left-field line that went between the pole and the limestone facing of the stands. It was ruled a foul ball by umpire Kerwin Danley. Red Sox manager Terry Francona asked about the ruling, so crew chief Tim Tschida looked at the replay and upheld the call. The gap between the pole and the wall is very narrow.

In the top of the ninth inning in Cleveland on August 6, 2010, pinch-hitter Jim Thome's fly hit the yellow stripe at the top of the left-center-field wall and caromed back onto the field. It was ruled in play but the Twins thought it was a home run. Crew chief Gerry Davis watched the replay and upheld the call. Twins manager Ron Gardenhire came on the field after the review and argued violently the about the ruling. Gardenhire was ejected by Davis, the first time someone was tossed objecting a replay decision. A complete list of all people ejected for arguing a replay decision is shown later in this article.

On August 29, 2010, the Marlins played in Atlanta. In the bottom of the ninth with two out and the score tied at six, Braves catcher Brian McCann hit a fly ball to right that hit over the top of the barrier wall, bounced off the back wall, and landed on the field. It was ruled in play but the Braves had started on the field to celebrate the victory. The umpires huddled then crew chief Tim McClelland watched the replay and overturned the call to a home run. It was the first game-ending homer reviewed.

On August 1, 2011, the Indians visited Boston. In the top of the eighth, Asdrubal Cabrera's fly ball hit what appeared to be the top of the wall just inside the right-field pole and rebounded onto the field. It was ruled in play but the umpires huddled. Crew chief Gerry Davis watched the replay and overturned the call to a home run. The ball had struck a fan in the front row and Davis changed the call when he saw the woman react to being hit. She had a large mark on her thigh later and the stitches of the ball were clearly visible in the bruise.

In the bottom of the third in Kansas City on August 17, 2011, Billy Butler's fly ball hit the top of the padding and caromed back onto the field. It was ruled a home run but Yankees manager Joe Girardi asked about the call. Crew chief Dana DeMuth watched the replay and upheld the call. The Yankees were upset by this. Mariano Rivera yelled from the dugout and was told to stop by plate umpire Chad Fairchild. When Rivera continued, coaches moved him away. Girardi went out to talk with DeMuth, insisting that the ground rule made this a ball in play. After the game, the four umpires were on the warning track with umpire supervisor Steve Palermo reviewing the ground rule.

On September 4, 2011, the Phillies were playing the Marlins in Florida. In the top of the sixth, Hunter Pence hit a fly ball to right, where Bryan Petersen made a leaping attempt to catch the ball. His glove was above the yellow stripe at the top of the wall but a fan reached over the wall with a Phillies cap and touched the ball. The ball was ruled in play, with Pence reaching second and Ryan Howard running from first to third. Both managers came out of the dugout. The umpires huddled and crew chief Joe West watched the replay and overturned the call to fan interference. Pence was called out and Howard returned to first base. The ball might have cleared the fence without the interference and it might have been caught. Phillies manager Charlie Manuel talked to West questioning the interpretation of using the replay system in this instance, not the decision made after watching the replay. Manuel was ejected by West. This process, including the review, took 13 minutes and the Phillies protested the game because of the use of the replay. At the time, the game was tied, 2-2 and the Marlins won the contest in 14 innings, 5-4.

In the eighth inning at Wrigley Field on September 18, 2011, a fly ball to left by the Cubs' Carlos Pena hit the yellow stripe on the front edge of the basket that hangs on the wall. There was an umbrella in the basket that moved as the ball hit, making it appear that the ball struck the umbrella and bounced back onto the field. The play was ruled a homer by umpire Marty Foster but when Astros manager Brad Mills asked about the call, acting chief Jeff Nelson watched the replay and overturned the call to a ball in play. The runners were placed at second and third. Cubs manager Mike Quade argued the ruling and was ejected by Foster.

The Red Sox were in Detroit on April 7, 2012 to play the Tigers. In the bottom of the fifth inning, Miguel Cabrera's fly ball landed behind the new left-field fence that was added in 2003 to shorten the distance for a home run. It hit the Tigers' bullpen seating area and rebounded to the chain-link fence. When it happened, it looked as if the ball got stuck in the fence and the Red Sox outfielders signaled as such; umpire CB Bucknor ran out, looked and signaled that it was a double. Tigers manager Jim Leyland talked with Bucknor and crew chief Dale Scott and Scott watched the replay The left-field camera angle showed that the ball went over the fence before coming back and getting tangled in the fencing. The call was overturned to a home run. It was Cabrera's second homer in the contest.

On June 18, 2012, Aramis Ramirez of the Brewers hit a fly ball in the bottom of the seventh inning that hit the edge of the pad on the left field wall. The play was ruled a foul ball by umpire Paul Nauert. Brewers manager Ron Roenicke asked about the call, so acting crew chief Kerwin Danley watched the replay and overturned the call to a home run. The ball glanced off the edge of the pad, which was not aligned straight up the foul line, and that ball might have been foul except for the incorrect alignment of the pad. The run from this solo homer was the decisive run in the Brewers' victory.

The Nationals were in St. Louis on September 29, 2012. In the top of the first inning, Michael Morse's fly hit a sign just above the right-field fence and caromed back onto the field. The ball was ruled in play. Bryce Harper scored from third and Ryan Zimmerman ran from second and stopped at third. Adam LaRoche, running from first, rounded second and realized that Zimmerman had stopped, so LaRoche headed back to second. Morse was almost to second and had to run back to first but was tagged out. First-base umpire Chris Guccione, who had ruled the ball in play, spoke briefly with acting crew chief Jeff Nelson, who had called Morse out. Nelson watched the replay and overturned the call to a home run. Since there had been some confusion on the bases, including a putout, Nelson sent all runners back to their original places and had them run the bases. To get back to the plate, Morse ran the bases backwards, retouching second and first on his way back. When he got to the plate, he heard his teammates in the dugout yelling for him to swing an imaginary bat. Catcher Yadier Molina repeated that, so Morse took a swing and all four runners scored on the recreated home run. Nationals television play-by-play announcer Bob Carpenter called the "homer" with his signature "See! You! Later!" as Morse's imaginary ball cleared the wall.

On May 8, 2013 in Cleveland, Adam Rosales of the Athletics hit a fly ball in the top of the ninth inning. The ball seemed to strike the metal fence

above and behind the yellow stripe at the top of the padded wall in left center. The ball was ruled in play but Athletics manager Bob Melvin asked about the call. Acting crew chief Angel Hernandez watched the replay and upheld the call. Melvin argued after the ruling and was ejected by Hernandez. The next day, a statement was released by the commissioner's office that the ruling was "improper" but that it would stand because the decision to reverse a call by use of instant replay is at the sole discretion of the crew chief.

In the top of the sixth inning on May 19, 2013, Matt Joyce of the Rays hit a fly ball down the right field line which was ruled fair and in play with Joyce reaching second. Orioles manager Buck Showalter talked to the umpires claiming it was a foul ball. The umpires huddled and Rays manager Joe Maddon came onto the field. Crew chief Gerry Davis watched the replay and overturned the call to a home run. The ball had actually struck the RF pole on the lowest part, which is painted black.

The Cubs played in Anaheim on June 5, 2013. In the bottom of the second inning, J.B. Shuck hit a fly ball off Matt Garza down the right-field line that was ruled a home run—the first of his first career. The Cubs claimed it was foul so the umpires huddled. Crew chief Jim Joyce watched the replay and over-turned the call to a foul ball. On July 29, the Angels were in Arlington to face Garza, who had been traded to the Rangers. In the fifth inning, Shuck hit his first career home run off Garza and this time it was not taken away by replay.

On July 27, 2013, the Red Sox played in Baltimore. In the top of the sixth inning, Stephen Drew's fly ball struck on top of the wall in right and caromed back onto the field. The ball was ruled in play by umpire Mike Estabrook. Jarrod Saltalamacchia scored and Drew trotted around third thinking he had a home run. The ball was relayed in to catcher Matt Wieters but Drew evaded Wieters and scored on what was ruled an inside-the-park home run by official scorer David Vincent. The Red Sox asked about the ruling on the ball in right, so crew chief Mike Winters watched the replay and overturned the call to a home run. This use of the review system changed the ruling on the field but did not change the result of the play or the statistical result!

There are a couple of replay instances that should be noted since they do not fall under the rules in place.

The first use of a television replay to change a call in major-league baseball happened nine years before it was legal to do so. On May 31, 1999, the Cardinals were playing the Marlins in Florida. In the bottom of the fifth inning, a fly ball by Cliff Floyd hit on or above the left-field scoreboard and was first ruled a double by second-base umpire Greg Gibson. Floyd and the Marlins argued the ball hit the facade behind the scoreboard and should be a homer. The umpires huddled and crew chief Frank Pulli changed the call to a home run. The Cardinals then argued and Pulli, who later said he was confused by the ground rules, decided to look at replays shown on a TV camera in the dugout. He overturned the call back to a double. The Marlins protested the game, but that protest was denied. Pulli was admonished by NL President Len Coleman, and a specific directive was issued barring future replays. The play would have been eligible for review under the replay rules adopted in 2008.

On June 25, 2009, after the replay system was put in place, the Phillies were playing in St. Petersburg against the Rays. In the bottom of the seventh inning, Pat Burrell came to the plate with a runner on first and two outs. He hit a fly ball which bounced into the left-center-field seats. Crew chief Gary Cederstrom watched a replay to determine if there was fan interference as the ball was leaving the field. After a one minute, 36 second delay, he said that the ball went into the seats cleanly and sent Carl Crawford, who had scored on the play, back to third. MLB Vice President Mike Port told Cederstrom the next day that he was not allowed to use replay in that circumstance.

Replay Expansion in 2014

On January 16, 2014, the owners unanimously approved an expanded use of the replay system to start in the 2014 season. This expansion covered the following play types:

- Book rule double (often incorrectly called "ground rule double")
- Fair/foul (outfield only)
- Fan interference
- Force play (except fielder's touching of second base on a double play)
- Grounds rule
- Hit by pitch
- Home plate collision
- Passing runners on the base path
- Plate collisions [new rule in 2014]
- Record keeping (such as ball/strike counts)
- Runners touching a base (appeal play)
- Stadium boundary calls (such as a fielder falling into the fan area to make a catch)
- Tag play
- Timing play (run scoring before the third out)
- Trap play (outfield only)

The following play types were not covered in the new version of the system:
- Balls and strikes
- Checked swings
- Fair/foul (infield only)
- Interference
- Obstruction
- Trap play (infield only)

This system allowed each manager one challenge per game. If a skipper challenged and was correct, he would get one more in that game. The umpires could not initiate a review until the seventh inning and only after a manager had used all his challenges. All plays would be reviewed by a staff of umpires at the review headquarters in New York once a review was requested.

Major League Baseball (MLB) agreed to hire six new umpires and create two more crews. The review headquarters would be staffed with current umpires, not retired umpires or umpire supervisors, thus the need for the additional crews. They would be able to overturn a call only if there was "clear and convincing evidence" that the ruling on the field was incorrect. The replay umpires had sole authority on runner placement if a call was overturned.

There were three outcomes defined:

- Confirmed—clear and convincing evidence that the call on the field was correct
- Stands—no clear and convincing evidence to confirm or overturn the call
- Overturned—clear and convincing evidence that the call on the field was incorrect

The home run review system already in place would remain essentially the same. The crew chief still made the decision to review a call just as in the past. However, the play would be reviewed by the replay umpires in New York, not by the crew chief at the ballpark.

MLB executive Tony LaRussa, one of the members of the committee that created the system, estimated that about 90 percent of all calls would be covered in the expanded system. The committee targeted what LaRussa called the "dramatic miss" type of call that had changed the outcome of a game in the past. The plan voted by the owners was what the committee announced as the first step, with changes expected to the new system for three years (2014 through 2016).

This system still allowed for missed calls to stand without review. For example, in addition to plays that are not reviewable, a manager might choose not to challenge a call early in a game, deciding to save his challenge for later. If a manager challenged one part of a play and a different part of the play is not correct, that second part is not reviewable. Limiting managers to one challenge and not allowing the umpires to initiate a review until that manager had used his was a decision based on MLB wanting to keep games moving and not let them get bogged down in innumerable reviews.

Teams were allowed to have a person in the clubhouse to monitor the game and look for plays to challenge but no television monitors were allowed in the dugout. Both teams would have the same video feed during a game and MLB standardized the technology in all ballparks. There would be 12 standard camera angles in each stadium made available to the replay umpires.

Challenges would have to be made before both the pitcher and batter are ready for the next pitch and teams would not be allowed to stall.

One interesting aspect of this expanded use of replay was the new rule in 2014 covering collisions at home plate. After spring training had started, MLB announced a new rule that the runner may not deviate from his path to the plate in order to initiate contact with the catcher. Also, the catcher could not block the plate unless he was in possession of the ball. The crew chief could use replay to determine if the rule was violated.

The first use of the newly-expanded system was on March 31, 2014, when it was used five times. In Pittsburgh in the top of the fifth inning, Cubs pitcher Jeff Samardzija bunted with runners on first and second. Pirates hurler Francisco Liriano fielded the ball and threw to third to force Nate Schierholtz. Pedro Alvarez' throw to first was ruled in time to get Samardzija but Cubs manager Rick Renteria challenged the call. After a 90-second review, the call was confirmed.

Later that afternoon in Milwaukee, the Brewers' Ryan Braun beat out an infield single. Braves manager Fredi Gonzalez challenged the call, which was overturned after a 58-second review. This was the first changed call under the new system and Braun was out.

That evening in Oakland, crew chief Mike Winters called for the first umpire review on a play at the plate. In the top of the sixth inning, Asdrubal Cabrera of the Indians hit a grounder to the mound. Sonny Gray threw to the plate and Michael Brantley was tagged out. Winters wanted to check that catcher John Jaso did not block the plate improperly on the play and the review confirmed that he did not.

The next day, April 1, one of the holes in the system was evident. In the bottom of the fourth inning in Phoenix, the Giants attempted to pick off A.J. Pollock at first base. Giants manager Bruce Bochy challenged the safe call, which was confirmed. After Geraldo Parra doubled Pollock to third, catcher

Buster Posey missed a pitch and Pollock scored. The call at the plate was controversial as it appeared Matt Cain tagged Pollock's foot. However, Bochy could not challenge the ruling as he has already used his one challenge. The umpires could not review the play since it was not after the sixth inning.

The Red Sox were at Yankee Stadium on April 12. In the bottom of the eighth inning, Dean Anna doubled to right. Sox manager John Farrell challenged the safe call at second, which was upheld by replay. The next day, Major League Baseball admitted that the call should have been overturned since Anna's foot came off the bag while Xander Bogaerts still had his glove on Anna's hip. In the game on April 13, Francisco Cervelli was called out at first on an apparent double play to end the bottom of the fourth. Yankees skipper Joe Girardi challenged the ruling, which was overturned by the replay officials. Farrell argued the changed ruling, which resulted in an automatic ejection. Farrell yelled about the two calls in two days, both of which were incorrect and went against his team.

The new plate-blocking rule caused a lot of confusion early in the 2014 season. On April 13, Phillies manager Ryne Sandberg thought Marlins catcher Jeff Mathis blocked the plate without the ball but the replay upheld the out call on Tony Gwynn, Jr. Later, MLB acknowledged that the call was incorrect. On June 18 in Pittsburgh, Devin Mesoraco was called out at home on a force play and the play was reviewed. The review official overturned the ruling, saying that Russell Martin blocked the plate without the ball. That call created a lot of controversy during and after the game. Pirates manager Clint Hurdle was ejected arguing the decision. The next day, MLB released a statement saying that the new rule was not intended to be used on a force play, since the catcher must have his foot on the plate in that instance.

On June 1 in Washington, the Rangers had runners on first and third with two out in the top of the first inning. On the 1-2 pitch to Donnie Murphy, Alex Rios attempted to steal second. Rios beat the throw but his foot came off the bag and he was tagged out. HP umpire Clint Fagan ruled that Elvis Andrus scored from third before the out was made at second. Nationals manager Matt Williams challenged the ruling at the plate and the call was overturned by replay. Rangers manager Ron Washington challenged the ruling at second. This call was upheld and the inning was over with no runs scoring. This was the first time both managers challenged a part of the same play.

The Indians were in Los Angeles on July 1. In the bottom of the fourth, the Dodgers had runners on first and third with no outs when Adrian Gonzalez hit a fly ball to left field that was caught. Dee Gordon attempted to score from third and was out on a close play at the plate. Yasiel Puig ran to second on the throw home and was called safe on a close play. Indians manager Terry Francona challenged the ruling at second and the call was overturned by replay. This meant the Indians completed a triple play. Then Dodgers field boss Don Mattingly challenged the call at home, which was upheld.

Replay Expansion in 2015

On February 20, 2015, Major League Baseball announced changes to the 2014 Expanded Replay system. The changes included the following points:

- Managers will no longer come onto the field to request a replay
- Managers will keep a challenge each time a call is overturned, not just once
- Managers can challenge new types of plays
  - Runners leaving a base too soon
  - Runners properly touching a base on a tag up play

A manager may stand on the top step of the dugout to hold play briefly while waiting for feedback from the team's video technician. In order to challenge an inning-ending call, the manager will be required to step onto the field so that the umpires can hold the defensive team on the field. This change was part of a larger pace-of-game initiative introduced at the same time, which is beyond the scope of this article.

A manager still had one challenge per game but could challenge again after each successful challenge. In post-season, regular season tie-breaker games and the All Star Game, a manager had two challenges to start the contest.

Through three years of expanded replay, there were 4,149 times the system had been used. Of these, 3,607 of them were manager challenges. Umpires requested 583 reviews without a manager challenge. Of the 583 umpire reviews, 41 were either a rules check or a ball/strike count check. The results of all reviews except the rule checks are listed in Table 1. The results of the manager challenges are listed in Table 2.

Result	Total	Percentage
Reviews	4149	
Confirmed	967	23.3%
Stands	1133	27.3%
Overturned	2049	49.3%

Table 1 — All Reviews by Result (2014-16)

Result	Total	Percentage
Challenges	3607	
Confirmed	686	19.0%
Stands	1022	28.3%
Overturned	1899	52.6%

Table 2 — Manager Challenges by Result (2014-16)

Managers have increased their number of challenges each season since 2014, when skippers challenged 1,062 calls. In 2015, that total increased to 1,188 and there was a large increase in 2016. That season, managers challenged 1,357 calls.

Those 3,607 challenges took place in 7,287 regular season and 103 post-season games, or one challenge every 2.05 games. With a turnover rate just over half, one call was overturned every 1.9 games. On a fully-scheduled day, there are 15 games played, so approximately four calls would be overturned on average in a fully-scheduled day. When one considers the number of reviewable calls made in each game, that is a small number of changed calls.

The overturn rate for all calls, including the umpire reviews (without the rule checks), is 49%. This is 2,049 out of 4,149 uses of the system in three years. This is a good baseline to look at individual umpires. Table 3 shows the umpires who have had the most calls reviewed in three seasons. These are all manager challenges and crew chief reviews except for rule checks. There is one minor league vacation substitute in this list marked as (AAA). The rest are major league staff umpires. The data are still small and trends will emerge as we acquire more data in future years. It is interesting that the umpires on this list have widely varying overturn rates, from Clint Fagan (43%) to Dan Iassogna (62%). The umpire who has been challenged the most times in three years has an overturn rate 6% lower than the league average. The number of games each man has umpired in the two years is listed in the right-most column.

Umpire	Total	Overturned	Confirmed	Stands	Overturned%	Games
Clint Fagan (AAA)	67	29	24	14	43%	363
Mark Carlson	65	31	18	16	48%	366
Tim Timmons	65	29	21	15	45%	350
Dan Iassogna	63	39	11	13	62%	355
Jim Reynolds	63	30	13	20	48%	359
Jerry Meals	61	34	12	15	56%	360
Doug Eddings	59	29	11	19	49%	338
D.J. Reyburn	59	31	13	15	53%	314
Chris Conroy	58	28	12	18	48%	360
Angel Hernandez	58	30	10	18	52%	361

Table 3 — Umpires with the Most Reviewed Calls (2014-16)

At the opposite end on this list are the umpires with the fewest calls reviewed. Table 4 shows the staff umpires who worked in 2014 through 2016 with the fewest reviews. To qualify for this list, an umpire must have worked at least 301 games over the three seasons, which is 62% of the three seasons games. David Rackley leads with just 25 reviewed calls and his overturn rate is very small as well.

Umpire	Total	Overturned	Confirmed	Stands	Overturned%
David Rackley	25	8	11	6	32%
Scott Barry	29	14	8	7	48%
Mike DiMuro	31	15	12	4	48%
Brian Gorman	31	16	9	6	52%
Alfonso Marquez	32	11	10	11	34%
Sam Holbrook	34	13	13	8	38%
Rob Drake	35	19	6	10	54%
Brian Knight	35	17	10	8	49%
Jim Joyce	36	18	7	11	50%
Jeff Kellogg	37	19	7	11	51%

Table 4 — Staff Umpires with the Fewest Reviewed Calls (2014-16)

Table 5 shows staff umpires with the highest overturn rate. The same qualifications apply as in Table 4.

Umpire	Total	Overturned	Confirmed	Stands	Overturned%
Phil Cuzzi	48	34	6	8	71%
Dan Iassogna	63	39	11	13	62%
Gabe Morales (AAA)	52	32	8	12	62%
Lance Barrett	55	33	8	14	60%
Gerry Davis	56	33	7	16	59%
Gary Cederstrom	52	30	12	10	58%
Andy Fletcher	53	31	6	16	58%
Todd Tichenor	40	23	7	10	58%
James Hoye	42	24	9	9	57%
Bob Davidson	57	32	7	18	56%
Jerry Meals	61	34	12	15	56%

Table 5 — Staff Umpires with the Highest Overturn Rate (2014-16)

The lowest overturn rates for staff umpires is shown in Table 6. The same qualifications apply as used in the two previous tables.

Umpire	Total	Overturned	Confirmed	Stands	Overturned%
Adam Hamari (AAA)	47	15	15	17	32%
David Rackley	25	8	11	6	32%
Chris Guccione	51	17	16	18	33%
Hunter Wendelstedt	40	13	13	14	33%
Alfonso Marquez	32	11	10	11	34%
Vic Carapazza	49	17	18	14	35%
Alan Porter	50	18	19	13	36%
Mike Estabrook	48	18	10	20	38%
Sam Holbrook	34	13	13	8	38%
Tom Hallion	42	17	9	16	40%
Pat Hoberg (AAA)	40	16	10	14	40%
Will Little	42	17	9	16	40%
Quinn Wolcott	48	19	13	16	40%

Table 6 — Staff Umpires with the Lowest Overturn Rate (2014–16)

Managers, coaches and players are not allowed to argue the result of a replay. This had not stopped some from doing so, however. There were six ejections during the years that home runs were reviewed. Since the expansion of replay, many more people have been ejected over a replay ruling. Since the 2014 expansion, all reviews are decided by umpires in the replay center, not the arbiters on the field. Someone who argues with the umpires on the field is not talking to the people who made the decision and thus it seems to be a waste of time. The following list shows all persons ejected for arguing replay rulings. Blue Jays manager John Gibbons has been ejected four times in three years of expanded replay, which is the most of anyone on the list.

Date	Ejectee	Team	Umpire
Home Run Replay			
08/06/2010	Ron Gardenhire	MIN	Gerry Davis
10/03/2010	Edwin Rodriguez	FLO	Joe West
08/18/2011	Ron Gardenhire	MIN	Brian O'Nora
09/04/2011	Charlie Manuel	PHI	Joe West
09/18/2011	Mike Quade	CHN	Marty Foster
05/08/2013	Bob Melvin	OAK	Angel Hernandez
Expanded Replay			
04/13/2014	John Farrell	BOS	Bob Davidson
04/14/2014	Ron Washington	TEX	Ted Barrett
04/27/2014	Bryan Price	CIN	Bill Miller
04/27/2014	Homer Bailey	CIN	Greg Gibson

Entrance to Replay Operations Center, New York City.

Replay Operations Center, interior.

Date	Ejectee	Team	Umpire
05/01/2014	Brian Butterfield	BOS	Dale Scott
05/02/2014	Joe Maddon	TBA	Brian O'Nora
05/25/2014	John Gibbons	TOR	Mark Carlson
06/07/2014	Ryne Sandberg	PHI	Tom Hallion
06/09/2014	Mike Scioscia	ANA	Bob Davidson
06/11/2014	Terry Collins	NYN	Gary Cederstrom
06/16/2014	Kirk Gibson	ARI	Ted Barrett
06/18/2014	Clint Hurdle	PIT	Jerry Layne
06/22/2014	Ron Washington	TEX	Bill Miller
06/23/2014	Buddy Black	SDN	Brian O'Nora
06/25/2014	Mike Moustakas	KCA	Brian Knight
07/02/2014	John Gibbons	TOR	Greg Gibson
07/07/2014	Fredi Gonzalez	ATL	Mike Everitt
07/26/2014	Brad Ausmus	DET	Jim Joyce
07/29/2014	Ron Gardenhire	MIN	Ted Barrett
07/31/2014	Mike Redmond	MIA	Mike Winters

Date	Ejectee	Team	Umpire
08/02/2014	Kirk Gibson	ARI	Ron Kulpa
08/10/2014	Buck Showalter	BAL	Jeff Nelson
08/13/2014	Robin Ventura	CHA	Fieldin Culbreth
08/14/2014	Buddy Black	SDN	Bob Davidson
08/17/2014	John Farrell	BOS	Doug Eddings
09/08/2014	Lloyd McClendon	SEA	Jeff Nelson
04/16/2015	Kevin Cash	TBA	Laz Diaz
04/26/2015	Jeff Banister	TEX	Manny Gonzalez
05/13/2015	Don Mattingly	LAN	Bob Davidson
06/17/2015	Walt Weiss	COL	Jerry Layne
06/20/2015	A.J. Hinch	HOU	Mike DiMuro
07/02/2015	John Gibbons	TOR	Gerry Davis
07/04/2015	Brayan Pena	CIN	Bill Welke
07/27/2015	Carlos Gomez	MIL	Gerry Davis
07/27/2015	Craig Counsell	MIL	Gerry Davis
08/02/2015	Joe Maddon	CHN	Hunter Wendelstedt

Date	Ejectee	Team	Umpire
08/15/2015	Craig Counsell	MIL	Fieldin Culbreth
08/15/2015	A.J. Hinch	HOU	Bill Miller
08/18/2015	Ned Yost	KCA	Mark Carlson
08/21/2015	Brad Ausmus	DET	Ron Kulpa
04/30/2016	Robin Ventura	CHA	Gerry Davis
05/11/2016	Clint Hurdle	PIT	Jeff Kellogg
05/11/2016	Starling Marte	PIT	Alan Porter
06/23/2016	Brian Snitker	ATL	Mike Everitt
06/28/2016	Jeff Francoeur	ATL	Hunter Wendelstedt
06/30/2016	Mike Matheny	SLN	Mike Everitt
07/30/2016	Terry Collins	NYN	Jeff Kellogg

Date	Ejectee	Team	Umpire
08/03/2016	Terry Francona	CLE	Fieldin Culbreth
08/03/2016	Mickey Callaway	CLE	Fieldin Culbreth
08/18/2016	Brian Butterfield	BOS	Scott Barry
09/11/2016	John Gibbons	TOR	Jim Joyce
09/16/2016	Bryan Price	CIN	Gerry Davis
09/19/2016	Jeff Banister	TEX	Joe West

NOTES

1   All game information is taken from the Retrosheet (www.retrosheet.org) web site. A complete list of the use of the replay system can be found at this site.

Larry Vanover—the first umpire to make a call at the Replay Operations Center

The first call ever made using baseball's new instant replay system was made on March 31, 2014 at the Replay Operations Center in New York. There had been four prior games. The Dodgers and Diamondbacks played two regulation games at the Sydney Cricket Grounds in Sydney, Australia on March 22 and 23. On Sunday night, the San Diego Padres hosted the Dodgers at Petco. There were no calls that resulted in challenges.

The Monday, March 31 game was a 1:14 PM game at Pittsburgh's PNC Park, the Cubs against the Pirates. The challenge came in the top of the fifth inning. The game was scoreless to that point. There was a single, then a walk, but Cubs pitcher Jeff Samardzija then bunted into what was ruled a 1-5-4 double play, with Pirates second baseman Neil Walker covering the bag at first base. The baserunner coming from second base was out at third base, and the Samardzija was thrown out at first. It was a close enough play that Chicago manager Rick Renteria challenged the play at first. Umpire Bob Davidson's call was upheld, the call being made from the Replay Operations Center in New York by Larry Vanover. It was the first use of the expanded instant replay system.

There was another call later in the game, which was still scoreless after nine. In the top of the 10th inning, the Cubs had a runner on first with one out, Emilio Bonifacio. Pitcher Bryan Morris threw to first to pick him off, but Davidson ruled that Bonifacio was safe. Pirates skipped Clint Hurdle challenged the

call and it was overturned from safe to out. The next Cubs batter struck out, and the Pirates won it in the bottom of the 10th when Neil Walker hit a walk-off home run.

BN: You were the first to make a call at the Replay Center.

LV: Yes.

BN: Did it strike you at the time as an historic decision of some sort?

LV: Well, I was aware of it, but at the time I wasn't. We came in Monday. I think there was four or five games Monday and we all came in and we got started. We came in kind of early because it was new to everybody.

As we were going along, everybody was noticing a whole lot of people in the room. Then the tech told me, "Well, we didn't have one Sunday night." It didn't set right then. Finally, I said, "You mean they didn't challenge anything the whole game?" He said, "No. We're waiting on the first one." It wasn't five minutes later my light went off and there it was.

BN: You were in the seat.

LV: Yeah. Luck of the draw.

BN: You upheld the decision on the field.

LV: I think it was, yeah. Yeah. And you know, the play where it happened—as we've done this for a year now, you look back on the first one and it really wasn't that close. I thought maybe they were doing to just see how the system works.

Interview with Larry Vanover by Bill Nowlin on September 1, 2015

Rich Rieker, Director of Umpire Development

By Bill Nowlin

For the past six-plus years, since before the 2011 season, Rick Rieker has been director of umpire development for Major League Baseball. Rieker umpired his first major-league game in 1992, and worked as both a National League and then major-league umpire through the 2001 season. In 2002 he began work as an umpire supervisor. For 16 years, he worked as an instructor at the Wendelstedt Umpire School.

He is responsible for administration of Major League Baseball Umpire Camps (MLBUC.com), based at MLB's Urban Youth Academy in California, and develops the *Virtual Umpire Camp* digital learning tool, available on CD-rom or flash drive. He coordinated the training and assignments of both major-league and international umpires for the World Baseball Classic. In short, through his position as director, umpire development, Rieker oversees a variety of training and educational initiatives.

Rieker start umpiring as early as age 11, working Little League games. He and his wife, Kathleen, first met in the St. Louis area; she was in Little League and they both worked in the same Khoury League Association. They met at an umpire meeting in the basement of a church. Many years later, they started dating.

Rich's father was a letter carrier, and the whole family were big St. Louis Cardinals fans. His brother Stephen officiated football for many years.

Rich officiated basketball, football, and baseball through high school and college, attending umpires school during his junior year—but it was actually working a flag-football tournament in 1982 that first introduced him to the Wendelstedt Umpire School. "They sent a crew down to Daytona Beach for the first annual flag-football tournament in 1982. When

we showed up for the tournament—we were there refereeing—unbeknownst to us, the umpire school was at the same complex. I saw what was going on over there and that's what got me the fever."[1]

He talked to Harry Wendelstedt and Randy Marsh and learned there were 90 students in the class, with likely 15 or 16 jobs available. Seeing some of the students in action, he not only thought that he could make it, but that that ratio of class to jobs was a pretty good percentage. Then when he showed up the following year, there were 262 students—the biggest class in history. But there were still only the 15 or 16 jobs. He did well: "Eddie Hickox and I graduated 1 and 2. I graduated number 1 and Hickox graduated number 2. I still give him trouble about that today."

Rieker got hired and worked in the Midwest League for two seasons and the Eastern League for two seasons. He worked his first big-league games in 1992, worked four seasons as a fill-in umpire, and was officially hired in 1996, just two weeks after umpire John McSherry died on the field.

He'd had a couple of neck surgeries while in the minor leagues, and when he herniated his third disk in 2001, he had to give up work on the field. He had worked in exactly 1,000 major-league games.

Still on salary, Rieker was fortunate that Ralph Nelson, then MLB's vice president for umpiring, asked him to work as a supervisor. It was a staff that included Marty Springstead, Frank Pulli, and Richie Garcia, and—later—Jim McKean and Steve Palermo.

"For the last six years, I've worked for Peter Woodfork [MLB's senior vice president for baseball operations] and Joe Torre [chief baseball officer]. Randy Marsh and myself became directors five or six years ago. In our offices, there are five directors—myself, Randy Marsh, Matt McKendry—who's director of administration. He's

Bruce Froemming and Ed Rapuano.

out of New York. He does all the admin and scheduling, stuff like that. The director of medical services is Mark Letendre. He's the best. And we have the director of replay the last three years, which is Justin Klemm, former minor-league umpire and former big-league call-up, who is out of New York.

"My responsibilities include major-league supervision. Randy Marsh is director of major-league umpires and I'm director of umpire development, but a lot of our stuff is overlapping, the major-league stuff, to where if we have to handle something with a club or through a manager if we're asked to do it. We evaluate the umpires like all the supervisors do. We help select umpires for the postseason. And under my side of the house is the Triple-A development side, which just finished the Fall League.

"Basically, when an umpire comes through the system, they have to work at every level. Instead of there being four levels — Rookie, A, Double A, and Triple A, like it was when I came in, now there's six levels. They divide Rookie into two levels and they divide A into two levels. So you can't go from the (New York-)Penn League to the Florida State League. You have to go through the South Atlantic League in between, even though they are all A leagues. To advance through those six levels generally takes between five and seven years. Then when they get to Triple A, we get them. Those five to seven years at the beginning, those are done by Minor League Baseball Umpire Development. Dusty Dellinger.

"Then the guys come up to us. We have several supervisors. Tom Lepperd. Cris Jones. Chuck

Meriwether. Ed Rapuano. We get some help from Larry Young and the major-league supervisors like Ed Montague, to see guys throughout the season in certain areas. We have a meeting in August where we have all the written reports, any video we need — every Triple-A game is broadcast in some way, shape, or form, whether it's a static camera or several cameras. We're able to evaluate, along with reports from league presidents, we're able to evaluate the Triple-A umpires.

"The top prospects go on to the Arizona Fall League, which is a six-week prospect league for both players and umpires. That's just concluded out in Scottsdale. There are six teams, and there's three games a day. We try to dispatch two supervisors — at least two, sometimes three — to cover these games in Arizona, to watch these umpires and their progress.

"We just had a conference call yesterday and now we've ranked them for spring training, so that when spring training comes out, we assign the umpires. Major-league guys get their names stuck on there first and then we look for holes for the Triple-A guys. In other words, if there's a need for an umpire in Jupiter, a Triple-A guy goes in there. We'll give the Triple-A guys a full schedule as well.

"They all get spring training. Major-league guys get a full schedule or a half-schedule. Major-league veterans who don't live in Florida or Arizona, they just take a half and the other guys take a full. It just depends on what the guys want to do that particular spring, but every major-league umpire has to work spring training.

"When we hire a guy, he has been purposefully vetted by all the games that he's worked. We have all of his plate data, his accuracy on the bases, replay data, situation-management data, all of his Triple-A reports. When we hire a guy, you can imagine any job out there and you put a camera over your employee 24/7, monitoring his whole shift, you're going to pick the right people. That's what we have the luxury of doing. We have everything these guys do, and we obviously take the best of the best. The supervisor recommends a name to me, I take the name to Peter

Woodfork and Joe Torre. They take it to the commissioner, and when he's cleared, the umpire is hired.

"Unfortunately, some of those umpires don't get hired. Some of the guys on the call-ups don't work out. They get released in the minor leagues. If you're in Triple A for three years, and there's no interest by the big leagues, then you are subsequently released from your minor-league contract.

"We have so much data, but it's important to know that data is just the starting point. When somebody's getting the same amount of pitches right as the big-league guys and somebody's getting the same number of plays right to our very high standards, you've got to look at what kind of employee this guy's going to be. How are they administratively? The same things you would consider for any other job. You want to make sure the reports are on time. That they're polite and courteous, that they handled their situations on the field in a professional fashion, and they've got to hope there's an opening. Some guys fall victims to the no-openings.

"Minor League Baseball told me that from '99 to 2008, I think there were three openings for minor-league umpires. From 2008 on, they told me, there were 20 that we've hired.

"That's on the major-league side. On the other side, we run our annual umpire camps. We have open tryouts from MLBUC — MLB Umpire Camps, which we started over 10 years ago. Using these camps in one way, shape, or form, we've helped place in the umpire schools [students who became] over 140 minor-league umpires. Our first two paybacks — our first two success stories — are Carlos Torres, who's working in the big leagues part-time, and Ramon DeJesus, the first Dominican umpire. Those guys were eight years ago. We're starting to see that these guys are coming back through our system. Last year — '15 — we had eight camps.

"We take our staffs to these one-day camps. The staffs help pick the people they think can walk and talk and display some athleticism during that three-to-five-hour camp — and the people who have the desire. They are subsequently interviewed by Cris Jones. They fill out a background check. They fill out

a lot of paperwork. And then of the people who pass that process, they will get a scholarship down to Fort Myers for December 27. Last year 35 people went. Twenty went on to umpire school. Eight of those were full scholarships paid for by MLB. The whole Fort Myers thing is paid for by MLB. So once you get invited from one of these free camps, you don't have any out-of-pocket.

"Out of those 20 who went to umpire schools out of our camps, 14 are working in the minor leagues, including our first female candidate from the camps. This year, we're looking at 25 to 26 down there in Fort Myers and we'll do the same thing all over again. This is our third year. It more or less makes us like a 31st ballclub to where we're actually scouting and prospecting, if you will. We're also offering opportunities for those in urban areas who can't afford it.

"It's fun to do the camps because that's the one day of the month and the four days in December that we roll up our sleeves and we help people go in the right direction with being ahead of the curve, helping to train people, and really, it's refreshing because it comes at no cost to them and my staff loves doing it.

"I don't get to do as much as I'd like to in the minor leagues — I went and saw a three-game series and they had three arguments on the bases. I think they got the calls right and they handled themselves fine. I talked to the guys after the games and I said, 'Those three arguments are more than you're ever going to have in your whole big-league career on the bases anymore, because of Replay.'

"What we've found is that if you have a 162-game season, and the pressure has to get let out of the tire somewhere before the tire explodes, it's a long season and arguments are part of the game, it's all going to be on balls and strikes and checked swings, really. Now the umpires are really engaged with all that. The bases are not a day off, but they are definitely not what they used to be. Our guys still try to get them right, because we record everything. They don't want to be standing there with the headset on, looking up at the big board, and finding out that they made a mistake in front of the full stands at Fenway.

"It's a dynamic that has really split the minor-league umpiring off from the major-league umpiring. But it's a good one for *us* to have because we can test their mettle more than just the ball-and-strike ejection, which is pretty much a check-box thing. You see the guys get upset about this, the umpire warns him, the player goes away, nothing happens. But if the player turns around, now he's going to get ejected and then the manager comes out: 'Why'd you eject him?' It doesn't have the open debate any more on the tag play at second base when the manager comes out and says, 'What have you got?' You have an open debate sometimes, and that's when situations are either squashed or they are accelerated. Those really don't exist anymore, save maybe for a random balk call or obstruction or interference maybe."

Rieker is responsible both for hiring people and letting people go, but for the people who get hired, he often has the chance to give them the good news.

"That's a great call, when you can finally do that with Joe [Torre]. Usually Randy Marsh is on the call. And Peter. Every call every year is different but we have to tell more people that they can't make it. I have heard that 55 percent of College World Series umpires are former professionals, so most of our guys that are call-ups can literally put in their résumé to a college in a major conference and those guys are almost always hired. Normally, they are going to four-umpire crews. There's a lot of opportunity now. You can make $2,000 a weekend, sometimes. A lot of our guys—three or four in just the last year or two—have gone on to major college conferences. That's what we encourage them to do. In effect, we are actually probably training more college umpires than we are major-league umpires.

"Now there's more money involved and college umpiring is much bigger and more traveled now than it ever has been. Bill McCallum is a former Triple-A umpire. He is now the NCAA supervisor for the Northeast region. He's working for us at the Fort Myers camp coming up. He instructed for 15 years, and we like to show students that there's other things available to them as well.

"We like to think we're one big brotherhood of umpiring and whether you work at the Little League, high school, college, or pro level, we're all basically doing the same job and we like to help whenever we can."

Rieker is the one who makes the decisions on the call-up umpires. How do they make use of the evaluations?

"We've got the four supervisors—Leppard, Jones, Meriwether, and Rapuano. Larry Young sees some of the guys. Ed Montague sees some of the guys. When they work in the big leagues, Steve Palermo, Randy Marsh, Charlie Reliford see the guys. We've got an extensive database of major-league and minor-league reports on our desktops. Each umpire in Triple A is seen an average of 25 to 30 games per year. When I was in the minors, you were lucky if you got seen five games. We now blanket the country and it's the responsibility of our guys to get every umpire seen and then we come up with cross-checking so we come up with a good idea of who might be the guys to move up. We've got all these reports in a database. Those are all in the same system.

"Umpire Observer Kevin O'Connor could actually evaluate a guy in Pawtucket and a week later, if the guys gets called up, he'll evaluate him in Boston. We try to have Kevin see all the guys in the (International League) who come through Pawtucket. That all goes into our desktop. These reports are combed over by supervisors. We try to look for deficiencies so we can try to help the umpire with these reports. We look for positives. We look for field presence. We look for judgment when we get the tapes. We look for mechanics. We look for mobility. All the different things that we would look for to stack these umpires up. Then we take all these reports and then over Labor Day weekend we meet and we pick the guys for the Fall League. So there's a bevy of data there. Not as much for a major-league umpire. If you've got a Gabe Morales or a Ben May, who's in the big leagues 200 or 300 games already, we've got all the big-league data on them, but we don't have the strike-zone data at the Triple-A level.

"One thing we do in the Fall League, by the way, we do shoot ZE—the strike-zone measurement—at them three or four games each, so we actually train them on that. We take one day and basically break the machine down and put them all upstairs and show them how it works, to train them because if we evaluate employees, we have a responsibility to train them, too.

"The other thing we do in the Fall League is we bring a high-def camera out, and our video director, and we bring a college team out and we throw as many close plays as we possibly can—it's banger after banger after banger—to try to get a baseline on the umpire's judgment, because until they get to the big-league level, we don't really have the cameras to decide whether he's getting all those plays right in the minor leagues or not. Maybe there's a judgment issue or a mechanical issue—that that umpire's not looking at the foot or the glove, or turning their head too soon off of a force-play throw. We try to look at all that, and that's another thing we do in the Fall League, to try to ramp that up and get that data.

"And then the phone call we had yesterday with all the supervisors who were at the Fall League, we selected the top three to five who are going to spring training. Based on all that data and all those reports."

It's Randy Marsh who selects the crew chiefs.

"Randy's a good partner in all this. He was my chief instructor at umpire school when I went, and then I worked with Randy at the school. Randy handles travel and all that."

How are umpires selected for the All-Star Game, and for the postseason?

"The supervisors—we have calls on that. We have a weekly call anyway and we generally know who's getting close for the All-Star Game. The supervisors, Randy, myself, and McKendry, who the supervisors recommend to Peter Woodfork and Joe Torre, and then they take those to the commissioner. So, yeah, we are the ones who push those things. We have a playoff meeting in September where we do the same thing. Again, we've got a year's worth of evaluations, conference calls, notes. Each major-league supervisor is assigned four or five crews that are in their pod—that they have to watch if there's an issue, you know, strike zone or situationally.

"With the instant replay and the data we collect on the strike zone, I challenge any profession to say they're as thoroughly evaluated as … maybe a physician or an air-traffic controller, I don't know, but there's not much umpires can do that's not evaluated now. And it's important that we do that. Obviously these guys maintain the integrity of the game and they do a great job doing it. It's our job to make sure that's all going well, and it is."

It is Matt McKendry who does the scheduling, working with somebody who does it. The schedules are done blindly, through 19 schedules, and then the crew chiefs—by seniority—select. Each umpire gets two or three weeks of replay and they get four weeks' vacation—you know that—but the schedules are done across the board blindly. Really, they're pretty generic. You could almost throw a dart, but I think some of the umpires look at "where am I coming out of vacation?" because this is where my crew is from. Maybe one guy's from Florida and one guy's from California. How does this benefit this person? They're all pretty close. Some of them might have a couple extra days in Replay. It's up to that crew chief and his crew's preferences. He'll consult with his crew and then make a selection out of those 19. The last guy, number 19, he gets what's left over, but since they're done blindly—I'm not saying they're all the same, but they try to balance out all the miles and seeing the clubs and all that sort of stuff.[2]

Rich Rieker, at the D.C. Urban Youth Academy Camp, 2016.

Rich Rieker.

"Guys can go two or three years without seeing a park. I've talked to umpires who, say, haven't been to Kansas City in a couple of years, or Detroit. It's just the way the schedule works out. And, his crew might have gone there but he might have had that week off. Injuries, all kinds of stuff plays into that."

In 2007 *St. Louis* magazine quoted Rieker in an article: "Basically we're the buffer between league management and umpires. We hear the umpires' problems and try to be counselors."[3]

But he clearly is management. "Obviously the umpires are in a union, and we are management. We get messages from our bosses and have to get them out to the umpires—whether it's an inconsistency on how to handle situations, or pace-of-games issues. Since we're former umpires, we have to take the message from Major League Baseball that we want enforced,

and get it out to the crews so that the commissioner's policies and procedures are adhered to. We are the deliverers of the messages in many cases. Likewise, we have to take some of the umpires' frustrations and take them back up the chain if it's worthwhile. That kind of buffer is still there, but we are management. Make no mistake about that.

"We're personal counselors, too. Marty Springstead—'Springer'—Marty was a great man. He spent 20 years in the field and 20 years in the office, and he insisted this is a human business. No matter how much automation, simulated training, and technology there is, he always said this is a people business and don't ever forget it. There's a lot of times when umpires have issues that we try to help them with, because we've been there. There aren't many people who aren't in the game that they can talk to about umpiring in the game today. So we're also sounding boards, if you will, and we try to counsel them and help them along the way, too.

"I love my job and I love working with the guys. Even though I'm not able to work the games anymore, I consider myself blessed to be able to do this part of the game and to be able to help these guys, to counsel these guys, and to help them succeed—to be able to put them in a position to really do the best they can. That's all we can ask for from the supervisors. Marty just would say, 'Remember, this is a people business. Don't ever forget it. There's all this technology that comes out, but number one, this is a people business and if you remember that, you'll be fine.'"

NOTES

1   Author interview with Rich Rieker on November 22, 2016. All quotations are from this interview unless otherwise indicated.

2   A study on the process of scheduling umpires is Michael A. Trick, Hakan Yildiz, and Tallys Yunes, "Scheduling Major League Baseball Umpires and the Traveling Umpire Problem," *Interfaces*, Vol. 42, No. 3, May-June 2012: 232-244.

3   Leslie Gibson McCarthy, *St. Louis* magazine, March 30, 2007.

Umpire Observer Kevin O'Connor

By Bill Nowlin

Major League Baseball wants its umpires to be the best that they can be. Toward this end, they have an extensive and lengthy process through which an umpire takes many years to reach the major-league level, and is individually graded at every step of development. Not only does MLB invest in umpire health and conditioning, but it maintains a group of evaluators and supervisors to monitor umpires, both new umpires and the most established ones. Major League Baseball is spending millions upon millions of dollars to make sure that umpires are performing their jobs as well as they can.

The MLB website, accessed in August 2015, lists the following individuals under the title "Umpire Executives." It appears the website may not have been updated since 2012. Because of the creation of the replay center in New York, the list is no doubt a more extensive one today.

At the top of the list are four men:
Joe Torre—Chief Baseball Officer
Peter Woodfork—Senior Vice President, Baseball Operations
Randy Marsh—Director, Major League Umpires
Rich Rieker—Director, Umpire Development

There follow seven Umpire Supervisors:
Cris Jones
Tom Lepperd
Chuck Meriwether
Ed Montague
Steve Palermo
Charlie Reliford
Larry Young

And a number of other staff:
Ed Rapuano—Umpire Evaluator

Bruce Froemming—Special Assistant, Umpiring
Matt McKendry—Director, Umpire Administration
Justin Klemm—Director, Instant Replay
Ross Larson—Instant Replay Coordinator
Mark A. Letendre—Director, Umpire Medical Services
Steven M. Erickson, M.D.—Medical Consultant
Cathy Davis—Specialist, Umpire Administration
Freddie Hernandez—Video Coordinator
Steve Mara—Coordinator, On-Field Operations
Michael Sansarran—Coordinator, On-Field Operations
Raquel Wagner—Coordinator, Umpire Administration

There are also 11 Umpire Observers:
Dave Buck (Chicago)
Terry Christman (San Francisco/Oakland)
Larry Hardy (Arlington)
Travis Katzenmaier (Phoenix)
Matt Malone (St. Louis)
Mitch Mele (New York)
Dr. Hank Nichols (Philadelphia/Baltimore)
Kevin O'Connor (Boston)
Rick Reed (Detroit)
Steve Rippley (South Florida)
Bill Russell (Los Angeles/Anaheim)

Many of the supervisors and evaluators have career backgrounds as former umpires working at the major-league level. All help to implement and oversee SURE, the Supervisor Umpire Review and Evaluation system, used to evaluate MLB umpires.

The Umpire Observers, as of the time the list was accessed, have a combined total of over 116 of umpiring experience, but also count years of experience as player, manager, scout, pitching coach, and officiating in other sports. One of the observers is Kevin O'Connor, who talked about his background and his work during a July 30, 2015 interview.

Kevin O'Connor: I was born in 1963. I've lived my whole life in Oxford, Massachusetts. Same town as Steve Palermo. I grew up with Steve's brother Mike. He was a year older. At a young age, I knew about umpiring because of Steve. [Steve Palermo umpired 152 American League games in 1977, when Kevin O'Connor was 14.]

We just lived sports. That's all we did since I was 10. Back in the day, at the basketball courts at the center of town, we played basketball with Jim McKean, Mike Reilly, and some of those guys. When they came to Boston, a lot of times they would stay at Steve's Mom's house. She was a fantastic cook. They always went down there, so we got to meet some of the guys at a young age. I knew that after high school I was going to go to umpire school.

I was the youngest of six, and I was always the catcher. And I would call balls and strikes when I was catching. We actually had a pitcher's mound—a legal pitcher's mound—which my dad built in my backyard. My father was a big sports fan. And my mother. One of my brothers was an extremely good pitcher. Played in college. If he had pursued it, I think he probably could have played in A ball. He wouldn't have gone further than that, but he was a very, very good pitcher. Dad was an accountant for Yankee Atomic Electric. And my mom was a schoolteacher, a fourth-grade teacher. And that's where I met my wife. My wife had my mother as a fourth-grade teacher, and my wife and I met in sixth grade.

BN: Did you do any umpiring work in Little League?

O'Connor: Yeah. When I was in Little League, I umpired minor league. $2.50 a game. It was one of the years that they first allowed girls to play in Little League. There was a rule that you had to have a female on the coaching staff. The head coach's wife was on the staff, and she was relentless. This was in minor league, 9-year-old league. I ended up throwing her out. She's like, "You can't do that" and the husband was so embarrassed. He just looked at her and said, "Yes, he can. Just leave." That was my first ejection.

A later ejection occurred in A ball, when O'Connor was working the June 26, 1985 Florida State League game in Clearwater, Florida between the Clearwater Phillies and the Osceola Astros. When a Clearwater coach got into an argument with first-base umpire John Golden over a double-play call, the 64-year-old organist, Wilbur Snapp, started playing the tune, "Three Blind Mice." Snapp was immediately ejected, not so much because any of the umpires had particularly thin skin but because Snapp had specifically asked whether it would be OK to play it, and was instructed not to.[1]

Another memorable ejection was on Opening Day in Pawtucket in 1992, when a reporter wouldn't shut off their Klieg light and it was interfering with play.

Asked about his professional development, O'Connor said:

I went to Joe Brinkman in 1983. It was the first year he owned it and I got in. There were 13 of us who went to the next school out of Brinkman's, and then we met the other guys from Harry Wendelstedt at the advanced school. Of like 450 kids between the schools, 33 of us went to the advanced school and 16 of us got spring training jobs. Those that passed muster went to the advanced school. That was run by Minor League Baseball. It was just a week-long evaluation. When we were told we made it, we literally got in a car

THE SABR BOOK ON UMPIRES AND UMPIRING

and drove to Bradenton and the next day we started.

Then I had a couple of weeks off and I got to go home, and then I went right back down for spring training. Tommy Hallion and Charlie Reliford, I was in their first spring training camp. I had some good teachers.

That year, I worked in the New York/ Penn League. I went to Instructional ball in Florida that fall. The next year, I was promoted to the Florida State League. I was there for two years. Then I went to the Eastern League—Double A — for three years. Then to Triple A, the International League, for four years.

In 1992, prior to the season, Marty Springstead, the head of the American League umpires told him, "I had planned on bringing you to spring training, but you know the situation. There's nowhere to go." There was no turnover, no major-league positions opening up, and Kevin's wife was pregnant. O'Connor worked the 1992 but then was released because there was indeed nowhere to advance. He had been in industrial sales during the offseasons, and now went full-time while also working as a substitute teacher in Oxford. In the late 1990s, he began to work in real estate and currently owns the ReMax franchise in Oxford.

How did he become an umpire observer?

O'Connor: It was in 2001. I had kept in touch with Jerry [Meals] and Jeff [Kellogg] and all those guys. Phil Cuzzi, all those guys I kept in touch with. And Jerry sent me an email. It was, "Hey, they're starting this new job. I don't know what it's about but I was just sent something."

O'Connor sent in his baseball resume and after some time was offered the position he still holds in 2015, 14 years later. It's officially a part-time job, for which he is paid on a per game basis. The only thing that's changed for him was around 2008 when Jim McKean

had a heart attack and O'Connor was asked to go to Pawtucket to look at some umpire crews working in the International League who needed to be seen. He filled in mid-year, and has covered both Triple-A games in Pawtucket and major-league games in Boston ever since. He's the only one in his position who covers both major-league and minor-league games. Between the Umpire Supervisors and the Umpire Observers, they cover virtually every major-league game.

Who does he report to?

O'Connor: In the big picture, it's Joe Torre. But my immediate guys…I consider any of the fulltime supervisors my boss. And then the head of the supervisors are Rich Rieker and Randy Marsh. But if Steve Palermo, Cris Jones, any of those—Charlie Reliford calls me—I consider them my bosses. For sure.

He arrives about an hour and a half before each game, and keeps himself busy with work until first pitch. He stays until the umpires have left the field and are out of his sight. What sort of reports does he provide? The actual reports, of course, are confidential and proprietary information.

O'Connor: They're reported on a daily basis. Each game has its own separate report. I have to have them in within 48 hours of the series' ending. I really don't have to have Friday night's game in on Saturday. I really have until Tuesday, but I normally have mine done and in the next day.

It's a combination of a form, checking things off, rating them, and using examples of plays and things that happened in the game. It's not a numeric rating.

BN: A couple of sentences on each umpire's work during the game?

O'Connor: It depends on what happened in the game. There are a lot of nights where the third-base umpire will have absolutely nothing. Just one of those nights where he might have a fair/foul by 10 feet and that's his only call, so it's very difficult to try to come up with stuff to talk about.

It's also hustle, though. We can comment on other things even if they don't have plays per se.

[Regarding communication with New York]

They'll send a number of plays after every game, to evaluate. Did they get plays right or wrong? And even review plays. We can say we disagree with the umpires in New York. If they uphold something and my angles show that they got it wrong, then I would say they got it wrong.

There is no contact or communication with the umpires themselves.

O'Connor: I'm not allowed to. Not allowed to. And it makes it tough, because I've worked with a number of the guys. And even in time between when I was off this field and I got this job, I'd come in and I'd see those guys. I'd stayed overnight with a few of them, and we'd go to dinner and the wives would come out and the whole thing, and now I can't talk to them. Impartiality.

Before submitting his report, how does he review plays on which he needs to comment?

O'Connor: I would come up after the ninth inning and I would get a tape from the Red Sox. I would make notes of anything close, and then I would check the tape later. Fair/ foul call. It looked like one thing from 10 rows off the field, but when you would get the tape, it wasn't even close. I still DVR all the games at home. If I have a question, I go back to it.

Do the umpire observers get together once a year to talk over how to best do their job?

O'Connor: We used to go to spring training every year and have meetings with films and slide show presentations and all, but now it's all done online. We'll have a presentation where we all log in. We'll talk about everything in the upcoming season—rules, new rules, interpretation, the whole shooting match. The whole staff, including all the big-league supervisors, will be on that. The evaluators, supervisors, and some of the office personnel.

This is our 14th year. I think the newest guy is probably three or four years in now. There's been a little bit of turnover, but over 14 years very little turnover. We all know what we're doing, so we're more just reviewing things. When we went to spring training, it was "this is how you do it." We just try to get the evaluators on the same page so one guy's not saying "that play is this rating and this play in your mind is this rating—to try and have some uniformity. Which makes sense.

We have a monthly conference call on the Triple-A part of my job. There's, I think, six of us on that call, and it's strictly about the Triple-A guys that we've seen.

Does he meet with the supervisors when one is in Boston?

O'Connor: If a supervisor's here, then I won't be here. They bump me. It used to be, the first few years, when it was Garcia, McKean, and those guys, they used to come to Boston a lot. We would both evaluate the game. A few years in, they said, "No, there's no need to have two there" so if someone would come in to Boston, I would get a call saying don't come in.

Come the postseason, the supervisors will work the games. Other work comes up from time to time, but O'Connor does not work games other than major-league or Triple-A teams.

O'Connor: We only do Triple A. Double A down has their own staff. They have sent me over the years just to a few different… They would send me out to the PCL and there was a guy from the PCL they would send out to the East Coast, to surprise the guys. There were times when crews didn't come to Pawtucket, so they would send me to a different International League city to see them. For the most part, the only traveling I will do now is that I will do a couple of the umpire camps that MLB puts on. I was out in Las Vegas earlier this year. Chicago.

We did it in Boston a few years ago. It's a free, one-day camp for local umpires. You work on positioning on the bases, on the plate. Bruce Froemming, when he's there, he and Eddie Rapuano, they'll do cage work for guys' stances and strike calls and things like that. In the two that I did this year, I was with Dusty Dellinger, who is a Triple-A umpire who was up and down but did not get a full-time job. He's now the head of the minor-league supervisors. We did how to take plays behind the plate and then we went down on how to take plays at first base for different situations.

I get calls from the media—even local associations—on rulings, my opinion on how something was handled.

Anyone observing umpire observer Kevin O'Connor at work or having the opportunity to talk with him has a deeper appreciation of the seriousness with which he approaches the work of officiating and the evaluations that are intended to help the umpires on the field improve their work.

SOURCES

Bill Nowlin conducted the interview with Kevin O'Connor at Fenway Park on July 30, 2015.

NOTES

1   UPI wrote up the story, which ran in the *Washington Post* under the headline "Umpire Hears All, Sees Red." *Washington Post*, June 28, 1985: E3.

Ross Larson, Instant Replay Coordinator

By Bill Nowlin

Major League Baseball's Replay Operations Center ("the ROC") is based at 75 Ninth Avenue, in the Chelsea Market Building. The building also houses MLB Advanced Media and other MLB offices.

Mike Teevan, Vice President for Communications, Major League Baseball: Ross is here every day. He and Justin [Klemm] work hand in hand.

Ross Larson: This is my second year in the department. It's been pretty interesting. It's *everyone's* second year, even Justin's, though he obviously has an extensive umpiring background. I do not. I have an operations background and that led me…I worked the Arizona Fall League and from there I went to help around the press box, so I got to meet several of the umpire supervisors. When this opened up, I reached out and they said they thought it would be a good fit.

What you see here mostly is our video technicians. We have about 25 or 30. On any given night, probably 20 will be working. The way the room is set up, we have stations. They're numbered at the top—1, 2, 3, 4, 5, 6. We have six stations. They will each run two games. So, right here (#3), the video technician sits on the left. The umpire sits on the right. When they get on the headsets on the field, they're on the headset with this umpire right here.

The technician will be here. They'll be watching the games together. They'll be watching two games at once.

If there's a day game, that umpire will come in and then he'll be done for the day after the day game. Either we have one or two extra who are not working a game at that time or they just worked a game earlier that day, depending on the day of the week.

The video technicians will come in about five hours before first pitch and setup everything. We check everything, every day. On site, everything gets unplugged every day—the cameras, the headphones, everything gets turned off.

We check everything multiple times before every game and multiple times in game as well. To make sure everything works. If stuff does go down, right next door are the guys who help us troubleshoot. Next door to that are guys who do other work for us. And then below us are guys who clip video for us. This is just the perfect area for it. We work hand in hand with every other department here.

This is what we call a multi-view, where we can see all the cameras at once. He'll be on the phone with someone at the ballpark, saying, "I see the center-field camera pointing at the backstop. Is that what you see?" And they'll say, "Yes." And if not, something's in the wrong place and we'll troubleshoot that.

What one ballpark might call a mid-third base camera, another ballpark might consider a high third base. That's been part of the learning process, working with the different ballparks, learning where the camera wells are, what they call them. The actual camera men are assigned to shoot different things sometimes. If you look at…when a close play happens sometimes…we'll take in 12 angles usually—six from the home team and six from the away team.

BN: Working from their commercial feeds.

RL: Correct. Out of those 12, maybe five catch the play. The other seven—one's in the dugout, one's on the stands, one's on the mascot or whatever. That's been an interesting learning curve, too. Sometimes we'll be like, "Did we not have a third-base shot on that?" There's a third-base camera but he was looking at the trail runner instead of the play at the plate, or something. That's been a good learning process for us, too, is to communicate. We're starting to have those open discussions with the regional networks saying, "This is what you guys need. This is what we want. Is there any way we can both get what we want out of all this?" That's a really nice thing we did starting this year where we're really opening up discussion with everyone else we're working with.

We're very aware that we're kind of seen as the people behind the black curtain but that's not the case at all. We love having people in here. We just want to be sure that we're communicating effectively all the time with everyone we work with, all the time, through media, through our technicians. Even down through the players on the team, with Joe Torre and whoever wants to communicate with these people.

BN: Everyone wants to make the right call. This just helps do that.

RL: Absolutely, yeah. The way it works is that this guy (points to umpire's chair) is on the headset with the guys on the field, but he's always welcome to turn to other umpires in the room and say, "This is what I have. Does anyone have anything different?"

Because we work every single game in here, I think sometimes we lose sight of the fact that there are some games that don't have any replays. We never go a day without one. I think it's happened once in two years. On a Monday or a Thursday without a full set of games, we might have one of those games with zero but on a day with 15 games we always have a few.

BN: Do you always have eight umpires assigned, even on those days that are very light?

RL: If we have an opportunity to give a day off, we will, but if there's a situation like yesterday (three postponements), or if there are games added, or we know there could be rain delays, we're going to say, "Hey, everybody's working because a guy might have a terribly long shift and we'll want to relieve him." The way the scheduling breaks down has also been a learning curve for us; how do we get what we need without holding these guys here—locked in here forever.

I think they enjoy the break from the field during the summer. They like to rest their bodies a little bit, too, I think. And obviously they like coming to New York City.

BN: And also staying in one place for seven days.

RL: That's longer than they usually do.

BN: I guess most crews come in for a full seven days. Do you have times they just come in for three or four days?

RL: If there's an injury and they need to pull someone, or an unexpected doubleheader down in Philadelphia, they sometimes will say, "Hey, we've got to pull a guy" from here. But then they'll always replace them with someone else. We're never short-staffed here. It has been kind of a nice accidental thing about Replay, that we're here as a resource to help out any last-ditch situation where they need to get someone to an East Coast city right away.

MT: The rainouts today affected how the umpires are staffed tomorrow. Sometimes guys get pulled out of replay and go elsewhere.

RL: We have a couple of what we call lines of defense. He and his technician are going to be sitting here watching the games. They'll watch every pitch. They'll be talking about what they do outside of baseball, what they do for fun. As soon as a close play happens, they'll start rewinding and looking at it again and you'll actually hear an alert go "Three!" and that means there's a close play at Station Three. Most of the room's aware at that point, and these guys are obviously aware. We also have extra technicians sitting back here at what we call the back wall. Those are not designated stations. Those guys will watch all the games going on and they'll get extra footage when we have a close play.

We also have, in the room next door, what's called the Logging Department. They'll log everything from broken bats…they'll have guys who will sit there and watch just one game and they'll log every event, including close plays. They're kind of our third line of defense. If they see a close play, they'll hit a close play button and we'll hear that same alert go off. So we have three sets of eyes on every single game, all the time.

BN: The umpires seem to be pretty generous in allowing the managers time to get the word from their replay coordinator.

RL: We'll wait for him to either go "No" or "Yes," and at that point we say, "OK, get ready. They're coming in. Put on your headset. Here's what we got."

They want to get the call right. I can't speak for them, but I think that's what it comes down to. They're willing to give them that extra five or 10 seconds just to be totally sure. If it really is a close play, they want to make sure.

One thing our numbers show us is that when they come on their own, after the seventh inning, we have a lot more of those that come back, "Yeah, the call's correct. Keep playing." They're overly willing to come check.

BN: It's still a surprise to me to see a challenge in the first inning. I saw one about a month ago, the first batter of the game—safe/out at first base. He was called out, and the call was in fact overturned, so the manager didn't lose his challenge, but still, what was so crucial about that?

MT: There was a 14-3 game after eight innings, and they challenged something in the ninth.

BN: There could be a reason for that—the manager considering the personality of one of the players, I suppose. And he still had a challenge in his pocket.

RL: Every team has a different strategy. It's not up to us to decide what's a right or wrong strategy. If they tell us, "Look at this," we're looking at it. There's clearly some teams that are going to hold onto theirs just in case they need it later, where there are some that say, "Uh, let's use it. If we don't get it, at least we tried."

BN: Obviously umpires get evaluated for their work on the field. I assume there have to be ways of evaluating the work of umpires in Replay.

RL: Sure. They all take it seriously. They all come in here and they're all focused. They want to get the call right. They see themselves as an extension of the crew on the field. They're the fifth man on that crew. So they want to be there for their guys there and make sure they're in tune for what's going on in the game. It's being built into their evaluations, right, but we're still learning how to exactly evaluate it. It's all brand new.

BN: This crew here, working this game (pointing to the monitor)—Jeff Kellogg's crew—do they know which umpire is sitting in this seat?

RL: If they don't know beforehand, they'll recognize the voice, definitely. But some of them will call in ahead and say, "Hey, just curious who we've got." Or sometime this guy (umpire in the seat) will text them beforehand and say, "Hey, I've got your game tonight. Good luck." That's encouraged. Any kind of communication like that's only going to help.

If we do get a particularly tricky play…the normal force outs and tag plays that we get, there's not a whole lot of conversation. It's "he tagged him" or he didn't. The throw beat him or it didn't. But if we get a hit by pitch or something where we need audio or they say, "Hey, this is what I had on this"—or it's a boundary call thing, that's when we'll probably have a little more back and forth. "OK, what exactly did you have? We're seeing this, but you have a better angle on this than we did. Did you have anything on that?"

But the normal force and tag plays, it's usually, "Hey, what have you got?" "OK, we're going to take a look at it. We'll get back to you."

BN: Do some parks have more cameras than others these days?

RL: Certainly. Sometimes there's only one broadcast. Oakland or Houston, maybe, won't be broadcasting their games sometimes. Half of these screens will be blue, and we'll only have six. We're at the mercy of those networks. We like it when there's more cameras. It's a big difference when you have Oakland and Houston playing each other versus the Yankees and Red Sox.

BN: What's the maximum number of cameras?

RL: We have taken 12, no matter what. They may have 20-something there, and at that point, we can pull from the broadcast whenever they're showing all the extra stuff. We have the 12 that we can pull on our own whenever we want, and then we'll be watching for anything else they show.

BN: So you'll also be in touch with the broadcast crews and if you want to request an extra angle, you can?

RL: We can't request it. That's up to them, to their producer as to what they're going to show but we have to have faith that they're going to show the best stuff. This guy will be manipulating the video frame-by-frame, and these guys will be looking at all the extra stuff and might say, "Hey, we found something new. Show this."

On a given night, it is a bit of a rotating door in here. People start coming in around noon to 2 PM and then we keep getting more and more. The umpires come in and it gets really full until about 11 PM and people then start to trickle out. We're here until the West Coast games are done, as late as 2 AM at times. Then we've got some record-keeping to do on the back end, and make sure everything adds up.

BN: Extra innings on the West Coast.

MT: There was a 17-inning game, I think, last year.

RL: Sometimes the broadcasters will say, "I wonder if they're still awake in New York." We're here.

BN: The official scorer usually announces the time of each replay. One minute and 52 seconds or something like that. Do you know when they start the clock?

MT: It's from the time the challenge is made. We've had good luck this year reducing the social exchange, compared to last year when the manager did the stroll and just waited to get the thumbs up. I think it's down about 80 percent this year.

RL: There's a lot less of that. It was not a sexy part of the game. They're sitting here watching this all real time. We try to have as little delay as possible.

BN: (indicating the people who sit at the desk in the middle of the room) What do these guys here do?

RL: These are who we call our administrators. The head technicians or engineers in charge. The umpire supervisors will be right here. (A couple of extra chairs on the center desk, closest to the real wall.)

BN: One or two supervisors.

RL: It depends on the week, yeah. During the week, our director Justin Klemm will work most of the shifts. On the weekend, one of the umpire supervisors will come in. They go out and watch games in stadium and they're responsible for several crews. They all split time doing work in here every month. They'll each come in for a few days every month and help us out. It's too much for just one guy to do all these, so we get help from the supervisors.

BN: Have you ever had a time the whole thing went down?

RL: We've never gone down. We have some backups in place. There's something similar to this in San Francisco. There's no umpires out there, but we do have some video guys out there who do the same thing so, God forbid a natural disaster strikes here, we could still do instant replay through the San Francisco location.

At each station, we have the rule book. A lot of times, midgame, the umpires will pull out a rule book. We endlessly play the "what if" game in here. Most of the time it's force and tag plays, pretty cut-and-dried, but if we get a funky play, that's been one of the benefits of this room—we'll get everyone together and we'll talk. "Hey, what if that ball had hit that rail right there? It didn't, but what if it did?" We have a supervisor on hand who'll say, "Thirty years ago, I had this play and this is what we did. I wish we'd done this" or something. It's just been a great education, especially for the young guys who are in here. All of a sudden, you can have 200 years of umpiring experience in the same room.

Previously, I think they only got together in the winter for their annual meeting. Now, every week we're getting together. It's been a really great by-product.

BN: You get the war stories, but game- and play-related.

RL: It's all baseball and as you know, you see new stuff all the time. There have been times we'll see something and all eight umpires here will say, "I've never seen that play." That's another cool moment every once in a while.

BN: I guess no one knows every nuance of every rule.

RL: Charlie Reliford's pretty close. He's incredible.

MT: Charlie Reliford is the one who, for their meetings, will compile the strange plays from throughout the year. "OK, on April 25 if the Angels/A's game, this happened...." He'll then walk through every facet of it in front of the whole group.

RL: It's really cool to see. And they all live for this stuff. We can sit here and talk about one play for three hours.

MT: They're so passionate about it.

RL: As someone who had no umpiring experience before this job, it's been very eye-opening. These guys, they live for this. The last thing they think about when they go to bed is umpiring and when they wake up, the first thing they think about is umpiring.

BN: And if they were in the wrong position to make a call, sometimes they don't get much sleep.

RL: That's very true. I lost some sleep over some plays last year and I wasn't even directly involved. That's another by-product. This is very real.

The room was designed by Booz Allen, who do a lot of government and military control centers, so that's obviously what it resembles. It is designed to make you lose track of time, so we joke sometimes that it's kind of like being in a casino. Pumping in oxygen, and you lose track of time. It may be sunny in LA but we forget that it's 11 PM here.

I hope this has been helpful. We think we do a good job, so we like showing off when we can. There's a lot of moving parts.

That schedule changes almost daily. By the time you go to the printer to grab it, it's already out of date. When we have the supervisors in here and we see an injury happen, or a game gets canceled and re-scheduled, we see it live—phone calls happening. There's a constant rotation of five or six guys who are in contact with each other.

MT: It seems like every year there are two or three guys who are hurt—their backs, often. Their knees.

RL: And then you've got to re-do weeks and weeks of the schedule. They're out there every day. Some of them will work 20 days before they get a day off. It's not like the players who get either a Monday or a Thursday off. These guys usually get neither. Maybe one or two days off a month.

I think the wives are the unsung heroes. They raise the kids all summer. Modern technology's great for these guys, though. They can face-time their kids on an i-Pad when they're traveling.

BN: And I guess some of them when they're here they can bring their families to New York.

RL: And we can show them that when they come into Replay, we're actually working.

BN: It must happen sometimes that, with overlapping times and extra innings, you've had 15 games going at one time.

RL: It has. This Sunday, all 15 games are starting at 3 o'clock and we'll be running all 15 games in their entirety, all at the same time. [Last day of the season.]

The playoffs — high intensity, but there's a little bit less going on.

BN: When you get down to the World Series, when there's one game going, how many umpires will you have in here?

RL: We'll have two. Two for one game, whereas usually we have one umpire for two games. We'll double up. And we'll have more supervisors than normal. It's a little quieter. There's one umpire on the phone, and when we're done, we're done. We'll have one replay maybe in a game, or two, instead of seven, eight, nine in a day. It's a lot less going on for sure.

BN: But many, many more people watching. And a lot more riding on it.

MT: It's kind of appropriate that Game Seven of the World Series last year had that one replay in the third inning.

RL: Made it worth all the 200 days we spent leading up to it.

Interview with Ross Larson and Mike Teevan conducted by Bill Nowlin on October 2, 2015

Replay Behind The Scenes—At The Ballpark

By Bill Nowlin

ANDY ANDRES, FIELD TIMING COORDINATOR

Interview on August 17, 2015

MLB approved replay and tested it out in the Arizona Fall League of 2013. In spring training 2014 they had all the technical stuff worked out, but when the broadcasters came in they realized the producers can't decide what to do with the third out. Third out, the regular producer's got like 10 seconds to wrap up, a minute 45 commercial, 10 seconds to talk, then the game. That's the producer's job. But on a third-out close play, the producers are like, "What do we do? Do we wait?" MLB realized they had forgot about that part.

So they hired Field Timing Coordinators to make the decision to go to commercial break or not. We watch the third out and both managers, to make the right decision. We also did clock management between innings. The umpires weren't supposed to start a pitch before we let them know. We had to coordinate with them. The original idea was that we would actually stand on the field with our own stopwatches and flash different colored cards—"go" or "don't go." Green was "go ahead." All 30 parks had a different spot, but we were all on the field. They backed off on that, so we were put just near the field, in the third-base photo well. The umpires were supposed to watch us. They hated it. They didn't want to do that. They were resistant. But then the Commissioner laid down the law and so they finally sort of got on board. Now, instead of flashing cards we operate the clock out of the press box.

The Commissioner really wants a 20-second pitch clock to increase the pace of play. Right now, it's hap-pening in Double A and Triple A and there's a real move to make that happen in major-league baseball. It's going to have to be negotiated, bargained between the owners and the players, but I give it a pretty high probability that it's going to happen because the lords of baseball want it to happen. It'll speed up the game. If it happens, the clock operator will be a part of that and become an official of the game.

I can see Dan Fish right now. He's the Replay Headset Coordinator. His whole job is to set up the headsets, make sure they're connected with the replay center in New York. There's an umpire crew there. The umpires know to look there if there's a replay in Fenway, and Dan's supposed to pop out and hand them headsets. Everyone's supposed to be connected. Last year, I was connected with the umpire headset chatter. I could hear them. There's usually one guy in New York as the talker. Last year we heard the chatter. They told us very clearly we're not supposed to talk about what was said.

Dan pops out with the headsets and make sure the umpires could chat with New York. The replay rules

Andy Andres.

336

are very specific. Call/not call. Who calls it when. The umpire crew on a challenge play.

Two guys always come over and they both get on the headsets. I think that's just redundancy so there's no screw-ups. I think baseball's very happy with replay. They see that peoples' interest spikes up. I think the time taken in replay is balanced by the time taken in arguing.

[One or two managers have been ejected for arguing a replay decision.] I think Scioscia was. Replay went against him, and he just kept railing and railing. His justification was, "I had to get a ruling, in case I have to protest." He had to know what the ruling was. That's how he justified his argument, that he needed a ruling for protest purposes. He was demonstratively vehement in his request for a ruling.

[There have been calls for replay even in the first inning.] The logic on that begins with the question: How many close plays are there in a game? If there's one, even if it happens in the first inning, you shouldn't not challenge just because you want to lose a challenge.

There's probabilities in all of these things. Everyone's measuring the probability of it being successful. I think there are fewer than one challenge per game, per team, which means "use it when you think you're close." If it's half a challenge per game, per team, when you get anything close, your probabilities go the other way. You should use it. If you do get screwed occasionally, it just happens. I'm sure someone has already analyzed how many challenges you can't make because you've already lost your right to challenge. I bet it's pretty infrequent.

If it's the seventh inning and you have a 10% likelihood of winning that challenge, I can see rolling the dice.

Dan Brooks and Harry Pavlidis, I think, wrote an article in spring 2014 about the strategy of calling a challenge from the manager's perspective.

With the emergence of PitchFX, fundamentally, if you think about the event of the pitch, there are four players—umpire, catcher, batter, and pitcher.

And they all have their own strike zone. That's not so clear to people. People think it's just "the strike zone."

The batter has a strike zone and there are tendencies there as to what gets called strikes for that batter. The pitcher has a strike zone. The catcher has a strike zone; that's "framing." Umpires obviously have a strike zone. You can evaluate each of those four impacts on the strike zone. If a pitch is here [indicates], that's probably going to be a strike if you know those pitcher/catcher/batter/umpire, you kind of know those probabilities.

When QuesTec came in, slowly but surely, the umpires' strike zones started conforming. Before that they were like…every guy was… all over the place.

Every game, they get a report. A disc that shows every one that they missed, or that they got.

I don't see the three-dimensional stuff here. But one thing to remember when you see the strike zone on Gameday or TV, you don't see the three-dimensional zone. If you're just looking at two dimensions, you're not seeing the full strike zone. If you're just looking at two dimensions, you're not seeing the full strike zone.

The real key is where the strike zone moved vertically. The guys in the PitchFX truck…MLB is telling them how to do it and that's driving the strike zone. The umpire gets a report, and he goes, "I've got to do this because this is what MLB is grading me on." Slowly but surely, umpires became more consistent vertically.

DAN FISH, REPLAY HEADSET COORDINATOR

Interview with Dan Fish, Replay Headset Coordinator, September 2, 2015

I worked the first games of replay here. I got the job through the military. I serve in the Reserves and one month while I was at drill, a representative from the Hero2Hired website came in and talk to our unit. I told her I was extremely interested and passionate about baseball, so she forwarded my information to MLB Network. A few weeks later I got a call from Erika Brockington in New York, the manager for

Dan Fish.

MLB, and here I am today, lucky enough to still be working with them.

I commute from East Brookfield, about 20 minutes away from the city of Worcester. I did most of the games last year and I've got about 50, 55 games this year so far, more than half. I split it with two other people. It's hourly pay. We get paid biweekly.

I usually get here at least three hours before the first pitch, get the headsets, and hook them up. They used to be in the umpires room, but we moved them to our little storage room known as the "hut," because it's a little easier to get to. It is where we keep all our camera stands, tripods, and other stuff we need for the day. I hook up the headsets, make sure they're all working. If the headset weren't working, the umpires would use the "legacy" backup set in the umpires room. One time, for some reason, it took a minute for the people in New York to respond. I was about to tell the umpires to go down to the legacy room. I was kind of nervous for a few seconds, didn't know what was going on, but then all of a sudden the people in New York started talking. It was a close call.

Before every series that I work, about 15 minutes before the first pitch, I go into the umpires room, introduce myself, let them know where I'm going to be standing so there's no confusion. I pay attention to the game. If it's a close call, I get a good idea if they're going to challenge it. If the umps flag me down, I'll just hop over the railing of the photo well here and give them the headsets. One set is for the crew chief and one is for the umpire whose call is challenged, unless it's the crew chief's call which is being challenged and then it's the number two man. I can't hear anything.

I really enjoy just being around the park, and the atmosphere. Being involved, seeing the professionals work to get better at what they do. Sometimes it's hot and sometimes it's cold, or raining. Have I ever had fans give me a hard time? I have, actually. Whenever a call doesn't go the Red Sox' way, the fans will boo me a few times.

But it's a great job for a baseball fan, someone who really enjoys baseball the way I do. I think it's a great opportunity, starting-wise. We have a replay tech, and a ballpark cam tech. I check in with the replay cam tech and I give him all my "fax" times - basically just my report times that I check to make sure all the equipment is working (headsets, field timing headset, PA headset, etc.) I think being the headset tech is a good way to get my foot in the door, maybe for some good opportunities in the future.

Being on the field during a game, watching the umpires waiting for a call, I'm trying to think of a word to describe the feeling, and I don't think I can come up with a word that truly describes how I feel. I remember how nervous I was for my first challenge, and just kept thinking not to screw it up in any way. I feel privileged to be able to be on the field with the best players in the world, and it just amazes me that I have this feeling of such excitement every time I'm out there, and these guys do this every day, 162 games a year. I almost feel like a player walking out with the headsets, and when everyone cheers because the manager challenged a play, that feels like my walk-up music. And I have an awesome view of the games.

JEREMY ALMAZAN, REPLAY HEADSET COORDINATOR

Interview with Jeremy Almazan done September 26, 2015

I grew up as a military kid. I was in the Air Force, a logistician, a 2S-071. Supply. 20 years, one month, seven days. I was stationed various places. I started at Dyess Air Force Base in Abilene, Texas, and I ended at Fort Meade, Maryland. I was at Balad (Iraq) in 2003-2004.

I consider myself a baseball junkie. I started on the Washington Nationals grounds crew. I'm a huge Pittsburgh Pirates fan and when they came to Washington last year, I was someplace I wasn't supposed to be. I snuck into the tunnel behind the dugout and I started bothering the headset people. I was asking them what it was like, how I could get involved. They gave me my boss's number just to get me to shut up.

Jeremy Almazan.

This is my first full season. I work for a consulting firm called Chris Fickes Consulting, which is contracted out to MLB. They are based out of Nashville, Tennessee.

I'm like the emergency guy, if they need a fill-in someplace, I'll go. This is my second series here. I did a series in June.

Love it. We're required to be here about four hours, but I come a little earlier because I like to have the ballpark to myself. I was an hour and a half early today. I appreciate the history and unless you go to Wrigley Field you can't get more historic than this. The last time I was here, I went into the Monster wall.

I feel like I'm part of the baseball game. I've been a part of baseball history this season. I was here when they had the ambidextrous pitcher (Pat Venditte), and I was the headset tech for the "no fans" game in Baltimore. (April 29, 2015 at Camden Yards, following rioting in the city) Hopefully we don't ever have to do that again. That was very weird.

Nobody got booed that day.

What I like is just being part of the game. I was lucky to make it into baseball another way. I feel like I'm part of the game. I don't make the calls. They make the calls in New York.

Replay's only going to get bigger. It's in its second year and, in my opinion, still in its infancy. I'm sure we're going to get some new things. I hope to continue on this path, and be part of it as long as my boss will have me. We don't get a report card or anything like that but I don't want to be that guy that sucks, and then somebody says something.

I'm part of a team of three, so there are other positions I could get. One is the instant replay tech, to make sure that all of the camera angles are good, and the other person runs the ballpark cam.

JOHN HERRHOLZ, BALLPARK CAMERA TECHNICIAN

Interview with John Herrholz done on September 27, 2015

I'm the ballpark camera technician. I work for Chris Fickes Consulting. I was on the initial crew

John Herrholz.

that put in the ballpark camera systems here, and I did the one in New York as well, at the old Yankee Stadium. That was done by our consulting team that installed them all for Major League Baseball Network. Following the installation, they said, "Well, OK, now we have to crew this. You're familiar with the system." So I got hired. I live north of Boston, in New Hampshire. I've worked in this park now for 32 years—local affiliates and all.

The first use of replay was in September 2008, and then we put the actual cameras in during the late spring of '09 and that's when I got involved.

Before 2014, it was almost only fair or foul. At that time, you had only one person—which was me –and you were working both for Major League Baseball Network doing ballpark cam, and for Major League Baseball.com ensuring they had in-bound feeds from the production trucks. That was all they had. It wasn't divided down into individual camera feeds. It was just a program feed, clean and dirty, with or without graphics, back to Major League Baseball.com. So you were a little bipolar—who are you working for and whose needs are you trying to address? It was a little ugly but we got through it.

Before the game, our job was simply to check out the replay monitor—the "legacy"—and make sure it was switching, make sure the sources were correct back from Major League Baseball.com. It's the same identical box now, same identical ringdown, all of that. It was more or less, OK, go in and make sure that technically it's working right. The problem we had was that you were downstream of getting the feeds from the truck set, so if there's any kind of hiccup with that…. At times that meant if you were delayed in doing that check, the umpires would get a little stress from that.

I'd just find a place inside the park where I'd like to be. You did not have to hang out near the box. There was virtually nothing for us to do except be available by phone should there be a problem.

The umpires would go out to left field, around the back door and then back to the umpires room. But if you're not at a dead run, that's time. A huge delay of the game.

It didn't happen often. And quite frankly what people were looking at from the team vantage point— to say do I have a challenge or I don't—was much more limited. You didn't have a bank of monitors of 14 different feeds to look at. It was, OK, from the top step, what do you think? Shall I challenge it or not?

You look at the human-ness of that argument (between a player or coach or manager, and an umpire) where in those days, for me as a fan, wow, there's somebody who's really passionate, and to see them go out and speak on behalf of their players, that to me was more exciting. More personal.

Now they get it right. Bring your anger down a little bit. They got it right.

Umpire Analytics

By Brian M. Mills

1. Introduction

Rule 9.02 of the official MLB rulebook states, "Any umpire's decision which involves judgment, such as, but not limited to, whether a batted ball is fair or foul, whether a pitch is a strike or a ball, or whether a runner is safe or out, is final. No player, manager, coach, or substitute shall object to any such judgment decisions." The importance of this authority is rooted in ensuring that the game proceeds smoothly and with integrity. MLB requires that umpires do not abuse their power and perform up to expectations as guided by the rules.

To ensure that rules are followed, the league monitors the behavior and performance of its umpires holding the integrity of the game in hand. Yet, precise measurements of performance, particularly for ball and strike calls, have not been readily available until recent technological innovations. The most important innovation was the introduction of ball-tracking technology to evaluate the called strike zone, but more recent additions include instant replay and tracking of umpire movements around the field. Various sabermetricians have used this data to apply the quantitative concepts to umpires that they have applied to player evaluation for years. The result has been a new and exciting understanding of the game of baseball and the role umpires play in those outcomes.

This article will start by giving a general overview of the evolution of technology used to monitor umpires and how this has been useful in developing an understanding of umpire behavior. While most readers are likely familiar with the use of *sabermetrics* to evaluate players and teams, player evaluation has been a part of the game since its inception. Much of this work on teams and players is known to a wide audience, but analysis of umpires has only recently become a topic of public conversation due to the availability of new data and technology. This article will therefore take the reader through many of approaches and findings of umpire analytics experts over the past 10 years to evaluate the performance and biases among umpires in MLB.

As the reader may well know, the history of umpires is one resistant to technological change and what is often seen as threatening oversight. However, recent advancements have encouraged the effective use of these technologies not only to monitor performance, but reduce bias and help train a new crop of high-performing umpires seemingly more open to receiving feedback on their work. The monitoring of umpires, however, is not the only proposed use of this technology. Using relatively simple analytics, paired with the influx of data on strike zones, many have proposed replacing the umpire with a machine to call balls and strikes. The possibility of replacement is uncertain, but we can be sure that analytics provide us with useful context in which to make more educated decisions about these types of policies.

2. The Evolution of Umpire Performance Monitoring Technology

Major League Baseball and its umpires have had a rather tumultuous history of labor strife, with performance standards, incentives, and salary considerations playing a central role in disagreements during the 1990s when the leagues were still separate (O'Neill, 1990; Chass, 1999). Umpires generally voiced interest in both autonomy and a seat at the table on rule and monitoring changes, but the commissioner's office issued directives in the 1990s related to strike-zone uniformity without much consultation with their umpires (Chass, 1999). The imposition of actual monitoring of umpire calls first became visible when the commissioner's office started its attempt at securing centralized control over umpires to create uniformity in the strike zone across the two leagues (Callan, 2012). While MLB refers to a single organization comprising the teams in both the American League and National League, these leagues operated as separate legal entities prior to 2000. There was a considerable effort to merge into a single group in the 1990s, and this merger had an important influence on the development of technology and umpire monitoring that would follow.

Specifically, the official strike zone had recently been amended in the rulebook in 1996, but Sandy Alderson, executive vice president for baseball operations at the time, had issued a memo calling for uniform enforcement of a zone slightly different from the newly described version (Weber, 2009). Most importantly, as part of this directive, Alderson asked team officials to manually chart pitches for umpires working their games (Callan, 2012), resulting in the first well-known direct evaluation of strike zones by the league. Manual charting, of course, did not provide substantial opportunities for in-depth statistical analysis of umpire performance. But it did give some level of monitoring and accountability to the arbiters of the strike zone as the commissioner's office looked to gain centralized control. This would set the stage for future disagreement and opportunities for more in-depth evaluation of umpire performance by baseball leadership and the public.

Around this same time, the commissioner's office had been experimenting with video simulations and other strategies to train and monitor umpires, largely driven by former minor-league umpire Philip Janssen and his research program (Weber, 2009).[1] The simulations—adapted from training of fighter pilots—provided umpires with opportunities to practice making calls on different types of pitches or areas of difficulty in the zone. This was the league's first real deep dive into using advanced technology to assist its umpires. But the endeavor did not get fully off the ground, with significant resistance from the umpires' union and limited funding from the commissioner's office.[2]

The league's attempt at gaining full control over umpires came to a boiling point in 1999 when the leader of the umpires' union, Richie Phillips, orchestrated a failed mass-resignation strategy. With a majority of major-league umpires sending resignation letters to the commissioner's office to gain leverage in negotiations for a new collective-bargaining agreement, the league unexpectedly accepted the resignations, quickly leading to a divide in the union and its ultimate collapse (Weber, 2009; Cyphers, 2012). This opened up an opportunity for MLB to gain leverage in negotiations, move to the league-controlled officiating we see today, and introduce new technology to monitor and evaluate their performance.

In 2001 the system now colloquially known as QuesTec was installed in a few major-league ballparks to track the accuracy of ball and strike calls on a trial basis. This expanded to 13 ballparks in subsequent seasons (Karegeannes, 2004). The system used video cameras mounted around stadiums to track pitches from the pitcher's hand to the plate, and identify where the ball crossed the front of the plate. The introduction of the system was not initially agreed upon by the umpires union, resulting in more unrest between the league and the umpires. Use of the system was ultimately ratified in 2004 during a new session of collective bargaining with a newer umpires union.

Umpires were sent a CD-ROM of the plotted data from their game(s) that included every pitch location and umpire call. However, in some cases, umpires did not receive the feedback at all, and there was little recourse for not paying attention to the discs (Karegeannes, 2004). And while the system could have been useful in improving umpires' performance, it is unclear whether many umpires used this information, as skepticism remained among them over whether the system would be useful in improving performance. For example, Jerry Crawford noted in an interview on *Real Sports* that he threw the discs in the trash immediately after receiving them (Frankel, 2016). And umpires were not the only ones unimpressed with the QuesTec monitoring. Players also had concerns over the accuracy and consistency of the system. In 2003, while walking off the field, pitcher Curt Schilling sought out and smashed a QuesTec camera (AP, 2003).

It should be noted that QuesTec did have issues with certain types of pitches and identifying a zone consistent with what umpires actually called (or what the league expected them to call). Given the possibility of error, umpires had various complaints about the technology relating both to its accuracy and its use to make employment decisions. The league ultimately gave umpires some leeway with the accuracy measurements, and agreed that any hiring or firing decisions would not be based solely on the technology (Chass, 2004). This system was used through 2008, when it was replaced by a new system from commercial provider Sportvision.

At about the time QuesTec was initially introduced in 2001, ESPN was working with Sportvision to add a strike-zone visual (known as K-Zone) on its television broadcasts for each pitch thrown and called by umpires (Gueziec, 2002). The two systems ultimately meant umpires were suddenly being judged not only by the league and its QuesTec technology, but also by every fan watching a game broadcast on ESPN. Unfortunately for the umpires, as with QuesTec the visual on broadcasts left substantial room for error, perhaps resulting in more fan backlash than was warranted (Fast, 2011a). While the error rate was relatively low using the camera technology, there are questions as to the proper placement of the top and bottom of the strike-zone boundaries and other problems. Umpires seemed to have good reason for loathing the additional scrutiny they faced every game.

As a new collective-bargaining agreement came together in 2009, it was clear that MLB would be shifting away from the proprietary QuesTec in favor of a new camera system from Sportvision known as PITCHf/x.[3] With PITCHf/x, umpires would receive direct and immediate feedback after each game through detailed reports accessible online at their convenience, avoiding some of the issues that plagued the QuesTec system early on. The new system, called Zone Evaluation, also used cameras to track ball movement and project the location of the ball as it crossed the front of the plate. This projection allowed both a two-dimensional and a three-dimensional representation of the strike zone. While presumably more accurate, the PITCHf/x system had some error in its data, measuring the location of the pitch within about a half-inch in either direction. Due to the error margin, umpires are allowed some leeway, though these adjustments are largely part of internal development and it is unclear whether the expected strike zone is evaluated precisely as the rulebook zone defines. But it is important to note that any performance that an analyst reports with this data may be slightly misleading without fully accounting for the error margin. And MLB is rather cagey about sharing the way in which it evaluates its umpires, or the strike-zone definition used to do so.

Luckily for sports analysts, PITCHf/x data had been available since mid-2007. By 2008 and beyond, anyone with the ability to scrape data from the internet had access to the location of every regular-season MLB pitch and the associated umpire call. This marked the beginning of a new era in analytics of baseball, and the start of analytics of umpires. Perhaps to the chagrin of umpires, this also meant that smart analysts had a way of publicly revealing relatively precise grades of ball-strike calls. As early work would show, umpires sometimes missed ball-strike calls in ways that revealed fallibility as arbiters of the truth, with notable biases in the patterns of these missed calls. However, analysts have shown that umpires have improved their accuracy since the system was put in place (Mills, 2016b).

Even more recently, a newer system developed by the Danish company, Trackman, has taken over data production across MLB. Trackman is a Doppler radar system that more precisely locates the ball and follows it on its entire path, rather than projecting its path to the plate (Nathan, Kensrud, Smith, & Lang, 2014). This information is combined with player and umpire movement tracking systems to form what is now well known as Statcast. As the league fully transitions to this new system it has started releasing some of the new information available from the radar system, including batted-ball trajectory and exit velocity and pitch spin rate and axis (Willman, 2016). Most of this information is more useful for player analysis, but has its place in understanding the effects of umpires on game play. Analysts have taken hold of much of this data and developed a new understanding of the work of baseball's umpires.

Interestingly, umpire *performance* itself is only one aspect of this work. There are various topics related to analysis of umpires, most of which are related to the strike zone, and include performance changes, effects on the game, biases, psychological phenomena, and (in the future) positioning. The next section will detail the data available to the analyst and recent work on how umpires perform, how they have improved, and how this can affect the game. Section 4 will detail a large literature on the performance of umpires, while Section 5 discusses biases and other psychological phenomena revealed through analyzing umpire data. Lastly, Section 6 will briefly discuss future directions of umpire analytics and the potential for replacement of home-plate umpires with machines.

3. Data Availability and Strike Zone Definitions

3.1 Data Availability, Methods, and Tools

At its core, umpire analytics have been about the strike zone, the shortcomings of the way it is called by umpires, and impact this has on the game. This interest calls for an in-depth understanding of not only what the data can tell us, but what it cannot. One of the largest drivers of the development of umpire analytics has been the availability of data to the public through the PITCHf/x system. This availability has shaped the focus of umpire analytics on the strike zone, given that information about positioning and video replay of individual calls elsewhere on the field is relatively limited to the outside analyst.

At the initial release of PITCHf/x data, only a few researchers had the technical ability to scrape the data and manipulate it on their own computers. However, analyst Mike Fast opened the flood gates by publicly releasing his Perl and SQL code to download data directly from the MLB Gameday website into a per-

sonal database.[4] Later, other engineers and computer savvy sabermetricians developed online databases that allow point-and-click access to large chunks of PITCHf/x and Statcast data. This data is now much more accessible, allowing for significant growth in the number of analysts evaluating umpire behavior.

Brooks Baseball (brooksbaseball.net), managed by Dan Brooks, was a pioneering site that allows close inspection of game data and visualization of ball and strike calls by umpires in each game. The most obvious benefit of this site is that it provides various options with which visitors can view and understand data on preprogrammed strike-zone maps. But there is also an option to download data at the game-pitcher level for use in Excel and statistical applications. For those who want large files of raw data for themselves, Daren Willman's Baseball Savant—now directly partnered with MLB—has been an excellent source of data downloads of individual pitch data.[5] The data can be downloaded using various queries, and includes umpire assignments within the data, and other information from Statcast like velocity of each hit, the exit angle, and other relevant variables.

Other applications have been developed for more experienced statistical programmers, such as the pitchRx package in the open-source programming language R, developed by Carson Sievert (2014). This package gives analysts the ability to download data directly into the R program from the MLB Gameday website and includes functions that make beautifully designed visuals of the strike zone. Other analysts are developing their own packages in R as well, such as Bill Petti's baseballr package that continues to be developed and improved (Petti, 2016).

While access to and organization of the data is a (sometimes long) process, it is only the first step in the analysis process. Although various quantitative techniques can be performed relatively simply in Excel, much of the impactful work in umpire analytics has used more advanced statistical and visualization tools. One of the most popular programs for doing so is the open-source statistical program known as R. Others have used Matlab and similar powerful programs to perform their sophisticated analyses. While this article will not get into the details of statistical methods and programming, it is clear that nonparametric statistical methods such as kernel density estimation and generalized additive models are becoming standard for measuring the strike zone and how it is impacted by the decisions of its arbiters.

Because PITCHf/x data begins as raw two-dimensional spatial coordinates of the pitch location, nonparametric methods can help to interpret locational properties of strike calls. Generalized additive models (Wood, 2006) have proved to be among the more useful methods in modeling the strike zone called by the umpire. These models use nonparametric regression to measure the probability of a strike call, given its two-dimensional location (and other factors). The most useful outcome of these models is the ability to visualize the strike zone using contour and heat maps. Heat maps are a color representation of the probability of a strike call, presented in a two-dimensional figure. Contours can help to visually identify a square or ellipsoidal boundary at which a strike and a ball call are equally likely to occur (or any other probability of a strike or ball). These models can then be used to compare strike zones of individual umpires or understand how the strike zone changes across different game situations, a key feature for estimating biases in umpire calls in a later section. Later, we'll take a look at the types of visuals that can be created from these methods. But first, it is important to define what we actually mean when referring to the strike zone itself.

3.2 Strike Zone Measurement and Definitions

As of 1996, the rulebook states that, "The STRIKE ZONE is that area over home plate, the upper limit of which is a horizontal line at the midpoint between the top of the shoulders and the top of the uniform pants, and the lower level is a line at the hollow beneath the knee cap. The Strike Zone shall be determined from the batter's stance as the batter is prepared to swing at a pitched ball." (MLB, 2010). However, most fans would agree that whatever the umpires are calling behind the plate, it does not look like the rectangle that K-Zone shows on television, or that would be expected from the description by MLB.

Early revelations that the called strike zone did not represent the rulebook zone brought about an important implication related to analysis of accuracy: The "correct" strike zone is a somewhat fluid concept. Hale (2007a) therefore suggests analyzing umpire accuracy and performance with great care (Josh Kalk [2009] and Mike Fast [2010; 2011d] echo this concern). This work set the stage for a deeper understanding of behavior of umpires relative to expectations of the league and general behavior of their peers, rather than a fixed rectangular strike zone.

Indeed, analysis of the data tells us that the shape of the strike zone called by umpires is more circular or ellipsoidal. And early work from John Walsh (2007a; 2007b) and Jonathan Hale (2007a) showed that its size and shape vary considerably depending on the umpire. Consistent with what fans and players suspected, it was clear that there were umpires with tighter strike zones than others.

There were three core points from this work that redefined how analysts might approach estimating strike zone accuracy: 1) the strike zone called by umpires tended to extend beyond the edges of the plate, 2) left-handed batters tend to have a strike zone shifted to the outside,[6] and 3) the top and bottom of the strike zone are not consistently called strikes, particularly at the corners. The apparent flexibility in the zone relative to the rulebook definition therefore opens up questions regarding the variation in performance of umpires across the league, whether they can improve and change their behavior, whether they have clear biases for or against certain players or in certain situations, and whether this impacts gameplay and fan interest in the sport.

In addition to the issues related to the called zone, there were data problems in measuring the top and bottom of the zone, particularly in earlier PITCHf/x data. These boundaries were manually drawn in by operators, and varied considerably depending on the at-bat and the person making the determination (Walsh, 2007a; Mills, 2011). For example, Walsh (2007a) finds that the total height of the strike zone varied by as much as nine inches from game to game for Derek Jeter in 2007 PITCHf/x data. Identifying the top and bottom of strike zones should therefore be done with care—particularly given the bias in measurement that came along with miscalibration in certain stadiums—but is made difficult without reliable information about each batter's stance in the data. Analysts have come up with ways to circumvent this issue in the data with a reasonably low loss in accuracy of the strike zone definition.

Mills (2016a; 2016b) uses a fixed strike zone to avoid these issues, using the average height of MLB players and setting the top and bottom of the zone congruent with anthropometric data from NASA (2000).[7] However, it is important to note that these fixed zone measurements will likely underestimate the accuracy of umpires, since they do not adjust for the height and stance of each batter at the plate. Roegele (2013) and Mills (2014) do attempt to adjust the strike zone by height, but there tend to be relatively small gains in understanding of accuracy by doing so at the aggregate level. Nevertheless, Roegele (2013) does find that taller players see both an upward shift and an upward expansion of the strike zone as might be expected, and more research is needed to further understand the best ways to integrate batter stances into umpire evaluation.

An additional complication with strike-zone measurement is that accuracy measures are generally tabulated using the location of the ball when it crosses the front of home plate using coordinates directly provided in the data. Yet, there is the question of whether the zone should be measured in two or three dimensions. And technically, if any part of the ball crosses over any part of the plate within the height boundaries of the zone, then it should be called a strike (Rule 2.00, A STRIKE (b) [MLB.com, 2007]). The limitations here are obvious: the ball does not have to cross the *front* of the plate to be a strike, and if only a small piece of the ball crosses through the zone, it is technically a strike. It is physically possible that the ball crosses the back corners of the plate or drops within the top border of the strike zone toward the back of the plate, while not having done so when

it crosses the rectangular two-dimensional plane at the front of the plate.

The issue related to having only a portion of the ball pass through the two-dimensional plane is relatively straight forward to fix. Since PITCHf/x data reports the location of the center of the ball as it passes through the plane, analysts can simply add the radius of the ball to identify additional pitches that should be called strikes. Aaron Baggett (2015) covers some of the intricacies of accounting for the radius of the ball (its diameter is between 2.86 and 2.94 inches) when calculating the width of the strike zone.[8] Figure 1 shows a bird's-eye view of the plate with the added radius of the ball on either side to make the strike zone slightly wider when measuring from PITCHf/x data.

Figure 1. *A bird's-eye view of strike zone width using PITCHf/x data. X-axis identifies the number of feet from the horizontal center of home plate.*

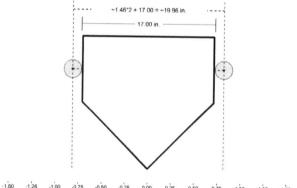

Bird's Eye View of Strike Zone Width

The three-dimensional representation is a bit more involved, using information from PITCHf/x on the trajectory of each pitch, rather than the provided coordinates. Recent work has attempted to evaluate the impact of accounting for these additional strikes (Lang, 2015; Mata, 2015). By representing the zone using a pentagonal (the shape of the plate) volume, rather than a rectangular plane, analysts allow for the movement of the pitch to enter the strike zone at different points as it crosses the plate. Specifically, the movement and path of the pitch can affect the likelihood that a pitch does not pass through the pentagonal volume while missing the plane at the front of the plate (back-door curveballs, for example). With respect to pitch height, Lang (2015) notes that a pitch can drop as much as two inches from the front to the back of the plate, leaving plenty of room for additional strike calls on pitches that were otherwise measured as balls. Both Lang (2015) and Mata (2015) show that strategies using physics of ball flight can actually improve upon our understanding of how umpires see the pitch and call it in the three-dimensional context.

To optimize the three-dimensional zone measurement as called by umpires, Mata (2015) creates an algorithm that improves upon the three-dimensional rulebook and two-dimensional plane representations.[9] Specifically, the back triangle of the plate is not especially helpful in improving our predictions of strike calls in the three-dimensional context. However, using the rectangular portion of the plate—along with height information—improves upon two-dimensional descriptions of umpire behaviors in the strike zone. Lang (2015) further informs us about the role of time in the three-dimensional context: The longer the path of a pitch spends inside this zone, the more likely it is that the umpire will call it a strike. We can presume that the longer the time a pitch is in the zone, the more time an umpire has to determine that it did, in fact, pass through that zone.

Nevertheless, the two-dimensional nature of the projection offers a useful glimpse into how umpires are performing generally. As Lang (2015) notes, pitches that do not cross the front of the plate are very unlikely to be called strikes in the first place, and Mata (2015) adds that two-dimensional plane representation gives a better approximation of the umpire-called strike zone than the true rulebook zone in three dimensions (rather than the simulated optimized zone). Therefore, in ranking umpire accu-

racy, the few pitches that do cross through the three-dimensional zone—but not the two-dimensional one—are unlikely to substantially affect our measures of the relative performance of umpires.[10]

The remainder of this article will therefore focus on the two-dimensional representation, particularly given that the bulk of the work analyzing the zone uses the coordinates of pitches provided by the PITCHf/x data. But it is important to note that future study of the differences in these two definitions is a fruitful area for expansion of umpire analytics work, particularly in the context of introducing automation behind the plate.

For exposition, Figure 2 presents various visualizations of the left-handed batter two-dimensional strike zone. The left panel presents raw 2014 PITCHf/x locational data in a scatterplot, colored by whether the pitch was called a ball (yellow triangles) or a strike (red circles). The center panel presents output from a generalized additive model estimating the boundary at which strikes are called 50 percent of the time. In other words, inside the ellipse, strikes are called at least half the time. Finally, the right panel presents a heat map to visualize various strike probabilities using the same model that was used to produce the contour visual. Again, this boundary approximates the equal blending of yellow triangles and red dots in the scatterplot. This is where there is the most uncertainty in the strike zone. As pitches move toward the center of the strike zone, red (dark color) is more prominent, indicating higher probabilities of strike calls in the heat map. The opposite is true as we move away from the center of the zone, with lighter and lighter yellow as the probability of a called strike approaches zero and the probability of a called ball reaches one. These types of visuals—from the umpire's view—will be used throughout this article to present some of the most interesting findings by analysts about the behavior and performance of umpires.

Figure 2. *Exposition of the called strike zone for left-handed batters.*

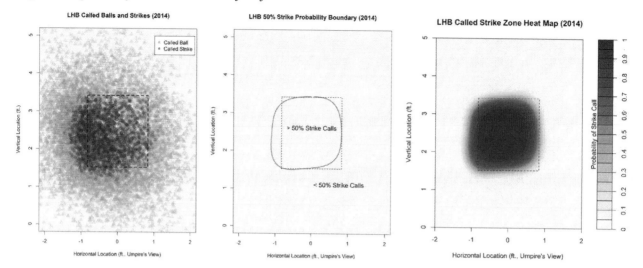

4. The Analytics of Umpire Performance

4.1 Who Are the Best Home-Plate Umpires?

As a primer on accuracy rates in general, I'll begin by presenting some basic statistics on the accuracy of major-league umpires from the 2015 season. The data come from Baseball Savant's Statcast Search tool, and include all pitches called by umpires during the season. Given that pitchouts and intentional balls do not require substantial judgment from the umpire, these are removed from the data, leaving us with just over 365,000 pitches to work with.[11]

I use the fixed strike zone definition created using the NASA information from Mills (2016b) to determine accuracy rates for the league and for individual umpires. This, of course, assumes that most umpires see a similar distribution of batter heights and pitch locations across a given season, an assumption required for simplicity of the exposition. I also note that the definition used here is more stringent than the one used by MLB. Specifically, umpires are given

some cushion around the edge of the strike zone in their Zone Evaluation grades, a practice that began with the implementation of QuesTec. The accuracy rates reported here are, therefore, likely to be underestimated relative to MLB standards.

For our purposes, "true strikes" will be defined as pitches that cross through the two-dimensional strike zone plane at the front of the plate (about 29.4 percent of the called pitch data), while "true balls" will be those that do not cross this plane (about 70.6 percent of the called pitch data). "Correct strikes" will consist of those true strikes that the umpire correctly calls a strike. Finally, "correct balls" will consist of true balls that the umpire correctly calls a ball. These simple classifications are pictured below in Figure 3. These can then be combined to find overall accuracy rates among umpires, as well as accuracy rates specific to pitches within zone and outside of the zone, respectively.

Figure 3. *Exposition of correct and incorrect ball and strike calls.*

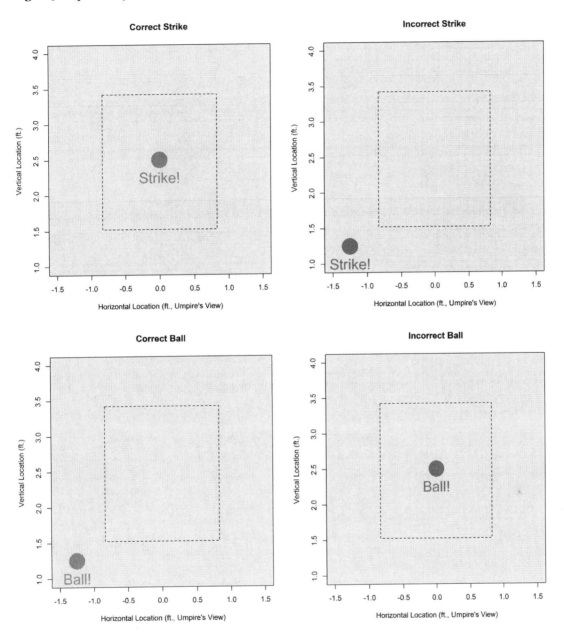

Using these definitions, we see that umpires correctly called 87.8 percent of true strikes and 90.7 percent of all true balls in 2015 (the correct strike rate and correct ball rate, respectively). The overall rate of correct calls was 89.9 percent. However, there is considerable variation in the correct call rates among umpires. Figure 4 below shows the distribution of correct strike and correct ball rates across umpires in 2015. While most umpires center around the mean accuracy rate, there are some extremes in in the distribution and considerable variation in favorability toward batters or pitchers (Fast, 2011c). As an additional exposition, Table 1 then ranks the 10 highest and 10 lowest overall accuracy rates among all 87 major-league umpires with at least 1,000 ball-strike calls in 2015. Interestingly, additional work shows that umpires' accuracy varies most up in the zone (Lindholm, 2014), though they all call strikes less often in the top and bottom corners (Figure 2).

Figure 4. *Distribution of correct call rates for MLB umpires in 2015.*

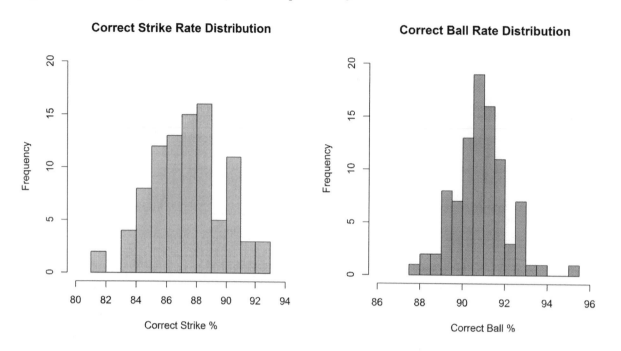

Table 1. *Highest and lowest accuracy rates for MLB umpires in 2015.*

Umpire	First Year	Total Calls	Correct Strike %	Correct Ball %	Accuracy %
1. Chris Conroy	2010	4,410	88.85	92.72	91.59
2. Toby Basner	2012	3,067	90.73	91.77	91.46
3. Lance Barksdale	2000	4,164	88.25	92.56	91.28
4. Will Little	2013	3,298	92.41	90.71	91.21
5. Al Porter	2010	4,543	90.04	91.67	91.20
6. Tom Woodring	2014	1,933	84.38	93.96	91.10
7. Phil Cuzzi	1991	4,555	91.41	90.95	91.09
8. Adam Hamari	2013	5,390	92.14	90.58	91.06
9. Quinn Wolcott	2013	3,603	90.02	91.47	91.06
10. Ryan Blakney	2015	3,226	87.25	92.58	91.01
78. Bruce Dreckman	1996	3,201	86.38	89.56	88.60
79. Adrian Johnson	2006	4,501	87.05	89.22	88.60
80. Gerry Davis	1982	4,460	83.51	90.77	88.59
81. Angel Hernandez	1991	4,955	90.21	87.93	88.56
82. Tom Hallion	1985	3,995	83.97	90.52	88.54
83. Jerry Layne	1989	1,481	85.75	89.65	88.52
84. Ed Hickox	1990	4,027	84.89	89.99	88.45
85. Mike DiMuro	1997	2,497	84.66	89.81	88.31
86. Paul Nauert	1995	3,804	85.28	89.13	88.07
87. Tim Welke	1983	4,344	85.15	88.51	87.52

Note: Minimum of 1,000 pitches called in 2015.

Let's put these numbers in perspective. Each game includes approximately 150 umpire-called pitches, meaning that even the best umpire misses about 12 to 13 pitches each game, presumably evenly against each of the two competing teams in the long run.[12] The least accurate umpire makes an *additional* six incorrect calls per game. And it is important to note that this accuracy rate has improved since the introduction of Zone Evaluation in 2009.[13] The net accuracy rates in Table 1 are considerably higher than they were just six years ago. It's no wonder we see players argue balls and strikes so often.

Explicit accuracy, however, is only one measure of performance for umpires. There are unresolved questions as to whether accuracy itself or *consistency* of calls is most representative of performance of an umpire. For example, it is entirely possible for one umpire to be more consistent than another but less accurate. To picture this, assume an umpire's zone center is shifted outside by six inches, but he calls every pitch inside some given boundary a strike, and every pitch outside that boundary a ball. This umpire would be perfectly consistent: there is no uncertainty over the calls he makes. But he would be very inaccurate: many of these calls would be well beyond the outside corner of the plate. On the other hand, picture a second umpire who has his strike zone centered perfectly around the center of the rulebook strike zone, but with "fuzzy" edges (the blending of red dots and yellow triangles we saw in Figure 2). This umpire will inherently have more uncertainty over calls as they move farther away from the center of the zone, resulting in more uncertainty, despite higher levels of accuracy.

In practice, it is unlikely that umpires differ to these extremes, but some players have noted that they would prefer predictability of strike calls over accuracy, making it easier to adjust their expectations (Cyphers, 2012). Peter Bonney takes our understanding of umpire performance in this direction with his article in the 2016 *Hardball Times Baseball Annual* (2016) using a machine learning algorithm.[14] Bonney notes that consistency itself is a skill among umpires that can be separated from simplistic binary accuracy

classifications. Given this skill, the question remains as to whether MLB should be encouraging its umpires to be more accurate, more consistent, or both. Some combination of both excellent accuracy and consistency—in academic research we call this validity and reliability—would probably be most optimal, assuming umpires cannot be perfect.

However, the league also needs to be cognizant of other factors related to umpire variability. Specifically, there is the question of uniformity: If all umpires are equally inaccurate and internally consistent, is this better than higher accuracy but less uniformity across umpires? Players may prefer the former, as they would not have to change their expectations of strike probabilities in each game officiated by a different home-plate umpire. Interestingly, there is evidence that umpires have continually become more uniform in their strike calls, particularly since MLB gained centralized control (Mills, 2015a), indicating that there is some higher level of predictability when players come to the plate. But the variation is still nontrivial in size, and it is unclear as to whether MLB incentivizes accuracy over consistency and uniformity in the training of umpires that will always be fallible. And there remain questions on just how good umpires can get. Analysts have begun evaluating whether the new technological systems have, in fact, improved accuracy over time.

4.2 Umpire Performance and Improvements

As noted earlier, the implementation of QuesTec and its successor, Zone Evaluation, was part of a long-term effort by MLB to enforce appropriate ball-strike calls based on the stated rules. Further, there has been a clear push to not only monitor the performance of umpires, but provide feedback and training through more precise measurement of accuracy over time. This raises the question as to whether the evaluation and training effort has been successful. With the release of PITCHf/x data, the answer to this question has been addressed in recent work both academically and among analysts writing for more popular sabermetric outlets.

Recent academic work has looked closely at the changes in performance among umpires during the Zone Evaluation era (Mills, 2016b), showing that based on a fixed definition of the strike zone based on the MLB rules, umpire accuracy increased by 3.65 percentage points from 2008 (85.35 percent correct) to 2014 (89.0 percent correct). Data in the previous section confirm that this path continued through at least 2015, with the overall rate approximately 89.9 percent. Other analysts (Davis and Lopez, 2015) have confirmed the improvement in accuracy, including some familiar names from Table 1 toward the top and bottom of the rankings.

One of the more interesting realizations from this work is that the accuracy rates in the strike zone are largely uncorrelated with postseason assignment, despite their supposed merit-based determination (Lindbergh, 2014). Although the strike zone is not the only aspect of evaluation for umpires when these assignments are made, it is surely the most salient measure of performance, hinting that postseason assignment might have more to do with seniority than merit. This raises the question as to why the monitoring would be successful: If there is no apparent reward or punishment for being a better (worse) ball-strike caller, then why have umpires bothered to try to improve their accuracy? Perhaps umpires are motivated professionals who take pride in their performance. Many people work in jobs that are rewarding in their own right, and calling balls and strikes well may be no different. But there are of course always some actors who need the extrinsic motivation. And theories from economics, psychology, and management generally predict that the simple act of being observed or monitored can reduce mistakes and biases, though there are limits to the success of these systems.

On the other hand, there is some evidence that umpires with less job security might be getting more calls right. Mills (2016b) finds that while all umpires have tended to improve their accuracy, newer umpires have outpaced their older, more experienced counterparts. This pattern is easily seen in Table 1, with eight of the 10 most accurate umpires making their debut in 2010 or later, and only one of the least accurate 10 making their debut after 1997 (Adrian Johnson in 2006). While sabermetricians do not have legal access to medical examinations of umpires' eyes,[15] it seems reasonable to expect that younger umpires—likely with higher average visual acuity—would perform better overall at the ball-strike-calling task. And these younger umpires are often competing for permanent contracts, introducing an additional incentive to perform at a high level.

Despite the noted improvement in overall accuracy, there are important caveats to the measured accuracy improvements. On an episode of *Real Sports*, economist Tobias Moskowitz noted that accuracy at the edges of the strike zone is considerably worse than the overall accuracy rate reported here and in many sabermetric studies. After all, pitches directly down the middle or well outside the strike zone are easy to judge even by a non-expert, and umpires call nearly all of these pitches correctly. This means the error comes from the fewer number of pitches at the edge of the strike zone where uncertainty over the location rises. Moskowitz estimates that within two inches of the edge of the strike zone umpires make less than 70 percent of calls correctly. Therefore, in judging accuracy by using all pitches, there is likely some information loss in using aggregate accuracy rates.

On the other hand, the accuracy increase found in Mills (2016b) and Davis and Lopez (2015) largely comes from higher strike rates in the bottom of the strike zone, between 18 and 21 inches (Roegele, 2013; Mills, 2016a). In previous seasons, umpires were especially poor at calling low pitches in the zone as strikes. This has left an imbalanced improvement in accuracy on balls and strikes. Umpires have improved their correct strike rate from approximately 78.7 percent to 87.8 percent in 2015, while correct ball rates improved only from 88.4 percent to 90.7 percent. In other words, the improvement is coming from expanding the strike zone in places where umpires almost never called strikes before. While a general increase in accuracy could point to neutral impacts on the game—and higher levels of consistency—the relative changes in these two rates could result in other effects on the game, like run scoring. As umpires call more strikes low in the zone, hitters fall behind more often in the count and are put at a disadvantage in the at-bat, likely resulting in worse offensive outcomes. The findings on the changes in the strike zone have, therefore, led to closer inspection of these effects in the analytics space to identify contributors to the decline in offense that began in the 2000s after the Steroid Era.

4.3 How Umpires Affect the Game

Given that umpires have been known to change their behavior—and as we will see in the next section, have various biases in strike calling—there are likely to be effects on the scoring environment in the game. Indeed, one of the primary complaints from MLB nearing the 1999 labor dispute was that strike zones were becoming too small and may have contributed to the large increases in scoring during the Steroid Era. Recent work has therefore shown substantial interest in estimating the influence of umpires on the run-scoring environment. If umpires have been a large contributor to inflated (or deflated) run scoring at certain points over the past 30 years, then this could weaken evidence that the Steroid Era scoring outburst was actually driven by steroids alone. This sort of revelation could presumably curb judgment related to certain players and their use of steroids prior to enforcement of any official policy on the matter.

Official enforcement of steroid policies at the MLB level began in 2006 through the Joint Drug Prevention and Treatment Program,[16] but it turns out that this was *not* the beginning of the reduced scoring we see in today's game. In fact, work by Rader and Winkle (2008) and Mills (2016b) showed that called-strike rates increased dramatically shortly after the installation of QuesTec, and run scoring decreased precipitously at the same time. From 2000 through 2002, MLB scoring decreased by 10 percent while called strike rates increased by 5 percent. While we do not have access to the QuesTec data itself, this was strong preliminary evidence that the so-called Steroid Era actually started to wane in 2001,[17] right about when we saw strike-zone enforcement become more uniform across the major leagues.[18]

More recently, PITCHf/x data have helped analysts understand the continued dramatic decrease in run scoring since 2008. Let's return to the extension of the zone downward from the previous section. In 2008 a pitch at the border of the hollow beneath the knee would have been called a strike approximately 25 percent of the time. By 2015, that number was more than 60 percent. Although umpires have reduced the amount of outside pitches they call strikes, the change in the bottom of the zone has resulted in a net increase in the size of the strike zone plane.[19]

For example, Mills (2016a) measured the strike zone as that area inside the boundary at which a pitch is equally likely to be called a ball or a strike. The area within this elliptical shape grew by 34 inches for right-handed batters and 30 inches for left-handed batters between 2008 and 2014. Roegele (2014a; 2014b) presents similar results. The effect is approximately equivalent to the size of six or seven baseballs lined up side-by-side across the bottom of the zone. Figure 5 shows the strike zone in 2008 compared with 2014 empirically derived from Mills (2015a) using a generalized additive model. The downward extension continued in 2015. As with Figure 2, the strike-zone border is defined as the point at which a ball and a strike are equally likely to be called.

Figure 5. *Comparison of called strike zone in 2008 vs. 2014.*

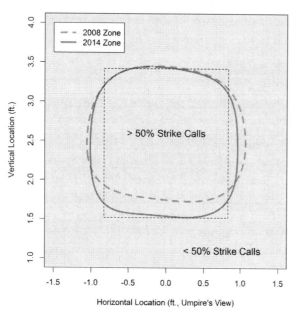

RHB 50% Strike Zone Comparison

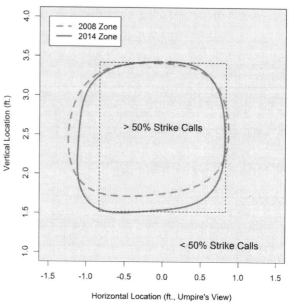

LHB 50% Strike Zone Comparison

Given a larger zone, and especially one where the increase comes in the low portion of the zone, any astute baseball fan would expect impacts on batters' ability to get hits and teams' chances to score runs. Indeed, both Mills (2016a) and Roegele (2014a)—as well as Ben Lindbergh (2014)—show that this increased strike-zone area has accounted for approximately 20 to 40 percent of the decrease in run scoring across MLB from 2009 through 2014. In 2008, two teams scored a combined average of 9.32 runs per nine innings. However, that number had decreased to 8.13 by 2014, a reduction of nearly 1.2 runs per game.[20] Of that 1.2 runs, estimates reveal that between 0.3 and 0.5 runs per game are directly attributable to umpire ball-strike calls. In other words, there are negative effects on the expected runs scored as umpires call more and more strikes. Throughout the game, this will put batters at a marginally higher disadvantage. For example, these results suggest that batters move from a 1-and-1 count to a 1-and-2 count instead of a 2-and-1 count on pitch 18 inches off the ground more often than they did before. Given that batters perform much worse in 1-and-2 counts, the result ends up being a net decrease in offense.

What's more, if batters and pitchers change their behavior strategically across seasons in response to umpire changes, then the regression method used in the paper may actually be conservative. Interestingly, however, Mills (2015a) shows that while umpires had an even larger effect on the reduction in walks across the league (as much as 71 percent of the reduction in walks per nine innings pitched), the effect on strikeouts was almost completely negligible at 3 to 9 percent of the overall increase in strikeouts per nine innings pitched.[21] In other words, high-velocity pitchers seem to be having an impact on some batter outcomes independent of these umpire changes.

Much of the work on umpire strike zone changes—and its apparent impact on scoring in baseball—got the attention of MLB, as reported by Jeff Passan (2015). As of 2015, there has been talk of enforcing new changes to the strike zone in an attempt to increase scoring back to levels more preferred by fans: a specific instance of where analytics have made clear contributions to policy considerations. Interestingly, scoring increased dramatically at the end of 2015 and through 2016, largely from an increase in home runs. But no official announcements were made regarding a change to the strike zone. This intrigued analysts, and Mills (2016c), Sullivan (2016), and Roegele (2015a; 2016) returned to the data to investigate changes in the zone. Each of these analysts found some evidence of small changes to the strike zone.

Figure 6 shows the differences in called strikes prior to and after the 2015 All-Star Game, when the changes began. As you can see, umpires have become less likely to call pitches low and away to both right- and left-handed batters, but show some increase in the propensity to call strikes up in the zone and inside to righties. Yet, the reduction in strike rate on pitches most difficult to hit—very low and away—could mean umpires exerted a new influence on offensive output.

Further, Mills (2016c) shows that pitchers and batters recognized this small change and changed their own behavior accordingly. However, after a comprehensive analysis of the effect of these changes on hitters' exit-velocity and home-run rates—a clear precursor to run scoring—there is scant evidence that these more recent changes have accounted for any of the sharp uptick in scoring since the 2015 All-Star break. In the coming seasons it will be important to keep an analytic eye on ball-strike calls to see if there is a continued trend toward a smaller zone, and how MLB might balance this with its attempt to reduce the length of games.

5. The Analytics of Umpire Biases

Some of the most interesting findings from analyzing umpires are related to biases in strike-zone calls. These biases generally fall under four different areas: 1) home-field advantage, 2) count-based and recent call biases, 3) superstar biases, and 4) framing and visual influences. A few individual works cover various biases found across these categories (Mills, 2014; Roegele, 2013; Turkenkopf, 2008). However, with revealed biases come various competing interpretations depending on the analyst or academic investigator. This section will break each down into their relevant contribution to the analytics of umpire performance in the strike zone and discuss the various ways to interpret the findings.

5.1 Home-Field Advantage

Home-field advantage is a well-documented phenomenon across various sports. MLB home teams won approximately 53 percent of the time in 2016, and only five of 30 teams had a higher winning percentage on the road than at home.[22] Contributors to this disparity may include fatigue and travel effects, team choices to rest top players on the road, spillover from excitement from the home crowd, comfort with the home park and its playing surfaces, and of course bias by umpires. Thanks to the availability of data, this last influence has been tested by various analysts.

Figure 6. *Change in Called Strike Probability After 2015 All-Star Game. Color scale in percentage points.*

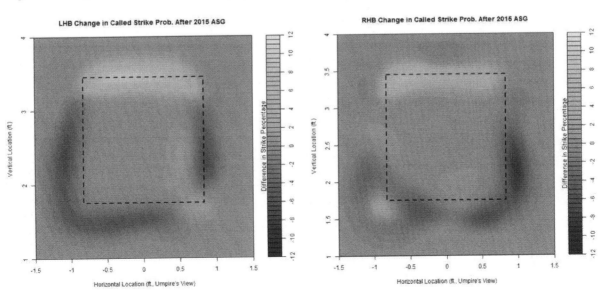

Economist Tobias Moskowitz and writer L. Jon Wertheim were among the first to document ball-strike-call bias in favor the home team in their popular book *Scorecasting* (2011). The work in *Scorecasting* begins by first evaluating strike-rate data from the QuesTec era. The authors find that there are more called strikes or balls called in favor of the home team, particularly in situations that are crucial to the outcome of the game. They continue by comparing the home-field advantage effect in stadiums with and without QuesTec, revealing that when umpires were monitored by the QuesTec system, the difference in ball-strike rates actually reversed: the strike-rate difference turned in favor of the visitors. In other words, when umpires were being closely watched, they no longer showed bias in favor of the home team, and perhaps overcompensated to avoid doing so. By counting up all the extra favorable calls that home teams get, and multiplying those by the changes in expected runs scored when transitioning from one ball-strike count to the next, Moskowitz and Wertheim propose that this umpire bias results in about 7.3 additional runs for the home team over the course of the season. They note that this accounts for more than two-thirds of the entire home-field advantage observed in the data.

John Walsh in the *2011 Hardball Times Baseball Annual* also finds the existence of umpire contributions to home-field advantage, calculating its effect as only one-third of the total run differential. And shortly after the release of *Scorecasting*, Jesse-Douglas Mathewson—writing for the sabermetric website Beyond the Box Score—finds results consistent with umpire ball-strike-call bias, too (2010a). However, there was even more disagreement on the size of the impact. Mathewson estimated that umpires account for only about 16 percent of the effect. It is important to note, however, that both Mathewson and Walsh do not break the data down for parks with and without QuesTec monitoring, and in fact use PITCHf/x data from seasons where this data is used to directly monitor umpires. So, assuming monitoring works well, it may simply be that much of the effect found in the QuesTec years—specific to non-

QuesTec parks—is no longer apparent in the Zone Evaluation era. However, Mills (2014) uses a larger sample of data from 2008 through 2010, and still finds evidence of home-team bias even in the face of Zone Evaluation monitoring. Controlling for location and a host of other factors, the odds of a strike call on a pitch thrown by a home pitcher were about 7 percent higher than for a visiting pitcher, a nontrivial effect. Taken together, there is clear evidence for a home-field advantage effect.

Yet, while many fans may malign the idea of umpire bias and home bias as a net negative to the integrity of the game, there is the possibility that the league has little incentive to enforce more equal calls. Specifically, fans tend to enjoy seeing winning teams when they play at home. This gives the league an incentive to have teams win more at home than on the road to maximize their revenues through increased fan interest (a proposition that echoes Price, Remer, and Stone [2012] in their work studying the National Basketball Association). This wouldn't necessarily affect the outcome of the season: all teams play 81 home and 81 away games so—leaving aside unbalanced scheduling—the bias should even out in the long run. Given this, any decrease in the propensity for home bias (if it exists) since the implementation of Zone Evaluation may not actually be optimal for MLB, despite its positive impact on the accuracy rates of umpires. But the impact on revenues is likely to be rather small relative to any loss in confidence from fans in the integrity of calls made by umpires down on the field. Still, there are other apparent biases that are not likely to play out this way.

5.2 The Ball-Strike Count and Make-Up Calls

Anyone familiar with baseball has heard of umpires widening their zone to speed up a game when a pitcher is struggling to hit the plate. As with home bias, PITCHf/x data has given us the tools to test whether umpires in fact behave in this way. Jonathan Hale (2009) and Dave Allen (2009a) were two of the first analysts to find the strike-zone variation across ball-strike counts. It turns out that umpires do in fact widen their zone when the batter is ahead in the count, and shrink it considerably when the pitcher is ahead. Ultimately, this behavior tends to extend at-bats longer than they otherwise would go. Experts have noted that the behavior is consistent with known behavioral biases, such as impact aversion or compassion and inequality aversion (Green & Daniels, 2015; Walsh, 2010; Mills, 2014). Impact aversion implies that umpires would prefer to "let the players play" than determine the outcome of an at-bat. Alternatively, umpires might have interest in making batters and pitchers more equal in the ball-strike count in some act of compassion.

Figure 7 shows the considerable differences in the size of the zone in 0-and-2 counts, where the pitcher is well ahead, and 3-and-0 counts when the batter is greatly advantaged. The area of the strike zone—measured as the 50 percent contour from before—is decreased by 117.4 square inches for left-handed batters and 124.7 square inches for right-handed batters when going from the 3-and-0 count to the 0-and-2 count. Ultimately, this can give players who tend to get behind in the count an undue performance advantage. This difference is pictured below in Figure 7.

While the idea that umpires act compassionately when calling balls and strikes may be intriguing, it doesn't seem consistent at first glance with their stated job definition: to get the call right. But as it turns out, it may be possible to reconcile this behavior with the goal of accuracy. Analysts have shown that the zone-size change behavior may be rational from an accuracy-maximizing standpoint using Bayes Theorem (Moore, 2009). Green and Daniels (2015) present a similar proposition.

Bayes Theorem rears its head in many fun applications of statistics, most notably in the Monty Hall problem featured in the 2008 movie *21*.[23] Specifically, Bayes tells us that we can more accurately assess the probability of an event by integrating prior knowledge about the likelihood that event takes place. So, if umpires know that in 0-and-2 counts the pitcher is more likely to throw a pitch outside of the strike zone—as pitchers are wont to do—then they know that calling a ball on pitches over which they're most uncertain may actually be their best bet. After all, determining whether a projectile traveling at 100 miles per hour crosses through an imaginary three-dimensional box is an inherently difficult and un-

Figure 7. *Strike-zone size difference in 0-and-2 count vs. 3-and-0 count in 2014.*

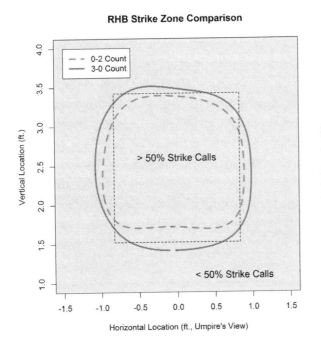

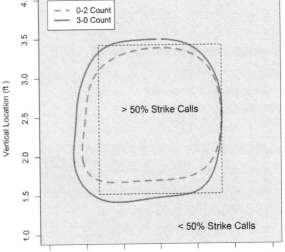

certain task. Even subconscious heuristics might be helpful in making the correct call.

Molyneux (2016) breaks down the data to show that the accuracy-rate data on pitches inside and outside of the strike zone are consistent with this Bayesian umpire hypothesis. In other words, umpires change their decision rule—whether to "lean" ball or "lean" strike—based on their prior knowledge about the probability that a pitch will be in the strike zone in the first place. Umpires have a lot of experience with this, and likely have a well-defined prior expectation for these probabilities. By "biasing" themselves, they can (admittedly counterintuitively) increase their accuracy rates.

The existence of makeup calls, however, would imply at least some level of compassion among umpires wanting to "make it right" after making what they know to have been an incorrect call. This behavior would not necessarily be consistent with Bayes. Fans certainly assume that umpires do this, yet much of this was subjective prior to data availability. But with this more recent data, there is some evidence for this phenomenon, with the size of the effect depending on the egregiousness of the previous incorrect call (Moskowitz & Wertheim, 2011). The jury is still out on the precise reason for the changes across ball-strike counts, but the influence of partially unconscious biases or knowledge continues to be especially interesting to academics.

One of these biases is known as the Gambler's Fallacy, defined by an individual's decision being negatively correlated with their past decisions. For example, imagine a roulette player. While at the casino, red has come up eight times in a row, and the gambler says, "It *has* to come up black this time," and puts all of her money on black. This is an irrational act: black is no more likely to come up than it has on any other spin of the wheel. This is a good way to lose all of your money at the casino, but most people can succumb to this type of problematic rationalization in many instances. It turns out that umpires tend to have negatively correlated ball and strike calls as well, though this effect was relatively small (Chen, Moskowitz, & Shue, 2016). In other

words, if an umpire made a strike call on a previous pitch—holding constant the ball-strike count and the pitch's location—then he is more likely to call the next one a ball. Similarly, if he called a ball on a previous pitch, the next one is more likely to be called a strike. While this doesn't mean the umpire is going to be losing thousands of dollars, it could mean that game outcomes are altered by these fallacies. And game outcomes lead to significant salary implications for players. The question is then: If umpires are subject to such biases, could they be subject to other biases that privilege certain players over others and costing some players millions?

5.3 Race and Status Bias

While home bias, inequality aversion, or compassion tend to be relatively harmless in practice, other subconscious biases can be a bit more problematic. While these biases could have negative impacts on individual players, they are not necessarily insidious in nature. For example, Mathewson (2011) showed that strike zones can vary considerably across pitchers, costing (or gaining) their teams precious runs, inviting the question as to whether there are identifiable causes of these discrepancies. In the years since, various analysts and academics have been particularly interested in umpire biases that could ultimately favor some players over, and why, with important impacts in the labor market for baseball players.

One of the more prominent investigations into umpire bias came from academic economists interested in racial discrimination (Parsons, Sulaeman, Yates, & Hamermesh, 2011). This work made the claim that umpires were more likely to call strikes for pitchers when their races were the same. Interestingly, they note that this bias is reduced when umpires are monitored either by QuesTec or by larger crowds at the game, a finding consistent with bias reduction found after monitoring in previous work. However, other researchers expanded the inquiry with larger and more comprehensive data sets, finding very little evidence of overt or implicit bias among umpires (Tainsky, Mills, & Winfree, 2015; Hamrick & Rasp, 2015). These authors note that much of the influence of the measured effect seemed to stem from very few minority umpires in the data set. Ultimately, if any bias does exist, it seems to be rather small as a whole.

Additional biases have been shown to be related to player star power and experience. Mathewson's (2011) work pointed toward the existence of favorable calls for higher-caliber and well-known pitchers. Indeed, Mills (2014) expands the investigation, estimating the impact of player age (experience) and performance (prominence) on the ball-strike calls of umpires. This work revealed evidence that younger batters got more strike calls, and younger pitchers more ball calls, after controlling for location. Higher-performing or better known players saw similar outcomes. Specifically, for each additional win above replacement,[24] a pitcher was 3 percent more likely to receive a strike call on a given pitch. And for each additional year of age, a pitcher was 2 percent more likely to receive a strike call on a given pitch. Each of these estimates controls for location, pitch type, ball-strike count, and other factors. Further, higher-performing teams, as a whole, were also found to receive favorable ball-strike calls for their pitchers.

Kim and King (2014) find similar results, noting that if a player was an All-Star in the previous season, he was more likely to receive favorable calls from the umpire. The results are reflective of a phenomenon known as the Matthew Effect, or the propensity for people to privilege high-status individuals external to the quality of the outcomes produced. These sorts of biases could enhance disparities in contracts for high-performing and low-performing players and make it more difficult for rookies to make a name for themselves. Although the bias is relatively small, it makes excellent rookie campaigns all the more impressive: Mike Trout was likely receiving fewer favorable calls than his teammate Albert Pujols when he posted a 10.5 WAR rookie season.

5.4 Other Strike Call Influences

Despite the interesting results related to psychological biases found in past work, it can be difficult to disentangle these from other characteristics of umpires' tasks behind the plate. For example, with star power and experience come higher levels of game play. Mariano Rivera and Greg Maddux were known to get the benefit of the doubt on many calls, but they also have another characteristic in common: They were both control artists, rarely missing their intended spot in the strike zone (Hale, 2007b; Allen, 2009b). Rivera was able to hit his spot like few others, painting corners with precision that is visible in the data. While data are not available for Maddux in his prime, he was known as a control artist as well. By hitting the catcher's glove without movement, these pitchers probably made it easier for the umpire to lean toward calling any given pitch a strike, using the still glove as a heuristic for their calls. It would be particularly interesting to assess how glove movement affects umpires' calls, but the data that has been collected is not publicly available.[25] Without this information, however, various analysts have found ways to measure catcher framing as a skill influencing the probability that umpires call strikes on borderline pitches (Fast, 2011f; Pavlidis & Brooks, 2014; Judge, Pavlidis, & Brooks, 2015; Carleton, 2016b; Carleton, 2016c).

Pitch type and velocity also tend to affect the probability of strike calls. For example, while fastballs are much more likely to be called strikes than off-speed pitches like curveballs and sliders. But the velocity of a pitch actually reduces the likelihood that it will be called a strike, holding constant location (Mills, 2014; Mathewson, 2010b). Despite the competing effects, this is not especially surprising, given the task at hand. Pitches traveling faster or with more movement will be more difficult to judge, and therefore might not look as much like a strike as something coming straight through the strike zone at a slightly slower speed. A portion of the discrepancy with respect to velocity could be related to higher-velocity pitchers not being control artists like Maddux and Rivera. Interestingly, there is little work investigating the *accuracy* of these calls, which might be more helpful in understanding how umpire accuracy keeps up with the ever-increasing average velocity of pitches in the major leagues and how these characteristics affect our estimates of umpire biases discussed here.

6. The Future of Umpire Analytics and the Automated Strike Zone

While this article has largely focused on analytics of the strike zone, analysis of other umpire behaviors could be just as interesting. As noted earlier, data availability limit these investigations, but recent implementation of instant replay provides useful data on overturned calls and biases that may result (such as home-field advantage) when replay is used. It is possible to evaluate umpires on the rate at which their replayed calls are overturned. Pairing this sort of analysis with video and expertise, along with more years of data, it is possible to develop an understanding of how well umpires make out and safe calls at the bases, or judge shoestring catches and fair or foul balls. It will be interesting to identify whether performance on these types of calls is correlated in any way with performance in the strike zone. A lack of (or negative) correlation in these skill sets could reveal why certain umpires are assigned to postseason games despite showing relatively low accuracy rates in the strike zone.

Additionally, a move to Statcast has allowed MLB to track everyone on the field during a game. Umpires' positioning and movement is especially important in evaluation, and this data could be used to begin new types of analytic understanding of umpires' ability to be in the right place at the right time. In fact, lessons currently being learned from Statcast data about outfielder routes could be applied in the umpire context to assess not only speed, but efficiency of movement. Of course, without publicly available data, much of this analysis will remain unseen by most of us.

We should also be careful in analyzing performance as outsiders, particularly in instances when we do not fully understand the expectations of umpires. In revealing various mistakes and biases among umpires, analysts and fans and analysts have begun to ask why the league does not just replace umpires with the machines that monitor them (Shultz, 2015; Frankel, 2016). In the pursuit of perfection in ball-strike calls, this would probably be the best choice. And it would mostly resolve the consistency and uniformity issues that can plague balls and strikes. Umpires may scoff

at this idea, but human umpires would not necessarily have to be replaced. They're still needed to call out and safe at home, balks, fair and foul balls, and maybe for players to argue with when they don't agree with Robo Ump. In this case, there would be just as many umpires as before and nobody would be out of a job. Umpire-union resistance would therefore seem misguided.

There are, of course, important caveats related to robot umpires that often go overlooked. Fans should remember that PITCHf/x and its successor, Trackman, are still fallible, and have their own problems with consistency across ballparks or operators drawing in the top and bottom of the strike zone for each batter. That doesn't mean this would make things worse, but it would not necessarily make things better. And the accuracy rates reported in this article could be underestimated due to these errors. What would a player do if a machine was miscalibrated and continued to call balls on pitches down the middle? What if the calibration is only slightly off and goes unseen? Can we rely on internal consistency in place of accuracy and uniformity? And where would all the fun we get from watching players arguing balls and strikes go?

But perhaps most importantly, the net impact on run scoring and game strategy is unclear with an automated strike zone. The league would certainly need to change its official definition and measurement if robot umpires took over for calling balls and strikes. Currently, umpires do not call strikes in the top and bottom corners very often, while a PITCHf/x robot would ring up a batter on all of them under the current definition. Although some of the zone growth would be offset by removing outside pitches previously called strikes, the increased strikes in the zone would come in areas where batters tend to get poor results. This could reduce run scoring substantially. On the other hand, if batters know what will and will not be called a strike, they may be able to focus more closely on the areas in which they should swing and make better contact on average. The net effect is, therefore, ambiguous.[26] Substantial research needs to take place before making a move like this. Lucky for us, umpire analytics experts are probably already working to understand this issue in more detail.

SOURCES

Allen, D. (2009a). Does the umpire know the count? *Baseball Analysts*. Retrieved January 7, 2017, from: baseballanalysts.com/ archives/2009/04/the_effect_of_t.php.

Allen, D. (2009b). Mariano Rivera: Another appreciation. *Baseball Analysts*. Retrieved January 8, 2017, from: baseballanalysts.com/ archives/2009/10/mariano_rivera.php.

Associated Press (2003). Schilling calls QuesTec system a joke. *ESPN Baseball*. Retrieved December 31, 2016, from: a.espncdn.com/ mlb/news/2003/0525/1558965.html.

Baggett, A. (2015). Conceptualizing the MLB strike zone using PITCHf/x data. *Exploring Baseball Data with R*. Retrieved January 8, 2017, from: baseballwithr.wordpress.com/2015/02/17/ conceptualizing-the-mlb-strike-zone-using-pitchfx-data/.

Bonney, P. (2016). Who watches the watchers? Introducing umpire consistency score. In *The Hardball Times Baseball Annual.* Joe Distelheim, Jason Linden, Greg Smions, & Paul Swydan (eds.), Fangraphs & The Hardball Times.

Brooks, D. Brooks Baseball: PITCHf/x tool. Retrieved December 19, 2016, from: brooksbaseball.net/pfxVB/pfx.php.

Callan, M. (2012). Called out: The forgotten baseball umpires strike of 1999. *The Classical*. Retrieved December 19, 2016, from: theclassical.org/articles/ called-out-the-forgotten-baseball-umpires-strike-of-1999.

Carleton, R. (2016a). Baseball therapy: The knee. *Baseball Prospectus*. Retrieved January 11, 2017, from: baseballprospectus.com/article. php?articleid=29358.

Carleton, R. (2016b). Baseball therapy: The dark side of pitch framing? *Baseball Prospectus*. Retrieved January 11, 2017 from: base-ballprospectus.com/article.php ?articleid=28350.

Carleton, R. (2016c). Baseball therapy: Framing the at-bat. *Baseball Prospectus*. Retrieved January 11, 2017, from: baseballprospectus.com/ article.php?articleid=29292.

Chass, M. (1999). Umpires giveth and taketh. *New York Times*. Retrieved December 19, 2016, from: nytimes.com/1999/03/10/sports/ baseball-umpires-giveth-and-taketh.html.

Chass, M. (2004). Baseball and umpires settle grading dispute. *New York Times*. Retrieved December 31, 2016, from: query.nytimes.com/ gst/fullpage.html?res=9E06E6 DB1E30F937A15751C1A9629C8B63.

Chen, D.L., Moskowitz, T. J., & Shue, K. (2016). Decision making under the gambler's fallacy: Evidence from asylum judges, loan officers, and baseball umpires. *Quarterly Journal of Economics*. DOI: 10.1093/qje/qjw017.

Cyphers, L. (2012). Players and umps think QuesTec stinks, they don't know the half. *ESPN*. Retrieved December

19, 2016, from: espn.com/espn/magazine/archives/ news/ story?page=magazine-20030804-article18.

Davis, N. & Lopez, M. (2015). Umpires are less blind than they used to be. *FiveThirtyEight*. Retrieved December 22, 2016, from: fivethir-tyeight.com/features/umpires-are-less-blind-than-they-used-to-be/.

Fast, M. (2010). The internet cried a little when you wrote that on it. *The Hardball Times*. Retrieved December 20, 2016, from: hardball-times.com/the-internet-cried-a-little-when-you-wrote-that-on-it/.

Fast, M. (2011a). Spinning yarn: How accurate is PitchTrax? *Baseball Prospectus*. Retrieved January 8, 2017, from: baseballprospectus.com/ article.php?articleid=13109.

Fast, M. (2011b). Spinning yarn: Home plate umpire positioning. *Baseball Prospectus*. Retrieved January 8, 2017, from: baseballprospec-tus.com/article.php?articleid=14951.

Fast, M. (2011c). NLCS umpire charts and data. *Baseball Prospectus*. Retrieved January 8, 2017, from: baseballprospectus.com/article. php?articleid=15269.

Fast, M. (2011d). Spinning yarn: The real strike zone Part 1. *Baseball Prospectus*. Retrieved December 20, 2016, from: baseballprospectus. com/article.php?articleid= 12965.

Fast, M. (2011e). Spinning yarn: The real strike zone Part 2. *Baseball Prospectus*. Retrieved December 20, 2016, from: baseballprospectus. com/article.php?articleid= 14098.

Fast, M. (2011f). Spinning yarn: Removing the mask encore presentation. *Baseball Prospectus*. Retrieved January 8, 2017, from: baseballprospectus.com/article.php?articleid =15093.

Frankel, J. (2016). Interview with Jerry Crawford. *Real Sports with Bryant Gumbel, Episode 234.* September 27, 2016.

Green, E.A. & Daniels, D.P. (2015). Impact aversion and arbitrator decisions. *SSRN Working Paper*, January 19, 2015: papers.ssrn.com/ sol3/papers.cfm?abstract_id=2391558.

Guziec, A. (2002). Tracking pitches for broadcast television. *IEEE Computer, 35*, 38-43.

Hale, J. (2007a). A zone of their own. *The Hardball Times*. Retrieved December 20, 2016, from: hardballtimes.com/a-zone-of-their-own/.

Hale, J. (2007b). A gentle massage. *The Hardball Times*. Retrieved January 8, 2017, from: bjays.wordpress.com/ archives/a-gentle-massage/.

Hale, J. (2009). Strikeouts are fascist (walks, too). *The Mockingbird*. Retrieved January 7, 2017, from: bjays.wordpress.com/2009/01/03/ strikeouts-are-fascist-walks-too/.

Hamrick, J. & Rasp, J. (2015). The connection between race and called strikes and balls. *Journal of Sports Economics, 16*, 714-734.

Janssen to speak at IHCC banquet. (2007). Retrieved January 11, 2017, from: dailyiowegian.com/janssen-to-speak-at-ihcc-banquet/ article_1ef5cce5-78c2-5e24-b4f1-64ac3a8d1605.html.

Judge, J., Pavlidis, H., & Brooks, D. (2015). Moving beyond WOWY: A mixed approach to measuring catcher framing. *The Hardball Times*.

Retrieved January 8, 2017, from: baseballprospectus.com/article.php?articleid=25514

Kalk, J. That was a strike? *The Hardball Times*. Retrieved December 20, 2016, from: hardballtimes.com/that-was-a-strike/.

Karegeannes, J. (2004). Confessions of a QuesTec operator: How the system works, how it can be improved. *Baseball Prospectus*. Retrieved December 19, 2016 from: baseballprospectus.com/article.php?articleid=3326.

Kim, J.W. & King, B.G. (2014). Seeing stars: Matthew effects and status bias in Major League Baseball umpiring. *Management Science*, 60, 2619-2644.

Lang, E. (2015). Analyzing the strike zone as a three-dimensional volume. *The Hardball Times*. Retrieved December 22, 2016, from: hardballtimes.com/analyzing-the-strike-zone-as-a-three-dimensional-volume/.

Lindbergh, B. (2014). Rung up: Are postseason umpires actually baseball's most accurate? *Grantland*. Retrieved December 22, 2016, from: grantland.com/the-triangle/postseason-umpires-mlb-accurate-joe-west/.

Lindholm, S. (2014). How well do umpires call balls and strikes? *Beyond the Box Score*. Retrieved January 8, 2017, from: beyondtheboxscore.com/2014/1/27/5341676/how-well-do-umpires-call-balls-and-strikes.

MLB.com. (2007). 2.00 Definitions of terms. Retrieved January 11, 2017, from:

mlb.mlb.com/mlb/downloads/y2007/02_definitions_of_terms.pdf.

Mata, M. (2015). On the nature of the strike zone in two and three dimensions. *The Hardball Times*. Retrieved December 22, 2016, from: hardballtimes.com/on-the-nature-of-the-strike-zone-in-two-and-three-dimensions/.

Mathewson, J.D. (2010a). Benefit of the doubt: Odd patterns in umpire compensation. *Beyond the Box Score*. Retrieved January 7, 2017, from: beyondtheboxscore.com/2010/12/24/1892898/benefit-of-the-doubt-odd-patterns-in-umpire-compensation.

Mathewson, J.D. (2010b). Benefit of the doubt: How pitch speed and movement affect the zone. *Beyond the Box Score*. Retrieved January 8, 2017, from: beyondtheboxscore.com/2010/12/15/1877296/benefit-of-the-doubt-how-pitch-speed-and-movement-affect-the-zone.

Mathewson, J.D. (2011). Benefit of the doubt: Mo and the wide zone. *Beyond the Box Score*. Retrieved January 8, 2017, from: beyondtheboxscore.com/2011/2/9/1970784/benefit-of-the-doubt-mo-and-the-wide-zone.

Mills, B.M. (2011). Data quality in Pitch f/x. *The Prince of Slides*. Retrieved December 22, 2016, from: princeofslides.blogspot.com/2011/03/data-quality.html.

Mills, B.M. (2014). Social pressure at the plate: Inequality aversion, status, and mere exposure.

Managerial and Decision Economics, 35, 387-403.

Mills, B.M. (2015a). Expert workers, performance standards, and on-the-job training: Evaluating Major League Baseball Umpires. *SSRN Working Paper*. Retrieved December 31, 2016, from: papers.ssrn.com/sol3/papers.cfm?abstract_id=2478447.

Mills, B.M. (2015b). Measuring strike zone contour areas. *Exploring Baseball Data with R*. Retrieved January 8, 2017, from: baseballwithr.wordpress.com/2015/05/12/ measuring-strike-zone-contour-areas/.

Mills, B.M. (2016a). Policy changes in Major League Baseball: Improved agent behavior and ancillary productivity outcomes. *Economic Inquiry*. DOI: 10.1111/ecin.12396.

Mills, B.M. (2016b). Technological innovations in monitoring and evaluation: Evidence of performance impacts among Major League Baseball umpires. *Labour Economics*. DOI: dx.doi.org/10.1016/j.labeco.2016.10.004.

Mills, B.M. (2016c). Are the umpires at it again? *The Hardball Times*. Retrieved December 31, 2016, from: hardballtimes.com/are-the-umpires-at-it-again/.

Molyneux, G. (2016). Umpires aren't compassionate, they're Bayesian. *Baseball Prospectus*. Retrieved January 7, 2017, from: baseballprospectus.com/article.php?articleid=28513.

Moore, C. (2009). Bayesian umpires. *Baseball Analysts*. Retrieved January 7, 2017, from: baseballanalysts.com/archives/2009/12/bayesian_umpire.php.

Moskowitz, T.J. & Wertheim, L.J. (2011). *Scorecasting*. New York: Crown Archetype.

NASA. (2000). Human integration design handbook. Retrieved February 4, 2014, from: msis.jsc.nasa.gov/sections/section03.htm.

Nathan, A., Kensrud, J., Smith, L., & Lang, E. (2014). Testing TrackMan. Retrieved January 11, 2017, from: baseballprospectus.com/article.php?articleid=23202 #commentMessage.

O'Neill, D. (1990). Umpires are victimized by lockout, too. *Chicago Tribune*. Retrieved March 20, 2014, from: articles.chicagotribune.com/1990-03-18/sports/9001230580_1_umpires-spring-training-lockout-dave-phillips.

Parsons, C.A., Sulaeman, J., Yates, M.C., & Hamermesh, D.S. (2011). Strike three: Discrimination, incentives, and evaluation. *American Economic Review, 101*, 1410-1435.

Passan, J. (2015). MLB could alter strike zone as response to declining offense. *Yahoo! Sports*. Retrieved December 31, 2016, from: sports.yahoo.com/news/sources—mlb-could-alter-strike-zone-as-response-to-declining-offense-232940947.html.

Pavlidis, H. & Brooks, D. (2014). Framing and blocking pitches: A regressed, probabilistic model. *Baseball Prospectus*. Retrieved January 8, 2017, from: baseballprospectus.com/article.php?articleid=22934.

Petti, B. (2016). Developing the baseballr package for R. *The Hardball Times*. Retrieved December 20, 2016, from: hardballtimes.com/developing-the-baseballr-package-for-r/.

Price, J., Remer, M., & Stone, D.F. (2012). Subperfect game: Profitable biases of NBA referees. *Journal of Economics and Management Strategy, 21*, 271-300.

Rader, B.G. & Winkle, K.J. (2008). Baseball's great hitting barrage of the 1990s (and beyond) reexamined. *NINE: A Journal of Baseball History and Culture, 17,* 70-96.

Roegele, J. (2014a). The strike zone during the PITCHf/x era. *The Hardball Times.* Retrieved December 31, 2016, from: hardballtimes.com/the-strike-zone-during-the-pitchfx-era/.

Roegele, J. (2014b). The strike zone expansion is out of control. *The Hardball Times.* Retrieved December 31, 2016, from: hardballtimes.com/the-strike-zone-expansion-is-out-of-control/.

Roegele, J. (2015a). The expanded strike zone: It's baaaack. *The Hardball Times.* Retrieved December 31, 2016, from: hardballtimes.com/the-expanded-strike-zone-its-baaaack/.

Roegele, J. (2015b). The commissioner speaks: Imagining a redefined strike zone. *The Hardball Times.* Retrieved December 31, 2016, from: hardballtimes.com/the-commissioner-speaks-imagining-a-redefined-strike-zone/.

Roegele, J. (2016). The 2016 strike zone. *The Hardball Times.* Retrieved December 31, 2016, from: hardballtimes.com/the-2016-strike-zone/.

Sievert, C. (2014). Taming PITCHf/x data with XML2R and pitchRx. *The R Journal, 6,* 5-19.

Steiner, N. (2009). Measuring the umpire's effect on the game. *The Hardball Times.* Retrieved December 31, 2016, from: hardballtimes.com/tht-live/measuring-the-umpires-effect-on-the-game/.

Tainsky, S., Mills, B.M., & Winfree, J.A. (2016). Further examination of potential discrimination among MLB umpires. *Journal of Sports Economics, 16,* 353-374.

Tango, T. (2015). Evaluating the effectiveness of an umpire … effectively. *Tangotiger Blog.* Retrieved January 8, 2017, from: tangotiger.com/index.php/site/article/evaluating-the-effectiveness-of-an-umpire-effectively.

Turkenkopf, D. (2008). A strike is a strike, right? *Beyond the Box Score.* Retrieved January 8, 2017, from: beyondtheboxscore.com/2008/4/24/459913/a-strike-is-a-strike-right.

Walsh, J. (2007a). Strike zone: Fact vs. fiction. *The Hardball Times.* Retrieved December 20, 2016, from: hardballtimes.com/strike-zone-fact-vs-fiction/.

Walsh, J. (2007b). The eye of the umpire. *The Hardball Times.* Retrieved December 20, 2016, from: hardballtimes.com/the-eye-of-the-umpire/.

Walsh, J. (2010). The compassionate umpire. *The Hardball Times.* Retrieved January 7, 2017, from: hardballtimes.com/the-compassionate-umpire/.

Walsh, J. (2011). That was a strike? In *The Hardball Times Baseball Annual 2011.* Joe Distelheim, Bryan Tsao, Jeremiah Oshan, & Carolina Bolado Hale (eds.), (Chicago: ACTA Sports).

Weber, B. (2009). *As They See 'Em: A Fan's Travels in the Land of Umpires.* New York: Scribner.

Weinstock, J. (2012). Which umpire has the largest strike zone. *The Hardball Times.* Retrieved January 8, 2017, from: hardballtimes.com/which-umpire-has-the-largest-strikezone/.

What is WAR? (2017). Retrieved January 11, 2017, from: fangraphs.com/library/misc/war/.

Willman, D. (2016). Baseball Savant: Statcast search. Retrieved December 19, 2016, from: baseballsavant.mlb.com/statcast_search.

Wood, S. (2006). *Generalized additive models: An introduction with R.* Boca Raton, Florida: Chapman Hall, Taylor & Francis Group, LLP.

NOTES

1 Janssen has a Ph.D. in Adult Education and looked to use these lessons to develop successful training programs for umpires ("Janssen to Speak," 2007).

2 Janssen did ultimately end up working with MLB — and later with World Umpires Association and minor-league umpires — in developing other evaluation and training programs for a number of years.

3 Data from this system had been publicly available since 2007, but not used for official evaluation of umpires.

4 Fast was hired by the Houston Astros shortly thereafter, and has served as the team's director of research and development as of 2015.

5 A previous website also allowed point-and-click downloads of raw data, developed by Joe Lefkowitz, but was taken down after he was hired within MLB.

6 Mike Fast (2011b) notes that some of this may be due to umpire positioning behind the plate.

7 Pairing this information with the stated rulebook strike zone, using an average batter height of 73.5 inches sets the bottom of the zone (just below the hollow of the knee) at 18.2 inches, and the top of the zone at 41 inches. This will be the preferred strike-zone definition for the data presentations in this article, and is relatively consistent with suggestions by PITCHf/x expert Mike Fast (2011e). However, as Carleton (2016) notes, knee shapes could result in varying zones, even for batters of the same height, so any measurement should be taken with caution.

8 The bird's-eye view of the plate in Figure 1 was created using Bagget's code from Github (github.com/aaronbaggett/baseball_blog).

9 The R code used to create these analyses are provided at pastebin.com/zMar7LUQ and pastebin.com/caZxe9y3.

10 Though it is certainly possible that they slightly underestimate performance as a whole.

11 Approximately 700,000 pitches were thrown in 2015 and recorded in the data with locational information.

12 As it turns out, there may be subconscious biases that influence the distribution of these incorrect calls such that they are not

evenly distributed across players and teams. I'll address this in the following section.

13 The relative missed ball and strike call rates also tell us about the *size* of individual umpire strike zones, as exhibited in Weinstock (2012). Mills (2015b) gives a comprehensive overview of how to analyze strike zone surface area in R.

14 MLBAM's senior database architect, Tom Tango (2015), also suggests this approach.

15 Analyzing umpires hardly seems worth committing a HIPAA violation.

16 However, MLB did begin implementing drug tests in 2003 with no explicit punishment for a failed test.

17 This makes the emergence of Barry Bonds as the all-time single-season home-run leader in 2001 all the more impressive.

18 Interestingly, minor-league scoring also decreased dramatically from 1999 to 2002, though the large drop started in 2000, rather than 2001, as it did in MLB. However, decreases in MLB scoring have outpaced minor-league scoring since 2006.

19 Both Mills (2016a; 2016b; 2016c) and Roegele (2014a; 2014b; 2015a; 2016) have ensured that these changes are well-documented.

20 Scoring had peaked in 2000 at 10.28 combined runs per game.

21 Much earlier work by Steiner (2009) also found that pitchers' walk rates could individually be affected by umpire mistakes on ball calls.

22 This varies from year to year. For example, in 2002 home-team win percentage was 0.542, and in 2009 it was 0.549.

23 It should be noted that Bayes Theorem has much more important applications than baseball and game shows, particularly in medicine, and the Monty Hall problem was known well before the release of this movie.

24 Wins Above Replacement (WAR) is a measure of player productivity developed by sabermetricians. While there are varying methods to reach the WAR value for a given player, the definition of the concept is relatively standard. WAR is defined as the number of additional wins provided to their team relative to a player available to replace them, such as a Triple-A player that could be moved up to the MLB roster in the event of injury. WAR can be negative if a player performs below what would be expected of a Triple-A player, with 10 wins being an unusually excellent season. As an example, in 2016 Mike Trout had the highest MLB WAR (as measured by Fangraphs ["What is WAR?" 2017]) at 9.4, while Carlos Correa produced 4.9 wins, and Denard Span produced 1.4 wins.

25 Sportvision built technology called COMMANDf/x with data back through the 2010 season. Mike Fast (2011f) attempts to analyze glove movement impacts by pairing video and PITCHf/x data.

26 Though this author notes for the record that he suspects run scoring would decrease substantially without a redefinition or some other under-the-hood tweak to the game.

The Chest Protector

By Bill Nowlin

Umpires have a fraternity of their own. Just as life in baseball seems like ballplayers and those who work closely with them are part of a big, sprawling family, so umpires are part of a close-knit group, albeit one where one umpire won't see another for a full season. They still feel like part of a tight, professional circle — as indeed they are — and they have great respect for those who have gone before.

Chris Guccione's chest protector offers evidence of an accumulation of personally meaningful patches and stickers that he has added over the years. The "Italia" sticker depicting the Italian flag is "for my heritage," he says. "I bought that in San Francisco in 1997 when I was working in the California league. That how old my protector is." The American flag is included, too. There are a number of patches honoring former umpires who have passed on - they honor Frank Pulli (FP), Harry Wendelstedt (HW), Marty Springstead (MS), Wally Bell (WB), John Kibler (JK), and Shag Crawford (SC). The red heart is for Sammy Holbrook's wife Susie, who lost a very long battle with cancer.

There are also four items for particular causes — the End It Movement, "Shining A Light on Slavery," the blue ribbon for prostate cancer awareness and

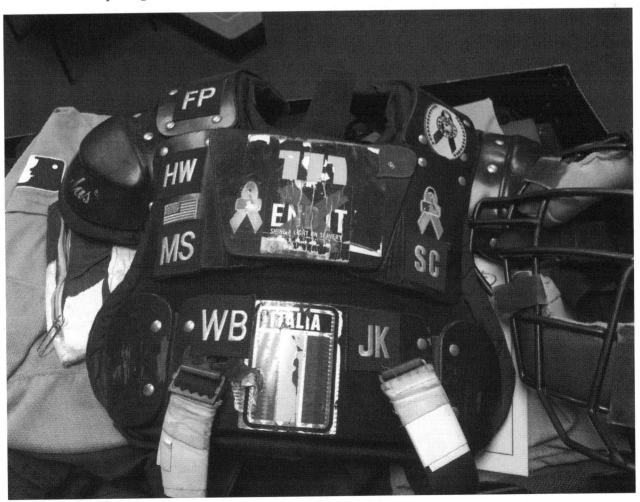

Chris Guccione's chest protector, July 2015, with stickers honoring various deceased umpires.

Laz Diaz and his equipment trunk, with his father's photograph.

the pink for breast cancer awareness. And there is the Newtown patch, one that umpires wore to honor the children and teachers that were killed in the Newtown, Connecticut school shooting at the Sandy Hook Elementary School in December 2012.

The decorations on his chest protector aren't seen during a game, of course, since they are covered by his uniform shirt, but they are there, a little closer to his heart.

Other umpires carry memories with them as well. Laz Diaz's equipment trunk, for instance, bears his father's photograph on the inside cover, as well as a

"42" Jackie Robinson patch (Chris Guccione has a few "42" patches on his trunk), and two umpire patches — MH and WB. The "WB" is for Wally Bell. The MH is actually an upside-down Harry Wendelstedt patch. Diaz had wanted to honor Michael Hirschbeck, the 27-year-old son of John Hirschbeck, who had died in 2014 of (ADL) adrenoleukodystrophy. "I worked with John together for so many years that I know his family very well, been in his house," explains Diaz. "That patch used to be for Harry Wendelstedt. It's upside down, because Michael Hirschbeck passed away last year. I looked at the patch and I turned it around. HW — MH. When I went around the league last year, I asked all the clubbies if they still had Harry Wendelstedt patches, which they did. That's a tribute to Michael Hirschbeck." Michael was the second child that John and Denise Hirschbeck lost to ADL; in 1992, they had lost their 8-year-old son, John.

One finds other trunks which bear dozens of photographs of family and friends. Each umpire brings his own memories with him on the road.

Photographs by Chris Guccione. Both Chris Guccione and Laz Diaz spoke with Bill Nowlin on July 3 & 5, 2015, and Chris provided additional information in emails later in July.

What's In the Water in Coldwater, Michigan?

By Bill Nowlin

Coldwater, Michigan had a population of 10,945 at the time of the 2010 United States census. Founded in 1861, the city is the county seat of Branch County and sits more or less 65 miles due north of Fort Wayne, Indiana on I-69. It is also the home of three major-league baseball umpires: Tim Welke, Bill Welke, and Jeff Kellogg.

Of the 76 big-league umpires, three came from the State of California, and three came from Coldwater.[1]

As it happens, so did Jim Curtiss who played center field in 27 games for the Cincinnati Reds back in 1891 and Alice Haylett who pitched for the Grand Rapids Chicks in the All-American Girls Professional Baseball League from 1946-49. Her 25-5 record in 1948 with an ERA of 0.77 earned her All-Star and Pitcher of the Year honors.

Tim Welke was born in Pontiac in 1957, but the family moved to Coldwater and he graduated from Coldwater High. Tim umpired his first major-league games in 1983 for the American League and worked 4,213 games through 2015. After having knee surgery in January 2016, and with surgery for the other knee scheduled for June, Tim was on the disabled list for all of 2016.

Tim's younger brother Bill was born in Coldwater itself, in 1967. His first of more than 2,000 games in the big leagues also came with the A.L., in 1999.

Jeff Kellogg is also a Coldwater native, born in 1961. Jeff was a National League umpire before the leagues merged, working his first four games in 1991. He's now worked over 3,000 games.

When Bill Welke married Jeff's younger sister Teri (Teresa), the families became united through marriage. 'But for the record," Bill points out, "I was dating her before Jeff went to umpire school. Small town. The Kellogg family and the Welke family, they had eight kids and we had seven kids."[2]

The three knew each other to some extent while growing up. Jeff and Teri's father Wayne Kellogg coached for many years and for the last 20 years or so has been athletic director at Coldwater High School. Jeff says, "I actually graduated with one of the Welke sisters and then I wrestled with one of the other brothers."[3]

All three went to Coldwater High. Tim, the eldest, played sports all through high school and went to umpire school at age 19. Following his retirement at the end of the 2016 season, one of his goals in life is to go back and finish getting a college degree. Tim said that his and Bill's father worked for the State Highway Department of Michigan. "He built roads and bridges and at the end of his career he was in charge of the entire department and worked out of Lansing. I got my work ethic from him."[4] Tim was the oldest of seven Welke children and Bill was the youngest. Coming up in baseball, with a brother who'd started umpiring in the majors 16 years earlier, a player might ask Bill if they were related. "I'd say, 'Distantly.' He'd say, 'Distantly?' and I'd say, 'Yeah, there's five kids between us.'"

With the age difference, Tim had left home to go to umpire school when Bill was only 8 years old. Bill said, "From the age of 8, I was more interested in following the umpires than following the teams. I've really been an umpire fan since I was 8 or 9 years old." But Bill didn't automatically follow in his brother's footsteps, and Tim certainly didn't encourage him. "I went to Western Michigan and got a business degree. I was thinking about quitting college to go to umpire school and give it a try. I had done some umpiring around home and I really enjoyed it, so I said something to Tim about it and he said, 'If you quit college, I'm not going to help you.'" That came about in time, after graduation. "He gave me a lot of good advice and some used uniforms, and I went off to umpire school."

When Bill joined Tim as fellow A.L. umpires, they were on the same crew for some time under crew chief Jim Evans. Bill knew he wanted to be seen as his own man, and shared that with Evans from the start. Evans told him, "I'd love to have you come and be one of us," but acknowledged, "It'll probably put you under more scrutiny."[5] There was remarkably little backlash. Bill recalls one story: "I was in Tampa and I had a chopper in front of the plate, the catcher came out to field it, and the batter ran into him and I called interference. Lou Piniella's managing Tampa. He came out and put on this little show. Tim's the chief and Tim walks out. I said, "There's a time for Lou to either get ejected if he wants to get ejected, or leave." So Tim comes down and talks to Lou and tried to get Lou going, and Lou starts and then stops and he says, "Oh, this is bullshit." He starts walking back and then he stops and turns and looks at Tim and I and goes, "I think I'm getting brothered here." And then just walked away."

Tim recalled, "We had a few years when we worked together as partners, which was good. We worked together for a few years and then I just kinda felt that maybe it would be better for his career if he worked with different people also, not just see it from his big brother's standpoint…Working with different people helps you become a better umpire because you see different ways to do things." It probably made the powers that be a little happier, Bill suggested: "I don't think baseball was crazy about it [being together on the same crew.]"

He added, "The first couple of years, I got called 'Tim' all the time. After about four or five years, someone would call Tim 'Bill' and I knew I'd arrived when they started calling Tim 'Bill.' I really enjoyed working with him, but I think it was time to move on. You don't want to be in anybody's shadow."

All in all, Bill said, "This is the best way to sum it up: when we're on the field, we're two umpires who happen to be brothers, and off the field we're two brothers who just happen to be umpires."

Jeff had known that Tim was umpiring, of course, but Tim was significantly older. "I knew him, but I didn't know him," he says. Jeff had gone to college at Central Michigan, then transferred into a Criminal Justice program at Ferris State. One day, he remembers, "I was watching the *Saturday Game of the Week* and the home plate umpire walked out to the mound to break up a conversation, and it was Tim. I was like, 'Holy cow! He's in the big leagues.'"

Jeff graduated and worked for about a year for the Sheriff's Department in Coldwater, but then decided he wanted to check out umpire school himself.

"I've worked postseason with Jeff a couple of times," says Tim. "We had a World Series together and a couple of other events, but we've never been on the same [regular-season] crew." Both are crew chiefs now.

Jeff says, regarding the three of them. "We all together over the holidays. We might talk a little shop, but otherwise we're talking about anything but baseball. Especially football season. We all enjoy football so we'll talk football. It depends on the time of year."

As it happens, there's a fourth major-league umpire in the area. Scott Barry was born in 1976 in Battle Creek, about 40 miles from Coldwater, but grew up in Quincy, which is, Jeff says, "right next door. It's right off Route 12, which runs right through Coldwater. It's 5-10 minutes away. It's right up the road." Scott umpired his first big-league games as a fill-in umpire in 2006 and joined the major-league staff in 2011. So three major-league umpires come from all of California, but four grew up within a short bicycle ride of each other in Branch County, Michigan.

Note: Midland isn't next door, but it's where Paul Emmel was born. He graduated from Central Michigan University. D. J. Reyburn was born in Grand Rapids and graduated from Olivet College.

NOTES

1   The California natives are Bill Miller, Mark Ripperger, and Mike Winters.

2   Author interview with Bill Welke, September 22, 2015. All quotations from Bill come from this interview.

3 Author interview with Jeff Kellogg, September 21, 2016. All quotations come from this interview.

4 Author interview with Tim Welke, July 30, 2015. All quotations come from this interview.

5 Author interview with Bill Welke.

One Umpire Crew's Schedule in 2016

In SABR's book on scouts and scouting, CAN HE PLAY? we printed the year 2007 schedules of a couple of baseball scouts: Damon Iannelli, Southeast Scouting Supervisor of the Colorado Rockies, and Leon Wurth, Pro Scout for the Milwaukee Braves. The schedules showed what each scout did on each day throughout his year. In Damon's case, it was so long we only included January into early June.

Through the courtesy of Major League Baseball, we were sent the full schedule for all umpires in 2016 after the season was over. What follows is one crew's schedule for the regular season in 2016. Needless to say, the umpires also worked in spring training and some in the postseason, not to mention work in umpire development and in many cases at umpire school or camps.

Within this particular crew (it was Crew I), there were individual comings and goings for one reason or another—individual vacations, injuries, and the like. This, however, is the schedule for this crew.

There is a great deal of travel involved. Crews aren't scheduled to work back-to-back series in a given ballpark; as one would expect, Major League Baseball doesn't want any given umpire to work too many games of one team throughout the course of the season. Umpires are seemingly always on the move. A typical crew will travel somewhere around 30,000 or more miles during the course of a season.

ONE SAMPLE CREW'S SCHEDULE IN 2016			
DAY OF WEEK	DATE	GAME	TIME
SUN	4/3	—-	
MON	4/4	MIN @ BAL	3:05
TUES	4/5	OPEN	
WED	4/6	MIN @ BAL	7:05
THURS	4/7	MIN @ BAL	7:05
FRI	4/8	STL @ ATL	7:35
SAT	4/9	STL @ ATL	7:10
SUN	4/10	STL @ ATL	1:35
MON	4/11	OPEN	
TUES	4/12	CLE @ TB	7:10
WED	4/13	CLE @ TB	7:10
THURS	4/14	CLE @ TB	1:10
FRI	4/15	SEA @ NYY	7:05
SAT	4/16	SEA @ NYY	1:05
SUN	4/17	SEA @ NYY	1:05
MON	4/18	REPLAY - NY	
TUES	4/19	REPLAY - NY	
WED	4/20	REPLAY - NY	

THURS	4/21	REPLAY - NY	
FRI	4/22	REPLAY - NY	
SAT	4/23	REPLAY - NY	
SUN	4/24	REPLAY - NY	
MON	4/25	OAK @ DET	7:10
TUES	4/26	OAK @ DET	7:10
WED	4/27	OAK @ DET	7:10
THURS	4/28	OAK @ DET	1:10
FRI	4/29	SD @ LAD	7:10
SAT	4/30	SD @ LAD	6:10
SUN	5/1	SD @ LAD	1:10
MON	5/2	VACATION	
TUES	5/3	VACATION	
WED	5/4	VACATION	
THURS	5/5	VACATION	
FRI	5/6	VACATION	
SAT	5/7	VACATION	
SUN	5/8	VACATION	
MON	5/9	OPEN	
TUES	5/10	PHI @ ATL	7:10
WED	5/11	PHI @ ATL	7:10
THURS	5/12	PHI @ ATL	7:10
FRI	5/13	CWS @ NYY	7:05
SAT	5/14	CWS @ NYY	1:05
SUN	5/15	CWS @ NYY	1:05
MON	5/16	TB @ TOR	7:07
TUES	5/17	TB @ TOR	7:07
WED	5/18	TB @ TOR	7:07
THURS	5/19	OPEN	
FRI	5/20	ARI @ STL	7:15
SAT	5/21	ARI @ STL	3:05
SUN	5/22	ARI @ STL	1:15
MON	5/23	SD @ SF	7:15
TUES	5/24	SD @ SF	7:15
WED	5/25	SD @ SF	12:45
THURS	5/26	OPEN	
FRI	5/27	MIN @ SEA	7:10
SAT	5/28	MIN @ SEA	7:10
SUN	5/29	MIN @ SEA	1:10
MON	5/30	CIN @ COL	2:10

TUES	5/31	CIN @ COL	6:40
WED	6/1	CIN @ COL	6:40
THURS	6/2	CIN @ COL	6:40
FRI	6/3	OAK @ HOU	7:10
SAT	6/4	OAK @ HOU	3:10
SUN	6/5	OAK @ HOU	1:10
MON	6/6	CHI @ PHI	7:05
TUES	6/7	CHI @ PHI	7:05
WED	6/8	CHI @ PHI	1:05
THURS	6/9	OPEN	
FRI	6/10	DET @ NYY	7:05
SAT	6/11	DET @ NYY	7:15
SUN	6/12	DET @ NYY	2:05
MON	6/13	OPEN	
TUES	6/14	BAL @ BOS	7:10
WED	6/15	BAL @ BOS	7:10
THURS	6/16	BAL @ BOS	7:10
FRI	6/17	ATL @ NYM	7:10
SAT	6/18	ATL @ NYM	8:15
SUN	6/19	ATL @ NYM	1:10
MON	6/20	REPLAY - NY	
TUES	6/21	REPLAY - NY	
WED	6/22	REPLAY - NY	
THURS	6/23	REPLAY - NY	
FRI	6/24	REPLAY - NY	
SAT	6/25	REPLAY - NY	
SUN	6/26	REPLAY - NY	
MON	6/27	CHI @ CIN	7:10
TUES	6/28	CHI @ CIN	7:10
WED	6/29	CHI @ CIN	12:35
THURS	6/30	BAL @ SEA	7:10
FRI	7/1	BAL @ SEA	7:10
SAT	7/2	BAL @ SEA	7:10
SUN	7/3	BAL @ SEA	1:10
MON	7/4	VACATION	
TUES	7/5	VACATION	
WED	7/6	VACATION	
THURS	7/7	VACATION	
FRI	7/8	VACATION	
SAT	7/9	VACATION	

SUN	7/10	VACATION		
MON	7/11	All-Star Break		
TUES	7/12	All-Star Break		
WED	7/13	All-Star Break		
THURS	7/14	All-Star Break		
FRI	7/15	TOR @ OAK	7:05	
SAT	7/16	TOR @ OAK	1:05	
SUN	7/17	TOR @ OAK	1:05	
MON	7/18	TEX @ LAA	7:05	
TUES	7/19	TEX @ LAA	7:05	
WED	7/20	TEX @ LAA	7:05	
THURS	7/21	ATL @ COL	6:40	
FRI	7/22	ATL @ COL	6:40	
SAT	7/23	ATL @ COL	6:10	
SUN	7/24	ATL @ COL	2:10	
MON	7/25	STL @ NYM		POSTPONED
TUES	7/26	STL @ NYM	7:10 DH	
WED	7/27	STL @ NYM	7:10	
THURS	7/28	OPEN		
FRI	7/29	PIT @ MIL	7:10	
SAT	7/30	PIT @ MIL	6:10	
SUN	7/31	PIT @ MIL	1:10	
MON	8/1	MIA @ CHI	7:05	
TUES	8/2	MIA @ CHI	7:05	
WED	8/3	MIA @ CHI	1:20	
THURS	8/4	OPEN		
FRI	8/5	BAL @ CWS	7:10	
SAT	8/6	BAL @ CWS	6:10	
SUN	8/7	BAL @ CWS	1:10	
MON	8/8	HOU @ MIN	7:10	
TUES	8/9	HOU @ MIN	7:10	
WED	8/10	HOU @ MIN		POSTPONED
THURS	8/11	HOU @ MIN	split DH	
FRI	8/12	SEA @ OAK	7:05	
SAT	8/13	SEA @ OAK	6:05	
SUN	8/14	SEA @ OAK	1:05	
MON	8/15	PIT @ SF	7:15	
TUES	8/16	PIT @ SF	7:15	
WED	8/17	PIT @ SF	12:45	
THURS	8/18	ARI @ SD	7:10	

FRI	8/19	ARI @ SD	7:40
SAT	8/20	ARI @ SD	5:40
SUN	8/21	ARI @ SD	1:40
MON	8/22	OPEN	
TUES	8/23	NYM @ STL	7:15
WED	8/24	NYM @ STL	7:15
THURS	8/25	NYM @ STL	6:15
FRI	8/26	COL @ WSH	7:05
SAT	8/27	COL @ WSH	1:05
SUN	8/28	COL @ WSH	1:35
MON	8/29	REPLAY - NY	
TUES	8/30	REPLAY - NY	
WED	8/31	REPLAY - NY	
THURS	9/1	REPLAY - NY	
FRI	9/2	REPLAY - NY	
SAT	9/3	REPLAY - NY	
SUN	9/4	REPLAY - NY	
MON	9/5	PHI @ MIA	1:10
TUES	9/6	PHI @ MIA	7:10
WED	9/7	PHI @ MIA	7:10
THURS	9/8	CIN @ PIT	7:05
FRI	9/9	CIN @ PIT	7:05
SAT	9/10	CIN @ PIT	7:05
SUN	9/11	CIN @ PIT	1:35
MON	9/12	VACATION	
TUES	9/13	VACATION	
WED	9/14	VACATION	
THURS	9/15	VACATION	
FRI	9/16	VACATION	
SAT	9/17	VACATION	
SUN	9/18	VACATION	
MON	9/19	HOU @ OAK	7:05
TUES	9/20	HOU @ OAK	7:05
WED	9/21	HOU @ OAK	12:35
THURS	9/22	SF @ SD	7:10
FRI	9/23	SF @ SD	7:40
SAT	9/24	SF @ SD	5:40
SUN	9/25	SF @ SD	1:40
MON	9/26	OPEN	
TUES	9/27	MIN @ KC	6:15

WED	9/28	MIN @ KC	6:15
THURS	9/29	MIN @ KC	6:15
FRI	9/30	TB @ TEX	7:05
SAT	10/1	TB @ TEX	7:05
SUN	10/2	TB @ TEX	2:05

We can see that this one crew traveled:
Home to Baltimore
Baltimore to Atlanta
Atlanta to Tampa Bay
Tampa Bay to NYC
NYC to Detroit
Detroit to LA
LA to vacation location
Vacation to Atlanta
Atlanta to NYC
NYC to Toronto
Toronto to St. Louis
St. Louis to San Francisco
San Francisco to Seattle
Seattle to Denver
Denver to Houston
Houston to Philadelphia
Philadelphia to NYC
NYC to Boston
Boston to NYC
NYC to Cincinnati
Cincinnati to Seattle
Seattle to vacation location
Vacation to Oakland
Oakland to LA
LA to Denver
Denver to NYC
NYC to Milwaukee
Milwaukee to Chicago
Chicago to Minneapolis/St. Paul
Minneapolis/St. Paul to Oakland
San Francisco to San Diego
San Diego to St. Louis
St. Louis to Washington DC
Washington DC to New York
New York to Miami
Miami to Pittsburgh
Pittsburgh to vacation location
Vacation to Oakland
Oakland to San Diego
San Diego to Kansas City
Kansas City to Dallas/Fort Worth
Dallas/Fort Worth to home.

While we could have created a listing of flight plans taken, with the mileage tabulated, and even provided a map showing the criss-crossing of the country reflected by the schedule, we chose to forego both ideas.

For a look at the process (and the algorithms that go into umpire scheduling of the 2,430 major-league games in 780 series throughout the regular season), please see the paper "Scheduling Major League Baseball Umpires and the Traveling Umpire Problem" by Michael A. Trick (Tepper School of Business, Carnegie Mello University), Hakan Yildiz (Eli Broad College of Business, Michigan State University), and Tallys Yunes (School of Business Administration, University of Miami). It was published online in *Articles in Advance* on June 1, 2011, and reprinted in *Interfaces* Vol. 42, No. 3, May-June 2012, pp. 232-244. http://pubsonline.informs.org/doi/abs/10.1287/inte.1100.0514

Thanks to Matt Levin for drawing our attention to this article.

Umpires and Health

By Eric Frost

In April 1996, 51-year-old major-league umpire John McSherry collapsed and died while working behind the plate a few pitches into the first game of the season at Riverfront Stadium in Cincinnati. McSherry's weight had been listed at 328 pounds by the league, but even Richie Phillips, the head of the major-league umpires union, estimated that McSherry may have reached 380 pounds. He had been diagnosed with a cardiac arrhythmia, for which he had a doctor's appointment scheduled for the day after his death.

More than 10 years before he died, McSherry first admitted to feeling ill. At the time, he had difficulty identifying when he was experiencing dizziness because he spent most of his waking hours feeling dizzy. Between 1991 and 1995 McSherry left three games early, experiencing heat prostration, dizziness, and dehydration, respectively. He had lost significant weight before, but it had always returned.[1]

McSherry's death sparked some conversation about the health status of the modern umpire. Umpire Jim Quick, who stood 6-feet tall and weighed 229 pounds, acknowledged that he was overweight, but he decried the fact that league officials were not in touch with the needs of umpires and criticized the poor condition of exercise equipment in dressing rooms across the league.[2] A piece in the *Chicago Tribune* contrasted the conditioning requirements for officials in baseball, hockey, and football. Major-league umpires simply had to pass a yearly physical, while NHL and NFL officials were also put through several days of agility and conditioning testing before the start of each season.[3]

Besides McSherry, other umpires were known to have weight or health problems. Perhaps most notably, Eric Gregg, a major-league umpire since the 1970s, stood 6-feet-3 and had a weight that sometimes approached 400 pounds. Gregg recalled that after games he would often eat from the umpire room spread at the stadium, enjoy several beers, and then leave the stadium for a large dinner, which included more alcohol. After his close friend McSherry died, Gregg was rattled. He decided to enter a weight management program and the National League agreed to pay for it. Taking a hiatus from umpiring until July, Gregg was able to lose 60 pounds. Gregg, who lost his job in the union-led mass resignations of 1999, died of a stroke seven years later at the age of 55.[4]

During Ford Frick's term as National League president, he required 270-pound umpire Dusty Boggess to lose 50 pounds before spring training in order to have his contract renewed. After the establishment of the major-league umpires union, their contract did not include weight restrictions for umpires, which limits the ability of league officials to hold umpires accountable for their weight.[5] After McSherry's death, a *Chicago Tribune* article said that 58 of the 64 active umpires exceeded American Heart Association guidelines for healthy weight in large-framed men; 25 of those umpires fell into the category of severely overweight. Phillips asserted that weight limits might be unfair because each person carried his weight differently, while NL Vice President Katy Feeney said that the league could not legally impose weight restrictions.[6]

Former Yankees and Giants athletic trainer Mark Letendre was hired as director of umpire medical services in 1999 to coordinate a new initiative for umpire health care. Letendre provides education to umpires on health-promotion topics.[7] He is also on call to address in-game and postgame issues such as concussions. Dr. Laurence M. Westreich serves as a consultant on behavioral health and addiction.

Though Major League Baseball has not been able to enact specific weight restrictions for its umpires, it seems that there is at least an awareness of the importance of health in umpire training. In 2017 the Harry Wendelstedt School for Umpires hired physician Steve Dorsey as its medical coordinator. Dorsey's responsibilities include teaching the school's students about fitness, injury prevention, and nutrition. Dorsey and his son were students at the school in 2016.[8]

In the early years of baseball, the game's umpires may have thought of assault as a much more pressing health risk than cardiovascular disease or obesity. Arbiters in the Deadball Era faced violence not only from upset fans, but from players and coaches. In an extreme case in 1905, Pacific Coast League umpire Bull Perrine was attacked by players in two separate incidents within two weeks. In the second incident, Perrine suffered cuts that required bandaging, and first baseman Marty Murphy was arrested and thrown out of the league.[9] Perrine later made the major leagues. Nearly 10 years before Perrine's incidents, Tom Lynch had left a major-league game after being assaulted by a player, Patsy Tebeau. Umpires were not always just on the receiving end of assaults, however. Two umpires were arrested during games for violent incidents (Tim Hurst in 1897 for throwing a bottle into the bleachers and Jack Sheridan in 1903 for fighting with a player).[10]

Serious in-game injuries and illnesses among umpires have been relatively rare throughout the game's history. Cal Drummond is thought to be the only major-league umpire whose death may be related to an on-field injury. In June 1969 Drummond was umpiring a game at Memorial Stadium in Baltimore when he was struck in the mask by a foul ball. He felt well enough to finish the game, but he was admitted to the hospital later that night with a head injury and he lapsed into unconsciousness for several days. After improving and flying home to South Carolina, Drummond became ill again and ultimately had surgery to remove a blood clot from his brain. He recovered and was umpiring in the minor leagues in preparation for a planned return to the majors. During a May 1970 game in Des Moines, Drummond suffered a stroke involving the injured portion of his brain and he died several days later.[11]

The minor leagues were unkind to at least one more former major-league umpire. Ziggy Sears umpired in the major leagues between 1934 and 1945; a broken foot forced his retirement from the majors. After his major-league service, Sears was able to

John McSherry.

return to the Texas League as an umpire. During a rainy 1951 exhibition game between Dallas and Milwaukee, Sears was struck in the eye by a baseball that had been errantly thrown past first base. The injury marked the end of his professional career. Sears later sued the Dallas club for allowing the game to continue in the rain and for not providing him with timely medical care.[12]

A Retrosheet database tracks instances in which umpires have had to leave major-league games that were in progress. The database provides some insight into the risks umpires face on the field. Between 1871 and 2016, more than 320 umpires have left games in progress. The list includes more than just injuries and illnesses, including a few umpires who had to catch trains out of town, several others who left to attend to family concerns, and one umpire who is described as leaving due to personal reasons. (In one case, an umpire exited with his health intact but his dignity probably injured: George Moriarty left a 1936 game after he ripped his pants while bending over to dust off home plate.) Some of the descriptions in the database are listed as unknown (13 players); more than a dozen of the entries are characterized as an unknown injury; and more than two dozen umpires were experiencing unknown illnesses.[13]

Perhaps not surprisingly, of the known injuries in the Retrosheet database, being struck by a baseball (either batted or thrown) was the most common mechanism of injury; this scenario felled more than 130 of the umpires and typically involved foul balls striking the man behind the plate. Seven umpires were also injured by baseball bats. These included Paul Emmel, who required stitches to his head after a bat flew out of the hands of Jefry Marte in 2016. Two umpires left games never to return to major-league umpiring, Billy Williams with a broken leg in 1987 and Charlie Reliford with a torn calf muscle in 2009. Williams, who collided with pitcher Zane Smith on a play at home plate, was one of at least 14 umpires to sustain a broken bone. In one of the more unusual injuries, Jerry Neudecker required 10 stitches after his chin came into contact with a catcher's head. Though several of the umpires injured by bats or balls took blows to the head, face or mask, only two entries (from 2008 and 2009) described the umpire as having suffered concussions. The known illnesses in the Retrosheet database are typically minor ailments like flulike illnesses. More than 20 umpires have left games early due to dehydration or heat-related issues.[14]

Working on stretching techniques, Wendelstedt Umpire School, January 2017.

The Retrosheet database indicates that August 26, 2009, was a particularly unusual day for umpires at a game in Toronto between the Blue Jays and the Tampa Bay Rays. The game required three men to don the home-plate gear. The original plate umpire, Jerry Crawford, left the game with back spasms, so second-base umpire Tom Hallion became the plate umpire. Hallion was struck in the chest by a ball in the seventh inning. He was able to return to the game after a short delay, but Brian O'Nora took over plate duties while Hallion went to first base.[15]

While the Retrosheet database provides a good overview of the typical risks of umpiring, it cannot capture every sequence of events that led to the downfall of an umpire in service to the game. Lou DiMuro, who had suffered from arthritis in his hip since a 1979 home-plate collision, went for a walk to exercise his hip after a 1982 game in Arlington. He was struck by a car and killed.[16]

Several active umpires have faced serious illnesses that did not present themselves on the baseball diamond. In 1999 National League umpire Wally Bell was in his mid-30s and working his seventh major-league season when he underwent quintuple-bypass surgery. Eleven weeks later, Bell returned to umpiring, and he later cited his return to the field as his proudest moment. He went on to umpire in the postseason several times, including the 2006 World Series. Bell was still umpiring when, after the end of the 2013 regular season, he became the first active major-league umpire to die since McSherry. The 48-year-old had suffered a heart attack in his hometown of Youngstown, Ohio.[17]

Cancer was fatal to one active major-league umpire. Bill Kunkel was in his mid-40s when he was diagnosed with cancer in 1981. A former major-league pitcher and NBA referee, Kunkel had been umpiring in the American League since 1968. He continued to umpire through the 1984 season, twice taking leaves of absence to have cancer-related surgeries. Kunkel died of cancer on May 5, 1985.[18]

Though Kunkel's story is a sad one, Lee Weyer, who entered the major leagues as one of the youngest umpires in NL history, may have experienced the most health-related misfortune during an umpiring career. In 1980 Weyer began to experience vision problems and shaking of the arms, legs, and hands. He was diagnosed with a life-threatening neurological disorder known as Guillain-Barre syndrome, which affects vision, muscle control, and motor function. After missing most of the 1980 season to rehabilitate from the illness, Weyer had recovered enough to return to umpiring, this time wearing eyeglasses.[19] Weyer later experienced more blurred vision, and he was diagnosed with diabetes, which he controlled with medication. On July 4, 1988, after umpiring an afternoon game, Weyer was playing basketball at the home of fellow umpire and close friend Ed Montague when he suffered shortness of breath. A short time later, Montague found Weyer unresponsive; he died of a heart attack at the age of 51.[20]

Other professional umpires have continued to work in the face of disabilities or serious chronic illnesses. After Eastern League umpire Max McLeary suffered a freak injury off the field in the 1970s that necessitated a prosthetic eye, he returned to umpiring 10 years later and ultimately spent several seasons in the independent Frontier League.[21] Henry Fanning, who had only one arm, became a well-respected umpire in the Pacific Coast League.[22] Current major-league crew chief (as of 2016) Tom Hallion is a type 1 diabetic.[23] Longtime umpire Bill McGowan also suffered from diabetes. Jim Honochick described the impact of McGowan's illness, saying, "There were days when he was so sick he shouldn't even have gone out on the ball field. … When the game ended, he was completely exhausted. He couldn't do anything on his own. You had to help him take his coat off. … He was drained, physically and emotionally drained, but he had given you the best game of umpiring you'd ever seen."[24]

Just as in the general population, health problems for umpires are not limited to physical ailments. A small number of major-league umpires have experienced mental-health concerns significant enough to lead to suicide, but in each case the umpire committed suicide after his retirement from the game. Six years after he was the victim of the two attacks in the Pacific Coast League, Bull Perrine was umpiring in the major leagues when he was said to have suffered sunstroke. He had a nervous breakdown and was admitted to an insane asylum in Napa, California; he committed suicide two years later.[25] Ron Luciano last umpired in the major leagues in 1979; he sought in-patient evaluation for depression in 1994 and committed suicide by carbon monoxide poisoning in January 1995.[26] Arthur Irwin, a baseball executive and former player, umpired in the National League for one month. Many years later, after being diagnosed with cancer, he boarded a steamer in Boston and is thought to have jumped overboard. Irwin's death was punctuated by the discovery that two wives and families survived him in separate cities.[27]

Umpires take the various challenges facing them seriously, and umpire Ted Barrett's doctoral dissertation for Trinity Theological Seminary surveyed major-league umpires and presented an overview of a number of such challenges.[28] NL umpire Jerry Dale did something similar in the 1970s, studying the personality traits of umpires for a master's thesis at Cal Poly Pomona. Dale found that common umpire traits included aggressiveness, assertiveness, and extroversion (the opposite of introversion). He said that successful umpires were also adept at managing difficult situations and that they adopted a forceful approach and thick skin early in their careers.[29]

When the National and American leagues combined into Major League Baseball, the new organization committed to make improvements in the health and conditioning of umpires, beginning with the hiring of Mark Letendre. In addition to addressing injuries, recommendations regarding nutrition, physical, and emotional health are all key to an ongoing program of wellness care.

NOTES

1   Dave Anderson, "Sports of the Times; Will Baseball Make the Call for Umpires?" *New York Times*, April 4, 1996.

2   Teddy Greenstein, "Baseball's Weighty Issue," *Chicago Tribune*, April 7, 1996.

3   Ibid.

4   Richard Goldstein, "Eric Gregg, Umpire Who Battled Weight Problems, Dies at 55," *New York Times*, June 6, 2006.

5   Anderson.

6   Greenstein.

7   Umpire Executives, MLB.com, mlb.mlb.com/mlb/official_info/ umpires/executives.jsp. Accessed January 17, 2017. See the article on Mark Letendre in this book.

8   Steven Dorsey, interview with Bill Nowlin, January 13, 2017.

9   Brian McKenna, *Early Exits: The Premature Endings of Baseball Careers* (Lanham, Maryland: Scarecrow Press, 2007), 56.

10 Umpire Changes During Games (Injury), Retrosheet, retrosheet. org/Research/VincentD/umpgmchg.htm. Accessed January 17, 2017.

11 Larry Gerlach, "Death on the Diamond: The Cal Drummond Story," *The National Pastime* 1, no. 24 (2004): 14-16.

12 "Ziggy Sears Sues Dallas Ball Club," *Bonham* (Texas) *Daily Favorite*, April 3, 1953.

13 Umpire Changes During Games (Injury).

14 Ibid.

15 Ibid.

16 David Vincent, "So, You Want to Be an Umpire?: Retrosheet, retrosheet.org/Research/VincentD/UmpireStories.pdf. Accessed January 22, 2017.

17 Alyson Footer, "Veteran MLB Umpire Bell, 48, Dies of Heart Attack," MLB.com, m.mlb.com/news/article/62954126//. October 15, 2013. Accessed January 17, 2017.

18 "Bill Kunkel, Former Pitcher and Umpire, Is Dead at 48," *New York Times*, May 5, 1985.

19 Ira Berkow, "Sports of the Times; Lee Weyer's Eyeglasses," *New York Times*, July 8, 1988.

20 Jerome Holtzman, "Weyer Had Ball Calling Ballgames," *Chicago Tribune*, July 7, 1988.

21 Ira Berkow, "Baseball; An Umpire with Everything in Perspective," *New York Times*, August 6, 2003.

22 Donald Wells, *Baseball's Western Front: The Pacific Coast League During World War II* (Jefferson, North Carolina: McFarland, 2004), 39.

23 Famous People with Diabetes, Diabetes Daily, diabetesdaily. com/learn-about-diabetes/diabetes-and-work-life-play/famous-people-with-diabetes/. Accessed January 17, 2017.

24 Larry R. Gerlach, *The Men in Blue: Conversations with Umpires* (Lincoln, Nebraska: University of Nebraska Press, 1980), 183-184.

25 McKenna, 81.

26 Barry Meisel, "No One Knows Forces That Drove Ex-Ump Luciano to Take His Life," *Seattle Times*, January 27, 1995.

27 Charlie Bevis, *The New England League: A Baseball History, 1885-1949* (Jefferson, North Carolina: McFarland, 2008), 139.

28 See the article on Ted Barrett in this book.

29 Holtzman.

Mark A. Letendre—Director, Umpire Medical Services

By Bill Nowlin

In October 1999, as part of the merging of the National League and American League into Major League Baseball, the decision was made to create a unified approach to look after the health and wellness of major-league umpires. Under the auspices of the Office of the Commissioner, Sandy Alderson and Ralph Nelson reached out to Mark Letendre and ask him to develop and oversee the first comprehensive athletic health care program for Major League Baseball umpires. It was, Letendre believes, the first such health and wellness program developed in any major professional sport.

Letendre had 22 years of experience at the time working as an athletic trainer for the New York Yankees (including four years in their minor-league system) and the San Francisco Giants. He had been a certified member of the National Athletic Trainers Association since 1979 and is a charter member of the Professional Baseball Athletic Trainers Society. Mark served as the

National League athletic trainer at the 1987 and 1994 All-Star Games.

The year before his appointment, in 1998, he had been honored by the National Spit Tobacco Education Program (NSTEP) for his efforts to educate players and umpires on the effects of spit tobacco.

Letendre is native of Manchester, New Hampshire and a 1978 graduate of the University of Maine—Orono, where he received a B.S. in Physical Education and Health, and immediately became involved in working in baseball.

He worked as athletic trainer for the Giants right through the 1999 season, its final season before moving to the new downtown stadium currently named AT&T Park; as Mark puts it, "I closed out Candlestick."[1]

This new program was an innovative one. It is Letendre's understanding that he was the first certified athletic trainer in the history of professional sports. The NBA now has a similar position, but they did not at the time. Major League Baseball was the first to make the move.

Leaving the Giants at the time he did means that Letendre cannot boast three recent World Championship rings. There had been a certain comfort in working for a team. But the new position was a challenge to which he looked forward. It was clear that umpires needed more attention to wellness and health, and as he says, philosophically, "You know, it's probably best. They've got a quality medical team that got them to the World Series."

Today's major-league umpires greatly appreciate the benefits the program has accorded them. Tim Welke, who has umpired in the major leagues since 1983, said, "The health and welfare of the umpires has just turned into something outstanding. It's a demanding job. The guys are healthier today. [Mark] oversees that. He's done a terrific job maintaining people. It's improved tenfold. He's done a terrific job at that. In the old days, when you'd get hit in the face mask with a foul ball, you'd just kind of blow it off. Now they're concerned about concussions. And guys' backs and necks and knees and all the components. And quality of life is mentioned; that's something that's really important."[2]

Letendre discusses the wear and tear of the job. "By nature, these guys don't break down. They wear down. That's due to the repetitive nature of the job. Now if I could extrapolate that, you begin in the minor leagues where they begin working every other day behind home plate, because there's only two umpires at Single A. They may be in a three-man crew at Double A. Sometimes four-man, before they get to the big leagues. The aggregate amount of squatting—and, more importantly, standing—3 ½ hours a day times 132 games at the major-league level. If you look at Tim Welke's career, how many years has he had at the major-league level? Plus his minor-league career. It's staggering to think that he could have squatted approaching a million times."

Indeed, MLB recognizes this aspect of umpiring with an annual Squats Crown. In the year 2014, there was a total of 707,176 squats by home plate umpires. The average number of pitches per game that year was 264.7. The 2014 Squats Champion was Tripp Gibson, with 10,757 home plate squats. He averaged 290.7 pitches per game in his 37 plate assignments that year. The 2015 *MLB Umpire Media Guide* presents past squats leaders:

Jeff Nelson (10,471) in 2003; Chuck Meriwether (11,570) in 2004; Jerry Layne (10,727) in 2005; Greg Gibson (11,075) in 2006; Randy Marsh (11,008) in 2007; Alfonso Marquez (11,254) in 2008; Tim McClelland (11,417) in 2009; Bob Davidson (11,064) in 2010; Joe West (10,914) in 2011; Gary Darling (11,216) in 2012; and Brian Knight (10,950) in 2013.

In 2015, Joe West again won the Squats Crown, with 10,331. West averaged 295.2 pitchers per game in his 35 plate assignments. And in 2016, West repeated with 9,814 squats (306.7 pitches per game) in 32 plate assignments.

Concussions have been receiving a great deal more attention throughout both amateur and professional sports in recent years, particularly in football and soccer.

Mark discusses the subject: "Head blows are obviously a concern, as well as the rest of the body. Soft tissue is the number one injury that occurs, from balls and bats going into the body." He noted that a good deal of what we have learned about concussions comes from medical experience from the military. A considerable number of soldiers suffer concussive events such as IED explosions. As we know, concussions may come from one big hit, but can also come from the frequency of many small hits.

Taking a ball off an arm is another example of soft tissue injury. "Yes, and though it would be painful and debilitating, it's not the same as with what we're learning about head assault." In late 2015, the U.S. Soccer Federation banned headers for players 10 and under. "There is a discernible difference between the myelinated brain, which has the adult hormone kicking in, and the pre-myelinated brain which is the young kid who hasn't quite had maturity yet. What we're finding is that it's more of a question mark. When you have questions, the safest thing to do is to eliminate what you think could be harmful—and that would be heading in youth sports, which I think is a wonderful idea. The term is 'no header/no-brainer.'

"I'm happy to see what we're doing with youth. It's more proactive, preventative. Even if we don't have the science to completely support, the science has started to lean that way; we're doing more harm than good [not to take action.]"

One of the things the MLB program does it to baseline each individual umpire. Letendre started doing that in the program in the year 2000. On the player side, neuro-psych baselining has been mandated for the past 10 years or so. For umpires, he says, "We baseline everybody. We also—and this is where it gets a little tricky, where some people get sensitive, on what we administer for our pre-employment physical. There's three domains to an injury now. There's the neuro-psych part, which is the brain. Vestibular balance, which is the inner ear. And there's a vision piece of it, because the cranial nerves to the brain come up the back of the head and control eye movement. The six movements of the eye are controlled by the cranial nerves that are exposed at the back of your head, so any kind of a head blow—and this is where things have taken quantum leaps in regards to understanding that there's three kinds of injuries that can occur to the head, not just brain injury.

"We do baseline pysch. We do baseline vestibular balance. We do baseline vision."

Because of the Triple-A call-up umpires, the program Letendre oversees includes more than just the 76-plus umpires working at the major-league level. With the call-ups, it may round out to between 90-100 umpires. He explains, however, that "the minor leagues have also hired a certified athletic trainer who is the coordinator of minor-league umpires. His name is Mark Stubblefield. Mark and I split duties between the minor-league callups."

The average major-league umpire has mandated vacation time built into his schedule these days; he works 132 games. The opportunity to work in Replay for a couple of weeks during the season helps, too.

"Replay has been an absolute guardian angel for the Medical Services Department. Now they're buying two more weeks of rest. Realistically, it's the demand of standing that's the #1 physically most demanding thing. Three and a half hours a day. It's unbelievable."

After all, no one ever sees an umpire sit down on the field for half any inning! "No, sir. I have had some well-meaning fans suggest that between innings, the ball or batboys run out the little walking stick seats that they can watch golf sitting on. We haven't had too much traction on that."

Asked about the spit tobacco campaign, Mark replied, "In the late '80's, I started the spit tobacco campaign in baseball, with the help of Al Rosen and owner Bob Lurie. They were the first team to kind of implement that. Since then, there's been major improvement in major-league and minor-league baseball, and NCAA and high school. Yet there's still addiction, so we can't say we've got our arms around everything."

Umpires are subject to the same pressures as the rest of us, and more. Ted Barrett, who has umpired in the majors beginning in 1994, wrote a doctoral dissertation for Trinity Theological Seminary which looked into some of the stressors attendant on the profession. To provide grounding for his dissertation, Barrett began with the words "It is said the job of the umpire is to start out perfect and get better." Umpires must work away from the ideally supportive environment of home, family, and neighbors. And with the games played out in front of large audiences, both in person and through television, it's fair to say, as he does, "The arbiters of major league games are under unprecedented scrutiny and pressure." Under all the stresses of the job, it is not surprising that in

their personal lives "some umpires fall into destructive behavior patterns."[3]

Major League Baseball has also worked to address the needs of umpires in this area as well. Dr. Laurence M. Westreich is the President of the American Academy of Addiction Psychiatry, and serves as the consultant on behavioral health and addiction to the Commissioner of Major League Baseball.

Umpires definitely appreciate the care and dedication Mark Letendre and his staff bring to their work. Umpire Paul Schrieber, whose first games in the majors were in 1997, says, "He's an amazing resource for us. Anything you call him about—anything—he's on top of it. 'My knee hurts.' 'OK, you've got to do this, this, this, this. I'm going to set you up with this doctor….' 'My filling fell out of my teeth.' 'OK, I've got the team dentist. You're going to meet at this time. Here are the directions. Give him a ring.' He's really a great resource. "

Mark's office will check in with any umpire who has been struck by a ball. "Yes, we have communications with the observers and supervisors in the stands. Of course, the replay department also notifies me if there is a blow to any part of the body." He will talk with the umpire, "and I'll refer out to our medical consultant, Dr. Steven Erickson. He is the primary care sports medicine physician based out of Phoenix. If an injury or illness should occur, [the home team physicians will get involved.] They're in charge of the emergent phase of that injury or illness. Then they contact me and Steve and I put together a plan of what is needed for the umpire. We have a virtual network from Seattle to Miami, from San Diego to Boston, and Toronto. And all parts in between."

And if a game is played overseas, such as when the Red Sox and Oakland A's opened in Tokyo in 2008? "Typically, the teams will take their own American physicians with them, but we're backed up there. We do have a good relationship with the Japanese league."

Major League Baseball seems to have all the bases covered, so to speak, and has given Letendre all the tools he has needed.

"We've been very blessed with their support. It's an organic program, though. It's not static. And it grows according to the roster. When we first took over, we had a lot of older umpires so we had to gauge our program for wellness and health to a more aged population. Now we've started to become younger and as we do that, we can go into more of a preventative type of program because they're younger."

Interviews with umpires show that they tend to select hotels which have a good exercise room and pool.

"Yes, gym facilities and swimming pools. We're trying to prevent them wearing down and in working out, swimming pools are our best ally because they're non-impact conditioning. They get enough pounding on the body during the game and during the season. It's a cumulative type of thing.

The results are incremental, of course, but it was suggested to Letendre that he must be gratified to see some of the results.

"It's a long-range approach to gratification, because I want to be sure that when they leave the game, there's quality of life on the back side.

"By and large, as we're seeing with replay, these guys have God-given talent you and I lack. They're seeing it one-time, real-time, fast-time, and still getting a preponderance of calls correct.

"I have yet to meet an umpire in my 16 years in this job who wants to go off the field without making sure that both teams got an honest game adjudicated and that every call was correct. And so, with the advent of replay, even though there is a kind of immediate blow to ego, that quickly resolves, because they know leaving the field that everything was adjudicated correctly."

In 2011, Letendre was honored with the prestigious PBATS President's Distinguished Service Award at the Baseball Winter Meetings in Dallas, Texas. In addition, he was inducted into the Hall of Fame of the Boys' and Girls Club of Manchester, New Hampshire. In 2011, Mark was the recipient of the President Abram W. Harris Outstanding Alumni Award by the University of Maine Foundation in 2014. He was recently recognized by the Professional Baseball Chiropractic Society with their Annual Visionary Award.

Mark is a member of the Scottsdale Charros, a civic group, and is on the board of Trustees for the Boys & Girls Club of Greater Scottsdale Foundation. Letendre also serves on the Board of Directors with the Baseball Assistance Team (B.A.T.), Major League Baseball's charitable organization dedicated to assisting members of the "baseball family" through financial grants, healthcare programs and rehabilitative counseling.

SOURCES

Thanks to the *2015* and *2016 MLB Umpire Media Guides,* edited by Michael Teevan and Donald Muller. Thanks as well to Mark Letendre and Mike Teevan for looking over this article.

NOTES

1   All quotations from Mark Letendre come from an interview on November 13, 2015, unless otherwise indicated.

2   Interview with Tim Welke, July 30, 2015.

3   Edward G. Barrett, *An Investigation of Faith As A Life Principle in the Lives of Major League Umpires* (Newburgh, Indiana: Trinity Theological Seminary, 2013), 2, 4, 6.

Interview with Kevin Gregg, Director of Media Relations, Boston Red Sox

Red Sox Director of Media Relations Kevin Gregg (since 2013) is son of former National League umpire Eric Gregg, who first worked in the majors in 1976 until the umpire strike in 1999. Eric Gregg's autobiography, *Working the Plate*, written with Marty Appel, provides the story of his life up to 1990, the year of its publication.

Kevin Gregg: I was born in April 1980. I'm the second of four in my family. An older brother, Eric, then a sister, Ashley, and another brother, Jamie.

BN: Your dad was well-established in the National League, then, by the time you were born.

The whole time you grew up, your father was a major-league umpire. What was that like growing up?

KG: Oh, my God. It was amazing. I loved every second of it because I was immersed in baseball. Totally. Spring training, regular season, postseason. My earliest memories were meeting other umpires, meeting players, taking pictures with players. As a kid, there was stuff I didn't realize was happening but I would later see in pictures—Pete Rose, Darryl Strawberry, Mike Schmidt—all these greats that I met. And also other umpires—Rich Garcia, Terry Tata, Frank Pulli, all these guys while I was growing up. It was just awesome.

Naturally, I gravitated toward baseball. I just wanted to do anything I could related to baseball. I loved it, absolutely loved it.

BN: Thinking of peer reaction as you were growing up, did all the kids think it was pretty cool that your dad was a big-league umpire?

KG: Oh, definitely. Definitely. I was always getting asked for tickets or baseball advice or stories. And Dad would always allow me to bring friends to

Veterans Stadium for games. Almost every time my dad would have a game at Shea Stadium, he would stay [at home] in Philly and drive. He'd take me out of school at about 2 PM, drive up to the game, and come home like 1 in the morning. Then I'd go back to school, and we'd do it again the next day.

BN: When you were young and your father was umpiring, did you hear some abuse hurled his way? What was that like, maybe having people say hurtful things about your own father?

KG: The comments I heard were at Shea Stadium or Veteran's Stadium, and it was just when something went against the home team. There was never anything personal. It was just like, "Well, that's a terrible call" or "This guy's blind." Stuff like that. At the time, when you're 10 years old, you're kind of….

BN: But you knew it was your father making the call.

KG: It was typically a play at home plate, or a call at one of the bases when he was there. There was one time in Philly—just a little thing—when a guy said, "That's a terrible call, Blue"—I hate when they call umpires "Blue," by the way. He said, "That's a terrible call, Blue." And somebody said, "Hey, that's the guy from Philly." I thought, "Well, at least they know who he is." I remember that sometimes I would look to see if I could see the person who was saying something, if they were near me. If my mom was with us, she'd say, "Don't pay them no mind." But I never heard anything that was so bad.

[Kevin said he never heard anything really over the top, but became aware later that his father "definitely got some death threats after the '97 NLCS. I remember seeing letters, from Braves fans after the '97 NLCS. I definitely saw some nasty stuff." His parents shielded their kids from that at the time.]

BN: You were in and out of the umpires' room….

Kevin Gregg, Director of Media Relations, Boston Red Sox.

KG: Oh, absolutely. All over the National League. I remember when I knew I was hooked on baseball is when I was 11 years old. My older brother—two years older than me—went to summer camp up here in New Hampshire on Lake Winnipesauke. I didn't want to go, because I knew I could travel with my dad. One summer we did a bunch of different trips. We did San Fran, San Diego—just he and I—then we did Atlanta, New York, Montreal....

My dad handed me 20 bucks at like 5 o'clock. I'd stand at the batting cage and throw balls, hit balls, go in the locker room, or go up in the stands and just wander around all by myself. I loved it. That's when I knew I wanted to be in baseball.

BN: Did you ever think about becoming an umpire?

KG: I thought about it. He and I never talked about it. I thought about it, but just like any kid, I just wanted to play.

BN: Of course, with the 1999 strike, he was gone.

KG: I was in college when that happened, yeah. I graduated high school in June 1998. I always wanted

to play. My younger brother did go to umpire school. He went out to that camp in Compton, California a few years back, but then decided it wasn't for him.

I was a sports management major at James Madison and I needed to do an internship to graduate. My dad knew the general manager at the time of the Sixers, Billy King, from his days at Duke. Billy went to Duke. My dad went to Duke Diet and Fitness Center to lose weight. He got me connected there, so I got a Sixers PR internship—the '02-'03 season.

The Phillies hired me in marketing as a merchandising intern in May 2003. I started two days after I graduated college, in 2003, the last year of Veterans Stadium, and then for the first year of Citizens Bank Park before I became their PR intern.

I PR interned for '04 and then three-quarters of the '05 season before the Sixers had a fulltime job. I went there and I was still at the Sixers when my dad passed [2006] so he never got to see me get back to baseball fulltime.

I was with the Phillies for six seasons. Phillies, from 2007 to '12. Those were great years. 2007 ended a 14-year playoff drought. We went to the World Series in '08 and back to the World Series in '09. Had the best record in the NL in '10 and '11, and then finished at .500 in '12. I was essentially the number two media relations person. Media Relations Assistant, Coordinator, and then Manager.

BN: I saw you come into the umpires' room the other day, to say hello to the umpires. Do you do that on a regular basis?

KG: Yeah, I do. It's two-fold. At baseball, in PR, at the Winter Meetings each year, they urge that the home media director check in with the umpires to make sure they're comfortable and in case there's any media questions after the game. And the other half is knowing the guys that I know. I saw Dan Iassogna the other day. Tom Hallion, the guys who used to work with my father. Gerry Davis. Phil Cuzzi, Angel Hernandez. It's always good to see those guys. CB Bucknor. Some guys have since retired, too—Ed Rapuano...but it's really good to see those guys.

Vic Carapazza, his father-in-law is Rich Garcia. I grew up with Stephanie Garcia, who is married to Vic. When we were kids in spring training, we spent time. This was mostly between the ages of 8-12 years old during spring trainings in Florida. My dad was always based in the Tampa/St. Pete area. We'd go to Richie's house or another umpire's for dinner and catch up then.

It was just so much fun growing up that way. I see what these guys do with their kids now and I grew up a similar way—running on the field after the game, getting chased by security for being in places we probably weren't supposed to be and stuff, collecting baseballs, broken bats, and stuff. A lot of the equipment I used, I got from players—cleats, gloves....

Interview with Kevin Gregg conducted by Bill Nowlin on September 8 and 22, 2015.

"Batter Ump": Basebrawls Involving Umpires

By Larry R. Gerlach

"Kill him! Kill the umpire!' shouted someone on the stand;
And it's likely they'd have killed him had not Casey raised his hand."

Even people not interested in the national pastime are familiar with that homicidal exhortation from Ernest Thayer's 1888 poem, "Casey at the Bat." While murderous rhetoric has never become a reality, umpires throughout history have been subjected to pejorative pronouncements as well as physical abuse. This essay is not concerned with the rhubarbs—the vituperative, often profane arguments that have so delighted and excited spectators. Neither is it about bodily harm suffered incident to the game—contusions, concussions and broken bones from being struck by thrown or batted balls. The concern here is with the violent physical assaults on and off the field inflicted upon the game's arbiters by players, managers and fans. And vice-versa.[1]

Bumped, jostled, punched, kicked, spiked, thrown to the ground, and spat upon, umpires have been subjected to far more corporeal abuse than officials in any other sport. It has always been thus.[2] Even during the game's formative years, the 1840s and 1850s, the club protocol of "gentlemanly behavior" was frequently breached as players were fined for swearing and disputing the umpire's decision—no doubt often redundant occurrences. Such transgressions increased as revisions of the rules in the 1850s transformed the umpire from an enforcer of decorum to a decision-maker of play itself. In the 1860 *Beadle's* guide, Henry Chadwick underscored newspaper commentary about "these days of finding fault with umpires" by lamenting: "[T]he position of an Umpire is an honorable one, but his duties are anything but agreeable, as it is next to impossible to give entire satisfaction to all parties concerned in a match." Within a genera-

tion the gentleman arbiter had become an enduring folk villain.[3]

Greater responsibility—e.g., calling balls and strikes after 1864—made the umpire an active participant in the game as well as an object of resentment and derision by pay-for-play professional players and the growing number of fans who paid to cheer on the home team. Rampant gambling, alcoholic inhibition, and competition between multiple "major leagues" increased the competitive stakes and thus "rowdy" behavior. Moreover, a single umpire could not always have a clear view of the action, and lack of frequent rotation promoted personal antagonisms. By 1884 it had become "perfectly disgraceful to see the manner in which the umpires are abused in the various cities throughout the United States," and "and unless some decided steps are taken to stop this mob business, it will soon be utterly impossible to find a man who is willing to risk his life in umpiring a game." Tim Hurst spoke for his fellow umpires in being disgusted with the frequency that players, employing "the worst language imaginable," would "kick, howl, threaten, and browbeat," even "threaten to lick an umpire after the game."[4]

While verbal vituperation and threats of violence far surpassed actual violence—perhaps because most umpires were former players and thus protected by a brotherhood code—physical altercations sporadically erupted. The most egregious early assault on an umpire occurred on July 11, 1886, when George "Foghorn" Bradley was first pelted with beer glasses and then viciously pummeled by both players and fans who descended onto the field. Umpires sometimes responded in kind because, as Hurst aptly put it: "Epithets have been hurled at umpires that no man could stand without offering resentment."[5] For example, on July 24, 1873, while serving as a substitute umpire, Bob "Death to Flying Things" Ferguson, player-manager of the New York Atlantics and also president of the National Association, ended a heated exchange with Nat Hicks of the New York Mutuals by breaking the catcher's arm with a bat.

The most combative arbiter was Hurst, a former boxer and fight referee, dubbed "Terrible Tim" for his temper and "Sir Timothy" for his umpiring ability. Never the aggressor but frequently the retaliator, in 1892 he flattened both an abusive player and a police officer with his mask, and in 1896 decked two Pirates players after the game with rights to the jaw. His most (in)famous encounter occurred on August 4, 1897, a few days after a fistfight with Reds catcher Henry "Heinie" Peitz when fans in Cincinnati showered him with beer steins. Struck in the back, Hurst fired one of the mugs back into the stands, skulling an innocent bystander. (He subsequently paid a fine for assault and battery.)

Berating umpires was actually encouraged. Nicholas "Nick" Young, a former umpire in the National Association from 1871-1873, admitted that during his tenure as president of the National League from 1885 to 1902, club owners, who routinely paid players' fines, "believed that to stop the players from baiting the umpire would be a detriment to the game" because "it amused the spectators to see an official hauled and pushed about by a lot of players, and when it was suggested that this sort of a practice be eliminated, it was argued that it would kill the sport."[6] (No doubt the contemporaneous popularity of football and prizefighting contributed to spectators' vicarious enjoyment of unabashed displays of violent behavior.)

Increased rowdyism prompted Henry Chadwick to rue in the 1895 *Spalding Guide* the increased "kicking," "blackguard language," and "brutal assaults on umpire and players." Sportswriter Tim Murnane predicted: "The time will soon come when no person above the rank of garrotter can be secured to umpire a game."[7] And Young admitted in 1897 that he had become "very badly off for umpires and don't know where to look for recruits."[8]

Not surprisingly, the league's laissez-faire attitude resulted in a period of unprecedented violence that continued through the turn of the twentieth century.[9] It began in 1897 when Jack Sheridan, who had been hit by rotten eggs in St. Louis and Pittsburgh, was cold-cocked by Pirates pitcher Emerson "Pink" Hawley; John Kelly and Hank O'Day were hit by balls thrown by angry players; and Tom Lynch, the target of glassware in Louisville, on August 8 smacked Baltimore's John "Dirty Jack" Doyle "fairly between the eyes" when the foul-mouthed player used an epithet "too much to be endured, even by an umpire."[10] Notable fracases in subsequent seasons included Doyle slugging Bob Emslie on July 4, 1900; Roger Bresnahan punching Bill Klem in the face on June 23, 1901; and Tommy Connolly being thrown to the ground by Detroit catcher Frederick "Fritz" Buelow on May 4, 1902, and, having to seek refuge in the Baltimore groundskeepers' office for over an hour after being mobbed by fans after a game on August 21. In 1905 Tiger fans on August 22 mobbed ump Jack Sheridan, chasing him to the clubhouse, whereupon he forfeited the game to the Senators, and on August 30 disgruntled fans punched and kicked Jim Johnstone in the face on his way to the ballpark. Norman "Kid" Elberfeld, dubbed "The Tabasco Kid," was reputedly "the dirtiest, scrappiest, most pestiferous, most cantankerous [sic], most rambunctious ball player that ever stood on spikes." Elberfeld once threw mud into the open mouth of an umpire, and in 1906 twice attacked umpire Silk O'Loughlin, trying to hit him with a bat on August 8 and on September 3 attempting six times to spike his foot in what the *New York Times* termed "one of the most disgraceful exhibitions of rowdyism ever witnessed on a baseball field."[11]

The umps sometimes lost control. On May 7, 1909, when Elberfeld jabbed Tim Hurst in the abdomen after being called out at home, the umpire smacked the player's jaw with his mask. (American League President Ban Johnson suspended Hurst until May 13.) Three months later, on August 3, Hurst was involved in a career-ending set-to with Philadelphia's Eddie Collins. The future Hall of Famer understandably argued being called out attempting to advance to second base after a fly out in the eighth inning of

Babe Pinelli in a rhubarb at Ebbets Field in 1943.

the second game of a doubleheader as the Boston second baseman had dropped the ball. The player's commentary is unknown, but the umpire, perhaps weary after 17 innings over nearly four hours, expectorated tobacco-laden saliva at Collins, causing a near-riot as fans poured onto the field. (Johnson, who had suspended Hurst indefinitely on August 5, fired him on August 18.)

In 1909 there were 355 physical assaults in professional baseball by players and fans.[12] League officials finally decided enough was enough.

Byron Bancroft "Ban" Johnson, president of the American League when it gained major-league status in 1901, continued his efforts begun as head of the Western League in 1893 to curb the rowdiness by investing umpires with increased on-field authority and support from league officials as well as demanding greater mutual respect from both players and arbiters. Subsequently, as president of the National League 1910-1913, Tom Lynch, a former major-league umpire (1888-1902), likewise pledged to curb rowdiness by supporting umpires and increasing penalties for of-

fending players and managers, a policy continued by another NL president, John Heydler (1918-1934), who also had umpired (1895-1898). Perhaps more important than official pronouncements was the adoption of a second umpire by the American League in 1909, standard in both leagues in 1912, followed by a three-man crew in 1933, which provided better positioning to make calls behind the plate and on the bases, thereby reducing controversies. (Note: The deferential title in box scores of single umpires as "Mr." and members of two-man crews as "Messrs." was dropped by the 1930s.)

Still, rowdyism remained an ingrained part of the game, eagerly anticipated and enjoyed by many fans. Incidents of umpire-baiting and fisticuffs declined appreciably in the American League, in no small measure due to the example of its diplomatic chief umpire, Tommy Connolly, but persisted to a significant degree in the National League, reflecting both the aggressive style and confrontational demeanor of the likes of John McGraw, Leo "The Lip" Durocher, and the pugnacious St. Louis Cardinals "Gashouse Gang" led by Frankie Frisch, as well as the authoritarian bearing of umpires like Bill Klem and John "Beans" Reardon. Reardon admitted that he responded in kind: "I'd give it back to them a little better than they gave it to me. I could use profanity, and I blasted them pretty good."[13]

Umpire responses to vituperative challenges were not only verbal. In 1915 when Buck Herzog on May 1 shoved Cy Rigler in the chest and spiked his foot, the ump hit the Cincinnati manager in the face with his mask, opening a gash over the right eye, and then decked him with a hard right; and on July 24 Ernie Quigley decked Johnny Evers after he spiked the umpire's foot. In a game on June 23, 1917, Clarence "Brick" Owens, who got his nickname after being skulled by a brick in the minor leagues, called four consecutive balls on the first batter. The incensed Red Sox pitcher, Babe Ruth, charged the plate, bellowing: "Throw me out and I'll punch ya right in the jaw." Owens did. So did the Babe. Reliever Ernie Shore then retired the baserunner and then the next 26 Washington batters

Umpire bearing the brunt of hostile fan reaction.

to complete a combined no-hitter, Ruth's errant start spoiling an otherwise perfect game.

Fisticuffs were not limited to the diamond. On September 24, 1911, Billy Evans, while heading to the clubhouse, was cursed and beaten by fans before being rescued by police. He was also involved in the best-known postgame pugilistic encounter. On September 15, 1921, Evans and Ty Cobb settled their disagreement over a third-strike call under the stands at Griffith Stadium in Washington. Cobb had threatened to "whip" Evans at home plate, but the umpire invited him to try after the game at the umpires' dressing room. Players from both teams encircled the combatants as they viciously bloodied each other before shaking hands, their manhood intact. Cobb was suspended for one game, while a bandaged Evans continued umpiring. On Memorial Day, May 30, 1932, umpire George Moriarty, a former boxer and combative player with the Detroit Tigers, took exception to the heckling of Chicago players as he left the field after a game in Cleveland, decking Mike Gaston, breaking his hand in the process, before being beaten badly by player-manager Lew Fonseca and catchers Charlie Berry and Frank Grube.

Tussles between umpires and fans on the diamond were infrequent due to increased security. The most notable incident occurred on September 16, 1940, when a Dodgers fan, 21-year-old Frank Germano, yelling, "Burglar! Burglar!" leaped onto the field and tackled first-base umpire George Magerkuth to the ground. Better known than the episode is the newspaper photo showing the combatants trading blows on the ground while security personnel stand by. It was not Maje's last altercation with a fan. On July 19, 1945, he went into the stands to retaliate for repeatedly being called a "thief" and a "robber," but regrettably struck the wrong man.

Missiles thrown from the stands, especially beer and pop bottles, endangered life and limb. Beans Reardon was right: "[I]t was like putting weapons in the hands of imbeciles."[14] On June 9, 1906, Klem escaped serious injury after being hit with seat cushions and pop bottles, but a year later, September 15, 1907, Evans suffered a near-fatal fractured skull when struck by a bottle in St. Louis. Connolly was hit in the mouth by a bottle during an argument with Ty Cobb on September 11, 1912. Among those struck by the barrage of bottles thrown in Cleveland on May 11, 1929, were Philadelphia Athletics shortstop Joe Boley, hit in the back of his head; umpire Emmett "Red" Ormsby, who suffered a severe concussion that almost killed him; and a fan, Lee Porter, who died three days later from his injury.

Talk of banning bottled beverages at ballparks came to naught. Bill Summers had to quit the field when struck in the groin by a whiskey bottle on July 26, 1936. Pop bottles continued to fly, sometimes a massive barrage, as in Cincinnati on July 17, 1935, and in Ebbets Field on July 26, 1938. In addition to glassware, fans hurled seat cushions, rotten fruit and vegetables, cans, and assorted debris including a woman's shoe hurled at Charlie Berry in September 1945. In Philadelphia on August 21, 1949, Lee Ballanfant was hit in the mouth by a pop bottle and Al Barlick in the leg by "an over-ripe tomato" during a 15-minute brawl that resulted in a forfeit to the New York Giants, the first in the major leagues since 1942.

The umpires stoically endured the hails of debris. On July 21, 1935, Joe Rue received "a shower of pop bottles, partly eaten fruit, half-smoked cigars, rolled newspapers and scorecards, the like of which has never before been seen either at the (Yankee) Stadium or the Polo Grounds." Although a bottle missed his head "by a scant inch or two," Rue said: "I stood my ground at the plate, maybe a bit foolishly, but only because I was so absolutely right in my decision."[15]

While commenting on the fusillade directed at Rue, sports columnist John Kieran decried bottle-tossing at games, but disingenuously said the problem was not bottles, but disorderly fans. Wiser heads prevailed. The lead in banning bottles from ballparks came, appropriately from St. Louis, where Sportsman's Park had long led the majors in bottle-tossing. In response to a massive bottle-throwing episode in the Browns-Yankees game on April 18, 1953, the Cardinals and Browns announced on May 2 that henceforth beverages at Busch Stadium would be sold in paper cups. Other clubs subsequently followed suit.[16]

Less hurtful, if disgusting, was spittle. When umpires donned white pants on Sundays in the late 1920s and early 1930s, players routinely decorated the back of their pants legs with tobacco juice, and on July 15, 1939, New York Giants shortstop Billy Jurges and George Magerkurth exchanged wads of saliva and clenched fists over a disputed foul-ball call.

Joe Rue, an AL umpire from 1938 to 1947, summed up the treatment and character of umpires during the rough-and tumble first half of the twentieth century: "I've been mobbed, cussed, booed, kicked in the ass, punched in the face, hit with mud balls and whiskey bottles, and had everything from shoes to fruits and vegetables thrown at me. I've been hospitalized with a concussion and broken ribs. I've been spit on and soaked with lime and water. I've probably experienced more violence than any other umpire who ever lived. But I've never been called a homer."[17]

Diamond disruptions declined dramatically after World War II. The advent of the four-man crew in 1952 further reduced questionable decisions on the basepaths, the advent of accredited umpire schools formalized professional conduct, and the onset of unionization for both players and umpires brought about increased salaries and greater job security. Confrontations between players soon devolved more to milling about and shouting than actual fighting, and the histrionic, often comically childish tantrums of managerial hotheads like Bobby Cox, Billy Martin, and Earl Weaver that replaced the spirited donnybrooks of yore ultimately were virtually eliminated by the advent of instant replay. Littering the field with debris, once commonplace, became rare, even after egregiously wrong calls such as Don Denkinger's in the 1985 World Series. Lengthy suspensions and substantial fines for even the slightest contact essentially eliminated attacks on umpires.

Mother, may I slug the umpire
May I slug him right away?
So he cannot be here, Mother
When the clubs begin to play?

Let me clasp his throat, dear Mother,
In a dear delightful grip
With one hand and with the other
Bat him several in the lip.

Let me climb his frame, dear Mother,
While the happy people shout;
I'll not kill him, dearest Mother
I will only knock him out.

Let me mop the ground up, Mother,
With his person, dearest do;
If the ground can stand it, Mother
I don't see why you can't, too.

Mother may I slug the umpire,
Slug him right between the eyes?
If you let me do it, Mother
You shall have the champion prize.

Chicago Daily Tribune, 1886.

Still, given the competitive nature of sport, confrontations periodically occurred.

In July 1960, a Kansas City fan jumped onto the field, tapped home-plate ump Bob Stewart on the shoulder and then decked him with a punch. Pittsburgh's Bill "Mad Dog" Madlock on May 1, 1980, shoved his glove into Jerry Crawford's face after being called out on strikes with the bases loaded. In the seventh inning of an AL East playoff game in New York City on October 9, 1981, a fan, upset by Mike Reilly's call at third base the previous inning, leaped over the railing and knocked the umpire to the ground. When Lanny Harris tried to separate Atlanta's Claudell Washington and Cincinnati's Mario Soto during a confrontation on June 16, 1984, he was mistakenly hit by a ball Soto intended for Washington, who then threw the umpire down. On April 30, 1988, Cincinnati manager Pete Rose shoved Dave Pallone several times, later erroneously claiming the umpire had poked him in the eye; Rose was suspended for 30 games and fined $10,000. The last on-field assault occurred on April 15, 2003, when a fan came out of the stands at Comiskey Park and tried unsuccessfully to tackle first-base umpire Laz Diaz.

During a time when several umpires were known for being quick-tempered, "Cowboy Joe" West was the most often involved in physical altercations. He was suspended for three days and fined $500 for shoving Atlanta manager Joe Torre outside the umpires' dressing room after a game on June 28, 1983; got involved in a postgame shoving match with Cincinnati player Ron Oester and manager Pete Rose on August 15, 1989; threw Philadelphia pitcher Dennis Cook to the ground during an on-field brawl on August 9, 1990; argued heatedly on July 23, 1991, with the Cubs' Andre Dawson, resulting in the player being suspended for one game and fined $1,000 for bumping the umpire; and on September 14, 2014, grabbed Philly pitcher Jonathan Papelbon's jersey during an argument.

During the first half of the twentieth century, umpire decisions not infrequently led to the disruption of play when irate fans strewed the field with thrown debris or stormed the field, occasionally resulting in forfeitures. Such occurrences, such as angry fans throwing promotional baseballs onto the field in Los Angeles on August 10, 1995, causing the first National League forfeited game in 41 years, and the October 14, 2015, littering of the diamond with trash including beer cans and water bottles in Toronto, are now rare.

On two other occasions not related to protests over decisions, umpires acted to quell far more serious instances of spectator violence. In the ninth inning of the Ten Cent Beer Night game in Cleveland on June 4, 1974, drunken fans, who had periodically thrown cups and other objects onto the field, poured out of the stands. The resultant uncontrollable melee prompted Nestor Chylak, who needed stitches after being hit in the head with a thrown chair, to forfeit the game to the Texas Rangers. Five years later, on July 12, 1979, during Disco Demolition Night at Comiskey Park in Chicago, fans threw music records, beer cans, and fireworks onto the field during the first game of a doubleheader, then came onto the field after a crate of records was exploded between games. Riot police restored order and groundskeepers cleared away the debris, but the umpires suspended the game because the explosion had torn a large hole in the outfield turf. The next day, AL President Lee MacPhail ruled the game forfeited to the Detroit Tigers because the White Sox had failed to provide suitable playing conditions.

None of the foregoing incidents remotely approached the seriousness of similar pre–World War II encounters. The no-holds-barred verbal and physical confrontations once commonplace on the diamond are now an arcane part of baseball history, and the exhortation "Kill the umpire!" a quaint rhetorical remnant of the game's folklore. But it is instructive to recall with admiration and respect the courage and dedication of the umpires who historically endured abusive behavior on the field and from the stands in order to make it possible to play the game in an orderly, efficient, and proficient manner.

NOTES

1   SABR member Alain Usereau has compiled an invaluable data base of over 3,300 "basebrawls" that chronicles, albeit incompletely, hundreds involving umpires.

2   For the history of umpires and umpiring, see James M. Kahn, *The Umpire Story* (New York: A.S. Barnes, 1947) and Larry R. Gerlach, "Umpires" in John Thorn and Pete Palmer, eds., *Total Baseball* (New York: Warner Books, 1989), 465-469, and "On Umpires: Historical Perspectives, Contemporary Observations," in *NINE: A Journal of Baseball History and Social Policy Perspectives*, 7 (Fall 1998), 16-45.

3   See David Q. Voigt, "America's Manufactured Villain—The Baseball Umpire," *Journal of Popular Culture*, 4 (Summer 1970), 1-21.

4   Quoted in Peter Morris, *Don't Kill the Umpire: How Baseball Escaped Its Violent Past* (Now and Then Reader eBook, 2012).

5   Ibid.

6   Ibid.

7   Rich Eldred, "Umpiring in the 1890s," *The Baseball Research Journal*, 18 (Cleveland: Society for American Baseball Research, 1989), 75.

8   Eldred, 76.

9   In addition to Eldred, 75-78, see David W. Anderson, *You Can't Beat the Hours: Umpires in the Dead Ball Era, 1901-1909* (CreateSpace Independent Publishing Platform, 2013).

10 Eldred, 75.

11 *New York Times*, September 4, 1906.

12 Charles Leerhsen, *Ty Cobb: A Terrible Beauty* (New York: Simon & Schuster, 2015), 331.

13 Larry R. Gerlach, ed., *The Men in Blue: Conversations with Umpires* (New York: Viking Press, 1980), 17.

14 Gerlach, *The Men in Blue*, 19.

15 *New York Times*, July 22, 1935.

16 Both the Cardinals and Browns played in Sportsman's Park; when August Busch bought the ballpark in February 1953, he renamed it Busch Stadium.

17 Gerlach, *The Men in Blue*, 51.

Death On The Diamond

The Cal Drummond Story

By Larry R. Gerlach

The collapse of umpire John McSherry at home plate on April 1, 1996, recalled immediately the fatal beaning death of Ray Chapman in 1920. The latter is, we are told, the lone instance of a game-related fatality in major-league history. To Chapman's fatality on the diamond should be added that of umpire Cal Drummond, who also succumbed to an injury suffered during a baseball game. That Drummond's story is little known is not surprising inasmuch as it received surprisingly little attention at the time, a neglect that is the umpire's lot.

Umpires know well that words will never harm them, but that bats and balls can break their bones. That's why the modern umpire wears steel-reinforced shoes, a chest protector, shin guards and mask when calling balls and strikes. Time and again such protective equipment has shielded the plate umpire from serious injury. Such was not the case with Cal Drummond.

Born on June 29, 1917, in Ninety Six, South Carolina, Calvin Troy Drummond was an outstanding three-sport athlete, playing football, basketball, and baseball at nearby Ninety Six High School, Class of 1938.[1] After serving for five years as an infantryman during World War II, he tried his hand at umpiring. Drummond attended Bill McGowan's umpiring school in 1948 and, after graduation, worked a season in the Class-D Alabama State League.

Drummond retired from baseball for the next three years, then donned the blue serge suit again in 1952. He advanced steadily through the professional ranks—the Georgia State League (Class D) 1952-1953, the South Atlantic League (Class A) 1954-1956, and the International League (Triple A) 1957-1959, reaching the American League in 1960.

Life in the bush leagues was not always pleasant. In 1952, after his partner made two close calls

in Fitzgerald, Georgia, irate fans slashed the tires of their car and poured sand into the gas tank; the deputy sheriff who attempted to prevent the vandalism was slugged.[2] When Drummond's partner in 1957 overruled him on a play at first base, the umpires were pelted with "stones, drinking cups and other debris" until the threat of forfeit restored order.[3]

The American League, following the lead of its supervisor of umpires, ex-professional football player Cal Hubbard, was known for fielding "big" arbiters, but Drummond, at an even 6 feet and 185 pounds, was one of the smaller junior circuit umpires. Nonetheless, he was known for a tough, no-nonsense demeanor, and thick skin. "The worst thing that can happen to a man is to be born without guts and be an umpire," he once said. "No umpire likes criticism, but you don't expect to be patted on the back. Nobody comes to see you. The managers are going to challenge you because that's their job. The writers and the announcers are going to criticize you. That's their job. What it amounts to is you've got your job and they've got theirs."[4]

Drummond was doing his job as the plate umpire on Tuesday, June 10, 1969, as the Baltimore Orioles hosted the California Angels. Sometime during the later innings of the game he was struck on the mask by a foul ball. (At the time umpires wore bar masks, which had no "give" like today's wire masks.) Drummond finished the game, but was later taken to Mercy Hospital, where he lost consciousness for more than a week. The particulars of the incident—the pitcher, the batter, the inning—are not known. Baltimore newspapers made no mention of the happening and did not even note Drummond's hospitalization for almost a week.[5]

Norman Macht's subsequent interviews in 1995 and 1996 with several Orioles who played in the game, including catcher Andy Etchebarren, produced no particulars about the incident.[6] However, Macht did obtain a critical recollection from crew member Larry Barnett; Barnett thought the foul ball occurred "probably late in the game," and said there was no break in the action as none of the umpires came in to check on Drummond. Barnett clearly recalled what happened in the dressing room after the game. "Drummond pulled his belt off and the two ball bags fell to the floor, balls rolling all over the floor. This was noteworthy because Drummond was a very neat, fastidious person who would take off one sock and carefully fold it before taking off the other one, and for him to just pull the belt out of the loops before taking off the ball bags was startling. But nothing was said; they [the umpires] just picked up the balls." Later that night, at the Lord Baltimore Hotel where the umpires were staying, Barnett got a call from crew chief Ed Runge: "I have to take Drummond to the hospital. His speech is slurred; something's wrong."[7]

Something was wrong. Drummond remained unconscious for about a week while doctors considered an operation to relieve the pressure on his brain.[8] Drummond's family rushed to Baltimore, and when his condition improved, had him flown home on June 22. His condition worsened after a few days and he was hospitalized again on June 30. This time doctors operated to remove a blood clot in Drummond's head.[9] Afterward he lay unconscious for two weeks in the intensive-care unit before beginning recuperation.[10]

By early spring 1970 Drummond had recovered enough to contemplate a return to baseball. "Really anxious to get back,"[11] he worked a few local college games as well as a dozen spring-training games in Florida to prepare himself for game conditions; he also threw out the first ball at the home opener of the Greenwood Braves of the Western Carolinas League. He was finally cleared by doctors to resume umpiring after the start of the major-league season. After talking with league President Joe Cronin, Drummond was set to resume his umpiring career by joining a major-league crew in Kansas City. Instead, he was sent to the American Association to work two games before joining his crew in Boston on Sunday, May 3.

Cal Drummond

It was 39 degrees on May Day in Des Moines, Iowa, when Drummond began his comeback by umpiring a series between the Iowa Oaks and the Oklahoma City 89ers.[12] His return was short-lived as he left the game in the second inning "complaining of illness" as well as some dizziness and numbness in the right side of his head. The next day, Saturday, he spoke with Joe Cronin on the telephone, assuring the league president that he was feeling fine and ready to umpire the plate that night.

Drummond called balls and strikes without incident until the end of the seventh inning. At the conclusion of the frame, he went to the Oklahoma City dugout "to rest," saying, "I feel dizzy. I think I'm going to pass out." He then collapsed. Attended to by the Iowa team physician, he gained semiconsciousness in the dressing room before again losing consciousness while being taken by ambulance to the hospital.[13]

Cal Drummond died some four hours later, in the early morning of May 3. An autopsy revealed that he "died of a cerebral infarction [stroke], a decreased blood supply to an area of the brain that required surgery last year."[14] The blow received in Baltimore in June 1969 proved fatal 11 months later. Thus came to an end an umpiring career of 19 years, 10 in the majors which included working the first of two All-Star games in 1961 and the 1966 World Series.

On Sunday, the day of Drummond's death, the American flag flew at half-staff at Des Moines' Sec Taylor Stadium in honor of the deceased arbiter. Iowa Oaks pitcher Fred Talbot, a former major leaguer, paid him the ultimate umpire's accolade: "He did one of the best umpiring jobs I've ever seen. He didn't miss a single pitch on me."[15] Obituaries appropriately did not mention the irony of his death: That 52-year-old Cal Drummond died on the day he had been scheduled to realize his dream of rejoining his American League crew.[16]

The Cal Drummond story is important aside from his tragic death and its place in the annals of baseball necrology. It is also the inspirational story of one man's personal commitment to the umpiring profession and determination to return to the major leagues after a life-threatening injury. It is likewise instructive in that the press, by ignoring the human-interest tale of an umpire who suffered a severe head injury and lay unconscious in the hospital, reflected the long-standing attitude of the public toward those who make playing the game possible.[17]

"Death on the Diamond" originally appeared in *The National Pastime* (2004), 14-16.

NOTES

1 Drummond's *Sporting News* umpire career card says he was born in Greenwood, but local newspapers say Ninety Six. Ninety Six was a small, rural town of 773 in 1920 so he probably regarded Greenwood as his experiential home

2 *The Sporting News*, July 30, 1952.

3 *The Sporting News*, August 14, 1957.

4 *The Sporting News*, May 16, 1970.

5 *Baltimore Evening Sun* and *Baltimore News American*, June 11, 1969; *Baltimore Evening Sun*, June 16, 1969. The *Washington Post* also failed to mention the incident or hospitalization. Veteran umpire Johnny Stevens replaced Drummond, although *The Sporting News* continued to list Drummond on the crew through June 16. Thanks to Joey Beretta for this information.

6 If the incident occurred in the later innings, Angels and Orioles scoresheets indicate that the pitchers and catchers involved were either Pedro Borbon and Ken Tatum, pitchers, and Jim Hicks, catcher for the Angels, or pitcher Marcelino Lopez and catcher Andy Etchebarren for the Orioles.

7 Norman Macht to Larry Gerlach, September 5, 1995.

8 *Baltimore Evening Sun*, June 16, 1969. This notice was the first piece to appear in the Baltimore press about Drummond's condition.

9 *Greenwood* (South Carolina) *Index-Journal*, June 21, July 1 and 12, August 5, 1969; *Baltimore Evening Sun*, July 1, 1969.

10 *Greenville* (South Carolina) *News*, May 4, 1970.

11 *Greenwood Index-Journal*, April 18 and 21, 1970.

12 *Des Moines Register*, May 2, 1970.

13 *Des Moines Register*, May 3, 1970.

14 *Des Moines Register*, May 4, 1970.

15 *Des Moines Register*, May 3 and 4, 1970.

16 The best obituaries are in the *Greenwood Journal-Index*, May 4, 1970; the *Greenville News*, May 4, 1970; and *The Sporting News*, May 16, 1970.

17 At the time of Drummond's hospitalization, the press gave widespread coverage to Jesus Alou's fractured jaw, Denny McLain's hospitalization for "nausea and a headache," Gates Brown's "respiratory infection," Wes Parker's appendectomy, and Reggie Smith's pulled shoulder muscle.

"Helping People Is An Easy Call": The Story of UMPS CARE Charities

By Kevin Cuddihy

UMPS CARE Charities, founded through the compassion of Major League Baseball Umpires, provides financial, in-kind, and emotional support for America's youth and families in need. The 501(c)(3) charity focuses on three main efforts:

1) Major League Baseball experiences for children awaiting adoption and at-risk young in mentoring programs.

2) Build-a-Bear Workshop experiences for children with cancer and other serious illnesses.

3) College scholarships for young adults who were adopted later in life.

The UMPS CARE mission puts into action its established creed, "Helping People Is an Easy Call." Through the youth-based programs, professional umpires enrich the lives of at-risk youth and children coping with serious illness by providing memorable baseball experiences. Through the scholarship initiatives, they offer financial support to children adopted later in life as well as current and former members of the military.

The Beginning: Helping Hands

UMPS CARE Charities started off, in part, as the Helping Hands Fund in 1999. A number of umpires lost their jobs in a negotiation strategy that year, and the fund was created to help out colleagues in financial distress. It was a way for umpires to give back to one of their own in a time of need.

In 2005, however, the group—led by Ted Barrett, Jim Reynolds, Larry Young, and Gary Darling—started looking at expanding its outreach. A conversation with former MLB Commissioner Fay Vincent convinced the umpires to investigate other avenues for giving back. That year also saw the first of the now-annual fundraiser, the Golf Classic, which raised $5,000.

At the same time, Young was in the process of completing the onerous paperwork involved with becoming an official 501(c)(3) charity. During the 2006 umpires union meeting, the charity, now called UMPSCARE, was voted as the official charity of MLB umpires. Young focused on the detail work: Articles of Incorporation, Letter of Exemption, Arizona Charitable Registration, By-Laws, Arizona Foreign Corporation Disclosure, etc.

The search for a new focal point continued as well, and soon attention centered on a charity called BLUE for Kids.

BLUE for Kids

BLUE for Kids got its genesis in 2004 with MLB umpire Marvin Hudson. Samuel Dearth, a former minor-league umpire with Hudson, asked Hudson if he could provide tickets to a game for him and his "little" in the Big Brothers/Big Sisters (BBBS) program. Hudson happily complied and his entire crew greeted the pair for a game and provided a VIP experience.

The following year, each of the umpires in Hudson's crew had moved to a different crew and wanted to recreate the same experience. So Hudson and Dearth reached out to BBBS programs in various MLB cities. "We weren't really doing it a lot, just occasional weekends," explained Dearth. But Hudson and his fellow umps, including Ted Barrett, Mark Wegner, and Mike DiMuro, pushed forward.

In 2006, the group incorporated BLUE for Kids. Around three or four different crews were involved by that time, and the tentacles kept spreading as umpires moved on to new crews. The organization reached out to the Dave Thomas Foundation that year and started the ticket program's focus that remains to this day: kids waiting for adoption.

The group also introduced a new charitable event in 2006, hospital visits with Build-a-Bear Workshops. An umpire crew and the local team's mascot would descend upon a hospital with a full Build-a-Bear Workshop for kids with cancer and other serious illnesses. The group's first hospital visit was at Johns Hopkins in Baltimore, and they did another five that year, nine the following year, and it continued to grow from there.

Coming Together

With UMPSCARE now an official 501(c)(3) charity and the official charity of MLB umpires—and with Fay Vincent's recommendation urging them forward—these two groups started talks about merging and combining resources. And in 2009, UMPSCARE (formerly Helping Hands) and BLUE for Kids merged to form UMPS CARE Charities, with the BLUE Crew ticket program and BLUE for Kids hospital program. Samuel Dearth was installed as the combined charity's first executive director.

Darling was excited about the opportunity. "The merger got us all pulling in the same direction," he said, "and it automatically gave us our programs to get behind." Darling, Young, Hudson, Reynolds, and DiMuro formed the backbone of the organization and soon focused everyone on moving forward.

Today, said Darling, "About 99 percent of the umpires are involved in some fashion, from providing tickets and the meet and greet, to participating in the hospital visits, to playing in or sponsoring the golf tournaments. It's really amazing how much everyone's come together." And with the charity well established, new umpires coming to the big leagues are jumping in with both feet, making for an even stronger charity every single year.

UMPS CARE Programs

As outlined at the start, UMPS CARE Charities focuses on three main programs; two were already in

full force at the merger, with the third to come into existence shortly after.

BLUE Crew Ticket Program

The program that started the original BLUE for Kids charity, the ticket program provides a special day for kids waiting for adoption—a reminder that special days are still possible and an opportunity for bonding between the youth and mentors. Depending on demand, the program provides experiences for kids in multiple stadiums each weekend throughout the entire MLB season.

Each BLUE Crew Ticket VIP experience includes great seats to the ballgame, a goody bag of "all things baseball," and the unique opportunity to step onto the field for a souvenir baseball and photo. The baseball experience is designed to strengthen relationships of at-risk youth and adult caregivers.

Since the program started in 2006, MLB umpires have welcomed more than 6,000 guests to games across the country, with great results. "This was the highlight of our activities together," said one Big Brother in Seattle, while a Big Sister in Colorado reported, "It's so cool that you are able to provide special opportunities like this. We had a really great time!"

BLUE for Kids Hospital Program

The BLUE for Kids Hospital Program remains one of the main programs for UMPS CARE

Umpires Chad Fairchild and Marvin Hudson outside the umpires room at Fenway Park with Big Brothers mentors and their little brothers, May 22, 2016.

Charities and a favorite of many of the umps. Begun in 2006, the charity held events at 13 children's hospitals during the 2016 regular season and then hosted a final event during the World Series.

The BLUE for Kids hospital program brings a crew of major-league umpires to the bedside of children with life-threatening illnesses, and they don't come empty-handed. Each crew brings a Build-a-Bear Workshop experience right to the hospital room!

While a hospital stay can be a frightening time for children and their families, the BLUE for Kids program lifts the spirits of all involved. Children outfit stuffed teddy bears, puppies, or monkeys while sharing high-fives and words of encouragement with the BLUE for Kids crew. When available, the home-team mascot tags along, making it a fun and memorable day.

Through this program UMPS CARE has delivered 1,200 to 1,400 bears annually, and during the 2015 season UMPS CARE put its 100,000th bear into a child's hands since the program's inception.

"Being able to possibly make a contribution and a difference for a day, or just a few moments, by putting a smile on someone's face … it's an honor and a privilege," said Jim Wolf after an event in 2015. "The kids are so great, and courageous."

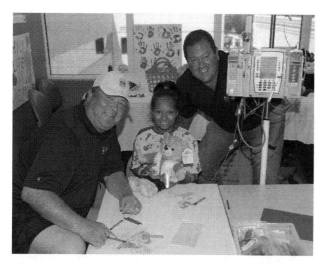

Gerry Davis and Sam Holbrook spend time with a patient at the Children's Hospital of Orange County while delivering Build-A-Bear Workshop experiences.

"This gives us a moment to step back, put everything in perspective and see what's really important," Chad Fairchild told MLB.com after a 2016 event. "It's a great day. Sometimes you feel helpless, but being here, you give back a little bit." The patients and their families, no doubt, would argue it's more than just "a little bit."

UMPS CARE All-Star Scholarship

The UMPS CARE All-Star Scholarship, which debuted in 2010, was the brainchild of Jim Reynolds. "It was definitely something he was passionate about," recalled Darling. For most parents, they start saving for their child's college education at birth. For those generous souls who adopt a child later in life—say, 15 or 16—the cost of college can be an even greater burden. That's why UMPS CARE Charities partnered with the Dave Thomas Foundation for Adoption for the scholarship program.

All-Star Scholarships are open to children adopted at the age of 10 or older to provide increased opportunities for advanced education. Each year one student will be selected to receive the All-Star Scholarship. This student will be eligible to receive up to $7,500 annually to go toward tuition, books, and other college-related expenses. In 2016 a total of $30,000 in scholarship funding was awarded to the multiple recipients still in school.

The year 2016 also saw a major milestone in the program: the first two graduates! Both reflected on the scholarship after their graduation. "This scholarship has been absolutely invaluable to me," said 2011 recipient Josh Perrin. "The financial support from the All-Star scholarship gave me the opportunity to fully focus on my academics. The community support from UMPS CARE Charities was just as valuable. … I have felt nothing but genuine support from my umpires family."

2012 recipient Candace "Zoe" Cottom commented on the importance of the scholarship to her journey. "Attending Butler had been my dream since I was about 12 years old," she said. "Unfortunately, it is a very expensive school so my chances of being able to afford it were slim. But once I found out I got the scholarship, I knew I could make my dream happen." The umpires continued to support her throughout her college years as well. She related how umpire Ted Barrett and his wife, Tina, sent her multiple care packages at college and how excited she was to go to a game and meet them. "They are two of the most gracious, generous, and caring people I've met. And it is because of people like them that I've had the opportunities I've had. I feel that it is both my duty and my privilege to give back to others so that they may succeed as well."

Family Care Program

Beyond those three main programs, UMPS CARE Charities also remains true to its original mission and core values, providing a "helping hand" to colleagues in need, including retired and minor-league umpires and the clubhouse attendants who cared for the umpire rooms.

Fund Raising

None of these programs are free, and UMPS CARE Charities continues thanks to its caring corporate sponsors and legion of supporters and volunteers. The charity also runs a number of fundraisers throughout the year, including:

- **UMPS CARE Golf Classic**, which includes a pre-event social, live auction, awards dinner, and the chance to golf with MLB and MiLB umpires.
- **100-Hole Golf Marathon**, an endurance event where MLB and MiLB umpires and supporters golf 100 holes in one day to raise money.
- **UMPS CARE Online Auction**, with autographed memorabilia from some of baseball's top players, premium MLB and UMPS CARE apparel, and one-of-a-kind "Experience Packages" at many of the minor- and major-league ballparks across the country.

Adrian Johnson brings a teddy bear and a much-needed smile to a young patient at the Children's Hospital of Philadelphia.

- And other events throughout the country, including a bowling tournament, a "run for bears" race to raise funds to purchase Build-a-Bears, a spring-training golf outing, and more.

Today and Tomorrow

Today, UMPS CARE Charities employs two full-time workers (an executive director and program director) while being led by a Board of Directors of umpires and supported by a volunteer wives' committee. Together the group pushes forward to improve the charity each and every year. "[Executive Director] Jenn Skolochenko-Platt and [Program Director] Jenn Jopling do a really great job," said Darling. "There's no way we could do this without their organization and structure, and they're making us better all the time."

If you'd like to get donate to UMPS CARE Charities, learn more, get involved, or participate in one of the charity's fundraisers, visit UmpsCare.com. You can also sign up for their quarterly newsletter or purchase UMPS CARE gear from the online store while you're there.

Helping people *is* an easy call. UMPS CARE Charities has been proving that for over a decade, and looks forward to living that phrase for many more years.

The Disqualification of Umpire Dick Higham

By Harold V. Higham

Any book about major-league umpiring would not be complete without a mention of Richard "Dick" Higham.[1] He was a professional player in the National Association of Professional Base Ball Players from 1871 through 1875, the National League in 1876, 1878 and 1879, as well as in the International Association in 1877 and the National Association in 1879. He had a .307 lifetime batting average and finished in a three-way tie in the National League for most doubles in 1876 and first in the National League in most doubles as well as total runs scored in 1878. He umpired a number of games during his playing career in the National Association, a not unusual task for a player in the predecessor professional league when it became necessary, and in the National League in 1881 and 1882. As an umpire he enjoyed a very good reputation for his knowledge of the rules. But on June 24, 1882, Dick Higham was adjudged guilty of involvement with gambling on games and was disqualified from again acting as an umpire in any National League contests. It is for being the lone major-league umpire ever expelled for colluding with gamblers to fix games that he is most often remembered.

Richard Higham was born on July 24, 1851, in Ipswich, County Suffolk, England, to James and Mary Higham. He had one brother, Frederick, born October 7, 1852, in Canterbury, Kent, England. The family arrived in America in 1854 and settled in Hoboken, New Jersey. They became close friends with Samuel Wright and his family, also then living in Hoboken. Sam Wright of the St. George Cricket Club and James Higham of the New York Cricket Club were teammates on the American All-Star Cricket Team which played against the Canadian All-Stars in the annual International Series from 1856 to 1860, their sons, Dick Higham and Harry, George and Sammy Wright, played professional baseball.

Efforts to determine the precise nature of the allegations against Higham previously have fallen short. As there was no television, radio, or motion pictures, nor game-action photographs, contemporary books and diaries of players, nor official game accounts available during the early to mid-nineteenth century, researchers have had to rely most often on the newspapers and periodicals of the day. Sometimes it appeared that some newspaper reports were not spot on or skewed based on some inclination or disposition of the reporter and/or the newspaper. It is, for example, well known that William A. Hulbert of the Chicago White Stockings, founder and later president of the National League, had a close relationship for some time with Lewis E. Meacham, a reporter for the *Chicago Tribune*.

Fortunately, in 2004 Miller Young, the great-grandson of Nicholas E. Young, who was the Secretary of the National League in June of 1882, located among his great-grandfather's papers the League's file of the "Hearing of League Umpire Richard Higham," held on June 24, 1882, beginning at 12 noon, at the Russell House in Detroit, Michigan.[2] The documents of the hearing, which is the most contemporary record, are presented here. This the first time that the original source material has been available and thus offers critical components of the historical record in assessing the appropriateness of Higham's singular disqualification. For that reason the text of relevant, handwritten documents are presented verbatim.

On June 20, 1882, A. H. Soden, acting president of the National League after the death of William A. Hulbert in April, sent a Western Union telegram from Boston to N.E. Young, Secretary of the National League:

"President Thompson [President of the Detroit Wolverines and Mayor of Detroit] will wire you preferring charges of crookedness against umpire Higham and will request you to convene board of directors at a time & and place he will name notify each member of the board also Higham who is at Buffalo of the time and place of meeting also concerning the charges and request prompt attendance either in person or by delegate. I shall be away until friday(sic) & all communications will be made to you direct."

That same day, June 20, William G. Thompson, President of the Detroit

Wolverines, sent a Western Union telegram from Detroit to Secretary Young:

"Detroit presents charges of crookedness against umpire Higham Call meeting of Directors here - Saturday when Brown [of Worcester] will be here."

On June 24, 1882, a Committee of the Board of Directors of the National League, consisting of Buffalo's James A. Mugridge chair, Gardner Earl of Troy and Worcester's Freeman Brown secretary, met in Detroit to assess the allegations against Higham. Two documents were offered as evidence.

The first was an accusatory telegram, designated Exhibit "A, which President Thompson sent to Board members from Detroit club headquarters on June 18, 1882:

"I hereby prefer charges against Umpire Richard Higham for having violated Section 45 of the Constitution and Playing Rule 67."

The second item, designated Exhibit "B," was letter Higham was alleged to have written to someone named James in care of the Brunswick Hotel on May 27 before leaving Detroit with the Wolverines to umpire games on an eastern road trip. That letter, also submitted by Thompson, was presented as incriminating evidence of collusion with gamblers.

"Friend James,

I just got word that we leave here at 3 o'clock p.m. for the East so won't be able to see you. J [illegible] play the Providence Club on tuesday(sic) that is the first game and I will telegraph you tuesday(sic) night what to do wednesday(sic) if I want you to play the Detroits I will telegraph you in this way buy all the Lumber you can get if you don't hear from me buy Providence sure. I think that will answer for all the games the Detroits will play on the trip. I will write you when I get to Boston. You can write me any time you want and direct your letters in care of Detroit B.B.C. and when you send me any money send a check for the amount. It will be all right. You can find out what city we are in by looking at that book I gave you the other day. I would not play every game if I were you. If I don't telegraph you tuesday(sic) don't play the game Wednesday.

Yours Truly
Dick"

The "REPORT OF THE PROCEEDINGS OF THE HEARING AND EXHIBITS THERETO" sets forth the evidence and rationale for the umpire's expulsion:

"The board of directors of the National League of Professional Base Ball Clubs met in special session, duly called by the Secretary of the League, at the Russell house at 12:30 noon, present W.G. Thompson of the Detroit Club, James A. Mugridge representing the Buffalo Club, Gardner Earl representing the Troy Club and Freeman Brown of the Worcester Club. In the absence of acting president A. H. Soden of the Boston Club, the meeting organized with Mr. Mugridge Chairman and Mr. Brown Secretary. Mr. Thompson was excused from acting with the board, the Detroit Club having presented the charges at issue.

Dick Higham, with the 1877 Syracuse Stars. Second row from the back, left to right, Higham is the third seated with arms crossed.

Mr. Thompson submitted the accompanying communication Marked "A" and in proof of his charges the accompanying letter Marked "B."

Mr. Richard Higham, League Umpire, against whom the charges were preferred was admitted to the meeting and an opportunity given him to present his defense. He denied the authorship of the letter Marked "B" and made a general denial of all complicity with any person or persons to cause any game of ball to result otherwise than on its merits under the playing rules. He was then permitted to retire.

The letter Marked "B" having been submitted with a letter, the authorship of which Mr. Higham acknowledged to be his own, to three of the best handwriting experts in Detroit and being pronounced identical with each other, it was

Voted - that the charges preferred by the Detroit Club against Richard Higham, League Umpire are fully sustained.

Voted - that Richard Higham, be forever disqualified from acting as Umpire of any game of ball participated in by a League Club.

No further business appearing, the meeting dissolved."

At the conclusion of the hearing Freeman Brown on June 24 sent a copy of the Report along with a covering letter to League Secretary Nick Young:

"Friend Young

I inclose(sic) report of the proceedings of the directors meeting held in this City today. The result as you will see is just what dear Mr. Hulbert predicted when Higham was elected an umpire. He knew him better than anybody Else(sic) and knew that as soon as the opportunity was offered Dick would go astray. The Evidence (sic) outside of the letter was circumstantial but wholly conclusive. Dick denied point blank, when questioned, that he knew a gambler in Detroit or in any other city, but each member of the board happened to know the men with whom he associated when in their respective cities. So we soon satisfied him that he was lying and We(sic) knew it. It appears that while in Detroit he associated with Todd and the proprietor of the Brunswick house says they passed notes at his hotel almost daily. Dick's defense was so weak and he acted throughout so much like a guilty man that we could not come to any other conclusion than the one reached. Dick was broke in pocket and we made up a purse of $15 to which the Detroit players added $12 and he started Saturday Evening for New York. Mr. Thompson is entitled to great credit for prosecuting the case. His Club has been benefited by Higham's umpiring and would have continued to have been in his favor, had not Mr. Thompson shown him up."

There are a number of points to supplement an understanding of the hearing's deliberations. First are the league bylaws. Sec. 45 of the Constitution of the National League states:

"Any person who shall be proven guilty of offering, agreeing, conspiring or attempting to cause any game of ball to result otherwise than on the merits under the Playing Rules, or who, while acting as umpire, shall willfully violate any part of the Constitution or the Playing Rules adopted hereunder, shall forever be disqualified from acting as umpire of any game of ball participated in by a League Club."

RULE 67 of the Playing Rules of the National League states:

"Any League Umpire who shall be convicted of selling, or offering to sell a game of which he is an Umpire, shall thereupon be removed from his official capacity and placed under the same disabilities inflicted on expelled players by the Constitution of the League." (italics added)

These Sections of the Constitution and the Playing Rules cited speak solely to the consequences of certain restricted activities as proven. Neither sets forth a charge or specification of any such activity having been engaged in by Higham. In addition, the exhibit "A" letter submitted by W. G. Thompson of the Detroit Wolverines sets forth only a reference to Secs. 45 & 67 with no charges in fact ever being made.

In his report, Secretary Brown alleged that the letter marked "B," also submitted by Thompson, is proof of "A." If "B" may be said to supply any support at all for the "A" letter, no foundation for "B" has been laid and it lacks credibility for that purpose. Thompson never states at the hearing how it came into his possession, from whom he received it and why it should be believed. It has been said in newspaper accounts that the letter was found by some unnamed clerk who handed it in to somebody and eventually it wound up with Thompson. Thompson never authenticates "B" and is never asked any authenticating questions. In addition, in his Official Report of the Hearing, Brown states that "B" had been submitted to "three of the best handwriting experts in Detroit" along with a letter that Higham acknowledged he had written and the experts pronounced them "identical." Who were these three handwriting experts? If they issued a report of their examination of and their findings with respect to the letters, where is the report? When did Higham make such an acknowledgement and where is the crucially important "acknowledgement" letter? It is well known that a person's handwriting is not "identical" from one exemplar to another.

The *Detroit Evening News*, on Monday, June 26, 1882, two days after the hearing, printed a letter dated May 27, shown to the paper and said to be Exhibit "B" but which differs in several respects:

> Friend Todd, I just got word we leave for the east(sic) on the 3 p.m. train, so I will not have a chance to see you. If you don't hear from me play the Providence Tuesday and if I want you to play the Detroits Wednesday I will telegraph in this way "Buy all the lumber you can." If you do not hear from me don't play the Detroits, but buy Providence sure-that is the first game. I think this will do for the eastern series. I will write you from Boston. You can write me at any time in care of the Detroit B.B. club. When you send me any money you can send check to me in care of the Detroit B.B. club, and it will be all right. You will see by that book I gave you the other day what city will (sic) be in. Yours truly, Dick.

Did the paper craft a letter based on second-hand accounts of the hearing or was there more than one letter?

The *Detroit Evening News*, in the same article, stated that "other letters" of his [Higham] were produced and that the signature "Dick" was declared by three bank examiners to be the same. It appears more than one letter of comparison was made available to the three bank "experts" who made no declaration that any of the writings were "identical." Where is this crucial "evidence?"

While SEC. 45 requires that the person "be proven guilty of offering, agreeing, conspiring or attempting to cause any game of ball to result otherwise than on the merits" and RULE 67 states that the Umpire must be "convicted of selling, or offering to sell, a game of which he is an umpire", neither threshold is

met in the wording of "B." The letter contains nothing offering, agreeing, conspiring, or attempting to cause any game to otherwise result than on its merits nor selling or offering to sell a game of which the writer is an umpire. Letter "B" does not contain any wording which gives rise to a violation of either SEC. 45 or RULE 67.

It appears the "Letter," either the one found in the "File" or the one given to the *Detroit Evening News*, sets out an arrangement between Todd and the author, who is traveling with the Detroits to Providence for a two-game series, to bet on both games in the order of Providence in the first and Detroit in the second. No mention is ever made of a guaranteed win in either game. As a fix always requires the purchase of the losing team to throw the game, the Detroit players would have to have been bought in the first game and Providence players would have to have been bought in the second game. An expensive proposition to be sure. Higham's umpiring of the first game won by Providence was highly praised and when Detroit won the second game no comments either way were made. It appears the "lumber" code of the conspirators was designed to give the one at the games an opportunity to pass on his personal observation of the morale and physical condition of the players after their long train ride and a completed game if, in his opinion, any comment would be helpful

Obviously it would be very foolish and very dangerous for a player, a manager, or an umpire to scheme with a gambler, in writing, to receive a check for money, having to do with the outcome of a game in which any one of them was engaged, addressed to them in care of one of the participating teams, such as here the Detroits, even if "it will be all right." Clearly someone, other than the manager, a player, and/or the umpire, also travelling with the Detroits, authored the letter marked "B" found in the "Hearing File." Although it would appear to be a smart matter to attempt to divert any inquiry arising from letter «B» to the umpire rather than the team manger or players or officers or executives of the team on the trip, nothing has been presented to establish how a single umpire, officiating at a game and acting alone, could cause a ball game "to result otherwise than on the merits."

Freeman Brown's cover letter to Secretary Young clearly shows that Brown knew the Directors were on shaky ground in their total reliance on the "B" letter in the face of Higham's continued denial that he had written it and the poor finding of the bank examiner experts who, according to the *Detroit Evening News*, found only the signatures "Dick" the same. Why would such experts say in one instance that the handwriting in "B" and the "acknowledged" writing were identical and then state in the item in the *Detroit Free Press* that only the signatures were the same? Perhaps these "experts" were not merely confused but, in fact, did not exist and someone else was confused.

Brown in his cover letter attempts to assure Secretary Young the decision of the Directors finding Higham guilty was a good one even outside of the Hearing and disregarding the "B" letter. Interestingly, in 1875 William Hulbert, an owner of the Chicago White Stockings, dispatched Nick Young to New York City to engage Dick Higham to manage the White Stockings. The wholly "circumstantial but conclusive evidence" Brown musters was never attested to in any way. In fact, Brown's reference to the personal knowledge of the Hearing Committee members as to what they might know about men with whom Higham "associated" in each of their respective cities raises the specter of their being prejudiced against him and the need for them to be disqualified to sit on the Committee. At the same time the alleged information from the proprietor of the Brunswick Hotel to someone about sealed, written communications with Todd; Brown's assurance that the directors had gotten to Higham in the face of his continued protestations of innocence, et. alia, do not appear in the Report of the Hearing. These and all similar slurs found in the cover letter are relied upon by Brown alone and are not part of the deliberations of all three directors in concert.

Secretary Young simply ignored Brown's cover letter and set forth Brown's enclosure as the full Minute of the Hearing in the "National League Minutes 1881-1890" which was published as such in 1883 in the *Spalding Guide* well after the news of Higham's disqualification had already been given to the newspapers, in violation of Article IV, Section 5 of the Constitution of the National League of Professional Base Ball Clubs.[3]

Brown makes it clear that the Committee Members and perhaps other Directors were pre-disposed against Higham, and did their best to hold him guilty in the face of his continuous denial of guilt and the actual lack of credibility of the "Evidence" they did consider. In light of the gravity of the charges and the implication for the future integrity of the game, it is surprising that only three of eight league clubs attended the hearing. (Detroit as an interested party was excused from deliberations.) The absence of Boston and Providence is understandable due to distance, but the absence of Cleveland and Chicago is curious.

Given the manner in which the hearing was conducted, lacking usual judicial procedures including representation, and the lack of presentation of specific charges, it is possible that Richard "Dick" Higham was not a crooked umpire and should not have been disqualified by the National League.

NOTES

1   For Higham's career, see Larry R. Gerlach and Harold V. Higham, "Dick Higham: Umpire at the Bar of History," *The National Pastime. A Review of Baseball History*, 20 (Cleveland. SABR 2000) 20-22 and "Dick Higham, Star of Baseball's Early Years," ibid, 21 (Cleveland: Society for American Research 2001, 72-80 as well as Harold V. Higham, "Dick Higham" in the SABR Baseball Biography Project.

2   A copy of the National League file "Case of Richard Higham League umpire" can be found in the file for Dick Higham maintained at the National Baseball Hall of Fame and Museum in Cooperstown, New York.

3   The "National League Minutes 1881-1890" may be found in the Archives of the National Baseball Hall of Fame and Museum in Cooperstown, New York.

Deadball Era Umpires: What They Did for Baseball

By David W. Anderson

Very little has been written about Deadball Era umpires who established the foundations of the modern umpiring profession—the implementation of umpire signals, the two-umpire system, and more support from league authorities for umpires. And yet this group of men who umpired during the Deadball Era established the traditions, rules, and procedures by which fans, sportswriters, managers, coaches, and players understand the game today.

In 1947 James M. Kahn wrote one of the first books detailing the development of umpires, *The Umpire Story*,[1] but he had to dig deep to get information. Historian John Durant offered to provide data on umpires but Kahn concluded, "No need returning to it until 2055, or so, I doubt if I'll ever write another line on the robbers."[2]

In the official history published on the 75th anniversary of the National League, not a word was written about umpires.[3] The development of umpires and umpiring didn't occur overnight; it took many years—decades—to implement, and the story needs to be told.

The use of signals by umpires

One of the major developments came when umpires signaled plays during the Deadball Era, to formalize communication between fellow umpires, players, and coaches and fans. Before the first public-address system arrived at the Polo Grounds in 1929, umpires would announce lineups or changes in lineups by using a megaphone. As for signals—safe, out, fair, foul, strike, ball, and others—history is not so clear.

Cy Rigler is credited with raising his right arm to call a strike, first doing it in 1905 in Evansville, Indiana, as an umpire in the Central League.[4] When he came to the majors in 1906, he found hand signals already in place.[5] In 1904 Bill Klem had begun using fair and foul signals in the minor leagues.[6] Klem asserted this in his interview with William J. Slocum, but there is no independent confirmation. Klem reached the majors in 1905. By 1906 many umpires, including Rigler, Klem, and others, were using signals, and the use of this communication was becoming more widespread.

In 1907 some publications began to push for more widespread adoption of umpire's signals in the major leagues. *Sporting Life*, citing an article from the *Chicago Tribune*, said: "The Tribune's agitation for a system of umpire's gestures to indicate decisions seems to be as far-reaching as popular. Chief Zimmer has been using signs for balls and strikes and delighting New Orleans patrons."[7]

The *Tribune* continued on April 14, 1907: "There is nothing but this habit of looking at baseball matters through the umpire's eyes to explain the failure of big league presidents to answer the public's demands by instructing their umpires to adopt a simple code of signals to indicate doubtful decisions on pitched balls, the same as on base decisions."[8]

But how signals came to be part of communication with managers, coaches, and fans remains a question. A 2009 film, *Signs of the Time*,[9] covers the matter by looking at the careers of William "Dummy" Hoy and Bill Klem. The bottom line in terms of hand signals is this: Some of the signs came from American Sign Language and deaf players including Ed Dundon and Hoy were able to use them to advance their game. Umpires came along slowly, with Klem, Rigler, and others playing a role in utilizing signs. *Signs of the Time* contributes to the dialogue about the use of signs and while one could say it's a nice story, there are many loose ends.

The first deaf player to reach the big leagues was Ed "Dummy" Dundon. He pitched in the major leagues for the American Association Columbus Buckeyes in 1883 and 1884. His deafness made it difficult for him to understand ball and strike calls and close plays on the bases. Dundon and the umpires in the Association reportedly worked out a set of uniform signs. "The fans in the stands loved the signs because for the first time they too knew the umpires' rulings instantaneously. Soon the umpires were using hand signs even when Dundon and Hoy weren't playing in the game."[10]

Dundon was on a winner in 1885. Former Columbus manager Gus Schmelz took him to the Southern League and won that year's pennant with Atlanta. Dundon had a 21-12 record with an earned-run average of 1.44. He finished out his career in the minors and died from tuberculosis on August 18, 1893.

American Sign Language provides some clue as to how signs developed. "The signal for 'out' in baseball is identical to the sign for the word *out* in ASL: A, or the thumbs down, is moved up and over. ... The signal for 'safe' in baseball is identical to the sign for the word for 'free' and is made with two open and flat hands with the palms down. ..."[11]

As Dundon's career was fading away, Hoy was emerging as a star player. According to baseball historian Richard Marazzi, "Hoy has been credited with initiating the practice of umpires raising their right hands on a called strike."[12]

That both Dundon and Hoy had a role in signaling is a fact, though there is a question as to how much of a role they played. Hoy's role might have been more important if only because he had a far lengthier career than did Dundon.

While deaf players were getting signs, most of the time umpires were calling games without signaling. As the twentieth century approached, there was an invisible wall between fans and umpires. Jim Hughes wrote, "No signals for strikes, no signals for safe, and no signals for out or foul. There were no electronic scoreboards, there were no announcers to interpret the game. The only signal was the umpire's voice, drowned out by the screams of thousands of excited fans."[13] The director and co-producer of the film, Don

THE UMP

Whose virtues do we seldom sing?
At whom do we our curses fling?
Who gets the blame for everything?
    The Ump!
Who never gets a word of praise,
Though right or wrong he calls the plays?
Who's sure to make our dander raise?
    The Ump!

Who's always wrong and never right?
Whom do we hail without delight,
And kid whene'er he heaves in sight?
    The Ump!
And if they game is twelve to two
Against us and the air is blue
With curses who gets blamed – O who?
    The Ump!

But who, upon the other hand,
Before us comes and takes his stand,
The coolest gent in all the land?
    The Ump!
And who's aloof from all of us?
Who smiles to hear us rave and fuss,
And doesn't care a tinker's cuss?
    The Ump!

C.P. McDonald
Chicago Daily Tribune, April 24, 1910: C3

Casper, said that whether or not Hoy initiated signals "is a little gray."[14]

Deaf ballplayers introduced signals so they could understand what was happening, but umpires did not universally adopt signs. Some did, but others did not. By the time signs were commonly used by major-league umpires, Hoy's major-league career was over.

Bill Klem, whose professional career began in 1902 said that by 1904 he was using signals for fair and foul balls. Klem claimed he invented the safe and out signals, even though another umpire, Cy Rigler, was using them in the previous year in the minor leagues

1912 World Series, with Jake Stahl and McGraw back to camera. Left to right – Cy Rigler, Silk O'Loughin, Bill Klem, and Billy Evans.

and, by 1905, according to the Hughes film, safe/out and fair/foul signs were already in use.

Klem said in his interview with *Collier's*, "I invented the standard 'safe' and 'out' signals used today by umpires in sandlots and in World Series games. The jerk of the thumb over the shoulder for 'out' and the palms-down gesture for 'safe.' These were innovations of convenience to me, but they were a boon to fans out of range of the umpire's voice."[15]

It is probably futile at this point to definitively establish the origin of hand signals. *Signs of the Time* said: "Although the legend of Bill Klem is literally cast in bronze at the Hall of Fame, many historians believe he had nothing to do with the innovation of hand signals."[16]

Coaches and umpires simply began to use signals on their own without any edict from the magnates of the game.

Though Hoy had a longer career, Dundon may have played more of a role in innovating hand signals. Dundon was called on to umpire a game while a member of the Acid Iron Earths of the four-team Gulf League in 1886. Bill Deane wrote, "Dundon, the deaf and dumb pitcher of the Acid Iron Earths, umpired a game between the Acids and Mobiles, on October 20. … He used the fingers of his right hand to indicate strikes, the fingers of the left to call balls, a shake of the head decided a man 'not out,' and a wave of the hand meant out."[17]

Deane may have read the *New York Clipper*, which wrote about signals, "Dundon, the deaf-mute pitcher, umpired a game in Mobile, Ala., and gave entire satisfaction."[18]

So what do we make of the Dundon, Hoy, and Klem ensemble? In the film *Signs of the Time*, myth is the first item mentioned. While Dundon and Hoy were getting signals, umpires didn't do the same until much later. In other words, it is tough to come to a conclusion over how signs became part of the game.

By 1908, hand signals were universally in use. "Umpire signals had been in practice prior to the 1908 season. … The *Reach* and *Spalding* guidebooks called the signals the umpire's semaphore system. Signaling strike, safe, and out calls was an important means of adding to the enjoyment of the game, noted the *Spalding Guide*. The signal system had been 'invaluable assistance' to the umpires in 'making their decisions understood when the size of the crowd is such that it is impossible to make the human voice carry distinctly to all parts of the field.'"[19]

Hoy died at the age of 99 in 1961. In a publication called *Silent Worker*, from Gallaudet University, Hoy said, "Coaches at third base kept me posted by lifting his right hand for strikes and his left for balls. This gave later day umpires an idea and they now raise their right … to emphasize an indisputable strike."[20]

Deane wrote, "This indicates that this practice was adopted after Hoy's career; and, as far as we know, Hoy merely assumed that his coaches' signals were the inspiration for this idea."[21]

As for Klem, it is another matter. Klem outlived all other Deadball Era umpires except one, fellow Hall of Famer Billy Evans. And since Evans was an American Leaguer, Klem could describe his career as he pleased with a mixture of fact and fiction. Baseball historian Peter Morris kindly said, "Somebody who had as long of an umpiring career as Bill Klem probably got asked questions a lot of times. I think you tend to shade your answer to giving people what they want to hear. So I think that Klem probably started to shade his story and before long he probably remembered it a little differently than how it actually happened."[22]

In *Signs of the Time*, pitching great Bob Feller told it like he saw it: "Bill Klem on his plaque said he invented hand signals. Of course, he didn't invent hand signals any more than I did. We live with myths every day, you can call them myths or lies or untruths or misquotes, whatever you want. But that's all part of life."[23]

The introduction of hand signals did a lot for baseball. Communication was a key to making the game more understandable and available to everyone. Today we know that hand signals facilitate communication with players, coaches, fans, and other umpires.

From one to multiple umpires

During the first eight years of the Deadball Era, most games were umpired by one man. The owners at that time believed only one umpire was needed, unless in a key game in a pennant race or another important contest. In 1908 the three contenders in the National League, the Cubs, Giants, and Pirates, had two-man crews a little over 80 percent of the time.[24] In the American League in 1908, games between Cleveland and the White Sox all had two-man crews. In 1909 both leagues effectively had two-man crews, but the major leagues did not formally adopt the two-man rule until the beginning of the 1912 season.

From the standpoint of both American and National League presidents and owners, augmentation of field staff to more than one umpire came slowly. In many ways having two umpires on the field, in very simple terms, involved money.

In the American League, Tommy Connolly and Jack Sheridan were two who remained through 1909, while in the National League Hank O'Day and Bob Emslie were permanent during that time. Most other umpires were basically part-timers as pressures from owners and players caused them to be, as they say, "one and done" as it concerned their major-league umpiring careers.

Until the umpire rolls added Silk O'Loughlin and Billy Evans in the American League and Jim Johnstone and Bill Klem in the National, major-league umpiring was not a long-term employment option for most. By 1909 several other umpires entered the league and had long careers: Jack Egan and Big Bill Dinneen in the American League, and Cy

Rigler in the National League. These new umpires helped both major leagues by establishing the umpire's role in the game and getting away from the "one and done" days. Connolly, Klem, Evans, and O'Day are in the Baseball Hall of Fame.

Ejections

While the American League's Ban Johnson and his counterpart Harry Pulliam in the National League were attempting to build the umpires' authority and status, they ran into problems from players, managers, and owners.

Many of the problems came from players. Owners were beginning to rein in vulgar and unseemly behavior by players. But umpires were still fair game.

Hall of Famer Sam Crawford said, "[W]e only had one umpire in a game, not four they have today. And you *know* that one umpire just can't see everything at once. He'd stand behind the catcher until a man got on base, and then he'd move out and call balls and strikes from behind the pitcher. … We'd run with one eye on the ball and the other on the umpire!"[25]

It would take almost a decade to remove difficult players from causing problems with umpires; managers were another problem. Connie Mack had been ejected by Hank O'Day when Mack was a catcher, but he rarely roused umpires as manager of the Philadelphia Athletics. Orioles and Giants manager John McGraw was one of the toughest on umpires, averaging several ejections a season. McGraw claimed that " 'artful kicking' to keep umpires aware of his

Smith - announcer, and Umpires Charles "Cy" Rigler, Bill Klem, Francis "Silk" O'Loughlin, Billy Evans, 1915 World Series.

presence gained his club as many as fifty extra runs a season."[26]

Other Deadball Era managers such as Frank Chance, Fielder Jones, Clark Griffith, Joe Kelley, and Fred Clarke were also tough managers in their attitude toward umpires. Clarke was flexible in his attitudes with umpires in 1908, when he decided that the best approach in a close race was to keep his players eligible and to leave umpires alone. Clarke told *Sporting Life*, "There's nothing to be gained by paying attention to the umpires but it may mean a big loss when men get put out of the game."[27] During the pennant race in 1908 the New York Giants led the league with 20 ejections, the Chicago Cubs had six, and Clarke's Pirates only three.[28]

Team owners

League presidents also had difficulty with team owners. While Andrew Freedman was president of the New York Giants, he was responsible for getting rid of umpires Billy Nash and Harry Colgan in 1901. During his presidency he also upset players, managers, sportswriters, and even fans. When Freedman was replaced by John T. Brush as Giants president, Brush became an opponent of National League President Pulliam until Pulliam killed himself in 1909.

In 1908 the owner of the Brooklyn Dodgers, Charles Ebbets, put enough evidence before Pulliam to get Frank Rudderham fired, after Rudderham stirred up a lot of bad press in the New York area.

In the American League, Ban Johnson had more leverage. When he formed the American League, he wanted it to penalize abusive behavior directed at umpires. Johnson was willing to face down owners as well as players and managers. But, as with the National League, it took years to repair the damage. League owners believed it increased attendance to have umpires the subject of vilification. The problem was that National League players came to the American League for a simple reason: The American League had money to spend on players. However, the former National Leaguers found Ban Johnson tough when it came to umpire abuse. Johnson said repeat-edly that it "was the number one crime an American Leaguer could commit."[29]

Johnson required umpires to file reports of serious incidents that occurred during games. If an umpire lied to Johnson, he was done as an umpire in the league. The league's first major-league season, 1901, was easily the worst in terms of umpire quality. The staff was "mediocre … the novelty of presidential support of umpires, and the influx of undisciplined National Leaguers guaranteed a certain amount of difficulty."[30]

The next step was to adopt a two-umpire system. The World Series already employed two umpires, one from each league. By 1908, many observers believed it was time for a change and Johnson declared that two umpires would officiate games in 1909 and thereafter. The National League finally adopted two umpires in 1912. The major leagues began three umpires in 1933 and in 1952 the current four-man setup was established.

Umpires themselves were split over the use of one man versus two men. O'Day, Connolly, and Hurst were strong supporters of a single-umpire system. O'Day believed it was more trouble working with another umpire because "in many cases he has not only [had to?] give his own decisions, but sometimes his mates' as well. …"[31] O'Day made the Merkle call after Bob Emslie said he did not see the play. His comment came after the Merkle play.

Sheridan and O'Loughlin were for the two-umpire system, as was Evans, who said that with just one umpire, "You did a lot of running, and let's face it, a lot of guessing."[32] *Sporting Life* weighed in with this editorial comment, during the 1908 season: "With batting cut down to a minimum, the slightest error by an umpire often deprives a team of victory. There is really too much for one man to watch in a ball game."[33]

While umpires had developed fundamental techniques, professionalization and standardization came with the establishment of formal umpire training schools. Schools for umpires did not come around until the mid-1930s; George Barr of the National League opened the first and was instrumental in handing down advice to those who wanted to take on the task. Four years later, Bill McGowan began his academy. Until then, individual umpires had to rely on on-the-job training.

The development of modern umpires comes down to three factors: creating signals that allowed fans, players, coaches, and umpires to understand what occurred on the diamond; giving greater authority over the game without fear of being unnecessarily overridden without cause; and finally the advent of more than one umpire on the field.

NOTES

1 James M. Kahn, *The Umpire Story* (New York: Putnam, 1947).

2 Larry R. Gerlach, "Umpires," in John Thorn and Pete Palmer, eds., *Total Baseball* (New York: Warner Books, 1989), 465.

3 Charles Segar, ed., *The Official History of the National League* (New York: Jay Publishing, 1951). The only mention of umpires was in the dedication, but nothing more.

4 Dan Krueckeberg, "The Forgotten Man," *Referee Magazine*, July 1983, 50.

5 Ibid.

6 Bill J. Klem and William J. Slocum, "Jousting With McGraw," *Collier's Magazine*, April 7, 1951: 31.

7 *Sporting Life*, March 30, 1907: 4.

8 Peter Morris, "Umpire's Signals," SABR-L Digest, April 2, 2003.

9 Jim Hughes, *Signs of the Time: the Myth, the Mystery, the Legend of Baseball's Greatest Innovation* (2009, Crystal Pix, Inc.).

10 Joseph Santry, "Columbus Buckeyes 1876-1899," *Anchors Aweigh*, July 1988: 15-16.

11 Randy Fisher and Jami N. Fisher, "The Deaf and the Origin of Hand Signals in Baseball," *The National Pastime*, 2008: 35.

12 Richard Marazzi, *The Rules and Lore of Baseball* (New York: Stein and Day, 1980), 21.

13 Jim Hughes, *Signs of the Time: The Myth, the Mystery, the Legend of Baseball's Greatest Innovation* (Documentary film script, Crystal Pix, Inc., 2009), 6.

14 Stuart Miller, "Umpires Signs: The Movie," *New York Times*, July 24, 2010.

15 William J. Klem and William J. Slocum, "Diamond Rhubarbs," *Collier's Magazine*, April 14, 1951: 31.

16 Hughes, 22.

17 Bill Deane, "Dummy Hoy, Inventor," SABR-L Digest, March 21, 2001.

18 Ibid.

19 David W. Anderson, *More Than Merkle* (Lincoln: University of Nebraska Press, 2000), 87-88.

20 Bill Deane, "Dummy Hoy, Inventor."

21 Ibid.

22 Hughes, *Signs of the Time*, interview with Peter Morris, 23.

23 Ibid.

24 Anderson, 230.

25 Lawrence S. Ritter, *The Glory of Their Times: The Story of the Early Days of Baseball Told by the Men Who Played It* (New York: Quill William Morrow, 1984), 55.

26 Robert F. Burk, *Never Just a Game: Players, Owners and American Baseball to 1920* (Chapel Hill, North Carolina: University of North Carolina Press, 1994), 134. Deane, SABR-L Digest, March 21, 2001.

27 "National League News," *Sporting Life*, July 18, 1908: 9.

28 Anderson, 232.

29 Eugene C. Murdock, *Ban Johnson: Czar of Baseball* (Westport, Connecticut: Greenwood Press, 1982), 80.

30 Murdock, 98.

31 "O'Day Differs," *Sporting Life*, October 24, 1908: 12.

32 Kahn, 75.

33 "Current Comment," *Sporting Life,* June 6, 1908: 4.

Major League Umpires and Unionization

By Chris Williams

Major-league baseball players and umpires are sometimes at odds, but both groups seemed to be thinking along the same lines around 1968. It was then that the Major League Baseball Players Association won the first collective bargaining agreement in professional sports, and umpires started on the road to formation of a union that would eventually be recognized as the official bargaining agent for major-league umpires.

Beginnings

Umpire Ernie Stewart started umpiring in the American League in 1940 but left baseball in 1945 after becoming embroiled in an effort to improve working conditions for umpires[1] and what was apparently a power struggle between Happy Chandler, then the relatively new commissioner of baseball, and Will Harridge, the president of the AL. According to Stewart, Chandler had concerns about the low pay for umpires and their poor working conditions and asked Stewart to write to the other umpires to determine their views and to "start the ball rolling for better conditions."[2] One of Stewart's letters found its way to Harridge, who was at odds with Chandler. Harridge considered Chandler's actions a challenge to his authority over the umpires and requested Stewart's resignation, asserting that Stewart had been disloyal to the umpires. Stewart denied any disloyalty and requested a meeting with both the commissioner and Harridge. At the meeting Chandler advocated for Stewart, but Harridge argued that his authority over the AL umpires gave him the power to demand Stewart's resignation,[3] and that the hiring and firing of umpires was exclusively within the purview of the league. Ultimately, Stewart was presented with a letter of resignation that Chandler told him to sign.[4] When the departure of Stewart was reported in the *St. Petersburg Evening Independent*, Stewart blamed his dismissal on his interest in trying to obtain higher salaries for umpires. When asked for comment, Harridge did not deny Stewart's version and merely stated: "If that's the way he prefers to have the story go out, that's perfect with me."[5] Chandler himself served only one term as commissioner, reportedly because, in part, the owners were unhappy with his perceived support for the unionization of umpires.[6]

Almost 20 years later, National League umpires began efforts to organize. At the 1963 owners' Winter Meetings, an attorney hired by the NL umpires, John J. Reynolds, was allowed to make a presentation about the umpires' concerns related to pensions and health insurance. A disappointingly small increase in pensions resulted and there was no movement on health insurance. In May 1964 the umpires informed the league that if there were no further negotiations the umpires would set a strike date. The league responded that unless the umpires' association was discontinued, all umpires would be fired. The strike was averted when the league agreed to allow the umpires' lawyer to make another presentation at the All-Star break. After the second presentation, the league agreed to pension increases and added life insurance to the umpires' benefits.[7] Off to what many might have considered a good start, the NL umpires' union was officially chartered in Illinois in 1964.[8] The directors included Augie Donatelli, Jocko Conlan, Al Barlick, Tom Gorman, and Shag Crawford.[9]

Donatelli, the son and brother of coal miners and himself a coal miner in his early days, spearheaded the efforts to unionize the NL umpires.[10] He had experienced the hardships of coal mining in Pennsylvania and saw the mine owners use their economic advantage to impose their will when establishing working conditions and pay. Donatelli was fired from a job as a "check weigh-man" assigned by the union to try to curb abuses at the weigh stations that determined miners' pay because he stood with the union and refused a company order to empty a coal car. He was later rehired after the company accepted the union's demands.[11] As an umpire, after a significant dispute with a player or manager, Donatelli would sometimes resume his position and, catching the eye of another umpire, mime shoveling coal to convey his belief that as hard as umpiring might be, it was better than the mines.[12] Donatelli had been a crew chief before he became active in organizing the umpires but was demoted supposedly for poor performance.[13] He was then assigned to work with Al Barlick, another union man, and the two used their time together to chart unionization efforts.[14]

Despite the successes with pensions and insurance, the union that was formed in 1964 was not recognized by the National League, which insisted on individual season-to-season contracts with each umpire, treating the umpires as independent contractors.[15] According to American League umpire Bill McKinley, the AL umpires lagged behind the NL umpires in their organizing efforts because the NL umpires had requested and gotten the league's permission for John J. Reynolds to attend the annual meeting to discuss unionization and moved on from there.[16] (Although the grant of permission might be seen as signaling a more open attitude by the league to unionization, National League umpire John Kibler recalled that in 1963 he was barred from a meeting of NL umpires by Barlick and Donatelli because Kibler was a rookie and they did not want Kibler to risk getting fired for attending the meeting.[17])

In 1964 Bill McKinley and other American League umpire crew chiefs approached league President Joe Cronin with their concerns and an outline of what they wanted. According to McKinley, Cronin said he would take the umpires' requests to the Winter Meetings. Subsequently, in 1965, McKinley was informed that he was being retired. McKinley had not planned to retire and believed his organizing efforts were the cause of his mandatory retirement, as well as the termination of two other AL umpires, Ed Runge and Joe Paparella.[18]

By September 1968, four years after the National League umpires union was formed, the NL umpires had better salaries and per diems than their AL counterparts. Al Salerno, Bill Valentine, and several other American League umpires attended a meeting with their National League counterparts in Chicago and proposed that the umpires of both leagues join together in one union. When the opinions of AL umpires were solicited by mail, most of them favored the union. Shortly after reportedly being told of the organizing efforts of Salerno and Valentine, Cronin called them and fired them, citing incompetence as the reason.[19] In response, the National League umpires voted to admit American League umpires to their union and the Major League Umpires Association (MLUA) was formed. AL umpire salaries were later increased to match NL salaries, but Salerno and Valentine were not reinstated, and the union ultimately voted not to support them in their efforts to be rehired.[20]

Union Recognition

In 1969 the new Major League Umpires Association (MLUA) petitioned the National Labor Relations Board to hold an election among the American League umpires to determine whether they wished to be represented by a union for purposes of negotiating with the league. The league opposed the petition, arguing that baseball did not involve interstate commerce, relying on a series of earlier court decisions upholding the sport's antitrust exemption on the basis that interstate commerce was not affected. The NLRB sided with the umpires and the MLUA was recognized as the official bargaining agent for the AL umpires. Later, membership in the MLUA was expanded to include all major-league umpires.[21]

In October 1970 the first umpires strike occurred, on the first day of the League Championship Series. The umpires sought more pay for working the extra games created by the addition of the League Championship Series to the postseason. Minor-league umpires worked the first National League game and minor-league and retired major-league umpires worked the first American League game.[22] Whether because of the quality of the officiating or because union workers at Three Rivers Stadium in Pittsburgh refused to cross the umpires' picket line, or for other reasons, by the start of the second games an agreement was in place and the umpires were back at work. They succeeded in getting a pay raise for working League Championship Series games from $2,500 to $4,000 and for World Series games from $6,500 to $8,000.[23]

In 1978 Richard G. Phillips, a lawyer from Philadelphia and "a renowned hardball negotiator,"[24] became executive director of the MLUA. Phillips had represented the referees in the American Basketball Association and "had some compassion for the umpires."[25] The collective bargaining agreement for 1977-1982 included basic terms that both sides had agreed on, but also some open clauses that were to be negotiated. The umpires felt that the commissioner's office was putting off those negotiations, and Phillips organized a one-day walkout in protest. A federal court ordered the umpires back to work.[26]

Despite the recognition of the MLUA as the umpires' bargaining agent, the leagues held fast to the requirement of individual contracts. Before the beginning of the 1979 season, the leagues sent letters to the umpires informing them that any umpire who had not signed his individual contract would not be allowed to work spring training. A short time later a second letter followed, threatening to hire replacements for any umpires who did not sign their contracts. On Opening Day the umpires began a strike that lasted until May 18, during which the umpires picketed the ballparks and, reportedly, Phillips persuaded several other unions to support the umpires. Eventually a settlement was reached, with an improved salary structure and a two-week in-season vacation. The minor-league umpires who had worked during the strike were shunned and eventually resigned.[27]

While the leagues and the umpires were at odds, the league presidents and the commissioner were in their own power struggles. In October 1984 the NL umpires threatened to walk out of the NL play-offs because talks with the league president, Chub Feeney, were not going well. To avoid a strike, Peter Ueberroth, who had been commissioner since March of that year, took a hand in the negotiations and offered terms that were more liberal than those Feeney had offered.[28] In 1991, Commissioner Fay Vincent took over negotiations with the NL umpires from league President Bill White.[29] Ultimately, after the 1999 season, Commissioner Bud Selig eliminated the offices of the league presidents and moved control of umpiring issues to the commissioner's office.[30]

1999: A Tumultuous Year

At the February 1999 meeting of the Major League Umpires Association, umpires Joe Brinkman, John Hirschbeck, and Tim Welke attempted to block the reappointment of Phillips as executive director, but failed.[31] The year before, Brinkman had asked Ronald M. Shapiro, a lawyer who represented numerous players in their contract negotiations with owners and who had worked with several umpires on matters not involving unionization, to challenge Phillips for the post of executive director of the MLUA.[32] Shapiro declined but agreed to advise Brinkman and other umpires who were dissatisfied with Phillips.

At the same time dissident umpires were busy trying to change their union, the commissioner's office was flexing its muscles. On February 19, 1999, in what was assumed by the umpires to be a show of strength, Sandy Alderson, a vice president of Major League Baseball, sent a memo stating a policy that the top of the strike zone was to be two inches above the top of the uniform pants. The umpires felt that the new policy contravened the official rules and were insulted that the commissioner had not sought umpire input. They also took exception to MLB's use of MLUA umpires for an exhibition game in Cuba without first negotiating with the MLUA.[33]

Adding fuel to the fire, on April 9 Alderson asked teams to chart pitches and report to the commissioner's office on strike zone consistency.[34] The umpires again felt disrespected. Then in June, umpire Tom Hallion was suspended for three games for bumping a player, the first-ever umpire suspension, and the umpires attributed it to Selig as part of his mission to control them.[35] The MLUA filed suit, alleging that the new policies from the commissioner's office violated the collective bargaining agreement.[36] Things then began to move fast.

On June 30, 1999, the MLUA Board of Directors discussed whether to strike to oppose the actions of the commissioner's office, but the suggestion was rejected because their contract included a no-strike clause and the umpires expected that if they went on strike, they would simply be ordered back to work by a federal court.[37] On July 14, 1999, at a special meeting of the MLUA membership during the All-Star Game break, Phillips proposed a mass resignation, apparently thinking that Major League Baseball would not want to have to use minor-league umpires nor would it want to pay the approximately $15 million in voluntary termination pay required under the contract if the resignations were accepted.[38] The plan was that each umpire would send a letter stating that he would resign effective September 5, 1999.[39] On July 15, 1999, 57 umpires major league umpires (out of a total of 68) signed resignation letters,[40] and Phillips announced the resignations at a press conference.[41] John Hirschbeck and Joe Brinkman opposed the massresignation strategy, and did not sign resignation letters.[42]

Some of the umpires who had sent resignation letters apparently had second thoughts, and 13 of them sent letters to MLB between July 18 and July 22 rescinding their resignations. On July 22 representatives of Major League Baseball decided not to negotiate with the union.[43] They also accepted the 13 rescission letters, effectively reinstating those umpires, and began replacing the umpires who had not rescinded. That same day, the National League made eight offers of employment to minor-league umpires and the American League made 12, all of which were accepted.[44]

The next day the MLUA filed suit in federal court seeking an order prohibiting the leagues from accepting the resignations, but on July 26, 1999 the court declined to grant the order.[45] On July 27, 1999 Phillips wrote to the two league presidents stating that all remaining resignation letters were rescinded.[46] However, by then the American League had no umpiring positions open and accepted the resignations of nine umpires, while the National League had 19 positions open with 32 umpires to fill them, and accepted the rescissions of 19 and the resignations of the remaining 13.[47] Major League Baseball had called the umpires' bluff and 22 umpires were out of work.

Decertification of the MLUA

On September 27, 1999, more than 40 umpires participated in a conference call with Brinkman, Shapiro, and several labor lawyers. The lawyers agreed that decertification of the MLUA and replacing it with a different union offered the best chance of resolving the conflict and getting the 22 terminated umpires back to work.[48] On October 3, on another conference call with umpires, Hirschbeck and Shapiro succeeded in obtaining $100,000 in funding from the umpires for the cost of a decertification campaign. The decertification petition was filed with the NLRB on October 16 and on November 30 the umpires voted 57 to 35 to decertify the Major League Umpires Association.

Perhaps predictably, the MLUA filed a petition with the NLRB in December of 1999 to overturn the decertification vote, arguing that Major League Baseball had violated federal labor law by negotiating with a union other than the MLUA. On February 20, 2000, the NLRB rejected the MLUA's request, finding that MLB had not improperly influenced the decertification election.[49]

On February 24, 2000 the umpires formally voted to certify the World Umpires Association (WUA), a newly formed organization, for all regular full-time major-league umpires.[50] With John Hirschbeck as its first president, the WUA went on to negotiate a five-year collective-bargaining agreement, covering 2000-2004.[51] Subsequent five-year contracts have been negotiated without further strikes, and eventually 11 of the 22 umpires who were terminated were reinstated.[52] The World Umpires Association now also represents International League and the Pacific Coast League umpires, as well as international umpires who work tournaments, including the World Baseball Classic, sanctioned by MLB.[53]

Arbitration

In an effort to reinstate the 22 umpires who had resigned and whose rescissions had not been accepted, on August 27, 1999, the Major League Umpires Association filed a demand for arbitration under the terms of the collective bargaining agreement.[54] The union alleged that MLB had conspired with Shapiro and an insurgent union movement in violation of the contract.[55] The court held a hearing on September 1 and the MLUA and MLB entered into a Memorandum of Understanding, under the terms of which the suit was withdrawn and the dispute would be taken to arbitration, with both sides allowed to put forth their procedural and substantive arguments, including MLB's position that the dispute was not subject to the contract's arbitration provisions.[56] The arbitration proceedings lasted approximately a year, with 17 days of testimony. When the decision was announced on May 11, 2001, the arbitrator found no evidence of a conspiracy but ordered reinstatement of two American League umpires (Drew Coble and Greg Kosc) and seven National League umpires (Garg Darling, Bill Hohn, Terry Tata, Frank Pulli, Larry Poncino, Joe West, and Larry Vanover), with full back pay and benefits.[57] The remaining umpires got no relief.

Federal Court

Unhappy with the arbitrator's decision, both sides filed suit in US District Court hoping to have the arbitrator's decision set aside.[58] The court confirmed the arbitrator's determinations that the dispute was subject to arbitration, that the leagues were entitled to rely on the resignation letters and to hire replacements, and that the six rescission letters submitted to the American League on July 27, 1999, were ineffective, as the AL umpire corps was fully staffed on that date.[59] Still unhappy, both sides appealed to the US Court of Appeals for the Third Circuit.[60] In March 2004 the appeals court affirmed the decision of the District Court[61] and in 2005 the US Supreme Court refused to hear the case.

State Court

As if the arbitration and the six years of litigation in federal court that followed weren't enough, on January 2, 2001, Phillips and his law firm, Richard G. Phillips Associates, filed suit in Pennsylvania state court against multiple defendants, including Selig; Robert Manfred, Alderson, and Francis X. Coonelly (all employees of the commissioner's office); the NL; the AL; Brinkman, Hirschbeck, David Phillips, and Tim Welke (all umpires); the World Umpires Association; and Shapiro and Shapiro's law firm.[62] The suit alleged ten separate claims, including tortious interference with existing and prospective contractual relations, defamation, false light invasion of privacy, commercial disparagement, injurious falsehood, fraudulent conveyance of property, conspiracy, unjust enrichment, and breach of contract.[63]

Although an allegation that the commissioner and the leagues had conspired with the umpires to be rid of Phillips and the MLUA might seem hard to believe, it may have been based, to some extent, on a perception that Major League Baseball would rather deal with Shapiro than Phillips. Shapiro, the author of *The Power of Nice: How to Negotiate So Everyone Wins—Especially You*, was often perceived as favoring a nonconfrontational negotiating style, while Phillips was noted for being especially contentious.[64] Phillips was thought by some to have intimidated MLB leaders to the extent that they were unwilling to discipline umpires who made mistakes,[65] and getting rid of Phillips might have been perceived by some owners as a positive step.

The defendants attempted to move Phillips' case to federal court, arguing that his claims arose under federal labor law. The case was sent back to state court, however, when the federal court ruled that the plaintiffs' claims arose solely under state law.[66]

Back in state court, on September 19, 2001, three of the claims asserted against the defendants (fraudulent conveyance of property, unjust enrichment, and breach of contract) were dismissed on legal grounds before trial.[67] Then, after five years during which the parties explored each other's claims and presented their legal arguments to the court, the judge ruled for the defendants without a trial on the remaining claims (tortious interference with existing and prospective contractual relations, defamation, false light invasion of privacy, commercial disparagement, injurious falsehood, and conspiracy).[68] Phillips appealed, but rather than relying on the original 10 claims, the only question presented on appeal was whether Shapiro and the other defendants had conspired to "interfere with the existing contractual attorney-client relationship between Plaintiffs and their client."[69] Phillips lost the appeal, and on March 24, 2009, the Pennsylvania Supreme Court declined review.[70]

Some Effects of Unionization

After the long strike in 1979, the umpires won an improved salary structure and a two-week in-season vacation.[71] The one-day strike on the first day of the 1970 League Championship Series resulted in better pay for postseason games. Over time there have been improvements in the umpires' pensions (including early retirement if an umpire wishes), travel accommodations, and per-diem expense money. In addition, the rotation of umpiring assignments for the All-Star Game and postseason games was negotiated by the union.

NOTES

1   Larry R. Gerlach, *The Men in Blue* (Lincoln: University of Nebraska Press, 1980), 122.

2   Gerlach, 124 (quoting Stewart).

3   John Bacchia, *Augie* (Bloomington: iUniverse, Inc., 2011), 194.

4   Gerlach, 124.

5   "American League Fires Umpire Ernie Stewart," *St. Petersburg Evening Independent*, August 16, 1945: 8, at news.google.com/newspapers?nid=PZE8UkGerEcC&dat=19450816&printsec=frontpage&hl=en .

6   Andrew Zimbalist, *Baseball and Billions* (New York: BasicBooks, 1992), 43.

7   Bacchia, 196-199.

8   Bacchia, 4.

9   Bacchia, 195.

10   Bacchia, 4.

11   Bacchia, 24-27.

12   Bacchia, xii-xiii, 151.

13   Bacchia, 196.

14   Bacchia, 191.

15   Ibid.

16   Gerlach, 169.

17   John C. Skipper, *Umpires* (Jefferson, North Carolina: McFarland & Company, Inc., 1997), 41.

18   Gerlach, 169.

19   Bacchia, 199-200.

20   Bacchia, 201.

21   Roger I. Abrams, *Legal Bases* (Philadelphia: Temple University Press, 1998), 79.

22   Gerlach, 211.

23   Bacchia, 203.

24   Ronald M. Shapiro, *The Power of Nice* (Hoboken: Wiley, Revised and Updated 2015), 238.

25   Ron Luciano, *The Umpire Strikes Back* (New York: Bantam Books, 1982), 232.

26   Luciano, 233.

27   Luciano, 234-238.

28   John Helyar, *Lords of the Realm* (New York: Ballantine Books, 1994), 332.

29   Helyar, 513.

30   See, e.g., ESPN Baseball, "Coleman Upset at Losing Authority," September 10, 1999, at a.espncdn.com/mlb/news/1999/0910/49189.html; Baseball Almanac, "Commissioners of Major League Baseball, American League Presidents and National League Presidents," at baseball-almanac.com/recbooks/officials.shtml; MLB.com, "The Commissionership: A Historical Perspective," at mlb.mlb.com/mlb/history/mlb_history_people.jsp?story=com; ESPN Baseball, "Four Umpire Evaluators to Be Fired," September 29, 1999, at a.espncdn.com/mlb/news/1999/0929/86052.html .

31   Shapiro, 239.

32   Shapiro, 58-59, 202-205, 239.

33   Major League Umpires Assoc. v. American League of Professional Baseball Clubs, 357 F.3d 272 (3d Cir. 2004), n. 1.

34   Matthew Callan, "Called Out: The Forgotten Baseball Umpires Strike of 1999," *The Classical*, October 2, 2012, at theclassical.org/articles/called-out-the-forgotten-baseball-umpires-strike-of-1999.

35   Matthew Callan, John H. Minan, and Kevin Cole, *The Little White Book of Baseball Law* (Chicago: ABA Publishing, 2009),

196; Major League Umpires Association v. American League of Professional Baseball Clubs, et al., 357 F.3d 272 (3d Cir. 2004).

36 Callan, Minan, and Cole, 196.

37 Phillips v. Selig, 959 A.2d 420 (2008).

38 Phillips v. Selig, 959 A.2d 420, 425 (2008).

39 Ibid.

40 Major League Umpires Assoc. v. American League of Professional Baseball Clubs, 357 F.3d 272, 276 (3d Cir. 2004).

41 Phillips v. Selig, 959 A.2d 420, 425 (2008).

42 Ibid.

43 Major League Umpires Assoc. v. American League of Professional Baseball Clubs, 357 F.3d 272, 276 (3d Cir. 2004).

44 Phillips v. Selig, 959 A.2d 420, 425 (2008).

45 Phillips v. Selig, 959 A.2d 420, 426 (2008).

46 Ibid.

47 Major League Umpires Assoc. v. American League of Professional Baseball Clubs, 357 F.3d 272, 277-78 (3d Cir. 2004).

48 Shapiro, 240.

49 Phillips v. Selig, 959 A.2d 420, 426 (2008).

50 Phillips v. Selig, 959 A.2d 420, 427 (2008).

51 Peter Schmuck, "Deal Calls Umpires Safe Through 2004," Baltimore Sun, September 2, 2000.

52 Barry M. Bloom and Tom Singer, "Umpires Ratify Labor Agreement," MLB.com, January 19, 2010, at m.mlb.com/news/article/7934990 .

53 Baseball-Reference.com, "World Umpires Association" at baseball-reference.com/bullpen/World_Umpires_Association .

54 Phillips v. Selig, 959 A.2d 420, 426 (2008).

55 Ibid.

56 Major League Umpires Assoc. v. American League of Professional Baseball Clubs, 357 F.3d 272, 278 (3d Cir. 2004).

57 Ibid.

58 Major League Umpires Assoc. v. American League of Professional Baseball Clubs, 357 F.3d 272, 275.

59 Major League Umpires Assoc. v. American League of Professional Baseball Clubs, 357 F.3d 272, 278 (3d Cir. 2004).

60 Major League Umpires Assoc. v. American League of Professional Baseball Clubs, 357 F.3d 272, 278-279 (3d Cir. 2004).

61 Major League Umpires Assoc. v. American League of Professional Baseball Clubs, 357 F.3d 272, 289 (3d Cir. 2004).

62 Phillips v. Selig, 2001 WL 1807951 (Ct. of Common Pleas, Phila. County, July Term 2000, No. 1550) (2001).

63 Phillips v. Selig, 2001 WL 1807951 at *2 (Ct. of Common Pleas, Phila. County, July Term 2000, No 1550) (2001).

64 Helyar, 332.

65 John Feinstein, Play Ball (New York: Villard Books, 1993), 195.

66 Phillips v. Selig, 157 F. Supp. 2d 419 (E.D. Pa. 2001).

67 Phillips v. Selig, 2001 WL 1807951 at *3-4 (Ct. of Common Pleas, Phila. County, July Term 2000, No. 1550) (2001).

68 Phillips v. Selig, 959 A.2d 420, 427 (2008).

69 Ibid.

70 Phillips v. Selig, 967 A.2d 960 (S. Ct. Pa., 2009).

71 Luciano, 234-238.

The Fates of "The 22"

By Chris Williams

In July 1999, as part of Richie Phillips' strategy to gain bargaining leverage against the leagues, 57 of 68 major-league umpires signed resignation letters and Phillips announced the resignations at a press conference on July 15, 1999.[1] Although many of the umpires attempted to rescind their resignations, the Leagues had been busy hiring replacements and ultimately 22 umpires were out of work.

On September 1, 1999 the umpires and MLB reached an interim agreement under the terms of which the umpires were paid for the remainder of the year but would not continue to work.[2] Also in September 1999 MLB offered to rehire 10 of the 22 umpires at the major-league level and three at the minor-league level, with buy-out offers for four, and five others allowed to retire, but the Major League Umpires Association, the Phillips union, rejected the offer.[3]

The grievances of the 22 were submitted to an arbitrator, Alan Symonette,[4] who ordered nine to be reinstated with full back pay and benefits.[5]

As appeals of the arbitrator's rulings made their way through the courts, MLB and some of the umpires agreed to a partial settlement in 2002.[6]

In 2004, as part of the negotiations for a new collective bargaining agreement, MLB agreed to rehire three of the 22 and pay a total of $2.3 million in severance pay to another six.[7]

Finally, in 2006, the last of the outstanding claims were resolved with an award of back pay to five umpires and pension contributions for two.[8] The 22, and their fates, follow.

Drew Coble (AL): Arbitrator ordered reinstatement with full back pay and benefits; retired with back pay[9]

Gary Darling (NL): Arbitrator ordered reinstatement with full back pay and benefits; rehired as part of 2002 partial settlement with issue of back pay left for resolution by courts; shared in court back pay award of $3.1 million with four others (Hohn, Poncino, Vanover, and West)[10]

Bob Davidson (NL): Arbitrator upheld discharge; worked as minor-league umpire; rehired as part of 2004 settlement[11]

Bruce Dreckman (NL): Arbitrator upheld discharge; federal court vacated arbitrator's decision and ordered new arbitration hearing; claim was settled—rehired without back pay in August 2004[12]

Jim Evans (AL): Arbitrator upheld discharge; received $400,000 severance pay and reinstatement to health benefits as part of 2004 settlement[13]

Dale Ford (AL): Arbitrator upheld discharge; received $400,000 severance pay and reinstatement to health benefits as part of 2004 settlement[14]

Rich Garcia (AL): Arbitrator upheld discharge; hired as umpire supervisor in 2002[15]

Eric Gregg (NL): Arbitrator upheld discharge; received $400,000 severance pay and reinstatement to health benefits as part of 2004 settlement[16]

Tom Hallion (NL): Arbitrator upheld discharge; worked as minor-league umpire; rehired as part of 2004 settlement[17]

Ed Hickox (AL): Arbitrator upheld discharge; worked as minor-league umpire; rehired as part of 2004 settlement[18]

Bill Hohn (NL): Arbitrator ordered reinstatement with full back pay and benefits; rehired as part of 2002 partial settlement with issue of back pay left for resolution by courts; shared in court back pay award of $3.1 million with four others (Darling, Poncino, Vanover, and West)[19]

Sam Holbrook (NL): Arbitrator upheld discharge; federal court vacated arbitrator's decision and ordered new arbitration hearing; claim was settled—rehired without back pay[20]

Mark Johnson (AL): Arbitrator upheld discharge; received $325,000 severance pay and reinstatement to health benefits as part of 2004 settlement[21]

Ken Kaiser (AL): Arbitrator upheld discharge; received $400,000 severance pay and reinstatement to health benefits as part of 2004 settlement[22]

Greg Kosc (AL): Ordered reinstated by arbitrator with full back pay and benefits; retired with back pay[23]

Larry McCoy (AL): Arbitrator upheld discharge; received $400,000 severance pay and reinstatement to health benefits as part of 2004 settlement[24]

Paul Nauert (NL): Arbitrator upheld discharge; federal court vacated arbitrator's decision and ordered new arbitration hearing; claim was settled—rehired without back pay[25]

Larry Poncino (NL): Arbitrator ordered reinstatement with full back pay and benefits; rehired as part of 2002 partial settlement with issue of back pay left for resolution by courts; shared in court back pay award of $3.1 million with four others (Darling, Hohn, Vanover, and West) and was awarded $47,422 pension contribution[26]

Frank Pulli (NL): Ordered reinstated by arbitrator with full back pay and benefits; retired with back pay[27]

Terry Tata (NL): Ordered reinstated by arbitrator with full back pay and benefits; retired with back pay[28]

Larry Vanover (NL): Arbitrator ordered reinstatement with full back pay and benefits; rehired as part of 2002 partial settlement with issue of back pay left for resolution by courts; shared in court back pay award of $3.1 million with four others (Darling, Hohn, Poncino, and West) and was awarded $42,356 pension contribution[29]

Joe West (NL): Arbitrator ordered reinstatement with full back pay and benefits; rehired as part of 2002 partial settlement with issue of back pay left for resolution by courts; shared in court back pay award of $3.1 million with four others (Darling, Hohn, Poncino, and Vanover)[30]

NOTES

1   Phillips v. Selig, 959 A.2d 420, 425 (2008).

2   Murray Chass, "Umpires; Arbitrator Named to Rule on 22 Jobs," *New York Times*, September 28, 1999, at http://www.nytimes.com/1999/09/28/sports/umpires-arbitrator-named-to-rule-on-22-jobs.html .

3   "Baseball; "Arbitrator Orders Baseball to Rehire 9 Umpires," *New York Times*, May 12, 2001, at http://www.nytimes.com/2001/05/12/sports/baseball-arbitrator-orders-baseball-to-rehire-9-umpires.html .

4   Murray Chass, "Umpires; Arbitrator Named to Rule on 22 Jobs," *New York Times*, September 28, 1999, at http://www.nytimes.com/1999/09/28/sports/umpires-arbitrator-named-to-rule-on-22-jobs.html .

5   "Baseball; "Arbitrator Orders Baseball to Rehire 9 Umpires," *New York Times*, May 12, 2001, at http://www.nytimes.com/2001/05/12/sports/baseball-arbitrator-orders-baseball-to-rehire-9-umpires.html .

6   "Umpires Awarded Back Pay," *Los Angeles* Times, August 26, 2006, at http://articles.latimes.com/print/2006/aug/26/sports/sp-bbnotes26 .

7   "Six More Will Split $2.3M in Severance Pay," ESPN.com at http://www.espn.com/mlb/news/story?id=1953109 .

8   "Umpires Awarded Back Pay," *Los Angeles* Times, August 26, 2006, at http://articles.latimes.com/print/2006/aug/26/sports/sp-bbnotes26 .

9   "Umpires Who Quit Lose Again in Court," *Cape Cod Times*, February 18, 2004, at http://www.capecodtimes.com/article/20040218/Sports/302189952 .

10 "Umpires Awarded Back Pay," *Los Angeles Times*, August 26, 2006.

11 "Six More Will Split $2.3M in Severance Pay," ESPN.com at http://www.espn.com/mlb/news/story?id=1953109 .

12 "Umpires Who Quit Lose Again in Court," *Cape Cod Times*, February 18, 2004, at http://www.capecodtimes.com/article/20040218/Sports/302189952 .

13 "Six More Will Split $2.3M in Severance Pay," ESPN.com at http://www.espn.com/mlb/news/story?id=1953109 .

14 "Six More Will Split $2.3M in Severance Pay," ESPN.com at http://www.espn.com/mlb/news/story?id=1953109 .

15 "Umpires Who Quit Lose Again in Court," *Cape Cod Times*, February 18, 2004, at http://www.capecodtimes.com/article/20040218/Sports/302189952 .

16 "Six More Will Split $2.3M in Severance Pay," ESPN.com at http://www.espn.com/mlb/news/story?id=1953109 .

17 "Six More Will Split $2.3M in Severance Pay," ESPN.com at http://www.espn.com/mlb/news/story?id=1953109 .

18 "Six More Will Split $2.3M in Severance Pay," ESPN.com at http://www.espn.com/mlb/news/story?id=1953109 .

19 "Umpires Awarded Back Pay," *Los Angeles Times*, August 26, 2006.

20 "Umpires Who Quit Lose Again in Court," *Cape Cod Times*, February 18, 2004, at http://www.capecodtimes.com/article/20040218/Sports/302189952 .

21 "Six More Will Split $2.3M in Severance Pay," ESPN.com at http://www.espn.com/mlb/news/story?id=1953109 .

22 "Six More Will Split $2.3M in Severance Pay," ESPN.com at http://www.espn.com/mlb/news/story?id=1953109 .

23 "Umpires Who Quit Lose Again in Court," *Cape Cod Times*, February 18, 2004, at http://www.capecodtimes.com/article/20040218/Sports/302189952 .

24 "Six More Will Split $2.3M in Severance Pay," ESPN.com at http://www.espn.com/mlb/news/story?id=1953109 .

25 "Umpires Who Quit Lose Again in Court," *Cape Cod Times*, February 18, 2004, at http://www.capecodtimes.com/article/20040218/Sports/302189952 .

26 "Umpires Awarded Back Pay," *Los Angeles Times*, August 26, 2006.

27 "Umpires Who Quit Lose Again in Court," *Cape Cod Times*, February 18, 2004, at http://www.capecodtimes.com/article/20040218/Sports/302189952 .

28 "Umpires Who Quit Lose Again in Court," *Cape Cod Times*, February 18, 2004, at http://www.capecodtimes.com/article/20040218/Sports/302189952 .

29 "Umpires Awarded Back Pay," *Los Angeles Times*, August 26, 2006, at http://articles.latimes.com/print/2006/aug/26/sports/sp-bbnotes26 .

30 "Umpires Awarded Back Pay," *Los Angeles Times*, August 26, 2006, at http://articles.latimes.com/print/2006/aug/26/sports/sp-bbnotes26 .

US Secret Service Agent Puts His Life on the Line Posing as a Major-League Umpire

By Bill Nowlin

I'd heard the story of a time that a US Secret Service agent borrowed major-league umpire garb and posed on the field at Yankee Stadium, ready to take a bullet if need be in order to protect the life of President George W. Bush.

It was the night that President Bush threw out the ceremonial first pitch before Game Three of the 2001 World Series — October 30, 2001. This made it less than two months after the 9/11 terrorist attacks.

I had myself been at the Stadium for three games against the Red Sox, on September 7, 8, and 9, and then headed back home to Boston. Less than 48 hours later, the Twin Towers were hit.

After the attacks, MLB postponed games across the country as the U.S. and the rest of the world grappled with the magnitude of the event, amid uncertainty as to what might happen next. Needless to say, a high-profile athletic event like a game at Yankee Stadium presented a prime target.

Baseball resumed a little over a week after the attacks. The Yankees had gone on the road, but returned home on September 25 for the first game held at the Stadium after 9/11. Ron Kulpa was the home-plate umpire that night. Wally Bell, Marty Foster, and Mark Hirschbeck were the base umpires. Ron holds vivid memories of the occasion.

"Everyone in the country was on edge, and going into Yankee Stadium was a thrill but there was a lot of emotion, a lot of tears being shed as far as fans and players — but you also knew we were probably in the safest place to be in the world. Security came in and briefed us on everything, and they told us, 'You're probably in the safest spot in the world right now.'"[1]

Roger Clemens had gone to visit a fire station earlier that day. A number of others had paid their respects one way or another. Both teams' players and the umpires were given special caps to wear, in honor of the first responders. For Kulpa, "It was an honor. It was an honor to be there and it was something I'll never forget."

The World Series, of course, is played in front of a massive worldwide television audience. And President Bush committed to throw out the first pitch prior to Game Three. Naturally, security was tight.

Steve Rippley was the crew chief of the six-man crew that night. In fact, he recalls, "My wife came to the Stadium with me, but because of Bush being there and all that, the security was so high that she didn't get in until the third inning."[2]

The other umpires on the crew were Dale Scott, Ed Rapuano, Jim Joyce, Dana DeMuth, and (again, as it happens) Mark Hirschbeck.

Rippley says that when he arrived at the umpires' dressing room, "I opened the door and here we've got a guy in there. In so many words, I said, 'Who the heck are you?' I believe his name was Jonathan Cherry. The guy was a phenomenal guy, a sweetheart of a guy. He said, 'I'm going to go out on the field with you and I'm going to stand next to you when the president throws out the first pitch.'

"Basically, he told me, 'I'm the bullet sponge. In other words, if anything happens to Bush on the field, I'm going to jump on top of him.'"

He was dressed in a way that resembled an umpire, but Rippley told him, "We've got to make it realistic. You have to dress like us. You can't just look like us." The other part of it was, there are six umpires who work World Series games. "If seven guys go on the field, somebody's going to realize something's out of

U.S. Secret Service agent bearing arms, umpires room, Yankee Stadium. October 30, 2001.

the ordinary, so I made one of the guys drop back so there were only six of us on the field."

That was Mark Hirschbeck. He said, "I'm fine. I'm fine to stay off the field."[3]

Rippley continued, "We made it as realistic as possible. In every dressing room, there's an extra kit. I think he drew from that and then the crew that was there, we gave him some of our stuff—kind of mixed and matched so he would look like us."

Of course the agent wore protective gear—bulletproof vest and all. And a pistol under his umpire's jacket. "Yeah, he was all covered up, but he was loaded for bear," Rippley said. "It was never in plain sight. There's probably other people who were around the field, but I don't know that there was anybody closer than he was."

The president himself came into the umpires' room about 20 minutes before the game and chatted with the umpires, signing baseballs for them and posing for a few personal photos.

A video on YouTube shows the agent, with his equipment. As Jim Joyce says in the clip, "He had communications. He had guns. He had things hooked on the back. He had things hooked on the front."[4] The clip also shows President Bush warming up before the game so he could make a proper first pitch.

Dana DeMuth was the number-two man on the crew. Before they went onto the field, they asked the agent where they should stand. "They had us stand on the line. Steve was the crew chief and I was the number-two man, so he says, 'I'll stand between you and Steve.' He was obviously there to protect the president, and what stands out in my mind about was when he said, 'If any sniper is going to take the president out, he'll take me out first.' I remember him saying that and Steve Rippley and I both looked at him, and we both took a step away from him."

Umpires themselves, of course, don't normally carry pistols onto the field, though Rippley joked, "I wish they would have given us grenades every once in a while!"

Everything proceeded as planned, without incident. The pitch was thrown—a good pitch, arcing right over the plate. Derek Jeter had warned Bush beforehand: "Don't bounce it. They'll boo you."

Rippley recalls, "As soon as the F-14s flew over, the Secret Service guy gave me a big shot in the ribs and he says, 'That's the sound of freedom.' It brought tears to your eyes, but it was kind of neat."

Thanks to Cathie Ross, Terry Samway, and Tim Samway.

NOTES

1 Author interview with Ron Kulpa on January 1, 2017.

2 Author interview with Steve Rippley on January 10, 2017.

3 Author interview with Dana DeMuth on January 13, 2017.

4 youtube.com/watch?v=evb489N11Q4.

Norman Rockwell's Umpire Paintings

By Larry R. Gerlach

Baseball has always been a favorite subject for artists wishing to portray popular aspects of American culture. Norman Rockwell (1894-1978), America's "Dickens with a paint brush," produced dozens of illustrations of the National Pastime for novels and magazine stories, commercial advertisements and magazine covers, notably 11 for the *Saturday Evening Post*. These paintings, which included *The Dugout* (1948) and *The Rookie* or *Red Sox Locker Room* (1957), were enormously influential as they conveyed an emotional sense of the game to a national audience decades before the appearance of multisport magazines featuring extensive color photography, *Sport* in 1946 and *Sports Illustrated* in 1954, and the onset of nationally televised major-league games in the 1950s.[1]

Rockwell's paintings, almost never titled and crafted from photographs of modeled scenes, were not intended as depictions of actual games, but as images of a story in progress that would draw viewers emotionally into baseball experiences and required their imagination to complete. Two of his more than 30 baseball magazine covers were devoted to umpires. *The Three Umpires* is his most famous painting, while *The Umpire* is virtually unknown.

The Three Umpires

On April 23, 1949, appeared the most clever, complex, confusing, and controversial painting of Rockwell's career. Now residing in the collection of the Hall of Fame in Cooperstown, it is known by four names: *Tough Call*, Rockwell's original title is spurious because no decision is called for; *Game Called Because of Rain* is nonsensical because it hasn't been; *Bottom of the Sixth* is logical because the scoreboard indicated that; and, for obvious reasons, *Three Umpires* is fitting. The best known of his baseball pictures,

it has assumed iconic status, widely reproduced as prints, collectibles, and decorations on a variety of commercial products ranging from whiskey bottles and ties, to cell phones and clothing.

The painting recalls the angst players, managers, and fans suffer when the vagaries of nature interferes with human design. Here he captures the moment when rain impacts a game between the Brooklyn Dodgers and the Pittsburgh Pirates at Ebbets Field. The painting is not about rendering a specific scene from an actual ballgame, but calls upon viewers to interpret baseball, calling upon viewers to interpret the unknown consequences of rain on any contest. And while presenting a detailed image for enjoyment and contemplation, Rockwell, as was his wont, cleverly inserted enigmatic elements into the picture to both confuse and amuse viewers.

Dominating the picture front and center are three umpires, their authoritative, even monumental presence magnified by the apparent elevated perspective of players in the dugout.[2] They are front and center because they have the responsibility to determine the fate, termination or suspension, of a game in progress. The veteran crew looks searchingly at the sky: John E. "Beans" Reardon, with the home plate umpire's chest protector commands the center; to his right, face uplifted, is Larry Goetz; to the left is Lou Jorda. It is not an accurate physical likeness of any of the arbiters, Reardon appears much too heavy, perhaps to emphasize authority; Goetz and, especially, Jorda look much older than their 53 and 56 years respectively.

Standing behind the men in blue are the team managers. Pittsburgh's Billy Meyer, then in his first year with the Pirates, is hunched over, hands fretfully clasped in despair, also looking much older than his 55 years. Who is the Brooklyn representative, obscured save for a grinning face, arm pointing skyward, and cap doffed as if to mock in delight his counterpart?

Norman Rockwell's "Three Umpires" watch for rain -- and also over the umpires' room at Coors Field in Denver.

Dodgers manager, Burt Shotton, the last big-league skipper to wear street clothes instead of a uniform, although he did usually don a Dodgers cap, was prevented by baseball rules from going onto the field. Besides, he always wore glasses. The figure is Clyde Sukeforth, the coach who represented the team on the field for discussions with players and arguments with umpires. Also visible are two Pirates outfielders. In right field stands Fred "Dixie" Walker, the team's leading hitter that season; in center is Johnny Hopp. The second baseman, hands on hips, is future Pirates manager, Danny Murtaugh

Rockwell staged the scene during the 1948 season at Ebbets Field. The date of modeling is unknown, but September 14, 1948, suggests itself. Reardon would have donned the balloon as the home plate

umpire for the first game of a doubleheader, the only time that season the portrayed trio umpired a Pirates-Dodgers game in Brooklyn. For the other games Reardon and Goetz umpired with Pittsburgh in Brooklyn, either Jocko Conlan replaced Jorda or Dusty Boggess worked as the fourth crew member. (The four-man crew became universal three years later in 1952, but there were some four-man crews in 1948.)

Despite on-site staging, this is a fictitious game as Rockwell intended not to document a specific incident or contest, but instead to evoke conflicting, uncertain emotions about possible outcomes. As usual, he provided touches of authenticity to make the situation believable. Reardon's use of the balloon chest protector worn outside the jacket was correct as he and Jocko Conlan bucked the National League's tradition of using the inside protector. And both wore polka-dot bow ties instead of the traditional hand-in-four neckties favored by all other umpires. The Dodgers batting order on the scoreboard lists uniform numbers 20, 35, and 42. That would be pitcher Phil Haugstad, left fielder Marv Rackley, and second baseman Jackie Robinson. Rackley leading off and Robinson hitting second was not the usual batting order in1948, but one that occurred enough to be credible. The view over the right-field fence, the portion of the Botany Ties sign visible on the fence to the left, "Electricity" at the top of the scoreboard, and the famous Abe Stark clothing store advertisement at the bottom are all accurate. On the other hand, fence signage to the right is SCM instead of GEM (razors), perhaps because of copyright concerns, and Meyers' uniform appears home team white instead of gray, and his stockings lack three yellow stripes, perhaps for artistic emphasis.[3]

Three crucial factual details have led to interpretive confusion. First, the scoreboard shows the game has reached the bottom of the sixth inning with Pittsburgh leading 1-0. Second, the Brooklyn "manager" is exuberantly gleeful, while the Pittsburgh skipper is dour and fretful. Third, because only seven scattered rain drops are falling, is rain beginning or ending and, in either case, what will be the result?

That the painting has four titles indicates confusion as to meaning and intention. And it is one of the very few Rockwell illustrations for which art experts have assigned interpretations. Christopher Finch variously posited two conflicting interpretations. He contended both that "the umpire is about to call the game as rain begins to fall from threatening skies" and that the Brooklyn manager is delighted because the "rain appears to be ending" so the game will continue with the Dodgers' cleanup hitter at the plate.[4] The brothers Stoltz claimed Rockwell "depicted that moment at which the ball game is brought to an early conclusion by foul weather" and that the Brooklyn manager is delighted because the Pittsburgh lead would not become official without the Dodgers getting to bat in the bottom half of the inning.[5] The artistic experts misread the painting and misunderstood baseball rules. Illustrative detail points clearly to rain beginning, not ending, and the scoreboard indicates the Brooklyn cleanup hitter is not due to bat. It was an official game because the teams had finished five innings, and umpires would never "call" or even delay a game when it just starts to rain.

Although the mix of dark clouds to the west and blue sky to the east makes it unclear as to whether rainfall is beginning or ending, Rockwell intended to suggest it was starting to rain. He originally painted dark clouds across the entire sky, but much to his chagrin *Post* editor Ken Stuart surreptitiously commissioned artist William H. Rapp to insert patches of blue on the right side. Rockwell was furious, saying it was "better as I conceived and painted it."[6] Unauthorized prepublication alteration aside, if the rain was about to stop, Pirates players, the umpires and managers would not be on the field. They would be, of course, if it were just starting. But, then, if a storm were arriving the center-field flag would be flapping in the wind, not hanging limp.

Each umpire looking skyward, Reardon's hand outstretched to capture a drop of rain, figuratively pose the question: What are the consequences of rain? The onset of rain, whether resulting in a delayed, called, or suspended game, does not at first blush explain the poses of the rival skippers. Why is the Pittsburgh manager upset? It was an official game as the teams had completed five innings, so according to rules, the Pirates, leading 1-0, would win if rain terminated the game. If the rain eventually stopped and the game continued, Pittsburgh still held the lead and might win, so there was no reason for such a worried reaction. The same is true if the game was suspended for completion at some future time. Why is the Brooklyn manager so happy? If the game were called, the Bums would lose as it was an official contest. If it were only temporarily halted then resumed, or suspended, the Dodgers might rally to win, but that uncertain eventuality does not warrant such exuberance.

However, the euphoric gesture makes sense if the Dodgers had just taken the lead with multiple runs in the bottom of the sixth, runs that according to custom in many ballparks, including Ebbets Field, would not be registered on the manual scoreboard until the end of the inning.[7] Should the game be called, Brooklyn would win the game. That the pitcher was the next batter, suggests the sixth inning in still in progress. Had Brooklyn not yet batted in the bottom of the inning, at that point in a one-run game a pinch hitter would likely been used.[8] Or perhaps he had not yet been announced. Since the Pirates are still in the field, could the umpires be assessing the onset of rain that might, should the game be called, mark a Brooklyn victory? As typical with Rockwell: Your call.

The much-beloved painting has been criticized by baseball aficionados for an unrealistic portrayal of the umpires huddled together on the field, the manner of assessing the nature of the rainfall, and the behavior of the managers. That confuses the creative license inherent in artistic representations with the accuracy required of documentary depictions: It is a painting, not a photograph, a fictional creation intended nothing other than eliciting emotions of the moment, leaving to the viewer to extrapolate various scenarios depending upon the implications of whether the rain is starting or stopping and the status of the game in progress. To criticize Rockwell for improbabilities is like criticizing Impressionist Claude Monet and Surrealist Salvador Dali for painting unrealistic images. Ironically, Rockwell's association with the umpires would lead him to the only major artistic faux pas of his career.

The Umpire

Rockwell's artistic creativity and desire to impart believability clashed as never before with *The Umpire*. As a follow-up to the *Three Umpires*, he envisioned a cover to celebrate the opening of the 1952 season that would feature an umpire. He was so enthusiastic about the project that he provided a rare explanation of what he intended to convey: "A brawny gorilla of an umpire was daintily dusting home plate with a little whisk broom while the batter and catcher waited. The contrast between the squatting umpire—

big, red-faced, square-jawed, broad-shouldered—and his finicky, housekeeping gesture seemed humorous to me."[9]

Since the Cardinals and Pirates were to open the season in St. Louis, he assembled a trio of local big leaguers at Sportsman's Park in early winter1951. Two St. Louis residents, Stan Musial in his Cardinals uniform with bat in hand, and Joe Garagiola, who had been traded to Pittsburgh on June 15, 1951, outfitted in catchers' gear, were positioned on either side of home plate. In between crouched veteran National League umpire Al Barlick, who had driven over from his home in nearby Springfield, Illinois.

As photographers took pictures of the posed trio, Garagiola mentioned that Rockwell had positioned Barlick the wrong way, his backside toward the grandstand. Tradition required umpires to face the spectators, not the pitcher, when brushing off home plate. But during the three days of posing and photographing, no one else said anything, not the half-dozen local newspaper reporters, the groundskeepers, Musial, or even Barlick. Thus when Rockwell returned to his studio in West Arlington, Vermont, and began painting the picture, he ignored Garagiola's comment. After all that would have countered the focal point of the painting, the uber-masculine expression on Barlick's face as he dusted off the plate. He was enthusiastic about the painting: "I had no doubts about this cover; it was a good one; I was sure of it."[10]

The painting was half-finished when a close friend and neighbor, Jim Edgerton, who had modeled for several Rockwell paintings, pointed out that the umpire's position was not correct. Rockwell frequently took minor liberties for artistic effect, but this was a major faux pas that violated a baseball custom that bordered on unwritten law. Taken aback by the gaffe, Rockwell submitted a revised painting, but the *Post* editors did not want readers looking at an umpire's backside. Rockwell was probably relieved inasmuch as a correctly posed painting would be both uninteresting and unable to convey his visual intent. As a result, he never published the painting, which after 1953 hung in his studio in Stockbridge, Massachusetts.[11]

Over the years baseball fans, even the most ardent among them, have paid scant attention to umpires save for controversial decisions. Thankfully Norman Rockwell recognized not only their conspicuous presence, but also the central place of umpires in the game. His most famous baseball painting, *The Three Umpires*, is a dramatic representation of their prominent position.

If *The Umpire* revealed Norman Rockwell's lack of familiarity with umpiring, he demonstrated an awareness of the conspicuous place of umpires in the game in *The Three Umpires*, a dramatic representation of their prominence that continues to provide baseball enthusiasts with visual and speculative enjoyment.

NOTES

1   For a complete account of Rockwell's baseball paintings, see Larry R. Gerlach, "Norman Rockwell and Baseball: Images of the National Pastime," *NINE: A Journal of Baseball History and Culture*, Vol. 23, no. 1 (Fall 2014).

2   Christopher Finch, *102 Favorite Paintings by Norman Rockwell* (New York: Crown Publishers, 1978), 96. incorrectly says the umpires are viewed from "about the height of the pitcher's mound" as the perspective from there would have been downward. He also misspelled Goetz as Gaetz.

3   Marc Okkonen, *Baseball Uniforms of the 20th Century: The Official Major League Baseball Guide* (New York: Sterling Publishing, 1991), 185.

4   Christopher Finch, *Rockwell: 332 Magazine Covers* (New York: Abbeville Press/Random House, 1979), 365 and Finch, *Norman Rockwell's America* (NY: Harry N. Abrams, 1975), 229.

5   Donald Stoltz and. Marshall Stoltz, *Norman Rockwell and the Saturday Evening Post, Vol. 3*, (New York: Fine Communications, 1997). 86.

6   See http://www.best-norman-rockwell-art.com/norman-rockwell-saturday-evening-post-cover-1949-04-23-game-called-because-of-rain-three-umpires.html#ixzz2kNB52tVy

7   Lyle Spatz, Dodgers fan and premier New York baseball historian, personally attested to when runs were posted on the Ebbets scoreboard in 1948.

8   *Referee* (March 1994): 9.

9   Norman Rockwell, *My Adventures as an Illustrator* (Garden City, New York: Doubleday & Company, Inc., 1960, 1972), 373-374.

10 Ibid., 373-375; and Oscar Ruhl, "From the Ruhl Book," *The Sporting News*, January 23, 1952, 14.

11 The painting was part of a Rockwell exhibit entitled "Flops" at the Norman Rockwell Museum in Stockbridge, Massachusetts. Garagiola was on hand to discuss the painting for a September 17, 1991, NBC *Today* show broadcast. Bea Snyder, "Today Show Broadcasts Live from Rockwell Museum," *The Portfolio*, vol. 8, no. 3 (Fall 1991), 1-2.

"Yer blind, Ump, Yer blind, Ump, Ya mus' be out-a yer mind, Ump!": Umpires on Screen... and Stage

By Rob Edelman

Most baseball fans would agree that the best umpire is the invisible umpire. Sure, the umps on the field ensure that the rules of the game are followed. They call balls and strikes. They determine if the fielder who dives for the fly ball has trapped the horsehide or made a clean catch. They call the runner out or safe at home. And if those umps are doing their job, the on-field squabbles and controversies will be minimal.

For this reason, umpires almost never are the central characters in fiction. Conflict is one of the essentials of stimulating storytelling; for this reason, a good ump who is unnoticed by the fans simply will not make a compelling character. So when an umpire is featured in a movie or on a TV show, that arbiter will be combative. He will be in conflict with the athletes and managers as well as the fans who are aligned with certain teams or players. It should be no surprise, then, that a documentary about umpires would be titled *The Men You Love to Hate*. This 1997 film opens with a definition of the word "umpire" followed by footage of umps making calls — and players or managers arguing those calls. (But the film is fair-minded, as it pays homage to arbiters. Soon after the opening, there is footage of Bill Klem, perhaps the most revered of all umps. "Do you honestly believe, Bill, that you never missed one?" Klem is asked. He responds, "Never missed one from here," and he points to his heart. "I maybe could've missed one, but never from here.")

Not all baseball-themed films or non-sports films with baseball sequences spotlight ballplayers. Occasionally, a scout may be the central character. One example here is *Trouble With the Curve* (2012), starring Clint Eastwood. So will a front-office type (2011's *Moneyball*, featuring Brad Pitt as Billy Beane) or a baseball writer (Spencer Tracy's Sam Craig in 1942's *Woman of the Year*, and Walter Matthau's Oscar Madison in 1968's *The Odd Couple*). Countless baseball films also highlight the antics of fan-atics. But the majority center on players: major leaguers; minor leaguers; Negro Leaguers; Little Leaguers; and even, on occasion, women. As for umpires, well, they may be present whenever there is on-field action, but they merely exist to yell "Strike three" (if the hero is a hurler who rescues his team with a stellar pitching performance) or "Safe" (if the lead character is the batter who has just bashed the horsehide and is sliding into second base).

The one exception— in a feature-length film, at least — dates from the midpoint of the 20th century: the appropriately titled *Kill the Umpire*, a 1950 farce whose title alone tells us that it does not offer a controversy-free depiction of an umpire. Two years after ingloriously impersonating the Bambino in *The Babe Ruth Story* — which arguably is the all-time worst baseball film — William Bendix is perfectly cast as Bill Johnson, a boorish ex-ballplayer and steadfast fan-atic. Johnson and his family conveniently live in St. Petersburg, which allows him access to spring training games. His obsession with the sport has prevented him from keeping a job; he spends his days

Lobby card, Kill the Umpire.

sneaking off to games, where he endlessly quarrels with umpires — and his voice floats above his fellow fans as he unkindly bellows his favored exhortation: "Kill the Umpire." Upon losing yet one more job, Johnson's frustrated spouse (Una Merkel) is set to end their marriage. To the rescue comes her father, Jonah Evans (Ray Collins), a retired big-league ump who proposes that he take up the profession. This way, a ball field will be his place of employment and he can be paid for attending endless games.

Johnson initially is aghast at the thought of becoming an arbiter. "Trying to make an umpire out of me, that's the lowest thing that can happen to a man," he gripes. However, in order to save his marriage, he enrolls in an umpire school run by Jimmy O'Brien (William Frawley), Jonah's old pal. Johnson is committed to failure and does all in his power to irritate O'Brien. But upon observing some ball-playing youngsters on a sandlot, he comes to appreciate the importance of the umpire. So he buckles down, graduates from O'Brien's school, and is hired to umpire in the Texas Interstate League. Here, Johnson must contend with fans who are clones of the loudmouth that he once was; collectively, they are akin to a lynch mob who just might murder an ump if they disagree with his call. So Bill Johnson experiences firsthand what it feels like to be the target of random name-calling — and, at the same time, is transformed into a competent, proud professional.

In so many baseball films, the villains are gamblers who scheme to throw the Big Game. Such is the case in *Kill the Umpire*. Here, some bettors plot to rope in Johnson, but he refuses to accept their bribe. The film's finale is a drawn-out chase sequence in which a resolute Johnson dodges a throng of irate fans and gun-toting hooligans before arriving at the ball yard to complete his professional obligations.

Bendix is at his comic best in *Kill the Umpire*. Indeed, his performance is the film's centerpiece. As Bill Johnson, baseball devotee, dashes onto the field to go head-to-head with an arbiter, he raises his beer bottle to strike his opponent but only succeeds in spilling the brew on himself. He wrecks the English language, pronouncing "ostracized" as "ostrichized." One of the comic highlights: Upon arriving at the umpire school, Johnson dons glasses and impersonates a blind man who is incapable of crossing a street, let alone umpiring a ballgame.

Ultimately, *Kill the Umpire* parodies the no-win plight of the umpire. If he calls a close pitch thrown to a home team batter a ball, the fans will disregard him and compliment the hitter for his sharp eye. If he calls the pitch a strike, he will expose himself to the hisses of the hometown faithful who surely will call him every name from ass to zombie.

On occasion, other shorter films have featured an arbiter as a central character. One, in fact, dates from 1916 and is a one-reel farce featuring Eddie Lyons and Lee Moran, a then-prolific comedy team. It also is titled *Kill the Umpire*. According to a brief synopsis and review published in the July 22, 1916 issue of *Moving Picture World*, this *Kill the Umpire* charts what happens when "Eddie goes to the game to bawl out the umpire. He slugs him with a pop bottle. Later they meet unexpectedly at dinner and trouble results. This will tickle baseball fans and others will enjoy it also." Another is *The Baseball Umpire* (1913), a split-reel (or, five-minute-long) comedy starring Fred Mace, a long-forgotten early screen farceur. *The Baseball Umpire* was one of almost 70 shorts featuring Mace that were released in 1913. The October 4, 1913 issue of *Moving Picture World* listed the title as *The Umpire* and noted that, in it, "Fred Mace disports himself as umpire at a Los Angeles ball game. The setting and photography are good, but more plot was needed."

There was plenty of plot in a second, earlier Fred Mace vehicle, this one produced on the stage, in which he also played an arbiter. Prior to coming to the movies — and, along with John Bunny and Ford Sterling, predating Fatty Arbuckle, Buster Keaton, Harold Lloyd, and Charlie Chaplin as a top silent screen comedy star — Mace earned kudos in *The Umpire*, a musical comedy with book and lyrics by Will M. Hough and Frank R. Adams and music by Joseph E. Howard. Here, Mace was an arbiter who incurs the wrath of fans after blowing a pair of calls at home plate because he is momentarily distracted by a pretty face in the stands. He flees the scene and ends up stranded in, of all places, Morocco.

The eternal plight of the arbiter is highlighted in one of the musical numbers. The title is "The Umpire Is A Most Unhappy Man," and the lyrics include the following:

An umpire is a cross between a bullfrog and a goat.

He has a mouth that's flannel-lined and brass tubes in his throat.

He needs a cool and level head that isn't hard to hit.

So when the fans beat up his frame, they'll have a nice place to sit.

The only job that worse,

Is driver on a hearse...

Mace, however, was not the first to star in *The Umpire*. The musical debuted at Chicago's La Salle Theatre on December 2, 1905, with local stage per-former Cecil Lean in the title role. A week after its premiere, the *New York Dramatic Mirror* reported that *The Umpire* "has drawn crowded houses ever since the opening and at the present time seems destined to be one of the most popular of the recent productions at the theatre. Joseph E. Howard has assembled a catchy, tuneful, effective score... Press criticism has been generally favorable." This prediction proved to be spot-on. Theater historian Gerald Bordman

noted that *The Umpire* was "far and away the big-gest musical hit the city had ever seen," adding that "the show established Lean as the leading musical comedy actor in Chicago and confirmed beyond any doubt the supremacy of Hough-Adams-Howard in the pecking order of Chicago's lyric stage." According to *Theatre Magazine*, *The Umpire* enjoyed "a run of over 300 nights at the La Salle Theatre..." While Lean remained with the original production, Mace took the lead when the show went on tour several months after its debut. He appeared in *The Umpire* off and on for the next three years, playing cities from San Francisco, Los Angeles, Atlanta, Denver, Philadelphia, Louisville, Des Moines, Winnipeg, and Portland, Oregon, to Muskogee, Oklahoma, Colfax, Washington, and Decatur, Joliet, and Jacksonville, Illinois. Curiously, *The Umpire* never opened in New York.

Near the start of the tour, Mace and his comi-cally-distorted mug were featured on the cover of *Billboard* (which then was known as *The Billboard*), an entertainment industry trade publication. The issue was dated August 18, 1906, and the caption un-derneath the image read: "Fred Mace; His Comedy Work in The Umpire, Placed Him in the Front Rank of Funny Men." Almost three years later, when *The Umpire* played the Princess Theater in San Francisco, it was advertised as "The Famous Baseball Musical Comedy Hit." Noted an anonymous *Los Angeles Herald* critic, reviewing the production during its Southern California run, "(The umpire's) description of his great game wherein he lets the home team lose by calling two 'safe' men out because he is entranced by a couple of pretty eyes in the stands, is an epic worthy of place beside that greatest of all baseball classics, 'Casey at the Bat'..."

The success of *The Umpire* did not result in a spate of fictional arbiter-heroes, either on stage or screen. But an umpire is likely to appear — albeit fleetingly — whenever a ballgame is depicted on celluloid. A textbook example of the abuse heaped on big-screen umps is found in the opening sequence in *Arsenic and Old Lace* (1944), based on the Joseph Kesselring stage play. The setting is the Brooklyn, New York of old: the Brooklyn of the dearly departed Dodgers. Here, the Bums are battling their New York rivals at Ebbets Field. A Dodger is at bat. The New York hurler, who wears #47, throws his pitch. "STEE-RIKE. Yer OUT!" roars the umpire. The batter — #43 — already has started making his way to first base, but he changes his course, approaches the ump, pulls off the arbiter's mask, and belts him in the kisser. As the dazed umpire runs his hand across his injured chin, Brooklyn and New York players — joined by the Ebbets Field faithful, who rush onto the field — commence a full-scale rhubarb. A similarly-depicted animated ump briefly materializes in *How to Play Baseball* (1942), in which Goofy, the beloved Disney character, demonstrates the art of pitching, batting, base running, and fielding. The umpire is introduced as "that impartial pillar of judicial dignity whose word is law," but a riot ensues when he calls a runner out at home plate.

Hullabaloos involving other screen umpires date from the earliest baseball films. For example, the initial celluloid *Casey at the Bat* (1899), filmed on the lawn of Thomas Edison's estate in West Orange, New Jersey, features a batter swinging wildly at a pair of pitches, which the home plate ump correctly calls strikes. The argumentative batter then pushes the arbiter to the ground, with bedlam ensuing as a jumble of bodies pile up at home plate. (The film's full title is *Casey at the Bat, or The Fate of a "Rotten" Umpire*. The arbiter is so-described not because he is incompetent but because "Casey" has no one else to blame for his lack of hitting prowess.)

Two other wacky umpire portrayals are found in *The Naked Gun: From the Files of Police Squad!* (1988) and *Dizzy and Daffy* (1934). In *The Naked Gun...*, bumbling Lieutenant Frank Drebin (Leslie Nielsen) is trying to thwart an assassination attempt on the Queen of England, who is attending a California Angels-Seattle Mariners game. Perhaps the killer is one of the players. Drebin knocks out and replaces the home-plate umpire and begins comically frisking players, as if they are being measured for suits. He over-theatrically calls strikes, at one point breaking into a Michael Jackson-inspired dance routine.

He wipes home plate first with a Dustbuster and then with a vacuum cleaner, and examines a bat by "opening" it as if he is removing a cork from a wine bottle. Meanwhile, *Dizzy & Daffy*, a two-reel comedy featuring Dizzy and Paul Dean, highlights a game between the Farmer White Sox and Shanty Town No Sox as well as some comic repartee between Lefty Howard (Shemp Howard, of Three Stooges fame), a hurler in desperate need of glasses, and Call 'Em Wrong Jones (Roscoe Ates), a stuttering arbiter. Lefty dubs Call 'Em Wrong the "world's worst umpire." Call 'Em Wrong responds, "Why, you just pitch 'em right and I'll call 'em..." Before he can complete the sentence with the word "right," Lefty breaks in with "wrong." Call 'Em Wrong stutters when calling a pitch a ball, so he deems it a strike instead — and vise-versa. Later on, Howard comically pokes at the eyes of the ump and tells him, "I'll get you a cup and some pencils."

Fictional umpires often go hand-in-hand with sightlessness. Such is the case even if the ump is mentioned but not seen onscreen. In "Six Months Out of Every Year," one of the musical numbers in *Damn Yankees*, the hit Broadway musical that was filmed in 1958, a fan's wife laments her mate's obsession with baseball. Mentioned in the lyrics are the Washington Senators, the (damn) New York Yankees, Willie Mays — and the fan's eternal roar of "Yer blind, Ump, Yer blind, Ump, Ya mus' be out-a yer mind, Ump!" This classic complaint might have been inspired by the umpire in *Porky's Baseball Broadcast* (1940), an animated short. Porky Pig is the play-by-play announcer for the "decisive World Series game." Pitching for the Giants is none other than "Carl Bubble," while one of the hitters is a pig with a face that is modeled after Babe Ruth. At one point, Porky reports, "Here comes the umpire out on the field." He is an unsmiling soul wearing dark glasses and clutching a cane who is guided by a seeing-eye dog. You guessed it. The ump is, quite literally, blind.

Not all fictional umpires are played for laughs, however. One of the more bizarre yet revealing onscreen umps is the central character in *A Prayer for the Umpire* (2009), which runs 16 minutes. Here, a chunky young arbiter named Jeremy faces an endless barrage of abuse while officiating a Little League playoff game. An oversexed mom pressures him to be "fair and unbiased," but what she really wants is for him to call pitches in favor of her son, who is one of the hurlers. Jeremy is chided and manipulated by the two petty, obnoxious coaches and, throughout, he is not so much an umpire as a receptacle of abuse. Eventually, Jeremy calls the game after the woman's son hits and bloodies a batter after being told to do so by his coach. The now-irate mom has the audacity to call Jeremy a "bully." She tells her son that Jeremy is "the definition of a loser," adding, "He can't play, so he has to ruin it for (the kids)." At the finale, while Jeremy is standing by his car and removing his chest protector, the woman sneaks up behind him and bashes him in the head with a bat.

A Prayer for the Umpire may be contrasted to the content of a TV series episode that dates from 43 years earlier. In "The Ball Game," an *Andy Griffith Show* episode that aired on October 3, 1966, Opie Taylor is about to play in a "big" Little League game pitting the Mayberry Giants against the Mt. Pilot Comets. "If we win, we get to go to Raleigh for the state championship," Opie explains. Because the regular ump is sick, Sheriff Andy Taylor, Opie's dad, is recruited as a replacement. "We know you'll be fair to both sides," Mayberry resident Goober declares, but trouble comes when the ever-honest Andy calls Opie out at home plate to end the game with Mayberry on the short end of a 6-5 score. So the sheriff incurs the wrath of the Mayberry populace. Goober is angry. So is Floyd the barber. Opie's pals snub him. An irate Aunt Bee tells him, "You were supposed to help," while Opie is depressed. "When that play happened, I was right on top of it," Andy explains to Opie. "And you were sliding, weren't you? Now all I was doing, I was looking right at the plate. So I was in the best position to see it, and I made my decision based on what I saw." Was Opie out or safe? That really isn't the point. The message here is that Andy's decision, right or wrong, should be accepted "in the spirit of good sportsmanship."

In vehicles from *Kill the Umpire* to "The Ball Game," arbiters are played by actors. On occasion, however, real umpires have appeared onscreen. For after all, why not cast a genuine ump as a celluloid arbiter whose only dialogue might be "Strike Three" or "Ball Four"? (It's a shame that George Moriarty, who umpired in the majors between 1917-1926 and 1929-1940, never had a role in a Hollywood movie — if only because he is the grandfather of actor Michael Moriarty, who starred as Henry Wiggen in the 1973 screen version of Mark Harris's *Bang the Drum Slowly*.)

Among real-life umps, John "Beans" Reardon represented his profession in *The Kid from Left Field* (1953). Joe Rue played an arbiter in *The Stratton Story* (1949). So did Bill Grieve in *The Kid from Cleveland* (1949) and Ziggy Sears in *The Babe Ruth Story* (1948) and *The Stratton Story*. Al Barlick and Augie Donatelli were respectively the home plate and first base umps in *The Odd Couple*. Appropriately, Emmett Ashford appeared as one in *The Bingo Long Traveling All-Stars & Motor Kings* (1976). More recently, Harry Wendelstedt umped at Shea Stadium in *Seven Minutes in Heaven* (1985). Joe West was the third-base umpire in *The Naked Gun: From the Files of Police Squad!* — and Ken Kaiser and Ron Luciano appeared as themselves. Jerry Crawford, Rich Garcia, and Rick Reed respectively were the second-base, first-base, and home-plate umps in *For Love of the Game* (1999); Reed also was credited as "Sheriff's

Lobby card, The Jackie Robinson Story.

Deputy" in *Real Bullets* (1990) and "Maintenance Man" in *Article 99* (1992). Doug Harvey umped in a couple of episodes of the TV series *A League of Their Own* that date from 1993.

Easily the busiest-in-show-biz ump was Art Passarella. He and Ashford were credited as "1st Umpire" and "2nd Umpire" in a 1969 episode of the TV series *Ironside*. Passarella also umped in several other shows, from *Guestward Ho!* (1961) to *Nichols* (1971) to the John Ford-directed "Flashing Spikes," a 1962 *Alcoa Premiere* episode featuring James Stewart as an ex-major leaguer banned from baseball for accepting a bribe. His fellow cast-members included Don Drysdale (playing a character named Gomer), Vin Scully, and Vern Stephens. Passarella's non-baseball roles included "Prison Guard #2" on *Sea Hunt* (1959) and "Officer Sekulovich" on four episodes of *The Streets of San Francisco* that aired between 1975 and 1977; the character was named for series star Karl Malden, whose birth name was Mladen Sekulovich. Passarella also umped on the big screen in *Critics Choice* (1963), a Bob Hope-Lucille Ball comedy. However, in his most memorable movie appearance, he mixed with a couple of other major stars as well as a trio of famous big leaguers. *That Touch of Mink* (1962), a romantic comedy, is the tale of Cathy Timberlake (Doris Day), an unemployed "computer machine" operator from Upper Sandusky, Ohio, who is making her way in the Big Apple. To her good fortune, she meets Philip Shayne (Cary Grant), a super-rich mover, shaker, and jet-setter who delivers speeches at the United Nations that even the Russians admire.

Shayne is attempting to charm Cathy, and he asks her: "What is a pretty girl offered in Upper Sandusky when the sun goes down?" After hesitating for a nanosecond, she utters the word "baseball," adding, "I went to a lot of baseball games. A friend of mine, Marvin Schwab, has a box behind the third base dugout.... Cougars won the pennant in '58." Given his status, Shayne can offer Cathy more than Marvin Schwab's box. Cut to Yankee Stadium. A game is in progress. Seated in the Yankee dugout are Cathy,

Shayne— and Roger Maris, Mickey Mantle, and Yogi Berra.

A Bronx Bomber is at bat, and the home plate ump (played by Passarella) has just called a strike. "STRIKE!" bellows Cathy, who loudly accuses Passarella of having an eyeball-related issue before adding, "It was a ball. It was THAT far from the plate." Passarella then approaches the dugout. "Little lady," he asks Cathy, "will you let me umpire this game? You been on my back all night."

Cathy looks to the Yankee sitting directly to her left. "Mickey," she says, "you saw that pitch. It was a ball, wasn't it?" "It looked like it," #7 responds — and Passarella tells him, "You're out of the game, Mantle."

A further-incensed Cathy turns to the player directly on her right. "Roger, how'd that pitch look to you?" "It could've missed the corner," Maris admits — and he too is tossed from the game.

Cathy then turns to Yogi, who needs no cajoling as he declares, "It's a perfect strike. The ump was right." But Passarella is not through. "I don't like sarcasm, Berra. You're out of the game, too."

Such is the power and authority of the umpire.

SOURCES

Books

Bordman, Gerald. *American Musical Theatre: A Chronicle*. (New York: Oxford University Press, 1978).

Edelman, Rob. *Great Baseball Films*. (New York: Citadel Press, 1994).

Newspapers/Magazines

Anthony, Walter. "'Umpire' Is Riot of Fun and Music: Catchy Production Charms Big Audience at the Princess Theater." *San Francisco Call*, April 14, 1909.

Cantwell, Robert. "Sport Was Box-office Poison." *Sports Illustrated*, September 15, 1969.

Mace, Fred. "Says His 'Head' Has Been Reduced." *Motion Picture*, March 1915.

Wall, H.C. "On Main Street: Looking Both Ways From Sewickley, Pennsylvania." *The Saturday Evening Post*, April 20, 1912.

"Fred Mace Won $11,000." *New York Times*, March 29, 1907.

"How Cecil Lean Won Fame Over Night." *Cambridge Sentinel*, September 4, 1909.

"LaSalle Theatre, Chicago." *The Poultry Tribune*, June 1906.

"Ridgeway Theater. 'The Umpire.'" *Colfax Gazette*, March 8, 1907.

"SAN FRANCISCO. Otis Skinner-Under Two Flags-Peter Pan-The New Orpheum-Classmates-Vaudeville Items," *New York Dramatic Mirror*, May 1, 1909.

"Telegraphic News." *New York Dramatic Mirror*, March 31, 1906.

"'Umpire' Mace on Stage." *The Sunday Oregonian*, February 17, 1907.

"'Umpire' Wins Close Decision." *Los Angeles Herald*, February 5, 1907.

"Universal Film Manufacturing Company."

Atlanta Constitution, April 28, 1907.

Chicago Daily Tribune, August 20, 1906.

Iowa City Daily Press, February 2, 1906.

Moving Picture World, October 4, 1913.

Moving Picture World, July 22, 1916.

Muskogee Times-Democrat, April 6, 1907.

New York Dramatic Mirror, December 9, 1905.

New York Star, November 7, 1908.

Photoplay, December 1912.

The Billboard, August 18, 1906.

The Theatre Magazine, December 1906.

———, February, 1907.

Variety, May 11, 1907.

Films

The Men You Love to Hate, 60 minutes, 1997. Directed by Verne Nobles, Sr.

Web Sites

http://www.imdb.com

http://www.loc.gov/item/ihas.100006523

Bowman's 1955 Umpire Baseball Cards

By Bill Nowlin

Many baseball fans of a certain age remember with some nostalgia the 1955 Bowman "TV set" of baseball cards, which featured a number of umpires. Television was new for many Americans at that time; it was maybe three years earlier that my family got the first set in the neighborhood I grew up in and neighbors came over to watch. In 1953 ABC had started televising *The Game of the Week* with Dizzy Dean and Buddy Blattner. In 1955 CBS took over the broadcast. Bowman was undoubtedly hoping to capitalize on the growing TV market by issuing the TV cards. Of course, the images were in black and white, unlike the Bowman cards.

Looking it up in an old book of baseball-card sets from the very end of the twentieth century, I found the set and the list of the umpires who had been featured.

The overall set numbered 320 different cards. Most of them were players, of course. That's what kids collected. But 30 of them featured umpires. Whose idea that was is something we probably can't reconstruct at this point.

Dean's Cards, a leading online baseball-card website, explains that all the player pictures were taken at Shibe Park, many of them featuring its "characteristic green wall." That's where Bowman was based, in Philadelphia. Using the television frame was a novelty at the time, one not repeated. Indeed, the 1955 set was Bowman's last set. Topps bought out Bowman at the end of the year.

The Dean's site says, "As for the umpire cards, they were, understandably, unpopular with kids, the primary purchasers of baseball cards. Part of what makes the umpire cards so difficult to find is that they were the first to be thrown away by kids looking for their baseball heroes. Curiously, the Bowman Company put the umpires in the last series, which historically competed with the football cards sets that were being released at the same time. Kids had already bought the previous two series full of players and had no interest in the coach- and umpire-heavy last series.

"The umpire cards themselves were similar to the other 1955 Bowman cards, but had a few key differences. As previously mentioned, the players' photographs were taken with Shibe Park as a background, while many of the umpires had head shots with a solid color background. On many of the players' cards, Bowman had the interesting idea to ask them to write about their biggest thrill in baseball, made famous by Eddie Waitkus' story that was the basis for *The Natural*, the most exciting game in which they had ever played, or the best pitcher or hitter they had faced. However, the umpire cards feature short biographies written by the Bowman Gum Company. The Bowman writers included facts such as the national heritage of the umpires as well as personal hobbies, family, and professional sports or umpiring experience." It's not surprising that young collectors favored, say, #1 Hoyt Wilhelm or #2 Al Dark, #10 Phil Rizzuto, #23 Al Kaline, #134 Bob Feller, #184 Willie Mays, or #202 Mickey Mantle, over — say — #284 William A. Jackowski or #297 Dusty Boggess. Kids who got a William Engeln card (#301) in their pack may have simply chucked it (no disrespect intended.) These umpire cards are rarer than many, though still not highly sought after.

Copies of these cards can still be purchased individually on eBay and similar sites. What follows is a listing of the umpire cards in the set.

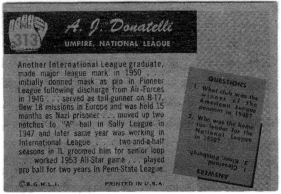

Augie Donatelli, Bowman card. (front & back)

Babe Pinelli, Bowman card (front & back)

Card #	Umpire
226	W F MCKINLEY
235	J A PAPARELLA
239	EDWIN A ROMMEL
250	LARRY NAPP
258	JOHN W STEVENS
260	EDWIN H HURLEY
265	AL BARLICK
267	GEORGE HONOCHICK
272	JOHN FLAHERTY
275	WILLIAM T GRIEVE
277	ED RUNGE
279	HANK SOAR
281	CHARLES BERRY
283	NESTOR CHYLAK
284	WILLIAM A JACKOWSKI
286	FRANK SECORY
289	ART GORE
291	FRANK DASCOLI
293	THOMAS D GORMAN
295	LEE BALLANFANT
297	DUSTY BOGGESS
299	LONNIE WARNEKE
301	WILLIAM ENGELN
303	JOCKO CONLAN
305	FRANK UMONT
307	BABE PINELLI
309	HAL DIXON
311	LARRY GOETZ
313	AUGIE DONATELLI
315	CAL HUBBARD
317	BILL SUMMERS

Thanks to Michael Curtin for the idea. He added, "As a high-school umpire for 15 years, I very much enjoy the artistic imagery of umpires over time." Thanks to Larry Gerlach as well.

An Umpire's Fan Club

By Larry Gerlach

Henry "Hank" Morgenweck had a brief but highly unusual major-league career (1970, 1972-1975). He has the unique distinction not only of beginning and ending his career umpiring a league championship game—in each league—but also having a national fan club. Morgenweck debuted in the National League on October 3, 1970, when as a International League umpire he was called upon to work second base in the first game of the Cincinnati and Pittsburg series owing to the one-day strike of the regular umpires. After joining the American League staff in 1972, he called two no-hitters—Dick Bosman in 1974 and Nolan Ryan in 1975—before his contract was not renewed without explanation after umpiring the 1975 championship series between Oakland and Boston.

Morgenweck wondered if the reason(s) for his dismissal may have been confrontations about pitcher Gaylord Perry allegedly throwing spitballs, the failure to eject anyone in 1975, a controversial base call late that season or simply that umpire supervisor Dick Butler didn't like him.[1] But he believed there was another factor: "I had a national fan club that started in Cleveland. At the end of one season, I was invited to Cleveland to speak to a group. Butler intervened, and Ron Luciano was sent in my place. I don't know why but I believe the fact I had a national fan club was one of the reasons the league did not renew my contract after 1975."[2] A fan club notwithstanding, his surname spelling was problematic. On May 3, while Morgenweck was positioned at second base, the Cleveland scoreboard welcomed the Hank "Morganweck" fan club; even his fan club, present with a banner, similarly misspelled his name. Then, at the beginning of the Oakland-Boston playoffs the Red Sox publicity department incorrectly spelled it "Norganweck."[3]

Virtually nothing is known about the fan club, but Morgenweck provided a few details in response to a letter of inquiry in 2003 about the club from John Toland, "a lifelong Indians fan."[4]

"Dear John,

The fan club start as a joke when one group took of picture of me and had it put on pins and another group had T-shirts made up—"Hank Morgenweck Fan Club."

Both groups got together and formed the club. Herb Score [Cleveland radio broadcaster] found about it and whenever I umpired a Cleveland game in another city he would mention it. The club as a result took off and became a National Fan Club.

It alienated me from members of the staff, but if that's what it took just being nice to fans, signing autographs, I could care less.

Hank Morgenweck"

NOTES

1   He had three ejections in 1972, four in 1973 and one in 1974.

2   "Hank Morgenweck" in John C. Skipper, *Umpires; Classic Baseball Stories from the Men Who Made the Calls* (Jefferson, North Carolina: McFarland, 1977), 112-113. See also his obituary in *The Record* [Bergen County, New Jersey], August 9, 2007.

3   *Cleveland Plain Dealer*, May 4 and October 5, 1975.

4   Photocopy provided by James Odenkirk.

Depicted here is Paul Horton of Connecticut obtaining an autograph from umpire James Hoye prior to the September 24, 2015 game at Fenway Park.

Horton comes up to about a dozen games a year and always asks for the umpires to autograph something for him. He says he has about 40 or 50 autographs of current umpires at this point. Some, of course, are friendlier than others.

He will also ask for player autographs, too, when he can.

Once in a while, he will see someone else ask the umpires to sign something, but very rarely.

He values their work as an integral part of the game, and finds himself sometimes watching the umpires more than the game. He enjoys watching them work, the different ways that umpires make strike calls, for instance.

He is a distant relative of Canadian hockey great Tim Horton.

The Umpire Band

As with any group of people, the individuals within the group have a number of talents, skills, and interests. Umpires are, of course, no exception.

Many express interest in fishing or hunting, golf and working out, and spending time with their families.

Among the varied interests that umpires have are boxing and motorcycling (Ted Barrett; Doug Eddings, Angel Hernandez, Ron Kulpa, Alfonso Marquez also enjoy motorcycling), working on classic cars (Scott Barry; Tim Timmons specializes in refurbishing vintage Porsches), winemaking and snowshoeing (Chris Guccione), piloting aircraft (Ed Hickox), woodworking (Marvin Hudson and Jerry Meals), Christmas lighting (Jim Joyce), training dogs (Brian O'Nora), and more.

Others, such as C. B. Bucknor, spend a considerable amount of time in the offseason doing charitable work. Several engage in mission work with their church.

It's a fair guess that any number of umpires took lessons on a various number of musical instruments as a child. Surely some played piano, and some played other instruments. The ones we know of, thanks to information gleaned through our research and talks with umpires, could come together and form a very interesting musical aggregation.

Envision a combo of this sort:

Bagpipes — Dan Iassogna
Banjo — Tripp Gibson
Euphonium — Quinn Wolcott
Guitar — Brian Knight
Trumpet — Mike Everitt (an All-State trumpet player in 1981-82)

In addition, Eric Cooper — who rings the bell for the Salvation Army each Christmas season — could chime in.

For vocals, we note that Paul Nauert enjoys singing in his spare time. With the right country songs on the agenda, who else but Country Joe West (who already has a couple of compact discs to his credit)?

A band like this would provide eclectic instrumentation, for sure. It's without a doubt safe to say there's never been a group like it.

Perhaps they will assemble the group one year at the annual golf tournament in January in Arizona.

—Bill Nowlin

By the Book: Writings By and About Umpires

By Reid Duffy

The annals of baseball prose include several memoirs and biographies from and about major-, minor-, and amateur-league umpires, well stocked with entertaining war stories from the diamond front, as well as numerous how-to-manuals for those pondering careers in this noble and unappreciated profession; and books inviting fans to offer their own interpretation of baseball's knottier problem calls, based on their impeccable knowledge of baseball rules and the inherent infallibility of their judgment. Here are some compelling selections.

Memoirs

Harry "Steamboat" Johnson, *Standing the Gaff: The Life & Hard Times of a Minor League Umpire* (Nashville: Parthenon Press, 1935; Bison Book Edition with Introduction by Larry R. Gerlach, University of Nebraska Press, 1994). The first book-length umpire memoir by one of its most colorful minor-league practitioners makes it clear that no arbiter stood the "gaff" with more flair, humor, courage, and resolute conviction than Steamboat Johnson. Steamboat, who called them as he saw them, primarily in the Southern Association, from 1909 to 1935, offers keen insights, observations, and fascinating tales of a career minor-league umpire. Gerlach's lengthy introduction provides a biographical portrait of the legendary arbiter.

Babe Pinelli as told to Joe King, *Mr. Ump* (Philadelphia: The Westminster Press, 1953). Ralph "Babe" Pinelli, former major-league player and National League ump from 1935 to 1956, after a brief major-league career in the 1920s as an infielder, best known as the plate umpire for Don Larsen's perfect game in the 1956 World Series. Alas, *Mr. Ump*, intended for younger readers, was published three years before that historic game.

Jocko Conlan and Robert Creamer, *Jocko* (New York: J.B. Lippincott Company, 1967). No shortage of colorful and amusing stories and opinions from Hall of Fame umpire John "Jocko" Conlan, NL umpire from 1941 to 1965.

Dusty Boggess as told to Ernie Helm, *Kill the Ump! My Life in Baseball* (San Antonio: Lone Star Brewing Company, 1966). This rare paperback is a surprisingly informative, entertaining, even controversial memoir considering it was published and distributed as a promotional giveaway by a Texas beer company that Lynton "Dusty" Boggess worked for after his retirement as a National League umpire from 1944 to 1962. Boggess augmented his colorful tales (related in third person by Ernie Helm) with strong opinions and suggestions on improving the national pastime, notably the unrelenting, if elusive, effort to speed up the game.

Tom Gorman as told to Jerome Holtzman, *Three and Two!* (New York: Charles Scribner's Sons, 1979). Tom Gorman was an NL umpire from 1951 to 1976, whose gregarious New York-cop-on-the-beat sensibility and well-honed Irish wit made him one of the more popular and respected umps of that era, both on the diamond and the banquet circuit. Thus funny anecdotes and keen observations abound in Gorman's autobiography, as cultivated by legendary Chicago sportswriter Jerome Holtzman.

Ron Luciano, *The Umpire Strikes Back* (New York: Bantam Books 1982), the first of four Luciano books written with veteran author David Fisher and published by Bantam Books. Luciano was an American League umpire from 1969 to 1979; his flamboyant style, gregarious witticisms, and basic insistence on having fun on the job made him a fan and media favorite, but not always appreciated by managers, players, and league executives. Luciano's most autobiographical book includes his exploits as an All-

American football lineman at Syracuse University and his unrelenting feud with Baltimore manager Earl Weaver. *Strike Two* (1984) basically culls anecdotes and assorted battlefield observations from fellow umpires. In *The Fall of the Roman Umpire* (1986), he chronicles his final years as an umpire and calls on several players to recall their lengthy struggles to make it to big leagues and stay there. *Remembrance of Swings Past* (1988) is crammed with more amusing anecdotes on strange plays and weird rules predicaments as well as the most intriguing characters he encountered, restrained, and debated with in the course of controlling the game.

Eric Gregg & Marty Appel, *Working the Plate: The Eric Gregg Story* (New York: William Morrow and Company, 1990). Gregg was a National League umpire, hired in 1975 as the third African-American umpire, and one of the youngest at 24. The popular ump, known for his upbeat and sunny demeanor, talks candidly about his tough childhood and his ongoing battles trying to control his weight. Published in his 15th year, the book doesn't cover the ill-fated controversies late in his career, the decision by the NL not to rehire Gregg after accepting his resignation as part of his union's bumbling labor action contract strategy, or his losing battle to control his weight that led to the stroke that took his life in 2006 at age 55.

Dave Pallone with Alan Steinberg, *Behind the Mask: My Double Life in Baseball* (New York: Viking, 1990). This best-selling memoir chronicles Pallone's turbulent major-league umpiring career from 1979, as a pariah to many fellow umps for crossing their picket lines to accept his first MLB umpiring job, to 1988, when he was basically "outed" and fired as a closeted gay man.

Pam Postema with Gene Wojciechowski, *You've Got to Have B*lls To Make It in This League: My Life as an Umpire* (New York: Simon & Shuster, 1992). A bittersweet memoir by the most successful woman umpire in professional baseball, starting in 1977 through 1989. Although Postema became a crew chief in Triple A and worked spring-training games, her efforts to become the first female ump in the major leagues fell short. As she saw it, an old-boys network was simply unable to put a woman on the major-league roster. The book is particularly interesting not only in relating the gender-based taunts she endured in her career, but also in depicting the intense competition within the minor-league umpiring community in pursuing the very few umpiring jobs available in the major leagues.

Durwood Merrill with Jim Dent, *You're Out and You're Ugly, Too!: Confessions of an Umpire with Attitude* (New York: St. Martin's Press, 1998). An AL umpire from 1977 to 1999, Merrill offers a book full of umpiring anecdotes and opinions, told with great relish from one of the game's most colorful and loquacious arbiters, especially when recounting his debating sessions with Earl Weaver, Lou Piniella, and Sparky Anderson, all of whom may have supplied the inspiration for the book's compelling title.

John Massaro, *Please Don't Kill the Umpire! Reminiscences of an Obscure Man in Blue* (Madison, Connecticut: Springbok Press, 1999). John Massaro toiled 24 years as a high-school and college umpire in the 1980s and '90s, and his memoir is designed to give the often emotional parental critics in the stands at that level keener insights into what is going on in the field, and better understanding of the calls the underappreciated men in blue make throughout the game.

Ken Kaiser & David Fisher, *Planet of the Umps: A Baseball Life from Behind the Plate* (New York: St. Martin Press, 2003). Kaiser was widely regarded as one the American League's most colorful umpires during his AL career from 1977 to 1999, with his wisecracking style, trademark minimalist "out" calls, and his background as a hefty professional wrestler from the villain ranks, wearing a black hood and nicknamed "The Hatchet Man." One of the funniest umpire memoirs for its bizarre anecdotes, it is impressively informative and incisive.

Dave Phillips with Rob Rains, *Center Field on Fire: An Umpire's Life with Pine Tar Bats, Spitballs, and Corked Personalities* (Chicago: Triumph Books, 2004). Widely praised as one of baseball's most respected umps in his 32-year career, primarily as an AL ump starting in 1971, Phillips was thrust into several of baseball's more bizarre controversies: the George Brett pine-tar saga, the Albert Belle corked-bat caper, being the first umpire to formally discover that Gaylord Perry included a spitball in his repertoire, and, as reflected in the source of the book's title, working the infamous Disco Demolition Night of 1979 in Chicago's Comiskey Park.

Bob Motley with Byron Motley, *Ruling Over Monarchs, Giants & Stars: Umpiring in the Negro Leagues & Beyond* (Champaign, Illinois: Sports Publishing LLC, 2007). Bob Motley is the last surviving Negro Leagues umpire, starting in 1947 through its final barnstorming days in 1958, and the first African-American trained in the Al Somers umpiring school. Written with son Byron Motley, this is an insightful, often rollicking memoir of traveling on the same buses carrying such legends as Satchel Paige, Willie Mays, Ernie Banks, and Henry Aaron, as the Negro Leagues started their final fade upon the formal and grudging integration of major-league baseball. Motley was known for his showmanship and acrobatic base calls; the cover photo shows impressive hang time while making a leaping out call at first base.

Al Clark with Dan Schlossberg, *Called Out But Safe: A Baseball Umpire's Journey* (Lincoln: University of Nebraska Press, 2014). The first Jewish AL umpire, Clark had a seemingly respected, if feisty, umpiring career in the AL and MLB (after the league umpiring staffs merged) for 25 years starting in 1976, before it came to an ignominious end when fired for misusing first-class plane tickets, and then briefly imprisoned and fined for his involvement in a baseball memorabilia scam. While clearly a reputation restoration project, Clark doesn't skimp on interesting and amusing anecdotes, insights, and relevant opinions.

Doug Harvey and Peter Golenbock, *They Called Me God: The Best Umpire Who Ever Lived* (New York: Gallery Books, 2014). This memoir came out shortly after Doug Harvey became the ninth umpire to be inducted into the Baseball Hall of Fame, on the basis of a 30-year career from 1962 to 1992 during which he was widely considered to be one of the best ever. Players bemusedly called him "God" in deference to

his Central Casting looks, his demeanor of umpiring rectitude, his sound judgment, and his no-nonsense approach to excess carping and chirping. The memoir is well stuffed with memorable calls and moments, interesting observations about players and managers, and keen insights into his Hall of Fame journey.

Biographies

Mary Bell Hubbard, *Strike 3! And You're Out: The Cal Hubbard Story* (self-published by Mary Bell Hubbard, 1976). A very rare, family-based biography of Cal Hubbard, the only person inducted into the College and Pro Football Halls of Fame and the Baseball Hall of Fame, reflecting his work as a legendary football lineman in the 1920s and '30s, and as a most imposing AL umpire from 1936 to 1951.

Mike Shannon, *Everything Happens in Chillicothe: A Summer in the Frontier League with Max McCleary, the One-Eyed Umpire* (Jefferson, North Carolina: McFarland and Company, 2004). This humorous, inspiring, and often poignant memoir recounts McCleary's 2000 season in the independent Frontier League. What set the veteran independent and collegiate umpire apart was that he was blind in one eye, the result of a freak accident that torpedoed his burgeoning minor-league umpiring career in 1977. But in 1986 he was able to get certified as an ump in the lower levels, glass right eye and all, with a productive career that spawned many amusing and intriguing stories and situations.

Bob Luke, *Dean of Umpires: A Biography of Bill McGowan* (Jefferson, North Carolina: McFarland & Company, 2005). A slim biography of Hall of Fame umpire Bill McGowan, a highly respected, if fiery and flamboyant AL arbiter, whose 30-year career from 1925 to 1954 was highlighted by 2,541 consecutive games, and the founding of an umpire training school subsequently operated by Al Somers and Harry Wendelstedt.

John Bacchia, *Augie: Stalag Luft VI to the Major Leagues* (Bloomington, Indiana: iUniverse, 2011). A compelling biography of Augie Donatelli, NL umpire from 1950 to 1973, with half of the book detailing his imprisonment in a World War II German prisoner of war camp after his B-17 bomber was shot down, that intriguingly serves as a launch to his umpiring career. The second half showcases his productive umpiring career in the '50s and '60s that saw him presiding over a record eight no-hitters.

Adrienne Cherie Ashford, *Strrr-ike!* (Bloomington, Indiana: Author House, 2004). A slim volume about Emmett Ashford, major-league baseball's first African-American umpire, written by his daughter. Hired by the AL in 1966, after considerable West Coast sports media pressure, at the advanced age of 51, he become a favorite of fans, if not always with players, for his hustling style, flamboyant strike and out calls, upbeat demeanor, and stylish dress.

History

James M. Kahn, *The Umpire Story* (New York: G.P. Putnam's Sons, 1953). This tome has long been the definitive history on the origins and development of major-league baseball umpiring, published as part of the 1940s and '50s-era Putnam Sports Series of baseball team histories and major figures. James Kahn chronicles the lot of umpires from the raucous and rowdy days of nineteenth-century professional baseball to the emergence of four-man crews and formal training of budding arbiters in umpiring schools. There is no shortage of great anecdotes and even greater photographs from this hard-to-find baseball classic.

Lee Gutkind, *The Best Seat in Baseball, But You Have to Stand: The Game as Umpires See It* (New York: Dial Press, 1975; Southern Illinois University Press reprint, 1999). In 1974 writer and college professor Lee Gutkind followed an umpiring crew—Doug Harvey, Harry Wendelstedt, Nick Colosi, and Art Williams (the first African-American umpire in the National League)—to produce an intriguing, controversial chronicle of their dedication and work ethic, all-too-candid thoughts on the players, managers, and sportswriters, and the pressures, insecurities, and chronic disrespect encountered in the course of the long season grind. The umpires were angered by the book's warts-and-all account, filled with profane

quotes from their locker room; Gutkind countered in the 1999 version that he gave an honest and ultimately positive portrayal of baseball's most difficult and least appreciated profession.

Larry R. Gerlach, *The Men in Blue: Conversations with Umpires* (New York: Viking Press, 1980; reprint with Afterword, University of Nebraska Press, 1994). The founding father of SABR's Umpires and Rules Research Committee conducted illuminating and candid interviews with a dozen "old-time" umpires: Beans Reardon, Lee Ballanfant, Joe Rue, George Pipgras, Ernie Stewart, Joe Paparella, Bill McKinley, Jim Honochick, Shag Crawford, Ed Sudol, Bill Kinnamon, and Emmett Ashford. The result is a series of autobiographies as well as an informal history of umpiring and the evolution of the profession from the 1920s to the 1970s.

John C. Skipper, *Umpires: Classic Baseball Stories from the Men Who Made the Calls* (Jefferson, North Carolina: McFarland and Company, paperback, 1997). Iowa newspaper editor John Skipper tapped the memories of 19 umpires on famous baseball moments, achievements, and controversies that occurred on their watch. Included are John "Red" Flaherty and Bill Kinnamon on Roger Maris's 61st home run in 1961; Bill Jackowski on Bill Mazeroski's 1960 World Series walk-off; Ed Runge on Don Larsen's World Series perfecto; and Don Denkinger on his ill-fated ninth-inning call in the 1985 World Series; and, yes, Steamboat Johnson on Ty Cobb.

Bruce Weber, *As They See 'Em: A Fan's Travels in the Land of Umpires* (New York: Scribner's, 2009). *New York Times* reporter Bruce Weber pursues insights into the contemporary world of umpires, putting himself through formal umpire training and working games in Little League and MLB spring training. His illuminating and informative account, replete with numerous interviews and anecdotes from umpires, players, and baseball executives, explores the challenges of umpiring amid the developments of instant replay, and the almost excruciating pressures and competition among minor-league umpires striving for inclusion in baseball's most exclusive fraternity, where many are called and few are chosen.

David W. Anderson, *You Can't Beat the Hours: Umpires in the Deadball Era from 1901–1909* (Create Space Independent Publishing, 2013). Anderson, an amateur umpire, pays homage to the MLB umpires who practiced their craft at a time when their profession was at its most challenging and dangerous, the first decade of the twentieth century. The book includes biographical sketches of all the NL and AL umpires.

Peter Morris, *A Game of Inches: The Game on the Field; The Stories Behind the Innovations that Shaped Baseball* (Cleveland: Ivan R. Dee, 2006). Pages 368 through 395 of the first volume of Morris's astounding and fascinating reference work contains all things related to umpiring from the first professional umpires to the use of Lena Blackburne's mud rubbing the gloss off the ball.

David W. Anderson, *More than Merkle: A History of the Best and Most Exciting Baseball Season in Human History* (Lincoln: University of Nebraska Press, 2006). This account of the thrilling 1908 season, historically defined by umpire Hank O'Day's delayed, dramatic, and utterly controversial ninth-inning call of the Giants' Fred Merkle out on a second-base force out that nullified the Giants' game-winning run in a September showdown game against the Chicago Cubs … all leading to the Cubs' last World Series championship (as of 2016) and lifetime scapegoating of "Merkle's Boner." Two other worthy accounts of this topic are Cait Murphy, *Crazy '08* (New York: Harper Collins, 2008) and G.H. Fleming, *The Unforgettable Season* (New York: Holt, Rinehart, and Winston, 1981).

Marilyn Kratz, U*mpire in a Skirt: The Amanda Clement Story* (South Dakota Historical Society, 2010). A brief book introducing young readers to Amanda Clement, who attracted national attention in 1904 when she became the first paid woman umpire for a South Dakota amateur baseball league.

Armando Galarraga and Jim Joyce, with Daniel Paisner, *Nobody's Perfect: Two Men, One Call, and a Game for Baseball History* (New York: Atlantic Monthly Press, 2011). A detailed account of the infamous first-base "safe" call by respected umpire Jim Joyce, depriving Detroit pitcher Armando Galarraga of a perfect game against Oakland on June 2, 2010. (It would have been the 27th and final out had Joyce called it correctly.) After viewing the replay after the game, a distraught and remorseful Joyce tearfully and poignantly apologized to a classy Galarraga, which led to chronicling the journey of the pitcher and the umpire in getting to that time and place, and a call that led to expansion of instant replay to cover virtually all judgment calls other than balls and strikes.

David Nemec and Eric Miklich, *Forfeits and Successfully Protested Games in Major League Baseball: A Complete Record, 1871–2013* (Jefferson, North Carolina: McFarland, 2014). This wonderfully researched book recounts the more than 50 successful appeals of games replayed, early on in their entirety and later from the point of the protest. And more than 130 forfeits are included, the vast majority before 1900, brought on by obstreperous player, manager, and fan behavior; no-show teams; and promotions-gone-bad, to wit, 1974's 10-cent Beer Night in Cleveland, the White Sox' Disco Demolition Night in 1979, and the Dodgers' Ball Night in 1995.

Filip Bondy, *The Pine Tar Game: The Kansas City Royals, the New York Yankees, and Baseball's Most Absurd and Entertaining Controversy* (New York: Scribner's, 2015). A detailed examination of the 1983 saga when Kansas City star George Brett's game-winning homer was nullified by the Yankees' claim that his bat had too much pine tar, only to be restored by AL President Lee McPhail on appeal.

The Art of Umpiring

There have been a number of books written on the fine art of umpiring at all professional and amateur levels, all stressing encyclopedic knowledge of baseball's rules, hustle, staying in shape, good positioning, and maintaining a level head when all around you are losing theirs. The following are of special note.

Billy Evans, *How to Umpire* (American Sports Publishing Company, 1920) launched the genre. An AL umpire from 1906 to 1927, the youngest ever hired at age 22, and the third umpire inducted into Baseball's Hall of Fame, Evans puts special emphasis on umpire deportment and maintaining control. He expounded more expansively on the fine art of umpiring in his self-published 1947 manual and grand umpiring thesis, *Umpiring from the Inside*, covering training, preparation, hustle, control of emotions, complete knowledge of rules, and interpretation of the "knotty problems" umpires confront that give official rules book a workout.

Joe Brinkman and Charlie Euchner, *The Umpire's Handbook* (Lexington, Massachusetts: The Stephen Greene Press, 1985). Brinkman, a respected if occasionally quirky MLB ump whose career spanned 35 years beginning in 1972, presided over his own umpiring school, from which this umpiring manual was spawned.

Carl Childress, *Baseball Umpires Encyclopedia* (Home Run Press, 2012). Childress, a longtime amateur ump from Texas, has written several books on umpiring technique, preparation, etiquette, and comportment. Childress, the editor of the website Officiating.com, has produced an encyclopedic account of all things umpiring, before, during, and after the game, with extensive expounding on rules interpretation, primarily geared to the amateur umpire.

Carl Childress, *The Umpire's List of Lists* (Home Run Press, 2013). This slim but enlightening and entertaining volume is a compendium of umpiring do's and don'ts before, during, and after the game designed to enhance to umpire competence, techniques, preparation, and credibility. Particularly compelling are his recommendations on dealing with managers and players, heading off potential trouble in the form of beanball wars and fights, dealing with the politics of umpire hiring and assignments, bonding and communicating with your fellow umpires on the field, and recognizing when your judgments and techniques are faltering. This is a good companion to Childress's 2012 opus from Home Run Press, *151 Ways to Ruin a Baseball Game*.

Rules of the Game

Official Rules of Major League Baseball (Chicago: Triumph Books). Published yearly in handbook format in the spring as an official publication of Major League Baseball, and revised as needed. The official rules also have a guide to umpires and official scorers on rules interpretations and odd circumstances.

Dan Formosa and Paul Hamburger, *Baseball Field Guide: An In-Depth Illustrated Guide to the Complete Rules of Baseball* (The Experiment, LLC, New York, 2006, 2008, 2016-3rd edition.) *Baseball Field Guide*, published in a handy paperback handbook format, fully lives up to its title with its lucid and comprehensive explanations and nuanced analysis of contemporary baseball rules in the video replay era, and the detailed roles of umpires, managers, coaches, players, and even spectators. The 20-page chapter on umpires is particularly informative and enlightening on the duties and challenges facing umpires practicing their craft amidst the technologies of the New Millennium, courtesy of book's 2016 third edition.

Glen Waggoner, Kathleen Moloney, and Hugh Howard, *Baseball by the Rules: Pine Tar, Spitballs, and Midgets: An Anecdotal Guide to America's Oldest and Most Complex Sport* (Dallas: Taylor Publishing Company, 1987; New York: Prentice Hall, 1990). A roundup of lively stories about the many and often bizarre controversies generated through baseball's decades by the official baseball rules that have bedeviled and beleaguered the men in blue, and generating the stormy debates with managers attempting to impose their own creative interpretations.

David Nemec, *The Official Rules of Baseball: An Anecdotal Look at the Rules of Baseball and How They Came to Be* (New York: Barnes & Noble Press, 1994 and 1999). This official MLB publication offers the official MLB rules and stories and motivations behind them.

"Knotty Problems"

In the final chapter of his 1920 seminal umpiring guide, *How to Umpire*, Billy Evans posed what he referred to as "knotty problems," or the unusual, puzzling, wacky situations that come up in baseball games that fully test and challenge the arbiter's knowledge and interpretation of the rules. Soon after, Evans' knotty problems became a popular feature of the yearly *Spalding Official Baseball Guide*. In 1949

Evans and the *The Sporting News* gave his feature its own literary showcase, *Knotty Problems of Baseball*, a paperback compilation of head-scratching diamond scenarios that popped up through the decades, and their judicious, and on occasions injudicious, solutions. The "Knotty Problems" books, now hard to come by, generated several similar books in recent years for the edification and pleasure of dedicated armchair umps including:

Harry Simmons, *So You Think You Know Baseball!* (New York: Fawcett, 1960). A best-selling collection of a popular baseball rules column appearing in the *Saturday Evening Post* from 1949 to 1961 that spawned at least three other similar books with the exact same title.

The Editorial Staff of Baseball America, *It's Your Call: Baseball's Oddest Plays* (New York: Collier Books, 1989). In addition to inviting readers to untangle baseball's oddball plays of yore, *Baseball America* asked several umpires from the 1980s and '90s to tell of the weirdest situations they had to untangle.

Richard Goldstein, *You Be the Umpire! The Baseball Controversy Quiz Book* (New York: Dell Publishing, 1993). An extensive question-and-answer format challenging readers on how they would have ruled on diamond history's controversial plays.

Ira L. Smith and H. Allen Smith, *Low and Inside* and *Three Men on Third* (Halcottsville, New York: Breakaway Books, 2001). These two volumes of baseball anecdotes and oddities prominently featuring umpires were originally published in the late 1940s and early '50's by sportswriter Ira L. Smith and humorist H. Allen Smith. *Low and Inside* focused on circumstances that tormented umps before World War I; *Three Men on Third* covers to the 1950s. These popular tomes are the most entertaining of this genre of baseball literature.

Peter E. Meltzer, *So You Think You Know Baseball? A Fan's Guide to the Official Rules* (New York: W.W. Norton and Company, 2013), the most extensive, best organized, and updated of the "So You Think You Know …" books.

Dom Forker, Wayne Stewart, and Robert Obojski, *The Big Book of Baseball Brainteasers* (New York: Main Street Books, 2004); Dom Forker, Wayne Stewart, and Mike Pellowski, *Baffling Baseball Trivia* (New York: Main Street Books, 2004), companion books of material culled from previous Sterling works by the assembled authors.

Miscellany

MLB Public Relations Department, *Major League Baseball Umpire Media Information Guide*. These annual media guides provide brief bios of each umpire's major- and minor-league career, World Series, and All-Star Game assignments, famous games umpired, and family and hobby information. They also include all-time umpire rosters, records, history time-lines, and lists of players-turned-umps; plate umps in each no-hitter; MLB rules that apply to umps; and each stadium's ground rules. The printed copies are not readily available to the general public, but easy accessed online on the umpire link on MLB's website (mlb.com) and the umpire website, stevetheump.com.

Derek Zumsteg, *The Cheater's Guide to Baseball* (New York: Houghton Mifflin Company, 2007), a *Baseball Prospectus* editor's report on how players and managers can, have, and continue to violate, abuse, mangle, and tweak the rules of baseball, all to gain an advantage, all under the scrutiny and gaze of the men in blue.

Ross Bernstein, *The Code: Unwritten Rules and Its Ignore-at-Your-Own Risk Code of Conduct* (Chicago: Triumph Books, 2008), two volumes discussing baseball's "unwritten rules," as mentally formulated by players and managers on assorted baseball etiquette and rituals.

Spike Vrusho, *Benchclearing: Baseball's Greatest Fights and Riots* (Guilford, Connecticut: The Lyons Press, 2008), a compilation of episodes brought on by perceived beanballs, basepath spikings, and mutual ill will, for which umpires served as referees, peacemakers, and prefects of discipline.

Paul Dickson, *The Unwritten Rules of Baseball: The Etiquette, Conventional Wisdom, and Axiomatic Codes of Our National Pastime* (New York: Collins, 2009), explores sundry behaviors—traditions, customs, rituals—apart from the official rules of the game.

Andrew Goldblatt, *Major League Umpires' Performance, 2007-2010* (Jefferson, North Carolina: McFarland and Company, 2011), a study of MLB umpire home-plate performances, habits and tendencies, employing various elements of sabrmetrics and Retrosheet to measure their strike zone and the possible impact on the games they umpired. Also reviewed are the player and manager ejection rates, and the circumstances that brought them about.

Novels

John Hough Jr., *The Conduct of the Game* (New York: Harcourt Brace Jovanovich, 1986), a well-reviewed novel of a young man in the early '60s pursuing a career as an MLB umpire, amid family turmoil, sexual awakenings, and moral dilemmas.

Pat Hines, *Making the Call* (New York: Avalon Books, 2001), from the Avalon Career Romance series in which a young woman named Wesley Garvin achieves her dream and goal to be MLB's first woman umpire, but soon encounters the complications that come when she develops a relationship with, and ultimately a passion for, a practicing first baseman from the Pittsburgh Pirates!

Jon L. Breen, *Kill the Umpire: The Calls of Ed Gorgon* (Norfolk, Virginia: Crippen & Landru, 2003). In 1970 veteran mystery writer Breen created veteran major-league umpire Ed Gorgon, the "Horsehide Sleuth," to solve crimes. The complete Gorgon canon is contained in this book, 16 stories in all, bearing such titles as "The Body in the Bullpen," "The Babe Ruth Murder Case," and, of course, "Kill The Umpire."

Laz Diaz, Chris Guccione, Cory Blaser, and fill-in umpire Clint Fagan

On July 3-5, 2015, the Houston Astros visited Boston's Fenway Park for a three-game series. Crew chief Jeff Nelson was on vacation, so Laz Diaz served as crew chief for the three games. Chris Guccione, Cory Blaser, and fill-in umpire Clint Fagan were the other umpires on the crew. Bill Nowlin sat down and talked with the crew.

Conversation in the Umpires Room at Fenway Park on July 3 and 5, 2015

Bill Nowlin: You guys answered one of the questions I had as you walked in just now. I wondered if you brought your gear with you.

Laz Diaz: DHL. They pick it up at the ballpark where we're at—we were at the Mets. Yesterday, Citi Field. It's waiting for us. Our clubhouse guy, Dean [Lewis], he opens it up. Whatever's underneath, we have in a bag, our dirty clothes. He washes all that and hangs it up here. He does our shoes and has everything ready once we get in.

LD: If you've got real fanatic fans, the ones that study baseball and study the umpires, they know who we are. But the regular Joe Blow, they won't know. I've gone with my friends at Wrigley and the first couple of times they came to Wrigley, I've taken a shower and gone and hung out at some of the bars around Wrigley, right in the neighborhood. Walk in and have my beer and hang out with them. They [other patrons] don't know who I am.

Chris Guccione: I think I've been recognized twice ever, having dinner or having a drink after the game. Once or twice.

BN: That's because you were wearing your face mask.

CG: Yeah, that's what it was. I had all my gear on.

BN: [to Clint] You're a Triple-A umpire right now?

Clint Fagan: Yeah.

BN: How does that work? You worked like 110 major-league games last year.

CF: I really don't know, ranking wise. You're given assignments. You're put on a list for callups.

BN: Mostly you're filling in, like for Jeff Nelson tonight.

CF: Yes. I fill in on replay, injuries, vacation.

BN: That's as many games as most regular guys work. You worked 119 games last year.

CF: I don't know the exact number.

LD: We're on our four weeks' vacation, where he goes first and gets his week [indicates Cory Blaser], then I got my week, then Jeff Nelson, and next week he goes [indicates Chris Guccione.] So he'll fill in [Clint] for the whole month for us. After he leaves us, Sunday, in Cleveland, when we have the All-Star break, there'll be another four guys, another crew, having their four-block, so he might go there and work with them for the whole four weeks. Yeah, he'll work maybe even more than what we work.

BN: You're the crew chief tonight?

LD: For the whole week.

BN: While Jeff Nelson's away.

LD: Yeah. These guys have been trembling the whole time.

BN: I imagine! It's a dictatorship, right?

LD: It's a dictatorship.

Cory Blaser: I was in his spot [Clint's] for four or five years and just recently got hired in January of last year, 2014.

BN: Did you all come together here just now, in a taxi or something?

LD: We have a car service that we use. We flew in last night, the car service picked us up at the airport, took us to the hotel. This morning, we did whatever we wanted to do during the day.

BN: Does MLB select the hotels for you?

LD: No, we pick our own hotels.

Laz Diaz and crew, L to R: Laz Diaz, Chris Guccione, Cory Blaser, Clint Fagan.

BN: You tend to stay together at the same hotel? This crew, anyhow?

LD: Yeah, we tend to stay at the same spot. We're all Hyatt guys; we like Hyatt. There's some other crews that like Marriott.

BN: If you get with one of their programs, you can build up points.

LD: Exactly. We're paying for our hotels, a daily per diem rate. Out of your per diem rate, you pay for your own hotels, so if you want to stay at Motel 6, you can, or you can stay at the Ritz.

LD: And when you're home, like when they're home in Denver [Guccione and Blaser are both from Colorado], of course, they don't use their per diem. It's real nice to be home and open the refrigerator.

GC: Like this city here, different cities have car services that we use—Toronto, New York, San Fran, Oakland, Chicago—both Cubs and White Sox, maybe that's it. All the rest, we get a rental car.

BN: One guy I talked to maybe 15 years ago, he just took the subway here. Which you could do if you don't get recognized.

CG: People don't recognize you.

LD: The only thing they see on the field is a black shirt.

CG: You know, it's funny, a lot of guys are staying at hotels and there's a lot of fans at the hotel. We'll leave the game and many times we're standing right in the same elevator. They're talking, "Oh, man, that

was an awesome game. This and that." And we'll say, "How was it? Who won? How'd the umpires do?" or something like that. And they're all, "It was great. They did this or that…"

BN: I wondered if you ever might have said, "Did you see that call at third base? What a…." You've heard it, but did you ever just goof on them?

CG: Oh yeah.

LD: I have, yeah. In Chicago, with a couple of guys that came see me, there was this one guy "Oh, the Cubbies won! The Cubbies won!" He was so happy. I said, "Yeah, but that second-base umpire"—I was working second base that day—"he blew that call." He said, "Yeah, he did" and he'd start to get all upset. I told him, "Listen, let's make a pact. If we ever see that umpire again, we're going to punch him right in the mouth, okay?" He said, "OK!" And all my buddies standing around me, they're all looking at me like, "You're crazy, man."

They don't know who we are.

BN: This room we're in is fairly new. You used to be up over the Red Sox clubhouse, right?

LD: Dean, how long we been here?

Dean Lewis, umpire room attendant: This room's been here since 2004.

BN: More than 10 years. A long time, now. When you go around the league, are most of the facilities relatively similar these days?

LD: The new ballparks are….

BN: Bigger than here?

LD: Yes. In the newer ballparks, but in San Diego—which is a new ballpark—that locker room is smaller than this one. Wouldn't you agree?

CG: Yeah.

Cory Blaser: But like Minnesota, that's enormous. Our dressing area, our living room area, the bathroom, everything….

LD: Philly's huge.

BN: What's the worst one?

LD: Wrigley?

CG: Wrigley's not bad, because they re-did that one also.

LD: I think the smallest one is San Diego.

CG: A lot of times when they build these new ballparks, they forget. At the last minute, someone will ask, "Where's the umpires room?"

CB: Miami's is not that big, either.

LD: Personally, what I look for is — especially in this area here [where the lockers and trunks are], where we get dressed, to have enough room.

BN: Not bumping in to each other.

LD: Not bumping into each other. Stretch. The one in Miami is very small. You could probably touch his hand. Where you are in front of me, that's how close we are.

BN: But they're similar enough these days. There must have been some really bad ones, 20, 25 years ago.

LD: Milwaukee.

BN: County Stadium?

LD: County Stadium was bad.

CG: Didn't that have a dirt floor?

LD: You had to lift up your trunk, because if it rained the clubhouse would get flooded.

[There was a little talk about Cuba, umpires walking in from the neighborhood around the ballpark.]

LD: I'm hoping to be in one of those games, if they have a spring training game next year. When I first heard of it, it would be 2017 but they've been pushing it for next year. [Diaz was the third-base umpire in the Tampa Bay vs. Cuba game at Estadio Latinamericano on March 22, 2016 in Havana.]

BN: Are you Cuban by ancestry?

LD: My dad came over in '61 and my mom in '62. They were already married in Cuba, and then when they got here, they found each other. I was there last week, to see my mom and dad's home town, in the north central part of the island. Where Livan Hernandez is from. Yuniesky Betancourt. That area.

BN: When you leave here to go to the field, do you go through the edge of the visitors' dugout?

LD: Yeah, we go through their dugout.

BN: Is that usually the way it is, through one team or another's dugout?

LD: It depends where we're at.

CB: Very rarely. There's maybe only three spots where we go through the dugout, right? It's usually separate.

BN: A lot of them are right behind home plate, right?

CB: Or a section right over from the dugout, where we go through a different tunnel.

CG: Just here and Toronto, really.

CB: What about Wrigley?

LD: Wrigley.

CB: There's only three, maybe four, that you still go through the dugout. A lot of them are right next to the dugout, but a separate tunnel.

BN: The positions you're working tonight, do you make that up, as the acting crew chief or does that come from New York?

LD: When the season starts, the crew chief will always have home plate. For the first game. The #2 guy will have first base, #3 guy second, and #4 guy at third base. And from that rotation, we just go. The whole year.

CG: It doesn't stay like 1, 2, 3, because like right now, let's see, it'll go him [Cory], he's the three guy now, then it'll be me, I'm at first — I'm the two guy,

Cory Blaser.

then it goes Clint. With guys leaving and everything, it gets mixed up. You keep the rotation pretty much intact. It might get a little bit skewed throughout the year but it stays pretty consistent.

BN: You get feedback from New York on a regular basis? Or from Kevin [O'Connor] upstairs?

CG: Kevin's a regional observer. There's supervisors and then there's regional observers.

BN: How often do you get feedback? After every series?

LD: After every series.

CB: Almost every day, you have video stuff to go over for calls that you had on the field. If New York believes that it's a close call—close enough—they'll put it in the system that's reviewed by a supervisor and put into a system that we log onto that says "Correct. Correct. Correct. Incorrect." They'll let you know. Obviously, if you go into replay and you get one overturned, it'll say "Incorrect" but there may be a lot of comments on positioning stuff.

BN: Do they do that with balls and strikes, too?

LD: We have what they call the ZE system.

CG: ZE. I don't even know what it means. [The technology (called Zone Enforcement or ZE) that was implemented in 2009 provided all home plate umpires a report after each game, showing them the accuracy of all of their ball and strike calls.]

LD: My game last night is posted, and all I do is log on and it'll tell me my percentage—raw—and then you'll have pitches that the catcher maybe butchered, and stuff like that. It might say my percentage, raw, in 93, and with adjustments, 94.

BN: So have a grade every day?

LD: Whether you're on the bases or on the plate, yeah.

CB: We get graded on everything. You know, a lot of times in the media you hear, "The umpires need to be held accountable." They have no idea. Every pitch and every play you have on the bases is graded.

BN: And promotions are tied into that.

CG: Sure. And postseason.

BN: It's a physically demanding job and you don't see—any more—umpires who seem to be as out of shape as some of them looked 20 or 30 years ago.

Do you guys end up working out on a regular kind of basis?

LD: He runs like six or seven miles every day.

CG: I just ran eight miles today. Go for a jog. I work out usually…try to do at least six, depending on travel. Sometimes five.

BN: Hotel gyms?

LD: That's one of the reasons we like the Hyatts. They have a pretty nice gym. This one has a nice gym and a pool. Minnesota has a real nice gym, big gym and a pool, and a basketball court and a boxing ring.

CB: Twenty-five years ago, they didn't have a medical director. We have a medical director, Mark Letendre. If you have a head blow, if you take a foul ball off the mask, you have a text message before you even get off the field, and you have to call and check in.

BN: For concussion.

CB: Concussions. Any time you have any injury, you have people from the ballpark who will stop by and check on you. They'll have different physical therapies for you. And the nutrition part of it's changed, I think night and day from 25 years ago. In the ballpark, most of the time it's healthier foods. Postgame meals, I think, are healthier. In the offseason, too, they'll have outfits if you're overweight and you need to see somebody—a nutritionist—they'll take care of all that. They want us to be healthy and in shape.

BN: It can be dangerous if you're not. And it also maybe doesn't look as good.

LD: There's also Mackie Shilstone out of New Orleans, who's kind of our guru nutritionist guy. In January, we go to a retreat. He has a place in New Orleans and if you need to go, you can stay there for a week. They have a hotel or something and you go through a training process and an eating process. And you can take your wife and you'll get up and you'll go through your different work exercises. Then you'll have a good breakfast, and a snack, and have a good lunch and then some more exercise. You get your routine, along with your wife—meals and exercise and all that, so that way when you get back home, you continue that same process. He's got several books out. He's trained boxers....

CG: Venus Williams.

LD: A lot of athletes go to him to get into shape.

BN: Did you ever work in the same ballpark in back-to-back series?

LD: Every series you're in a different park. We used to do that in the minor leagues, but not here.

CB: The only time would be if we're working San Francisco, Oakland. We won't work in the same park.

LD: Maybe we'll have a three-game set here and Monday will be a day game where they'll start a four-game set—Monday, Tuesday, Wednesday, Thursday. Let's say the Yankees are coming in and they're playing an afternoon game on Monday at 1, and the crew that's coming in for that four-game set is not able to make it, we'll stay for that one game and then we'll leave for wherever we're going to go for Tuesday, Wednesday, Thursday.

CG: It's pretty rare that you will see the same team even within the next two weeks. We won't see Boston for at least two more weeks; we might not even see them for the rest of the year.

BN: This is the second time you've been here this year and you might be back....

CG: This is it. We're not coming back to Boston.

LD: We miss seven stadiums this year. We miss Wrigley, Yankee Stadium, Philly, Tampa, Houston, Atlanta, and DC. We miss those seven stadiums this year.

BN: I'm surprised you're missing that many.

LD: Usually, it's not that many. Usually it's three or four, but this year we miss seven.

BN: You guys all go to New York for replay?

LD: Yes.

BN: As a crew?

LD: As a crew.

BN: When you're there, will all of you be....

LD: In the room together?

BN: Or maybe just or three of you.

LD: There's two crews in there. Every Tuesday and Wednesday, Friday, Saturday, and Sunday, there are 15 games.

BN: There's a lot of games, and there's East Coast games and West Coast games.

LD: Mondays and Thursdays are usually travel days/off days. But Tuesday, Wednesday, Friday, Saturday, and Sunday, everybody plays. I'd say Tuesdays and Fridays are the most hectic days in there because everybody starts to play.

CB: We work in shifts, four to five hours. Or if you're working the West Coast...I call them the graveyards, they're start at 10 or 11 and you go 15, 16 innings, you're in there until 4 in the morning.

LD: We're in Miami Labor Day weekend, and we go in to replay Labor Day Monday. I've already talked to the people at replay. I'm driving home from Miami to Orlando and I'm going to get up at 6 o'clock in the morning and catch the first flight out to be there for 1 o'clock, because there'll be a lot of day games. I told them already, I'll take the West Coast games, the late shift. That way, I can get up at 8 o'clock, 9 o'clock.

CG: Here's the whole schedule for the year. [Displays schedule.]

BN: I'm not supposed to see that.

CG: After the first night, they know you're in town anyway.

LD: Sometimes they post it anyway, right on the scoreboard.

CB: Minor leagues.

LD: Umpire hotel sponsored by....

BN: [to Laz] You started as an American League umpire. [To Chris] And you started as a Major League umpire.

CG: The first year, 2000, through spring training, I worked National League and American. That's the year they combined the two.

BN: You talked about wearing a black uniform. What's the last year you actually wore blue? American League umpires were wearing red jackets for a while there.

LD: We wore dark blue and red, in the American League.

BN: You always hear people yell, "Hey, Blue!" And I'm thinking, yeah, maybe 20 years ago.

LD: We still got the blue... [indicated shirt hanging in locker]. We always wear black. I remember

Clint Fagan.

being at first base one time and, "Hey, Blue! You missed that call." I look at him, like, "I missed the call?" "Yeah." "You say I'm blind?" "Yeah, Blue, you missed it." "You're one who's blind, because I'm wearing black." After that, they don't say anything.

OK, now, can we call them black?

BN: Well, you don't want people calling *you* black, because that causes another problem.

LD: If they're going to call me Blue, but I've got a black shirt. There's some guys that are, "You know what? You're right. Hey, Black, you missed that call!"

BN: What made you first get into umpiring? What made you choose this as a profession?

Clint Fagan: I went to a college umpire camp because I wanted to learn how to umpire. I played high-school ball. I started doing it through college as a part-time profession, just to help pay bills and tuition. I ended up running into a major-league umpire, Eddie Hickox, and David Rackley. They asked me if I ever thought about going to umpire school. I said, "No, I'm just graduating college and I don't know what I'm going to do." I said, "Sure, I'll go." I got a business degree from the University of Houston. After that, it was all downhill. They gave me all the information. I graduated in December and I went the next month, in January. 2005.

BN: When you say it's all downhill, then there's a long uphill. One you're still going through right now. And I guess, Cory, you say you spent like five years or so doing what Clint's doing now?

CB: Yeah, I spent 12 full years in the minor leagues. In his position, four or five years. [Before that] lower minor leagues, working your way up.

BN: When you're here working in the major leagues, you get the same per diem everybody else gets.

CF: Yeah. The per diem rate is the same across the board.

BN: What about when you're in the minor leagues?

CF: Different. It's a different contract.

BN: When you first came up and joined a major-league crew, was there any kind of hazing or anything? Here you're a tighter and smaller crew than on a ball team.

CF: No. No type of hazing. You get your chops busted a little bit because you're the young guy, but no hazing. It's all in fun.

BN: What do they do to bust your chops? You don't wear pink backpacks or anything like that.

LD: Mostly talk. In here. In years past, the young guy…they're supposed to get all the towels. So if there's a young guy here, one of us will go get all the towels. "Don't worry about it, I'll get the towels." Then the other guys will say later, "You let the crew chief go get the towels?"

That was a big thing back in the day, especially in the National League. In the National League, the young umpire had to go get the towels. The young umpire was the last one to shower. The young umpire was the last one to sit at the table and eat. Routine. Not so much in the American League, but in the National League.

BN: That's one of the things I want to talk with Ted Barrett about next weekend, what it was like between the two leagues. I guess there used to be some rivalry between the two leagues. It almost doesn't make sense.

LD: It used to be.

CG: That's called pride.

BN: But basically you find that the more senior umpires are really helping you learn the ropes.

CF: Absolutely. Absolutely. There's no way you can work in the big leagues without getting advice from the guys who have been here. You wouldn't survive.

BN: You'd go to different cities you hadn't been to before, so you'd just sort of tag along and go where people suggest.

CF: Absolutely.

BN: And you're working in a brighter spotlight, too.

CF: That's true. Very true. It's a lot different than working in Triple A. Absolutely.

BN: What are one or two of the ways you say it might be different?

CF: I'd say the play is better. There's not as many mental mistakes that the players go through, or the manager. As to yourself, you don't want to make those type of mental mistakes. The physical is the same, but the mental aspect of the game is more…captivating. You've got to be on every pitch, every play. You can't drop a second while you're out there.

BN: And every game is televised, which probably isn't always true in the minor leagues. I guess it depends on the level.

CF: I think Triple A they have a video on every game, but it's just for in-house. It's not broadcast nationally, or regionally.

BN: Have you already worked some games in the minors this year?

CF: Yes, I worked a couple.

BN: And you may work another few as things progress?

CF: Yeah, I kind of move around.

LD: Hopefully not!

CF: Yeah, hopefully not, but sometimes you're switching crews and there's breaks and stuff and sometimes you just go down for a while. It's part of the system.

When you go down, you work twice as hard.

BN: Why?

CF: Because you set an example for young guys. You set an example. This is a profession that's seniority-based. You don't want to come down and big-league it or anything like that, so you work twice as hard when you go down.

BN: That makes a lot of sense. There are guys who have never been up.

CF: Exactly. And you want to teach them the ropes and give them the opportunity, and pass down what was passed down to you.

LD: And shame on the guys who go down to Triple A and don't do that. A lot of guys when I came up, they would go down and would not pass on the information, being that they were probably uncertain of themselves or whatever the case might be.

BN: Well, going back in history with ballplayers, the veteran ballplayers would almost always freeze out the young guys because they were afraid of having their job taken. I was wondering about that here, the way you get graded on everything. You're all trying to get better. They want you to get better, or stay at the level that works for them. But with the grading system, do you find that some people don't get promoted?

CB: Are you talking about from the minor leagues to the big leagues, or up the big-league ladder?

BN: I'm talking about actually once you're in the major leagues and you're being graded. Or if you're filling in and being graded. What happens if you get bad grades? I know what can happen in other jobs.

LD: A bad grade for us, when you average it out, is still a 96 or a 97. Doctors aren't that good.

Somebody's got to be at the bottom of the barrel. And if you're at the bottom of the barrel with a 95, it's kind of hard for them to say, "Hey, you're 95. You're going to get fired." If you're 85 and the next one above you is 93, then there's a gap. But when you've got 95.2, 95.3, 95.7, 96, 97, and the highest one is 98, and you've got 76 of us….

BN: So there's not that many guys who wash out, because that would have happened well before.

CG: There's never been an umpire fired, ever, within the recent…for performance.

BN: That says a lot for getting to this point. Let me ask you, Cory, how you got started umpiring.

CB: I was 14 or 15 when my dad said, "If you want to get a car when you're 16, you've got to get a job." So I got a job at Target. I was working at Target, working eight-hour days or more and making very little money after taxes. I was working inside, and didn't really care for it. My dad was a longtime high-school umpire in the State of Colorado for 20-plus years and he asked why I don't umpire. I said I never really thought about it. I took a course and got into umpiring and I was 14 or 15, working Little League games. I worked eight-hour days there and made a heck of a lot more money doing that. I really liked the job. The next summer, I started getting into high-school ball, in the summer leagues. I promised my dad two years of college before I decided to go to umpire school or not. I wanted to go right out of high school but he said, "Go to college for a couple of years and make that decision." I went to Colorado State University and then two years later went to umpire school in 2002, and here I am, 14 years later.

BN: It worked out.

CB: Yeah. Luckily.

BN: Economic questions can be kind of touchy sometimes. If you don't mind, what is the per diem you all are getting? Are food and hotels separate?

CB: No, it's four something, but we get taxed.

LD: 52% of our per diem is taxed. Let's say we get an even number of $400 a day. Fifty-two percent of that is taxed, which is $208. So we get $192 cash money and the other money is taxed.

CB: It sounds like a really large number, but after tax we get close to 4. It's the high 390s, I think. The first night here, we stayed at this hotel, with us working out that multiple people would be staying here…$299 for the first night.

CG: $340 with taxes.

BN: That's pretty close to breakeven, then, with food and all.

All: Yeah.

CB: It sounds like a large number and people think you're going to pocket some of that money, but in the bigger cities—Boston, New York…it evens out. You may go over your per diem.

BN: It's the same per diem regardless of the city.

All: Yeah.

CB: So you may have a little extra from Cincinnati and St. Louis but then when you come to bigger cities, you're paying more than your per diem. It

evens out. You don't really make any money off the per diem.

LD: Any umpire that thinks he's going to make… you can, but you're going to be staying at a Comfort Inn, a Holiday Inn Express, places like that.

CB: Another thing. We pay the clubhouse guy. We pay him between $60 and $100 a day. Per guy.

BN: That's a pretty good job.

CG: Real good pay.

BN: He was telling me how he brings in food and all that, all on his own dime. He pays for all that.

CB: You're making $300 a day or more. Up to $400, depending on the service.

BN: That's why he's been doing this since 1990, I guess.

CG: Yeah.

BN: You've got these chairs [pointing to chairs in the room, each of which has the Red Sox logo on their back and on the seat cushion], with the team logo on them.

CF: I didn't notice that.

BN: I just wondered, why wouldn't they have neutral chairs in here?

CB: We don't care. It's just a chair.

LD: They probably just order a whole bunch.

BN: Sure, but I thought MLB might frown on it.

LD: MLB doesn't have to pay for it. These chairs are paid for by the Red Sox. They [MLB] don't care where we sit.

BN: It's just the visual, seeing team logos. I realize that…I've talked to a few umpires who, if you ask them after the game is over, it might take them a moment to remember which team won.

CB: Yeah. We don't care.

LD: You come in here after the game, you take a shower, you go back to the hotel. You might sit at the hotel bar for a minute and the bartender…the bartender probably didn't see the game, and he'd ask, "Who won?" Who did win? "What was the score?"

CB: It's funny, too. We'll get to the next city and you'll get asked, "Where are you guys coming from?" We'll all be looking at each other. We can't even remember what city we were just in.

LD: We know more where we're going next than where we just were.

BN: Your pay now is much better—maybe even double—what it was when you were starting off [asked of Laz]?

LD: When I started, it was 75 [thousand] for a first-year guy. 72. I don't know what it is now. One something. [Over $100,000]

BN: So when you're working in the major leagues and you were working in the minor leagues, that's a big jump?

LD: Drastic.

CB: Probably quadruple.

CG: What would a Triple-A umpire, if you worked every game at Triple A….

CB: $3,400 is the max you can make a month.

CG: Times April, May, June, July, August, and a little bit of September.

CB: You don't get paid in the winter. It's just the months you're working.

CG: $15,000.

CB: Yeah, it's like, max.

CG: And you get a per diem of $40?

CF: You max out at $55.

LD: My last year at Triple A was $34.

CB: And Triple A is the highest you can go in the minor leagues. We all started out in rookie ball.

BN: That's when *you* pay *them* per diem!

CF: Ed Hickox told me that when you reach the majors, it's kind of like you're getting back pay.

BN: So, let me ask you, Gooch—how'd you get started? You told me a little before.

CG: I grew up in a small town in Colorado. We didn't have much baseball. We didn't have any baseball in high school. Our last year of baseball was like a Babe Ruth at age 15, but in between then, I was already at the ballpark anyway with my brother, who was four years younger than me. I was umpiring Babe Ruth baseball even into high school. I was already there because my brother was playing and it was easy money. It was enough to buy fishing lures or fishing poles or whatever else garbage I could buy. So I did that for a lot of years. My best friend in high school, Chris Carson, his dad said, "Why don't you guys go

to umpire school?" I'd never heard of umpire school, didn't know what it was about, never knew where it was. So he and I and his brother C.P., we all ended up taking a bus 52 hours from Salida, Colorado, to Kissimmee, Florida. That's kind of how I started umpiring. The shorter version.

BN: You probably get asked this question a lot, but I better ask it. Sometimes you guys are out there four or more hours a night. What happens if you've gotta go?

CG: You leave. You just leave. You just run off. It takes you longer than the inning goes, you wait 'til the next half-inning. And you work three-man. Very rarely, but it's happened. You just wait out the half-inning.

BN [to Laz Diaz]: I wanted to ask you about the town in Cuba, if you could spell it for me.

LD: La Panchita.

BN: Are your parents still living?

LD: My mom is. My dad passed away three years ago.

BN: Did she go with you?

LD: Yeah. I was 15 years old the first time I went back. Then I joined the Marine Corps and I didn't dare to go back until….

BN: Not in uniform anyway.

LD: Until now. This is the fourth time I've been.

BN: You're fluent in Spanish.

LD: Yeah.

BN: What did your parents do before they came over here?

LD: My dad worked the sugar cane.

BN: Cutter?

LD: Yeah.

BN: That's about as tough work as you can get. [Shows on Google Maps, shows where his parents grew up, and even found a baseball field.]

BN: You like going back?

LD: I like it. There's nothing to do. Your day consists of waking up and having a coffee, having breakfast, going on the porch and having a cigar. Then in the afternoon your cousins, they all come over from work or wherever they're at. My uncle's retired now so he'll come by. You go to the little store that's nearby, you buy a case of beer and bring it back to the house, you sit on the porch and have another cigar and tell stories and drink a couple of beers.

Havana's about four or five hours away from my mom and dad were at. We used to fly to Havana. Now we fly into Santa Clara, which is an hour away.

BN: You mentioned Mackie Shilstone. He seems to cater to all sorts of athletes, but does he offer some umpire-specific programs?

CB: Fat camp.

LD: I've never been but from what they tell me the place he has is immaculate. They have a kitchen area. They've got cooks that can teach you and your wife how to cook. You just go down for a week, maybe 10 days.

BN: Mark Letendre who you mentioned, does he travel?

LD: No, he sees most of the crews when they go through Phoenix. He used to travel more but he slipped and fell and had a head injury. He had trouble with his equilibrium so he's not traveling as much.

BN: It kind of impressed me. I went to look him up and I got onto an MLB umpires page and I saw the list of people, from Joe Torre on down, there's a long list of people. That's quite an investment they're making to make sure that umpires are on the field and doing their job well.

LD: Mark Letendre has his hands full. When we get sick or we get hurt, they're going to try to put us back on the field. When we're not able to do that, they're going to bring up minor-league guys to replace us, which dilutes the staff a little bit. They'll keep pushing—"Hey, you need to get Clint on the field? What's wrong with Cory?" He's constantly calling—"Cory, how's your knee? Have you been going to rehab? Have you been taking your pills?" He's constantly calling Cory trying to get him back on the field. He's getting pressure from the top to get him back on the field. He's got a very difficult job. He's between a rock and a hard place.

BN: Tell me how you got started.

LD: Well, I played high-school ball. Played college ball, and I played in the minor leagues, with the Twins organization. Shortstop/outfield. In '84.

I got released at the end. In '85 I tried out with the Cardinals. Got hurt and left. Sat out '86. In '87 I went to spring training with the Yankees. They let me go and I said, "OK, I'm done." That's when I started umpiring. One of my best friends that I played baseball with, he was going through a divorce and he needed to make some extra money so he said, "Why don't we do umpiring?" We were good friends. I said, "OK, we'll go umpire." We started with slow-pitch softball. We did beer leagues on weekends. Then we got into high-school ball and from high school we got into college. When I got my divorce, one of the guys who helped after I was going through my divorce said, "Hey, now that you're divorced, you don't have anything holding you back. Why don't you go to umpire school?" And like Gooch, I didn't know anything about umpire school. Didn't know anything about nothing. I knew there was one in Cocoa. Joe Brinkman School. And the Harry Wendelstedt in Daytona. I knew what Cocoa was all about because that's where there was minor-league spring training for the Twins. There was nothing there. No way I'm going back to Cocoa. It's closer to Miami than Daytona, but you know what, if I'm going to go do this I'm at least going to have fun.

So I went to Daytona. I got lucky and blessed and came out of there as one of the top students and got a job, worked my way up, and here I am.

BN: How often do you go to replay?

LD: We go twice. We went in May and now we go in the middle part of September. There's some crews, they go….

CB: Max is three weeks. When you go, it's a week at a time. The crew chiefs can bid on what ones they want, by seniority. Some of those have three weeks. Some have two. One or two have two and a half.

BN: Now you three guys were on the same crew—were you on the same crew last year?

LD: No. I was with Jeff Nelson last year. He was the crew chief. Gooch, who were you with?

CG: Hallion.

CB: I was with Jimmy Joyce.

BN: And is that…can you assume that next year, you'll all be on different crews?

CG: You can assume that. We could all four be back together, but it's highly unlikely.

LD: Yeah. He'll [CG] probably be a two man somewhere. Most definitely, he'll be a two man somewhere. With his skills and everything, he'll be a two man somewhere.

BN: You're a number three right now.

CG: Yeah.

LD: Last year Mark Carlson was number three and now he's a two man on another crew.

BN: They probably want to mix it up anyhow.

CB: Yeah.

LD: See, that's one thing sometimes I don't understand. If you've got a crew that gets along and you do well off the field, on the field, unless you're going to promote him from three man to number-two man, why don't you keep the same crew together?

If we're gelling, we get along on the field, we get along off the field, we have fun, and we're a good crew.

BN: The only reason I think they might want to do that is that they thought you might get stale somehow, or that there'd be some funny business going on. There was a thing with someone selling memorabilia some time ago.

LD: No, trust me, with Cory around, nothing gets….

CG, pointing to his chest protector: This is kind of my thing here. These are all the patches for people who have passed that have been umpires. Frank Pulli, Harry Wendelstedt, Marty Springstead, Wally Bell….

BN: People you worked with at one time or another.

CG: No, I never worked with Frank. I never worked with Harry. I never worked with Marty. Never worked with Wally. Shag Crawford, Sammy Holbrook.

LD: Those are just people who passed. [Points to the inside top of his trunk.] That's a picture of my dad there, a patch for Wally Bell. And that patch used to be for Harry Wendelstedt. It's upside down, because Michael Hirschbeck passed away last year. John Hirschbeck and I…worked with John together for so many years that I know his family very well, been in his house. So I looked at the patch and I turned it around. HW—MH. That's a tribute to Michael Hirschbeck [John's son]. When I went around the league last year, I asked all the clubbies if they still had Harry Wendelstedt patches, which they did. And I shipped them to….

CB: [talking about posing for a photo] I'll get one rubbing a baseball.

CG: (laughs) You haven't rubbed a baseball since Double A.

CB: Shall I do one with my mask on, since I usually work the plate?

BN: Fine with me! Fool around. You can take one in the shower. No…

LD: Sitting on the pot.

BN: Yeah, right. Thank you all again.

Ted Barrett, Angel Hernandez, Chris Conroy, Pat Hoberg

Conversation in the Umpires Room, Fenway Park, July 11, 2015, with Bill Nowlin

Bill Nowlin: Mainly, I wanted to talk to you about being a crew chief. Your last crew, you had a couple of different people from now.

Ted Barrett: We're on our individual vacations now, so Pat's in for Scott [Barry]. And in Chicago, they brought in a guy to assist us with the double-header. Tom Woodring.

BN: Marcus Pattillo?

TB: Marcus was there because Angel had to cover another crew. Someone was out so they had to beef up the crew so they took Angel.

BN: So your normal crew is you three and Scott. He's on vacation now. [to Pat] This is your first year now?

Pat Hoberg: Second.

BN: In this room, you've got all the Hall of Fame umpires. Most of the rooms you go to around baseball, is there some kind of historical recognition, or is it kind of hit and miss?

TB: Hit and miss, yeah. Detroit's got plaques of every one of them. Interesting story on that, there was these pictures of old ballplayers in Oakland, back to the Philadelphia A's, and Ernie Harwell would always come in the umpires' locker room and say hi. There were no captions, so I had no idea who these old players were. He's looking and saying, "That's Ed Rommel, and…" he's going on and on. I thought Ernie's losing it. He looks at me and says, "You know why these are up here" and I said, "Yeah, they're the A's and we're in Oakland." He said, "No, these are players who became umpires." I thought that was kind of cool. Last one was….the guy whose son played in the National League.

Angel Hernandez: Kunkel?

TB: Yeah, Bill Kunkel.

BN: You've been a crew chief for a while now?

TB: This is my third season.

BN: Obviously, you've got to put in a few years to get there.

TB: Yeah, it's seniority driven.

BN: (to Angel) I was wondering how that works. You started a few years earlier than Ted, but have you been a crew chief yet?

AH: I have no recollection of it. I don't really follow those things.

TB: He's a crew chief a lot of times when crew chiefs go, and he fills in. Bob Davidson is the other one.

AH: When a crew chief goes on vacation, the #2 guy basically just runs the crew. He's the intern.

BN: What do you do as a crew chief?

TB: Basically, it's just—probably the biggest thing is when it rains. That's the biggest thing, is trying to coordinate with…

BN: Dave next door? [Dave Mellor, head groundskeeper]

TB: Yeah, and the ballpark personnel. Even now, with the technology. Other than that, it's just on the field. Replay's brought a whole new dimension to it.

BN: There's two guys who go on the headsets.

TB: Always the crew chief and the other one's the calling umpire. If that's me, then the two-man, Angel, would go with me.

BN: If you were the calling umpire.

TB: Yeah.

BN: And the other two stand around.

Chris Conroy: Make sure everybody's…

TB: There's actually a lot of responsibility. They're doing a lot. There can't be any conferences, changes, and they also are thinking through what happens if a play gets flipped—what's the count, what are the outs, where are the runners? When we come off the headsets, there's a lot of information. If there's something wrong, the runner's in the wrong spot, or the count's wrong on the board, I rely on these guys to come over, "Hey, wait a minute, wait a minute…" before we start.

BN: It's a whole new world, I guess. I don't know how you feel about it. Some of the fans…it used to be kind of fun to see a good argument.

TB: Baseball purists, from the feedback I'm getting, they don't like it. But it seems like our society's so tech-driven now that they love it. And they want the machine to call balls and strikes, and I think eventually that's going to happen.

BN: Well, if they get it just right, in three dimensions, it probably could.

TB: I think they would rather have it in its present state than us. But people who been around baseball a little more appreciate what we do a little more. I think this younger generation doesn't….

BN: Did the crew chief used to handle things like hotel and flight arrangements?

TB: Not since I've been umpiring.

BN: There's an agency that makes the arrangements for the flights, but you all make the arrangements with the agency?

TB: Yeah, we all individually do that. We have a guy—Chris handles our hotels. There's a lot of leg work and Angel helps him. They're on the phone constantly. Even on the way over here today, we were talking about our future reservations.

When I came up, the crew chief was a little more domineering. We would always get two rental cars and he would always take one that was at his disposal. You couldn't take the chief's car. The old-timers tell me that you didn't answer the phone when it rang in the locker room. Only the crew chiefs did. The real old-timers—the chief showered first. These seem like ridiculous rules; that's all kind of out of the window. We're all really respectful of the crew chiefs, but there's no more of that domineering stuff going on.

BN: Do you get paid a little extra?

Angel Hernandez.

TB: A hundred dollars a game. So when I'm gone, Angel will get the hundred dollars. It adds up over the course of the season.

BN: Are you guys all staying at the same hotel?

TB: This time we are, yeah.

BN: Do you think the role of the crew chief has changed over time? I'm not talking about what you already addressed, but umpiring on the field, or anything at all.

TB: I think, especially for younger guys—people like Pat—when Angel and I came up, the crew chief was the one who would really critique you, who would give you advice. Now, it's more the supervisory staff. And we really almost have to stay out of their way because as we transitioned into that, we would tell them some things that might be counter to what they [supervisory staff] were saying. Then we're just messing them up. So we try to stay out of their way and be a kind of support system.

BN: Do you hear directly from the umpire observers, or from the supervisors?

TB: The observers we don't hear from. We get evaluations through the computer, from the observers. But the supervisors we'll hear directly from. He'll hear [indicating Pat] directly from the supervisory staff. We have a supervisor assigned to us. For our crew, it's Ed Montague. So if we have an issue, we call him or he calls us. Our supervisor will look at the observer's reports, and we'll get them, too, but we don't have any contact with him.

BN: But what he puts on the computer, you'll see the exact same thing.

TB: Yeah.

BN: You don't filter any of that information, as crew chief. It's just there on the computer.

TB: Only in the case of somebody like Pat, somebody that is filling in. They might call me and say something like, "Pass this on to him" or Work with him on this." But not with these guys [points to Chris and Angel]. They would contact them directly.

BN: [to Chris] Are you officially a major-league umpire now?

CC: Yes.

BN: And you're a minor-league umpire [Pat]. That would be the dividing line.

TB: Yeah. There's some crew chiefs that might maybe be a little more hands-on with that, but for me with on-the-field stuff, these guys are so good that….

AH: In my opinion, he's a major-league umpire when he's here. Because that's what he's doing. He's working a major-league game.

BN: And he's getting all the benefits of being a major-league umpire, too, while he's here.

AH: And that's exactly why they called him, because otherwise they wouldn't have called him.

BN: [to Pat] How many games did you work last year?

PH: 120-something.

BN: That's about as much as almost anybody works, right? So you're basically just paying your dues, so to speak.

AH: This is his chance. He's getting his exposure. That's how everybody started. Vacation or injury, they'll call the next guy that they're looking at - a prospect. You're looking at one. He's right in front of you.

BN: What do you call them—"fill-in umpires"?

CC: Up-and-down umpires.

AH: Fill-ins. Call-ups. Prospects is what I say. The future.

BN: You were born in Cuba?

AH: Havana. I left when I was 11 months old. Yes, sir.

BN: I was just there a few months ago. Have you ever had occasion to go back at all?

AH: I never have. [Hernandez was selected to serve as the first-base umpire in the Tampa Bay vs. Cuba game at Estadio Latinamericano on March 22, 2016 in Havana. That became his second trip. In the 2015-16 offseason, Angel joined Ted Barrett on a mission to Cuba.]

TB: I've been there. I was there last year.

BN: International umpiring?

TB: No, actually on a mission trip. Religious visit, but then I ended up hooking up with the umpires through that.

BN: They have a woman umpire there, and one up in Canada, too. Yanet Moreno in Cuba—I didn't get a chance to meet her.

TB: I did. She came to the clinic that we did. She did a good job. You know what, they didn't have uniforms and last year when we went, we took them pants and shirts. Now they match. They were wearing…one had a blue shirt and one had a black shirt. One had a jacket.

BN: I think I saw five games this last trip and everybody I saw was in uniform.

TB: Maybe that's the uniforms we took them.

BN: Could be. Actually, I noticed that some of them had something that looked like MLB logos on them and I wondered where they got them from.

TB: Yeah, we brought a lot of our extra old shirts.

AH: But I am not the first. The first was Armando Rodriguez. Mr. Richie Garcia was born in Key West, in the States. And Laz Diaz as well. Armando was the first. For the record.

BN: It's all black and gray now pretty much, right?

AH: They kept the light powder blue color for hot games. So we still have them. For hot games, it's needed.

BN: That could be tomorrow.

AH: I will be wearing it. You can assure yourself. [Indeed, game time temperature on July 12 was 86 degrees and the crew all wore their blue shirts.]

BN: Are you working the plate tomorrow?

AH: God willing. If He will allow me to, I will be, yes.

BN: You [Ted] were an American League umpire, and you [Angel] were a National League umpire before they came together. I asked you [Ted, on an earlier phone call] if there was kind of a rivalry between the two leagues, even though there was no interleague play until 1997, so you hardly would see each other. You said, yeah, there was, and I said something like just a joking rivalry, and you said sometimes it had a little bite to it.

TB: Yeah.

BN: And I was wondering, what's that all about?

TB: I don't know. I never understood that myself. I think it was just kind of a pride thing. I'd always kind of equate it to my son's in the Army and the other's in the Air Force, and they tease each other.

BN: Sure.

TB: And if anybody knows a Marine, they tease the other three mercilessly.

BN: Right.

TB: I thought it was like that, but there were occasions that I think it carried into a little more of a prideful thing. That's gone now, now that we're all together.

AH: Look at the history of it. They were really different. American League umpires wore the balloon, the outside chest protector. The National League umpires never wore that. They always wanted to be different. And they were different.

BN: And of course since the DH. You'd only meet each other in the offseasons, postseason, or the All-Star Game.

TB: Union meetings.

BN: Did people really say stuff like, "Our league's better"?

TB: Yeah. There's stories of fist fights.

BN: You were a boxer. Nobody's going to pick a fist fight with you!

TB: By the time I showed up that was kind of gone, but there was still the teasing.

BN: Maybe one or two people were a little too thin-skinned?

TB: Back then, it was so different. Like Angel said, with the uniforms, the equipment, philosophies....

AH: Higher strike zone, lower strike zone because of the positions they worked with the different equipment. When we'd get together, there'd just be arguments about different rules and theories.

TB: Our way's the right way.

BN: Obviously there weren't brawls all the time, but once or twice somebody hit somebody?

TB: Yeah.

AH: The DH versus the no-DH, why the American League games were longer, why the National League games were shorter. Just discussions like that.

BN: The pace of game has come down some this year, but I don't think it's due to replay. I think it's due to the clocks between innings and on the relievers and....

AH: There's really no data for that yet. We'll see at the end of the season. You've got to love all the changes that they're making. They're trying to make it better for the fans as well as the game and for everybody to enjoy. The beauty is, the gate's always open for you. You pay to watch entertainment. If you don't like it, you can always leave. You pay to go watch a movie. I'm a big moviegoer, but if I don't like it, I leave. It's entertainment.

BN: With the comings and goings throughout the season, you get into a working rhythm if things are working right. Is it a little disruptive, in a way... though you only typically have one person gone at any given time.

TB: Usually that's not too bad when you've got one guy coming in. it's when you have massive turnover—you look at some crews, they've just completely blown out. Injuries.

BN: On top of vacations.

TB: Yeah. And that can be disruptive. But when you just have one of our guys, like Pat, slide in for a few weeks, that's usually pretty seamless. It's refreshing to get a young guy in and try to help him out, too.

BN: Maybe it helps you guys, too, in a way. I mean, you all came up once, too.

TB: Yup.

AH: To give back, exactly. We remember, like I do, our first game. Excited. You never forget your first game. Where it was at, who you worked with, the score, et cetera. That's a memory-filer, for sure.

BN: You guy who are major-league umpires, when's the last time you actually rubbed up a baseball?

CC: It would have been back in Double A. You get to Triple A and the teams…ball boy, or whoever, start doing that. Double A was the last time I remember rubbing up a baseball.

BN: Was that your experience, too, Pat?

PH: Yeah.

TB: I did it until about the late 90s.

AH: Special mud. It's really special.

BN: You've got some of it right over there inside that cabinet.

TB: I don't miss it. You get tired of it. In the minor leagues, it wasn't bad. It's a couple of dozen and it's kind of your routine. In the big leagues, there's so many. You're rubbing up seven or eight dozen and it'll take a while.

BN: Dean [Lewis] says he does 12 or 14 dozen.

TB: Yeah, he probably does.

CC: When I was in Double A just four or five years ago, we were doing seven or eight dozen.

AH: Back in the day, and I don't go that far back, the pitchers would be upset if the catcher…[many people talking at once] they would toss that ball out. Now you see it where every ball gets thrown out. Even take notice of the ball the catcher will throw to second and is short-hopped. The hitting coach is yelling at you, "Hey, change the ball!" So just to save

Chris Conroy.

time, we don't even wait for them—we know it's coming, so we go to the catcher, "Here's a new one." It's such a habit that when they're throwing it around to the third baseman, as opposed to tossing it to the pitcher, he's throwing it to the third-base coach or throwing it to a kid.

BN: It's good for the fans.

AH: It's very costly, when you think of it.

BN: Working with the groundskeepers—and that is you, primarily, as the crew chief…?

TB: Yeah. He'll usually stop in and give us the lowdown, what's going on, and then if there's a delay I'll go over to his office to look at the radar. [Dave Mellor's office is immediately adjacent to the umpires' room.]

BN: [pointing to the closed door behind which is the home run replay equipment] Do you use this home run thing anymore?

TB: That's in case of emergency. That's a backup, if the system goes down.

BN: If the current replay system goes down.

TB: Yeah.

BN: But you used to use that for a couple of years.

TB: A couple of years, yeah, for home runs. We call that The Legacy. The techs refer to that as The Legacy.

BN: Nobody uses It anymore.

TB: No. If the system completely crashes down there…

BN: Has that ever happened yet?

TB: No.

BN: Let me ask the other three of you. [To Angel] How'd you first get interested in umpiring?

AH: My dad. Credit my dad for everything he did. He came from Cuba. He brought us up…I have five brothers…he brought us up playing baseball. He loved the game. Long story short, when I was old enough to start umpiring, I wanted to hit the streets, but in his mind there was no way I was going to hit the streets and catch up with my friends. Hialeah, Florida. Near Miami. So he started a program for umpires in the Little League organization. There's where I started to umpire.

BN: What age?

AH: 14. Over 60,000 kids played there.

TB: How many major-league players came out of there?

AH: A lot. A lot of major-league players. Alex Fernandez. Ricky Gutierrez. Johnny Cangelosi. Palmeiro. That's where it started, and I can thank him for that.

BN: Did you ever play ball, too?

AH: Just high school. My brother was a first-round, eighth pick in the nation, for the Brewers. Nick Hernandez. But he just basically quit. [Catcher out of Hialeah High School, in the 1978 draft.]

BN: Did you ever, at any level, happen to work a game he was in?

AH: No, that was before I went to school. I went to school in '81.

It's happened. We have an active umpire who umpired while his brother was playing, but they would change him. They would change the cities for him. It's a no-win situation. Jim Wolf. His brother is Randy Wolf.

TB: When I was in A ball, one of the guys in the league, his brother was the pitching coach for the Angels. Another guy's brother played on an independent team. But the story I always tell when it comes to managers, there was an umpire in Triple A in the Coast League named Zack Bevington. His brother was Terry Bevington. He would do his games and everybody thought that… but as it came out, they hated each other. They wouldn't talk. He ejected him one night. "You've always been a butthole." They just quit talking.

AH: As a matter of fact, that question came up at umpire school. I went to Bill Kinnamon's Umpire School. One of the umpires asked me, "So, if you get a chance to call your brother out on a strike…" I said, "I would have to be doing my job, so hopefully that would happen one day."

BN: [to Chris] How about yourself?

CC: I can remember back when I was playing Little League baseball as a kid. For a reason I can't explain, I can remember being fascinated and my eyes being drawn to what umpires did on the field. I thought it was neat. I thought the uniforms were cool.

Pat Hoberg.

I thought the way they made calls…I used to find it amusing how different guys had a different kind of strike mechanic. From that point on, it always stuck in the back of my head that it looks like it would be something neat to do. I maybe worked a handful of games as a teenager just because I maybe happened to be going by the Little League field and nobody showed up and it was like, "Hey, could you help us out?" I liked doing that but I didn't do a ton of it.

Then I was in about my mid-20s and I was single and just one day, I was like, "You know what? If I'm ever going to give this a shot, now's the time in my life to try it and if it works out, great, if it doesn't, then I tried and I know and I'll move on with my life. I got in, and here I am. I was 25 when I went to umpire school.

BN: Which one?

CC: I went to Evans. I went in 2000.

PH: My dad was big into Little League. He did a little umpiring, so I started when I was 12, 14, somewhere around there, doing Little League games. I actually played basketball in college. My summer job was umpiring high school and college baseball, four games a day Monday through Friday. I decided when I was a sophomore in college that I wanted to do it so I did the research, graduated, and then went to umpire school. Grandview University in Des Moines.

BN: [to Chris] What were you doing until you were 25?

CC: I went to college. Graduated there in '96. I had a couple of jobs when I first got out of college. I

Ted Barrett.

was working for a YMCA. Then I spent a couple of years back in my hometown working on a youth recreation center. I was like 23, 24, making like 30 grand a year. It was OK for me but I just wanted more. In the back of my head. It was a time in my life I was just like if I try this now, it only impacts me. I'm not married, I have no kids. It's as good a time as any to try it. They gave me a leave of absence from the job to go five weeks to umpire school. It's all worked out OK.

AH: It's the best experience of my life. I went at 18 and it was like a boot camp. Set up like a boot camp. They had lots of umpires there, trying to get into the game. And I never thought I would be one. Very competitive from the start. I remember calling my dad on a rotary phone back then, a pay phone, and he says, "Son, you're young, so if you don't get a job…." I said, "Dad, I'm up against men here. I shouldn't even be here." He said, "Give it the best you can." The instructors were all major-league umpires and that was a phenomenal thing being in the presence of these guys. It was overwhelming—the experience and everything you learn. Besides the rules, they

taught you positioning. You didn't even really need to have umpired when you went to umpire school. They literally taught you everything to know about the game.

BN: It's a pretty small percentage of people who go to umpire school and actually make it to the major leagues.

AH: Oh, yes, sir. The percentage is very low.

CC: I can remember the first day, you're sitting in a big room with 120 or 150 other guys and they'd say, "Statistically speaking, in this entire room, one, maybe two, will be a major-league umpire someday."

AH: And then you've got to endure the years in the minor leagues. I've worked with a lot of really good officials in the minor leagues. The opportunity was just never there for them when they were around, and they had the years in so they just passed them over, but they were quite deserving of working as well. I've worked with a lot of good umpires, guys who would go out there and work the job day in and day out.

Then there were the guys who found out it just wasn't for them. The loneliness, the travel, the heckling. When you missed a call, back then they taught you, you never admitted it. The game's changed a lot there now. It's different.

BN: Did you enjoy the heckling sometimes?

AH: No. And it kind of scarred you. It made who you were. Those years in the minor leagues is what made you who you were. If you endured that.

There was a spectator in the Carolina League, and he called us all "muleheads." You wanted to laugh but you couldn't laugh. I wanted to grin and I had to bite my teeth together. He was hilarious.

[On the other hand, AH talked about anti-Latino slurs being thrown his way.]

Jim Joyce, Greg Gibson, Chad Fairchild, Carlos Torres

Conversation in the umpires room, Fenway Park, September 26, 2015, with Bill Nowlin.

Bill Nowlin: I notice that a lot of umpires have family photos on the inside of their trunks.

Jim Joyce: Absolutely.

BN: You joined the major-league staff in 1989, I guess. Was that a tradition which goes back that far?

JJ: Oh yeah. Every bit of that. You bring your family on the road. We're on the road so much that you bring your family with you. We have these little cutouts that usually sit on top of our clothes and a lot of times we'll use that and just do a collage. I have pictures going back to when I started. I keep those on there just to remind me where it all came from. Like I said, we bring our families on the road with us.

BN: It's a tough life, obviously. You don't get to play half your games at home.

JJ: Exactly. And every time we walk in here, that reminds us of, really, part of the reason we do this.

BN: Well, if you make it this far, you begin to make a decent living but it's the years you put in to get here that are the biggest struggle.

JJ: Without a doubt.

BN: That's one of the things I wanted to ask you about. You went to the Kinnamon School?

JJ: Yes, I did.

BN: What is it like today…do you go back once in a while to instruct, or look in on one of the schools to visit?

JJ: Never have. Gibby [Greg Gibson] has, in the past.

BN: I'm just curious how different it is. The curriculum is probably relatively similar, but presumably more refined. More use of video, certainly, and digital media.

Greg Gibson: Hunter Wendelstedt took over the school from his dad. Hunter and I have been friends.

I've worked for Harry. I sat at the feet of Harry Wendelstedt for 10 years. One of the things about it, you want to get a real perspective of where we all get started, you should call Hunter—he's at um-pireschool.com—and make a trip down to umpire school to see. Because one of the things we do, we treat—even if a guy…there's been lots of times we get a guy with experience, and then we get the 18-year-old kid that he doesn't really know what he wants to do and mom and dad don't want to waste money on college. Three grand is a better investment to see if he wants to do that. They treat everybody [the same]. He starts with the basics. Obviously things change and you have to teach the system that is sent down from Umpire Development as far as coverage and things like that. Things change with the way they want to do things, depending upon who's in charge.

GG: The basic fundamentals that they teach at umpire schools is one of the things that I remind Triple-A guys when they get here. What's your first responsibility? Fair/foul, catch/no catch. The things that we teach from day one are the things you build on no matter what level you're at. One of the things that I enjoy going back is to be around not only the kids who want to learn but the kids who teach. When you go to umpire school and you're an instructor, most of the staff is made up of minor-league umpires with the supervision and help of…Hunter will bring in…Jerry Layne's always there. David Rackley's still there. Eddie Hickox is still there. Jordan Baker comes down. Kids that have went through the school as instructors, made it as major-league umpires. I haven't been down for three years now.

BN: One of the things you said you'd heard of umpires who had to sleep in their cars when they were starting off.

JJ: Oh, yeah. Actually, the way I got started is that I was a player and I wanted to stay in the game. I got hurt and I couldn't play anymore. There was a guy back in Toledo, Ohio by the name of Tom Raveshear who was a long-time minor-league umpire. He worked for the Toledo Recreation Division and I was 16 years old and I used to listen to his stories about umpiring while I was playing. When my playing days were over, I went back to him and asked him about it. He told me how tough the life was and everything, but you know what? It was still professional baseball.

BN: You played in college.

JJ: Yeah. Bowling Green State University. The Falcons. I was a pitcher.

BB: One thing I thought was interesting was that three of you on this crew were all born in Ohio. On this particular crew.

JJ: Yeah. On this particular crew.

BN: And one from Venezuela. Only you [to Carlos Torres]. You missed.

JJ: By a few miles. And a few countries.

BN: There seem to be little clusters. There's a group of umpires that came from Connecticut. A group from Ohio. Michigan.

JJ: We were talking about that the other day. Chad was talking about how many guys are from Ohio. I don't know how many we ended up coming up with, but there were quite a few. It's kind of funny. We all kind of placed somewhere else, though. We met our wives or whatever.

BN: Your dad worked at Jeep? What kind of work did he do?

JJ: My dad was in charge of payroll. He went way back. He started back when it was still Willys Overland after the war when they built the Willys Jeep. Then it went to Kaiser Jeep, then it went to American Motors, and then it finally ended up Chrysler. He put in like 36 years. My mom actually worked there, too. And so did I.

BN: I knew you worked there. Greasing tie rods or something?

JJ: Yes, I greased tie rods. I worked in the press shop. I worked in the paint shop. The body shop. My dad would always get me in during spring break or summer breaks in college. Over at least five years.

BN: And fulltime for at least six months or so.

JJ: Yeah, yeah.

BN: I read your book, that's how I knew that. You also have a special interest in Christmas lighting?

JJ: Absolutely.

BN: You put up one of those monster displays at home?

JJ: Absolutely. Absolutely. And my son has developed a knack for it. To this day, I'll put up—well, we live in a different house now, but at my second house, I was putting up over 30,000 lights. This house, it's scaled down to about 10,000.

BN: Your father did some umpiring?

JJ: Yes, he did. He was an amateur umpire for a while. I would follow him around a little bit. I don't know if he just lost the interest in it or whatever, but he abruptly quit. Just quit doing it.

BN: You had already started by that time?

JJ: No, no. This was when I was just in high school ball. I never umpired until I went to umpire school. I never umpired. I just watched him. It was kind of interesting. It was a way to stay in baseball. That's the reason I pursued it.

BN: You just decided to go to umpire school and they thought you were good enough, and you got the bug a little bit.

JJ: Yeah. That's exactly how it goes. I spent 11 years in the minor leagues.

BN: In the early years before the leagues united, I heard that there was some real rivalry between the National League umpires and the American League umpires.

JJ: It was kind of funny because we all became—in 1982 is when they did away with the outside protector. I always wore the inside, anyway. I think it came from that. The way the two different leagues developed. American League umpires were considered high-ball umpires and National League umpires were considered low-ball umpires. When we went to the inside protector, uniform all the way across the board, there became a friendly rivalry between the American League and the National League. They were always called the Senior League. When I came up, we were a much younger staff that the National League and it was a competitive drive a little bit to show that the

American League was just as good as the National League. And the National League never believed it.

BN: And the AL had the DH, too.

JJ: Exactly. That was a big thing, and it was a big thing only because with the addition of the designated hitter, the American League games increasingly started getting longer and longer. There was more offense. The National League always had the belief that their games were always shorter. I was an American League umpire for 13 years and one of our arguments was that our pitchers don't hit and we have more offense in the game. The National League always claimed that their game was better. Without the DH.

We all came from the same place, though. We all ended up in the major leagues. And we're all doing the same thing. I like to think it was more of a friendly rivalry.

BN: You actually saved a woman's life one time.

JJ: Yes, I did.

BN: Jayne Powers. Do you keep in touch with her?

JJ: All the time. It's been three years now. What was it? 2012. August 20. I just saw her three weeks ago.

It's really strange. There's a lot of eerie coincidences. Her birthday and my wife's birthday are at the same time. We're all of us very Irish. She had a vision that she was going to have a heart attack. The day before, we left late to the ballpark and I told my crew the next day that we're leaving 20 minutes earlier because we were a little bit late. If we hadn't left early that day, I wouldn't have been walking down the tunnel.

She actually had a heart episode, not a heart attack *per se*, that only five percent of the people survive even with CPR. Everybody should know CPR. Everybody. Tanner, Chad's son, could do CPR. You're going to be 13? He's going to be 13 and he could do it. I think it should be a prerequisite in school. I'm pushing for that in Oregon.

BN: I do have one question that I guess is kind of the obvious one. I would suspect that you wish that there had been replay at the time of the Galarraga game.

JJ: It would have been very beneficial. It would have spared me a lot of death threats.

BN: You really had death threats.

JJ: My whole family.

BN: I didn't realize it had reached that point.

JJ: I've said ever since the incident, it was my worst day in baseball but it was also my best day in baseball. Actually, in my life. I always look at outcomes. I always look at things done for a reason. I still don't know the reason, but a lot of good has come from it. More good than bad.

BN: Besides becoming a published author. Before that time, were you in favor of replay at all, or just really not that interested?

JJ: Probably not that interested. At that time, we already had the replay with the box for boundary calls of home runs and stuff. I think we all knew that eventually replay would evolve into what it is today. And I'll be honest with you—I'm a fan.

BN: I think we know that the technology exists that could even call balls and strikes.

JJ: If that happens, I'm not so sure that you'll need us.

[some interruption that prevented continuing to talk to Carlos Torres]

BN [asking Greg Gibson]: When you first joined the major-league staff, was that a result of the big transition that occurred in 1999?

GG: I'd rather not answer questions about that.

BN: OK. But that's when you first got your opportunity.

GG: My first opportunity was when I went up in '97. But I got hired in '99.

BN: I mentioned to Jim before that it caught my eye that three of you guys were born in Ohio.

GG: I was born there, but I was raised in Kentucky.

BN: OK. Well, part of Ohio was just across the river. I notice you were involved in a couple of replay firsts.

GG: The very first one, with Frank Pulli. [May 31, 1999, in Florida, Cardinals versus Marlins] Cliff Floyd hit a ball that went off the wall; Frank called it a home run. I went to the minor leagues with Cliff Floyd and I was at second base. Cliff got to second base and he said, "Gibby, that was a home run." And I said, "No, the ball hit the wall." Cliff ran right to Frank. Frank was working third. Frank whistled (GG gestures the circular motion indicating rounding the bases) and gave a home run.

Well, there's kind of a thing in the umpiring world where everybody comes out of the dugout and starts yelling at you—chances are, you might have missed it. This was back in the days before replay or anything. Frank was an old National League guy, and you just didn't huddle. You made the call, that was the call, and that was it. We huddled.

BN: Frank overruled you?

GG: No, it was Frank's call. It was Frank's call all the way. But Cliff got to second base and he talked to me. Cliff and I had known each other since A ball. Cliff and I had been together for eight years, every level up through.

Cliff ran to Frank and Frank called it a home run. So we huddled. Frank was big on seniority and Greg Bonin had the plate. He said, "What have you got, Peewee?" "Ah, I don't know, Frank." Ed Rapuano was at first base. "What have you got, Eddie Rap?" "I don't know, Frank. I'm not real sure, Frank." Frank called me Hoot. Hoot Gibson. Frank had a big Italian… "Hoot, what have you got?" I said, "The ball hit the wall, Frank." "*What*?" I said, "The ball hit the wall, Frank." He said, "Where?" I said, "What do you want me to do, go out there and climb it?" I remember it like it was yesterday. I said, "What do you want me to do, go out there and draw you a big X on the scoreboard?" I said, "It hit the scoreboard."

He said, "There's only one way to fix this. And, with that, he turned and he started walking toward the Marlins dugout, with Greg Bonin. And I looked at Eddie Rap and I said, "Is he going to do what I think he's going to do?" And Rap said back to me, "Like you're going to stop him?" (laughs)

So Frank goes to the Marlins' first-base dugout and he literally asks one of the technicians to turn the camera and around and give him the look. Well, some photographer is trying to take pictures of the whole thing. Greg Bonin grabs the guy's camera and slams it to the ground. Breaks this guy's real expen-

sive camera. Anyway, it was just a mess, the whole thing was just a mess. That was the first use of instant replay.

John Boles was sick and not there. Fredi Gonzalez was the bench coach and actually the fill-in manager for the Marlins. And I had gone through the minor leagues with Fredi as a manager. So we're getting ready to go and Fredi comes out and goes, "I want to protest. I want to play this game under protest." We huddle again and Frank looks at me and he goes, "You're the rules guy. What have you got?" "There's nothing to cover this." I said, "Frank, you're using technology. There's nothing to cover this." Anyway, Frank marks up the protest. We can't even get off the field. Runge was the supervisor. This was back and I was the only guy who had a cellphone. The first year I had a cellphone. Let's just say it was a major, major, major…it was a big deal.

BN: You had two other firsts.

GG: Well, we had replay come into effect on boundary calls [in 2008]. I was with Charlie Reliford. Brian Runge had the call. Jerry Layne was at first base and I was at the plate. Tropicana was weird; they had these two…lines. (gestures toward roof) We huddled. Charlie looks at me and says, "What have you got?" and I said, "Brian got it right, but we've got it. We might as well use it." And Charlie was like, "Okay." So I stayed on the field, and Jerry and Charlie and Runge went off the field and used it.

And then last year, I was the infamous one. I was with Ted Barrett and kicked the crap out of a call at first base. I was the first guy to get overturned.

[March 31, 2014 at Miller Field, Braves vs. Brewers. Bottom of the sixth: BREWERS 6TH: Braun grounded out (third to first); Braves manager Fredi Gonzalez challenged the call at 1B when Ryan Braun was ruled safe; the review overturned the call, which was the first time a call was changed in the newly expanded replay system.]

So I hit the trifecta. What I want to point out is this: I was 2-for-3 with all the firsts on replay. As Meatloaf said, "Two out of three ain't bad." Well, that's been me. I got two out of three right.

BN: Do you know who was in the chair at the replay center?

GG: Brian O'Nora. Mine was the first one flipped. People know I had the first one overturned but they didn't know that I also had the first unofficial and the first official and I had both of them right.

BN: And probably 99% of all the other calls you've made, too.

GG: Well, they only remember you for the ones you miss. They don't remember you for the ones you get right.

BN: You did work behind the plate for Randy Johnson's perfect game.

GG: I did.

BN: That must have been quite a thrill in a way.

GG: Well, it's one of those things that you really don't think about it until it's over.

BN: And you worked Kershaw's no-hitter, too.

GG: Kershaw's no-hitter, yeah.

BN: Some guys work their whole career and never have a no-hitter from behind the plate.

GG: A lot of guys.

BN: Mexico City. World Baseball Classic. Was that a different experience?

GG: Just the culture. It was fun to go and do that. The World Baseball Classic, there's three major-league umpires and four amateur picked by the international committee. So that's fun. You get to work with those guys and they enjoy being around us. It's a lot of fun.

BN: Those are all the specific questions I have for you right now. Maybe I can catch up with the other guys another time. I know it's running late.

GG: I'll be honest with you. One of the most important things—and one of the things I enjoy most—is playing cards before the game.

BN: When you go to replay, do you usually show up there about an hour and a half before the games?

GG: No. Thirty minutes.

BN: At least you don't have to change beforehand.

GG: It's a nice break. It's intense, though. It's one of those things where you might not have anything going on and then all of a sudden you've got something going on over here and something going on over there. It's a break, but when they come to the headset and they're needing info, it gets intense. We are all about getting it right, whether we're on the field or off the field. Our job is the integrity of the game and our job is to get it right.

No matter what a fan thinks. As a fan, you can look at a replay and I can look at a replay and you can have your opinion and I can have my opinion. But at the end of the day, what our guys do, we get it right.

BN: Chad, I wanted to ask you one question. You're #4.

CF: Yes.

BN: Do the numbers mean anything to people?

CF: Some people, they do; some people, they don't. Me, they don't.

BN: That was Tim Tschida's number.

CF: If I had a number to pick and everything's available, I'll take 24. Other than that, I have no….i don't care what my number is. Is that Jerry Layne?

JJ: Yes.

CF: So if he retires and I'm able to, I'll take 24. Other than that, I don't care what my number is.

BN: So they just gave it to you.

CF: Something like that, yeah.

[A fuller interview with Chad Fairchild was conducted on April 20, 2016.]

Contributors

DAVID W. ANDERSON is the author of *More than Merkle*, a detailed history about the 1908 season published by the University of Nebraska Press in 2000, he also wrote *You Can't Beat the Hours*. He was a member of the Society of American Baseball Research from 1988 until 2016. He lives in Olathe, Kansas with his wife Judy. They have three adult children—Karin, Erik, and Julia. They spend most of their spare time baby-sitting their triplet grand-children Robert, David, and Hadley.

MARK ARMOUR is the founder and former director (2002-2016) of the Baseball Biography Project, and currently a Co-Chair of SABR's Baseball Cards Committee. The author of several books and dozens of articles on baseball history, Mark lives in Oregon's Willamette Valley with Jane, Maya, and Drew.

PERRY BARBER started umpiring Little League with her identical twin sister Warren in 1981 when women on the diamond were few and far between. Since then, she has umpired all levels of amateur and professional baseball including major-league exhibitions in the United States and Japan, the fabled Cape Cod League, the independent Atlantic League, and international competitions abroad. From her origins as a New York City debutante to *Jeopardy!* champion at the tender age of 19 to a 10-year career as a singer/songwriter who opened shows for Bruce Springsteen and Billy Joel, Perry's path to the dia-mond has been long and winding, primarily in pur-suit of avoiding getting a real job. Her goal now is to ensure that the women who follow in her plate shoes will have the opportunities and support they'll need to make it where she did not: the major leagues.

JOHN BEHREND started umpiring when he was 16 after one of the umpires didn't show up for a high school baseball game, and has been hooked ever since that day in 1963. He says, "I've loved the game of baseball ever since I could walk. I played

American Legion baseball and in 1965 went to the 40th annual Legion World Series, held in Aberdeen, South Dakota where I had the pleasure of meeting Ted Williams, Bob Feller, and Burleigh Grimes." Behrend served in the Marine Corps from 1967-1994, including service in Vietnam in 1968-69 with 3/7 as an infantryman. A resident of South Korea since 1994, he has been member of the ABUA since Jim Evans invited him to join in 2007. John umpires Korean youth leagues and semipro baseball in the amateur league in Korea, selected to umpire in the Asian Pacific Pony Baseball World Series in Seoul, South Korea, July 2016. Three times he has been se-lected to umpire in the DODEA, Far East NFHS baseball championships held in Korea with 13 teams from the Pacific region, including teams from Korea, Guam, and Japan. He is married and currently living in Daegu, Korea.

DENNIS BINGHAM served as a writer, editor, and historian for the Chicago Police Department for three decades and now works free-lance. A long-time umpire, he works more than 150 games a year in the Chicagoland area at various levels. His passions include reading, attending White Sox games, and the study of baseball rules. In 1988, he co-founded SABR's Umpires and Rules Committee with Larry Gerlach and Bob McConnell. He lives with wife Diane on Chicago's south side; both are delighted whenever the cutest grandson in the world visits them. Their sons Sean and Kevin have escaped the household and third son Rocky is about to.

ALAN COHEN has been a SABR member since 2011. He has written more than 30 biographies for SABR's bio-project, and has contributed to several SABR books. He is expanding his research into the Hearst Sandlot Classic (1946-1965), an annual youth All-Star game which launched the careers of 88 major-league players. He graduated from Franklin and Marshall College with a degree in history. He has four children and six grandchildren and resides in West Hartford, Connecticut with his wife Frances, one cat, and two dogs.

REYNALDO CRUZ is the founder and head editor of the Cuban-based magazine *Universo Béisbol*, which is hosted in MLBlogs. He is a language graduate in the University of Holguin, in his hometown, and has been leading the aforementioned magazine since March 2010. A SABR member since the summer of 2014, he writes, translates, and photographs baseball and was in the first row of the Barack Obama game in Havana, shooting from the Tampa Bay Rays dugout. In spite of the rich history of Cuban baseball, his favorite player happens to be no other than Ichiro Suzuki, whom he expects to meet and interview. A retro lover, he envisions Fenway Park, Wrigley Field, Koshien Stadium, and Estadio Palmar de Junco as the can't-miss places in baseball.

KEVIN CUDDIHY is an advocacy writer for the Air Line Pilots Association and a former sports acquisitions editor for Potomac Books, Inc. He was a member of SABR and attendee of multiple SABR Conventions while with Potomac, and recently rejoined the organization. Kevin has been a volunteer with UMPS CARE Charities since 2009. He lives in Fairfax, Virginia, with his wife and son.

REID DUFFY has been a SABR member since 1985 and a former chairman of its Umpires & Rules Committee. He lives in Indianapolis, and is retired after a long career as a television news reporter.

ROB EDELMAN has authored the books *Great Baseball Films*, *Baseball on the Web* and (with Audrey Kupferberg) *Meet the Mertzes* and *Matthau: A Life*. He often contributes to *Base Ball: A Journal of the Early Game*; he offers film commentary on WAMC Northeast Public Radio and is a longtime Contributing Editor of *Leonard Maltin's Movie Guide*. His byline appears in dozens of publications (from *Total Baseball* to *NINE: A Journal of Baseball History and Culture*) and on the DVD *Reel Baseball: Baseball Films from the Silent Era, 1899-1926*. He is an interviewee on documentaries on the director's cut DVD of *The Natural* and teaches film courses at the University at Albany. He currently is coediting (with Bill Nowlin) a book on baseball players and the movies.

ERIC FROST is a neonatal intensive care nurse at a Houston children's hospital. Lacking any natural athletic prowess as a Little Leaguer many years ago, he tried to learn as much as possible about baseball strategy and rules. He spent two seasons as a very mediocre amateur umpire, and the experience left him with a deep appreciation for the men who do this thankless job.

LARRY GERLACH, a member since 1979, has served SABR as president and founder of the Umpires and Rules Committee. Emeritus Professor of History, University of Utah, he has written extensively on his two historical loves, the American Revolution and baseball. The latter work includes *The Men in Blue: Conversations With Umpires*.

DENNIS GOODMAN is an amateur umpire and professional statistician. A SABR member since 2002, he spends his spring and summer nights on ball fields umpiring all levels from youth to high school varsity. His 2015 book *RuleGraphics: Professional Baseball* was praised by readers for making the baseball rules easier to understand and research. A lifelong Cubs fan, he lives outside of Indianapolis, Indiana with his wife and two sons.

LESLIE HEAPHY is an associate professor of history at Kent State University and has been a SABR member since 1988. She is the chair of the Women in Baseball Committee and serves on the committee for the Annual Jerry Malloy Negro League Conference. She is the author/editor of six books on baseball history and editor of *Blackball*, a national peer reviewed journal on black baseball.

HAROLD V. HIGHAM is the great grandson of nineteenth century National League player and umpire Richard "Dick" Higham. During 40 years of practicing law he has succeeded in researching and publishing pieces about his great grandfather and exposing serious questions about his career as a player and umpire especially surrounding his disqualification.

JOANNE HULBERT - Boston Chapter co-chair and Baseball and the Arts Committee co-chair, is a resident of Mudville, a venerable old neighborhood of Holliston MA., where she satisfies her baseball obsession by scanning hundreds of newspapers, old and new, searching for the ultimate in baseball poetry, has amassed thousands of forgotten baseball masterpieces, and has rescued these nearly forgotten literary gems from neglect and obscurity in order to remember and to celebrate the bards of baseball.

BOB HURTE, of Stewartsville, New Jersey has been a member of SABR since 1998. He was one of the early writers for its Baseball Biography Project. Over his tenure he has authored 18 bios for the BioProject website, and contributed to three others to appear in future publications. He is a Volunteer Coordinator for Catholic Charities, and has been active in your sports in his community, serving as its vice president for 10 years, coached baseball and soccer for 14 years. It is an honor to write the bio for Tom Gorman, and be a part of this book. When he was 10, he attended a banquet at Rutgers University where Tom was a speaker along with Jeff Torborg, Al Downing, and Monte Irvin. Bob has never forgot being regaled by Tom's baseball stories, especially those involving Leo Durocher. He has been married to Barbara for 27 years and they have raised three children: Matthew (deceased), Tegan (22), and Samuel (18).

GIL IMBER is the founder of Close Call Sports (www.closecallsports.com) and chief commissioner of the Umpire Ejection Fantasy League, dedicated to the objective analysis of close and controversial calls in sport with great regard for the rules and spirit of the game; in addition to extensive rules analysis, specialties include replay review, ejections, and interpretation of pitch f/x location data. During the off-season, Gil serves as organist for hockey's Anaheim Ducks and previously worked with baseball's Los Angeles Dodgers. He may be reached via e-mail at gil@closecallsports.com.

CHUCK JOHNSON has been a SABR member since 1991 and is a co-founder of Arizona's Flame Delhi Chapter. Chuck has provided minor-league content for such media outlets as MLB.com, SB Nation, and Bleacher Report and is a frequent contributor to SABR's Bio and Game Projects. A member of the Minor League Alumni Association through his work with the Eastern League, Chuck lives with his wife and daughter in Surprise, Arizona where he works as an official scorer for the Arizona Rookie League.

RODNEY JOHNSON is one of the founders of Arizona's Flame Delhi (Arizona) SABR chapter. He has served in chapter leadership since 1992 and also served on the national SABR Board of Directors for five years. He is the co-chair of the Umpires and Rules Committee. Rodney has written many published articles about baseball history. Since 2001 he has worked for Major League Baseball as an official scorer and is also the Coordinator of Official Scorers for the affiliated rookie-level Arizona League.

STEPHEN JOHNSON is a retired public school band director. He has been member of SABR since 1992. He served one three-year term as president of the Jack Graney Chapter and was the coordinator for the 2008 Cleveland SABR Convention. He has spent over 20 years researching the career of player/coach/umpire Charlie Berry, who was a friend of his father. He wrote the bio of Rudy Regalado for the SABR book, *Pitching to the Pennant*.

BOB LEMOINE grew up in Maine and has followed his beloved Red Sox for most of his life. Bob joined SABR in 2013 and has contributed to several projects. In 2016 he co-edited with Bill Nowlin *Boston's First Nine: the 1871-75 Boston Red Stockings*. Bob has recently discovered a fascination with 19th Century baseball, including the fact that umpires would sometimes, instead of a right thumb, give a player a right cross to help restore order. Bob lives in Barrington, New Hampshire and works as a high school librarian.

LEN LEVIN served as an umpire once — in junior high school — an assignment that helped him appreciate the work umpires do. When not umpiring, he is a retired newspaper editor and a copy editor for SABR publications.

HANK LEVY is a CPA in Berkeley, California. He started umpiring in 2001 as a volunteer for his son's Little League team, working progressively more difficult and older ages, and working with District 4. He moved to high school umpiring in 2005 with two, then a third, high school umpires' association. He is currently a Board member of the NorthEast Bay Umpires Association. He has umpired at the Community College level as well as preseason games for Division I Colleges. Most of his umpiring now is at the high school, men's senior leagues, Vintage baseball, and some semipro summer leagues. His umpiring has taken him to the Dream Park in Cooperstown, New York, and to San Quentin Prison. His dream is to go to Cuba to umpire. Hank was a former journalist, and plans to write more about his umpiring experience for both non-fiction and fiction venues.

BOB LUKE took up writing baseball books after retiring from a 40 year career in Human Resource Development. His first was *Dean of Umpires: A Biography of Bill McGowan, 1896-1954* published by McFarland. Others are *Willie Wells: "El Diablo" of the Negro Leagues* (University of Texas), *The Baltimore Elite Giants: Sport and Society in the Age of Negro League Baseball* (Johns Hopkins University), *The Most Famous Woman in Baseball: Effa Manley and the Negro Leagues* (Potomac Books), and *Integrating the Orioles: Baseball and Race in Baltimore* (McFarland.) He lives in Garrett Park, Maryland with his wife Judy Wentworth.

SHAUN MCCREADY is employed as a full time Police Officer who lives in Hollidaysburg, Pennsylvania. He holds a Bachelor's Degree in Criminology with a minor in Psychology from Mount Aloysius College in Cresson, Pennsylvania. He is a 2013 graduate of the Wendelstedt Umpire School and has been working as an amateur umpire since 2010. He currently umpires high school baseball as well as several local teenage and adult baseball leagues. He has previously umpired in the Nine Baseball Futures Game at Penn State University, two Altoona Curve Classic High School Championship Games, and the Altoona Regionals of the AAABA Baseball Tournament. He is a Boston Red Sox fan and has had a lifelong passion for baseball.

CLARK G. "RED" MERCHANT; 72 years old, and no longer officiating as physical disabilities have taken their toll. Officiated for 37 years, from pee-wee up thru AA and Division I baseball and softball; pee-wee thru Division II football; military soccer, volleyball, and basketball. Retired from the USAF in 1988 with 50% disability from service in Viet Nam. Now living in TX and have been married to Evelyn for 51 years now, celebrating our 50th last year.

BRIAN MILLS is an Assistant Professor at the University of Florida. His research encompasses sports analytics and managerial sports economics, with a focus in labor and personnel economics and industrial organization. Brian is also the creator of a course on pitching analytics at DataCamp called "Exploring Pitch Data with R." He holds a PhD and MA in Sport Management, an MA in Economics, and an MA in Statistics from the University of Michigan. Prior to his time in Ann Arbor, Brian earned a BA in Psychology from St. Mary's College of Maryland where he played Division III baseball. He still holds out hope of being the inspiration for a sequel to *The Rookie* once he gets his elbow put back together.

BILL NOWLIN, known to none as "The Old Arbiter" since he has never worked a game behind the plate, still favors the balloon chest protector for its nostalgic aesthetics. Aside from a dozen years as a college professor, his primary life's work was as a co-founder of Rounder Records (it got him inducted into the Bluegrass Music Hall of Fame). He's written or edited more than 50 books, mostly on baseball, and has been on the Board of Directors of SABR since the magic Red Sox year of 2004.

ALBERT PIACENTE has taught philosophy at several colleges and universities in New York and is presently at NYU. He has authored and co-authored several books, on political philosophy and the philosophy of education, but is at present focused on the philosophy of sport (especially baseball). A lifelong fan of baseball, ever since attending his first Yankees game in the original Yankees Stadium (pre-1970's renovations), he is in the process of completing several projects related to baseball, and sport generally.

BILL PRUDEN has been a teacher and administrator, primarily at the high school level, for almost 35 years. A SABR member since 2001, he has contributed to both the Bio and Games Projects. A lifetime baseball fan, he also loves to read, research, and write American History of all kinds, passions undoubtedly fueled by the fact that as a 7-year-old, at only his second major-league game, he witnessed Roger Maris hit his historic 61st home run.

DAVID VINCENT was presented the Bob Davids Award, SABR's highest honor, in 1999. Vincent is an official scorer for Major League Baseball in Washington and in the Carolina League. The 2016 season was his 29th in professional baseball and he has been an official scorer at all levels of pro ball, from rookie to both major leagues.

BOB WEBSTER grew up in Northwest Indiana and has been a Cubs fan since 1963. Earned a BS in Accounting from Linfield College and an MBA from Marylhurst University. Now living in Portland, Oregon and recently retired from Intel, Bob is currently working on the History of the Northwest League as well as writing about the West Coast League along with the many other wooden-bat, collegiate leagues. In 2015, was a stats stringer for MLB Gameday at the Hillsboro Hops (Short-Season Single-A) games. He is a member of the Northwest Chapter of SABR, on the Board of Executives of the Old-Timers Baseball Association of Portland, and a manager in the Great American Fantasy League.

CHRIS WILLIAMS is a lawyer in the employee benefits group at Perkins Coie LLP in Los Angeles and a long-time member of SABR. Having lived in Baltimore for many years her first love is the Orioles, but now that she's in SoCal she also roots for the Angels and Dodgers.

HERB WILSON was born in North Carolina but has lived in Waterville, Maine with his wife for the past 27 years. He is a Professor of Biology at Colby College. His research specialty is ornithology. He regularly teaches a course on the Science of Baseball. He is the Chair of the Educational Resources Committee of SABR. He is an avid member of Red Sox Nation.

SABR BIOPROJECT TEAM BOOKS

In 2002, the Society for American Baseball Research launched an effort to write and publish biographies of every player, manager, and individual who has made a contribution to baseball. Over the past decade, the BioProject Committee has produced over 6,000 biographical articles. Many have been part of efforts to create theme- or team-oriented books, spearheaded by chapters or other committees of SABR.

THE 1986 BOSTON RED SOX:
THERE WAS MORE THAN GAME SIX
One of a two-book series on the rivals that met in the 1986 World Series, the Boston Red Sox and the New York Mets, including biographies of every player, coach, broadcaster, and other important figures in the top organizations in baseball that year. .
Edited by Leslie Heaphy and Bill Nowlin
$19.95 paperback (ISBN 978-1-943816-19-4)
$9.99 ebook (ISBN 978-1-943816-18-7)
8.5"X11", 420 pages, over 200 photos

THE 1986 NEW YORK METS:
THERE WAS MORE THAN GAME SIX
The other book in the "rivalry" set from the 1986 World Series. This book re-tells the story of that year's classic World Series and this is the story of each of the players, coaches, managers, and broadcasters, their lives in baseball and the way the 1986 season fit into their lives.
Edited by Leslie Heaphy and Bill Nowlin
$19.95 paperback (ISBN 978-1-943816-13-2)
$9.99 ebook (ISBN 978-1-943816-12-5)
8.5"X11", 392 pages, over 100 photos

SCANDAL ON THE SOUTH SIDE:
THE 1919 CHICAGO WHITE SOX
The Black Sox Scandal isn't the only story worth telling about the 1919 Chicago White Sox. The team roster included three future Hall of Famers, a 20-year-old spitballer who would win 300 games in the minors, and even a batboy who later became a celebrity with the "Murderers' Row" New York Yankees. All of their stories are included in Scandal on the South Side with a timeline of the 1919 season.
Edited by Jacob Pomrenke
$19.95 paperback (ISBN 978-1-933599-95-3)
$9.99 ebook (ISBN 978-1-933599-94-6)
8.5"x11", 324 pages, 55 historic photos

WINNING ON THE NORTH SIDE
THE 1929 CHICAGO CUBS
Celebrate the 1929 Chicago Cubs, one of the most exciting teams in baseball history. Future Hall of Famers Hack Wilson, '29 NL MVP Rogers Hornsby, and Kiki Cuyler, along with Riggs Stephenson formed one of the most potent quartets in baseball history. The magical season came to an ignominious end in the World Series and helped craft the future "lovable loser" image of the team.
Edited by Gregory H. Wolf
$19.95 paperback (ISBN 978-1-933599-89-2)
$9.99 ebook (ISBN 978-1-933599-88-5)
8.5"x11", 314 pages, 59 photos

DETROIT THE UNCONQUERABLE:
THE 1935 WORLD CHAMPION TIGERS
Biographies of every player, coach, and broadcaster involved with the 1935 World Champion Detroit Tigers baseball team, written by members of the Society for American Baseball Research. Also includes a season in review and other articles about the 1935 team. Hank Greenberg, Mickey Cochrane, Charlie Gehringer, Schoolboy Rowe, and more.
Edited by Scott Ferkovich
$19.95 paperback (ISBN 9978-1-933599-78-6)
$9.99 ebook (ISBN 978-1-933599-79-3)
8.5"X11", 230 pages, 52 photos

THE TEAM THAT TIME WON'T FORGET:
THE 1951 NEW YORK GIANTS
Because of Bobby Thomson's dramatic "Shot Heard 'Round the World" in the bottom of the ninth of the decisive playoff game against the Brooklyn Dodgers, the team will forever be in baseball public's consciousness. Includes a foreword by Giants outfielder Monte Irvin.
Edited by Bill Nowlin and C. Paul Rogers III
$19.95 paperback (ISBN 978-1-933599-99-1)
$9.99 ebook (ISBN 978-1-933599-98-4)
8.5"X11", 282 pages, 47 photos

A PENNANT FOR THE TWIN CITIES:
THE 1965 MINNESOTA TWINS
This volume celebrates the 1965 Minnesota Twins, who captured the American League pennant in just their fifth season in the Twin Cities. Led by an All-Star cast, from Harmon Killebrew, Tony Oliva, Zoilo Versalles, and Mudcat Grant to Bob Allison, Jim Kaat, Earl Battey, and Jim Perry, the Twins won 102 games, but bowed to the Los Angeles Dodgers and Sandy Koufax in Game Seven.
Edited by Gregory H. Wolf
$19.95 paperback (ISBN 978-1-943816-09-5)
$9.99 ebook (ISBN 978-1-943816-08-8)
8.5"X11", 405 pages, over 80 photos

MUSTACHES AND MAYHEM: CHARLIE O'S THREE TIME CHAMPIONS:
THE OAKLAND ATHLETICS: 1972-74
The Oakland Athletics captured major league baseball's crown each year from 1972 through 1974. Led by future Hall of Famers Reggie Jackson, Catfish Hunter and Rollie Fingers, the Athletics were a largely homegrown group who came of age together. Biographies of every player, coach, manager, and broadcaster (and mascot) from 1972 through 1974 are included, along with season recaps.
Edited by Chip Greene
$29.95 paperback (ISBN 978-1-943816-07-1)
$9.99 ebook (ISBN 978-1-943816-06-4)
8.5"X11", 600 pages, almost 100 photos

SABR Members can purchase each book at a significant discount (often 50% off) and receive the ebook editions free as a member benefit. Each book is available in a trade paperback edition as well as ebooks suitable for reading on a home computer or Nook, Kindle, or iPad/tablet.
To learn more about becoming a member of SABR, visit the website: sabr.org/join

THE SABR DIGITAL LIBRARY

The Society for American Baseball Research, the top baseball research organization in the world, disseminates some of the best in baseball history, analysis, and biography through our publishing programs. The SABR Digital Library contains a mix of books old and new, and focuses on a tandem program of paperback and ebook publication, making these materials widely available for both on digital devices and as traditional printed books.

GREATEST GAMES BOOKS

TIGERS BY THE TALE:
GREAT GAMES AT MICHIGAN AND TRUMBULL
For over 100 years, Michigan and Trumbull was the scene of some of the most exciting baseball ever. This book portrays 50 classic games at the corner, spanning the earliest days of Bennett Park until Tiger Stadium's final closing act. From Ty Cobb to Mickey Cochrane, Hank Greenberg to Al Kaline, and Willie Horton to Alan Trammell.
Edited by Scott Ferkovich
$12.95 paperback (ISBN 978-1-943816-21-7)
$6.99 ebook (ISBN 978-1-943816-20-0)
8.5"x11", 160 pages, 22 photos

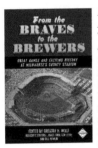

FROM THE BRAVES TO THE BREWERS: GREAT GAMES AND HISTORY AT MILWAUKEE'S COUNTY STADIUM
The National Pastime provides in-depth articles focused on the geographic region where the national SABR convention is taking place annually. The SABR 45 convention took place in Chicago, and here are 45 articles on baseball in and around the bat-and-ball crazed Windy City: 25 that appeared in the souvenir book of the convention plus another 20 articles available in ebook only.
Edited by Gregory H. Wolf
$19.95 paperback (ISBN 978-1-943816-23-1)
$9.99 ebook (ISBN 978-1-943816-22-4)
8.5"X11", 290 pages, 58 photos

BRAVES FIELD:
MEMORABLE MOMENTS AT BOSTON'S LOST DIAMOND
From its opening on August 18, 1915, to the sudden departure of the Boston Braves to Milwaukee before the 1953 baseball season, Braves Field was home to Boston's National League baseball club and also hosted many other events: from NFL football to championship boxing. The most memorable moments to occur in Braves Field history are portrayed here.
Edited by Bill Nowlin and Bob Brady
$19.95 paperback (ISBN 978-1-933599-93-9)
$9.99 ebook (ISBN 978-1-933599-92-2)
8.5"X11", 282 pages, 182 photos

AU JEU/PLAY BALL: THE 50 GREATEST GAMES IN THE HISTORY OF THE MONTREAL EXPOS
The 50 greatest games in Montreal Expos history. The games described here recount the exploits of the many great players who wore Expos uniforms over the years—Bill Stoneman, Gary Carter, Andre Dawson, Steve Rogers, Pedro Martinez, from the earliest days of the franchise, to the glory years of 1979-1981, the what-might-have-been years of the early 1990s, and the sad, final days.and others.
Edited by Norm King
$12.95 paperback (ISBN 978-1-943816-15-6)
$5.99 ebook (ISBN978-1-943816-14-9)
8.5"x11", 162 pages, 50 photos

ORIGINAL SABR RESEARCH

CALLING THE GAME:
BASEBALL BROADCASTING FROM 1920 TO THE PRESENT
An exhaustive, meticulously researched history of bringing the national pastime out of the ballparks and into living rooms via the airwaves. Every play-by-play announcer, color commentator, and ex-ballplayer, every broadcast deal, radio station, and TV network. Plus a foreword by "Voice of the Chicago Cubs" Pat Hughes, and an afterword by Jacques Doucet, the "Voice of the Montreal Expos" 1972-2004.
by Stuart Shea
$24.95 paperback (ISBN 978-1-933599-40-3)
$9.99 ebook (ISBN 978-1-933599-41-0)
7"X10", 712 pages, 40 photos

BIOPROJECT BOOKS

WHO'S ON FIRST:
REPLACEMENT PLAYERS IN WORLD WAR II
During World War II, 533 players made the major league debuts. More than 60% of the players in the 1941 Opening Day lineups departed for the service and were replaced by first-times and oldsters. Hod Lisenbee was 46. POW Bert Shepard had an artificial leg, and Pete Gray had only one arm. The 1944 St. Louis Browns had 13 players classified 4-F. These are their stories.
Edited by Marc Z Aaron and Bill Nowlin
$19.95 paperback (ISBN 978-1-933599-91-5)
$9.99 ebook (ISBN 978-1-933599-90-8)
8.5"X11", 422 pages, 67 photos

VAN LINGLE MUNGO:
THE MAN, THE SONG, THE PLAYERS
40 baseball players with intriguing names have been named in renditions of Dave Frishberg's classic 1969 song, Van Lingle Mungo. This book presents biographies of all 40 players and additional information about one of the greatest baseball novelty songs of all time.
Edited by Bill Nowlin
$19.95 paperback (ISBN 978-1-933599-76-2)
$9.99 ebook (ISBN 978-1-933599-77-9)
8.5"X11", 278 pages, 46 photos

NUCLEAR POWERED BASEBALL
Nuclear Powered Baseball tells the stories of each player—past and present—featured in the classic Simpsons episode "Homer at the Bat." Wade Boggs, Ken Griffey Jr., Ozzie Smith, Nap Lajoie, Don Mattingly, and many more. We've also included a few very entertaining takes on the now-famous episode from prominent baseball writers Jonah Keri, Joe Posnanski, Erik Malinowski, and Bradley Woodrum
Edited by Emily Hawks and Bill Nowlin
$19.95 paperback (ISBN 978-1-943816-11-8)
$9.99 ebook (ISBN 978-1-943816-10-1)
8.5"X11", 250 pages

SABR Members can purchase each book at a significant discount (often 50% off) and receive the ebook edtions free as a member benefit. Each book is available in a trade paperback edition as well as ebooks suitable for reading on a home computer or Nook, Kindle, or iPad/tablet.
To learn more about becoming a member of SABR, visit the website: sabr.org/join

SABR BioProject Books

In 2002, the Society for American Baseball Research launched an effort to write and publish biographies of every player, manager, and individual who has made a contribution to baseball. Over the past decade, the BioProject Committee has produced over 2,200 biographical articles. Many have been part of efforts to create theme- or team-oriented books, spearheaded by chapters or other committees of SABR.

THE YEAR OF THE BLUE SNOW:
THE 1964 PHILADELPHIA PHILLIES
Catcher Gus Triandos dubbed the Philadelphia Phillies' 1964 season "the year of the blue snow," a rare thing that happens once in a great while. This book sheds light on lingering questions about the 1964 season—but any book about a team is really about the players. This work offers life stories of all the players and others (managers, coaches, owners, and broadcasters) associated with this star-crossed team, as well as essays of analysis and history.
Edited by Mel Marmer and Bill Nowlin
$19.95 paperback (ISBN 978-1-933599-51-9)
$9.99 ebook (ISBN 978-1-933599-52-6)
8.5"X11", 356 PAGES, over 70 photos

DETROIT TIGERS 1984:
WHAT A START! WHAT A FINISH!
The 1984 Detroit tigers roared out of the gate, winning their first nine games of the season and compiling an eye-popping 35-5 record after the campaign's first 40 games—still the best start ever for any team in major league history. This book brings together biographical profiles of every Tiger from that magical season, plus those of field management, top executives, the broadcasters—even venerable Tiger Stadium and the city itself.
Edited by Mark Pattison and David Raglin
$19.95 paperback (ISBN 978-1-933599-44-1)
$9.99 ebook (ISBN 978-1-933599-45-8)
8.5"x11", 250 pages (Over 230,000 words!)

SWEET '60: THE 1960 PITTSBURGH PIRATES
A portrait of the 1960 team which pulled off one of the biggest upsets of the last 60 years. When Bill Mazeroski's home run left the park to win in Game Seven of the World Series, beating the New York Yankees, David had toppled Goliath. It was a blow that awakened a generation, one that millions of people saw on television, one of TV's first iconic World Series moments.
Edited by Clifton Blue Parker and Bill Nowlin
$19.95 paperback (ISBN 978-1-933599-48-9)
$9.99 ebook (ISBN 978-1-933599-49-6)
8.5"X11", 340 pages, 75 photos

RED SOX BASEBALL IN THE DAYS OF IKE AND ELVIS: THE RED SOX OF THE 1950s
Although the Red Sox spent most of the 1950s far out of contention, the team was filled with fascinating players who captured the heart of their fans. In *Red Sox Baseball*, members of SABR present 46 biographies on players such as Ted Williams and Pumpsie Green as well as season-by-season recaps.
Edited by Mark Armour and Bill Nowlin
$19.95 paperback (ISBN 978-1-933599-24-3)
$9.99 ebook (ISBN 978-1-933599-34-2)
8.5"X11", 372 PAGES, over 100 photos

THE MIRACLE BRAVES OF 1914
BOSTON'S ORIGINAL WORST-TO-FIRST CHAMPIONS
Long before the Red Sox "Impossible Dream" season, Boston's now nearly forgotten "other" team, the 1914 Boston Braves, performed a baseball "miracle" that resounds to this very day. The "Miracle Braves" were Boston's first "worst-to-first" winners of the World Series. Refusing to throw in the towel at the midseason mark, George Stallings engineered a remarkable second-half climb in the standings all the way to first place.
Edited by Bill Nowlin
$19.95 paperback (ISBN 978-1-933599-69-4)
$9.99 ebook (ISBN 978-1-933599-70-0)
8.5"X11", 392 PAGES, over 100 photos

THAR'S JOY IN BRAVELAND!
THE 1957 MILWAUKEE BRAVES
Few teams in baseball history have captured the hearts of their fans like the Milwaukee Braves of the 1950s. During the Braves' 13-year tenure in Milwaukee (1953-1965), they had a winning record every season, won two consecutive NL pennants (1957 and 1958), lost two more in the final week of the season (1956 and 1959), and set big-league attendance records along the way.
Edited by Gregory H. Wolf
$19.95 paperback (ISBN 978-1-933599-71-7)
$9.99 ebook (ISBN 978-1-933599-72-4)
8.5"x11", 330 pages, over 60 photos

NEW CENTURY, NEW TEAM:
THE 1901 BOSTON AMERICANS
The team now known as the Boston Red Sox played its first season in 1901. Boston had a well-established National League team, but the American League went head-to-head with the N.L. in Chicago, Philadelphia, and Boston. Chicago won the American League pennant and Boston finished second, only four games behind.
Edited by Bill Nowlin
$19.95 paperback (ISBN 978-1-933599-58-8)
$9.99 ebook (ISBN 978-1-933599-59-5)
8.5"X11", 268 pages, over 125 photos

CAN HE PLAY?
A LOOK AT BASEBALL SCOUTS AND THEIR PROFESSION
They dig through tons of coal to find a single diamond. Here in the world of scouts, we meet the "King of Weeds," a Ph.D. we call "Baseball's Renaissance Man," a husband-and-wife team, pioneering Latin scouts, and a Japanese-American interned during World War II who became a successful scout—and many, many more.
Edited by Jim Sandoval and Bill Nowlin
$19.95 paperback (ISBN 978-1-933599-23-6)
$9.99 ebook (ISBN 978-1-933599-25-0)
8.5"X11", 200 PAGES, over 100 photos

SABR Members can purchase each book at a significant discount (often 50% off) and receive the ebook editions free as a member benefit. Each book is available in a trade paperback edition as well as ebooks suitable for reading on a home computer or Nook, Kindle, or iPad/tablet.
To learn more about becoming a member of SABR, visit the website: sabr.org/join

THE SABR DIGITAL LIBRARY

The Society for American Baseball Research, the top baseball research organization in the world, disseminates some of the best in baseball history, analysis, and biography through our publishing programs. The SABR Digital Library contains a mix of books old and new, and focuses on a tandem program of paperback and ebook publication, making these materials widely available for both on digital devices and as traditional printed books.

CLASSIC REPRINTS

BASE-BALL: HOW TO BECOME A PLAYER
by John Montgomery Ward
John Montgomery Ward (1860-1925) tossed the second perfect game in major league history and later became the game's best shortstop and a great, inventive manager. His classic handbook on baseball skills and strategy was published in 1888. Illustrated with woodcuts, the book is divided into chapters for each position on the field as well as chapters on the origin of the game, theory and strategy, training, base-running, and batting.
$4.99 ebook (ISBN 978-1-933599-47-2)
$9.95 paperback (ISBN 978-0910137539)
156 PAGES, 4.5"X7" replica edition

BATTING by F. C. Lane
First published in 1925, *Batting* collects the wisdom and insights of over 250 hitters and baseball figures. Lane interviewed extensively and compiled tips and advice on everything from batting stances to beanballs. Legendary baseball figures such as Ty Cobb, Casey Stengel, Cy Young, Walter Johnson, Rogers Hornsby, and Babe Ruth reveal the secrets of such integral and interesting parts of the game as how to choose a bat, the ways to beat a slump, and how to outguess the pitcher.
$14.95 paperback (ISBN 978-0-910137-86-7)
$7.99 ebook (ISBN 978-1-933599-46-5)
240 PAGES, 5"X7"

RUN, RABBIT, RUN
by Walter "Rabbit" Maranville
"Rabbit" Maranville was the Joe Garagiola of Grandpa's day, the baseball comedian of the times. In a twenty-four-year career that began in 1912, Rabbit found a lot of funny situations to laugh at, and no wonder: he caused most of them! The book also includes an introduction by the late Harold Seymour and a historical account of Maranville's life and Hall-of-Fame career by Bob Carroll.
$9.95 paperback (ISBN 978-1-933599-26-7)
$5.99 ebook (ISBN 978-1-933599-27-4)
100 PAGES, 5.5"X8.5", 15 rare photos

MEMORIES OF A BALLPLAYER
by Bill Werber and C. Paul Rogers III
Bill Werber's claim to fame is unique: he was the last living person to have a direct connection to the 1927 Yankees, "Murderers' Row," a team hailed by many as the best of all time. Rich in anecdotes and humor, Memories of a Ballplayer is a clear-eyed memoir of the world of big-league baseball in the 1930s. Werber played with or against some of the most productive hitters of all time, including Babe Ruth, Ted Williams, Lou Gehrig, and Joe DiMaggio.
$14.95 paperback (ISNB 978-0-910137-84-3)
$6.99 ebook (ISBN 978-1-933599-47-2)
250 PAGES, 6"X9"

ORIGINAL SABR RESEARCH

INVENTING BASEBALL: THE 100 GREATEST GAMES OF THE NINETEENTH CENTURY
SABR's Nineteenth Century Committee brings to life the greatest games from the game's early years. From the "prisoner of war" game that took place among captive Union soldiers during the Civil War (immortalized in a famous lithograph), to the first intercollegiate game (Amherst versus Williams), to the first professional no-hitter, the games in this volume span 1833–1900 and detail the athletic exploits of such players as Cap Anson, Moses "Fleetwood" Walker, Charlie Comiskey, and Mike "King" Kelly.
Edited by Bill Felber
$19.95 paperback (ISBN 978-1-933599-42-7)
$9.99 ebook (ISBN 978-1-933599-43-4)
302 PAGES, 8"x10", 200 photos

NINETEENTH CENTURY STARS: 2012 EDITION
First published in 1989, *Nineteenth Century Stars* was SABR's initial attempt to capture the stories of baseball players from before 1900. With a collection of 136 fascinating biographies, SABR has re-released *Nineteenth Century Stars* for 2012 with revised statistics and new form. The 2012 version also includes a preface by **John Thorn**.
Edited by Robert L. Tiemann and Mark Rucker
$19.95 paperback (ISBN 978-1-933599-28-1)
$9.99 ebook (ISBN 978-1-933599-29-8)
300 PAGES, 6"X9"

GREAT HITTING PITCHERS
Published in 1979, *Great Hitting Pitchers* was one of SABR's early publications. Edited by SABR founder Bob Davids, the book compiles stories and records about pitchers excelling in the batter's box. Newly updated in 2012 by Mike Cook, *Great Hitting Pitchers* contain tables including data from 1979-2011, corrections to reflect recent records, and a new chapter on recent new members in the club of "great hitting pitchers" like Tom Glavine and Mike Hampton.
Edited by L. Robert Davids
$9.95 paperback (ISBN 978-1-933599-30-4)
$5.99 ebook (ISBN 978-1-933599-31-1)
102 PAGES, 5.5"x8.5"

THE FENWAY PROJECT
Sixty-four SABR members—avid fans, historians, statisticians, and game enthusiasts—recorded their experiences of a single game. Some wrote from inside the Green Monster's manual scoreboard, the Braves clubhouse, or the broadcast booth, while others took in the essence of Fenway from the grandstand or bleachers. The result is a fascinating look at the charms and challenges of Fenway Park, and the allure of being a baseball fan.
Edited by Bill Nowlin and Cecilia Tan
$9.99 ebook (ISBN 978-1-933599-50-2)
175 pages, 100 photos

SABR Members can purchase each book at a significant discount (often 50% off) and receive the ebook editions free as a member benefit. Each book is available in a trade paperback edition as well as ebooks suitable for reading on a home computer or Nook, Kindle, or iPad/tablet.
To learn more about becoming a member of SABR, visit the website: sabr.org/join

Society for American Baseball Research

Cronkite School at ASU
555 N. Central Ave. #416, Phoenix, AZ 85004
602.496.1460 (phone)
SABR.org

Become a SABR member today!

If you're interested in baseball — writing about it, reading about it, talking about it — there's a place for you in the Society for American Baseball Research. Our members include everyone from academics to professional sportswriters to amateur historians and statisticians to students and casual fans who enjoy reading about baseball and occasionally gathering with other members to talk baseball. What unites all SABR members is an interest in the game and joy in learning more about it.

SABR membership is open to any baseball fan; we offer 1-year and 3-year memberships. Here's a list of some of the key benefits you'll receive as a SABR member:

- Receive two editions (spring and fall) of the *Baseball Research Journal*, our flagship publication
- Receive expanded e-book edition of *The National Pastime*, our annual convention journal
- 8-10 new e-books published by the SABR Digital Library, all FREE to members
- "This Week in SABR" e-newsletter, sent to members every Friday
- Join dozens of research committees, from Statistical Analysis to Women in Baseball.
- Join one of 70 regional chapters in the U.S., Canada, Latin America, and abroad
- Participate in online discussion groups
- Ask and answer baseball research questions on the SABR-L e-mail listserv
- Complete archives of *The Sporting News* dating back to 1886 and other research resources
- Promote your research in "This Week in SABR"
- Diamond Dollars Case Competition
- Yoseloff Scholarships

- Discounts on SABR national conferences, including the SABR National Convention, the SABR Analytics Conference, Jerry Malloy Negro League Conference, Frederick Ivor-Campbell 19th Century Conference
- Publish your research in peer-reviewed SABR journals
- Collaborate with SABR researchers and experts
- Contribute to Baseball Biography Project or the SABR Games Project
- List your new book in the SABR Bookshelf
- Lead a SABR research committee or chapter
- Networking opportunities at SABR Analytics Conference
- Meet baseball authors and historians at SABR events and chapter meetings
- 50% discounts on paperback versions of SABR e-books
- 20% discount on MLB.TV and MiLB.TV subscriptions
- Discounts with other partners in the baseball community
- SABR research awards

We hope you'll join the most passionate international community of baseball fans at SABR! Check us out online at SABR.org/join.

- - - ✂ -

SABR MEMBERSHIP FORM

	Annual	3-year	Senior	3-yr Sr.	Under 30
U.S.:	☐ $65	☐ $175	☐ $45	☐ $129	☐ $45
Canada/Mexico:	☐ $75	☐ $205	☐ $55	☐ $159	☐ $55
Overseas:	☐ $84	☐ $232	☐ $64	☐ $186	☐ $55

Add a Family Member: $15 each family member at same address (list names on back)
Senior: 65 or older before 12/31 of the current year
All dues amounts in U.S. dollars or equivalent

Participate in Our Donor Program!

Support the preservation of baseball research. Designate your gift toward:
☐ General Fund   ☐ Endowment Fund   ☐ Research Resources   ☐ _____
☐ I want to maximize the impact of my gift; do not send any donor premiums
☐ I would like this gift to remain anonymous.

Note: Any donation not designated will be placed in the General Fund.
SABR is a 501 (c) (3) not-for-profit organization & donations are tax-deductible to the extent allowed by law.

Name _____

E-mail* _____

Address _____

City _____ ST _____ ZIP _____

Phone _____ Birthday _____

* Your e-mail address on file ensures you will receive the most recent SABR news.

Dues $_____

Donation $_____

Amount Enclosed $_____

Do you work for a matching grant corporation? Call (602) 496-1460 for details.

If you wish to pay by credit card, please contact the SABR office at (602) 496-1460 or visit the SABR Store online at SABR.org/join. We accept Visa, Mastercard & Discover.

Do you wish to receive the *Baseball Research Journal* electronically?: ☐ Yes   ☐ No
Our e-books are available in PDF, Kindle, or EPUB (iBooks, iPad, Nook) formats.

Mail to: SABR, Cronkite School at ASU, 555 N. Central Ave. #416, Phoenix, AZ 85004